XHTML™
in Plain English

XHTML™
in Plain English

Sandra E. Eddy

M&T Books
An imprint of IDG Books Worldwide, Inc.

Foster City, CA • Chicago, IL • Indianapolis, IN • New York, NY

XHTML™ in Plain English

Published by
M&T Books
An imprint of IDG Books Worldwide, Inc.
919 E. Hillsdale Blvd., Suite 400
Foster City, CA 94404
www.idgbooks.com (IDG Books Worldwide Web site)

ISBN: 0-7645-4743-7

Printed in the United States of America

10 9 8 7 6 5 4 3 2 1

1O/SX/RQ/QQ/FC

Distributed in the United States by IDG Books Worldwide, Inc.

Distributed by CDG Books Canada Inc. for Canada; by Transworld Publishers Limited in the United Kingdom; by IDG Norge Books for Norway; by IDG Sweden Books for Sweden; by IDG Books Australia Publishing Corporation Pty. Ltd. for Australia and New Zealand; by TransQuest Publishers Pte Ltd. for Singapore, Malaysia, Thailand, Indonesia, and Hong Kong; by Gotop Information Inc. for Taiwan; by ICG Muse, Inc. for Japan; by Intersoft for South Africa; by Eyrolles for France; by International Thomson Publishing for Germany, Austria, and Switzerland; by Distribuidora Cuspide for Argentina; by LR International for Brazil; by Galileo Libros for Chile; by Ediciones ZETA S.C.R. Ltda. for Peru; by WS Computer Publishing Corporation, Inc., for the Philippines; by Contemporanea de Ediciones for Venezuela; by Express Computer Distributors for the Caribbean and West Indies; by Micronesia Media Distributor, Inc. for Micronesia; by Chips Computadoras S.A. de C.V. for Mexico; by Editorial Norma de Panama S.A. for Panama; by American Bookshops for Finland.

For general information on IDG Books Worldwide's books in the U.S., please call our Consumer Customer Service department at 800-762-2974. For reseller information, including discounts and premium sales, please call our Reseller Customer Service department at 800-434-3422.

For information on where to purchase IDG Books Worldwide's books outside the U.S., please contact our International Sales department at 317-596-5530 or fax 317-572-4002.

For consumer information on foreign language translations, please contact our Customer Service department at 800-434-3422, fax 317-572-4002, or e-mail rights@idgbooks.com.

For information on licensing foreign or domestic rights, please phone + 1-650-653-7098.

For sales inquiries and special prices for bulk quantities, please contact our Order Services department at 800-434-3422 or write to the address above.

For information on using IDG Books Worldwide's books in the classroom or for ordering examination copies, please contact our Educational Sales department at 800-434-2086 or fax 317-572-4005.

For press review copies, author interviews, or other publicity information, please contact our Public Relations department at 650-653-7000 or fax 650-653-7500.

For authorization to photocopy items for corporate, personal, or educational use, please contact Copyright Clearance Center, 222 Rosewood Drive, Danvers, MA 01923, or fax 978-750-4470.

Library of Congress Cataloging-in-Publication Data

Eddy, Sandra E.
   XHTML in plain english / Sandra E. Eddy.
      p. cm.
   ISBN 0-7645-4743-7 (alk. paper)
   1. XHTML (Document markup language)
I. Title.
QA76.76.H94 E35 2000
005.7'2--dc21   00-061347

 is a registered trademark or trademark under exclusive license to IDG Books Worldwide, Inc. from International Data Group, Inc. in the United States and/or other countries.

 is a trademark of IDG Books Worldwide, Inc.

ABOUT IDG BOOKS WORLDWIDE

Welcome to the world of IDG Books Worldwide.

IDG Books Worldwide, Inc., is a subsidiary of International Data Group, the world's largest publisher of computer-related information and the leading global provider of information services on information technology. IDG was founded more than 30 years ago by Patrick J. McGovern and now employs more than 9,000 people worldwide. IDG publishes more than 290 computer publications in over 75 countries. More than 90 million people read one or more IDG publications each month.

Launched in 1990, IDG Books Worldwide is today the #1 publisher of best-selling computer books in the United States. We are proud to have received eight awards from the Computer Press Association in recognition of editorial excellence and three from Computer Currents' First Annual Readers' Choice Awards. Our best-selling ...For Dummies® series has more than 50 million copies in print with translations in 31 languages. IDG Books Worldwide, through a joint venture with IDG's Hi-Tech Beijing, became the first U.S. publisher to publish a computer book in the People's Republic of China. In record time, IDG Books Worldwide has become the first choice for millions of readers around the world who want to learn how to better manage their businesses.

Our mission is simple: Every one of our books is designed to bring extra value and skill-building instructions to the reader. Our books are written by experts who understand and care about our readers. The knowledge base of our editorial staff comes from years of experience in publishing, education, and journalism — experience we use to produce books to carry us into the new millennium. In short, we care about books, so we attract the best people. We devote special attention to details such as audience, interior design, use of icons, and illustrations. And because we use an efficient process of authoring, editing, and desktop publishing our books electronically, we can spend more time ensuring superior content and less time on the technicalities of making books.

You can count on our commitment to deliver high-quality books at competitive prices on topics you want to read about. At IDG Books Worldwide, we continue in the IDG tradition of delivering quality for more than 30 years. You'll find no better book on a subject than one from IDG Books Worldwide.

John J. Kilcullen

John Kilcullen
Chairman and CEO
IDG Books Worldwide, Inc.

*Eighth Annual
Computer Press
Awards ≥1992*

*Ninth Annual
Computer Press
Awards ≥1993*

*Tenth Annual
Computer Press
Awards ≥1994*

*Eleventh Annual
Computer Press
Awards ≥1995*

IDG is the world's leading IT media, research and exposition company. Founded in 1964, IDG had 1997 revenues of $2.05 billion and has more than 9,000 employees worldwide. IDG offers the widest range of media options that reach IT buyers in 75 countries representing 95% of worldwide IT spending. IDG's diverse product and services portfolio spans six key areas including print publishing, online publishing, expositions and conferences, market research, education and training, and global marketing services. More than 90 million people read one or more of IDG's 290 magazines and newspapers, including IDG's leading global brands — Computerworld, PC World, Network World, Macworld and the Channel World family of publications. IDG Books Worldwide is one of the fastest-growing computer book publishers in the world, with more than 700 titles in 36 languages. The "...For Dummies®" series alone has more than 50 million copies in print. IDG offers online users the largest network of technology-specific Web sites around the world through IDG.net (http://www.idg.net), which comprises more than 225 targeted Web sites in 55 countries worldwide. International Data Corporation (IDC) is the world's largest provider of information technology data, analysis and consulting, with research centers in over 41 countries and more than 400 research analysts worldwide. IDG World Expo is a leading producer of more than 168 globally branded conferences and expositions in 35 countries including E3 (Electronic Entertainment Expo), Macworld Expo, ComNet, Windows World Expo, ICE (Internet Commerce Expo), Agenda, DEMO, and Spotlight. IDG's training subsidiary, ExecuTrain, is the world's largest computer training company, with more than 230 locations worldwide and 785 training courses. IDG Marketing Services helps industry-leading IT companies build international brand recognition by developing global integrated marketing programs via IDG's print, online and exposition products worldwide. Further information about the company can be found at www.idg.com.   1/26/00

Credits

Acquisitions Editor
Debra Williams Cauley

Project Editor
Andy Marinkovich

Technical Editor
Simon St.Laurent

Copy Editors
Gabrielle Chosney
Kathi Duggan
Kevin Kent

Proof Editor
Neil Romanosky

Project Coordinators
Danette Nurse
Marcos Vergara

Graphics and Production Specialists
Bob Bihlmayer
Jude Levinson
Michael Lewis
Victor Pérez-Varela
Ramses Ramirez

Quality Control Technician
Dina F Quan

Book Designers
London Road Design
Kurt Krames

Illustrator
Gabriele McCann

Proofreading and Indexing
York Production Services

Cover Image
© Noma/Images.com

About the Author

Sandra E. Eddy specializes in writing how-to and reference books about the Internet, Internet applications and technologies, Windows, and Windows applications. Her first book was published in 1991. Until she became a full-time freelance writer in 1993, Ms. Eddy was a documentation manager and technical writer for a major software company. From 1984 to 1993, she wrote and edited user and technical manuals for both PC- and mainframe-based computer programs. Ms. Eddy is the author of the following books from IDG Books Worldwide: *XHTML in Plain English, HTML in Plain English, TeachYourself XML, Teach Yourself ASP,* and *The GIF Animator's Guide.*

For E. A. S.

"He that has patience may compass anything."

— Rabelais

Preface

Welcome to *XHTML in Plain English*. I hope you enjoy using this book as much as I have enjoyed researching and writing it. I have crafted this reference and tutorial to provide you with quick yet comprehensive information about all XHTML 1.0 elements (commonly known as *tags*), the elements of its predecessors, HTML 4.0, HTML 3.2, HTML 2.0, and earlier versions; Netscape, Microsoft, and WebTV extensions; and the Universal Character Set (UCS), or Unicode 2.0, the supported character set. Also, I include all associated attributes and many examples that you can use as templates for coding World Wide Web pages.

Although you can find comprehensive XHTML (and HTML) references and tutorials on the Web and in many other XHTML books, this handbook cuts to the heart of XHTML. When you want to write an XHTML document, you don't need to learn about the background; all you need is the element name and purpose, its syntax, attributes, and illustrated examples of how it works. Are you writing a page specifically for Netscape Navigator or the Microsoft Internet Explorer browser or a WebTV site? Or are you creating a document that you want the whole online world to be able to view? *XHTML in Plain English* identifies elements and attributes that are tailored for particular browsers or ones that you can safely use for a much wider audience.

Although *XHTML in Plain English* does not cover CGI scripting and Java programming, it leads you right to those levels. So, this book is for all levels of XHTML page creators, from first-time users to the most advanced.

XHTML in Plain English is the essential XHTML handbook that should have a special place next to your personal computer.

How This Book Is Organized

Finding XHTML information online or in a book can be daunting. *XHTML in Plain English* is designed to be easy to use, regardless of your level of experience.

XHTML in Plain English is organized into three parts: *Part I: XHTML Reference, Part II: XHTML Tutorial,* and *Appendixes.*

If you want to use a comprehensive reference and cross-references to the tutorial, browse through *Part I: XHTML Reference,* which includes the following sections:

- *XHTML in Plain English.* If you know what you want to do but can't remember the element name, view this thumbnail list of plain-English tasks and related elements. Then use the cross-reference to find the appropriate page in the reference or tutorial part.

- *XHTML A to Z.* If you know the name of the element you want to use, scan this alphabetically arranged list with brief descriptions. Once you have located a particular element, flip to a reference or tutorial page cited in the cross-reference.

- *XHTML Syntax.* If you know the element name but want to learn more about it or how to use one of its attributes, browse through these pages of elements and extensions. In this part, you'll find each element along with its purpose; its complete syntax and attributes; the element set or extension set that supports it; usage notes; related elements; and plenty of examples and illustrations of the results.

- *Cascading Style Sheets in Plain English.* If you know how you want to style an element but have not memorized the CSS property name, view this thumbnail list of plain-English styles.

- *Cascading Style Sheets A to Z*. If you think you know the name of the property you want to use, verify it by looking through this alphabetically arranged list with brief descriptions. Once you have located a particular property, go to a cross-referenced page.

- *Cascading Style Sheet Syntax*. Throughout most of personal computing history, individuals creating word processor documents have set standard paragraph formats using style sheets. Then they have applied individual properties, or styles, from the style sheets to paragraphs in both new and old documents. Now you can use style sheets to employ formats for XHTML documents. This section provides an introduction to and overview of cascading style sheets. You'll find each property along with its purpose, its complete syntax, usage notes, and related properties.

If you want to learn XHTML or to compare XHTML with HTML, use the tutorial, which also contains cross-references to the reference, browse through *Part II: XHTML Tutorial*, which includes the following chapters:

- *Chapter 1: Introducing XHTML*. This chapter introduces you to markup languages, narrates the history of hypertext, and presents XHTML in the context of its close relatives, XML and HTML.

- *Chapter 2: Constructing a Basic Document*. An accurate XHTML document combines character data with elements, attributes, entities, and so on, following XML rules and standards. This chapter shows you how to create simple XHTML documents — their structure and content.

- *Chapter 3: Using Lists in Documents*. The main reasons for inserting lists in documents are to organize related information and to relieve the presentation of paragraphs and paragraphs of text. This chapter covers the structure and presentation of four types of lists in XHTML documents.

- *Chapter 4: Adding Tables to Documents*. Tables, which organize and manage data into rows and columns, enable you to present related information in a clear and concise way. This chapter shows you the details of constructing each component in a table — from simple to detailed.

- *Chapter 5: Framing Documents*. Framesets and their frames enable you to combine fixed and dynamic information in a single computer desktop. This chapter presents the four framing elements and explains how to use them easily and effectively.

- *Chapter 6: Linking to Other Resources*. Hyperlinks, or links, make Web documents unique. Without links, users would most likely read through a document from top to bottom. By clicking links, users can research a particular topic using documents from worldwide sites. This chapter explains how to create a local or remote textual or graphical link and how to add it to a document.

- *Chapter 7: Using Interactive Forms*. As the Web becomes more commercial, developers need to know how to gather information from users to better serve the customer. This chapter presents a variety of form controls, shows how to construct a form, and provides information about testing and processing forms.

- *Chapter 8: Styling Documents with CSS*. When you associate a style sheet with a document or apply style properties to an element, you can control the look and format of a document more easily than you can with formatting attributes. This chapter shows you various ways of applying styles to elements and provides an overview of popular CSS styling properties.

- *Chapter 9: Testing and Maintaining Documents*. Because XHTML 1.0 redefines HTML 4.0 as an application of XML 1.0, XHTML must follow XML rules and standards. Because XHTML processing is more stringent than HTML processing, testing and correcting is extremely important. This chapter covers testing, processing, and maintaining documents.

- *Chapter 10: Creating Dynamic Documents*. XHTML documents can contain scripts written in scripting languages such as JavaScript, JScript, and VBScript. Scripts enable a document to become dynamic: when a user moves the mouse, clicks a mouse button, or presses a key, a script can change the look of a document or display an entirely new document. This chapter provides an overview of writing scripts and inserting them in your documents.

- *Chapter 11: Customizing XHTML*. Because XHTML combines XML and HTML, you can take advantage of the assets of both languages. For example, you can use XML rules to declare new elements and attributes or use an existing language created under XML, thereby customizing XHTML for a document or set of documents. This chapter shows you how to refer to a custom XML-based language and how to declare your own.

The appendixes provide subsidiary information that helps you build your XHTML knowledge and better understand the history of markup languages, including SGML, HTML, XML, and XHTML. The *Appendixes* section includes the following:

- *Appendix A: Elements by Version and Activity*. This appendix provides lists of elements organized under HTML versions and extensions. It also provides lists of the elements that are deprecated and obsolete in XHTML 1.0.

- *Appendix B: Unicode Characters and Character Sets*. XHTML emphasizes *internationalization,* the use of many languages in documents. When you create international documents, you use different alphabets and symbols, all supported by XHTML. This appendix provides illustrated tables of characters and character sets (especially those commonly used by English-speakers) and specifies non-English characters and character sets.

- *Appendix C: Internationalization*. When you create documents for an international audience, you must name a language for an XHTML document using a two-letter language code or specify country codes and subcodes, which name a particular country's version of a language. This appendix contains tables of language and country codes.

- *Appendix D: EBNF Reference*. The XML 1.0 recommendation uses Extended Backus-Naur Form (EBNF) notation to define XML documents and DTD syntax. To develop a custom language or to understand the XHTML DTD in which elements and attributes are declared, you should understand EBNF. This appendix contains tables of syntax and symbols.

- *Glossary*. XHTML and the Internet have their own unique vocabularies. If you have never seen a term or you want a clarification, browse through this glossary of XHTML and Internet terms.

- *Appendix E: Attributes in Depth*. XHTML 1.0 includes many attributes for every element and extension. This bonus appendix, which is posted at www.mandtbooks.com/extras/xhtmlipe, lists XHTML 1.0 attributes alphabetically. Each entry describes the attribute, tells how it works, and names valid and default values. To get comprehensive attributed information, download this file today!

Conventions Used in This Book

The conventions used in *XHTML in Plain English* are as follows:

- Throughout the book, element names are in lowercase or **boldface lowercase**.

- Elements and attributes to be typed into an XHTML document are displayed in a monospaced typeface.

- *Italics* are used to identify both new terms and variables (such as file names, paths, colors, numbers, or URLs) that you name and enter. For example, in the following syntax BGCOLOR="#*rrggbb*"|"*color*"], *rrggbb* and *color* represent a hexadecimal code and color name, respectively, for a page background color. Substitute a code (such as "#FFFFFF") or color ("white") for the italicized text.

- Default values, which are automatically supplied when you do not use a particular attribute, are <u>underlined</u>.

- ⊖ Indicates that Microsoft Internet Explorer can read and use the element.

- N Indicates that Netscape Navigator can read and use the element.

- 📺 Indicates that an element is unique to WebTV.

Web indicates a cross-reference to Appendix E on the Web.

Any element not preceded by one of these icons is supported by the XHTML 1.0 recommendation.

● **NOTE** ──────────────────────────────────

At the beginning of "HTML Syntax" in Part I, you will find a complete explanation of the syntax conventions for the elements documented in that part. In Appendix D, "EBNF Reference," you will find an explanation of Extended Backus-Naur Form notation, with which you can define DTD syntax.

Acknowledgments

In almost every acknowledgments section of any computer book, you can read a reference to a support team of editors, experts, family, and friends. However, there's no getting around it: producing the best possible book is a team effort. When you're "deadlined out" and trying to make sense of what's displayed on your computer screen in the middle of an all-nighter or you're attempting to understand and then explain a technical concept that is way over your head, it's great to know that you have a group of people urging you on and helping you in many ways. In this section, I'd like to thank all those whose support has been so important.

Very special thanks go to Acquisitions Editor Debra Williams Cauley, who is always a joy to work with.

Thanks to Project Editor Andy Marinkovich for keeping things moving, and to the copyediting team of Gabrielle Chosney, Kathi Duggan, and Kevin Kent for their diligence with the details.

For his expertise and attention to detail, an enthusiastic thank you to the technical editor, Simon St.Laurent, who has been with me as co-author and technical editor on many other projects.

As always, a special thank you for the patience and persistence of my agent, Matt Wagner of Waterside Productions.

For their continued encouragement, thanks to my family and friends.

> *"A friend may well be reckoned the masterpiece*
> *of Nature."*

> — *Ralph Waldo Emerson*

For his special and continuing contributions — Eli — and a very warm welcome to Grace. Always in loving memory of Indy, Bart, and Toni.

> *"Recollect that the Almighty, who gave the dog to*
> *be companion of our pleasures and our toils,*
> *hath invested him with a nature noble and*
> *incapable of deceit."*

> — *Sir Walter Scott*

Finally, thank you to the readers of this book. I hope you'll let me know what you think of the book and how I can make the next edition even better.

Contents at a Glance

Contents

XHTML Reference

Part One presents a comprehensive reference to XHTML and its associated style sheet language, Cascading Style Sheets. Each major section within is accompanied by its own table of contents. If you know the task you want to perform or style you want to apply but don't remember the element or property name, review the tasks in "XHTML in Plain English" or "Cascading Style Sheets in Plain English" and find the appropriate page in either Part One or Part Two. On the other hand, if you know the element or property name but want to find it in either Part One or Part Two, browse through the alphabetical lists in "XHTML A to Z" or "Cascading Style Sheets A to Z." In addition, "Cascading Style Sheets by Category" enables you to look up styling properties by category type. Again, find the desired property by going to one of the cross-referenced pages.

IN THIS PART

- XHTML in Plain English
- XHTML A to Z
- XHTML Syntax
- Cascading Style Sheets in Plain English
- Cascading Style Sheets A to Z
- Cascading Style Sheets by Category
- Cascading Style Sheet Syntax

XHTML in Plain English

If a writer's worst nightmare is a blank sheet of paper, a Web page designer's bad dream is a blank computer screen. To compound the terror, XHTML elements are not always easy to remember. For example, what do ol and ul do? Are dl, dt, dd, and dh related? What about th and thead? What's the difference between caption and legend? You get the idea.

The following table is for those of you who know what XHTML can do but don't always remember the names of the elements or extensions. This table is composed of four columns:

- The first column lists tasks to be performed, with italicized key words.
- The second column contains the element or extension with which you can accomplish the specified task.
- The third column lists the page number in Part I, *"XHTML Reference"* where you'll find a complete description of the element or extension, its syntax, its attributes, and more.
- The last column lists the page number in Part II, *"XHTML Tutorial"* where you can learn how to use a particular element or extension.

● — **NOTE** ———————————————————————————

Special characters are listed in Appendix B, *"Unicode Characters and Character Sets."*

If you want to . . .	Use this element	Located on this reference page	Located on this tutorial page
write an *abbreviation*	abbr	**29 – 30**	
identify an *acronym*	acronym	**31 – 33**	
provide author *address* information	address	**33 – 37**	
anchor a hypertext link	a	**24 – 29**	**599 – 604**
embed a Java *applet*	applet	**37 – 41**	**600**
define an image map *area*	area	**41 – 45**	**523**
create an *audioscope*	⎁audio scope	**45 – 46**	
include a *background sound*	☺⎁ bgsound	**56 – 57**	
define the *base* (default) *font size*	basefont	**51 – 52**	
define the *base* (absolute) *URL*	base	**49 – 50**	
change to a *bigger* font	big	**57 – 60**	
apply very bold *blackface* to selected text	⎁ blackface	**61**	
blink text on and off	ⓝblink	**61**	
define the *body* of the document	body	**65 – 70**	**528**
specify *boldface* text	b	**46 – 49**	**521, 617, 619**

If you want to . . .	Use this element	Located on this reference page	Located on this tutorial page
break a line of text	br	**70–72**	**523**
break a word or line in a nonbreak line	⊖Ⓝwbr	**339–340**	
insert a *button* in a form	button	**72–75**	**610**
place a *table caption*	caption	**76–79**	**557, 558–559**
place a form control's *caption*	legend	**195–198**	**616, 617**
center a line of text between the margins	center	**79–83**	
cite a book or other source	cite	**83–86**	
define a *column group*	colgroup	**92–94**	**565–566**
align a table *column*	col	**90–92**	**565–566**
insert a nondisplaying *comment*	!	**23–24**	**528–529**
insert a nondisplaying *comment*	comment	**94**	
insert a *definition*	dfn	**101–104**	
insert a *definition description* in a definition list (glossary)	dd	**95–98**	**542, 549–551**
start a *definition list*	dl	**112–116**	**542, 549–551**
insert a *definition term* in a definition list	dt	**116–119**	**542, 549–551**

Continued

If you want to . . .	Use this element	Located on this reference page	Located on this tutorial page
indicate *deleted* text	del	**98–100**	
specify text *direction*	bdo	**52–56**	
start a *directory* list	dir	**104–108**	
mark a *division* in a document	div	**108–112**	
state the *document type*	!DOCTYPE	**24**	**516**
embed an object	⊖N 🖥 embed	**123–127**	
code *embed alternates* for nonembed browsers	N🖥 noembed	**221–222**	
emphasize text	em	**120–123**	**563**
specify an *input* field in a form	input	**167–181**	**609–617**
mark a *field set*	fieldset	**127–131**	**616–618**
insert an *inline floating frame*	iframe	**158–160**	**579, 588**
assign a *font* characteristic	font	**131–135**	**509**
insert a fill-out *form*	form	**135–139**	**611–620**
specify a *frame*	frame	**139–141**	**579, 582–588**
code *frame alternates* for nonframe browsers	noframes	**222–223**	**589–590**
specify a *frames set*	frameset	**141–144**	**579, 581–587**
place a *horizontal rule*	hr	**149–153**	
create a unique *identifier*	⊖nextid	**217–219**	

If you want to . . .	Use this element	Located on this reference page	Located on this tutorial page
specify an inline *image*	img	162–167	523, 531–532
define an *inflow layer*	N ilayer	160–162	
indicate *inserted* text	ins	181–184	
specify *italicized* text	i	154–158	
generate a public *key*	N keygen	190	
indicate *keyboard input*	kbd	186–189	
label an input control	label	190–194	614, 615
define a *layer* of XHTML content	N layer	194–195	
code a *layer* alternate for nonlayer browsers	N nolayer	223–224	
make a *level 1* heading	h1	144–148	521–522
make a *level 2* heading	h2	144–148	521–522
make a *level 3* heading	h3	144–148	521–522
make a *level 4* heading	h4	144–148	521–522
make a *level 5* heading	h5	144–148	521–522
make a *level 6* heading	h6	144–148	521–522
document a *link* to another document	link	202–204	625
define a *list item*	li	198–202	543–544, 545–546

Continued

If you want to . . .	Use this element	Located on this reference page	Located on this tutorial page
define an image *map*	map	**205 – 207**	
add a scrolling *marquee*	⊖🖥 marquee	**208 – 212**	
identify a *menu list*	menu	**212 – 215**	
provide *meta* information	meta	**216 – 217**	**525, 527 – 528, 651**
format *multiple columns*	Ⓝ multicol	**217**	
specify an area with *no line breaks*	Ⓝ🖥 nobr	**219 – 221**	
embed a *multimedia object*	object	**225 – 230**	
insert an *option* in a form's menu	option	**236 – 238**	**616**
group *options* in a form's menu	optgroup	**234 – 236**	
specify an *ordered* (numbered) *list*	ol	**230 – 234**	**543 – 545**
specify a *paragraph*	p	**238 – 241**	**521 – 522**
define *parameters* for a Java applet	param	**241 – 242**	
specify a *predefined* layout and font	pre	**242 – 245**	
identify a long block-level *quotation*	blockquote	**61 – 65**	**628**
identify a short inline *quotation*	q	**246 – 248**	
select *ruby text*	⊖ rt	**248 – 251**	
specify *ruby text* interpretation	⊖ ruby	**251 – 254**	

If you want to . . .	Use this element	Located on this reference page	Located on this tutorial page
display text as *sample* computer output	samp	**258–262**	
define a client- or server-side *script*	script	**262–263**	**655–671**
include a LiveWire-compiled *script*	Ⓝ server	**267–268**	
code *script alternates* for nonscript browsers	noscript	**224–225**	
identify a simple *search index*	isindex	**184–186**	
produce a *selection menu* in a form	select	**263–267**	**616**
change to a *smaller* font	small	**268–271**	
display as *source program code*	code	**87–89**	
mark a *span* of text	span	**272–276**	
specify *strikethrough* text	s **or** strike	**254–258**	
strongly emphasize text	strong	**276–280**	
define a *style* or style sheet	style	**280–281**	**626–627**
specify *subscript* text	sub	**281–284**	
specify *superscript* text	sup	**284–288**	
define an entire *table*	table	**288–293**	**555–576**
define the *table body*	tbody	**293–297**	**565–566**

Continued

If you want to . . .	Use this element	Located on this reference page	Located on this tutorial page
indicate a *table data cell*	td	**297 – 302**	**561 – 562**
define a *table footer*	tfoot	**307 – 310**	**565 – 566**
define a *table header*	thead	**315 – 318**	**565 – 566**
define a *table heading* cell	th	**310 – 315**	**560 – 561**
define a *table row*	tr	**319 – 323**	**560**
specify *teletype* (monospaced) *text*	tt	**324 – 327**	
define a multiline *text* field in a form	textarea	**302 – 306**	**610 – 612**
specify an HTML document *title*	title	**318 – 319**	**520 – 521** **527 – 528**
specify *underlined* text	u	**327 – 331**	
specify an *unordered* (bulleted) *list*	ul	**331 – 335**	**543, 545 – 546**
display text indicating a *variable*	var	**335 – 338**	
insert a *white-space* area	N ⏏ spacer	**271 – 272**	
describe an *XHTML document*	head	**148 – 149**	**527 – 528**
start and end an *XHTML document*	html	**153 – 154**	**517, 581**
indicate *XML content* in an XHTML document	℮ xml	**339 – 340**	

in plain english in p
sh in plain english in
glish in plain english
in plain english in p
sh in plain english in
glish in plain english
in plain english in p
glish in plain english
in plain english in p
sh in plain english in
glish in plain english
in plain english in p
sh in plain english in
glish in plain english
in plain english in p
lish in plain english
in plain english in p
sh in plain english in
glish in plain english
in plain english in p
sh in plain english in
lish in plain english
in plain english in p
glish in plain english

XHTML A to Z

The following table is an alphabetically arranged master list of XHTML elements. This table is composed of three columns:

- The first column lists elements and extensions with which you can perform certain tasks.

- The second column lists the page number in Part I, "XHTML Reference" where you'll find a complete description of the element or extension, its syntax, its attributes, and more.

- The last column lists the page number in Part II, "XHTML Tutorial" where you can learn how to use a particular element or extension.

Element	Located in this reference page	Located in this tutorial page
!	23–24	
!DOCTYPE	24	516
a	24–29	599–604
abbr	29–30	
acronym	31–33	
address	33–37	
applet	37–41	600
area	41–45	523
⏹audioscope	45–46	
b	46–49	521, 617, 619
base	49–50	
basefont	51–52	
bdo	52–56	
☺⏹bgsound	56–57	
big	57–60	
⏹blackface	61	
Ⓝblink	61	
blockquote	61–65	628
body	65–70	528
br	70–72	523
button	72–75	610
caption	76–79	557, 558–559
center	79–83	
cite	83–86	
code	87–89	
col	90–92	565–566
colgroup	92–94	565–566
comment	94	
dd	95–98	542, 549–551
del	98–100	
dfn	101–104	
dir	104–108	
div	108–112	

Continued

XHTML Syntax

This section is the cornerstone of *XHTML in Plain English*. Here you will find detailed information about each element and entity in HTML 4.0 as well as Microsoft, Netscape, and WebTV extensions. Some extensions may be added to the next version of XHTML.

Using This Section

This section is arranged by element. The element heading includes the name of the element and a very brief description, followed by the element's purpose, syntax, and attributes (listed under the "Where" heading). In addition, notes about using the element, and, optionally, a list of related elements are included.

● **NOTE** ─────────────────────────────────

If you need more information about how an element or extension works, be sure to check Part II, "XHTML Tutorial."

The following conventions are used to describe the syntax and attributes of an element:

- Required attributes are listed alphabetically before optional attributes, which are also listed alphabetically. Note that optional attributes are enclosed within [] brackets within the syntax listing.

- If there are {} braces surroundiøng a set of objects, you must choose one of the attributes, values, or punctuation marks within the braces.

- If there are [ ] brackets surrounding a set of objects, you can choose one or more of the attributes, values, or punctuation marks within the brackets.

- A | pipe symbol indicates an OR. You can choose only one of the given attributes or values.

- An ellipsis (...) indicates a continuation of the preceding attribute and that the next attribute is the end of the series.

- If an attribute or value is <u>underlined</u>, it is the default. If you do not specify a different attribute or value, your browser will automatically use the default.

- *Italicized* text represents a variable (such as a file name, path, color, number, URI, and so on) that you enter. Most times, you enclose a variable within double quotes (" ") or single quotes (' '); do not mix double and single quotes.

XHTML Syntax

●—**NOTE**————————————————————————

Appendix E, "Attributes in Depth," which you'll find at www.mandtbooks.com/extras/xhtmlipe describes all attributes in the HTML 4.0 standard, and for Microsoft, Netscape, and WebTV extensions. With each entry, you'll find valid values and usage notes.

For More Information

The following icons are used to identify attributes that are supported exclusively by Microsoft Internet Explorer, Netscape Navigator, or WebTV:

  ⓔ   Indicates that Microsoft Internet Explorer can read and use the element or attribute but most other browsers cannot. Use this element or attribute sparingly or not at all.

  Ⓝ   Indicates that Netscape Navigator can read and use the element or attribute but most other browsers cannot. Use this element or attribute sparingly or not at all.

⌷   Indicates that an element or attribute is unique to WebTV but most browsers do not support it. Use this element or attribute sparingly or not at all.

Any element or attribute not preceded by one of these icons is supported by the XHTML 1.0 recommendation, which sets the standards for XHTML documents. It is best to use XHTML elements rather than extensions in your documents.

●─NOTE

HTML 2.0, which was a major and long-lasting version of HTML, is the base from which the elements in this section start. So, if you see that an element originated in HTML 2.0, the developers of HTML actually might have introduced it in an earlier version of the language.

XHTML Elements

The remainder of this section consists of an alphabetically arranged list of HTML elements along with important information about each.

!	Comment

Purpose
Places a comment in the document.

Syntax
```
<!- comment text ->
```

Where
- *comment text* is the text comprising the comment

Notes
- Comments are an XML standard — not defined by XHTML 1.0 itself.
- Use a comment to document a line or part of an XHTML document. For example, you can state the reason for using one particular element instead of another. Or, for someone who will maintain this document, you can describe how you created a complex table or form. Comments are very useful if one individual creates an XHTML document and another maintains it.
- You can see the comment in the source file but not in the published document.
- You cannot nest a comment within another comment.

Related Element
comment (94)

XHTML Syntax

For More Information

Learn how to use comments on page 528 in Chapter 2.

!DOCTYPE	**Document Declaration**

Purpose

Identifies the type of document.

Syntax

```
<!DOCTYPE html PUBLIC "-//W3C//DTD
    XHTML 1.0 level//lang" "URI">
```

Where

- *lang* is the two-letter HTML DTD language. For example, EN represents English.
- *level* represents one of three DTDs: Strict, Transitional, or Frameset.
- *URI* is the URI of the DTD that contains element, attribute, and entity declarations.

Notes

- This declaration first appeared in HTML 2.0 but is actually an SGML and XML standard. HTML 4.0 and XHTML 1.0 documents use <!DOCTYPE declarations to identify the kind of markup that they contain.
- This element originated in HTML 2.0 but is actually an SGML standard, not part of HTML 4.0.
- The <!DOCTYPE declaration is automatically placed at the top of a new XHTML document created using an HTML editor. This line is not required; however, it is a good idea to include it so that individual users, browser software, validation software, and other programs know that you are using HTML 4.0.
- You can see this comment in the source file but not in the published document.

For More Information

Learn more about the !DOCTYPE declaration on page 516 in Chapter 2.

a	**Hypertext Link**

Purpose

Specifies a link and/or *anchor* (a location to which you can jump either within the current XHTML document or to another XHTML document).

Syntax

```
<a[ accesskey="shortcut_key"]
    [ charset="ISO-8859-1"]["char_set"]
    [ class="class_name"]
```

```
[ contenteditable="edit_string"]
[ coords="coords_1, coords_2, coords_3
[..., coords_n"][ datafld="ds_col_name"]
[ datasrc="ds_identifier"][ dir="ltr"|"rtl"]
[ disabled="disabled"][ href="link_uri"]
[ hreflang="link_lang"][ id="id_name"]
[ lang="lang_code"][ language="javascript"|"jscript"
|"vbs[cript]"][ methods="functions_perf"]
[ name="anchor_name"][ nohref]
[ onbeforecopy="bc_script"]
[ onbeforecut="bt_script"]
[ onbeforeeditfocus="bef_script"]
[ onbeforefocusenter="bfe_script"]
[ onbeforefocusleave="bfl_script"]
[ onbeforepaste="bp_script"][ onblur="bl_script"]
[ onclick="cl_script"][ oncontextmenu="cm_script"]
[ oncontrolselect="ctl_script"][ oncopy="cp_script"]
[ oncut="ct_script"][ ondblclick="dc_script"]
[ ondrag="d_script"][ ondragend="dd_script"]
[ ondragenter="de_script"][ ondragleave="dl_script"]
[ ondragover="do_script"][ ondragstart=ds_script"]
[ ondrop="dr_script"][ onfocus="fc_script"]
[ onfocusenter="fe_script"]
[ onfocusleave="fl_script"][ onhelp="hlp_script"]
[ onkeydown="kd_script"][ onkeypress="kp_script"]
[ onkeyup="ku_script"][ onlosecapture="lc_script"]
[ onmousedown="md_script"]
[ onmouseenter="me_script"]
[ onmouseleave="ml_script"]
[ onmousemove="mm_script"][ onmouseout="mo_script"]
[ onmouseover="mov_script"][ onmouseup="mu_script"]
[ onpaste="p_script"][ onpropertychange="pc_script"]
[ onreadystatechange="rse_script"]
[ onresizeend="ree_script"]
[ onresizestart="res_script"]
[ onselectstart="ss_script"]
[ rel="contents"|"index"|"glossary"|"copyright"
|"next"|"prev[ious]"|"start"|"help"|"bookmark"
|"stylesheet"|"alternate"|"chapter"|"section"
|"subsection"|"appendix"|"same"|"parent"
|"link_type_1"[ "link_type_2"[..."link_type_n"]]]
[ rev="contents"|"index"|"glossary"|"copyright"
|"next"|"prev[ious]"|"start"|"help"|"bookmark"
```

```
|"stylesheet"|"alternate"|"chapter"|"section"
|"subsection"|"appendix"|"same"|"parent"
|"link_type_3"[ "link_type_4"[..."link_type_m"]]]
[ selected="selected"][ shape="rect[angle]"
|"circ[le]"|"poly[gon]"|"def[ault]"]
[ style="name_1: value_1"
[; "name_2: value_2"][...; "name_n: value_n"]]
[ tabindex="position_number"][ target="window"
|"_blank"|"_parent"|"_search"|"_self"|"_top"]
[ title="title"][ type="Internet_Media_Type"]
[ urn="urn"]>anchor</a>
```

Where

- accesskey (Web) assigns a shortcut key to the link to focus on it.
- charset (Web) specifies the character set for the hypertext link.
- class (Web) specifies a class identification for the link.
- ⊖ contenteditable (Web) specifies or obtains a value that indicates whether a user can edit the element content.
- coords (Web) is a list containing the coordinates of a shape.
- ⊖ datafld (Web) specifies the column name from the file that contains the data source object for the link.
- ⊖ datasrc (Web) names the identifier of the data source object for the link.
- dir (Web) specifies the direction in which the link text is displayed: left-to-right or right-to-left.
- ⊖ disabled (Web) is a keyword that prevents a user from using the element.
- href (Web) specifies a URI for the link.
- hreflang (Web) specifies the base language of the href link.
- nohref (Web) indicates that the area does not have a link associated with it.
- id (Web) provides a unique identifier name for the link.
- ⊖ lang (Web) specifies the code for the language used for the link text.
- ⊖ language (Web) declares the scripting language of the current script.
- ⊖ methods (Web) names the functions to be run on the data source object.
- name (Web) is the unique name of the anchor. In XHTML, name is deprecated; use id instead.
- Ⓝ ⊖ onbeforecopy (Web) names a script to run when a user starts copying a selection to the Clipboard but before any action actually takes place.
- ⊖ onbeforecut (Web) names a script to run when a user starts cutting a selection to the Clipboard but before any action actually takes place.
- ⊖ onbeforeeditfocus (Web) names a script to run when a user starts activating an object but before the object actually becomes active.
- ⊖ onbeforefocusenter (Web) names a script to run when a user starts focusing on an object but before the object actually gains focus.

- ☺ onbeforefocusleave (Web) names a script to run when a user starts leaving an object but before the object actually loses focus.
- ☺ onbeforepaste (Web) names a script to run when a user starts pasting an object but before any action actually takes place.
- onblur (Web) names a script to run when the object loses focus.
- onclick (Web) names a script to run when a user moves the mouse pointer or other pointing device over the link and clicks the button.
- ☺ oncontextmenu (Web) names a script to run when a user clicks the right mouse button to open a shortcut menu.
- ☺ oncontrolselect (Web) names a script to run when a user selects a control.
- ☺ oncopy (Web) names a script to run when a user copies a selection to the Clipboard.
- ☺ oncut (Web) names a script to run when a user cuts a selection to the Clipboard.
- ondblclick (Web) names a script to run when a user moves the mouse pointer or other pointing device over the link and double-clicks the button.
- ☺ ondrag (Web) names a script to run when a user drags a selection.
- ☺ ondragend (Web) names a script to run after a user completes a drag-and-drop operation.
- ☺ ondragenter (Web) names a script to run when a user drags a selection into an area in which it can be dropped.
- ☺ ondragleave (Web) names a script to run when a user drags a selection beyond an area in which it can be dropped.
- ☺ ondragover (Web) names a script to run when a user drags a selection over an area in which it can be dropped.
- ☺ ondrop (Web) names a script to run when a user releases the mouse button to drop a dragged selection.
- onfocus (Web) names a script to run when a user points the mouse pointer or other pointing device to focus on the current element.
- ☺ onfocusenter (Web) names a script to run when a user focuses on the current element in any way.
- ☺ onfocusleave (Web) names a script to run when a user inactivates the current element in any way.
- ☺ onhelp (Web) names a script to run when a user presses the F1 or Help key over the current element.
- onkeydown (Web) names a script to run when a user presses and holds down a key over the link.
- onkeypress (Web) names a script to run when a user presses and releases a key over the link.
- onkeyup (Web) names a script to run when a user releases a key that is currently held down over the link.
- ☺ onlosecapture (Web) names a script to run when a user releases a selection that has been captured by the mouse.
- onmousedown (Web) names a script to run when a user moves the mouse pointer or other pointing device over the link and presses and holds down the button.

- ☺ onmouseenter (Web) names a script to run when a user moves the mouse pointer onto the object.
- ☺ onmouseleave (Web) names a script to run when the mouse pointer leaves the object.
- onmousemove (Web) names a script to run when a user moves the mouse pointer or other pointing device over the link.
- onmouseout (Web) names a script to run when a user moves the mouse pointer or other pointing device away from the link.
- onmouseover (Web) names a script to run the first time a user moves the mouse pointer or other pointing device over the link.
- onmouseup (Web) names a script to run when a user moves the mouse pointer or other pointing device over the link and releases a mouse button that is currently held down.
- ☺ onpaste (Web) names a script to run when a user pastes the Clipboard contents onto the object.
- ☺ onpropertychange (Web) names a script to run when a property changes on the selected object in any way.
- ☺ onresizeend (Web) names a script to run after the object has been resized.
- ☺ onresizestart (Web) names a script to run as a user resizes the object.
- ☺ onselectstart (Web) names a script to run when a user starts selecting an object.
- rel (Web) specifies a forward link type from the current link to the target anchor.
- rev (Web) specifies a backward link type from the target anchor to its originating link.
- ☑ selected (Web) is a keyword that indicates that a URI has been selected.
- shape (Web) is the shape of an area within a client-side image-map link.
- style (Web) sets styles for the link.
- tabindex (Web) defines the position of the current element in all the elements that a user can navigate to using a Tab or Shift + Tab key.
- target (Web) loads a linked and named document in a particular window. This attribute is deprecated; use the id attribute instead .
- title (Web) provides a title for the link.
- type (Web) specifies a valid Internet Media Type (that is, MIMETYPE) of the link.
- ☺ urn (Web) names a uniform resource name (URN) for the target document specified with the target attribute.
- anchor is a named location within the document to which you can jump.

Notes

- This inline element originated in the earliest version of HTML.
- Any text or element within the a element becomes a link. If you want to link to a document in the same folder as the current document, there is no need to enter the complete URI. Simply enter the file name (for example, child.html).

- You cannot nest links and anchors within the a element. In XHTML, a cannot contain nested a elements.
- If the link is on the current page, don't use its complete address; doing so tells the browser to reload the page, which is costly in time and resources.
- URIs to which you can link — depending on the browser that you are using — include files on your computer (file), on the World Wide Web (http), at a file transfer protocol (FTP) site (ftp), at a Gopher site (gopher), at a Usenet newsgroup (news), on a WAIS site (wais), or a Telnet connection (telnet).
- When creating a text link, use meaningful words, such as the title of the page or the top-level heading. Do not use "Click here" or even "here." Make a text link part of the text on a page rather than breaking the flow for a reader. All but the newest users can identify a link without being prompted to click.
- The `target` attribute allows a user to visit a target window without leaving your site. For example, a user can click on an advertising icon at your site and return to your site without retyping your URI.
- WebTV supports the following attributes for a: `class`, `href`, `id`, `name`, `onclick`, `onmouseout`, `onmouseover`, `rel`, `selected`, `style`, `target`, and `title`.

Related Element
link (202–204)

For More Information
Learn more about the a element on page 599 in Chapter 6.

| abbr | Abbreviation |

Purpose
Indicates an abbreviation.

Syntax
```
<abbr[ class="class_name"][ dir="ltr"|"rtl"]
  [ id="id_name"][ lang="lang_code"]
  [ onclick="cl_script"][ ondblclick="dc_script"]
  [ onkeydown="kd_script"][ onkeypress="kp_script"]
  [ onkeyup="ku_script"][ onmousedown="md_script"]
  [ onmousemove="mm_script"][ onmouseout="mo_script"]
  [ onmouseover="mov_script"][ onmouseup="mu_script"]
  [ style="name_1: value_1"[; "name_2: value_2"]
  [...; "name_n: value_n"]][ title="title"]>abbr_text</abbr>
```

Where
- `class` (Web) specifies a class identification for the abbreviation.

- dir (Web) specifies the direction in which the abbreviation text is displayed: left-to-right or right-to-left.
- id (Web) provides a unique identifier name for the abbreviation.
- lang (Web) specifies the code for the language used for the abbreviation.
- onclick (Web) names a script to run when a user moves the mouse pointer or other pointing device over the abbreviation and clicks the button.
- ondblclick (Web) names a script to run when a user moves the mouse pointer or other pointing device over the abbreviation and double-clicks the button.
- onkeydown (Web) names a script to run when a user presses and holds down a key over the abbreviation.
- onkeypress (Web) names a script to run when a user presses and releases a key over the abbreviation.
- onkeyup (Web) names a script to run when a user releases a key that is currently held down over the abbreviation.
- onmousedown (Web) names a script to run when a user moves the mouse pointer or other pointing device over the abbreviation and presses and holds down the button.
- onmousemove (Web) names a script to run when a user moves the mouse pointer or other pointing device over the abbreviation.
- onmouseout (Web) names a script to run when a user moves the mouse pointer or other pointing device away from the abbreviation.
- onmouseover (Web) names a script to run the first time a user moves the mouse pointer or other pointing device over the abbreviation.
- onmouseup (Web) names a script to run when a user moves the mouse pointer or other pointing device over the abbreviation and releases a mouse button that is currently held down.
- style (Web) sets styles for the abbreviation.
- title (Web) provides a title for the abbreviation.
- *abbr_text* is abbreviation text.

Notes

- This inline element originated in HTML 4.0.
- abbr is one of the elements in the %phrase entity. The other %phrase elements are acronym, cite, code, dfn, em, kbd, samp, strong, and var.
- Do not confuse abbreviations (abbr) with acronyms (acronym). According to the *Random House Dictionary of the English Language*, an abbreviation is "a shortened or contracted form of a word or phrase," and an acronym is "a word formed from the initial letters or groups of letters of words in a set phrase."

Related Elements

acronym (31), cite (83), code (87), dfn (101), kbd (186), samp (258), tt (324), var (335)

acronym	Acronym

Purpose

Indicates an acronym, such as FBI, CIA, FTP, URI, WWW, and so on.

Syntax

```
<acronym[ accesskey="shortcut_key"]
  [ class="class_name"]
  [ contenteditable="edit_string"]
  [ dir="ltr"|"rtl"][ disabled="disabled"]
  [ id="id_name"][ lang="lang_code"]
  [ language="javascript"|"jscript"|"vbs[cript]"]
  [ onbeforefocusenter="bfe_script"]
  [ onbeforefocusleave="bfl_script"]
  [ onblur="bl_script"][ onclick="cl_script"]
  [ oncontrolselect="ctl_script"]
  [ ondblclick="dc_script"][ ondrag="d_script"]
  [ ondragend="dd_script"][ ondragenter="de_script"]
  [ ondragleave="dl_script"][ ondragover="do_script"]
  [ ondragstart="ds_script"][ ondrop="dr_script"]
  [ onfocus="fc_script"][ onfocusenter="fe_script"]
  [ onfocusleave="fl_script"][ onkeydown="kd_script"]
  [ onkeypress="kp_script"][ onkeyup="ku_script"]
  [ onmousedown="md_script"]
  [ onmouseenter="me_script"]
  [ onmouseleave="ml_script"]
  [ onmousemove="mm_script"][ onmouseout="mo_script"]
  [ onmouseover="mov_script"][ onmouseup="mu_script"]
  [ onreadystatechange="rsc_script"]
  [ onresizeend="ree_script"]
  [ onresizestart="res_script"]
  [ onselectstart="ss_script"]
  [ style="name_1: value_1"[; "name_2: value_2"]
  [...; "name_n: value_n"]]
  [ tabindex="position_number"]
  [ title="title"]>acronym_text</acronym>
```

Where

- class (Web) specifies a class identification for the acronym.
- dir (Web) specifies the direction in which the acronym text is displayed: left-to-right or right-to-left.
- id (Web) provides a unique identifier name for the acronym.
- lang (Web) specifies the code for the language used for the acronym.

- ⊖ onbeforefocusenter (Web) names a script to run when a user starts focusing on an object but before the object actually gains focus.
- ⊖ onbeforefocusleave (Web) names a script to run when a user starts leaving an object but before the object actually loses focus.
- ⊖ onblur (Web) specifies that the referred-to script runs when the acronym loses focus (that is, it is no longer the active element).
- onclick (Web) names a script to run when a user moves the mouse pointer or other pointing device over the acronym and clicks the button.
- ⊖ oncontrolselect (Web) names a script to run when a user selects a control.
- ondblclick (Web) names a script to run when a user moves the mouse pointer or other pointing device over the acronym and double-clicks the button.
- ⊖ ondrag (Web) names a script to run when a user drags a selection.
- ⊖ ondragend (Web) names a script to run after a user completes a drag-and-drop operation.
- ⊖ ondragenter (Web) names a script to run when a user drags a selection into an area in which it can be dropped.
- ⊖ ondragleave (Web) names a script to run when a user drags a selection beyond an area in which it can be dropped.
- ⊖ ondragover (Web) names a script to run when a user drags a selection over an area in which it can be dropped.
- ⊖ ondragstart (Web) names a script to run when a user starts dragging a selection or element.
- ⊖ ondrop (Web) names a script to run when a user releases the mouse button to drop a dragged selection.
- ⊖ onfocus (Web) names a script to run when a user points the mouse pointer or other pointing device to focus on the current element.
- ⊖ onfocusenter (Web) names a script to run when a user focuses on the current element in any way.
- ⊖ onfocusleave (Web) names a script to run when a user inactivates the current element in any way.
- onkeydown (Web) names a script to run when a user presses and holds down a key over the acronym.
- onkeypress (Web) names a script to run when a user presses and releases a key over the acronym.
- onkeyup (Web) names a script to run when a user releases a key that is currently held down over the acronym.
- onmousedown (Web) names a script to run when a user moves the mouse pointer or other pointing device over the acronym and presses and holds down the button.
- ⊖ onmouseenter (Web) names a script to run when a user moves the mouse pointer onto the object.
- ⊖ onmouseleave (Web) names a script to run when the mouse pointer leaves the object.
- onmousemove (Web) names a script to run when a user moves the mouse pointer or other pointing device over the acronym.

- onmouseout (Web) names a script to run when a user moves the mouse pointer or other pointing device away from the acronym.
- onmouseover (Web) names a script to run the first time a user moves the mouse pointer or other pointing device over the acronym.
- onmouseup (Web) names a script to run when a user moves the mouse pointer or other pointing device over the acronym and releases a mouse button that is currently held down.
- ⊖ onreadystatechange (Web) names a script to run when the status of an element has changed (for example, the element receives data).
- ⊖ onresizeend (Web) names a script to run after the object has been resized.
- ⊖ onresizestart (Web) names a script to run as a user resizes the object.
- ⊖ onselectstart (Web) names a script to run when a user starts selecting an object.
- style (Web) sets styles for the acronym.
- ⊖ tabindex (Web) defines the position of the current element in all the elements that a user can navigate to using a Tab or Shift + Tab key.
- title (Web) provides a title for the acronym.
- acronym_text is the acronym.

Note

- This inline element originated in HTML 4.0.
- acronym is one of the elements in the %phrase entity. The other %phrase elements are abbr, cite, code, dfn, em, kbd, samp, strong, and var.
- Do not confuse acronyms (acronym) with abbreviations (abbr). According to the *Random House Dictionary of the English Language*, an acronym is "a word formed from the initial letters or groups of letters of words in a set phrase," and an abbreviation is "a shortened or contracted form of a word or phrase."

Related Elements

abbr (29), cite (83), code (87), dfn (101), em (120), kbd (186), samp (258), strong (276), tt (324), var (335)

address   Address

Purpose

Shows address information, usually e-mail addresses.

Syntax

```
<address[ accesskey="shortcut_key"]
  [ class="class_name"]
  [ contenteditable="edit_string"][ dir="ltr"|"rtl"]
```

```
[ disabled="disabled"][ id="id_name"]
[ lang="lang_code"][ language="javascript"|"jscript"
|"vbs[cript]"][ onbeforecopy="bc_script"]
[ onbeforecut="bt_script"]
[ onbeforefocusenter="bfe_script"]
[ onbeforefocusleave="bfl_script"]
[ onbeforepaste="bp_script"][ onblur="bl_script"]
[ onclick="cl_script"][ oncontextmenu="cm_script"]
[ oncontrolselect="ctl_script"][ oncopy="cp_script"]
[ oncut="ct_script"][ ondblclick="dc_script"]
[ ondrag="d_script"][ ondragend="dd_script"]
[ ondragenter="de_script"][ ondragleave="dl_script"]
[ ondragover="do_script"][ ondragstart="ds_script"]
[ ondrop="dr_script"][ onfocus="fc_script"]
[ onfocusenter="fe_script"]
[ onfocusleave="fl_script"]
[ onhelp="hlp_script"][ onkeydown="kd_script"]
[ onkeypress="kp_script"][ onkeyup="ku_script"]
[ onlosecapture="lc_script"]
[ onmousedown="md_script"]
[ onmouseenter="me_script"]
[ onmouseleave="ml_script"]
[ onmousemove="mm_script"][ onmouseout="mo_script"]
[ onmouseover="mov_script"][ onmouseup="mu_script"]
[ onpaste="p_script"][ onpropertychange="pc_script"]
[ onreadystatechange="rsc_script"]
[ onresize="rsz_script"][ onresizeend="ree_script"]
[ onresizestart="res_script"]
[ onselectstart="ss_script"]
[ style="name_1: value_1"[; "name_2: value_2"]
[...; "name_n: value_n"]]
[ tabindex="position_number"][ title="title"]>
text</address>
```

Where

- class (Web) specifies a class identification for the address.
- dir (Web) specifies the direction in which the address text is displayed: left-to-right or right-to-left.
- id (Web) provides a unique identifier name for the address.
- lang (Web) specifies the code for the language used for the address.
- ⊖ language (Web) declares the scripting language of the current script.
- ⊖ onbeforecopy (Web) names a script to run when a user starts copying a selection to the Clipboard but before any action actually takes place.

- ⊖ onbeforecut (Web) names a script to run when a user starts cutting a selection to the Clipboard but before any action actually takes place.
- ⊖ onbeforefocusenter (Web) names a script to run when a user starts focusing on an object but before the object actually gains focus.
- ⊖ onbeforefocusleave (Web) names a script to run when a user starts leaving an object but before the object actually loses focus.
- ⊖ onbeforepaste (Web) names a script to run when a user starts pasting an object but before any action actually takes place.
- ⊖ onblur (Web) names a script to run when the address loses focus (that is, it is no longer the active element).
- onclick (Web) names a script to run when a user moves the mouse pointer or other pointing device over the address and clicks the button.
- ⊖ oncontextmenu (Web) names a script to run when a user right-clicks the mouse to open a shortcut menu.
- ⊖ oncontrolselect (Web) names a script to run when a user selects a control.
- ⊖ oncopy (Web) names a script to run when a user copies a selection to the Clipboard.
- ⊖ oncut (Web) names a script to run when a user cuts a selection to the Clipboard.
- ondblclick (Web) names a script to run when a user moves the mouse pointer or other pointing device over the address and double-clicks the button.
- ⊖ ondrag (Web) names a script to run when a user drags a selection.
- ⊖ ondragend (Web) names a script to run after a user completes a drag-and-drop operation.
- ⊖ ondragenter (Web) names a script to run when a user drags a selection into an area in which it can be dropped.
- ⊖ ondragleave (Web) names a script to run when a user drags a selection beyond an area in which it can be dropped.
- ⊖ ondragover (Web) names a script to run when a user drags a selection over an area in which it can be dropped.
- ⊖ ondragstart (Web) names a script to run when a user starts dragging a selection or element.
- ⊖ ondrop (Web) names a script to run when a user releases the mouse button to drop a dragged selection.
- ⊖ onfocus (Web) names a script to run when a user points the mouse pointer or other pointing device to focus on the current element.
- ⊖ onfocusenter (Web) names a script to run when a user focuses on the current element in any way.
- ⊖ onfocusleave (Web) names a script to run when a user inactivates the current element in any way.
- ⊖ onhelp (Web) names a script to run when a user presses the F1 or Help key over the address.
- onkeydown (Web) names a script to run when a user presses and holds down a key over the address.

XHTML Syntax

- onkeypress (Web) names a script to run when a user presses and releases a key over the address.
- onkeyup (Web) names a script to run when a user releases a key that is currently held down over the address.
- ⊖ onlosecapture (Web) names a script to run when a user release a selection that has been captured by the mouse.
- onmousedown (Web) names a script to run when a user moves the mouse pointer or other pointing device over the address and presses and holds down the button.
- ⊖ onmouseenter (Web) names a script to run when a user moves the mouse pointer onto the object.
- ⊖ onmouseleave (Web) names a script to run when the mouse pointer leaves the object.
- onmousemove (Web) names a script to run when a user moves the mouse pointer or other pointing device over the address.
- onmouseout (Web) names a script to run when a user moves the mouse pointer or other pointing device away from the address.
- onmouseover (Web) names a script to run the first time a user moves the mouse pointer or other pointing device over the address.
- onmouseup (Web) names a script to run when a user moves the mouse pointer or other pointing device over the address and releases a mouse button that is currently held down.
- ⊖ onpaste (Web) names a script to run when a user pastes the Clipboard contents onto the object.
- ⊖ onpropertychange (Web) names a script to run when a property changes on the selected object in any way.
- ⊖ onreadystatechange (Web) names a script to run when the status of an element has changed (for example, the element receives data).
- ⊖ onresize (Web) names a script to run when a user resizes the selected object.
- ⊖ onresizeend (Web) names a script to run after the object has been resized.
- ⊖ onresizestart (Web) names a script to run as a user resizes the object.
- ⊖ onselectstart (Web) names a script to run when a user starts selecting an object.
- style (Web) sets styles for the address.
- ⊖ tabindex (Web) defines the position of the current element in all the elements that a user can navigate to using a Tab or Shift + Tab key.
- title (Web) provides a title for the address.
- text represents one or more characters.

Notes

- This inline element originated in HTML 2.0.
- The HTML 4.0 DTD categorizes address as an inline element. However, the cascading style sheet specification categorizes address as a block-level element.

- For the address element, WebTV supports the class attribute.

Related Elements

acronym (31), b (46), cite (83), code (87), dfn (101), em (120),
i (154), kbd (186), pre (242), samp (258), strong (276), tt (324),
var (335)

---

applet   Applet

Purpose

Indicates a Java applet that is embedded in the current document.

Syntax

```
<applet height="height_pix"|height_%
    width="width_pix"|width_%
    [ accesskey="shortcut_key" ]
    [ align="bottom"|"middle"|"top"|"left"|"right"
    |"absmiddle"|"absbottom"|"texttop"|"baseline"
    |"center" ][ alt="alternate_name" ]
    [ archive="preload_archive_1[, preload_archive_2
    [..., preload_archive_n" ][ class="class_name" ]
    [ code="subclass_resource_uri" ]
    [ codebase="base_uri" ]
    [ contenteditable="edit_string" ]
    [ datafld="ds_col_name" ]
    [ datasrc="ds_identifier" ][ disabled="disabled" ]
    [ hspace="horiz_pix ]
    [ id="id_name" ][ lang="lang_code" ]
    [ language="javascript"|"jscript"|"vbs[cript]" ]
    [ mayscript ][ name="applet_name" ]
    [ object="serial_resource" ]
    [ onbeforecut="bt_script" ]
    [ onbeforeeditfocus="bef_script" ]
    [ onbeforefocusenter="bfe_script" ]
    [ onbeforefocusleave="bfl_script" ]
    [ onbeforepaste="bp_script" ][ onblur="bl_script" ]
    [ oncellchange="cc_script" ][ onclick="cl_script" ]
    [ oncontextmenu="cm_script" ]
    [ oncontrolselect="ctl_script" ]
    [ oncut="ct_script" ][ ondataavailable="da_script" ]
    [ ondatasetchanged="dsc_script" ]
    [ ondatasetcomplete="dsf_script" ]
```

XHTML Syntax

```
[ ondblclick="dc_script"][ onfocus="fc_script"]
[ onfocusenter="fe_script"]
[ onfocusleave="fl_script"]
[ onhelp="hlp_script"][ onkeydown="kd_script"]
[ onkeypress="kp_script"][ onkeyup="ku_script"]
[ onload="ol_script"][ onlosecapture="lc_script"]
[ onmousedown="md_script"]
[ onmouseenter="me_script"]
[ onmouseleave="ml_script"]
[ onmousemove="mm_script"][ onmouseout="mo_script"]
[ onmouseover="mov_script"][ onmouseup="mu_script"]
[ onpaste="p_script"][ onpropertychange="pc_script"]
[ onreadystatechange="rsc_script"]
[ onresize="rsz_script"][ onresizeend="ree_script"]
[ onresizestart="res_script"]
[ onrowenter="re_script"][ onrowexit="rex_script"]
[ onrowsdelete="rd_script"]
[ onrowsinserted="rn_script"]
[ onscroll="sc_script"][ src="object_uri"]
[ style="name_1: value_1"[; "name_2: value_2"]
[...; "name_n: value_n"]]
[ tabindex="position_number"][ title="title_text"]
[ vspace="vert_pix"]>applet</applet>
```

Where

- height (Web) specifies the height, in pixels, of the window in which the applet will run.
- width (Web) specifies the width, in pixels, of the window in which the applet will run.
- ⊕ accesskey (Web) assigns a shortcut key to the object in order to focus on it.
- align (Web) aligns the applet window with the surrounding area of the XHTML document.
- alt (Web) specifies alternate text that will replace the Java applet if the browser does not support Java applets. Some browsers display alternate text as a tool tip.
- archive (Web) names archives containing resources that will be loaded before the applet runs.
- class (Web) specifies a class identification for the element.
- code (Web) names the resource containing the compiled applet subclass for the applet.
- codebase (Web) specifies the base URI of the applet.
- ⊕ contenteditable (Web) specifies or obtains a value that indicates whether a user can edit the element content.

XHTML Syntax

- ⊖ dataf ld (Web) specifies the column name from the file that contains the data source object.
- ⊖ datasrc (Web) specifies the identifier of the data source object.
- ⊖ disabled (Web) is a keyword that prevents a user from using the element.
- hspace (Web) specifies a horizontal gutter, in pixels, between the left margin of the page and the left margin of the applet window.
- id (Web) provides a unique identifier name for the element.
- ⊖ lang (Web) specifies the code representing the language used for the element.
- ⊖ language (Web) declares the scripting language of the current script.
- Ⓝ mayscript (Web) allows the applet to access JavaScript.
- name (Web) names the current applet. In XHTML, name is deprecated; use id instead.
- object (Web) names the resource containing a serialized version of the current applet.
- ⊖ onblur (Web) names a script to run when the applet loses focus (that is, it is no longer the active element).
- ⊖ onclick (Web) names a script to run when a user moves the mouse pointer or other pointing device over the applet and clicks the device button.
- ⊖ ondatasetchanged (Web) names a script to run when a user changes a data set from the data resource.
- ⊖ ondatasetcomplete (Web) names a script to run when all data has been received from the data resource.
- ⊖ ondblclick (Web) names a script to run when a user moves the mouse pointer or other pointing device over the applet and double-clicks the device button.
- ⊖ ondragstart (Web) names a script to run when a user starts dragging a selection or element.
- ⊖ onfocus (Web) names a script to run when a user points the mouse pointer or other pointing device to focus on the current element.
- ⊖ onhelp (Web) names a script to run when a user presses the F1 or Help key over the current element.
- ⊖ onkeydown (Web) names a script to run when a user presses and holds down a key over the applet.
- ⊖ onkeypress (Web) names a script to run when a user presses and releases a key over the applet.
- ⊖ onkeyup (Web) names a script to run when a user releases a key that is currently held down over the applet.
- ⊖ onload (Web) names a script to run after the active browser has finished loading the applet.
- ⊖ onmousedown (Web) names a script to run when a user moves the mouse pointer or other pointing device over the applet and presses and holds down the device button.
- ⊖ onmouseenter (Web) names a script to run when a user moves the mouse pointer onto the object.

- ⊖ onmouseleave (Web) names a script to run when the mouse pointer leaves the object.
- ⊖ onmousemove (Web) names a script to run when a user moves the mouse pointer or other pointing device over the applet.
- ⊖ onmouseout (Web) names a script to run when a user moves the mouse pointer or other pointing device away from the applet.
- ⊖ onmouseover (Web) names a script to run the first time a user moves the mouse pointer or other pointing device over the applet.
- ⊖ onmouseup (Web) names a script to run when a user moves the mouse pointer or other pointing device over the applet and releases a pressed-down device button.
- ⊖ onpaste (Web) names a script to run when a user pastes the Clipboard contents onto the object.
- ⊖ onpropertychange (Web) names a script to run when a property changes on the selected object in any way.
- ⊖ onreadystatechange (Web) names a script to run when the status of an element has changed (for example, the element receives data).
- ⊖ onresize (Web) names a script to run when a user resizes the selected object.
- ⊖ onresizeend (Web) names a script to run after the object has been resized.
- ⊖ onresizestart (Web) names a script to run as a user resizes the object.
- ⊖ onrowenter (Web) names a script to run after the data in the current row has changed.
- ⊖ onrowexit (Web) names a script to run as a data source attempts to load data into the current row.
- ⊖ onrowsdelete (Web) names a script to run when a user starts to delete one or more rows from a set of records but before the deletion actually takes place.
- ⊖ onrowsinserted (Web) names a script to run when a user inserts one or more rows in the current set of records.
- ⊖ onscroll (Web) names a script to run when a user moves the scroll box within the scroll bar.
- ⊖ src (Web) specifies an object, such as a sound or video file, embedded in the current page.
- style (Web) sets styles for the element.
- ⊖ tabindex (Web) defines the position of the current element in all the elements that a user can navigate to using a Tab or Shift + Tab key.
- title (Web) inserts title information about the applet.
- vspace (Web) is the vertical area, in pixels, between the top margin of the page and the top margin of the applet window.
- *applet* represents a Java applet.

Notes

- This inline element originated in HTML 3.2.

- Although `applet` is supported by HTML 4.0, it has been deprecated (that is, it will eventually be obsolete). So, `applet` does not appear in the Strict DTD. Use the `object` element instead.
- The `param` element is a child element of `applet`.

Related Elements
`area` (41), `img` (162), `map` (205), `noscript` (224), `object` (225), `param` (241), `script` (262)

For More Information
Learn more about the `applet` element on page 600 in Chapter 6.

area   Area

Purpose
Defines coordinates, actions, and shapes of clickable areas within client-side image maps.

Syntax
```
<area alt="alternate_name"[ accesskey="shortcut_key"]
  [ class="class_name"]
  [ contenteditable="edit_string"]
  [ coords="coords_1, coords_2,
  coords_3[..., coords_n]"][ dir="ltr"|"rtl"]
  [ disabled="disabled"][ href="link_uri"]
  [ id="id_name"][ lang="lang_code"]
  [ language="javascript"|"jscript"|"vbs[cript]"]
  [ name="map_name"][ nohref][ notab]
  [ onbeforecopy="bc_script"]
  [ onbeforecut="bt_script"]
  [ onbeforeeditfocus="bef_script"]
  [ onbeforefocusenter="bfe_script"]
  [ onbeforefocusleave="bfl_script"]
  [ onbeforepaste="bp_script"][ onblur="bl_script"]
  [ onclick="cl_script"][ oncontextmenu="cm_script"]
  [ oncontrolselect="ctl_script"][ oncopy="cp_script"]
  [ oncut="ct_script"][ ondblclick="dc_script"]
  [ ondrag="d_script"][ ondragend="dd_script"]
  [ ondragenter="de_script"][ ondragleave="dl_script"]
  [ ondragover="do_script"][ ondragstart="ds_script"]
  [ ondrop="dr_script"][ onfocus="fc_script"]
  [ onfocusenter="fe_script"]
  [ onfocusleave="fl_script"][ onhelp="hlp_script"]
  [ onkeydown="kd_script"][ onkeypress="kp_script"]
```

XHTML Syntax

```
[ onkeyup="ku_script"][ onlosecapture="lc_script"]
[ onmousedown="md_script"]
[ onmouseenter="me_script"]
[ onmouseleave="ml_script"]
[ onmousemove="mm_script"][ onmouseout=mo_script]
[ onmouseover=mov_script] [ onmouseup="mu_script"]
[ onpaste="p_script"][ onpropertychange="pc_script"]
[ onreadystatechange="rsc_script"]
[ onresizeend="ree_script"]
[ onresizestart="res_script"]
[ onselectstart="ss_script"]
[ shape="rect[angle]"|"circ[le]"|"poly[gon]"
|"def[ault]"][ style="name_1: value_1"
[; "name_2: value_2"][...; "name_n: value_n"]]
[ tabindex="position_number"][ target="window"
|"_blank"|"_parent"|"_search"|"_self"|"_top"]
[ title="title_text"]>image_map{ /></area>}
```

Where

- alt (Web) describes the image for text-only browsers, temporarily describes an image as it loads, or displays a tool tip.
- accesskey (Web) assigns a shortcut key to the element in order to focus on it.
- class (Web) specifies a class identification for the area.
- ⊖ contenteditable (Web) specifies or obtains a value that indicates whether a user can edit the element content.
- coords (Web) is a list containing the coordinates of a shape.
- ⊖ dir (Web) specifies the direction in which the current text is displayed: left-to-right or right-to-left.
- ⊖ disabled (Web) is a keyword that prevents a user from using the element.
- href (Web) specifies a URI for a link.
- id (Web) provides a unique identifier name for the element.
- lang (Web) specifies the code representing the language used for the element.
- ⊖ language (Web) declares the scripting language of the current script.
- Ⓝ name (Web) labels the current area.
- nohref (Web) is a keyword that specifies that the area does not have a link associated with it.
- ⊖ onbeforecopy (Web) names a script to run when a user starts copying a selection to the Clipboard but before any action actually takes place.
- ⊖ onbeforecut (Web) names a script to run when a user starts cutting a selection to the Clipboard but before any action actually takes place when a user starts cutting a selection to the Clipboard but before any action actually takes place.

- ⊖ onbeforeeditfocus (Web) names a script to run when a user starts activating an object but before the object actually becomes active when a user starts activating an object but before the object actually becomes active.
- ⊖ onbeforefocusenter (Web) names a script to run when a user starts focusing on an object but before the object actually gains focus.
- ⊖ onbeforefocusleave (Web) names a script to run when a user starts leaving an object but before the object actually loses focus.
- ⊖ onbeforepaste (Web) names a script to run when a user starts pasting an object but before any action actually takes place.
- onblur (Web) names a script to run when the area loses focus (that is, it is no longer the active element).
- onclick (Web) names a script to run when a user moves the mouse pointer or other pointing device over the area and clicks the device button.
- ⊖ oncontextmenu (Web) names a script to run when a user clicks the right mouse button to open a shortcut menu.
- ⊖ oncontrolselect (Web) names a script to run when a user selects a control.
- ⊖ oncopy (Web) names a script to run when a user copies a selection to the Clipboard.
- ⊖ oncut (Web) names a script to run when a user cuts a selection to the Clipboard.
- ondblclick (Web) names a script to run when a user moves the mouse pointer or other pointing device over the area and double-clicks the device button.
- ⊖ ondrag (Web) names a script to run when a user drags a selection.
- ⊖ ondragend (Web) names a script to run after a user completes a drag-and-drop operation.
- ⊖ ondragenter (Web) names a script to run when a user drags a selection into an area in which it can be dropped.
- ⊖ ondragleave (Web) names a script to run when a user drags a selection beyond an area in which it can be dropped.
- ⊖ ondragover (Web) names a script to run when a user drags a selection over an area in which it can be dropped.
- ⊖ ondragstart (Web) names a script to run when a user starts dragging a selection or element.
- ⊖ ondrop (Web) names a script to run when a user releases the mouse button to drop a dragged selection.
- onfocus (Web) names a script to run when a user points the mouse pointer or other pointing device to focus on the current element.
- ⊖ onfocusenter (Web) names a script to run when a user focuses on the current element in any way.
- ⊖ onfocusleave (Web) names a script to run when a user inactivates the current element in any way.
- ⊖ onhelp (Web) names a script to run when a user presses the F1 or Help key over the current element.

- onkeydown (Web) names a script to run when a user presses and holds down a key over the area.
- onkeypress (Web) names a script to run when a user presses and releases a key over the area.
- onkeyup (Web) names a script to run when a user releases a key that is currently held down over the area.
- ☺ onlosecapture (Web) names a script to run when a user releases a selection that has been captured by the mouse.
- onmousedown (Web) names a script to run when a user moves the mouse pointer or other pointing device over the area and presses and holds down the device button.
- ☺ onmouseenter (Web) names a script to run when a user moves the mouse pointer onto the object.
- ☺ onmouseleave (Web) names a script to run when the mouse pointer leaves the object.
- onmousemove (Web) names a script to run when a user moves the mouse pointer or other pointing device over the area.
- onmouseout (Web) names a script to run when a user moves the mouse pointer or other pointing device away from the object.
- onmouseover (Web) names a script to run the first time a user moves the mouse pointer or other pointing device over the object.
- onmouseup (Web) names a script to run when a user moves the mouse pointer or other pointing device over the area and releases a pressed-down device button.
- ☺ onpaste (Web) names a script to run when a user pastes the Clipboard contents onto the object.
- ☺ onpropertychange (Web) names a script to run when a property changes on the selected object in any way.
- ☺ onreadystatechange (Web) names a script to run when the status of an element has changed (for example, the element receives data).
- ☺ onresizeend (Web) names a script to run after the object has been resized.
- ☺ onresizestart (Web) names a script to run as a user resizes the object.
- ☺ onselectstart (Web) names a script to run when a user starts selecting an object.
- shape (Web) is the shape of the area.
- style (Web) sets styles for the area.
- tabindex (Web) defines the position of the current element in all the elements that a user can navigate to using a Tab or Shift + Tab key.
- target (Web) loads a linked and named document in a particular window. This attribute is deprecated; use id instead.
- title (Web) inserts a balloon help title.
- *image_map* is the image map defined by the current **area** element.

Notes

- This element originated in HTML 3.2.
- area is an empty element.
- area is a child element of the map element.
- Most maps contain multiple area statements.
- You can mix the content of an area element with the content of block-level elements.
- WebTV supports the following attributes for area: coords, href, id, name, nohref, onmouseout, onmouseover, shape, and target.

Related Elements

img (162), map (205), object (225)

For More Information

Learn more about the area element on page 523 in Chapter 2.

▣ audioscope   Audioscope

Purpose

Creates an audioscope, which shows the amplitude of the current sound for the left and right channels.

Syntax

```
<audioscope[ align="absbottom"|"absmiddle"|"baseline"
 |"bottom"|"left"|"middle"|"right"|"texttop"|"top"]
 [ border="border_pix"][ gain="gain_multiplier"]
 [ height="height_pix"][ leftcolor="#rrggbb"|"color"]
 [ leftoffset="l_offset"][ maxlevel="1"]
 [ rightcolor="#rrggbb"|"color"]
 [ rightoffset="r_offset"][ width="width_pix"]
 { /></audioscope>}
```

Where

- ▣ align (Web) horizontally or vertically aligns the audioscope with the adjacent text.
- ▣ border (Web) sets the width, in pixels, of the object.
- ▣ gain (Web) sets the gain value for the amplitude.
- ▣ height (Web) specifies the height, in pixels, of the audioscope.
- ▣ leftcolor (Web) is the color given to the line of the left audio channel.
- ▣ leftoffset (Web) sets the vertical offset of the left audio channel.
- ▣ maxlevel (Web) enables lines that indicate the minimum and maximum levels of the audioscope waveform.
- ▣ rightcolor (Web) is the color given to the line of the right audio channel.
- ▣ rightoffset (Web) sets the vertical offset of the right audio channel.
- ▣ width (Web) specifies the width, in pixels, of the audioscope.

Note

audioscope animates the sounds played in a WebTV document.

---

b   **Bold**

Purpose

Applies boldface to selected text.

Syntax

```
<b[ accesskey="shortcut_key"][ class="class_name"]
   [ contenteditable="edit_string"][ dir="ltr"|"rtl"]
   [ disabled="disabled"][ id="id_name"]
   [ lang="lang_code"][ language="javascript"|"jscript"
   |"vbs[cript]"][ onbeforecopy="bc_script"]
   [ onbeforecut="bt_script"]
   [ onbeforefocusenter="bfe_script"]
   [ onbeforefocusleave="bfl_script"]
   [ onbeforepaste="bp_script"][ onblur="bl_script"]
   [ onclick="cl_script"][ oncontextmenu="cm_script"]
   [ oncontrolselect="ctl_script"][ oncopy="cp_script"]
   [ oncut="ct_script"][ ondblclick="dc_script"]
   [ ondrag="d_script"][ ondragend="dd_script"]
   [ ondragenter="de_script"][ ondragleave="dl_script"]
   [ ondragover="do_script"][ ondragstart="ds_script"]
   [ ondrop="dr_script"][ onfocus="fc_script"]
   [ onfocusenter="fe_script"]
   [ onfocusleave="fl_script"][ onhelp="hlp_script"]
   [ onkeydown="kd_script"][ onkeypress="kp_script"]
   [ onkeyup="ku_script"][ onlosecapture="lc_script"]
   [ onmousedown="md_script"]
   [ onmouseenter="me_script"]
   [ onmouseleave="ml_script"]
   [ onmousemove="mm_script"][ onmouseout="mo_script"]
   [ onmouseover="mov_script"][ onmouseup="mu_script"]
   [ onpaste="p_script"][ onpropertychange="pc_script"]
   [ onreadystatechange="rsc_script"]
   [ onresize="rsz_script"][ onresizeend="ree_script"]
   [ onresizestart="res_script"]
   [ onselectstart="ss_script"]
   [ style="name_1: value_1"[; "name_2: value_2"]
```

```
[...; "name_n: value_n"]]
[ tabindex="position_number"][ title="title"]>
text</b>
```

Where

- ⊖ `accesskey` (Web) assigns a shortcut key to the object in order to focus on it.
- `class` (Web) specifies a class identification for the current text.
- ⊖ `contenteditable` (Web) specifies or obtains a value that indicates whether a user can edit the element content.
- `dir` (Web) specifies the direction in which the current text is displayed: left-to-right or right-to-left.
- ⊖ `disabled` (Web) is a keyword that prevents a user from using the element.
- `id` (Web) provides a unique identifier name for the current text.
- `lang` (Web) specifies the code for the language used for the current text.
- ⊖ `language` (Web) declares the scripting language of the current script.
- ⊖ `onbeforecopy` (Web) names a script to run when a user starts copying a selection to the Clipboard but before any action actually takes place.
- ⊖ `onbeforecut` (Web) names a script to run when a user starts cutting a selection to the Clipboard but before any action actually takes place.
- ⊖ `onbeforefocusenter` (Web) names a script to run when a user starts focusing on an object but before the object actually gains focus.
- ⊖ `onbeforefocusleave` (Web) names a script to run when a user starts leaving an object but before the object actually loses focus.
- ⊖ `onbeforepaste` (Web) names a script to run when a user starts pasting an object but before any action actually takes place.
- ⊖ `onblur` (Web) names a script to run when the element loses focus (that is, it is no longer the active element).
- `onclick` (Web) names a script to run when a user moves the mouse pointer or other pointing device over the boldface text and clicks the button.
- ⊖ `oncontextmenu` (Web) names a script to run when a user right-clicks the mouse to open a shortcut menu.
- ⊖ `oncontrolselect` (Web) names a script to run when a user selects a control.
- ⊖ `oncopy` (Web) names a script to run when a user copies a selection to the Clipboard.
- ⊖ `oncut` (Web) names a script to run when a user cuts a selection to the Clipboard.
- `ondblclick` (Web) names a script to run when a user moves the mouse pointer or other pointing device over the boldface text and double-clicks the button.
- ⊖ `ondrag` (Web) names a script to run when a user drags a selection.
- ⊖ `ondragend` (Web) names a script to run after a user completes a drag-and-drop operation.

- ☺ ondragenter (Web) names a script to run when a user drags a selection into an area in which it can be dropped.
- ☺ ondragleave (Web) names a script to run when a user drags a selection beyond an area in which it can be dropped.
- ☺ ondragover (Web) names a script to run when a user drags a selection over an area in which it can be dropped.
- ☺ ondragstart (Web) names a script to run when a user starts dragging a selection or element.
- ☺ ondrop (Web) names a script to run when a user releases the mouse button to drop a dragged selection.
- ☺ onfocus (Web) names a script to run when a user points the mouse pointer or other pointing device to focus on the current element.
- ☺ onfocusenter (Web) names a script to run when a user focuses on the current element in any way.
- ☺ onfocusleave (Web) names a script to run when a user inactivates the current element in any way.
- ☺ onhelp (Web) names a script to run when a user presses the F1 or Help key over the boldface text.
- onkeydown (Web) names a script to run when a user presses and holds down a key over the boldface text.
- onkeypress (Web) names a script to run when a user presses and releases a key over the boldface text.
- onkeyup (Web) names a script to run when a user releases a key that is currently held down over the boldface text.
- ☺ onlosecapture (Web) names a script to run when a user releases a selection that has been captured by the mouse.
- onmousedown (Web) names a script to run when a user moves the mouse pointer or other pointing device over the boldface text and presses and holds down the button.
- ☺ onmouseenter (Web) names a script to run when a user moves the mouse pointer onto the object.
- ☺ onmouseleave (Web) names a script to run when the mouse pointer leaves the object.
- onmousemove (Web) names a script to run when a user moves the mouse pointer or other pointing device over the boldface text.
- onmouseout (Web) names a script to run when a user moves the mouse pointer or other pointing device away from the boldface text.
- onmouseover (Web) names a script to run the first time a user moves the mouse pointer or other pointing device over the boldface text.
- onmouseup (Web) names a script to run when a user moves the mouse pointer or other pointing device over the boldface text and releases a mouse button that is currently held down.
- ☺ onpaste (Web) names a script to run when a user pastes the Clipboard contents onto the object.
- ☺ onpropertychange (Web) names a script to run when a property changes on the selected object in any way.

- ⊖ onreadystatechange (Web) names a script to run when the status of an element has changed (for example, the element receives data).
- ⊖ onresize (Web) names a script to run when a user resizes the selected object.
- ⊖ onresizeend (Web) names a script to run after the object has been resized.
- ⊖ onresizestart (Web) names a script to run as a user resizes the object.
- ⊖ onselectstart (Web) names a script to run when a user starts selecting an object.
- style (Web) sets styles for the boldface text.
- ⊖ tabindex (Web) defines the position of the current element in all the elements that a user can navigate to using a Tab or Shift + Tab key.
- title (Web) provides a title for the boldface text.
- *text* represents one or more characters.

Notes

- This inline element originated in HTML 2.0.
- b is one of the elements in the %fontstyle entity. The other %fontstyle elements are big, i, small, and tt. Deprecated elements in the %fontstyle entity are s, strike, and u.
- The b and i elements are physical styles, which specifically command a browser to apply boldface and italics, respectively. Their counterpart logical style elements are em and strong, which allow a browser to emphasize selected text in the way in which it is programmed to do.
- For the b element, WebTV supports the class and style attributes.

Related Elements

big (57), blackface (61), em (120), font (131), i (154), s (254), small (268), strike (254), strong (276), sub (281), sup (284), tt (324), u (327)

For More Information

Learn more about the b element on page 526 in Chapter 2.

Learn more about the b element on page 526 in Chapter 2.

base   Base URI

Purpose

Specifies the URI of the home page of the current document.

Syntax

```
<base href="base_URI"
    [ contenteditable="edit_string"]
    [ disabled="disabled"][ id="id_name"]
    [ onlayoutcomplete="la_script"]
    [ onmouseenter="me_script"]
```

```
[ onmouseleave="ml_script"]
[ onreadystatechange="rsc_script"]
[ target="window"|"_blank"|"_parent"|"_search"
|"_self"|"_top"][ title="title"]{ />|</base>}
```

Where

- href (Web) specifies an absolute URI for the current document.
- ⊖ contenteditable (Web) specifies or obtains a value that indicates whether a user can edit the element content.
- ⊖ disabled (Web) is a keyword that prevents a user from using the element.
- ⊖ id (Web) provides a unique identifier name for the text.
- ⊖ onlayoutcomplete (Web) names a script to run when a user lays out a selection using Print or Print Preview.
- ⊖ onmouseenter (Web) names a script to run when a user moves the mouse pointer onto the object.
- ⊖ onmouseleave (Web) names a script to run when the mouse pointer leaves the object.
- ⊖ onreadystatechange (Web) names a script to run when the status of an element has changed (for example, the element receives data).
- target (Web) loads a linked and named document in a particular window or frame. This attribute is deprecated; use the id attribute instead.
- ⊖ title (Web) provides a title or title information about the base URI.

Notes

- This element originated in HTML 2.0.
- base is an empty element.
- base is valid only at the top of the document within the HEAD section.
- The target attribute, which is deprecated and appears only in the Transitional DTD, allows a user to visit a target window without actually leaving your site. For example, a user can click on an advertising icon at your site, automatically open a window, view its contents, close the window, and be able to return to your site without retyping your URI.
- For the base element, WebTV supports the href, target, and title attributes.

Related Elements

head (148), isindex (184), link (202), meta (216), script (262), style (280), title (318)

basefont   Base Font

Purpose

Defines the size of the font for the entire current document from the basefont start tag to the end of the document.

Syntax

```
<basefont size="[+|-]1|2|3|4|5|6|7"
   [ class="class_name"][ color="#rrggbb"|"color"]
   [ contenteditable="edit_string"]
   [ disabled="disabled"][ face="typeface"]
   [ id="id_name"][ lang="lang_code"]
   [ onlayoutcomplete="la_script"]
   [ onmouseenter="me_script"]
   [ onmouseleave="ml_script"]
   [ onreadystatechange="rsc_script"]
   [ title="title"]{ /></basefont>}
```

Where

- size (Web) indicates that you will change the actual (1-7) size of the text.
- ⊕ class (Web) specifies a class identification for the text.
- color (Web) is the color of the text.
- ⊕ contenteditable (Web) specifies or obtains a value that indicates whether a user can edit the element content.
- ⊕ disabled (Web) is a keyword that prevents a user from using the element.
- face (Web) specifies the name of a typeface to be applied to the selected text. Note that the typeface must be installed on your computer.
- ⊕ id (Web) provides a unique identifier name for the text.
- ⊕ lang (Web) specifies the code for the language used for the text.
- ⊕ onlayoutcomplete (Web) names a script to run when a user lays out a selection using Print or Print Preview.
- ⊕ onmouseenter (Web) names a script to run when a user moves the mouse pointer onto the object.
- ⊕ onmouseleave (Web) names a script to run when the mouse pointer leaves the object.
- ⊕ onreadystatechange (Web) names a script to run when the status of an element has changed (for example, the element receives data).
- ⊕ title (Web) provides a title for the text.

Notes

- This inline HTML 4.0 element was originally a Netscape extension and a Microsoft extension.
- basefont is an empty element.

XHTML Syntax

- Although basefont is supported by HTML 4.0 in the Transitional DTD, it has been deprecated (that is, it will eventually be obsolete). basefont does not appear in the Strict DTD. Use style sheets to specify font attributes.
- You can use the font element, which is also deprecated, to change the typeface, size, and/or color of the base font. However, because font is deprecated, it is best to use style sheets to specify font attributes.
- For the basefont element, WebTV supports the class and size attributes.

Related Element
font (131)

bdo	Bidirectional Text

Purpose
Changes the direction of selected text.

Syntax
```
<bdo dir="ltr"|"rtl"[ accesskey="shortcut_key"]
  [ class="class_name"]
  [ contenteditable="edit_string"]
  [ disabled="disabled"]
  [ id="id_name"][ lang="lang_code"]
  [ language="javascript"|"jscript"|"vbs[cript]"]
  [ onafterupdate="au_script"]
  [ onbeforecopy="bc_script"]
  [ onbeforecut="bt_script"]
  [ onbeforefocusenter="bfe_script"]
  [ onbeforefocusleave="bfl_script"]
  [ onbeforepaste="bp_script"]
  [ onbeforeupdate="bu_script"][ onclick="cl_script"]
  [ oncontextmenu="cm_script"]
  [ oncontrolselect="ctl_script"][ oncopy="cp_script"]
  [ oncut="ct_script"][ ondblclick="dc_script"]
  [ ondrag="d_script"][ ondragend="dd_script"]
  [ ondragenter="de_script"][ ondragleave="dl_script"]
  [ ondragover="do_script"][ ondragstart="ds_script"]
  [ ondrop="dr_script"][ onerrorupdate="eu_script"]
  [ onfilterchange="f_script"][ onfocus="fc_script"]
  [ onfocusenter="fe_script"]
  [ onfocusleave="fl_script"][ onhelp="hlp_script"]
```

```
[ onkeydown="kd_script"][ onkeypress="kp_script"]
[ onkeyup="ku_script"][ onlosecapture="lc_script"]
[ onmousedown="md_script"]
[ onmouseenter="me_script"]
[ onmouseleave="ml_script"]
[ onmousemove="mm_script"][ onmouseout="mo_script"]
[ onmouseover="mov_script"][ onmouseup="mu_script"]
[ onpaste="p_script"][ onpropertychange="pc_script"]
[ onreadystatechange="rsc_script"]
[ onresizeend="ree_script"]
[ onresizestart="res_script"][ onscroll="sc_script"]
[ onselectstart="ss_script"]
[ style="name_1: value_1"[; "name_2: value_2"]
[...; "name_n: value_n"]]
[ tabindex="position_number"][ title="title"]>
text</bdo>
```

Where

- dir (Web) specifies the direction in which the selected text is displayed: left-to-right or right-to-left. (For example, English is displayed from left to right, and Hebrew is displayed from right to left.)
- ⊖ accesskey (Web) assigns a shortcut key to the element in order to focus on it.
- class (Web) specifies a class identification for the selected text.
- ⊖ contenteditable (Web) specifies or obtains a value that indicates whether a user can edit the element content.
- ⊖ disabled (Web) is a keyword that prevents a user from using the element.
- id (Web) provides a unique identifier name for the selected text.
- lang (Web) specifies the code for the language used for the selected text.
- ⊖ language (Web) declares the scripting language of the current script.
- ⊖ onafterupdate (Web) names a script to run after data has been transferred from the element to the data resource.
- ⊖ onbeforecopy (Web) names a script to run when a user starts copying a selection to the Clipboard but before any action actually takes place.
- ⊖ onbeforecut (Web) names a script to run when a user starts cutting a selection to the Clipboard but before any action actually takes place.
- ⊖ onbeforefocusenter (Web) names a script to run when a user starts focusing on an object but before the object actually gains focus.
- ⊖ onbeforefocusleave (Web) names a script to run when a user starts leaving an object but before the object actually loses focus.
- ⊖ onbeforepaste (Web) names a script to run when a user starts pasting an object but before any action actually takes place.
- ⊖ onbeforeupdate (Web) names a script to run before data is transferred from the element to the data resource.

- 😊 onblur (Web) names a script to run when the selected text loses focus (that is, it is no longer the active element).
- 😊 oncellchange (Web) names a script to run when data is modified in the data resource.
- 😊 onclick (Web) names a script to run when a user moves the mouse pointer or other pointing device over the big text and clicks the button.
- 😊 oncontextmenu (Web) names a script to run when a user right-clicks the mouse to open a shortcut menu.
- 😊 oncontrolselect (Web) names a script to run when a user selects a control.
- 😊 oncopy (Web) names a script to run when a user copies a selection to the Clipboard.
- 😊 oncut (Web) names a script to run when a user cuts a selection to the Clipboard.
- 😊 ondblclick (Web) names a script to run when a user moves the mouse pointer or other pointing device over the selected text and double-clicks the button.
- 😊 ondrag (Web) names a script to run when a user drags a selection.
- 😊 ondragend (Web) names a script to run after a user completes a drag-and-drop operation.
- 😊 ondragenter (Web) names a script to run when a user drags a selection into an area in which it can be dropped.
- 😊 ondragleave (Web) names a script to run when a user drags a selection beyond an area in which it can be dropped.
- 😊 ondragover (Web) names a script to run when a user drags a selection over an area in which it can be dropped.
- 😊 ondragstart (Web) names a script to run when a user starts dragging a selection or element.
- 😊 ondrop (Web) names a script to run when a user releases the mouse button to drop a dragged selection.
- 😊 onerrorupdate (Web) names a script to run when an error occurs while data is updated in the data resource.
- 😊 onfilterchange (Web) names a script to run when a visual filter changes in any way.
- 😊 onfocus (Web) names a script to run when a user points the mouse pointer or other pointing device to focus on the current element.
- 😊 onfocusenter (Web) names a script to run when a user focuses on the current element in any way.
- 😊 onfocusleave (Web) names a script to run when a user inactivates the current element in any way.
- 😊 onhelp (Web) names a script to run when a user presses the F1 or Help key over the current element.
- 😊 onkeydown (Web) names a script to run when a user presses and holds down a key over the selected text.
- 😊 onkeypress (Web) names a script to run when a user presses and releases a key over the selected text.

- ⊖ onkeyup (Web) names a script to run when a user releases a key that is currently held down over the selected text.
- ⊖ onlosecapture (Web) names a script to run when a user releases a selection that has been captured by the mouse.
- ⊖ onmousedown (Web) names a script to run when a user moves the mouse pointer or other pointing device over the selected text and presses and holds down the button.
- ⊖ onmouseenter (Web) names a script to run when a user moves the mouse pointer onto the object.
- ⊖ onmouseleave (Web) names a script to run when the mouse pointer leaves the object.
- ⊖ onmousemove (Web) names a script to run when a user moves the mouse pointer or other pointing device over the selected text.
- ⊖ onmouseout (Web) names a script to run when a user moves the mouse pointer or other pointing device away from the selected text.
- ⊖ onmouseover (Web) names a script to run the first time a user moves the mouse pointer or other pointing device over the selected text.
- ⊖ onmouseup (Web) names a script to run when a user moves the mouse pointer or other pointing device over the selected text and releases a mouse button that is currently held down.
- ⊖ onpaste (Web) names a script to run when a user pastes the Clipboard contents onto the object.
- ⊖ onpropertychange (Web) names a script to run when a property changes on the selected object in any way.
- ⊖ onreadystatechange (Web) names a script to run when the status of an element has changed (for example, the element receives data).
- ⊖ onresizeend (Web) names a script to run after the object has been resized.
- ⊖ onresizestart (Web) names a script to run as the object is resized.
- ⊖ onscroll (Web) names a script to run when a user moves the scroll box within the scroll bar.
- ⊖ onselectstart (Web) names a script to run when a user starts selecting an object.
- style (Web) sets styles for the selected text.
- ⊖ tabindex (Web) defines the position of the current element in all the elements that a user can navigate to using a Tab or Shift + Tab key.
- title (Web) provides a title for the selected text.
- text represents one or more characters.

Notes

- This inline element originated in HTML 4.0.
- Use bdo to manually set text direction. This element is part of the internationalization effort of the World Wide Web Consortium (W3C). With bdo, you can use languages that flow from left to right as well as those that flow from right to left.

- You can change the direction of text by inserting the Unicode characters: LEFT-TO-RIGHT OVERRIDE (hexadecimal code 202D), RIGHT-TO-LEFT OVERRIDE (hexadecimal code 202E). You can end the effect of these codes by inserting the POP DIRECTIONAL FORMATTING character (hexadecimal 202C). However, if you use these characters while the dir attribute is in effect, you may experience unusual results. For more information about Unicode, go to http://www.unicode.org.

Related Elements

br (70), q (246), span (272), sub (281), sup (284)

Related Attribute

dir (Web)

⊖ 📺 bgsound   Background Sound

Purpose

Defines a sound file, in .WAV, .AU, or .MID format, that plays when a user opens a page.

Syntax

```
<bgsound src="sound_name"[ balance="bal_num"]
  [ class="class_name"]
  [ contenteditable="edit_string"]
  [ disabled="disabled"][ id="id_name"]
  [ lang="lang_code"][ loop="number_of_plays"
  |"infinite"][ onlayoutcomplete="la_script"]
  [ onmouseenter="me_script"]
  [ onmouseleave="ml_script"]
  [ onreadystatechange="rsc_script"]
  [ title="title"][ volume="vol_num"]
  { />|[</bgsound>}
```

Where

- ⊖📺 src (Web) specifies the name of the sound file.
- ⊖ balance (Web) specifies the balance of volume for the left and right speakers.
- ⊖ class (Web) specifies a class identification for the element.
- ⊖ contenteditable (Web) specifies or obtains a value that indicates whether a user can edit the element content.
- ⊖ disabled (Web) is a keyword that prevents a user from using the element.

- ⊝ id (Web) provides a unique identifier name for the element.
- ⊝ lang (Web) specifies the code for the language used for the element.
- ⊝📺 loop (Web) indicates the number of times that the sound file will play.
- ⊝ onlayoutcomplete (Web) names a script to run when a user lays out a selection using Print or Print Preview.
- ⊝ onmouseenter (Web) names a script to run when a user moves the mouse pointer onto the object.
- ⊝ onmouseleave (Web) names a script to run when the mouse pointer leaves the object.
- ⊝ onreadystatechange (Web) names a script to run when the status of an element has changed (for example, the element receives data).
- ⊝ title (Web) provides a title for the element.
- ⊝ volume (Web) specifies how loud or soft the background sound file will play.

Notes

- Place this element within the HEAD section of the document.
- bgsound is an empty element.
- According to the *WebTV HTML For More Information Guide* (http://developer.webtv.net/authoring/main.htm), "this element is now generally considered obsolete."
- For the bgsound extension, WebTV supports the loop and src attributes.

big   Big Text

Purpose

Displays text in a larger font than the base font or than the current font.

Syntax

```
<big[ accesskey="shortcut_key"][ class="class_name"]
  [ contenteditable="edit_string"][ dir="ltr"|"rtl"]
  [ disabled="disabled"][ id="id_name"]
  [ lang="lang_code"][ language="javascript"|"jscript"
  |"vbs[cript]"][ onbeforecopy="bc_script"]
  [ onbeforecut="bt_script"]
  [ onbeforefocusenter="bfe_script"]
  [ onbeforefocusleave="bfl_script"]
  [ onbeforepaste="bp_script"][ onblur="bl_script"]
  [ onclick="cl_script"][ oncontextmenu="cm_script"]
  [ oncontrolselect="ctl_script"][ oncopy="cp_script"]
  [ oncut="ct_script"][ ondblclick="dc_script"]
  [ ondrag="d_script"][ ondragend="dd_script"]
```

```
[ ondragenter="de_script"]
[ ondragleave="dl_script"]
[ ondragover="do_script"]
[ ondragstart="ds_script"][ ondrop="dr_script"]
[ onfocus="fc_script"][ onfocusenter="fe_script"]
[ onfocusleave="fl_script"][ onhelp="hlp_script"]
[ onkeydown="kd_script"][ onkeypress="kp_script"]
[ onkeyup="ku_script"][ onlosecapture="lc_script"]
[ onmousedown="md_script"]
[ onmouseenter="me_script"]
[ onmouseleave="ml_script"]
[ onmousemove="mm_script"][ onmouseout="mo_script"]
[ onmouseover="mov_script"][ onmouseup="mu_script"]
[ onpaste="p_script"][ onpropertychange="pc_script"]
[ onreadystatechange="rsc_script"]
[ onresize="rsz_script"][ onresizeend="ree_script"]
[ onresizestart="res_script"]
[ onselectstart="ss_script"]
[ style="name_1: value_1"[; "name_2: value_2"]
[...; "name_n: value_n"]]
[ tabindex="position_number"][ title="title"]>
text</big>
```

Where

- ⊕ accesskey (Web) assigns a shortcut key to the object in order to focus on it.
- class (Web) specifies a class identification for the big text.
- ⊕ contenteditable (Web) specifies or obtains a value that indicates whether a user can edit the element content.
- dir (Web) specifies the direction in which the big text is displayed: left-to-right or right-to-left.
- ⊕ disabled (Web) is a keyword that prevents a user from using the element.
- id (Web) provides a unique identifier name for the big text.
- lang (Web) specifies the code for the language used for the big text.
- ⊕ language (Web) declares the scripting language of the current script.
- ⊕ onbeforecopy (Web) names a script to run when a user starts copying a selection to the Clipboard but before any action actually takes place.
- ⊕ onbeforecut (Web) names a script to run when a user starts cutting a selection to the Clipboard but before any action actually takes place.
- ⊕ onbeforefocusenter (Web) names a script to run when a user starts focusing on an object but before the object actually gains focus.
- ⊕ onbeforefocusleave (Web) names a script to run when a user starts leaving an object but before the object actually loses focus.

- ☺ onbeforepaste (Web) names a script to run when a user starts pasting an object but before any action actually takes place.
- ☺ onblur (Web) names a script to run when the big text loses focus (that is, it is no longer the active element).
- onclick (Web) names a script to run when a user moves the mouse pointer or other pointing device over the big text and clicks the button.
- ☺ oncontextmenu (Web) names a script to run when a user right-clicks the mouse to open a shortcut menu.
- ☺ oncontrolselect (Web) names a script to run when a user selects a control.
- ☺ oncopy (Web) names a script to run when a user copies a selection to the Clipboard.
- ☺ oncut (Web) names a script to run when a user cuts a selection to the Clipboard.
- ondblclick (Web) names a script to run when a user moves the mouse pointer or other pointing device over the big text and double-clicks the button.
- ☺ ondrag (Web) names a script to run when a user drags a selection.
- ☺ ondragend (Web) names a script to run after a user completes a drag-and-drop operation.
- ☺ ondragenter (Web) names a script to run when a user drags a selection into an area in which it can be dropped.
- ☺ ondragleave (Web) names a script to run when a user drags a selection beyond an area in which it can be dropped.
- ☺ ondragover (Web) names a script to run when a user drags a selection over an area in which it can be dropped.
- ☺ ondragstart (Web) names a script to run when a user starts dragging a selection or element.
- ☺ ondrop (Web) names a script to run when a user releases the mouse button to drop a dragged selection.
- ☺ onfocus (Web) names a script to run when a user points the mouse pointer or other pointing device to focus on the current element.
- ☺ onfocusenter (Web) names a script to run when a user focuses on the current element in any way.
- ☺ onfocusleave (Web) names a script to run when a user inactivates the current element in any way.
- ☺ onhelp (Web) names a script to run when a user presses the F1 or Help key over the current element.
- onkeydown (Web) names a script to run when a user presses and holds down a key over the big text.
- onkeypress (Web) names a script to run when a user presses and releases a key over the big text.
- onkeyup (Web) names a script to run when a user releases a key that is currently held down over the big text.
- ☺ onlosecapture (Web) names a script to run when a user releases a selection that has been captured by the mouse.

XHTML Syntax

- onmousedown (Web) names a script to run when a user moves the mouse pointer or other pointing device over the big text and presses and holds down the button.
- ⊕ onmouseenter (Web) names a script to run when a user moves the mouse pointer onto the object.
- ⊕ onmouseleave (Web) names a script to run when the mouse pointer leaves the object.
- onmousemove (Web) names a script to run when a user moves the mouse pointer or other pointing device over the big text.
- onmouseout (Web) names a script to run when a user moves the mouse pointer or other pointing device away from the big text.
- onmouseover (Web) names a script to run the first time a user moves the mouse pointer or other pointing device over the big text.
- onmouseup (Web) names a script to run when a user moves the mouse pointer or other pointing device over the big text and releases a mouse button that is currently held down.
- ⊕ onpaste (Web) names a script to run when a user pastes the Clipboard contents onto the object.
- ⊕ onpropertychange (Web) names a script to run when a property changes on the selected object in any way.
- ⊕ onreadystatechange (Web) names a script to run when the status of an element has changed (for example, the element receives data).
- ⊕ onresize (Web) names a script to run when a user resizes the selected object.
- ⊕ onresizeend (Web) names a script to run after the object has been resized.
- ⊕ onresizestart (Web) names a script to run as a user resizes the object.
- ⊕ onselectstart (Web) names a script to run when a user starts selecting an object.
- style (Web) sets styles for the big text.
- ⊕ tabindex (Web) defines the position of the current element in all the elements that a user can navigate to using a Tab or Shift + Tab key.
- title (Web) provides a title for the big text.
- *text* represents one or more characters.

Notes

- This inline element originated in HTML 3.2.
- big is one of the elements in the %fontstyle entity. The other %fontstyle elements are b, I, small, and tt. Deprecated elements in the %fontstyle entity are s, strike, and u.
- For the big element, WebTV supports the class and style attributes.

Related Elements

b (46), em (120), font (131), i (154), s (254), small (268), strike (254), strong (276), sub (281), sup (284), tt (324), u (327)

blackface   Blackface Text

Purpose

Applies very bold blackface to selected text.

Syntax

```
<blackface>text</blackface>
```

Where

text represents one or more words.

Related Elements

b (46), big (57), em (120), strong (276), u (327)

blink   Blink Text

Purpose

Turns the display of a block of text on and off.

Syntax

```
<blink>text</blink>
```

Where

text represents one or more words.

Note

Use this element sparingly or not at all; many users dislike blinking text.

blockquote   Block Quote

Purpose

Formats a long block-level quotation.

Syntax

```
<blockquote[ accesskey="shortcut_key"]
  [ cite="cite_uri"][ class="class_name"]
  [ contenteditable="edit_string"]
  [ dir="ltr"|"rtl"][ disabled="disabled"]
```

```
[ id="id_name"][ lang="lang_code"]
[ language="javascript"|"jscript"|"vbs[cript]"]
[ onbeforecopy="bc_script"]
[ onbeforecut="bt_script"]
[ onbeforefocusenter="bfe_script"]
[ onbeforefocusleave="bfl_script"]
[ onbeforepaste="bp_script"][ onblur="bl_script"]
[ onclick="cl_script"][ oncontextmenu="cm_script"]
[ oncontrolselect="ctl_script"]
[ oncopy="cp_script"][ oncut="ct_script"]
[ ondblclick="dc_script"][ ondrag="d_script"]
[ ondragend="dd_script"][ ondragenter="de_script"]
[ ondragleave="dl_script"][ ondragover="do_script"]
[ ondragstart="ds_script"][ ondrop="dr_script"]
[ onfocus="fc_script"][ onfocusenter="fe_script"]
[ onfocusleave="fl_script"][ onhelp="hlp_script"]
[ onkeydown="kd_script"][ onkeypress="kp_script"]
[ onkeyup="ku_script"][ onlosecapture="lc_script"]
[ onmousedown="md_script"]
[ onmouseenter="me_script"]
[ onmouseleave="ml_script"]
[ onmousemove="mm_script"][ onmouseout="mo_script"]
[ onmouseover="mov_script"][ onmouseup="mu_script"]
[ onpaste="p_script"]
[ onpropertychange="pc_script"]
[ onreadystatechange="rsc_script"]
[ onresize="rsz_script"][ onresizeend="ree_script"]
[ onresizestart="res_script"]
[ onselectstart="ss_script"]
[ style="name_1: value_1"[; "name_2: value_2"]
[...; "name_n: value_n"]]
[ tabindex="position_number"][ title="title"]>
text</blockquote>
```

Where

- ⊖ accesskey (Web) assigns a shortcut key to the object in order to focus on it.
- cite (Web) provides a URI for a document or message that contains information about a quote.
- class (Web) specifies a class identification for the current text.
- ⊖ contenteditable (Web) specifies or obtains a value that indicates whether a user can edit the element content.
- dir (Web) specifies the direction in which the current text is displayed: left-to-right or right-to-left.

- ⊖ disabled (Web) is a keyword that prevents a user from using the element.
- id (Web) provides a unique identifier name for the current text.
- lang (Web) specifies the code for the language used for the current text.
- ⊖ language (Web) declares the scripting language of the current script.
- ⊖ onbeforecopy (Web) names a script to run when a user starts copying a selection to the Clipboard but before any action actually takes place.
- ⊖ onbeforecut (Web) names a script to run when a user starts cutting a selection to the Clipboard but before any action actually takes place.
- ⊖ onbeforefocusenter (Web) names a script to run when a user starts focusing on an object but before the object actually gains focus.
- ⊖ onbeforefocusleave (Web) names a script to run when a user starts leaving an object but before the object actually loses focus.
- ⊖ onbeforepaste (Web) names a script to run when a user starts pasting an object but before any action actually takes place.
- ⊖ onblur (Web) names a script to run when the object loses focus (that is, it is no longer the active element).
- onclick (Web) names a script to run when a user moves the mouse pointer or other pointing device over the quote and clicks the button.
- ⊖ oncontextmenu (Web) names a script to run when a user right-clicks the mouse to open a shortcut menu.
- ⊖ oncontrolselect (Web) names a script to run when a user selects a control.
- ⊖ oncopy (Web) names a script to run when a user copies a selection to the Clipboard.
- ⊖ oncut (Web) names a script to run when a user cuts a selection to the Clipboard.
- ondblclick (Web) names a script to run when a user moves the mouse pointer or other pointing device over the quote and double-clicks the button.
- ⊖ ondrag (Web) names a script to run when a user drags a selection.
- ⊖ ondragend (Web) names a script to run after a user completes a drag-and-drop operation.
- ⊖ ondragenter (Web) names a script to run when a user drags a selection into an area in which it can be dropped.
- ⊖ ondragleave (Web) names a script to run when a user drags a selection beyond an area in which it can be dropped.
- ⊖ ondragover (Web) names a script to run when a user drags a selection over an area in which it can be dropped.
- ⊖ ondragstart (Web) names a script to run when a user starts dragging a selection or element.
- ⊖ ondrop (Web) names a script to run when a user releases the mouse button to drop a dragged selection.
- ⊖ onfocus (Web) names a script to run when a user points the mouse pointer or other pointing device to focus on the current element.
- ⊖ onfocusenter (Web) names a script to run when a user focuses on the current element in any way.

XHTML Syntax

- ⊖ onfocusleave (Web) names a script to run when a user inactivates the current element in any way.
- ⊖ onhelp (Web) names a script to run when a user presses the F1 or Help key over the current element.
- onkeydown (Web) names a script to run when a user presses and holds down a key over the quote.
- onkeypress (Web) names a script to run when a user presses and releases a key over the quote.
- onkeyup (Web) names a script to run when a user releases a key that is currently held down over the quote.
- ⊖ onlosecapture (Web) names a script to run when a user releases a selection that has been captured by the mouse.
- onmousedown (Web) names a script to run when a user moves the mouse pointer or other pointing device over the quote and presses and holds down the button.
- ⊖ onmouseenter (Web) names a script to run when a user moves the mouse pointer onto the object.
- ⊖ onmouseleave (Web) names a script to run when the mouse pointer leaves the object.
- onmousemove (Web) names a script to run when a user moves the mouse pointer or other pointing device over the quote.
- onmouseout (Web) names a script to run when a user moves the mouse pointer or other pointing device away from the quote.
- onmouseover (Web) names a script to run the first time a user moves the mouse pointer or other pointing device over the quote.
- onmouseup (Web) names a script to run when a user moves the mouse pointer or other pointing device over the quote and releases a mouse button that is currently held down.
- ⊖ onpaste (Web) names a script to run when a user pastes the Clipboard contents onto the object.
- ⊖ onpropertychange (Web) names a script to run when a property changes on the selected object in any way.
- ⊖ onreadystatechange (Web) names a script to run when the status of an element has changed (for example, the element receives data).
- ⊖ onresize (Web) names a script to run when a user resizes the selected object.
- ⊖ onresizeend (Web) names a script to run after the object has been resized.
- ⊖ onresizestart (Web) names a script to run as a user resizes the object.
- ⊖ onselectstart (Web) names a script to run when a user starts selecting an object.
- style (Web) sets styles for the quote.
- ⊖ tabindex (Web) defines the position of the current element in all the elements that a user can navigate to using a Tab or Shift + Tab key.
- title (Web) provides a title for the quote.
- *text* represents one or more characters.

Notes

- This block-level element originated in HTML 2.0.
- Within quotes, text is indented from the left margin and is ragged on the right margin.
- blockquote causes a paragraph break.
- For the blockquote element, WebTV supports the class and style attributes.

Related Elements

code (87), kbd (186), pre (242), q (246), samp (258), tt (324)

For More Information

Learn more about the blockquote element on page 628 in Chapter 8.

body	Document Body

Purpose

Indicates the start and end of the body, or the contents, of the document.

Syntax

```
<body[ accesskey="shortcut_key"]
  [ alink="#rrggbb"|"color"]
  [ background="picture_uri"]
  [ bgcolor="#rrggbb"|"color"][ bgproperties="fixed"]
  [ bottommargin="bot_mar_pix"][ class="class_name"]
  [ contenteditable="edit_string"]
  [ credits="credits_uri"][ datafld="ds_col_name"]
  [ dataformatas="html"|"text"]
  [ datasrc="ds_identifier"][ dir="ltr"|"rtl"]
  [ disabled="disabled"][ id="id_name"]
  [ instructions=="instruct_uri"][ lang="lang_code"]
  [ language="javascript"|"jscript"|"vbs[cript]"]
  [ leftmargin="lmar-num"] [ link="#rrggbb"|"color"]
  [ logo=="logo_uri"][ nowrap="nowrap"]
  [ onafterprint="ap_script"]
  [ onbeforecut="bt_script"]
  [ onbeforefocusenter="bfe_script"]
  [ onbeforefocusleave="bfl_script"]
  [ onbeforepaste="bp_script"]
  [ onbeforeprint="bpr_script"]
  [ onbeforeunload="bul_script"][ onblur="bl_script"]
  [ onclick="cl_script"][ oncontextmenu="cm_script"]
  [ oncontrolselect="ctl_script"][ oncut="ct_script"]
  [ ondblclick="dc_script"][ ondrag="d_script"]
```

```
[ ondragend="dd_script"][ ondragenter="de_script"]
[ ondragleave="dl_script"][ ondragover="do_script"]
[ ondragstart="ds_script"][ ondrop="dr_script"]
[ onfilterchange="f_script"][ onfocus="fc_script"]
[ onfocusenter="fe_script"]
[ onfocusleave="fl_script"][ onkeydown="kd_script"]
[ onkeypress="kp_script"][ onkeyup="ku_script"]
[ onload="ol_script"][ onlosecapture="lc_script"]
[ onmousedown="md_script"]
[ onmouseenter="me_script"]
[ onmouseleave="ml_script"]
[ onmousemove="mm_script"][ onmouseout="mo_script"]
[ onmouseover="mov_script"][ onmouseup="mu_script"]
[ onpaste="p_script"][ onpropertychange="pc_script"]
[ onreadystatechange="rsc_script"]
[ onresizeend="ree_script"]
[ onresizestart="res_script"][ onscroll="sc_script"]
[ onselect="sl_script"][ onselectstart="ss_script"]
[ onunload="un_script"][ rightmargin="rmar-num"]
[ scroll="yes"|"no"][ style="name_1: value_1"
[; "name_2: value_2"][...; "name_n: value_n"]]
[ tabindex="position_number"]
[ text="#rrggbb"|"color"][ title="title"]
[ topmargin="tmar-num"][ vlink="#rrggbb"|"color"]>
body-contents</body>
```

Where

- ⊕ accesskey (Web) assigns a shortcut key to the element in order to focus on it.
- alink (Web) defines the color of the text and graphics borders of the link that has just been clicked. This attribute is deprecated; consider using style sheets instead.
- background (Web) specifies an image file that is displayed in the background of each page of the current document. This attribute is deprecated; use style sheets instead.
- bgcolor (Web) specifies the background color for the document body. This attribute is deprecated; use style sheets instead.
- ⊕ bgproperties (Web) specifies that the background picture does not move when you scroll the document.
- ⊕ bottommargin (Web) specifies the measurement, in pixels, of the bottom margin of the document.
- class (Web) specifies a class identification for the document body.
- ⊕ contenteditable (Web) specifies or obtains a value that indicates whether a user can edit the element content.
- ⛶ credits (Web) is the URI of the document that contains credits.

- ⊝ datafld (Web) specifies the column name from the file that contains the data source object.
- ⊝ dataformatas (Web) indicates whether the data for this element is formatted as plain text (that is, unformatted ASCII) or HTML.
- ⊝ datasrc specifies the identifier of the data source object.
- dir (Web) specifies the direction in which the document body text is displayed: left-to-right or right-to-left.
- ⊝ disabled (Web) is a keyword that prevents a user from using the element.
- id (Web) provides a unique identifier name for the document body.
- ⛶ instructions (Web) is the URI of the document that contains instructions for using the current document.
- lang (Web) specifies the code for the language used for the body text.
- ⊝ language (Web) declares the scripting language of the current script.
- ⊝ leftmargin (Web) specifies the left margin, in pixels, of the document.
- link (Web) defines the color of the text and graphics borders of links that have not been visited or that have been visited but have been made inactive again from within the user's browser. This attribute is deprecated; use style sheets instead.
- ⛶ logo (Web) is the URI of the document that contains the thumbnail logo for the current document.
- ⊝ nowrap (Web) disables word wrap within the current object.
- ⊝ onafterprint (Web) names a script to run after the document prints.
- ⊝ onbeforecut (Web) names a script to run when a user starts cutting a selection to the Clipboard but before any action actually takes place.
- ⊝ onbeforefocusenter (Web) names a script to run when a user starts focusing on an object but before the object actually gains focus.
- ⊝ onbeforefocusleave (Web) names a script to run when a user starts leaving an object but before the object actually loses focus.
- ⊝ onbeforepaste (Web) names a script to run when a user starts pasting an object but before any action actually takes place.
- ⊝ onbeforeprint (Web) names a script to run after a user acts to print a document but before the document actually prints.
- ⊝ onbeforeunload (Web) names a script to run after a user acts to display another document but before the page is actually unloaded.
- Ⓝ onblur (Web) names a script to run when the object loses focus (that is, it is no longer the active element).
- onclick (Web) names a script to run when a user moves the mouse pointer or other pointing device over the document body and clicks the button.
- ⊝ oncontextmenu (Web) names a script to run when a user right-clicks the mouse to open a shortcut menu.
- ⊝ oncontrolselect (Web) names a script to run when a user selects a control.
- ⊝ oncut (Web) names a script to run when a user cuts a selection to the Clipboard.

- ondblclick (Web) names a script to run when a user moves the mouse pointer or other pointing device over the document body and double-clicks the button.
- ⊖ ondrag (Web) names a script to run when a user drags a selection.
- ⊖ ondragend (Web) names a script to run after a user completes a drag-and-drop operation.
- ⊖ ondragenter (Web) names a script to run when a user drags a selection into an area in which it can be dropped.
- ⊖ ondragleave (Web) names a script to run when a user drags a selection beyond an area in which it can be dropped.
- ⊖ ondragover (Web) names a script to run when a user drags a selection over an area in which it can be dropped.
- ⊖ ondragstart (Web) names a script to run when a user starts dragging a selection or element.
- ⊖ ondrop (Web) names a script to run when a user releases the mouse button to drop a dragged selection.
- ⊖ onfilterchange (Web) names a script to run when a visual filter changes in any way.
- Ⓝ onfocus (Web) names a script to run when a user points the mouse pointer or other pointing device to focus on the current element.
- ⊖ onfocusenter (Web) names a script to run when a user focuses on the current element in any way.
- ⊖ onfocusleave (Web) names a script to run when a user inactivates the current element in any way.
- onkeydown (Web) names a script to run when a user presses and holds down a key over the document body.
- onkeypress (Web) names a script to run when a user presses and releases a key over the document body.
- onkeyup (Web) names a script to run when a user releases a key that is currently held down over the document body.
- onload (Web) names a script to run after the active browser has finished loading the window.
- onmousedown (Web) names a script to run when a user moves the mouse pointer or other pointing device over the document body and presses and holds down the button.
- ⊖ onmouseenter (Web) names a script to run when a user moves the mouse pointer onto the object.
- ⊖ onmouseleave (Web) names a script to run when the mouse pointer leaves the object.
- onmousemove (Web) names a script to run when a user moves the mouse pointer or other pointing device over the document body.
- onmouseout (Web) names a script to run when a user moves the mouse pointer or other pointing device away from the document body.
- onmouseover (Web) names a script to run the first time a user moves the mouse pointer or other pointing device over the document body.

- onmouseup (Web) names a script to run when a user moves the mouse pointer or other pointing device over the document body and releases a mouse button that is currently held down.
- ⊖ onpaste (Web) names a script to run when a user pastes the Clipboard contents onto the object.
- ⊖ onpropertychange (Web) names a script to run when a property changes on the selected object in any way.
- ⊖ onreadystatechange (Web) names a script to run when the status of an element has changed (for example, the element receives data).
- ⊖ onscroll (Web) names a script to run when a user moves the scroll box within the scroll bar.
- ⊖ onselect (Web) names a script to run when a user selects some text in the input control.
- ⊖ onselectstart (Web) names a script to run when a user starts selecting an object.
- onunload (Web) names a script to run after the active browser has removed the document from a window.
- ⊖ scroll (Web) turns on or off document scrollbars.
- style (Web) sets styles for the entire document body.
- ⊖ tabindex (Web) defines the position of the current element in all the elements that a user can navigate to using a Tab or Shift + Tab key.
- text (Web) defines the color of all nonlink text in the current document. This attribute is deprecated; use a style sheet instead.
- title (Web) provides a title for the document body.
- ⊖ topmargin (Web) specifies the top margin, in pixels, of this document.
- vlink (Web) defines the color of the text and graphics borders of links that have been visited. This attribute is deprecated; use a style sheet instead.
- *body-contents* is the contents of the BODY section of the document.

Notes

- This inline element originated in HTML 2.0.
- If you use the body element, the starting element should be immediately after the </head> end tag, and the </body> end tag should be immediately above the </html> end tag.
- If you omit the quotation marks from the color values or the picture file URI, some HTML editors automatically insert them. However, XHTML processors may issue an error message instead.
- Background pictures can take time to load and can interfere with a user's ability to view text and links, so use them carefully.
- If you do not accept the default colors for links, try to specify a bright color for links that have not been visited and a darker, duller color for visited links. Make sure that the text, links, and body colors are compatible.
- Both Netscape and Microsoft provide many more color names. However, keep in mind that many other browsers do not support Netscape and Microsoft attributes.

- For the body element, WebTV supports the background, bgcolor, credits, instructions, link, logo, onload, onunload, text, and vlink attributes.

Related Element
head (148)

For More Information
Learn more about the body element on page 528 in Chapter 2.

---

br   Line Break

Purpose
Starts a new line of text.

Syntax
```
text<br[ class="class_name"][ clear="none"|"left"
    |"all"|"right"][ contenteditable="edit_string"]
    [ dir="ltr"|"rtl"][ disabled="disabled"]
    [ id="id_name"][ lang="lang_code"]
    [ language="javascript"|"jscript"|"vbs[cript]"]
    [ onclick="cl_script"][ ondblclick="dc_script"]
    [ onkeydown="kd_script"][ onkeypress="kp_script"]
    [ onkeyup="ku_script"]
    [ onlayoutcomplete="la_script"]
    [ onlosecapture="lc_script"]
    [ onmousedown="md_script"][ onmousemove="mm_script"]
    [ onmouseout="mo_script"][ onmouseover="mov_script"]
    [ onmouseup="mu_script"]
    [ onreadystatechange="rsc_script"]
    [ style="name_1: value_1"
    [; "name_2: value_2"][...; "name_n: value_n"]]
    [ title="title"]{ />|</br>}
```

Where
- text represents one or more characters.
- class (Web) specifies a class identification for the break.
- clear (Web) clears previous alignment settings depending on the location of floating images (placed with the img element (Web)). This attribute is deprecated; use a style sheet instead.
- ⊖ contenteditable (Web) specifies or obtains a value that indicates whether a user can edit the element content.
- dir (Web) specifies the direction in which the current text is displayed: left-to-right or right-to-left.

- ⊖ disabled (Web) is a keyword that prevents a user from using the element.
- id (Web) provides a unique identifier name for the break.
- lang (Web) specifies the code for the language used for the current text.
- ⊖ language (Web) declares the scripting language of the current script.
- onclick (Web) names a script to run when a user moves the mouse pointer or other pointing device over the current text and clicks the button.
- ondblclick (Web) names a script to run when a user moves the mouse pointer or other pointing device over the current text and double-clicks the button.
- onkeydown (Web) names a script to run when a user presses and holds down a key over the current text.
- onkeypress (Web) names a script to run when a user presses and releases a key over the current text.
- onkeyup (Web) names a script to run when a user releases a key that is currently held down over the current text.
- ⊖ onlayoutcomplete (Web) names a script to run when a user lays out a selection using Print or Print Preview.
- ⊖ onlosecapture (Web) names a script to run when a user releases a selection that has been captured by the mouse.
- onmousedown (Web) names a script to run when a user moves the mouse pointer or other pointing device over the current text and presses and holds down the button.
- onmousemove (Web) names a script to run when a user moves the mouse pointer or other pointing device over the current text.
- onmouseout (Web) names a script to run when a user moves the mouse pointer or other pointing device away from the current text.
- onmouseover (Web) names a script to run the first time a user moves the mouse pointer or other pointing device over the current text.
- onmouseup (Web) names a script to run when a user moves the mouse pointer or other pointing device over the current text and releases a mouse button that is currently held down.
- ⊖ onreadystatechange (Web) names a script to run when the status of an element has changed (for example, the element receives data).
- style (Web) sets styles for the break.
- title (Web) provides a title for the break.

Notes

- This inline element originated in HTML 2.0. However, the clear attribute is an HTML 3.2 feature.
- br is an empty element, which looks like this in an XHTML document: <br />.
- For the br element, WebTV supports the clear attribute.

Related Elements

bdo (52), p (238), q (246), span (272), sub (281), sup (284)

For More Information

Learn more about the br element on page 523 in Chapter 2.

button	Push Button

Purpose

Creates a script-operated button.

Syntax

```
<button[ accesskey="shortcut_key"]
    [ class="class_name"]
    [ contenteditable="edit_string"]
    [ datafld="ds_col_name"]
    [ dataformatas="html"|"text"]
    [ datasrc="ds_identifier"][ dir="ltr"|"rtl"]
    [ disabled="disabled"][ id="id_name"]
    [ lang="lang_code"][ language="javascript"|"jscript"
    |"vbs[cript]"][ name="button_name"]
    [ onbeforecut="bt_script"]
    [ onbeforeeditfocus="bef_script"]
    [ onbeforefocusenter="bfe_script"]
    [ onbeforefocusleave="bfl_script"]
    [ onbeforepaste="bp_script"][ onblur="bl_script"]
    [ onclick="cl_script"][ oncontextmenu="cm_script"]
    [ oncontrolselect="ctl_script"][ oncut="ct_script"]
    [ ondblclick="dc_script"][ ondragenter="de_script"]
    [ ondragleave="dl_script"][ ondragover="do_script"]
    [ ondrop="dr_script"][ onfilterchange="f_script"]
    [ onfocus="fc_script"][ onfocusenter="fe_script"]
    [ onfocusleave="fl_script"][ onhelp="hlp_script"]
    [ onkeydown="kd_script"][ onkeypress="kp_script"]
    [ onkeyup="ku_script"][ onlosecapture="lc_script"]
    [ onmousedown="md_script"]
    [ onmouseenter="me_script"]
    [ onmouseleave="ml_script"]
    [ onmousemove="mm_script"]
    [ onmouseout="mo_script"][ onmouseover="mov_script"]
    [ onmouseup="mu_script"][ onpaste="p_script"]
    [ onpropertychange="pc_script"]
    [ onreadystatechange="rsc_script"]
    [ onresize="rsz_script"][ onresizeend="ree_script"]
```

```
[ onresizestart="res_script"]
[ onselectstart="ss_script"]
[ style="name_1: value_1"[; name_2: value_2"]
[...; name_n: value_n"]]
[ tabindex="position_number"][ title="title"]
[ type="submit"|"button"|"reset"]
[ value="button_value"]>input_data</button>
```

Where

- accesskey (Web) assigns a shortcut key to the button in order to focus on it.
- class (Web) specifies a class identification for the button.
- ⊖ contenteditable (Web) specifies or obtains a value that indicates whether a user can edit the element content.
- ⊖ datafld (Web) specifies the column name from the file that contains the data source object.
- ⊖ dataformatas (Web) indicates whether the data for this element is formatted as plain text (that is, unformatted ASCII) or HTML.
- ⊖ datasrc (Web) specifies the identifier of the data source object.
- dir (Web) specifies the direction in which the button text is displayed: left-to-right or right-to-left.
- disabled (Web) is a keyword that prevents a user from clicking on the button. disabled is unavailable for this element but may be available in the future.
- id (Web) provides a unique identifier name for the button.
- lang (Web) specifies the code representing the language used for the button text.
- ⊖ language (Web) declares the scripting language of the current script.
- name (Web) labels the button.
- ⊖ onbeforecut (Web) names a script to run when a user starts cutting a selection to the Clipboard but before any action actually takes place.
- ⊖ onbeforeeditfocus (Web) names a script to run when a user starts activating an object but before the object actually becomes active.
- ⊖ onbeforefocusenter (Web) names a script to run when a user starts focusing on an object but before the object actually gains focus.
- ⊖ onbeforefocusleave (Web) names a script to run when a user starts leaving an object but before the object actually loses focus.
- ⊖ onbeforepaste (Web) names a script to run when a user starts pasting an object but before any action actually takes place.
- onblur (Web) names a script to run when the button loses focus.
- onclick (Web) names a script to run when a user moves the mouse pointer or other pointing device over the button and clicks the device button.
- ⊖ oncontextmenu (Web) names a script to run when a user right-clicks the mouse to open a shortcut menu.

- ⊝ oncontrolselect (Web) names a script to run when a user selects a control.
- ⊝ oncut (Web) names a script to run when a user cuts a selection to the Clipboard.
- ondblclick (Web) names a script to run when a user moves the mouse pointer or other pointing device over the button and double-clicks the device button.
- ⊝ ondragenter (Web) names a script to run when a user drags a selection into an area in which it can be dropped.
- ⊝ ondragleave (Web) names a script to run when a user drags a selection beyond an area in which it can be dropped.
- ⊝ ondragover (Web) names a script to run when a user drags a selection over an area in which it can be dropped.
- ⊝ ondrop (Web) names a script to run when a user releases the mouse button to drop a dragged selection.
- ⊝ onfilterchange (Web) names a script to run when a visual filter changes in any way.
- onfocus (Web) names a script to run when a user points the mouse pointer or other pointing device to focus on the current element.
- ⊝ onfocusenter (Web) names a script to run when a user focuses on the current element in any way.
- ⊝ onfocusleave (Web) names a script to run when a user inactivates the current element in any way.
- ⊝ onhelp (Web) names a script to run when a user presses the F1 or Help key over the current element.
- onkeydown (Web) names a script to run when a user presses and holds down a key over the button.
- onkeypress (Web) names a script to run when a user presses and releases a key over the button.
- onkeyup (Web) names a script to run when a user releases a key that is currently held down over the button.
- ⊝ onlosecapture (Web) names a script to run when a user releases a selection that has been captured by the mouse.
- onmousedown (Web) names a script to run when a user moves the mouse pointer or other pointing device over the button and presses and holds down the device button.
- ⊝ onmouseenter (Web) names a script to run when a user moves the mouse pointer onto the object.
- ⊝ onmouseleave (Web) names a script to run when the mouse pointer leaves the object.
- onmousemove (Web) names a script to run when a user moves the mouse pointer or other pointing device over the button.
- onmouseout (Web) names a script to run when a user moves the mouse pointer or other pointing device away from the button.

- onmouseover (Web) names a script to run the first time a user moves the mouse pointer or other pointing device over the button.
- onmouseup (Web) names a script to run when a user moves the mouse pointer or other pointing device over the button and releases a pressed-down device button.
- ⊖ onpaste (Web) names a script to run when a user pastes the Clipboard contents onto the object.
- ⊖ onpropertychange (Web) names a script to run when a property changes on the selected object in any way.
- ⊖ onreadystatechange (Web) names a script to run when the status of an element has changed (for example, the element receives data).
- ⊖ onresize (Web) names a script to run when a user resizes the selected object.
- ⊖ onresizeend (Web) names a script to run after the object has been resized.
- ⊖ onresizestart (Web) names a script to run as a user resizes the object.
- ⊖ onselectstart (Web) names a script to run when a user starts selecting an object.
- style (Web) sets styles for the button.
- tabindex (Web) defines the position of the button in all the elements that a user can navigate to using a Tab or Shift + Tab key.
- title (Web) provides a title for the button.
- type (Web) specifies the type of button.
- value (Web) sets the initial value for a button.
- *input_data* is the data submitted when the button is clicked.

Notes
- This block-level and inline element originated in HTML 4.0.
- A browser should display the button as three-dimensional with a potential of appearing to be pressed down when clicked.
- Do not use an image map with an img embedded within a button element.
- In XHTML, a button element cannot contain nested button, fieldset, form, iframe, input, isindex, label, select, or textarea elements.
- XHTML automatically labels buttons created by button. Most browsers label buttons using the value of the value attribute.

Related Elements
fieldset (127), form (135), img (162), input (167), isindex (184), label (190), legend (195), optgroup (234), option (236), select (263), textarea (302)

For More Information
Learn more about the button element on page 610 in Chapter 7.

caption   Caption

Purpose

Adds a caption above or below a table.

Syntax

```
<caption[ accesskey="shortcut_key"]
   [ align="top"|"bottom"|"left"|"right"|"center"]
   [ class="class_name"]
   [ contenteditable="edit_string"]
   [ dir="ltr"|"rtl"][ disabled="disabled"]
   [ id="id_name"][ lang="lang_code"]
   [ language="javascript"|"jscript"|"vbs[cript]"]
   [ onbeforecopy="bc_script"]
   [ onbeforecut="bt_script"]
   [ onbeforefocusenter="bfe_script"]
   [ onbeforefocusleave="bfl_script"]
   [ onbeforepaste="bp_script"][ onblur="bl_script"]
   [ onclick="cl_script"][ oncontextmenu="cm_script"]
   [ oncontrolselect="ctl_script"]
   [ oncopy="cp_script"][ oncut="ct_script"]
   [ ondblclick="dc_script"][ ondrag="d_script"]
   [ ondragend="dd_script"][ ondragenter="de_script"]
   [ ondragleave="dl_script"][ ondragover="do_script"]
   [ ondragstart="ds_script"][ ondrop="dr_script"]
   [ onfocus="fc_script"][ onfocusenter="fe_script"]
   [ onfocusleave="fl_script"][ onhelp="hlp_script"]
   [ onkeydown="kd_script"][ onkeypress="kp_script"]
   [ onkeyup="ku_script"][ onlosecapture="lc_script"]
   [ onmousedown="md_script"]
   [ onmouseenter="me_script"]
   [ onmouseleave="ml_script"]
   [ onmousemove="mm_script"][ onmouseout="mo_script"]
   [ onmouseover="mov_script"][ onmouseup="mu_script"]
   [ onpaste="p_script"][ onpropertychange="pc_script"]
   [ onreadystatechange="rsc_script"]
   [ onresizeend="ree_script"]
   [ onresizestart="res_script"]
   [ onselectstart="ss_script"]
   [ style="name_1: value_1"[; "name_2: value_2"]
   [...; "name_n: value_n"]]
   [ tabindex="position_number"][ title="title"]
   [ valign="top"|"bottom"]>caption_text</caption>
```

Where

- ⊝ accesskey (Web) assigns a shortcut key to the object in order to focus on it.
- align (Web) indicates the alignment of the caption: above, below, to the left, or to the right of the table. By default, captions are left-aligned. Note that the center value is a Netscape-defined attribute, which is also supported by Internet Explorer. align is a deprecated attribute; use a style sheet instead.
- class (Web) specifies a class identification for the caption.
- ⊝ contenteditable (Web) specifies or obtains a value that indicates whether a user can edit the element content.
- dir (Web) specifies the direction in which the caption text is displayed: left-to-right or right-to-left.
- ⊝ disabled (Web) is a keyword that prevents a user from using the element.
- id (Web) provides a unique identifier name for the caption.
- lang (Web) specifies the code for the language used for the caption.
- ⊝ language (Web) declares the scripting language of the current script.
- ⊝ onbeforecopy (Web) names a script to run when a user starts copying a selection to the Clipboard but before any action actually takes place.
- ⊝ onbeforecut (Web) names a script to run when a user starts cutting a selection to the Clipboard but before any action actually takes place.
- ⊝ onbeforefocusenter (Web) names a script to run when a user starts focusing on an object but before the object actually gains focus.
- ⊝ onbeforefocusleave (Web) names a script to run when a user starts leaving an object but before the object actually loses focus.
- ⊝ onbeforepaste (Web) names a script to run when a user starts pasting an object but before any action actually takes place.
- ⊝ onblur (Web) names a script to run when the object loses focus (that is, it is no longer the active element).
- onclick (Web) names a script to run when a user moves the mouse pointer or other pointing device over the caption and clicks the device button.
- ⊝ oncontextmenu (Web) names a script to run when a user right-clicks the mouse to open a shortcut menu.
- ⊝ oncontrolselect (Web) names a script to run when a user selects a control.
- ⊝ oncopy (Web) names a script to run when a user copies a selection to the Clipboard.
- ⊝ oncut (Web) names a script to run when a user cuts a selection to the Clipboard.
- ondblclick (Web) names a script to run when a user moves the mouse pointer or other pointing device over the caption and double-clicks the device button.
- ⊝ ondrag (Web) names a script to run when a user drags a selection.

- Ⓔ ondragend (Web) names a script to run after a user completes a drag-and-drop operation.
- Ⓔ ondragenter (Web) names a script to run when a user drags a selection into an area in which it can be dropped.
- Ⓔ ondragleave (Web) names a script to run when a user drags a selection beyond an area in which it can be dropped.
- Ⓔ ondragover (Web) names a script to run when a user drags a selection over an area in which it can be dropped.
- Ⓔ ondragstart (Web) names a script to run when a user starts dragging a selection or element.
- Ⓔ ondrop (Web) names a script to run when a user releases the mouse button to drop a dragged selection.
- Ⓔ onfocus (Web) names a script to run when a user points the mouse pointer or other pointing device to focus on the current element.
- Ⓔ onfocusenter (Web) names a script to run when a user focuses on the current element in any way.
- Ⓔ onfocusleave (Web) names a script to run when a user inactivates the current element in any way.
- Ⓔ onhelp (Web) names a script to run when a user presses the F1 or Help key over the current element.
- onkeydown (Web) names a script to run when a user presses and holds down a key over the caption.
- onkeypress (Web) names a script to run when a user presses and releases a key over the caption.
- onkeyup (Web) names a script to run when a user releases a key that is currently held down over the caption.
- Ⓔ onlosecapture (Web) names a script to run when a user releases a selection that has been captured by the mouse.
- onmousedown (Web) names a script to run when a user moves the mouse pointer or other pointing device over the caption and presses and holds down the device button.
- Ⓔ onmouseenter (Web) names a script to run when the mouse pointer is moved onto the object.
- Ⓔ onmouseleave (Web) names a script to run when the mouse pointer leaves the object.
- onmousemove (Web) names a script to run when a user moves the mouse pointer or other pointing device over the caption.
- onmouseout (Web) names a script to run when a user moves the mouse pointer or other pointing device away from the caption.
- onmouseover (Web) names a script to run the first time a user moves the mouse pointer or other pointing device over the caption.
- onmouseup (Web) names a script to run when a user moves the mouse pointer or other pointing device over the caption and releases a pressed-down device button.
- Ⓔ onpaste (Web) names a script to run when a user pastes the Clipboard contents onto the object.

- ⊖ onpropertychange (Web) names a script to run when a property changes on the selected object in any way.
- ⊖ onreadystatechange (Web) names a script to run when the status of an element has changed (for example, the element receives data).
- ⊖ onresizeend (Web) names a script to run after the object has been resized.
- ⊖ onresizestart (Web) names a script to run as a user resizes the object.
- ⊖ onselectstart (Web) names a script to run when a user starts selecting an object.
- style (Web) sets styles for the caption.
- ⊖ tabindex (Web) defines the position of the current element in all the elements that a user can navigate to using a Tab or Shift + Tab key.
- title (Web) provides a title for the caption.
- ⊖ valign (Web) indicates the vertical alignment of the caption, above or below the table.
- *caption_text* represents one or more words.

Notes

- This inline element originated in HTML 3.2.
- caption is a child element of the table element.
- caption must immediately follow the <table> start tag.
- Tables do not require captions.
- For the caption element, WebTV supports the align, class, and style attributes.

Related Elements

col (90), colgroup (92), table (288), tbody (293), td (297), tfoot (307), th (310), thead (315), tr (319)

For More Information

Learn more about the caption element on page 558 in Chapter 4.

center   Center Text

Purpose

Centers a line of text between the left margin and the right margin.

Syntax

```
<center[ accesskey="shortcut_key"]
    [ class="class_name"]
    [ contenteditable="edit_string"][ dir="ltr"|"rtl"]
    [ disabled="disabled"][ id="id_name"]
    [ lang="lang_code"][ language="javascript"|"jscript"
    |"vbs[cript]"][ onbeforecopy="bc_script"]
    [ onbeforecut="bt_script"]
```

```
[ onbeforefocusenter="bfe_script"]
[ onbeforefocusleave="bfl_script"]
[ onbeforepaste="bp_script"][ onblur="bl_script"]
[ onclick="cl_script"][ oncontextmenu="cm_script"]
[ oncontrolselect="ctl_script"][ oncopy="cp_script"]
[ oncut="ct_script"][ ondblclick="dc_script"]
[ ondrag="d_script"][ ondragend="dd_script"]
[ ondragenter="de_script"][ ondragleave="dl_script"]
[ ondragover="do_script"][ ondragstart="ds_script"]
[ ondrop="dr_script"][ onfocus="fc_script"]
[ onfocusenter="fe_script"]
[ onfocusleave="fl_script"]
[ onhelp="hlp_script"][ onkeydown="kd_script"]
[ onkeypress="kp_script"][ onkeyup="ku_script"]
[ onlosecapture="lc_script"]
[ onmousedown="md_script"]
[ onmouseenter="me_script"]
[ onmouseleave="ml_script"]
[ onmousemove="mm_script"]
[ onmouseout="mo_script"][ onmouseover="mov_script"]
[ onmouseup="mu_script"][ onpaste="p_script"]
[ onpropertychange="pc_script"]
[ onreadystatechange="rsc_script"]
[ onresize="rsz_script"][ onresizeend="ree_script"]
[ onresizestart="res_script"]
[ onselectstart="ss_script"]
[ style="name_1: value_1"[; "name_2: value_2"]
[...; "name_n: value_n"]]
[ tabindex="position_number"][ title="title"]>
text-line</center>
```

Where

- ⊖ accesskey (Web) assigns a shortcut key to the object in order to focus on it.
- class (Web) specifies a class identification for the current text.
- ⊖ contenteditable (Web) specifies or obtains a value that indicates whether a user can edit the element content.
- dir (Web) specifies the direction in which the current text is displayed: left-to-right or right-to-left.
- ⊖ disabled (Web) is a keyword that prevents a user from using the element.
- id (Web) provides a unique identifier name for the current text.
- lang (Web) specifies the code for the language used for the current text.
- ⊖ language (Web) declares the scripting language of the current script.

- ⊖ onbeforecopy (Web) names a script to run when a user starts copying a selection to the Clipboard but before any action actually takes place.
- ⊖ onbeforecut (Web) names a script to run when a user starts cutting a selection to the Clipboard but before any action actually takes place.
- ⊖ onbeforefocusenter (Web) names a script to run when a user starts focusing on an object but before the object actually gains focus.
- ⊖ onbeforefocusleave (Web) names a script to run when a user starts leaving an object but before the object actually loses focus.
- ⊖ onbeforepaste (Web) names a script to run when a user starts pasting an object but before any action actually takes place.
- ⊖ onblur (Web) names a script to run when the object loses focus (that is, it is no longer the active element).
- onclick (Web) names a script to run when a user moves the mouse pointer or other pointing device over the centered text and clicks the button.
- ⊖ oncontextmenu (Web) names a script to run when a user right-clicks the mouse to open a shortcut menu.
- ⊖ oncontrolselect (Web) names a script to run when a user selects a control.
- ⊖ oncopy (Web) names a script to run when a user copies a selection to the Clipboard.
- ⊖ oncut (Web) names a script to run when a user cuts a selection to the Clipboard.
- ondblclick (Web) names a script to run when a user moves the mouse pointer or other pointing device over the centered text and double-clicks the button.
- ⊖ ondrag (Web) names a script to run when a user drags a selection.
- ⊖ ondragend (Web) names a script to run after a user completes a drag-and-drop operation.
- ⊖ ondragenter (Web) names a script to run when a user drags a selection into an area in which it can be dropped.
- ⊖ ondragleave (Web) names a script to run when a user drags a selection beyond an area in which it can be dropped.
- ⊖ ondragover (Web) names a script to run when a user drags a selection over an area in which it can be dropped.
- ⊖ ondragstart (Web) names a script to run when a user starts dragging a selection or element.
- ⊖ ondrop (Web) names a script to run when a user releases the mouse button to drop a dragged selection.
- ⊖ onfocus (Web) names a script to run when a user points the mouse pointer or other pointing device to focus on the current element.
- ⊖ onfocusenter (Web) names a script to run when a user focuses on the current element in any way.
- ⊖ onfocusleave (Web) names a script to run when a user inactivates the current element in any way.
- ⊖ onhelp (Web) names a script to run when a user presses the F1 or Help key over the current element.

XHTML Syntax

- onkeydown (Web) names a script to run when a user presses and holds down a key over the centered text.
- onkeypress (Web) names a script to run when a user presses and releases a key over the centered text.
- onkeyup (Web) names a script to run when a user releases a key that is currently held down over the centered text.
- ⊝ onlosecapture (Web) names a script to run when a user releases a selection that has been captured by the mouse.
- onmousedown (Web) names a script to run when a user moves the mouse pointer or other pointing device over the centered text and presses and holds down the button.
- ⊝ onmouseenter (Web) names a script to run when a user moves the mouse pointer onto the object.
- ⊝ onmouseleave (Web) names a script to run when the mouse pointer leaves the object.
- onmousemove (Web) names a script to run when a user moves the mouse pointer or other pointing device over the centered text.
- onmouseout (Web) names a script to run when a user moves the mouse pointer or other pointing device away from the centered text.
- onmouseover (Web) names a script to run the first time a user moves the mouse pointer or other pointing device over the centered text.
- onmouseup (Web) names a script to run when a user moves the mouse pointer or other pointing device over the centered text and releases a mouse button that is currently held down.
- ⊝ onpaste (Web) names a script to run when a user pastes the Clipboard contents onto the object.
- ⊝ onpropertychange (Web) names a script to run when a property changes on the selected object in any way.
- ⊝ onreadystatechange (Web) names a script to run when the status of an element has changed (for example, the element receives data).
- ⊝ onresize (Web) names a script to run when a user resizes the selected object.
- ⊝ onresizeend (Web) names a script to run after the object has been resized.
- ⊝ onresizestart (Web) names a script to run as a user resizes the object.
- ⊝ onselectstart (Web) names a script to run when a user starts selecting an object.
- style (Web) sets styles for the centered text.
- ⊝ tabindex (Web) defines the position of the current element in all the elements that a user can navigate to using a Tab or Shift + Tab key.
- title (Web) provides a title for the centered text.
- *text-line* represents a line of text.

Notes

- This block-level element originated in HTML 3.2.

- Although center is supported by HTML 4.0, it has been deprecated (that is, it will eventually be obsolete) and appears only in the Transitional DTD — not the Strict DTD. Use style sheets to lay out documents instead.
- Some browsers do not recognize center; some HTML editors convert this element to <center><p>*text*</p></center>.
- Using center is analogous to starting a text selection with <p align= "center">. Remember that the align attribute is deprecated; use a style sheet instead.
- For the center element, WebTV supports the class and style attributes.

Related Attribute
align (763)

cite   Citation

Purpose
Indicates a citation — such as a book, paper, or the name of an expert — by emphasizing it, usually with italics.

Syntax
```
<cite[ accesskey="shortcut_key"][ class="class_name"]
  [ contenteditable="edit_string"][ dir="ltr"|"rtl"]
  [ disabled="disabled"][ id="id_name"]
  [ lang="lang_code"][ language="javascript"|"jscript"
  |"vbs[cript]"][ onbeforecopy="bc_script"]
  [ onbeforecut="bt_script"]
  [ onbeforefocusenter="bfe_script"]
  [ onbeforefocusleave="bfl_script"]
  [ onbeforepaste="bp_script"][ onblur="bl_script"]
  [ onclick="cl_script"][ oncontextmenu="cm_script"]
  [ oncontrolselect="ctl_script"][ oncopy="cp_script"]
  [ oncut="ct_script"][ ondblclick="dc_script"]
  [ ondrag="d_script"][ ondragend="dd_script"]
  [ ondragenter="de_script"][ ondragleave="dl_script"]
  [ ondragover="do_script"][ ondragstart="ds_script"]
  [ ondrop="dr_script"][ onfocus="fc_script"]
  [ onfocusenter="fe_script"]
  [ onfocusleave="fl_script"]
  [ onhelp="hlp_script"][ onkeydown="kd_script"]
  [ onkeypress="kp_script"][ onkeyup="ku_script"]
  [ onlosecapture="lc_script"]
```

XHTML Syntax

```
[ onmousedown="md_script"]
[ onmouseenter="me_script"]
[ onmouseleave="ml_script"]
[ onmousemove="mm_script"][ onmouseout="mo_script"]
[ onmouseover="mov_script"][ onmouseup="mu_script"]
[ onpaste="p_script"][ onpropertychange="pc_script"]
[ onreadystatechange="rsc_script"]
[ onresize="rsz_script"][ onresizeend="ree_script"]
[ onresizestart="res_script"]
[ onselectstart="ss_script"]
[ style="name_1: value_1"[; "name_2: value_2"]
[...; "name_n: value_n"]]
[ tabindex="position_number"][ title="title"]>
text</cite>
```

Where

- ⊖ accesskey (Web) assigns a shortcut key to the object in order to focus on it.
- class (Web) specifies a class identification for the current text.
- ⊖ contenteditable (Web) specifies or obtains a value that indicates whether a user can edit the element content.
- dir (Web) specifies the direction in which the current text is displayed: left-to-right or right-to-left.
- ⊖ disabled (Web) is a keyword that prevents a user from using the element.
- id (Web) provides a unique identifier name for the current text.
- lang (Web) specifies the code for the language used for the current text.
- ⊖ language (Web) declares the scripting language of the current script.
- ⊖ onbeforecopy (Web) names a script to run when a user starts copying a selection to the Clipboard but before any action actually takes place.
- ⊖ onbeforecut (Web) names a script to run when a user starts cutting a selection to the Clipboard but before any action actually takes place.
- ⊖ onbeforefocusenter (Web) names a script to run when a user starts focusing on an object but before the object actually gains focus.
- ⊖ onbeforefocusleave (Web) names a script to run when a user starts leaving an object but before the object actually loses focus.
- ⊖ onbeforepaste (Web) names a script to run when a user starts pasting an object but before any action actually takes place.
- ⊖ onblur (Web) names a script to run when the object loses focus (that is, it is no longer the active element).
- onclick (Web) names a script to run when a user moves the mouse pointer or other pointing device over the citation and clicks the button.
- ⊖ oncontextmenu (Web) names a script to run when a user right-clicks the mouse to open a shortcut menu.
- ⊖ oncontrolselect (Web) names a script to run when a user selects a control.

- ⊖ oncopy (Web) names a script to run when a user copies a selection to the Clipboard.
- ⊖ oncut (Web) names a script to run when a user cuts a selection to the Clipboard.
- ondblclick (Web) names a script to run when a user moves the mouse pointer or other pointing device over the citation and double-clicks the button.
- ⊖ ondrag (Web) names a script to run when a user drags a selection.
- ⊖ ondragend (Web) names a script to run after a user completes a drag-and-drop operation.
- ⊖ ondragenter (Web) names a script to run when a user drags a selection into an area in which it can be dropped.
- ⊖ ondragleave (Web) names a script to run when a user drags a selection beyond an area in which it can be dropped.
- ⊖ ondragover (Web) names a script to run when a user drags a selection over an area in which it can be dropped.
- ⊖ ondragstart (Web) names a script to run when a user starts dragging a selection or element.
- ⊖ ondrop (Web) names a script to run when a user releases the mouse button to drop a dragged selection.
- ⊖ onfocus (Web) names a script to run when a user points the mouse pointer or other pointing device to focus on the current element.
- ⊖ onfocusenter (Web) names a script to run when a user focuses on the current element in any way.
- ⊖ onfocusleave (Web) names a script to run when a user inactivates the current element in any way.
- ⊖ onhelp (Web) names a script to run when a user presses the F1 or Help key over the current element.
- onkeydown (Web) names a script to run when a user presses and holds down a key over the citation.
- onkeypress (Web) names a script to run when a user presses and releases a key over the citation.
- onkeyup (Web) names a script to run when a user releases a key that is currently held down over the citation.
- ⊖ onlosecapture (Web) names a script to run when a user releases a selection that has been captured by the mouse.
- onmousedown (Web) names a script to run when a user moves the mouse pointer or other pointing device over the citation and presses and holds down the button.
- ⊖ onmouseenter (Web) names a script to run when a user moves the mouse pointer onto the object.
- ⊖ onmouseleave (Web) names a script to run when the mouse pointer leaves the object.
- onmousemove (Web) names a script to run when a user moves the mouse pointer or other pointing device over the citation.
- onmouseout (Web) names a script to run when a user moves the mouse pointer or other pointing device away from the citation.

- onmouseover (Web) names a script to run the first time a user moves the mouse pointer or other pointing device over the citation.
- onmouseup (Web) names a script to run when a user moves the mouse pointer or other pointing device over the citation and releases a mouse button that is currently held down.
- ⊖ onpaste (Web) names a script to run when a user pastes the Clipboard contents onto the object.
- ⊖ onpropertychange (Web) names a script to run when a property changes on the selected object in any way.
- ⊖ onreadystatechange (Web) names a script to run when the status of an element has changed (for example, the element receives data).
- ⊖ onresize (Web) names a script to run when a user resizes the selected object.
- ⊖ onresizeend (Web) names a script to run after the object has been resized.
- ⊖ onresizestart (Web) names a script to run as a user resizes the object.
- ⊖ onselectstart (Web) names a script to run when a user starts selecting an object.
- style (Web) sets styles for the citation.
- ⊖ tabindex (Web) defines the position of the current element in all the elements that a user can navigate to using a Tab or Shift + Tab key.
- title (Web) provides a title for the citation.
- *text* represents one or more characters.

Notes

- This inline element originated in HTML 2.0.
- cite is one of the elements in the %phrase entity. The other %phrase elements are abbr, acronym, code, dfn, em, kbd, samp, strong, and var.
- cite is a logical element, in which particular browsers are programmed to apply a certain style to the selected text. This is in contrast to a physical element in which you "code" the styles yourself.
- Many browsers use italics to format the i, cite, em, and var elements.
- The HTML 4.0 DTD categorizes this as an inline element.
- For the cite element, WebTV supports the class and style attributes.

Related Elements

abbr (29), acronym (31), b (46), code (87), dfn (101), em (120), i (154), kbd (186), pre (242), s (254), samp (258), strike (254), strong (276), tt (324), u (327), var (335)

code   Source Code

Purpose
Applies a computer code (monospace) font to selected text.

Syntax
```
<code[ class="class_name"]
  [ contenteditable="edit_string"][ dir="ltr"|"rtl"]
  [ disabled="disabled"][ id="id_name"]
  [ lang="lang_code"][ language="javascript"|"jscript"
  |"vbs[cript]"][ onbeforecopy="bc_script"]
  [ onbeforecut="bt_script"]
  [ onbeforepaste="bp_script"][ onclick="cl_script"]
  [ oncontextmenu="cm_script"][ oncopy="cp_script"]
  [ oncut="ct_script"][ ondblclick="dc_script"]
  [ ondrag="d_script"][ ondragend="dd_script"]
  [ ondragenter="de_script"][ ondragleave="dl_script"]
  [ ondragover="do_script"][ ondragstart="ds_script"]
  [ ondrop="dr_script"][ onhelp="hlp_script"]
  [ onkeydown="kd_script"][ onkeypress="kp_script"]
  [ onkeyup="ku_script"][ onlosecapture="lc_script"]
  [ onmousedown="md_script"]
  [ onmouseenter="me_script"]
  [ onmouseleave="ml_script"]
  [ onmousemove="mm_script"][ onmouseout="mo_script"]
  [ onmouseover="mov_script"][ onmouseup="mu_script"]
  [ onpaste="p_script"][ onpropertychange="pc_script"]
  [ onreadystatechange="rsc_script"]
  [ onresize="rsz_script"][ onselectstart="ss_script"]
  [ style="name_1: value_1"[; "name_2: value_2"]
  [...; "name_n: value_n"]][ title="title"]>
  text</code>
```

Where
- class (Web) specifies a class identification for the current text.
- ⊖ contenteditable (Web) specifies or obtains a value that indicates whether a user can edit the element content.
- dir (Web) specifies the direction in which the current text is displayed: left-to-right or right-to-left.
- ⊖ disabled (Web) is a keyword that prevents a user from using the element.
- id (Web) provides a unique identifier name for the current text.
- lang (Web) specifies the code for the language used for the current text.
- ⊖ language (Web) declares the scripting language of the current script.

- ⊜ onbeforecopy (Web) names a script to run when a user starts copying a selection to the Clipboard but before any action actually takes place.
- ⊜ onbeforecut (Web) names a script to run when a user starts cutting a selection to the Clipboard but before any action actually takes place.
- ⊜ onbeforepaste (Web) names a script to run when a user starts pasting an object but before any action actually takes place.
- onclick (Web) names a script to run when a user moves the mouse pointer or other pointing device over the source code and clicks the button.
- ⊜ oncontextmenu (Web) names a script to run when a user right-clicks the mouse to open a shortcut menu.
- ⊜ oncopy (Web) names a script to run when a user copies a selection to the Clipboard.
- ⊜ oncut (Web) names a script to run when a user cuts a selection to the Clipboard.
- ondblclick (Web) names a script to run when a user moves the mouse pointer or other pointing device over the source code and double-clicks the button.
- ⊜ ondrag (Web) names a script to run when a user drags a selection.
- ⊜ ondragend (Web) names a script to run after a user completes a drag-and-drop operation.
- ⊜ ondragenter (Web) names a script to run when a user drags a selection into an area in which it can be dropped.
- ⊜ ondragleave (Web) names a script to run when a user drags a selection beyond an area in which it can be dropped.
- ⊜ ondragover (Web) names a script to run when a user drags a selection over an area in which it can be dropped.
- ⊜ ondragstart (Web) names a script to run when a user starts dragging a selection or element.
- ⊜ ondrop (Web) names a script to run when a user releases the mouse button to drop a dragged selection.
- ⊜ onhelp (Web) names a script to run when a user presses the F1 or Help key over the current element.
- onkeydown (Web) names a script to run when a user presses and holds down a key over the source code.
- onkeypress (Web) names a script to run when a user presses and releases a key over the source code.
- onkeyup (Web) names a script to run when a user releases a key that is currently held down over the source code.
- ⊜ onlosecapture (Web) names a script to run when a user releases a selection that has been captured by the mouse.
- onmousedown (Web) names a script to run when a user moves the mouse pointer or other pointing device over the source code and presses and holds down the button.
- ⊜ onmouseenter (Web) names a script to run when a user moves the mouse pointer onto the object.

- ⊖ onmouseleave (Web) names a script to run when the mouse pointer leaves the object.
- onmousemove (Web) names a script to run when a user moves the mouse pointer or other pointing device over the source code.
- onmouseout (Web) names a script to run when a user moves the mouse pointer or other pointing device away from the source code.
- onmouseover (Web) names a script to run the first time a user moves the mouse pointer or other pointing device over the source code.
- onmouseup (Web) names a script to run when a user moves the mouse pointer or other pointing device over the source code and releases a mouse button that is currently held down.
- ⊖ onpaste (Web) names a script to run when a user pastes the Clipboard contents onto the object.
- ⊖ onpropertychange (Web) names a script to run when a property changes on the selected object in any way.
- ⊖ onreadystatechange (Web) names a script to run when the status of an element has changed (for example, the element receives data).
- ⊖ onresize (Web) names a script to run when a user resizes the selected object.
- ⊖ onselectstart (Web) names a script to run when a user starts selecting an object.
- style (Web) sets styles for the source code.
- title (Web) provides a title for the source code.
- text represents one or more characters.

Notes

- This inline element originated in HTML 2.0.
- code is one of the elements in the %phrase entity. The other %phrase elements are abbr, acronym, cite, dfn, em, kbd, samp, strong, and var.
- code is a logical element, in which particular browsers are programmed to apply a certain style to the selected text. This is in contrast to a physical element in which you "code" the styles yourself.
- Many browsers use the same font for the following elements: code, kbd, pre, samp, and tt.
- To display two or more lines of preformatted text, use the pre element.
- For the code element, WebTV supports the class and style attributes.

Related Elements

abbr (29), acronym (31), b (46), cite (83), dfn (101), em (120), i (154), kbd (186), pre (242), s (254), samp (258), strike (254), strong (276), tt (324), u (327), var (335)

col   Column Properties

Purpose

Specifies alignment for one or more columns in a table.

Syntax

```
<col[ align="left"|"center"|"right"|"justify"
   |"char"][ bgcolor="#rrggbb"|"color"]
   [ char="character"][ charoff="offset"]
   [ class="class_name"][ dir="ltr"|"rtl"]
   [ disabled="disabled"][ id="id_name"]
   [ lang="lang_code"][ onclick="cl_script"]
   [ ondblclick="dc_script"][ onkeydown="kd_script"]
   [ onkeypress="kp_script"][ onkeyup="ku_script"]
   [ onlayoutcomplete="la_script"]
   [ onmousedown="md_script"]
   [ onmousemove="mm_script"][ onmouseout="mo_script"]
   [ onmouseover="mov_script"][ onmouseup="mu_script"]
   [ onreadystatechange="rsc_script"]
   [ SPAN="num_cols"|"1"|"0"][ style="name_1: value_1"
   [; "name_2: value_2"][...; "name_n: value_n"]]
   [ title="title"][ valign="middle"|"top"|"bottom"
   |"baseline"][ width="width_pix"|"width_%"|"0*"|"n*"]
   { />|</col>}
```

Where

- align (Web) indicates the alignment of the text within the column: aligned with the left or right margin, centered between the left and right margins, or aligned with a particular character.
- ⊝ bgcolor (Web) specifies the background color for the column group.
- char (Web) names a character with which column text is aligned in both directions.
- charoff (Web) sets the horizontal distance between the left or right margin and the first occurrence of the char character.
- class (Web) specifies a class identification for the column.
- dir (Web) specifies the direction in which the column contents are displayed: left-to-right or right-to-left.
- ⊝ disabled (Web) is a keyword that prevents a user from using the element.
- id (Web) provides a unique identifier name for the column.
- lang (Web) specifies the code for the language used for the column.
- onclick (Web) names a script to run when a user moves the mouse pointer or other pointing device over the column and clicks the device button.

- ondblclick (Web) names a script to run when a user moves the mouse pointer or other pointing device over the column and double-clicks the device button.
- onkeydown (Web) names a script to run when a user presses and holds down a key over the column.
- onkeypress (Web) names a script to run when a user presses and releases a key over the column.
- onkeyup (Web) names a script to run when a user releases a key that is currently held down over the column.
- ⊖ onlayoutcomplete (Web) names a script to run when a user lays out a selection using Print or Print Preview.
- onmousedown (Web) names a script to run when a user moves the mouse pointer or other pointing device over the column and presses and holds down the device button.
- onmousemove (Web) names a script to run when a user moves the mouse pointer or other pointing device over the column.
- onmouseout (Web) names a script to run when a user moves the mouse pointer or other pointing device away from the column.
- onmouseover (Web) names a script to run the first time a user moves the mouse pointer or other pointing device over the column.
- onmouseup (Web) names a script to run when a user moves the mouse pointer or other pointing device over the column and releases a pressed-down device button.
- ⊖ onreadystatechange (Web) names a script to run when the status of an element has changed (for example, the element receives data).
- span (Web) specifies the number of columns over which the col attributes are set.
- style (Web) sets styles for the column.
- title (Web) provides a title for the column.
- valign (Web) indicates the vertical alignment of the column, from the top to the bottom.
- width (Web) indicates the absolute width of the column, in pixels or as a percentage of the full-screen width, or the relative width of the column to other columns in the current table.

Notes

- This is an HTML 4.0 element. Previously, it was a Microsoft extension.
- col is an empty element.
- col is a child element of the table and colgroup elements.
- Use col to specify attributes for several columns in a column group.
- The attributes set by col override those set by the colgroup element.
- A column group may or may not contain columns.

Related Elements

caption (76), colgroup (92), table (288), tbody (293), td (297), tfoot (307), th (310), thead (315), tr (319)

For More Information

Learn more about the col element on page 565 in Chapter 4.

colgroup	Column Group

Purpose

Groups and formats one or more columns in a table.

Syntax

```
<colgroup [ align="left"|"center"|"right"|"justify"
  |"char"|"bleedleft"|"bleedright"]
  [ bgcolor="#rrggbb"|"color"][ char="character"]
  [ charoff="offset"][ class="class_name"]
  [ dir="ltr"|"rtl"][ disabled="disabled"]
  [ Halign="center"|"left"|"right"]
  [ id="id_name"][ lang="lang_code"]
  [ onclick="cl_script"][ ondblclick="dc_script"]
  [ onkeydown="kd_script"][ onkeypress="kp_script"]
  [ onkeyup="ku_script"][ onmousedown="md_script"]
  [ onmousemove="mm_script"][ onmouseout="mo_script"]
  [ onmouseover="mov_script"][ onmouseup="mu_script"]
  [ onreadystatechange="rsc_script"]
  [ SPAN="num_cols"|"1"|"0"]
  [ style="name_1: value_1"[; "name_2: value_2"]
  [...; "name_n: value_n"]][ title="title"]
  [ valign="middle"|"top"|"bottom"|"baseline"]
  [ width="width_pix"|"width_%"|"0*"]>
columns-contents</colgroup>
```

Where

- align (Web) indicates the alignment of the text within the column group: aligned with the left or right margin, centered between the left and right margins, or aligned with a particular character.
- ⊝ bgcolor (Web) specifies the background color for the column group.
- char (Web) names a character from which text is aligned in both directions.
- charoff (Web) sets the horizontal distance between the left or right margin and the first occurrence of the char character.
- class (Web) specifies a class identification for the column group.
- dir (Web) specifies the direction in which the column group contents are displayed: left-to-right or right-to-left.
- ⊝ disabled (Web) is a keyword that prevents a user from using the element.

- ⓝ `halign` (Web) horizontally aligns the text within the cells in the column group.
- `id` (Web) provides a unique identifier name for the column group.
- `lang` (Web) specifies the code for the language used within the column group.
- `onclick` (Web) names a script to run when a user moves the mouse pointer or other pointing device over the column group and clicks the device button.
- `ondblclick` (Web) names a script to run when a user moves the mouse pointer or other pointing device over the column group and double-clicks the device button.
- `onkeydown` (Web) names a script to run when a user presses and holds down a key over the column group.
- `onkeypress` (Web) names a script to run when a user presses and releases a key over the column group.
- `onkeyup` (Web) names a script to run when a user releases a key that is currently held down over the column group.
- `onmousedown` (Web) names a script to run when a user moves the mouse pointer or other pointing device over the column group and presses and holds down the device button.
- `onmousemove` (Web) names a script to run when a user moves the mouse pointer or other pointing device over the column group.
- `onmouseout` (Web) names a script to run when a user moves the mouse pointer or other pointing device away from the column group.
- `onmouseover` (Web) names a script to run the first time a user moves the mouse pointer or other pointing device over the column group.
- `onmouseup` (Web) names a script to run when a user moves the mouse pointer or other pointing device over the column group and releases a pressed-down device button.
- ⊜ `onreadystatechange` (Web) names a script to run when the status of an element has changed (for example, the element receives data).
- `span` (Web) specifies the number of columns over which the `colgroup` attributes are set.
- `style` (Web) sets styles for the column group.
- `title` (Web) provides a title for the column group.
- `valign` (Web) indicates the vertical alignment of the column group, from the top to the bottom.
- `width` (Web) indicates the absolute width of the column group, in pixels or as a percentage of the full-screen width, or the relative width of the column group to other column groups in the current table.
- *columns-contents* represents the contents of the column group.

Notes

- This is an HTML 4.0 element. Previously, it was a Microsoft extension.
- The attributes set by the `col` element override those set by `colgroup`.
- `colgroup` is a child element of the `table` element and is the parent of the `col` element.

Related Elements

caption (76), col (90), table (288), tbody (293), td (297), tfoot (307), th (310), thead (315), tr (319)

For More Information

Learn more about the colgroup element on page 565 in Chapter 4.

⊖ comment	Comment

Purpose

Places a comment in the document.

Syntax

```
<comment[ disabled="disabled"][ id="id_name"]
   [ lang="lang_code"]
   [ onpropertychange="pc_script"]
   [ onreadystatechange="rsc_script"]>
```

Where

- disabled (Web) prevents a user from using the current element.
- id (Web) provides a unique identifier name for the comment.
- lang (Web) specifies the code representing the language used for the comment.
- onpropertychange (Web) names a script to run when a property changes on the selected object in any way.
- onreadystatechange (Web) names a script to run when the status of an element has changed (for example, the element receives data).

Notes

- Use a comment to document a line or part of an XHTML document. For example, you can state the reason for using a particular element rather than another. Or, for someone who will maintain this document, you can describe how you created a complex table or form. Comments are very useful if one individual creates an XHTML document and another maintains it.
- You can see the comment in the source file but not in the published document.
- You cannot nest a comment within another comment.
- According to the *WebTV HTML Reference Guide* (http://developer. webtv.net/authoring/main.htm), "this element is now generally considered obsolete."

Related Element

! (23)

dd	Definition Description

Purpose
Marks the beginning and end of a description in a definition list.

Syntax
```
<dd[ accesskey="shortcut_key"][ class="class_name"]
  [ contenteditable="edit_string"][ dir="ltr"|"rtl"]
  [ disabled="disabled"][ id="id_name"]
  [ lang="lang_code"][ language="javascript"|"jscript"
  |"vbs[cript]"][ nowrap="nowrap"]
  [ onbeforecopy="bc_script"]
  [ onbeforecut="bt_script"]
  [ onbeforefocusenter="bfe_script"]
  [ onbeforefocusleave="bfl_script"]
  [ onbeforepaste="bp_script"][ onblur="bl_script"]
  [ onclick="cl_script"][ oncontextmenu="cm_script"]
  [ oncontrolselect="ctl_script"][ oncopy="cp_script"]
  [ oncut="ct_script"][ ondblclick="dc_script"]
  [ ondrag="d_script"][ ondragend="dd_script"]
  [ ondragenter="de_script"][ ondragleave="dl_script"]
  [ ondragover="do_script"][ ondragstart="ds_script"]
  [ ondrop="dr_script"][ onfocus="fc_script"]
  [ onfocusenter="fe_script"]
  [ onfocusleave="fl_script"]
  [ onhelp="hlp_script"][ onkeydown="kd_script"]
  [ onkeypress="kp_script"][ onkeyup="ku_script"]
  [ onlayoutcomplete="la_script"]
  [ onlosecapture="lc_script"]
  [ onmousedown="md_script"]
  [ onmouseenter="me_script"]
  [ onmouseleave="ml_script"]
  [ onmousemove="mm_script"][ onmouseout="mo_script"]
  [ onmouseover="mov_script"][ onmouseup="mu_script"]
  [ onpaste="p_script"][ onpropertychange="pc_script"]
  [ onreadystatechange="rsc_script"]
  [ onresize="rsz_script"][ onresizeend="ree_script"]
  [ onresizestart="res_script"]
  [ onselectstart="ss_script"]
  [ style="name_1: value_1"[; "name_2: value_2"]
  [...; "name_n: value_n"]]
  [ tabindex="position_number"]
  [ title="title"]>
  definition</dd>
```

Where

- ⊖ accesskey (Web) assigns a shortcut key to the element in order to focus on it.
- class (Web) specifies a class identification for the description.
- ⊖ contenteditable (Web) specifies or obtains a value that indicates whether a user can edit the element content.
- dir (Web) specifies the direction in which the description is displayed: left-to-right or right-to-left.
- ⊖ disabled (Web) is a keyword that prevents a user from using the element.
- id (Web) provides a unique identifier name for the description.
- lang (Web) specifies the code for the language used for the description text.
- ⊖ language (Web) declares the scripting language of the current script.
- ⊖ nowrap (Web) disables word wrap within the current object.
- ⊖ onbeforecopy (Web) names a script to run when a user starts copying a selection to the Clipboard but before any action actually takes place.
- ⊖ onbeforecut (Web) names a script to run when a user starts cutting a selection to the Clipboard but before any action actually takes place.
- ⊖ onbeforefocusenter (Web) names a script to run when a user starts focusing on an object but before the object actually gains focus.
- ⊖ onbeforefocusleave (Web) names a script to run when a user starts leaving an object but before the object actually loses focus.
- ⊖ onblur (Web) names a script to run when the object loses focus (that is, it is no longer the active element).
- onclick (Web) names a script to run when a user moves the mouse pointer or other pointing device over the description and clicks the button.
- ⊖ oncontextmenu (Web) names a script to run when a user right-clicks the mouse to open a shortcut menu.
- ⊖ oncontrolselect (Web) names a script to run when a user selects a control.
- ⊖ oncopy (Web) names a script to run when a user copies a selection to the Clipboard.
- ⊖ oncut (Web) names a script to run when a user cuts a selection to the Clipboard.
- ondblclick (Web) names a script to run when a user moves the mouse pointer or other pointing device over the description and double-clicks the button.
- ⊖ ondrag (Web) names a script to run when a user drags a selection.
- ⊖ ondragend (Web) names a script to run after a user completes a drag-and-drop operation.
- ⊖ ondragenter (Web) names a script to run when a user drags a selection into an area in which it can be dropped.
- ⊖ ondragleave (Web) names a script to run when a user drags a selection beyond an area in which it can be dropped.
- ⊖ ondragover (Web) names a script to run when a user drags a selection over an area in which it can be dropped.

- ⊖ `ondragstart` (Web) names a script to run when a user starts dragging a selection or element.
- ⊖ `ondrop` (Web) names a script to run when a user releases the mouse button to drop a dragged selection.
- ⊖ `onfocus` (Web) names a script to run when a user points the mouse pointer or other pointing device to focus on the current element.
- ⊖ `onfocusenter` (Web) names a script to run when a user focuses on the current element in any way.
- ⊖ `onfocusleave` (Web) names a script to run when a user inactivates the current element in any way.
- ⊖ `onhelp` (Web) names a script to run when a user presses the F1 or Help key over the description.
- `onkeydown` (Web) names a script to run when a user presses and holds down a key over the description.
- `onkeypress` (Web) names a script to run when a user presses and releases a key over the description.
- `onkeyup` (Web) names a script to run when a user releases a key that is currently held down over the description.
- ⊖ `onlayoutcomplete` (Web) names a script to run when a user lays out a selection using Print or Print Preview.
- ⊖ `onlosecapture` (Web) names a script to run when a user releases a selection that has been captured by the mouse.
- `onmousedown` (Web) names a script to run when a user moves the mouse pointer or other pointing device over the description and presses and holds down the button.
- ⊖ `onmouseenter` (Web) names a script to run when a user moves the mouse pointer onto the object.
- ⊖ `onmouseleave` (Web) names a script to run when the mouse pointer leaves the object.
- `onmousemove` (Web) names a script to run when a user moves the mouse pointer or other pointing device over the description.
- `onmouseout` (Web) names a script to run when a user moves the mouse pointer or other pointing device away from the description.
- `onmouseover` (Web) names a script to run the first time a user moves the mouse pointer or other pointing device over the description.
- `onmouseup` (Web) names a script to run when a user moves the mouse pointer or other pointing device over the description and releases a mouse button that is currently held down.
- ⊖ `onpaste` (Web) names a script to run when a user pastes the Clipboard contents onto the object.
- ⊖ `onpropertychange` (Web) names a script to run when a property changes on the selected object in any way.
- ⊖ `onreadystatechange` (Web) names a script to run when the status of an element has changed (for example, the element receives data).
- ⊖ `onresize` (Web) names a script to run when a user resizes the selected object.

XHTML Syntax

- ⊝ onresizeend (Web) names a script to run after the object has been resized.
- ⊝ onresizestart (Web) names a script to run as a user resizes the object.
- ⊝ onselectstart (Web) names a script to run when a user starts selecting the definition.
- style (Web) sets styles for the description.
- ⊝ tabindex (Web) defines the position of the current element in all the elements that a user can navigate to using a Tab or Shift + Tab key.
- title (Web) provides a title for the description.
- *definition* represents a definition description (dd) paired with a definition term (dt).

Notes

- This element originated in HTML 2.0.
- Each dd element in a definition list must be paired with a dt element.
- Pairs of terms (dt) and descriptions (dd) are embedded within dl elements.
- To present multiple terms in a definition description, insert line breaks using the br element (70).
- A paragraph break automatically occurs at the end of a dd element and its contents.
- For the dd element, WebTV supports the class and style attributes.

Related Elements

dir (104), dl (112), dt (116), li (198), menu (212), ol (230), ul (331)

For More Information

Learn more about the dd element on page 549 in Chapter 3.

---

del   Mark Deletion

Purpose

Marks document sections that have been deleted since the original document was created and posted.

Syntax

```
<del[ accesskey="shortcut_key"][ CITE="uri"]
   [ class="class_name"]
   [ contenteditable="edit_string"]
   [ datetime="YYYY-MM-DD[Thh:mm:ssTZD]"]
   [ dir="ltr"|"rtl"][ disabled="disabled"]
   [ id="id_name"][ lang="lang_code"]
   [ language="javascript"|"jscript"
   |"vbs[cript]"][ onblur="bl_script"]
   [ onclick="cl_script"][ ondblclick="dc_script"]
```

```
[ ondrag="d_script"][ ondragend="dd_script"]
[ ondragenter="de_script"][ ondragleave="dl_script"]
[ ondragover="do_script"][ ondragstart="ds_script"]
[ ondrop="dr_script"][ onfocus="fc_script"]
[ onkeydown="kd_script"][ onkeypress="kp_script"]
[ onkeyup="ku_script"][ onmousedown="md_script"]
[ onmousemove="mm_script"][ onmouseout="mo_script"]
[ onmouseover="mov_script"][ onmouseup="mu_script"]
[ onreadystatechange="rsc_script"]
[ onselectstart="ss_script"]
[ style="name_1: value_1"[; "name_2: value_2"]
[...; "name_n: value_n"]]
[ tabindex="position_number"][ title="title"]>
deleted-section</del>
```

Where

- ⊖ `accesskey` (Web) assigns a shortcut key to the object in order to focus on it.
- `cite` (Web) provides a URI for a document that contains the reason for a document change.
- `class` (Web) specifies a class identification for the marked text.
- ⊖ `contenteditable` (Web) specifies or obtains a value that indicates whether a user can edit the element content.
- `datetime` (Web) specifies the date and time at which a change in the document was made.
- `dir` (Web) specifies the direction in which the marked text is displayed: left-to-right or right-to-left.
- ⊖ `disabled` (Web) is a keyword that prevents a user from using the element.
- `id` (Web) provides a unique identifier name for the text marked as deleted.
- `lang` (Web) specifies the code for the language used for the marked text.
- ⊖ `language` (Web) declares the scripting language of the current script.
- ⊖ `onblur` (Web) names a script to run when the object loses focus (that is, it is no longer the active element).
- `onclick` (Web) names a script to run when a user moves the mouse pointer or other pointing device over the marked text and clicks the button.
- `ondblclick` (Web) names a script to run when a user moves the mouse pointer or other pointing device over the marked text and double-clicks the button.
- ⊖ `ondrag` (Web) names a script to run when a user drags a selection.
- ⊖ `ondragend` (Web) names a script to run after a user completes a drag-and-drop operation.
- ⊖ `ondragenter` (Web) names a script to run when a user drags a selection into an area in which it can be dropped.

- ⊜ ondragleave (Web) names a script to run when a user drags a selection beyond an area in which it can be dropped.
- ⊜ ondragover (Web) names a script to run when a user drags a selection over an area in which it can be dropped.
- ⊜ ondragstart (Web) names a script to run when a user starts dragging a selection or element.
- ⊜ ondrop (Web) names a script to run when a user releases the mouse button to drop a dragged selection.
- ⊜ onfocus (Web) names a script to run when a user points the mouse pointer or other pointing device to focus on the current element.
- onkeydown (Web) names a script to run when a user presses and holds down a key over the text marked as deleted.
- onkeypress (Web) names a script to run when a user presses and releases a key over the text marked as deleted.
- onkeyup (Web) names a script to run when a user releases a key that is currently held down over the text marked as deleted.
- onmousedown (Web) names a script to run when a user moves the mouse pointer or other pointing device over the text marked as deleted and presses and holds down the button.
- onmousemove (Web) names a script to run when a user moves the mouse pointer or other pointing device over the text marked as deleted.
- onmouseout (Web) names a script to run when a user moves the mouse pointer or other pointing device away from the text marked as deleted.
- onmouseover (Web) names a script to run the first time a user moves the mouse pointer or other pointing device over the text marked as deleted.
- onmouseup (Web) names a script to run when a user moves the mouse pointer or other pointing device over the marked text and releases a mouse button that is currently held down.
- ⊜ onreadystatechange (Web) names a script to run when the status of an element has changed (for example, the element receives data).
- ⊜ onselectstart (Web) names a script to run when a user starts selecting an object.
- style (Web) sets styles for the text marked as deleted.
- ⊜ tabindex (Web) defines the position of the current element in all the elements that a user can navigate to using a Tab or Shift + Tab key.
- title (Web) provides a title for the text marked as deleted.
- *deleted-section* is the text marked as deleted.

Notes
- This element originated in HTML 4.0.
- Browsers may mark deleted text in various ways, such as changing the text to a special font or striking it through.

Related Element
ins (181)

dfn   Definition

Purpose
Identifies a definition term in a definition list.

Syntax

```
<dfn[ accesskey="shortcut_key"][ class="class_name"]
[ contenteditable="edit_string"][ dir="ltr"|"rtl"]
[ disabled="disabled"][ id="id_name"]
[ lang="lang_code"][ language="javascript"|"jscript"
|"vbs[cript]"][ onbeforecopy="bc_script"]
[ onbeforecut="bt_script"]
[ onbeforefocusenter="bfe_script"]
[ onbeforefocusleave="bfl_script"]
[ onbeforepaste="bp_script"][ onblur="bl_script"]
[ onclick="cl_script"][ oncontextmenu="cm_script"]
[ oncontrolselect="ctl_script"][ oncopy="cp_script"]
[ oncut="ct_script"][ ondblclick="dc_script"]
[ ondrag="d_script"][ ondragend="dd_script"]
[ ondragenter="de_script"][ ondragleave="dl_script"]
[ ondragover="do_script"][ ondragstart="ds_script"]
[ ondrop="dr_script"][ onfocus="fc_script"]
[ onfocusenter="fe_script"]
[ onfocusleave="fl_script"]
[ onhelp="hlp_script"][ onkeydown="kd_script"]
[ onkeypress="kp_script"][ onkeyup="ku_script"]
[ onlosecapture="lc_script"]
[ onmousedown="md_script"]
[ onmouseenter="me_script"]
[ onmouseleave="ml_script"]
[ onmousemove="mm_script"][ onmouseout="mo_script"]
[ onmouseover="mov_script"][ onmouseup="mu_script"]
[ onpaste="p_script"][ onpropertychange="pc_script"]
[ onreadystatechange="rsc_script"]
[ onresize="rsz_script"][ onresizeend="ree_script"]
[ onresizestart="res_script"]
[ onselectstart="ss_script"]
[ style="name_1: value_1"[; "name_2: value_2"]
[...; "name_n: value_n"]]
[ tabindex="position_number"][ title="title"]>
text</dfn>
```

Where

- ⊖ `accesskey` (Web) assigns a shortcut key to the object in order to focus on it.
- `class` (Web) specifies a class identification for the definition.
- ⊖ `contenteditable` (Web) specifies or obtains a value that indicates whether a user can edit the element content.
- `dir` (Web) specifies the direction in which the definition text is displayed: left-to-right or right-to-left.
- ⊖ `disabled` (Web) is a keyword that prevents a user from using the element.
- `id` (Web) provides a unique identifier name for the definition.
- `lang` (Web) specifies the code for the language used for the definition text.
- ⊖ `language` (Web) declares the scripting language of the current script.
- ⊖ `onbeforecopy` (Web) names a script to run when a user starts copying a selection to the Clipboard but before any action actually takes place.
- ⊖ `onbeforecut` (Web) names a script to run when a user starts cutting a selection to the Clipboard but before any action actually takes place.
- ⊖ `onbeforefocusenter` (Web) names a script to run when a user starts focusing on an object but before the object actually gains focus.
- ⊖ `onbeforefocusleave` (Web) names a script to run when a user starts leaving an object but before the object actually loses focus.
- ⊖ `onbeforepaste` (Web) names a script to run when a user starts pasting an object but before any action actually takes place.
- ⊖ `onblur` (Web) names a script to run when the object loses focus (that is, it is no longer the active element).
- `onclick` (Web) names a script to run when a user moves the mouse pointer or other pointing device over the definition and clicks the button.
- ⊖ `oncontextmenu` (Web) names a script to run when a user right-clicks the mouse to open a shortcut menu.
- ⊖ `oncontrolselect` (Web) names a script to run when a user selects a control.
- ⊖ `oncopy` (Web) names a script to run when a user copies a selection to the Clipboard.
- ⊖ `oncut` (Web) names a script to run when a user cuts a selection to the Clipboard.
- `ondblclick` (Web) names a script to run when a user moves the mouse pointer or other pointing device over the definition and double-clicks the button.
- ⊖ `ondrag` (Web) names a script to run when a user drags a selection.
- ⊖ `ondragend` (Web) names a script to run after a user completes a drag-and-drop operation.
- ⊖ `ondragenter` (Web) names a script to run when a user drags a selection into an area in which it can be dropped.
- ⊖ `ondragleave` (Web) names a script to run when a user drags a selection beyond an area in which it can be dropped.

- ⊝ `ondragover` (Web) names a script to run when a user drags a selection over an area in which it can be dropped.
- ⊝ `ondragstart` (Web) names a script to run when a user starts dragging a selection or element.
- ⊝ `ondrop` (Web) names a script to run when a user releases the mouse button to drop a dragged selection.
- ⊝ `onfocus` (Web) names a script to run when a user points the mouse pointer or other pointing device to focus on the current element.
- ⊝ `onfocusenter` (Web) names a script to run when a user focuses on the current element in any way.
- ⊝ `onfocusleave` (Web) names a script to run when a user inactivates the current element in any way.
- ⊝ `onhelp` (Web) names a script to run when a user presses the F1 or Help key over the current element.
- `onkeydown` (Web) names a script to run when a user presses and holds down a key over the definition.
- `onkeypress` (Web) names a script to run when a user presses and releases a key over the definition.
- `onkeyup` (Web) names a script to run when a user releases a key that is currently held down over the definition.
- ⊝ `onlosecapture` (Web) names a script to run when a user releases a selection that has been captured by the mouse.
- `onmousedown` (Web) names a script to run when a user moves the mouse pointer or other pointing device over the definition and presses and holds down the button.
- ⊝ `onmouseenter` (Web) names a script to run when the mouse pointer is moved onto the object.
- ⊝ `onmouseleave` (Web) names a script to run when the mouse pointer leaves the object.
- `onmousemove` (Web) names a script to run when a user moves the mouse pointer or other pointing device over the definition.
- `onmouseout` (Web) names a script to run when a user moves the mouse pointer or other pointing device away from the definition.
- `onmouseover` (Web) names a script to run the first time a user moves the mouse pointer or other pointing device over the definition.
- `onmouseup` (Web) names a script to run when a user moves the mouse pointer or other pointing device over the definition and releases a mouse button that is currently held down.
- ⊝ `onpaste` (Web) names a script to run when a user pastes the Clipboard contents onto the object.
- ⊝ `onpropertychange` (Web) names a script to run when a property changes on the selected object in any way.
- ⊝ `onreadystatechange` (Web) names a script to run when the status of an element has changed (for example, the element receives data).
- ⊝ `onresize` (Web) names a script to run when a user resizes the selected object.

XHTML Syntax

- ⊕ onresizeend (Web) names a script to run after the object has been resized.
- ⊕ onresizestart (Web) names a script to run as a user resizes the object.
- ⊕ onselectstart (Web) names a script to run when a user starts selecting an object.
- style (Web) sets styles for the definition.
- ⊕ tabindex (Web) defines the position of the current element in all the elements that a user can navigate to using a Tab or Shift + Tab key.
- title (Web) provides a title for the definition.
- *text* represents one or more characters.

Notes

- This inline element originated in HTML 3.2.
- dfn is one of the elements in the %phrase entity. The other %phrase elements are abbr, acronym, cite, code, em, kbd, samp, strong, and var.
- dfn is a logical element, in which particular browsers are programmed to apply a certain style to the selected text. This is in contrast to a physical element in which you "code" the styles yourself.
- For the dfn element, WebTV supports the class and style attributes.

Related Elements

abbr (29), acronym (31), b (46), cite (83), code (87), em (120), i (154), kbd (186), pre (242), s (254), samp (258), strike (254), strong (276), tt (324), u (327), var (335)

---

dir   Directory List

Purpose

Displays a word list.

Syntax

```
<dir [ accesskey="shortcut_key"][ class="class_name"]
  [ compact="compact"][ contenteditable="edit_string"]
  [ dir="ltr"|"rtl"][ id="id_name"][ lang="lang_code"]
  [ language="javascript"|"jscript"|"vbs[cript]"]
  [ onbeforecopy="bc_script"]
  [ onbeforecut="bt_script"]
  [ onbeforefocusenter="bfe_script"]
  [ onbeforefocusleave="bfl_script"]
  [ onbeforepaste="bp_script"][ onblur="bl_script"]
  [ onclick="cl_script"][ oncontextmenu="cm_script"]
  [ oncontrolselect="ctl_script"][ oncopy="cp_script"]
  [ oncut="ct_script"][ ondblclick="dc_script"]
```

```
[ ondrag="d_script"][ ondragend="dd_script"]
[ ondragenter="de_script"][ ondragleave="dl_script"]
[ ondragover="do_script"][ ondragstart="ds_script"]
[ ondrop="dr_script"][ onfocus="fc_script"]
[ onfocusenter="fe_script"]
[ onfocusleave="fl_script"]
[ onhelp="hlp_script"][ onkeydown="kd_script"]
[ onkeypress="kp_script"][ onkeyup="ku_script"]
[ onlosecapture="lc_script"]
[ onmousedown="md_script"]
[ onmouseenter="me_script"]
[ onmouseleave="ml_script"]
[ onmousemove="mm_script"]
[ onmouseout="mo_script"][ onmouseover="mov_script"]
[ onmouseup="mu_script"][ onpaste="p_script"]
[ onpropertychange="pc_script"]
[ onreadystatechange="rsc_script"]
[ onresize="rsz_script"][ onresizeend="ree_script"]
[ onresizestart="res_script"]
[ onselectstart="ss_script"]
[ style="name_1: value_1"[; "name_2: value_2"]
[...; "name_n: value_n"]]
[ tabindex="position_number"][ title="title"]>
directory-list</dir>
```

Where

- ⊖ **accesskey** (Web) assigns a shortcut key to the object in order to focus on it.
- **class** (Web) specifies a class identification for the directory list.
- **compact** (Web) indicates that a browser might decrease the size of the space between a number or bullet and the list item.
- ⊖ **contenteditable** (Web) specifies or obtains a value that indicates whether a user can edit the element content.
- **dir** (Web) specifies the direction in which the directory list text is displayed: left-to-right or right-to-left.
- **id** (Web) provides a unique identifier name for the directory list.
- **lang** (Web) specifies the code for the language used for the directory list text.
- ⊖ **language** (Web) declares the scripting language of the current script.
- ⊖ **onbeforecopy** (Web) names a script to run when a user starts copying a selection to the Clipboard but before any action actually takes place.
- ⊖ **onbeforecut** (Web) names a script to run when a user starts cutting a selection to the Clipboard but before any action actually takes place.
- ⊖ **onbeforefocusenter** (Web) names a script to run when a user starts focusing on an object but before the object actually gains focus.

- ⊝ `onbeforefocusleave` (Web) names a script to run when a user starts leaving an object but before the object actually loses focus.
- ⊝ `onbeforepaste` (Web) names a script to run when a user starts pasting an object but before any action actually takes place.
- ⊝ `onblur` (Web) names a script to run when the object loses focus (that is, it is no longer the active element).
- `onclick` (Web) names a script to run when a user moves the mouse pointer or other pointing device over the directory list and clicks the button.
- ⊝ `oncontextmenu` (Web) names a script to run when a user right-clicks the mouse to open a shortcut menu.
- ⊝ `oncontrolselect` (Web) names a script to run when a user selects a control.
- ⊝ `oncopy` (Web) names a script to run when a user copies a selection to the Clipboard.
- ⊝ `oncut` (Web) names a script to run when a user cuts a selection to the Clipboard.
- `ondblclick` (Web) names a script to run when a user moves the mouse pointer or other pointing device over the directory list and double-clicks the button.
- ⊝ `ondrag` (Web) names a script to run when a user drags a selection.
- ⊝ `ondragend` (Web) names a script to run after a user completes a drag-and-drop operation.
- ⊝ `ondragenter` (Web) names a script to run when a user drags a selection into an area in which it can be dropped.
- ⊝ `ondragleave` (Web) names a script to run when a user drags a selection beyond an area in which it can be dropped.
- ⊝ `ondragover` (Web) names a script to run when a user drags a selection over an area in which it can be dropped.
- ⊝ `ondragstart` (Web) names a script to run when a user starts dragging a selection or element.
- ⊝ `ondrop` (Web) names a script to run when a user releases the mouse button to drop a dragged selection.
- ⊝ `onfocus` (Web) names a script to run when a user points the mouse pointer or other pointing device to focus on the current element.
- ⊝ `onfocusenter` (Web) names a script to run when a user focuses on the current element in any way.
- ⊝ `onfocusleave` (Web) names a script to run when a user inactivates the current element in any way.
- ⊝ `onhelp` (Web) names a script to run when a user presses the F1 or Help key over the current element.
- `onkeydown` (Web) names a script to run when a user presses and holds down a key over the directory list.
- `onkeypress` (Web) names a script to run when a user presses and releases a key over the directory list.

- onkeyup (Web) names a script to run when a user releases a key that is currently held down over the directory list.
- ⊖ onlosecapture (Web) names a script to run when a user releases a selection that has been captured by the mouse.
- onmousedown (Web) names a script to run when a user moves the mouse pointer or other pointing device over the directory list and presses and holds down the button.
- ⊖ onmouseenter (Web) names a script to run when a user moves the mouse pointer onto the object.
- ⊖ onmouseleave (Web) names a script to run when the mouse pointer leaves the object.
- onmousemove (Web) names a script to run when a user moves the mouse pointer or other pointing device over the directory list.
- onmouseout (Web) names a script to run when a user moves the mouse pointer or other pointing device away from the directory list.
- onmouseover (Web) names a script to run the first time a user moves the mouse pointer or other pointing device over the directory list.
- onmouseup (Web) names a script to run when a user moves the mouse pointer or other pointing device over the directory list and releases a mouse button that is currently held down.
- ⊖ onpaste (Web) names a script to run when a user pastes the Clipboard contents onto the object.
- ⊖ onpropertychange (Web) names a script to run when a property changes on the selected object in any way.
- ⊖ onreadystatechange (Web) names a script to run when the status of an element has changed (for example, the element receives data).
- ⊖ onresize (Web) names a script to run when a user resizes the selected object.
- ⊖ onresizeend (Web) names a script to run after the object has been resized.
- ⊖ onresizestart (Web) names a script to run as a user resizes the object.
- ⊖ onselectstart (Web) names a script to run when a user starts selecting an object.
- style (Web) sets styles for the directory list.
- title (Web) provides a title for the directory list.
- *directory-list* represents one or more li (list item) elements containing one or more characters.

Notes

- This block-level element originated in HTML 2.0.
- Although dir is supported by HTML 4.0, it has been deprecated (that is, it will eventually be obsolete) and appears only in the Transitional DTD — not the Strict DTD. Use other list elements (ol or ul) instead.
- Some browsers arrange dir lists in columns, which is the element's intended format.
- Directory list words cannot be longer than 20 characters each.

- Items on a directory list may or may not be preceded with bullets, depending on the browser.

Related Elements

menu (212), ol (230), ul (331)

---

div   Division

Purpose

Marks the beginning of a new division in a document.

Syntax

```
<div[ accesskey="shortcut_key"]
   [ align="left"|"center"|"right"|"justify"]
   [ class="class_name"]
   [ contenteditable="edit_string"]
   [ datafld="ds_col_name"]
   [ dataformatas="html"|"text"]
   [ datasrc="ds_identifier"][ dir="ltr"|"rtl"]
   [ disabled="disabled"][ id="id_name"]
   [ lang="lang_code"][ language="javascript"|"jscript"
   |"vbs[cript]"][ nowrap="nowrap"]
   [ onbeforecopy="bc_script"]
   [ onbeforecut="bt_script"]
   [ onbeforeeditfocus="bef_script"]
   [ onbeforefocusenter="bfe_script"]
   [ onbeforefocusleave="bfl_script"]
   [ onbeforepaste="bp_script"][ onblur="bl_script"]
   [ onclick="cl_script"][ oncontextmenu="cm_script"]
   [ oncontrolselect="ctl_script"][ oncopy="cp_script"]
   [ oncut="ct_script"][ ondblclick="dc_script"]
   [ ondrag="d_script"][ ondragend="dd_script"]
   [ ondragenter="de_script"][ ondragleave="dl_script"]
   [ ondragover="do_script"][ ondragstart="ds_script"]
   [ ondrop="dr_script"][ onfilterchange="f_script"]
   [ onfocus="fc_script"][ onfocusenter="fe_script"]
   [ onfocusleave="fl_script"][ onhelp="hlp_script"]
   [ onkeydown="kd_script"][ onkeypress="kp_script"]
   [ onkeyup="ku_script"]
   [ onlayoutcomplete="la_script"]
   [ onlosecapture="lc_script"]
   [ onmousedown="md_script"]
   [ onmouseenter="me_script"]
```

```
[ onmouseleave="ml_script"]
[ onmousemove="mm_script"]
[ onmouseout="mo_script"][ onmouseover="mov_script"]
[ onmouseup="mu_script"][ onpaste="p_script"]
[ onpropertychange="pc_script"]
[ onreadystatechange="rsc_script"]
[ onresize="rsz_script"][ onresizeend="ree_script"]
[ onresizestart="res_script"]
[ onscroll="sc_script"][ onselectstart="ss_script"]
[ style="name_1: value_1"[; "name_2: value_2"]
[...; "name_n: value_n"]]
[ tabindex="position_number"][ title="title"]>
text</div>
```

Where

- ⊖ accesskey (Web) assigns a shortcut key to the object in order to focus on it.
- align (Web) horizontally aligns the contents of the entire division. This attribute is deprecated; use a style sheet instead.
- class (Web) specifies a class identification for the division.
- ⊖ contenteditable (Web) specifies or obtains a value that indicates whether a user can edit the element content.
- ⊖ datafld (Web) specifies the column name from the file that contains the data source object.
- ⊖ dataformatas (Web) indicates whether the data for this element is formatted as plain text (that is, unformatted ASCII) or HTML.
- ⊖ datasrc (Web) specifies the identifier of the data source object.
- dir (Web) specifies the direction in which the text in the division is displayed: left-to-right or right-to-left.
- ⊖ disabled (Web) is a keyword that prevents a user from using the element.
- id (Web) provides a unique identifier name for the division.
- lang (Web) specifies the code for the language used for the division text.
- ⊖ language (Web) declares the scripting language of the current script.
- ⊖ onbeforecopy (Web) names a script to run when a user starts copying a selection to the Clipboard but before any action actually takes place.
- ⊖ onbeforecut (Web) names a script to run when a user starts cutting a selection to the Clipboard but before any action actually takes place.
- ⊖ onbeforeeditfocus (Web) names a script to run when a user starts activating an object but before the object actually becomes active.
- ⊖ onbeforefocusenter (Web) names a script to run when a user starts focusing on an object but before the object actually gains focus.
- ⊖ onbeforefocusleave (Web) names a script to run when a user starts leaving an object but before the object actually loses focus.

- ⊕ onbeforepaste (Web) names a script to run when a user starts pasting an object but before any action actually takes place.
- ⊕ onblur (Web) names a script to run when the object loses focus (that is, it is no longer the active element).
- onclick (Web) names a script to run when a user moves the mouse pointer or other pointing device over the division and clicks the button.
- ⊕ oncontextmenu (Web) names a script to run when a user right-clicks the mouse to open a shortcut menu.
- ⊕ oncontrolselect (Web) names a script to run when a user selects a control.
- ⊕ oncopy (Web) names a script to run when a user copies a selection to the Clipboard.
- ⊕ oncut (Web) names a script to run when a user cuts a selection to the Clipboard.
- ondblclick (Web) names a script to run when a user moves the mouse pointer or other pointing device over the division and double-clicks the button.
- ⊕ ondrag (Web) names a script to run when a user drags a selection.
- ⊕ ondragend (Web) names a script to run after a user completes a drag-and-drop operation.
- ⊕ ondragenter (Web) names a script to run when a user drags a selection into an area in which it can be dropped.
- ⊕ ondragleave (Web) names a script to run when a user drags a selection beyond an area in which it can be dropped.
- ⊕ ondragover (Web) names a script to run when a user drags a selection over an area in which it can be dropped.
- ⊕ ondragstart (Web) names a script to run when a user starts dragging a selection or element.
- ⊕ ondrop (Web) names a script to run when a user releases the mouse button to drop a dragged selection.
- ⊕ onfilterchange (Web) names a script to run when a visual filter changes in any way.
- ⊕ onfocus (Web) names a script to run when a user points the mouse pointer or other pointing device to focus on the current element.
- ⊕ onfocusenter (Web) names a script to run when a user focuses on the current element in any way.
- ⊕ onfocusleave (Web) names a script to run when a user inactivates the current element in any way.
- ⊕ onhelp (Web) names a script to run when a user presses the F1 or Help key over the current element.
- onkeydown (Web) names a script to run when a user presses and holds down a key over the division.
- onkeypress (Web) names a script to run when a user presses and releases a key over the division.
- onkeyup (Web) names a script to run when a user releases a key that is currently held down over the division.

XHTML Syntax

- ⊖ `onlayoutcomplete` (Web) names a script to run when a user lays out a selection using Print or Print Preview.
- ⊖ `onlosecapture` (Web) names a script to run when a user releases a selection that has been captured by the mouse.
- `onmousedown` (Web) names a script to run when a user moves the mouse pointer or other pointing device over the division and presses and holds down the button.
- ⊖ `onmouseenter` (Web) names a script to run when a user moves the mouse pointer onto the object.
- ⊖ `onmouseleave` (Web) names a script to run when the mouse pointer leaves the object.
- `onmousemove` (Web) names a script to run when a user moves the mouse pointer or other pointing device over the division.
- `onmouseout` (Web) names a script to run when a user moves the mouse pointer or other pointing device away from the division.
- `onmouseover` (Web) names a script to run the first time a user moves the mouse pointer or other pointing device over the division.
- `onmouseup` (Web) names a script to run when a user moves the mouse pointer or other pointing device over the division and releases a mouse button that is currently held down.
- ⊖ `onpaste` (Web) names a script to run when a user pastes the Clipboard contents onto the object.
- ⊖ `onpropertychange` (Web) names a script to run when a property changes on the selected object in any way.
- ⊖ `onreadystatechange` (Web) names a script to run when the status of an element has changed (for example, the element receives data).
- ⊖ `onresize` (Web) names a script to run when a user resizes the selected object.
- ⊖ `onresizeend` (Web) names a script to run after the object has been resized.
- ⊖ `onresizestart` (Web) names a script to run as a user resizes the object.
- ⊖ `onscroll` (Web) names a script to run when a user moves the scroll box within the scroll bar.
- ⊖ `onselectstart` (Web) names a script to run when a user starts selecting an object.
- `style` (Web) sets styles for the division.
- ⊖ `tabindex` (Web) defines the position of the current element in all the elements that a user can navigate to using a Tab or Shift + Tab key.
- `title` (Web) provides a title for the division.
- *text* represents one or more characters.

Notes

- This block-level element originated in HTML 3.2.
- `div` simply marks the location of a new chapter or section within a document; it does not change or reset alignment, enhancements, or anything else in the document unless you specify the alignment using the

align attribute. However, note that align is deprecated; it appears only in the Transitional DTD.

- You can use div to apply styles to a particular section of a document.
- div usually causes a line break.
- You cannot use div within a paragraph set with the p element (238); it will terminate the paragraph.
- For the div element, WebTV supports the align, class, id, and title attributes.

Related Element

body (65)

dl   **Definition List**

Purpose

Defines a definition list.

Syntax

```
<dl[ accesskey="shortcut_key"][ class="class_name"]
   [ compact="compact"][ contenteditable="edit_string"]
   [ dir="ltr"|"rtl"][ disabled="disabled"]
   [ id="id_name"][ lang="lang_code"]
   [ language="javascript"|"jscript"|"vbs[cript]"]
   [ onbeforecopy="bc_script"]
   [ onbeforecut="bt_script"]
   [ onbeforefocusenter="bfe_script"]
   [ onbeforefocusleave="bfl_script"]
   [ onbeforepaste="bp_script"][ onblur="bl_script"]
   [ onclick="cl_script"][ oncontextmenu="cm_script"]
   [ oncontrolselect="ctl_script"][ oncopy="cp_script"]
   [ oncut="ct_script"][ ondblclick="dc_script"]
   [ ondrag="d_script"][ ondragend="dd_script"]
   [ ondragenter="de_script"][ ondragleave="dl_script"]
   [ ondragover="do_script"][ ondragstart="ds_script"]
   [ ondrop="dr_script"][ onfocus="fc_script"]
   [ onfocusenter="fe_script"]
   [ onfocusleave="fl_script"][ onhelp="hlp_script"]
   [ onkeydown="kd_script"][ onkeypress="kp_script"]
   [ onkeyup="ku_script"]
   [ onlayoutcomplete="la_script"]
   [ onlosecapture="lc_script"]
   [ onmousedown="md_script"]
```

XHTML Syntax

```
[ onmouseenter="me_script"]
[ onmouseleave="ml_script"]
[ onmousemove="mm_script"][ onmouseout="mo_script"]
[ onmouseover="mov_script"][ onmouseup="mu_script"]
[ onpaste="p_script"][ onpropertychange="pc_script"]
[ onreadystatechange="rsc_script"]
[ onresize="rsz_script"][ onresizeend="ree_script"]
[ onresizestart="res_script"]
[ onselectstart="ss_script"]
[ style="name_1: value_1"[; "name_2: value_2"]
[...; "name_n: value_n"]]
[ tabindex="position_number"][ title="title"]>
definition-list</dl>
```

Where

- ⊖ `accesskey` (Web) assigns a shortcut key to the object in order to focus on it.
- `class` (Web) specifies a class identification for the definition list.
- `compact` (Web) indicates that a browser might decrease the size of the space between the term and its definition. This attribute is deprecated; use a style sheet instead.
- ⊖ `contenteditable` (Web) specifies or obtains a value that indicates whether a user can edit the element content.
- `dir` (Web) specifies the direction in which the text in the definition list is displayed: left-to-right or right-to-left.
- ⊖ `disabled` (Web) is a keyword that prevents a user from using the element.
- `id` (Web) provides a unique identifier name for the definition list.
- `lang` (Web) specifies the code for the language used for the definition list text.
- ⊖ `language` (Web) declares the scripting language of the current script.
- ⊖ `onbeforecopy` (Web) names a script to run when a user starts copying a selection to the Clipboard but before any action actually takes place.
- ⊖ `onbeforecut` (Web) names a script to run when a user starts cutting a selection to the Clipboard but before any action actually takes place.
- ⊖ `onbeforefocusenter` (Web) names a script to run when a user starts focusing on an object but before the object actually gains focus.
- ⊖ `onbeforefocusleave` (Web) names a script to run when a user starts leaving an object but before the object actually loses focus.
- ⊖ `onbeforepaste` (Web) names a script to run when a user starts pasting an object but before any action actually takes place.
- ⊖ `onblur` (Web) names a script to run when the object loses focus (that is, it is no longer the active element).

XHTML Syntax

- onclick (Web) names a script to run when a user moves the mouse pointer or other pointing device over the definition list and clicks the button.
- ⊖ oncontextmenu (Web) names a script to run when a user right-clicks the mouse to open a shortcut menu.
- ⊖ oncontrolselect (Web) names a script to run when a user selects a control.
- ⊖ oncopy (Web) names a script to run when a user copies a selection to the Clipboard.
- ⊖ oncut (Web) names a script to run when a user cuts a selection to the Clipboard.
- ondblclick (Web) names a script to run when a user moves the mouse pointer or other pointing device over the definition list and double-clicks the button.
- ⊖ ondrag (Web) names a script to run when a user drags a selection.
- ⊖ ondragend (Web) names a script to run after a user completes a drag-and-drop operation.
- ⊖ ondragenter (Web) names a script to run when a user drags a selection into an area in which it can be dropped.
- ⊖ ondragleave (Web) names a script to run when a user drags a selection beyond an area in which it can be dropped.
- ⊖ ondragover (Web) names a script to run when a user drags a selection over an area in which it can be dropped.
- ⊖ ondragstart (Web) names a script to run when a user starts dragging a selection or element.
- ⊖ ondrop (Web) names a script to run when a user releases the mouse button to drop a dragged selection.
- ⊖ onfocus (Web) names a script to run when a user points the mouse pointer or other pointing device to focus on the current element.
- ⊖ onfocusenter (Web) names a script to run when a user focuses on the current element in any way.
- ⊖ onfocusleave (Web) names a script to run when a user inactivates the current element in any way.
- ⊖ onhelp (Web) names a script to run when a user presses the F1 or Help key over the current element.
- onkeydown (Web) names a script to run when a user presses and holds down a key over the definition list.
- onkeypress (Web) names a script to run when a user presses and releases a key over the definition list.
- onkeyup (Web) names a script to run when a user releases a key that is currently held down over the definition list.
- ⊖ onlayoutcomplete (Web) names a script to run when a user lays out a selection using Print or Print Preview.
- ⊖ onlosecapture (Web) names a script to run when a user releases a selection that has been captured by the mouse.

- `onmousedown` (Web) names a script to run when a user moves the mouse pointer or other pointing device over the definition list and presses and holds down the button.
- ⊖ `onmouseenter` (Web) names a script to run when a user moves the mouse pointer onto the object.
- ⊖ `onmouseleave` (Web) names a script to run when the mouse pointer leaves the object.
- `onmousemove` (Web) names a script to run when a user moves the mouse pointer or other pointing device over the definition list.
- `onmouseout` (Web) names a script to run when a user moves the mouse pointer or other pointing device away from the definition list.
- `onmouseover` (Web) names a script to run the first time a user moves the mouse pointer or other pointing device over the definition list.
- `onmouseup` (Web) names a script to run when a user moves the mouse pointer or other pointing device over the definition list and releases a mouse button that is currently held down.
- ⊖ `onpaste` (Web) names a script to run when a user pastes the Clipboard contents onto the object.
- ⊖ `onpropertychange` (Web) names a script to run when a property changes on the selected object in any way.
- ⊖ `onreadystatechange` (Web) names a script to run when the status of an element has changed (for example, the element receives data).
- ⊖ `onresize` (Web) names a script to run when a user resizes the selected object.
- ⊖ `onresizeend` (Web) names a script to run after the object has been resized.
- ⊖ `onresizestart` (Web) names a script to run as a user resizes the object.
- ⊖ `onselectstart` (Web) names a script to run when a user starts selecting an object.
- `style` (Web) sets styles for the definition list.
- ⊖ `tabindex` (Web) defines the position of the current element in all the elements that a user can navigate to using a Tab or Shift + Tab key.
- `title` (Web) provides a title for the definition list.
- *definition-list* represents one or more pairs of definition terms (`dt` (116)) and definition descriptions (`dd` (95)).

Notes

- This block-level element originated in HTML 2.0.
- Each definition term (`dt`) in a definition list is paired with a definition description (`dd`).
- You can nest other lists within a definition list.
- Not all browsers recognize the `compact` attribute. `compact` has been deprecated (that is, it will eventually be obsolete) and appears only in the Transitional DTD — not in the Strict DTD.

- Embed the dd, dl, and dt elements within dl. However, some browsers do not support the nesting of elements.
- For the dl element, WebTV supports the class and style attributes.

Related Elements

dd (95), dt (116)

For More Information

Learn more about the dl element on page 549 in Chapter 3.

dt	Definition Term

Purpose

Names a term in a definition list.

Syntax

```
<dt[ accesskey="shortcut_key"][ class="class_name"]
  [ contenteditable="edit_string"][ dir="ltr"|"rtl"]
  [ disabled="disabled"][ id="id_name"]
  [ lang="lang_code"][ language="javascript"|"jscript"
  |"vbs[cript]"][ nowrap="nowrap"]
  [ onbeforecopy="bc_script"]
  [ onbeforecut="bt_script"]
  [ onbeforefocusenter="bfe_script"]
  [ onbeforefocusleave="bfl_script"]
  [ onbeforepaste="bp_script"][ onblur="bl_script"]
  [ onclick="cl_script"][ oncontextmenu="cm_script"]
  [ oncontrolselect="ctl_script"]
  [ oncopy="cp_script"][ oncut="ct_script"]
  [ ondblclick="dc_script"][ ondrag="d_script"]
  [ ondragend="dd_script"][ ondragenter="de_script"]
  [ ondragleave="dl_script"][ ondragover="do_script"]
  [ ondragstart="ds_script"][ ondrop="dr_script"]
  [ onfocus="fc_script"][ onfocusenter="fe_script"]
  [ onfocusleave="fl_script"][ onhelp="hlp_script"]
  [ onkeydown="kd_script"][ onkeypress="kp_script"]
  [ onkeyup="ku_script"]
  [ onlayoutcomplete="la_script"]
  [ onlosecapture="lc_script"]
  [ onmousedown="md_script"]
  [ onmouseenter="me_script"]
  [ onmouseleave="ml_script"]
  [ onmousemove="mm_script"]
  [ onmouseout="mo_script"][ onmouseover="mov_script"]
```

```
[ onmouseup="mu_script"][ onpaste="p_script"]
[ onpropertychange="pc_script"]
[ onreadystatechange="rsc_script"]
[ onresize="rsz_script"][ onresizeend="ree_script"]
[ onresizestart="res_script"]
[ onselectstart="ss_script"]
[ style="name_1: value_1"[; "name_2: value_2"]
[...; "name_n: value_n"]]
[ tabindex="position_number"][ title="title"]>
definition-term</dt>
```

Where

- ⊖ `accesskey` (Web) assigns a shortcut key to the object in order to focus on it.
- `class` (Web) specifies a class identification for the definition term.
- ⊖ `contenteditable` (Web) specifies or obtains a value that indicates whether a user can edit the element content.
- `dir` (Web) specifies the direction in which the definition term text is displayed: left-to-right or right-to-left.
- ⊖ `disabled` (Web) is a keyword that prevents a user from using the element.
- `id` (Web) provides a unique identifier name for the definition term.
- `lang` (Web) specifies the code for the language used for the definition term text.
- ⊖ `language` (Web) declares the scripting language of the current script.
- ⊖ `nowrap` (Web) disables word wrap within the current object.
- ⊖ `onbeforecopy` (Web) names a script to run when a user starts copying a selection to the Clipboard but before any action actually takes place.
- ⊖ `onbeforecut` (Web) names a script to run when a user starts cutting a selection to the Clipboard but before any action actually takes place.
- ⊖ `onbeforefocusenter` (Web) names a script to run when a user starts focusing on an object but before the object actually gains focus.
- ⊖ `onbeforefocusleave` (Web) names a script to run when a user starts leaving an object but before the object actually loses focus.
- ⊖ `onbeforepaste` (Web) names a script to run when a user starts pasting an object but before any action actually takes place.
- ⊖ `onblur` (Web) names a script to run when the object loses focus (that is, it is no longer the active element).
- `onclick` (Web) names a script to run when a user moves the mouse pointer or other pointing device over the definition term and clicks the button.
- ⊖ `oncontextmenu` (Web) names a script to run when a user right-clicks the mouse to open a shortcut menu.
- ⊖ `oncontrolselect` (Web) names a script to run when a user selects a control.

- ⊖ oncopy (Web) names a script to run when a user copies a selection to the Clipboard.
- ⊖ oncut (Web) names a script to run when a user cuts a selection to the Clipboard.
- ondblclick (Web) names a script to run when a user moves the mouse pointer or other pointing device over the definition term and double-clicks the button.
- ⊖ ondrag (Web) names a script to run when a user drags a selection.
- ⊖ ondragend (Web) names a script to run after a user completes a drag-and-drop operation.
- ⊖ ondragenter (Web) names a script to run when a user drags a selection into an area in which it can be dropped.
- ⊖ ondragleave (Web) names a script to run when a user drags a selection beyond an area in which it can be dropped.
- ⊖ ondragover (Web) names a script to run when a user drags a selection over an area in which it can be dropped.
- ⊖ ondragstart (Web) names a script to run when a user starts dragging a selection or element.
- ⊖ ondrop (Web) names a script to run when a user releases the mouse button to drop a dragged selection.
- ⊖ onfocus (Web) names a script to run when a user points the mouse pointer or other pointing device to focus on the current element.
- ⊖ onfocusenter (Web) names a script to run when a user focuses on the current element in any way.
- ⊖ onfocusleave (Web) names a script to run when a user inactivates the current element in any way.
- ⊖ onhelp (Web) names a script to run when a user presses the F1 or Help key over the current element.
- onkeydown (Web) names a script to run when a user presses and holds down a key over the definition term.
- onkeypress (Web) names a script to run when a user presses and releases a key over the definition term.
- onkeyup (Web) names a script to run when a user releases a key that is currently held down over the definition term.
- ⊖ onlayoutcomplete (Web) names a script to run when a user lays out a selection using Print or Print Preview.
- ⊖ onlosecapture (Web) names a script to run when a user releases a selection that has been captured by the mouse.
- onmousedown (Web) names a script to run when a user moves the mouse pointer or other pointing device over the definition term and presses and holds down the button.
- ⊖ onmouseenter (Web) names a script to run when a user moves the mouse pointer onto the object.
- ⊖ onmouseleave (Web) names a script to run when the mouse pointer leaves the object.

XHTML Syntax

- `onmousemove` (Web) names a script to run when a user moves the mouse pointer or other pointing device over the definition term.
- `onmouseout` (Web) names a script to run when a user moves the mouse pointer or other pointing device away from the definition term.
- `onmouseover` (Web) names a script to run the first time a user moves the mouse pointer or other pointing device over the definition term.
- `onmouseup` (Web) names a script to run when a user moves the mouse pointer or other pointing device over the definition term and releases a mouse button that is currently held down.
- ⊖ `onpaste` (Web) names a script to run when a user pastes the Clipboard contents onto the object.
- ⊖ `onpropertychange` (Web) names a script to run when a property changes on the selected object in any way.
- ⊖ `onreadystatechange` (Web) names a script to run when the status of an element has changed (for example, the element receives data).
- ⊖ `onresize` (Web) names a script to run when a user resizes the selected object.
- ⊖ `onresizeend` (Web) names a script to run after the object has been resized.
- ⊖ `onresizestart` (Web) names a script to run as a user resizes the object.
- ⊖ `onselectstart` (Web) names a script to run when a user starts selecting an object.
- `style` (Web) sets styles for the definition term.
- ⊖ `tabindex` (Web) defines the position of the current element in all the elements that a user can navigate to using a Tab or Shift + Tab key.
- `title` (Web) provides a title for the definition term.
- *definition-term* represents a definition term (`dt`), which will be paired with a definition description (`dd`).

Notes

- This element originated in HTML 2.0.
- Each `dd` element in a definition list must be paired with a `dt` element.
- Pairs of terms (`dt`) and descriptions (`dd`) are embedded within `dl` elements.
- A paragraph break automatically occurs at the end of a `dt` element and its contents.
- For the `dt` element, WebTV supports the `class` and `style` attributes.

Related Elements

`dd` (95), `dir` (104), `dl` (112), `li` (198), `menu` (212), `ol` (230), `ul` (331)

For More Information

Learn more about the `dt` element on page 549 in Chapter 3.

em	Emphasis

Purpose
Emphasizes selected text, usually with italics.

Syntax
```
<em[ accesskey="shortcut_key"][ class="class_name"]
   [ contenteditable="edit_string"][ dir="ltr"|"rtl"]
   [ disabled="disabled"][ id="id_name"]
   [ lang="lang_code"][ language="javascript"|"jscript"
   |"vbs[cript]"][ onbeforecopy="bc_script"]
   [ onbeforecut="bt_script"]
   [ onbeforefocusenter="bfe_script"]
   [ onbeforefocusleave="bfl_script"]
   [ onbeforepaste="bp_script"][ onblur="bl_script"]
   [ onclick="cl_script"][ oncontextmenu="cm_script"]
   [ oncontrolselect="ctl_script"][ oncopy="cp_script"]
   [ oncut="ct_script"][ ondblclick="dc_script"]
   [ ondrag="d_script"][ ondragend="dd_script"]
   [ ondragenter="de_script"]
   [ ondragleave="dl_script"]
   [ ondragover="do_script"]
   [ ondragstart="ds_script"][ ondrop="dr_script"]
   [ onfocus="fc_script"][ onfocusenter="fe_script"]
   [ onfocusleave="fl_script"][ onhelp="hlp_script"]
   [ onkeydown="kd_script"][ onkeypress="kp_script"]
   [ onkeyup="ku_script"][ onlosecapture="lc_script"]
   [ onmousedown="md_script"]
   [ onmouseenter="me_script"]
   [ onmouseleave="ml_script"]
   [ onmousemove="mm_script"][ onmouseout="mo_script"]
   [ onmouseover="mov_script"][ onmouseup="mu_script"]
   [ onpaste="p_script"][ onpropertychange="pc_script"]
   [ onreadystatechange="rsc_script"]
   [ onresize="rsz_script"][ onresizeend="ree_script"]
   [ onresizestart="res_script"]
   [ onselectstart="ss_script"]
   [ style="name_1: value_1"[; "name_2: value_2"]
   [...; "name_n: value_n"]]
   [ tabindex="position_number"][ title="title"]>
text</em>
```

Where

- ⊖ `accesskey` (Web) assigns a shortcut key to the object in order to focus on it.
- `class` (Web) specifies a class identification for the emphasized text.
- ⊖ `contenteditable` (Web) specifies or obtains a value that indicates whether a user can edit the element content.
- `dir` (Web) specifies the direction in which the current text is displayed: left-to-right or right-to-left.
- ⊖ `disabled` (Web) is a keyword that prevents a user from using the element.
- `id` (Web) provides a unique identifier name for the emphasized text.
- `lang` (Web) specifies the code for the language used for the emphasized text.
- ⊖ `language` (Web) declares the scripting language of the current script.
- ⊖ `onbeforecopy` (Web) names a script to run when a user starts copying a selection to the Clipboard but before any action actually takes place.
- ⊖ `onbeforecut` (Web) names a script to run when a user starts cutting a selection to the Clipboard but before any action actually takes place.
- ⊖ `onbeforefocusenter` (Web) names a script to run when a user starts focusing on an object but before the object actually gains focus.
- ⊖ `onbeforefocusleave` (Web) names a script to run when a user starts leaving an object but before the object actually loses focus.
- ⊖ `onbeforepaste` (Web) names a script to run when a user starts pasting an object but before any action actually takes place.
- ⊖ `onblur` (Web) names a script to run when the object loses focus (that is, it is no longer the active element).
- `onclick` (Web) names a script to run when a user moves the mouse pointer or other pointing device over the emphasized text and clicks the button.
- ⊖ `oncontextmenu` (Web) names a script to run when a user right-clicks the mouse to open a shortcut menu.
- ⊖ `oncontrolselect` (Web) names a script to run when a user selects a control.
- ⊖ `oncopy` (Web) names a script to run when a user copies a selection to the Clipboard.
- ⊖ `oncut` (Web) names a script to run when a user cuts a selection to the Clipboard.
- `ondblclick` (Web) names a script to run when a user moves the mouse pointer or other pointing device over the emphasized text and double-clicks the button.
- ⊖ `ondrag` (Web) names a script to run when a user drags a selection.
- ⊖ `ondragend` (Web) names a script to run after a user completes a drag-and-drop operation.

- ☺ ondragenter (Web) names a script to run when a user drags a selection into an area in which it can be dropped.
- ☺ ondragleave (Web) names a script to run when a user drags a selection beyond an area in which it can be dropped.
- ☺ ondragover (Web) names a script to run when a user drags a selection over an area in which it can be dropped.
- ☺ ondragstart (Web) names a script to run when a user starts dragging a selection or element.
- ☺ ondrop (Web) names a script to run when a user releases the mouse button to drop a dragged selection.
- ☺ onfocus (Web) names a script to run when a user points the mouse pointer or other pointing device to focus on the current element.
- ☺ onfocusenter (Web) names a script to run when a user focuses on the current element in any way.
- ☺ onfocusleave (Web) names a script to run when a user inactivates the current element in any way.
- ☺ onhelp (Web) names a script to run when a user presses the F1 or Help key over the current element.
- onkeydown (Web) names a script to run when a user presses and holds down a key over the emphasized text.
- onkeypress (Web) names a script to run when a user presses and releases a key over the emphasized text.
- onkeyup (Web) names a script to run when a user releases a key that is currently held down over the emphasized text.
- ☺ onlosecapture (Web) names a script to run when a user releases a selection that has been captured by the mouse.
- onmousedown (Web) names a script to run when a user moves the mouse pointer or other pointing device over the emphasized text and presses and holds down the button.
- ☺ onmouseenter (Web) names a script to run when a user moves the mouse pointer onto the object.
- ☺ onmouseleave (Web) names a script to run when the mouse pointer leaves the object.
- onmousemove (Web) names a script to run when a user moves the mouse pointer or other pointing device over the emphasized text.
- onmouseout (Web) names a script to run when a user moves the mouse pointer or other pointing device away from the emphasized text.
- onmouseover (Web) names a script to run the first time a user moves the mouse pointer or other pointing device over the emphasized text.
- onmouseup (Web) names a script to run when a user moves the mouse pointer or other pointing device over the emphasized text and releases a mouse button that is currently held down.
- ☺ onpaste (Web) names a script to run when a user pastes the Clipboard contents onto the object.
- ☺ onpropertychange (Web) names a script to run when a property changes on the selected object in any way.

- ⊖ onreadystatechange (Web) names a script to run when the status of an element has changed (for example, the element receives data).
- ⊖ onresize (Web) names a script to run when a user resizes the selected object.
- ⊖ onresizeend (Web) names a script to run after the object has been resized.
- ⊖ onresizestart (Web) names a script to run as a user resizes the object.
- ⊖ onselectstart (Web) names a script to run when a user starts selecting an object.
- style (Web) sets styles for the emphasized text.
- ⊖ tabindex (Web) defines the position of the current element in all the elements that a user can navigate to using a Tab or Shift + Tab key.
- title (Web) provides a title for the emphasized text.
- *text* represents one or more characters.

Notes

- This inline element originated in HTML 2.0.
- em is one of the elements in the %phrase entity. The other %phrase elements are abbr, acronym, cite, code, dfn, kbd, samp, strong, and var.
- The em and strong elements are logical styles, which allow a browser to emphasize selected text in the way in which it is programmed to do. Their counterpart physical style elements are i and b, which specifically command a browser to apply italics and boldface, respectively.
- For the em element, WebTV supports the class and style attributes.

Related Elements

acronym (31), b (46), cite (83), code (87), dfn (101), i (154) kbd (186), pre (242), s (254), samp (258), strike (254), strong (276), tt (324), u (327), var (335)

For More Information

Learn more about the em element on page 563 in Chapter 4.

⊖ Ⓝ 📺 embed   Embed Object

Purpose

Embeds an object into an XHTML document.

Syntax

```
<embed{ src="object_uri"|type="Internet_Media_Type"}
   [ accesskey="shortcut_key"][ align="left"|"right"
   |"top"|"bottom"|"absbottom"|"absmiddle"|"baseline"
   |"middle"|"texttop"][ alt="alternate_name" ]
   [ border="border_pix"][ class="class_name" ]
```

```
[ code="subclass_resource_uri"]
[ contenteditable="edit_string"]
[ dir="ltr"|"rtl"][ disabled="disabled"]
[ frameborder="no"]
[ height="height_pix"|"height_meas"]
[ hidden="false"|"true"][ hspace="horiz_pix"]
[ id="id_name"][ lang="lang_code"]
[ name="object_name"]
[ onbeforecut="bt_script"]
[ onbeforefocusenter="bfe_script"]
[ onbeforefocusleave="bfl_script"]
[ onbeforepaste="bp_script"]
[ onblur="bl_script"][ onclick="cl_script"]
[ oncontextmenu="cm_script"]
[ oncontrolselect="ctl_script"]
[ oncut="ct_script"][ ondblclick="dc_script"]
[ onfocus="fc_script"][ onfocusenter="fe_script"]
[ onfocusleave="fl_script"][ onhelp="hlp_script"]
[ onload="ol_script"][ onlosecapture="lc_script"]
[ onmousedown="md_script"]
[ onmouseenter="me_script"]
[ onmouseleave="ml_script"]
[ onmousemove="mm_script"][ onmouseout="mo_script"]
[ onmouseover="mov_script"][ onmouseup="mu_script"]
[ onpaste="p_script"][ onpropertychange="pc_script"]
[ onreadystatechange="rsc_script"]
[ onresize="rsz_script"][ onresizeend="ree_script"]
[ onresizestart="res_script"][ onscroll="sc_script"]
[ palette="background"|"foreground"]
[ pluginspage="plug_in_uri"
| pluginspage="plug_in_uri" pluginurl="plug_in_uri"]
[ src="source_uri"][ style="name_1: value_1"
[; "name_2: value_2"][...; "name_n: value_n"]]
[ tabindex="position_number"][ title="title"]
[ units="pixels"|"en"][ vspace="vert_pix"]
[ width="width_pix"|"width_meas"]{ />|<embed>}
```

Where

- ⊖Ⓝ src (Web) specifies an object, such as a sound or video file, embedded on the current page.
- Ⓝ type (Web) specifies a valid Internet Media Type (that is, MIME-TYPE) of the object.
- ⊖Ⓝ⅍ align (Web) horizontally or vertically aligns the object with the adjacent text.

- ⊖ `alt` (Web) specifies alternate text that will replace the embedded object if the browser does not support the `embed` element (Web) or temporarily describes the object as it loads. Some browsers display alternate text as a tool tip.
- Ⓝ☐ `border` (Web) sets the width, in pixels, of the object.
- ⊖ `class` (Web) specifies a class identification for the element.
- ⊖ `code` (Web) names the resource containing the compiled object subclass for the applet.
- Ⓝ `frameborder` (Web) turns off the border of the object.
- ⊖Ⓝ☐ `height` (Web) specifies the height, in pixels or the unit of measure specified with the Microsoft-defined `units` attribute (Web), of the window in which the object is placed.
- Ⓝ☐ `hidden` (Web) indicates whether a plug-in application appears in the window.
- ⊖Ⓝ☐ `hspace` (Web) is the horizontal area, in pixels, of the left and right sides of the object and other text, graphics, and links on the current page.
- ⊖☐ `id` (Web) provides a unique identifier name for the element.
- ⊖Ⓝ☐ `name` (Web) labels the object.
- ⊖ `onbeforecut` (Web) names a script to run when a user starts cutting a selection to the Clipboard but before any action actually takes place.
- ⊖ `onbeforefocusenter` (Web) names a script to run when a user starts focusing on an object but before the object actually gains focus.
- ⊖ `onbeforefocusleave` (Web) names a script to run when a user starts leaving an object but before the object actually loses focus.
- ⊖ `onbeforepaste` (Web) names a script to run when a user starts pasting an object but before any action actually takes place.
- ⊖ `onblur` (Web) names a script to run when the object loses focus (that is, it is no longer the active element).
- ⊖ `onclick` (Web) names a script to run when a user moves the mouse pointer or other pointing device over the form and clicks the device button.
- ⊖ `oncontextmenu` (Web) names a script to run when a user right-clicks the mouse to open a shortcut menu.
- ⊖ `oncontrolselect` (Web) names a script to run when a user selects a control.
- ⊖ `oncut` (Web) names a script to run when a user cuts a selection to the Clipboard.
- ⊖ `ondblclick` (Web) names a script to run when a user moves the mouse pointer or other pointing device over the form and double-clicks the device button.
- ⊖ `onfocus` (Web) names a script to run when a user points the mouse pointer or other pointing device to focus on the current element.
- ⊖ `onfocusenter` (Web) names a script to run when a user focuses on the current element in any way.
- ⊖ `onfocusleave` (Web) names a script to run when a user inactivates the current element in any way.

- ⊖ onhelp (Web) names a script to run when a user presses the F1 or Help key over the current element.
- ⊖ onload (Web) names a script to run after the active browser has finished loading the frameset.
- ⊖ onlosecapture (Web) names a script to run when a user releases a selection that has been captured by the mouse.
- ⊖ onmousedown (Web) names a script to run when a user moves the mouse pointer or other pointing device over the form and presses and holds down the device button.
- ⊖ onmouseenter (Web) names a script to run when a user moves the mouse pointer onto the object.
- ⊖ onmouseleave (Web) names a script to run when the mouse pointer leaves the object.
- ⊖ onmousemove (Web) names a script to run when a user moves the mouse pointer or other pointing device over the form.
- ⊖ onmouseout (Web) names a script to run when a user moves the mouse pointer or other pointing device away from the form.
- ⊖ onmouseover (Web) names a script to run the first time a user moves the mouse pointer or other pointing device over the form.
- ⊖ onmouseup (Web) names a script to run when a user moves the mouse pointer or other pointing device over the form and releases a pressed-down device button.
- ⊖ onpaste (Web) names a script to run when a user pastes the Clipboard contents onto the object.
- ⊖ onpropertychange (Web) names a script to run when a property changes on the selected object in any way.
- ⊖ onreadystatechange (Web) names a script to run when the status of an element has changed (for example, the element receives data).
- ⊖ onresize (Web) names a script to run when a user resizes the selected object.
- ⊖ onresizeend (Web) names a script to run after the object has been resized.
- ⊖ onresizestart (Web) names a script to run as a user resizes the object.
- ⊖ onscroll (Web) names a script to run when a user moves the scroll box within the scroll bar.
- Ⓝ palette (Web) specifies that the palette used by the plug-in object becomes the background or foreground palette for the current page.
- ⊖Ⓝ pluginspage (Web) specifies the URI of the plug-in file (for Internet Explorer) or, in combination with pluginurl, the URI of the file that instructs how to install a plug-in for Netscape Navigator.
- Ⓝ pluginurl (Web) specifies the URI of the plug-in file for Netscape Navigator.
- ♻ src (Web) specifies the source file displayed within the embedded object.
- ⊖ style (Web) sets styles for the element.
- ⊖ title (Web) provides a title for the element.

- ⊖🅽 units (Web) specifies the unit of measure for the height (Web) and width (Web) attributes.
- ⊖🅽⌨ vspace (Web) is the vertical area, in pixels, of the top and bottom of the object and other text, graphics, and links on the current page.
- ⊖🅽⌨ width (Web) specifies the width, in pixels or the unit of measure specified with the Microsoft-defined units attribute (Web), of the window in which the object is placed.

Notes

- embed is an empty extension, which is not part of any XHTML or HTML recommendation.
- The object element serves the same purpose as embed. Therefore, it is preferable to use object rather than embed.
- If you intend to use embed for Netscape Navigator-compatible browsers, the src attribute (883) is required. If you intend to use embed for Microsoft Internet Explorer-compatible browsers, either src or type (894) is required.
- You can double-click an embedded object to edit it in its original application or plug-in module.
- WebTV supports the following attributes for embed: align, border, height, hidden, hspace, id, name, src, vspace, and width.

Related Elements

img (162), object (225)

fieldset · Grouped Controls

Purpose

Groups related input controls.

Syntax

```
<fieldset[ accesskey="shortcut_key"]
  [ align="left"|"center"|"right"]
  [ class="class_name"]
  [ contenteditable="edit_string"]
  [ dir="ltr"|"rtl"][ disabled="disabled"]
  [ id="id_name"][ lang="lang_code"]
  [ language="javascript"|"jscript"|"vbs[cript]"]
  [ onbeforecopy="bc_script"]
  [ onbeforecut="bt_script"]
  [ onbeforeeditfocus="bef_script"]
  [ onbeforefocusenter="bfe_script"]
  [ onbeforefocusleave="bfl_script"]
  [ onbeforepaste="bp_script"][ onblur="bl_script"]
  [ onclick="cl_script"]
```

```
[ oncontextmenu="cm_script"]
[ oncontrolselect="ctl_script"]
[ oncopy="cp_script"][ oncut="ct_script"]
[ ondblclick="dc_script"][ ondrag="d_script"]
[ ondragend="dd_script"][ ondragenter="de_script"]
[ ondragleave="dl_script"][ ondragover="do_script"]
[ ondragstart="ds_script"][ ondrop="dr_script"]
[ onfilterchange="f_script"][ onfocus="fc_script"]
[ onfocusenter="fe_script"]
[ onfocusleave="fl_script"][ onhelp="hlp_script"]
[ onkeydown="kd_script"][ onkeypress="kp_script"]
[ onkeyup="ku_script"][ onlosecapture="lc_script"]
[ onmousedown="md_script"]
[ onmouseenter="me_script"]
[ onmouseleave="ml_script"]
[ onmousemove="mm_script"][ onmouseout="mo_script"]
[ onmouseover="mov_script"][ onmouseup="mu_script"]
[ onpaste="p_script"][ onpropertychange="pc_script"]
[ onreadystatechange="rsc_script"]
[ onresize="rsz_script"][ onresizeend="ree_script"]
[ onresizestart="res_script"]
[ onselectstart="ss_script"]
[ style="name_1: value_1"
[; name_2: value_2][...; name_n: value_n"]]
[ tabindex="position_number"][ title="title"]>
controls_group</fieldset>
```

Where

- ⊖ accesskey (Web) assigns a shortcut key to the object in order to focus on it.
- ⊖ align (Web) horizontally aligns the object.
- class (Web) specifies a class identification for the controls group.
- ⊖ contenteditable (Web) specifies or obtains a value that indicates whether a user can edit the element content.
- dir (Web) specifies the direction in which the controls text is displayed: left-to-right or right-to-left.
- ⊖ disabled (Web) is a keyword that prevents a user from using the element.
- id (Web) provides a unique identifier name for the controls group.
- lang (Web) specifies the code representing the language used for the controls text.
- ⊖ language (Web) declares the scripting language of the current script.
- ⊖ onbeforecopy (Web) names a script to run when a user starts copying a selection to the Clipboard but before any action actually takes place.

- ☻ onbeforecut (Web) names a script to run when a user starts cutting a selection to the Clipboard but before any action actually takes place.
- ☻ onbeforeeditfocus (Web) names a script to run when a user starts activating an object but before the object actually becomes active.
- ☻ onbeforefocusenter (Web) names a script to run when a user starts focusing on an object but before the object actually gains focus.
- ☻ onbeforefocusleave (Web) names a script to run when a user starts leaving an object but before the object actually loses focus.
- ☻ onbeforepaste (Web) names a script to run when a user starts pasting an object but before any action actually takes place.
- ☻ onblur (Web) names a script to run when the object loses focus (that is, it is no longer the active element).
- onclick (Web) names a script to run when a user moves the mouse pointer or other pointing device over the controls group and clicks the device button.
- ☻ oncontextmenu (Web) names a script to run when a user right-clicks the mouse to open a shortcut menu.
- ☻ oncontrolselect (Web) names a script to run when a user selects a control.
- ☻ oncopy (Web) names a script to run when a user copies a selection to the Clipboard.
- ☻ oncut (Web) names a script to run when a user cuts a selection to the Clipboard.
- ondblclick (Web) names a script to run when a user moves the mouse pointer or other pointing device over the controls group and double-clicks the device button.
- ☻ ondrag (Web) names a script to run when a user drags a selection.
- ☻ ondragend (Web) names a script to run after a user completes a drag-and-drop operation.
- ☻ ondragenter (Web) names a script to run when a user drags a selection into an area in which it can be dropped.
- ☻ ondragleave (Web) names a script to run when a user drags a selection beyond an area in which it can be dropped.
- ☻ ondragover (Web) names a script to run when a user drags a selection over an area in which it can be dropped.
- ☻ ondragstart (Web) names a script to run when a user starts dragging a selection or element.
- ☻ ondrop (Web) names a script to run when a user releases the mouse button to drop a dragged selection.
- ☻ onfilterchange (Web) names a script to run when a visual filter changes in any way.
- ☻ onfocus (Web) names a script to run when a user points the mouse pointer or other pointing device to focus on the current element.
- ☻ onfocusenter (Web) names a script to run when a user focuses on the current element in any way.
- ☻ onfocusleave (Web) names a script to run when a user inactivates the current element in any way.

- ☺ onhelp (Web) names a script to run when a user presses the F1 or Help key over the current element.
- onkeydown (Web) names a script to run when a user presses and holds down a key over the controls group.
- onkeypress (Web) names a script to run when a user presses and releases a key over the controls group.
- onkeyup (Web) names a script to run when a user releases a key that is currently held down over the controls group.
- ☺ onlosecapture (Web) names a script to run when a user releases a selection that has been captured by the mouse.
- onmousedown (Web) names a script to run when a user moves the mouse pointer or other pointing device over the controls group and presses and holds down the device button.
- ☺ onmouseenter (Web) names a script to run when a user moves the mouse pointer onto the object.
- ☺ onmouseleave (Web) names a script to run when the mouse pointer leaves the object.
- onmousemove (Web) names a script to run when a user moves the mouse pointer or other pointing device over the controls group.
- onmouseout (Web) names a script to run when a user moves the mouse pointer or other pointing device away from the controls group.
- onmouseover (Web) names a script to run the first time a user moves the mouse pointer or other pointing device over the controls group.
- onmouseup (Web) names a script to run when a user moves the mouse pointer or other pointing device over the controls group and releases a pressed-down device button.
- ☺ onpaste (Web) names a script to run when a user pastes the Clipboard contents onto the object.
- ☺ onpropertychange (Web) names a script to run when a property changes on the selected object in any way.
- ☺ onreadystatechange (Web) names a script to run when the status of an element has changed (for example, the element receives data).
- ☺ onresize (Web) names a script to run when a user resizes the selected object.
- ☺ onresizeend (Web) names a script to run after the object has been resized.
- ☺ onresizestart (Web) names a script to run as a user resizes the object.
- ☺ onselectstart (Web) names a script to run when a user starts selecting an object.
- style (Web) sets styles for the controls group.
- ☺ tabindex (Web) defines the position of the current element in all the elements that a user can navigate to using a Tab or Shift + Tab key.
- title (Web) provides a title for the controls group.
- *controls_group* represents a group of input controls.

Notes

- This block-level element originated in HTML 4.0.
- A fieldset is analogous to a division (div) or section (span) of a document.
- Use the legend element to add a caption to a fieldset.

Related Elements

button (72), div (108), form (135), input (167), isindex (184), label (190), legend (195), optgroup (234), option (236), select (263), span (272), textarea (302)

For More Information

Learn more about the fieldset element on page 616 in Chapter 7.

font   Font

Purpose

Changes the size, color, and/or typeface of selected text.

Syntax

```
<font[ accesskey="shortcut_key"][ class="class_name"]
[ color="#rrggbb"|"color"]
[ contenteditable="edit_string"][ dir="ltr"|"rtl"]
[ disabled="disabled"]
[ effect="emboss"|"relief"|"shadow"]
[ face="typeface"][ id="id_name"][ lang="lang_code"]
[ language="javascript"|"jscript"|"vbs[cript]"]
[ onbeforecut="bt_script"]
[ onbeforefocusenter="bfe_script"]
[ onbeforefocusleave="bfl_script"]
[ onbeforepaste="bp_script"][ onblur="bl_script"]
[ onclick="cl_script"][ oncontextmenu="cm_script"]
[ oncontrolselect="ctl_script"][ oncut="ct_script"]
[ ondblclick="dc_script"][ ondrag="d_script"]
[ ondragend="dd_script"][ ondragenter="de_script"]
[ ondragleave="dl_script"][ ondragover="do_script"]
[ ondragstart="ds_script"][ ondrop="dr_script"]
[ onfocus="fc_script"][ onfocusenter="fe_script"]
[ onfocusleave="fl_script"][ onhelp="hlp_script"]
[ onkeydown="kd_script"][ onkeypress="kp_script"]
[ onkeyup="ku_script"]
[ onlayoutcomplete="la_script"]
[ onlosecapture="lc_script"]
[ onmousedown="md_script"]
```

XHTML Syntax

```
[ onmouseenter="me_script"]
[ onmouseleave="ml_script"]
[ onmousemove="mm_script"][ onmouseout="mo_script"]
[ onmouseover="mov_script"][ onmouseup="mu_script"]
[ onpaste="p_script"][ onpropertychange="pc_script"]
[ onreadystatechange="rsc_script"]
[ onresizeend="ree_script"]
[ onresizestart="res_script"]
[ onselectstart="ss_script"][ point-size=nn]
[ size="[+|-]1|2|3|4|5|6|7"]
[ style="name_1: value_1"[; "name_2: value_2"]
[...; "name_n: value_n"]]
[ tabindex="position_number"][ title="title"]
[ transparency="trans_value"]
[ weight="100"|"200"|"300"|"400"|"500"|"600"
|"700"|"800"|"900"]> text</font>
```

Where

- ⊕ `accesskey` (Web) assigns a shortcut key to the object in order to focus on it.
- `class` (Web) specifies a class identification for the element.
- `color` (Web) is the color of the selected text.
- ⊕ `contenteditable` (Web) specifies or obtains a value that indicates whether a user can edit the element content.
- ⊕ `dir` (Web) specifies the direction in which the current text is displayed: left-to-right or right-to-left.
- ⊕ `disabled` (Web) is a keyword that prevents a user from using the element.
- ⊠ `effect` (Web) decorates the selected font.
- `face` (Web) specifies the name of a typeface to be applied to the selected text. Note that the typeface must be installed on your computer.
- `id` (Web) provides a unique identifier name for the element.
- `lang` (Web) specifies the code for the language used for the element.
- ⊕ `language` (Web) declares the scripting language of the current script.
- ⊕ `onbeforecut` (Web) names a script to run when a user starts cutting a selection to the Clipboard but before any action actually takes place.
- ⊕ `onbeforefocusenter` (Web) names a script to run when a user starts focusing on an object but before the object actually gains focus.
- ⊕ `onbeforefocusleave` (Web) names a script to run when a user starts leaving an object but before the object actually loses focus.
- ⊕ `onbeforepaste` (Web) names a script to run when a user starts pasting an object but before any action actually takes place.
- ⊕ `onblur` (Web) names a script to run when the object loses focus (that is, it is no longer the active element).

- ⊜ onclick (Web) names a script to run when a user moves the mouse pointer or other pointing device over the selected text and clicks the button.
- ⊜ oncontextmenu (Web) names a script to run when a user right-clicks the mouse to open a shortcut menu.
- ⊜ oncontrolselect (Web) names a script to run when a user selects a control.
- ⊜ oncut (Web) names a script to run when a user cuts a selection to the Clipboard.
- ⊜ ondblclick (Web) names a script to run when a user moves the mouse pointer or other pointing device over the selected text and double-clicks the button.
- ⊜ ondrag (Web) names a script to run when a user drags a selection.
- ⊜ ondragend (Web) names a script to run after a user completes a drag-and-drop operation.
- ⊜ ondragenter (Web) names a script to run when a user drags a selection into an area in which it can be dropped.
- ⊜ ondragleave (Web) names a script to run when a user drags a selection beyond an area in which it can be dropped.
- ⊜ ondragover (Web) names a script to run when a user drags a selection over an area in which it can be dropped.
- ⊜ ondragstart (Web) names a script to run when a user starts dragging a selection or element.
- ⊜ ondrop (Web) names a script to run when a user releases the mouse button to drop a dragged selection.
- ⊜ onfocus (Web) names a script to run when a user points the mouse pointer or other pointing device to focus on the current element.
- ⊜ onfocusenter (Web) names a script to run when a user focuses on the current element in any way.
- ⊜ onfocusleave (Web) names a script to run when a user inactivates the current element in any way.
- ⊜ onhelp (Web) names a script to run when a user presses the F1 or Help key over the current element.
- ⊜ onkeydown (Web) names a script to run when a user presses and holds down a key over the selected text.
- ⊜ onkeypress (Web) names a script to run when a user presses and releases a key over the selected text.
- ⊜ onkeyup (Web) names a script to run when a user releases a key that is currently held down over the form.
- ⊜ onlayoutcomplete (Web) names a script to run when a user lays out a selection using Print or Print Preview.
- ⊜ onlosecapture (Web) names a script to run when a user releases a selection that has been captured by the mouse.
- ⊜ onmousedown (Web) names a script to run when a user moves the mouse pointer or other pointing device over the selected text and presses and holds down the button.

- ⊖ onmouseenter (Web) names a script to run when a user moves the mouse pointer onto the object.
- ⊖ onmouseleave (Web) names a script to run when the mouse pointer leaves the object.
- ⊖ onmousemove (Web) names a script to run when a user moves the mouse pointer or other pointing device over the selected text.
- ⊖ onmouseout (Web) names a script to run when a user moves the mouse pointer or other pointing device away from the selected text.
- ⊖ onmouseover (Web) names a script to run the first time a user moves the mouse pointer or other pointing device over the selected text.
- ⊖ onmouseup (Web) names a script to run when a user moves the mouse pointer or other pointing device over the selected text and releases a mouse button that is currently held down.
- ⊖ onpaste (Web) names a script to run when a user pastes the Clipboard contents onto the object.
- ⊖ onpropertychange (Web) names a script to run when a property changes on the selected object in any way.
- ⊖ onreadystatechange (Web) names a script to run when the status of an element has changed (for example, the element receives data).
- ⊖ onresizeend (Web) names a script to run after the object has been resized.
- ⊖ onresizestart (Web) names a script to run as a user resizes the object.
- ⊖ onselectstart (Web) names a script to run when a user starts selecting an object.
- Ⓝ point-size (Web) sets the actual point size of the selected text.
- size (Web) indicates that you will change the relative (+ or –) or actual (1-7) size of the selected text. For Netscape Navigator, use size to set the relative size (1 to 7).
- style (Web) sets styles for the selected text.
- ⊖ tabindex (Web) defines the position of the current element in all the elements that a user can navigate to using a Tab or Shift + Tab key.
- title (Web) provides a title for the selected text.
- ⍁ transparency (Web) sets the level of transparency or opaqueness of the selected text.
- Ⓝ weight (Web) sets the level of boldness of the selected text.
- text represents one or more characters.

Notes

- This inline element originated in HTML 3.2.
- Although font is supported by HTML 4.0, it has been deprecated (that is, it will eventually be obsolete) and appears only in the Transitional DTD — not in the Strict DTD. Use style sheets to specify font attributes instead of the font element.
- If you select a typeface not found on your computer system, the browser substitutes the default font, usually Times Roman.

- If you omit the quotation marks from the color values or the typeface, some HTML editors automatically insert them.
- For the font element, WebTV supports the color, effect, size, and transparency attributes.

Related Elements
basefont (51), big (57), small (268)

For More Information
Learn more about the font element on page 509 in Chapter 1.

form	Form

Purpose
Produces a fill-in form that will be processed by an HTTP server.

Syntax
```
<form action="submit_url"[ accept="MIME_type_1"
 [,MIME_type_2][...,MIME_type_n]]
 [ accept-charset=["unknown"]|[["charset_1"]
 [{ |,}"charset_2"][...{ |,}"charset_n"]]]
 [ autocomplete="off"|"on"][ class="class_name"]
 [ contenteditable="edit_string"][ dir="ltr"|"rtl"]
 [ disabled="disabled"]
 [ enctype="Internet_Media_Type"][ id="id_name"]
 [ lang="lang_code"][ language="javascript"|"jscript"
 |"vbs[cript]"][ method="get"|"post"]
 [ name="form_name"][ onbeforecopy="bc_script"]
 [ onbeforecut="bt_script"]
 [ onbeforefocusenter="bfe_script"]
 [ onbeforefocusleave="bfl_script"]
 [ onbeforepaste="bp_script"][ onblur="bl_script"]
 [ onclick="cl_script"][ oncontextmenu="cm_script"]
 [ oncontrolselect="ctl_script"]
 [ oncopy="cp_script"][ oncut="ct_script"]
 [ ondblclick="dc_script"][ ondrag="d_script"]
 [ ondragend="dd_script"][ ondragenter="de_script"]
 [ ondragleave="dl_script"][ ondragover="do_script"]
 [ ondragstart="ds_script"][ ondrop="dr_script"]
 [ onfocus="fc_script"][ onfocusenter="fe_script"]
 [ onfocusleave="fl_script"][ onhelp="hlp_script"]
 [ onkeydown="kd_script"][ onkeypress="kp_script"]
 [ onkeyup="ku_script"][ onlosecapture="lc_script"]
 [ onmousedown="md_script"]
```

```
[ onmouseenter="me_script"]
[ onmouseleave="ml_script"]
[ onmousemove="mm_script"][ onmouseout="mo_script"]
[ onmouseover="mov_script"][ onmouseup="mu_script"]
[ onpaste="p_script"][ onpropertychange="pc_script"]
[ onreadystatechange="rsc_script"]
[ onreset="rs_script"][ onresize="rsz_script"]
[ onresizeend="ree_script"]
[ onresizestart="res_script"]
[ onselectstart="ss_script"][ onsubmit="su_script"]
[ style="name_1: value_1"[; name_2: value_2"]
[...; name_n: value_n"]]
[ tabindex="position_number"]
[ target="window"|"_blank"|"_parent"|"_search"
|"_self"|"_top"][ title="title"]>fill-in-form</form>
```

Where

- action (Web) specifies a server-side cgi-bin program or HTTP script that processes the filled-in information.
- accept (Web) is a list of one or more Internet Media Types (MIMETYPE) that this part of the form and the form-processing server will accept.
- accept-charset (Web) lists one or more character sets supported by the server processing the submitted forms.
- ⊖ autocomplete (Web) suggests ("yes") or does not suggest ("no") values for a particular text field in a form.
- class (Web) specifies a class identification for the form.
- ⊖ contenteditable (Web) specifies or obtains a value that indicates whether a user can edit the element content.
- dir (Web) specifies the direction in which the form text is displayed: left-to-right or right-to-left.
- ⊖ disabled (Web) is a keyword that prevents a user from using the element.
- enctype (Web) specifies an Internet Media Type (MIMETYPE) for encoding user responses to be submitted to the server.
- id (Web) provides a unique identifier name for the form.
- lang (Web) specifies the code representing the language used for the form.
- ⊖ language (Web) declares the scripting language of the current script.
- method (Web) specifies the HTTP method used to send the form to the server.
- name (Web) labels the form for the use of scripts. In XHTML, name is deprecated; use id instead.
- ⊖ onbeforecopy (Web) names a script to run when a user starts copying a selection to the Clipboard but before any action actually takes place.

- ℮ `onbeforecut` (Web) names a script to run when a user starts cutting a selection to the Clipboard but before any action actually takes place.
- ℮ `onbeforefocusenter` (Web) names a script to run when a user starts focusing on an object but before the object actually gains focus.
- ℮ `onbeforefocusleave` (Web) names a script to run when a user starts leaving an object but before the object actually loses focus.
- ℮ `onbeforepaste` (Web) names a script to run when a user starts pasting an object but before any action actually takes place.
- ℮ `onblur` (Web) names a script to run when the object loses focus (that is, it is no longer the active element).
- `onclick` (Web) names a script to run when a user moves the mouse pointer or other pointing device over the form and clicks the device button.
- ℮ `oncontextmenu` (Web) names a script to run when a user right-clicks the mouse to open a shortcut menu.
- ℮ `oncontrolselect` (Web) names a script to run when a user selects a control.
- ℮ `oncopy` (Web) names a script to run when a user copies a selection to the Clipboard.
- ℮ `oncut` (Web) names a script to run when a user cuts a selection to the Clipboard.
- `ondblclick` (Web) names a script to run when a user moves the mouse pointer or other pointing device over the form and double-clicks the device button.
- ℮ `ondrag` (Web) names a script to run when a user drags a selection.
- ℮ `ondragend` (Web) names a script to run after a user completes a drag-and-drop operation.
- ℮ `ondragenter` (Web) names a script to run when a user drags a selection into an area in which it can be dropped.
- ℮ `ondragleave` (Web) names a script to run when a user drags a selection beyond an area in which it can be dropped.
- ℮ `ondragover` (Web) names a script to run when a user drags a selection over an area in which it can be dropped.
- ℮ `ondragstart` (Web) names a script to run when a user starts dragging a selection or element.
- ℮ `ondrop` (Web) names a script to run when a user releases the mouse button to drop a dragged selection.
- ℮ `onfocus` (Web) names a script to run when a user points the mouse pointer or other pointing device to focus on the current element.
- ℮ `onfocusenter` (Web) names a script to run when a user focuses on the current element in any way.
- ℮ `onfocusleave` (Web) names a script to run when a user inactivates the current element in any way.
- ℮ `onhelp` (Web) names a script to run when a user presses the F1 or Help key over the current element.
- `onkeydown` (Web) names a script to run when a user presses and holds down a key over the form.

- onkeypress (Web) names a script to run when a user presses and releases a key over the form.
- onkeyup (Web) names a script to run when a user releases a key that is currently held down over the form.
- ⊖ onlosecapture (Web) names a script to run when a user releases a selection that has been captured by the mouse.
- onmousedown (Web) names a script to run when a user moves the mouse pointer or other pointing device over the form and presses and holds down the device button.
- ⊖ onmouseenter (Web) names a script to run when a user moves the mouse pointer onto the object.
- ⊖ onmouseleave (Web) names a script to run when the mouse pointer leaves the object.
- onmousemove (Web) names a script to run when a user moves the mouse pointer or other pointing device over the form.
- onmouseout (Web) names a script to run when a user moves the mouse pointer or other pointing device away from the form.
- onmouseover (Web) names a script to run the first time a user moves the mouse pointer or other pointing device over the form.
- onmouseup (Web) names a script to run when a user moves the mouse pointer or other pointing device over the form and releases a pressed-down device button.
- ⊖ onpaste (Web) names a script to run when a user pastes the Clipboard contents onto the object.
- ⊖ onpropertychange (Web) names a script to run when a property changes on the selected object in any way.
- ⊖ onreadystatechange (Web) names a script to run when the status of an element has changed (for example, the element receives data).
- onreset (Web) names a script to run when a user clicks the Reset button to clear the form.
- ⊖ onresize (Web) names a script to run when a user resizes the selected object.
- ⊖ onresizeend (Web) names a script to run after the object has been resized.
- ⊖ onresizestart (Web) names a script to run as a user resizes the object.
- ⊖ onselectstart (Web) names a script to run when a user starts selecting an object.
- onsubmit (Web) names a script to run when a user clicks the Submit button to submit the current form.
- style (Web) sets styles for the form.
- ⊖ tabindex (Web) defines the position of the current element in all the elements that a user can navigate to using a Tab or Shift + Tab key.
- target (Web) loads a linked and named document in a particular window or frame. This attribute is deprecated; use the id attribute instead.
- title (Web) provides a title for the form.

XHTML Syntax

- *fill-in-form* represents a form, which includes its input, select, and textarea elements, other embedded elements, text, and graphics.

Notes
- This block-level element originated in HTML 2.0.
- form contains all the form *controls* (that is, the parts of the form with which the user interacts).
- form controls the form layout.
- When a user submits a form, it is sent to a form-processing program.
- In XHTML, you cannot nest one form within another form.
- The default action attribute is the base address of the document.
- WebTV supports the following attributes for form: action, class, enctype, id, method, name, onreset, onload, script, and target. The script attribute, which is considered to be obsolete, is not covered in this book.

Related Elements
fieldset (127), input (167), isindex (184), keygen (190), label (190), legend (195), optgroup (234), option (236), select (263), textarea (302)

For More Information
Learn more about the form element on page 611 in Chapter 7.

frame   Frame

Purpose
Defines one pane within the computer desktop.

Syntax
```
<frame[ align="left"|"center"|"right"|"top"|"bottom"]
  [ application="off"|"on"]
  [ bordercolor=#rrggbb"|"color"][ class="class_name"]
  [ datafld="ds_col_name"][ datasrc="ds_identifier"]
  [ disabled="disabled"][ frameborder="1"|"0"]
  [ id="id_name"]
  [ lang="lang_code"][ language="javascript"|"jscript"
  |"vbs[cript]"][ longdesc="description_uri"]
  [ marginheight="height_pix"]
  [ marginwidth="width_pix"][ name="frame_name"
  |"_blank"|"_parent"|"_self"|"_top"]
  [ noresize="noresize"[|resize="resize"]]
  [ onbeforefocusenter="bfe_script"]
```

```
[ onbeforefocusleave="bfl_script"]
[ onblur="bl_script"][ oncontrolselect="ctl_script"]
[ onfocus="fc_script"][ onfocusenter="fe_script"]
[ onfocusleave="fl_script"][ onresize="rsz_script"]
[ onresizeend="ree_script"]
[ onresizestart="res_script"]
[ scrolling="auto"|"yes"|"no"][ src="source_uri"]
[ style="name_1: value_1"[; "name_2: value_2"]
[...; "name_n: value_n"]]
[ tabindex="position_number"][ title="title"]
[ width="width_pix"|width_%]{ />|</frame>}
```

Where

- ⊕ `align` (Web) aligns an object with the surrounding text.
- ⊕ `application` (Web) indicates whether content is an HTML application ("yes") or not ("no").
- ⊕🅽 `bordercolor` (Web) specifies the color for the borders of the current frame.
- `class` (Web) specifies a class identification for the element.
- ⊕ `datafld` (Web) specifies the column name from the file that contains the data source object.
- ⊕ `datasrc` (Web) specifies the identifier of the data source object.
- ⊕ `disabled` (Web) is a keyword that prevents a user from using the element.
- `frameborder` (Web) specifies whether the current frame will have a border.
- `id` (Web) provides a unique identifier name for the element.
- ⊕ `lang` (Web) specifies the code representing the language used for the controls text.
- ⊕ `language` (Web) declares the scripting language of the current script.
- `longdesc` (Web) provides the URI of a long alternate description.
- `marginheight` (Web) is the space, in pixels, between the top and bottom margins of the frame and the contents of the frame.
- `marginwidth` (Web) is the space, in pixels, between the left and right margins of the frame and the contents of the frame.
- `name` (Web) labels the current frame. Microsoft supports the use of the `_blank`, `_parent`, `_self`, and `_top` reserved words. In XHTML, name is deprecated; use `id` instead.
- `noresize|resize` (Web) freezes the current frame at its current height and width or allows resizing of the frame.
- ⊕ `onbeforefocusenter` (Web) names a script to run when a user starts focusing on an object but before the object actually gains focus.
- ⊕ `onbeforefocusleave` (Web) names a script to run when a user starts leaving an object but before the object actually loses focus.
- ⊕ `onblur` (Web) names a script to run when the object loses focus (that is, it is no longer the active element).

- ⊖ oncontrolselect (Web) names a script to run when a user selects a control.
- ⊖ onfocus (Web) names a script to run when a user points the mouse pointer or other pointing device to focus on the current element.
- ⊖ onfocusenter (Web) names a script to run when a user focuses on the current element in any way.
- ⊖ onfocusleave (Web) names a script to run when a user inactivates the current element in any way.
- ⊖ onresize (Web) names a script to run when a user resizes the selected object.
- ⊖ onresizeend (Web) names a script to run after the object has been resized.
- ⊖ onresizestart (Web) names a script to run as a user resizes the object.
- scrolling (Web) specifies whether the current frame contains scrollbars.
- src (Web) specifies the source file displayed within the current frame.
- style (Web) sets styles for the element.
- ⊖ tabindex (Web) defines the position of the current element in all the elements that a user can navigate to using a Tab or Shift + Tab key.
- title (Web) provides a title for the element.
- ⊖ width (Web) specifies the width, in pixels or as a percentage of the entire height of the computer screen, of a frame.

Notes

- This HTML 4.0 element was originally a Netscape extension and a Microsoft extension.
- frame is an empty element.
- Embed one or more frame elements within a <frameset> start tag and </frameset> end tag.
- The contents of a frame cannot be within the same document as the definition of a frame.
- WebTV supports the following attributes for frame: align, frameborder, marginheight, marginwidth, name, and src.

Related Elements

frameset (141), iframe (158), noframes (222)

For More Information

Learn more about the frame element on page 582 in Chapter 5.

frameset   Frame Set

Purpose

Defines a set of frames that make up the current document.

Syntax

```
<frameset[ border="border_pix"]
  [ bordercolor="#rrggbb"|"color"]
  [ class="class_name"][ cols="col_value_1
  [, col_value_2[..., col_value_n]]"]
  [ disabled="disabled"]
  [ frameborder="yes"|"no"|"1"|"0"]
  [ framespacing="frame_space"][ id="id_name"]
  [ lang="lang_code"][ language="javascript"|"jscript"
  |"vbs[cript]"][ onafterprint="ap_script"]
  [ onbeforefocusenter="bfe_script"]
  [ onbeforefocusleave="bfl_script"]
  [ onbeforeprint="bpr_script"]
  [ onbeforeunload="bul_script"]
  [ onblur="bl_script"][ oncontrolselect="ctl_script"]
  [ onfocus="fc_script"][ onfocusenter="fe_script"]
  [ onfocusleave="fl_script"][ onload="ol_script"]
  [ onresizeend="ree_script"]
  [ onresizestart="res_script"][ onunload="un_script"]
  [ rows="row_value_1[, row_value_2
  [..., row_value_n]]"][ tabindex="position_number"]
  [ title="title"]>frames</frameset>
```

Where

- **N🖮 border** (Web) turns on a border and sets the width of the frameset.
- **N bordercolor** (Web) specifies the color for the borders of the current frameset.
- **class** (Web) specifies a class identification for the element.
- **cols** (Web) is a left-to-right measurement of the frameset.
- ⊖ **disabled** (Web) is a keyword that prevents a user from using the element.
- ⊖N🖮 **frameborder** (Web) specifies whether frames in the frameset will have borders.
- 🖮 **framespacing** (Web) sets spacing, in pixels, between all the frames in a frameset.
- **id** (Web) provides a unique identifier name for the element.
- ⊖ **lang** (Web) specifies the code representing the language used for the element.
- ⊖ **language** (Web) declares the scripting language of the current script.
- ⊖ **onafterprint** (Web) names a script to run after the document prints.
- ⊖ **onbeforefocusenter** (Web) names a script to run when a user starts focusing on an object but before the object actually gains focus.

- ⊖ `onbeforefocusleave` (Web) names a script to run when a user starts leaving an object but before the object actually loses focus.
- ⊖ `onbeforeprint` (Web) names a script to run after a user acts to print a document but before the document actually prints.
- ⊖ `onbeforeunload` (Web) names a script to run after a user acts to display another document but before the page is actually unloaded.
- ⊖🅽 `onblur` (Web) names a script to run when the object loses focus (that is, it is no longer the active element).
- ⊖ `oncontrolselect` (Web) names a script to run when a control is selected.
- ⊖🅽 `onfocus` (Web) names a script to run when the current element receives focus (that is, is made active) by the mouse pointer or other pointing device.
- ⊖ `onfocusenter` (Web) names a script to run when a user focuses on the current element in any way.
- ⊖ `onfocusleave` (Web) names a script to run when a user inactivates the current element in any way.
- `onload` (Web) names a script to run after the active browser has finished loading the frameset.
- ⊖ `onresizeend` (Web) names a script to run after the object has been resized.
- ⊖ `onresizestart` (Web) names a script to run as a user resizes the object.
- `onunload` (Web) names a script to run after the active browser has removed a document from the frameset.
- `rows` (Web) is a top-to-bottom measurement of the frameset.
- ⊖ `tabindex` (Web) defines the position of the current element in all the elements that a user can navigate to using a Tab or Shift + Tab key.
- `title` (Web) provides a title for the element.
- *frames* are the frames within the frame set.

Notes

- This HTML 4.0 element was originally a Netscape extension and a Microsoft extension.
- In a document with frames, `frameset` elements must precede `body` elements and elements that are usually embedded within a document body. Improper placement of a `body` element causes `frameset` to be disregarded.
- `frame`, `frameset`, and `noframes` are child elements of `frameset`, so you can embed those elements within a frame set.
- Once you have defined a `frameborder`, it is applied to all proceeding frames until you set new `frameborder` values.
- A `body` element following a `frameset` element is equivalent to a `noframes` section.
- If you specify an absolute value for the `rows` and/or `cols` in a frameset, you run the risk of setting widths and heights that are too large or small. It is best to use a combination of percentages and values.

- If you specify a percentage value for the rows and/or cols in a frame set and the total is not 100%, the editor will scale the rows and/or cols to reach 100%.
- Once you have defined a frameborder or framespacing, its value is applied to all proceeding frames until you set a new value for frame borders or spacing.
- For the frameset element, WebTV supports the border, cols, frameborder, framespacing, and rows attributes.

Related Elements
frame (133), iframe (158), noframes (222)

For More Information
Learn more about the frameset element on page 581 in Chapter 5.

h*n*	Heading Number

Purpose
Applies one of six heading characteristics to selected text.

Syntax

```
<hn[ accesskey="shortcut_key"]
   [ align="left"|"center"|"right"|"justify"]
   [ class="class_name"]
   [ contenteditable="edit_string"]
   [ dir="ltr"|"rtl"][ disabled="disabled"]
   [ id="id_name"][ lang="lang_code"]
   [ language="javascript"|"jscript"|"vbs[cript]"]
   [ onbeforecopy="bc_script"]
   [ onbeforecut="bt_script"]
   [ onbeforefocusenter="bfe_script"]
   [ onbeforefocusleave="bfl_script"]
   [ onbeforepaste="bp_script"][ onblur="bl_script"]
   [ onclick="cl_script"][ oncontextmenu="cm_script"]
   [ oncontrolselect="ctl_script"][ oncopy="cp_script"]
   [ oncut="ct_script"][ ondblclick="dc_script"]
   [ ondrag="d_script"][ ondragend="dd_script"]
   [ ondragenter="de_script"][ ondragleave="dl_script"]
   [ ondragover="do_script"][ ondragstart="ds_script"]
   [ ondrop="dr_script"][ onfocus="fc_script"]
   [ onfocusenter="fe_script"]
   [ onfocusleave="fl_script"][ onhelp="hlp_script"]
   [ onkeydown="kd_script"][ onkeypress="kp_script"]
   [ onkeyup="ku_script"][ onlosecapture="lc_script"]
```

```
[ onmousedown="md_script"]
[ onmouseenter="me_script"]
[ onmouseleave="ml_script"]
[ onmousemove="mm_script"][ onmouseout="mo_script"]
[ onmouseover="mov_script"][ onmouseup="mu_script"]
[ onpaste="p_script"][ onpropertychange="pc_script"]
[ onreadystatechange="rsc_script"]
[ onresize="rsz_script"][ onresizeend="ree_script"]
[ onresizestart="res_script"]
[ onselectstart="ss_script"]
[ style="name_1: value_1"[; "name_2: value_2"]
[...; "name_n: value_n"]]
[ tabindex="position_number"]
[ title="title"]>
heading-text</hn>
```

Where

- *n* represents a heading level from 1 to 6.
- ⊝ accesskey (Web) assigns a shortcut key to the object in order to focus on it.
- align (Web) horizontally aligns the heading. This attribute is deprecated; use a style sheet instead.
- class (Web) specifies a class identification for the current heading.
- ⊝ contenteditable (Web) specifies or obtains a value that indicates whether a user can edit the element content.
- dir (Web) specifies the direction in which the heading text is displayed: left-to-right or right-to-left.
- ⊝ disabled (Web) is a keyword that prevents a user from using the selected element.
- id (Web) provides a unique identifier name for the heading.
- lang (Web) specifies the code for the language used for the heading text.
- ⊝ language (Web) declares the scripting language of the current script.
- ⊝ onbeforecopy (Web) names a script to run when a user starts copying a selection to the Clipboard but before any action actually takes place.
- ⊝ onbeforecut (Web) names a script to run when a user starts cutting a selection to the Clipboard but before any action actually takes place.
- ⊝ onbeforefocusenter (Web) names a script to run when a user starts focusing on an object but before the object actually gains focus.
- ⊝ onbeforefocusleave (Web) names a script to run when a user starts leaving an object but before the object actually loses focus.
- ⊝ onbeforepaste (Web) names a script to run when a user starts pasting an object but before any action actually takes place.
- ⊝ onblur (Web) names a script to run when the object loses focus (that is, it is no longer the active element).
- onclick (Web) names a script to run when a user moves the mouse pointer or other pointing device over the heading and clicks the button.

- ⊕ oncontextmenu (Web) names a script to run when a user right-clicks the mouse to open a shortcut menu.
- ⊕ oncontrolselect (Web) names a script to run when a user selects a control.
- ⊕ oncopy (Web) names a script to run when a user copies a selection to the Clipboard.
- ⊕ oncut (Web) names a script to run when a user cuts a selection to the Clipboard.
- ondblclick (Web) names a script to run when a user moves the mouse pointer or other pointing device over the heading and double-clicks the button.
- ⊕ ondrag (Web) names a script to run when a user drags a selection.
- ⊕ ondragend (Web) names a script to run after a user completes a drag-and-drop operation.
- ⊕ ondragenter (Web) names a script to run when a user drags a selection into an area in which it can be dropped.
- ⊕ ondragleave (Web) names a script to run when a user drags a selection beyond an area in which it can be dropped.
- ⊕ ondragover (Web) names a script to run when a user drags a selection over an area in which it can be dropped.
- ⊕ ondragstart (Web) names a script to run when a user starts dragging a selection or element.
- ⊕ ondrop (Web) names a script to run when a user releases the mouse button to drop a dragged selection.
- ⊕ onfocus (Web) names a script to run when a user points the mouse pointer or other pointing device to focus on the current element.
- ⊕ onfocusenter (Web) names a script to run when a user focuses on the current element in any way.
- ⊕ onfocusleave (Web) names a script to run when a user inactivates the current element in any way.
- ⊕ onhelp (Web) names a script to run when a user presses the F1 or Help key over the current element.
- onkeydown (Web) names a script to run when a user presses and holds down a key over the heading.
- onkeypress (Web) names a script to run when a user presses and releases a key over the heading.
- onkeyup (Web) names a script to run when a user releases a key that is currently held down over the heading.
- ⊕ onlosecapture (Web) names a script to run when a user releases a selection that has been captured by the mouse.
- onmousedown (Web) names a script to run when a user moves the mouse pointer or other pointing device over the heading and presses and holds down the button.
- ⊕ onmouseenter (Web) names a script to run when a user moves the mouse pointer onto the object.
- ⊕ onmouseleave (Web) names a script to run when the mouse pointer leaves the object.

- `onmousemove` (Web) names a script to run when a user moves the mouse pointer or other pointing device over the heading.
- `onmouseout` (Web) names a script to run when a user moves the mouse pointer or other pointing device away from the heading.
- `onmouseover` (Web) names a script to run the first time a user moves the mouse pointer or other pointing device over the heading.
- `onmouseup` (Web) names a script to run when a user moves the mouse pointer or other pointing device over the heading and releases a mouse button that is currently held down.
- ⊖ `onpaste` (Web) names a script to run when a user pastes the Clipboard contents onto the object.
- ⊖ `onpropertychange` (Web) names a script to run when a property changes on the selected object in any way.
- ⊖ `onreadystatechange` (Web) names a script to run when the status of an element has changed (for example, the element receives data).
- ⊖ `onresize` (Web) names a script to run when a user resizes the selected object.
- ⊖ `onresizeend` (Web) names a script to run after the object has been resized.
- ⊖ `onresizestart` (Web) names a script to run as a user resizes the object.
- ⊖ `onselectstart` (Web) names a script to run when a user starts selecting an object.
- `style` (Web) sets styles for the selected heading.
- ⊖ `tabindex` (Web) defines the position of the current element in all the elements that a user can navigate to using a Tab or Shift + Tab key.
- `title` (Web) provides a title for the selected heading.
- *heading-text* represents a section or page heading.

Notes

- These block-level elements originated in HTML 2.0.
- The number representing the heading level must be the same in both the start tag and the end tag.
- An h1 element is at the highest level and has the largest font size; an h6 element is at the lowest level and has the smallest font size.
- By default, all h*n* headings have line spaces above and below.
- The h*n* start and end tags both cause a line break.
- When planning a document, be sure to select the proper heading elements. At the top of the document, place an h1 heading. As a rule, don't skip heading levels (for example, from h1 to h3). Think of how you would outline your document, and use the outline levels to plan your heading levels.
- The h1, h2, h3, h4, h5, and h6 elements are simply headings; place the paragraphs under the headings within <p> and </p> tags and other page elements within other appropriate tags.
- Some browsers can create tables of contents using the heading elements.

- For the h*n* elements, WebTV supports the `align`, `class`, and `id` attributes.

For More Information

Learn more about the h*n* elements on page 521 in Chapter 2.

head	Document Head

Purpose

Introduces and describes an XHTML document, including its title.

Syntax

```
<head[ class="class_name"][ dir="ltr"|"rtl"]
  [ disabled="disabled"][ id="id_name"]
  [ lang="lang_code"]
  [ onlayoutcomplete="la_script"]
  [ onreadystatechange="rsc_script"]
  [ profile="prof_uri_1"[ "prof_uri_2"
  [..."prof_uri_n"]]][ title="title"]>]
  head-section</head>
```

Where

- ⊝ `class` (Web) specifies a class identification for the element.
- `dir` (Web) specifies the direction in which the text in the HEAD section is displayed: left-to-right or right-to-left.
- ⊝ `disabled` (Web) is a keyword that prevents a user from using the element.
- ⊝ `id` (Web) provides a unique identifier name for the element.
- `lang` (Web) specifies the code for the language used for the text in the HEAD section.
- ⊝ `onlayoutcomplete` (Web) names a script to run when a user lays out a selection using Print or Print Preview.
- ⊝ `onreadystatechange` (Web) names a script to run when the status of an element has changed (for example, the element receives data).
- `profile` (Web) lists one or more URIs of files containing meta information, which describes the current document.
- *head-section* includes the title and other introductory lines of text.

Notes

- This element originated in HTML 2.0.
- An XHTML document is composed of a HEAD section and a BODY section, headed by the following elements: `head` and `body`. All other elements are included in one of these sections. Frames documents use the `frameset` element and its contents rather than the `body` element and its contents.

XHTML Syntax

- The HEAD section of a document includes information that is not displayed when you open the document.
- Many documents have only a `title` element in the HEAD section. However, you can also embed the following elements within the HEAD section: `base`, `isindex`, `link`, `meta`, `script`, and `style`.
- The `head` element is embedded within the `html` element, which is the root element.

Related Elements

`base` (49), `body` (65), `frameset` (141), `html` (153), `isindex` (184), `link` (202), `meta` (216), `script` (262), `style` (280), `title` (318)

For More Information

Learn more about the `head` element on page 527 in Chapter 2.

hr — Horizontal Rule

Purpose

Inserts a horizontal rule line between sections of a document.

Syntax

```
<hr[ accesskey="shortcut_key"]
   [ align="center"|"left"|"right"]
   [ class="class_name"][ color="#rrggbb"|"color"]
   [ contenteditable="edit_string"]
   [ disabled="disabled"][ id="id_name"]
   [ invertborder][ lang="lang_code"]
   [ language="javascript"|"jscript"|"vbs[cript]"]
   [ noshade="noshade"][ onbeforecut="bt_script"]
   [ onbeforefocusenter="bfe_script"]
   [ onbeforefocusleave="bfl_script"]
   [ onbeforepaste="bp_script"][ onblur="bl_script"]
   [ onclick="cl_script"][ oncontextmenu="cm_script"]
   [ oncontrolselect="ctl_script"][ oncopy="cp_script"]
   [ oncut="ct_script"][ ondblclick="dc_script"]
   [ ondrag="d_script"][ ondragend="dd_script"]
   [ ondragenter="de_script"][ ondragleave="dl_script"]
   [ ondragover="do_script"][ ondragstart="ds_script"]
   [ ondrop="dr_script"][ onfocus="fc_script"]
   [ onfocusenter="fe_script"]
   [ onfocusleave="fl_script"][ onhelp="hlp_script"]
   [ onkeydown="kd_script"][ onkeypress="kp_script"]
   [ onkeyup="ku_script"]
   [ onlayoutcomplete="la_script"]
```

```
[ onlosecapture="lc_script"]
[ onmousedown="md_script"]
[ onmouseenter="me_script"]
[ onmouseleave="ml_script"]
[ onmousemove="mm_script"][ onmouseout="mo_script"]
[ onmouseover="mov_script"][ onmouseup="mu_script"]
[ onpaste="p_script"][ onpropertychange="pc_script"]
[ onreadystatechange="rsc_script"]
[ onresize="rsz_script"]
[ onresizeend="ree_script"]
[ onresizestart="res_script"]
[ onselectstart="ss_script"][ size="rule_height"]
[ style="name_1: value_1"[; "name_2: value_2"]
[...; "name_n: value_n"]]
[ tabindex="position_number"][ title="title"]
[ width="width_pix"|"width_%"]{ />|</hr>}
```

Where

XHTML Syntax

- ⊖ accesskey (Web) assigns a shortcut key to the object in order to focus on it.
- align (Web) horizontally aligns the horizontal rule. This attribute is deprecated; use a style sheet instead.
- class (Web) specifies a class identification for the horizontal rule.
- ⊖ color (Web) defines the color of the horizontal rule.
- ⊖ contenteditable (Web) specifies or obtains a value that indicates whether a user can edit the element content.
- ⊖ disabled (Web) is a keyword that prevents a user from using the element.
- id (Web) provides a unique identifier name for the horizontal rule.
- ⌘ invertborder (Web) embosses the border, which is usually in relief, of the horizontal rule.
- lang (Web) specifies the code for the language used for the element.
- ⊖ language (Web) declares the scripting language of the current script.
- noshade (Web) removes the shading from the rule. This attribute is deprecated; use a style sheet instead.
- ⊖ onbeforecut (Web) names a script to run when a user starts cutting a selection to the Clipboard but before any action actually takes place.
- ⊖ onbeforefocusenter (Web) names a script to run when a user starts focusing on an object but before the object actually gains focus.
- ⊖ onbeforefocusleave (Web) names a script to run when a user starts leaving an object but before the object actually loses focus.
- ⊖ onbeforepaste (Web) names a script to run when a user starts pasting an object but before any action actually takes place.
- ⊖ onblur (Web) names a script to run when the object loses focus (that is, it is no longer the active element).

- onclick (Web) names a script to run when a user moves the mouse pointer or other pointing device over the horizontal rule and clicks the button.
- Ⓔ oncontextmenu (Web) names a script to run when a user right-clicks the mouse to open a shortcut menu.
- Ⓔ oncontrolselect (Web) names a script to run when a user selects a control.
- Ⓔ oncopy (Web) names a script to run when a user copies a selection to the Clipboard.
- Ⓔ oncut (Web) names a script to run when a user cuts a selection to the Clipboard.
- ondblclick (Web) names a script to run when a user moves the mouse pointer or other pointing device over the horizontal rule and double-clicks the button.
- Ⓔ ondrag (Web) names a script to run when a user drags a selection.
- Ⓔ ondragend (Web) names a script to run after a user completes a drag-and-drop operation.
- Ⓔ ondragenter (Web) names a script to run when a user drags a selection into an area in which it can be dropped.
- Ⓔ ondragleave (Web) names a script to run when a user drags a selection beyond an area in which it can be dropped.
- Ⓔ ondragover (Web) names a script to run when a user drags a selection over an area in which it can be dropped.
- Ⓔ ondragstart (Web) names a script to run when a user starts dragging a selection or element.
- Ⓔ ondrop (Web) names a script to run when a user releases the mouse button to drop a dragged selection.
- Ⓔ onfocus (Web) names a script to run when a user points the mouse pointer or other pointing device to focus on the current element.
- Ⓔ onfocusenter (Web) names a script to run when a user focuses on the current element in any way.
- Ⓔ onfocusleave (Web) names a script to run when a user inactivates the current element in any way.
- Ⓔ onhelp (Web) names a script to run when a user presses the F1 or Help key over the current element.
- onkeydown (Web) names a script to run when a user presses and holds down a key over the horizontal rule.
- onkeypress (Web) names a script to run when a user presses and releases a key over the horizontal rule.
- onkeyup (Web) names a script to run when a user releases a key that is currently held down over the horizontal rule.
- Ⓔ onlayoutcomplete (Web) names a script to run when a user lays out a selection using Print or Print Preview.
- Ⓔ onlosecapture (Web) names a script to run when a user releases a selection that has been captured by the mouse.

- onmousedown (Web) names a script to run when a user moves the mouse pointer or other pointing device over the horizontal rule and presses and holds down the button.
- ☺ onmouseenter (Web) names a script to run when a user moves the mouse pointer onto the object.
- ☺ onmouseleave (Web) names a script to run when the mouse pointer leaves the object.
- onmousemove (Web) names a script to run when a user moves the mouse pointer or other pointing device over the horizontal rule.
- onmouseout (Web) names a script to run when a user moves the mouse pointer or other pointing device away from the horizontal rule.
- onmouseover (Web) names a script to run the first time a user moves the mouse pointer or other pointing device over the horizontal rule.
- onmouseup (Web) names a script to run when a user moves the mouse pointer or other pointing device over the horizontal rule and releases a mouse button that is currently held down.
- ☺ onpaste (Web) names a script to run when a user pastes the Clipboard contents onto the object.
- ☺ onpropertychange (Web) names a script to run when a property changes on the selected object in any way.
- ☺ onreadystatechange (Web) names a script to run when the status of an element has changed (for example, the element receives data).
- ☺ onresize (Web) names a script to run when a user resizes the selected object.
- ☺ onresizeend (Web) names a script to run after the object has been resized.
- ☺ onresizestart (Web) names a script to run as a user resizes the object.
- ☺ onselectstart (Web) names a script to run when a user starts selecting an object.
- size (Web) is the height of the rule, in pixels. This attribute is deprecated; use a style sheet instead.
- style (Web) sets styles for the horizontal rule.
- ☺ tabindex (Web) defines the position of the current element in all the elements that a user can navigate to using a Tab or Shift + Tab key.
- title (Web) provides a title for the horizontal rule.
- width (Web) represents the width of the rule, in pixels or as a percentage of the width of the window. This attribute is deprecated; use a style sheet instead.

Notes

- This block-level element originated in HTML 2.0.
- hr is an empty element, which looks like this in an XHTML document (without any attributes added): <hr />.
- hr causes a paragraph break.
- The default horizontal rule is 600 pixels wide based on a 640×480 screen resolution.

- You cannot align a rule that is the full width of the computer screen.
- For the `hr` element, WebTV supports the `align`, `invertborder`, `noshade`, `size`, and `width` attributes.

Related Element
img (162)

| **html** | **XHTML Document** |

Purpose
Defines an XHTML (HyperText Markup Language, a subset of XML) document.

Syntax
```
<html[ class="class_name"][ dir="ltr"|"rtl"]
   [ disabled="disabled"][ id="id_name"]
   [ lang="lang_code"]
   [ onlayoutcomplete="la_script"]
   [ onmouseenter="me_script"]
   [ onmouseleave="ml_script"]
   [ onreadystatechange="rsc_script"]
   [ title="title"][ version="dtd_uri"]
   [[ xmlns: xmlns_prefix_1][ xmlns: xmlns_prefix_2]
   [ ...xmlns: xmlns_prefix_n ]]>
   XHTML-document</html>
```

Where
- ⊖ class (Web) specifies a class identification for the document.
- ⊖ contenteditable (Web) specifies or obtains a value that indicates whether a user can edit the element content.
- dir (Web) specifies the direction in which the XHTML document text is displayed: left-to-right or right-to-left.
- ⊖ disabled (Web) is a keyword that prevents a user from using the element.
- ⊖ id (Web) provides a unique identifier name for the document.
- lang (Web) specifies the code for the language used for the text in the XHTML document.
- ⊖ onlayoutcomplete (Web) names a script to run when a user lays out a selection using Print or Print Preview.
- ⊖ onmouseenter (Web) names a script to run when a user moves the mouse pointer onto the object.
- ⊖ onmouseleave (Web) names a script to run when the mouse pointer leaves the object.
- ⊖ onreadystatechange (Web) names a script to run when the status of an element has changed (for example, the element receives data).

- ⊖ `title` (Web) provides a title for the element.
- `version` (Web) specifies the URI for the Document Type Definition (DTD) of the HTML standard for the elements and attributes of the current document. This attribute is deprecated; use the `!DOCTYPE` declaration instead.
- ⊖ `xmlns` (Web) declares an XML-based namespace for a custom XHTML element.
- *HTML–document* represents an entire document.

Notes

- This inline element originated in HTML 2.0.
- `html` is the root element of the document. The `<html>` start tag should be the first in a document, and the `</html>` end tag should be the last.
- You can embed the `head` and `body` elements within the `html` start and end tags, but they are not required. However, if you are working on a frames document, the `<frameset>` start tag and `</frameset>` end tag are required.

Related Elements

`body` (65), `frameset` (141), `head` (148)

For More Information

Learn more about the `html` element on page 517 in Chapter 2.

---

i   Italic Text

Purpose

Applies italics to selected text.

Syntax

```
<i[ accesskey="shortcut_key"][ class="class_name"]
  [ contenteditable="edit_string"][ dir="ltr"|"rtl"]
  [ disabled="disabled"][ id="id_name"]
  [ lang="lang_code"][ language="javascript"|"jscript"
  |"vbs[cript]"][ onbeforecopy="bc_script"]
  [ onbeforecut="bt_script"]
  [ onbeforefocusenter="bfe_script"]
  [ onbeforefocusleave="bfl_script"]
  [ onbeforepaste="bp_script"][ onblur="bl_script"]
  [ onclick="cl_script"][ oncontextmenu="cm_script"]
  [ oncontrolselect="ctl_script"][ oncopy="cp_script"]
  [ oncut="ct_script"][ ondblclick="dc_script"]
  [ ondrag="d_script"][ ondragend="dd_script"]
```

XHTML Syntax

```
[ ondragenter="de_script"][ ondragleave="dl_script"]
[ ondragover="do_script"][ ondragstart="ds_script"]
[ ondrop="dr_script"][ onhelp="hlp_script"]
[ onkeydown="kd_script"][ onkeypress="kp_script"]
[ onkeyup="ku_script"][ onlosecapture="lc_script"]
[ onmousedown="md_script"]
[ onmouseenter="me_script"]
[ onmouseleave="ml_script"]
[ onmousemove="mm_script"][ onmouseout="mo_script"]
[ onmouseover="mov_script"][ onmouseup="mu_script"]
[ onpaste="p_script"][ onpropertychange="pc_script"]
[ onreadystatechange="rsc_script"]
[ onresize="rsz_script"][ onresizeend="ree_script"]
[ onresizestart="res_script"]
[ onselectstart="ss_script"]
[ style="name_1: value_1"[; "name_2: value_2"]
[...; "name_n: value_n"]]
[ tabindex="position_number"][ title="title"]>
text</i>
```

Where

- 🌐 `accesskey` (Web) assigns a shortcut key to the object in order to focus on it.
- `class` (Web) specifies a class identification for the italicized text.
- 🌐 `contenteditable` (Web) specifies or obtains a value that indicates whether a user can edit the element content.
- `dir` (Web) specifies the direction in which the italicized text is displayed: left-to-right or right-to-left.
- 🌐 `disabled` (Web) is a keyword that prevents a user from using the element.
- `id` (Web) provides a unique identifier name for the italicized text.
- `lang` (Web) specifies the code for the language used for the italicized text.
- 🌐 `language` (Web) declares the scripting language of the current script.
- 🌐 `onbeforecopy` (Web) names a script to run when a user starts copying a selection to the Clipboard but before any action actually takes place.
- 🌐 `onbeforecut` (Web) names a script to run when a user starts cutting a selection to the Clipboard but before any action actually takes place.
- 🌐 `onbeforefocusenter` (Web) names a script to run when a user starts focusing on an object but before the object actually gains focus.
- 🌐 `onbeforefocusleave` (Web) names a script to run when a user starts leaving an object but before the object actually loses focus.
- 🌐 `onbeforepaste` (Web) names a script to run when a user starts pasting an object but before any action actually takes place.
- 🌐 `onblur` (Web) names a script to run when the object loses focus (that is, it is no longer the active element).

- `onclick` (Web) names a script to run when a user moves the mouse pointer or other pointing device over the italicized text and clicks the button.
- ⊖ `oncontextmenu` (Web) names a script to run when a user right-clicks the mouse to open a shortcut menu.
- ⊖ `oncontrolselect` (Web) names a script to run when a user selects a control.
- ⊖ `oncopy` (Web) names a script to run when a user copies a selection to the Clipboard.
- ⊖ `oncut` (Web) names a script to run when a user cuts a selection to the Clipboard.
- `ondblclick` (Web) names a script to run when a user moves the mouse pointer or other pointing device over the italicized text and double-clicks the button.
- ⊖ `ondrag` (Web) names a script to run when a user drags a selection.
- ⊖ `ondragend` (Web) names a script to run after a user completes a drag-and-drop operation.
- ⊖ `ondragenter` (Web) names a script to run when a user drags a selection into an area in which it can be dropped.
- ⊖ `ondragleave` (Web) names a script to run when a user drags a selection beyond an area in which it can be dropped.
- ⊖ `ondragover` (Web) names a script to run when a user drags a selection over an area in which it can be dropped.
- ⊖ `ondragstart` (Web) names a script to run when a user starts dragging a selection or element.
- ⊖ `ondrop` (Web) names a script to run when a user releases the mouse button to drop a dragged selection.
- ⊖ `onfocus` (Web) names a script to run when a user points the mouse pointer or other pointing device to focus on the current element.
- ⊖ `onfocusenter` (Web) names a script to run when a user focuses on the current element in any way.
- ⊖ `onfocusleave` (Web) names a script to run when a user inactivates the current element in any way.
- ⊖ `onhelp` (Web) names a script to run when a user presses the F1 or Help key over the current element.
- `onkeydown` (Web) names a script to run when a user presses and holds down a key over the italicized text.
- `onkeypress` (Web) names a script to run when a user presses and releases a key over the italicized text.
- `onkeyup` (Web) names a script to run when a user releases a key that is currently held down over the italicized text.
- ⊖ `onlosecapture` (Web) names a script to run when a user releases a selection that has been captured by the mouse.
- `onmousedown` (Web) names a script to run when a user moves the mouse pointer or other pointing device over the italicized text and presses and holds down the button.

- ⊖ onmouseenter (Web) names a script to run when a user moves the mouse pointer onto the object.
- ⊖ onmouseleave (Web) names a script to run when the mouse pointer leaves the object.
- onmousemove (Web) names a script to run when a user moves the mouse pointer or other pointing device over the italicized text.
- onmouseout (Web) names a script to run when a user moves the mouse pointer or other pointing device away from the italicized text.
- onmouseover (Web) names a script to run the first time a user moves the mouse pointer or other pointing device over the italicized text.
- onmouseup (Web) names a script to run when a user moves the mouse pointer or other pointing device over the italicized text and releases a mouse button that is currently held down.
- ⊖ onpaste (Web) names a script to run when a user pastes the Clipboard contents onto the object.
- ⊖ onpropertychange (Web) names a script to run when a property changes on the selected object in any way.
- ⊖ onreadystatechange (Web) names a script to run when the status of an element has changed (for example, the element receives data).
- ⊖ onresize (Web) names a script to run when a user resizes the selected object.
- ⊖ onresizeend (Web) names a script to run after the object has been resized.
- ⊖ onresizestart (Web) names a script to run as a user resizes the object.
- ⊖ onselectstart (Web) names a script to run when a user starts selecting an object.
- style (Web) sets styles for the italicized text.
- title (Web) provides a title for the italicized text.
- text represents one or more characters.

Notes
- This inline element originated in HTML 2.0.
- i is one of the elements in the %fontstyle entity. The other %fontstyle elements are b, big, small, and tt. Deprecated elements in the %fontstyle entity are s, strike, and u.
- The i and b elements are physical styles, which specifically command a browser to apply italics and boldface, respectively. Their counterpart logical style elements are em and strong, which allow a browser to emphasize selected text in the way in which it is programmed to do.

Related Elements
b (46), big (57), cite (83), em (120), font (131), s (254), small (268), strike (254), strong (276), sub (281), sup (284), tt (324), u (327), var (335)

iframe — Inline Frame

Purpose

Defines a floating frame within an XHTML document.

Syntax

```
<iframe[ align="top"|"middle"|"bottom"|"left"|"center"
  |"right"|"absbottom"|"absmiddle"|"baseline"
  |"texttop"][ application="off"|"on"]
  [ bgcolor="#rrggbb"|"color"]
  [ border="0"|"border_pix"][ class="class_name"]
  [ contenteditable="edit_string"]
  [ datafld="ds_col_name"][ datasrc="ds_identifier"]
  [ disabled="disabled"][ frameborder="1"|"0]
  [ framespacing="frame_space"][ height="height_pix"]
  [ hspace="horiz_pix"][ id="id_name"]
  [ longdesc="description_uri"]
  [ marginheight="height_pix"]
  [ marginwidth="width_pix"][ name="frame-name"
  |"_blank"|"_parent"|"_self"|"_top"]
  [ noresize="noresize"[|resize="resize"]]
  [ onbeforefocusenter="bfe_script"]
  [ onbeforefocusleave="bfl_script"]
  [ onblur="bl_script"][ oncontrolselect="ctl_script"]
  [ onfocus="fc_script"][ onfocusenter="fe_script"]
  [ onfocusleave="fl_script"]
  [ onresizeend="ree_script"]
  [ onresizestart="res_script"]
  [ scrolling="auto"|"yes"|"no"]
  [ src="source_uri"][ style="name_1: value_1"
  [; "name_2: value_2"][...; "name_n: value_n"]]
  [ tabindex="position_number"]
  [ title="title"][ vspace="vert_pix"]
  [ width="width_pix"|"width_%"]>
  alternate_contents</iframe>
```

Where

- align (Web) aligns the frame or the surrounding text.
- ⊖ application (Web) indicates whether content is an HTML application ("yes") or not ("no").
- ⊖ bgcolor (Web) specifies the background color for the object.
- ⊖ border (Web) turns on a border and/or sets the width, in pixels, of the inline frame.

- `class` (Web) specifies a class identification for the element.
- ⊖ `contenteditable` (Web) specifies or obtains a value that indicates whether a user can edit the element content.
- ⊖ `datafld` (Web) specifies the column name from the file that contains the data source object.
- ⊖ `datasrc` (Web) specifies the identifier of the data source object.
- ⊖ `disabled` (Web) is a keyword that prevents a user from using the element.
- `frameborder` (Web) specifies whether the current frame will have a border.
- ⊖ `framespacing` (Web) sets spacing, in pixels, between all the frames in a frameset.
- `height` (Web) specifies the height of the current inline frame.
- ⊖🖰 `hspace` (Web) is the horizontal area, in pixels, of the left and right sides of the frame and its contents.
- `id` (Web) provides a unique identifier name for the element.
- `longdesc` (Web) provides the URI of a long alternate description.
- `marginheight` (Web) is the space, in pixels, between the top and bottom margins of the frame and the contents of the frame.
- `marginwidth` (Web) is the space, in pixels, between the left and right margins of the frame and the contents of the frame.
- `name` (Web) labels the current frame. Microsoft Internet Explorer supports the use of the `_blank`, `_parent`, `_self`, and `_top` reserved words. In XHTML, `name` is deprecated; use `id` instead.
- ⊖ `noresize|resize` (Web) freezes the current frame at its current height and width or allows resizing of the frame.
- ⊖ `onbeforefocusenter` (Web) names a script to run when a user starts focusing on an object but before the object actually gains focus.
- ⊖ `onbeforefocusleave` (Web) names a script to run when a user starts leaving an object but before the object actually loses focus.
- ⊖ `onblur` (Web) names a script to run when the object loses focus (that is, it is no longer the active element).
- ⊖ `oncontrolselect` (Web) names a script to run when a user selects a control.
- ⊖ `onfocus` (Web) names a script to run when a user points the mouse pointer or other pointing device to focus on the current element.
- ⊖ `onfocusenter` (Web) names a script to run when a user focuses on the current element in any way.
- ⊖ `onfocusleave` (Web) names a script to run when a user inactivates the current element in any way.
- ⊖ `onresizeend` (Web) names a script to run after the object has been resized.
- ⊖ `onresizestart` (Web) names a script to run as a user resizes the object.
- `scrolling` (Web) specifies whether the current frame contains scrollbars.
- `src` (Web) specifies the source file displayed within the current frame.
- `style` (Web) sets styles for the element.

- ⊖ `tabindex` (Web) defines the position of the current element in all the elements that a user can navigate to using a Tab or Shift + Tab key.
- `title` (Web) provides a title for the element.
- ⊖ `vspace` (Web) is the vertical area, in pixels, between the top margin of the page and the top margin of the frame. This attribute is deprecated; use a style sheet instead.
- `width` (Web) specifies the width of the current inline frame.
- `alternate_contents` represents text that will print if a browser does not support inline frames.

Notes

- This inline and block-level element was formerly a Microsoft extension and is now part of HTML 4.0.
- If a browser supports inline frames, the contents of the source file will appear within the frame. If a browser does not support inline frames, the text inserted between the start and end tags will appear in the XHTML document.
- According to the World Wide Web Consortium (W3C), "inserting an inline frame within a section of text is much like inserting an object via the `object` element; they both allow you to insert an XHTML document in the middle of another, they may both be aligned with surrounding text, etc."
- Use `iframe` to insert a frame within a block of text in the same way that you would insert a graphic.
- For the `iframe` element, WebTV supports the `align`, `height`, `hspace`, `id`, `name`, `src`, `vspace`, and `width` attributes.

Related Elements

`frame` (139), `frameset` (141), `noframes` (222), `object` (225)

For More Information

Learn more about the `iframe` element on page 579 in Chapter 5.

N ilayer   **Inflow Layer**

Purpose

Defines opaque or transparent blocks of XHTML content that overlap other content in the current document.

Syntax

```
<ilayer[ above="top_layer_name"]
  [ background="picture_uri"]
  [ below="below_layer_name"]
  [ bgcolor="#rrggbb"|"color"]
```

```
[ clip=[0|"l_pix,0|t_pix,]r_pix,b_pix"]
[ height="height_pix"][ id="id_name"]
[ left="left_pos_pix"][ name="layer_name"]
[ onblur="bl_script"][ onfocus="fc_script"]
[ onload="ol_script"][ onmouseout="mo_script"]
[ onmouseover="mov_script"][ pagex="horz_pos_pix"]
[ pagey="vert_pos_pix"][ src="source_uri"]
[ top="top_pos_pix"][ visibility="inherit"|"show"
|"hide"][ width="width_pix"][ z-index="order_num"]
{ />|</ilayer>}
```

Where

- **N** above (Web) names the layer that is the top layer in the stack of layers.
- **N** background (Web) specifies an image file that is displayed in the background of the current layer.
- **N** below (Web) names the layer that is immediately below the newest layer in the stack.
- **N** bgcolor (Web) specifies the background color for the layer.
- **N** clip (Web) specifies the dimensions of the layer window.
- **N** height (Web) specifies the height, in pixels, of the layer window.
- **N** id (Web) provides a unique identifier name for the layer.
- **N** left (Web) specifies the leftmost position, in pixels, of the left side of a layer window.
- **N** name (Web) provides a unique identifier name for the layer. In XHTML, name is deprecated; use id instead.
- **N** onblur (Web) names a script to run when the layer loses focus.
- **N** onfocus (Web) names a script to run when a user points the mouse pointer or other pointing device to focus on the current element.
- **N** onload (Web) names a script to run after the active browser has finished loading a layer.
- **N** onmouseout (Web) names a script to run when a user moves the mouse pointer or other pointing device away from the layer.
- **N** onmouseover (Web) names a script to run the first time a user moves the mouse pointer or other pointing device over the layer.
- **N** pagex (Web) specifies the horizontal position, in pixels, of the top left corner of the layer window within the current XHTML document.
- **N** pagey (Web) specifies the vertical position, in pixels, of the top left corner of the layer window within the current XHTML document.
- **N** src (Web) specifies a source file that contains the contents of a layer window.
- **N** top (Web) specifies the topmost position, in pixels, of the top of a layer window.
- **N** visibility (Web) specifies whether a layer is visible or hidden.
- **N** width (Web) specifies the width, in pixels, of the layer window.
- **N** z-index (Web) specifies the numerical order of the current layer.

Notes

- This extension is supported only within Netscape Navigator 4.0 or greater.
- ilayer is an empty element.
- By default, a layer is transparent.
- You can use layers to animate a page or to modify a page almost instantly.
- You can stack multiple layers on a page, and you can nest layers.
- Use JavaScript to move, hide, expand, contract, rearrange, and change the color and image characteristics of layers.

Related Elements

layer (194), nolayer (223)

---

img   Inline Image

Purpose

Inserts an inline image in the document.

Syntax

```
<img src="image_uri" alt="alternate_name"
  [ accesskey="shortcut_key"][ align="bottom"
  |"middle"|"top"|"left"|"right"|"absmiddle"
  |"absbottom"|"texttop"|"baseline"|"center"]
  [ border="border_pix"][ class="class_name"]
  [ contenteditable="edit_string"]
  [ datafld="ds_col_name"][ datasrc="ds_identifier"]
  [ dir="ltr"|"rtl"][ disabled="disabled"]
  [ dynsrc="dynamic_uri"][ height="height_pix"]
  [ hspace="horiz_pix"][ id="id_name"]
  [ ismap="ismap"["ismap_name"]][ lang="lang_code"]
  [ language="javascript"|"jscript"|"vbs[cript]"]
  [ longdesc="description_uri"]
  [ loop="number_of_plays"][ lowsrc="low_res_uri"]
  [ name="image_name"][ onabort="a_script"]
  [ onbeforecopy="bc_script"]
  [ onbeforecut="bt_script"]
  [ onbeforefocusenter="bfe_script"]
  [ onbeforefocusleave="bfl_script"]
  [ onbeforepaste="bp_script"]
  [ onblur="bl_script"][ onclick="cl_script"]
  [ oncontextmenu="cm_script"]
  [ oncontrolselect="ctl_script"][ oncopy="cp_script"]
  [ oncut="ct_script"][ ondblclick="dc_script"]
  [ ondrag="d_script"][ ondragend="dd_script"]
```

```
[ ondragenter="de_script"][ ondragleave="dl_script"]
[ ondragover="do_script"][ ondragstart="ds_script"]
[ ondrop="dr_script"][ onerror="e_script"]
[ onfilterchange="f_script"][ onfocus="fc_script"]
[ onfocusenter="fe_script"]
[ onfocusleave="fl_script"][ onhelp="hlp_script"]
[ onkeydown="kd_script"][ onkeypress="kp_script"]
[ onkeyup="ku_script"][ onload="ol_script"]
[ onlosecapture="lc_script"]
[ onmousedown="md_script"]
[ onmouseenter="me_script"]
[ onmouseleave="ml_script"]
[ onmousemove="mm_script"][ onmouseout="mo_script"]
[ onmouseover="mov_script"][ onmouseup="mu_script"]
[ onresize="rsz_script"][ onpaste="p_script"]
[ onpropertychange="pc_script"]
[ onreadystatechange="rsc_script"]
[ onresize="rsz_script"][ onresizeend="ree_script"]
[ onresizestart="res_script"]
[ onselectstart="ss_script"]
[ selected="x_axis,y_axis"]
[ style="name_1: value_1"[; "name_2: value_2"]
[...; "name_n: value_n"]][ suppress="true"|"false"]
[ tabindex="position_number"][ title="title"]
[ transparency="trans_value"][ usemap="map_uri"]
[ vspace="vert_pix"][ width="width_pix"]{ />|</img>}
```

Where

- `src` (Web) specifies the URI of an image file.
- `alt` (Web) permanently describes the image for text-only browsers or temporarily describes an image as it loads. Some browsers display alternate text as a tool tip.
- ⊖ `accesskey` (Web) assigns a shortcut key to the object in order to focus on it.
- `align` (Web) aligns the image with the surrounding area of the XHTML document. This is a deprecated attribute; use a style sheet instead.
- `border` (Web) turns on a border and sets the width, in pixels, of the image. This is a deprecated attribute; use a style sheet instead.
- `class` (Web) specifies a class identification for the image.
- ⊖ `contenteditable` (Web) specifies or obtains a value that indicates whether a user can edit the element content.
- ⊖ `datafld` (Web) specifies the column name from the file that contains the data source object.
- ⊖ `datasrc` (Web) specifies the identifier of the data source object.

- dir (Web) specifies the direction in which the current text is displayed: left-to-right or right-to-left.
- ⊝ disabled (Web) is a keyword that prevents a user from using the element.
- ⊝ dynsrc (Web) names the URI of a video clip or multimedia file to be inserted in an image.
- height (Web) specifies the height, in pixels, of the window in which the image will be placed. For Internet Explorer, the height can also be measured as a percentage of the parent object's height.
- hspace (Web) is the horizontal area, in pixels, between the left margin of the page and the left margin of the image. This attribute is deprecated; use a style sheet instead.
- id (Web) provides a unique identifier name for the image.
- ismap (Web) indicates that the image is a server-side image map. For Microsoft Internet Explorer and compatible browsers, you can name the image.
- lang (Web) specifies the code representing the language used with text associated with the image.
- longdesc (Web) provides the URI of a long alternate description.
- ⊝ loop (Web) indicates the number of times that an embedded video clip will play.
- ⊝N lowsrc (Web) specifies the URI of a low-resolution graphic to be loaded in the same location as the image named with the src attribute.
- name (Web) labels the current image for the use of one or more associated scripts. In XHTML, name is deprecated; use id instead.
- ⊝N onabort (Web) names a script to run when a user stops the current image from loading.
- ⊝ onbeforecopy (Web) names a script to run when a user starts copying a selection to the Clipboard but before any action actually takes place.
- ⊝ onbeforecut (Web) names a script to run when a user starts cutting a selection to the Clipboard but before any action actually takes place.
- ⊝ onbeforefocusenter (Web) names a script to run when a user starts focusing on an object but before the object actually gains focus.
- ⊝ onbeforefocusleave (Web) names a script to run when a user starts leaving an object but before the object actually loses focus.
- ⊝ onbeforepaste (Web) names a script to run when a user starts pasting an object but before any action actually takes place.
- ⊝ onblur (Web) names a script to run when the object loses focus (that is, it is no longer the active element).
- onclick (Web) names a script to run when a user moves the mouse pointer or other pointing device over the image and clicks the device button.
- ⊝ oncontextmenu (Web) names a script to run when a user clicks the right mouse button to open a shortcut menu.
- ⊝ oncontrolselect (Web) names a script to run when a user selects a control.

- ⊖ oncopy (Web) names a script to run when a user copies a selection to the Clipboard.
- ⊖ oncut (Web) names a script to run when a user cuts a selection to the Clipboard.
- ondblclick (Web) names a script to run when a user moves the mouse pointer or other pointing device over the image and double-clicks the device button.
- ⊖ ondrag (Web) names a script to run when a user drags a selection.
- ⊖ ondragend (Web) names a script to run after a user completes a drag-and-drop operation.
- ⊖ ondragenter (Web) names a script to run when a user drags a selection into an area in which it can be dropped.
- ⊖ ondragleave (Web) names a script to run when a user drags a selection beyond an area in which it can be dropped.
- ⊖ ondragover (Web) names a script to run when a user drags a selection over an area in which it can be dropped.
- ⊖ ondragstart (Web) names a script to run when a user starts dragging a selection or element.
- ⊖ ondrop (Web) names a script to run when a user releases the mouse button to drop a dragged selection.
- ⊖Ⓝ onerror (Web) specifies a script to run when the referred-to script experiences an error.
- ⊖ onfilterchange (Web) names a script to run when a visual filter changes in any way.
- ⊖ onfocus (Web) names a script to run when a user points the mouse pointer or other pointing device to focus on the current element.
- ⊖ onfocusenter (Web) names a script to run when a user focuses on the current element in any way.
- ⊖ onfocusleave (Web) names a script to run when a user inactivates the current element in any way.
- ⊖ onhelp (Web) names a script to run when a user presses the F1 or Help key over the current element.
- onkeydown (Web) names a script to run when a user presses and holds down a key over the image.
- onkeypress (Web) names a script to run when a user presses and releases a key over the image.
- onkeyup (Web) names a script to run when a user releases a key that is currently held down over the image.
- ⊖Ⓝ⌘ onload (Web) names a script to run after the active browser has finished loading an image.
- ⊖ onlosecapture (Web) names a script to run when a user releases a selection that has been captured by the mouse.
- onmousedown (Web) names a script to run when a user moves the mouse pointer or other pointing device over the image and presses and holds down the device button.
- ⊖ onmouseenter (Web) names a script to run when a user moves the mouse pointer onto the object.

- ☺ onmouseleave (Web) names a script to run when the mouse pointer leaves the object.
- onmousemove (Web) names a script to run when a user moves the mouse pointer or other pointing device over the image.
- onmouseout (Web) names a script to run when a user moves the mouse pointer or other pointing device away from the image.
- onmouseover (Web) names a script to run the first time a user moves the mouse pointer or other pointing device over the image.
- onmouseup (Web) names a script to run when a user moves the mouse pointer or other pointing device over the image and releases a pressed-down device button.
- ☺ onpaste (Web) names a script to run when a user pastes the Clipboard contents onto the object.
- ☺ onpropertychange (Web) names a script to run when a property changes on the selected object in any way.
- ☺ onreadystatechange (Web) names a script to run when the status of an element has changed (for example, the element receives data).
- ☺ onresize (Web) names a script to run when a user resizes the selected object.
- ☺ onresizeend (Web) names a script to run after the object has been resized.
- ☺ onresizestart (Web) names a script to run as a user resizes the object.
- ☺ onselectstart (Web) names a script to run when a user starts selecting an object.
- ☒ selected (Web) sets the starting cursor position of the ismap or usemap attribute.
- style (Web) sets styles for the image.
- Ⓝ suppress (Web) specifies whether a placeholder icon and tool tip are active while the image is loading.
- ☺ tabindex (Web) defines the position of the current element in all the elements that a user can navigate to using a Tab or Shift + Tab key.
- title (Web) provides a title for the image.
- ☒ transparency (Web) sets the level of transparency or opaqueness of the selected text.
- usemap (Web) specifies a client-side image map that is an embedded image within a document.
- vspace (Web) is the vertical area, in pixels, between the top margin of the page and the top margin of the image. This attribute is deprecated; use a style sheet instead.
- width (Web) specifies the width, in pixels, of the window in which the image will be placed. For Internet Explorer, the width can also be measured as a percentage of the parent object's width.

Notes

- This inline element originated in HTML 2.0.
- img is an empty element.

- Consider displaying the file size next to a large image file, so that users can decide whether to wait for downloading.
- As a rule, JPEG image files are smaller than GIF image files. This means that JPEG images load more quickly than GIF images.
- Netscape Navigator supports GIF, JPEG, XPM (X PixMap), and XBM (X BitMap) image files.
- For a faster loading site, consider limiting images to 70 kilobytes or less and using fewer colors.
- When an `img` is embedded in an `a` element, browsers must access `longdesc` and `src` URIs differently.
- GIF animations are single GIF files with individual frames inserted within them. For more information about GIF animations, refer to *The GIF Animator's Guide,* also written by Sandra E. Eddy and published by IDG Books Worldwide.
- The `align` attribute is limited in its page formatting abilities. Use style sheets instead.
- WebTV supports the following attributes for `img`: `align`, `border`, `class`, `height`, `hspace`, `id`, `ismap`, `name`, `onabort`, `onerror`, `onload`, `selected`, `src`, `style`, `transparency`, `usemap`, `vspace`, and `width`.

Related Elements

a (24), `link` (202)

For More Information

Learn more about the `img` element on page 531 in Chapter 2.

---

input   **Input Form Field**

Purpose

Provides a way to accept various forms of input, using text boxes, check boxes, radio buttons, images, command buttons, or image maps.

● NOTE

The syntax for various input types are arranged as follows: text boxes (the default), button, check box, file, hidden, image, password, radio buttons, reset button, and submit.

Syntax (Text Box)

```
<input name="input_name"
 [ accept="MIME_type_1"[,MIME_type_2]
 [...,MIME_type_n]][ accesskey="shortcut_key"]
 [ align="top"|"middle"|"bottom"|"left"|"right"]
 [ alt="alternate_name"][ autocomplete="off"|"on"]
```

XHTML Syntax

```
[ bgcolor="#rrggbb"|"color"][ class="class_name"]
[ contenteditable="edit_string"]
[ CURSOR="#rrggbb"|"color"][ datafld="ds_col_name"]
[ datasrc="ds_identifier"][ dir="ltr"|"rtl"]
[ disabled="disabled"][ id="id_name"]
[ lang="lang_code"][ language="javascript"|"jscript"
|"vbs[cript]"][ maxlength="max_length"]
[ onafterupdate="au_script"]
[ onbeforecut="bt_script"]
[ onbeforeeditfocus="bef_script"]
[ onbeforefocusenter="bfe_script"]
[ onbeforefocusleave="bfl_script"]
[ onbeforepaste="bp_script"]
[ onbeforeupdate="bu_script"][ onblur="bl_script"]
[ onchange="ch_script"][ onclick="cl_script"]
[ oncontextmenu="cm_script"]
[ oncontrolselect="ctl_script"][ oncut="ct_script"]
[ ondblclick="dc_script"][ ondrag="d_script"]
[ ondragend="dd_script"][ ondragenter="de_script"]
[ ondragleave="dl_script"][ ondragover="do_script"]
[ ondragstart="ds_script"][ ondrop="dr_script"]
[ onerrorupdate="eu_script"]
[ onfilterchange="f_script"]
[ onfocus="fc_script"][ onfocusenter="fe_script"]
[ onfocusleave="fl_script"][ onhelp="hlp_script"]
[ onkeydown="kd_script"][ onkeypress="kp_script"]
[ onkeyup="ku_script"][ onlosecapture="lc_script"]
[ onmousedown="md_script"]
[ onmouseenter="me_script"]
[ onmouseleave="ml_script"]
[ onmousemove="mm_script"][ onmouseout="mo_script"]
[ onmouseover="mov_script"][ onmouseup="mu_script"]
[ onpaste="p_script"][ onpropertychange="pc_script"]
[ onreadystatechange="rsc_script"]
[ onresize="rsz_script"][ onresizeend="ree_script"]
[ onresizestart="res_script"][ onselect="sl_script"]
[ onselectstart="ss_script"][ readonly="readonly"]
[ size="input_control_size"]
[ style="name_1: value_1"[; name_2: value_2"]
[...; name_n: value_n"]]
[ tabindex="position_number"][ title="title"]
[ type="text"][ value="initial_value"]
[ vcard_name="vCard_value"]
[ width="width_pix"]{ />|</input>}
```

Syntax (Button)

```
<input name="input_name"[ accept="MIME_type_1"
[,MIME_type_2][...,MIME_type_n]]
[ accesskey="shortcut_key"]
[ align="top"|"middle"|"bottom"|"left"|"right"]
[ alt="alternate_name"][ class="class_name"]
[ contenteditable="edit_string"]
[ datasrc="ds_identifier"]
[ dir="ltr"|"rtl"][ disabled="disabled"]
[ id="id_name"][ lang="lang_code"]
[ language="javascript"|"jscript"|"vbs[cript]"]
[ onbeforecut="bt_script"]
[ onbeforeeditfocus="bef_script"]
[ onbeforefocusenter="bfe_script"]
[ onbeforefocusleave="bfl_script"]
[ onbeforepaste="bp_script"][ onblur="bl_script"]
[ onclick="cl_script"][ oncontextmenu="cm_script"]
[ oncontrolselect="ctl_script"][ oncut="ct_script"]
[ ondblclick="dc_script"][ ondrag="d_script"]
[ ondragend="dd_script"][ ondragenter="de_script"]
[ ondragleave="dl_script"][ ondragover="do_script"]
[ ondragstart="ds_script"][ ondrop="dr_script"]
[ onfilterchange="f_script"][ onfocus="fc_script"]
[ onfocusenter="fe_script"]
[ onfocusleave="fl_script"]
[ onhelp="hlp_script"][ onkeydown="kd_script"]
[ onkeypress="kp_script"][ onkeyup="ku_script"]
[ onlosecapture="lc_script"]
[ onmousedown="md_script"]
[ onmouseenter="me_script"]
[ onmouseleave="ml_script"]
[ onmousemove="mm_script"]
[ onmouseout="mo_script"][ onmouseover="mov_script"]
[ onmouseup="mu_script"][ onpaste="p_script"]
[ onpropertychange="pc_script"]
[ onreadystatechange="rsc_script"]
[ onresize="rsz_script"][ onresizeend="ree_script"]
[ onresizestart="res_script"][ onselect="sl_script"]
[ onselectstart="ss_script"]
[ size="input_control_size"]
[ style="name_1: value_1"[; name_2: value_2"]
[...; name_n: value_n"]]
[ tabindex="position_number"]
```

```
[ title="title"][ type="button"]
[ value="initial_value"]
[ width="width_pix"]{ />|</input>}
```

Syntax (Check Box)

```
<input name="input_name"[ accept="MIME_type_1"
[,MIME_type_2][...,MIME_type_n]]
[ accesskey="shortcut_key"]
[ align="top"|"middle"|"bottom"|"left"|"right"]
[ alt="alternate_name"][ checked="checked"]
[ class="class_name"]
[ contenteditable="edit_string"]
[ datafld="ds_col_name"][ datasrc="ds_identifier"]
[ dir="ltr"|"rtl"][ disabled="disabled"]
[ id="id_name"][ lang="lang_code"]
[ language="javascript"|"jscript"|"vbs[cript]"]
[ onbeforecut="bt_script"]
[ onbeforeeditfocus="bef_script"]
[ onbeforefocusenter="bfe_script"]
[ onbeforefocusleave="bfl_script"]
[ onbeforepaste="bp_script"][ onblur="bl_script"]
[ onchange="ch_script"][ onclick="cl_script"]
[ oncontextmenu="cm_script"]
[ oncontrolselect="ctl_script"][ oncut="ct_script"]
[ ondblclick="dc_script"][ ondrag="d_script"]
[ ondragend="dd_script"][ ondragenter="de_script"]
[ ondragleave="dl_script"][ ondragover="do_script"]
[ ondragstart="ds_script"][ ondrop="dr_script"]
[ onfilterchange="f_script"][ onfocus="fc_script"]
[ onfocusenter="fe_script"]
[ onfocusleave="fl_script"]
[ onhelp="hlp_script"][ onkeydown="kd_script"]
[ onkeypress="kp_script"][ onkeyup="ku_script"]
[ onlosecapture="lc_script"]
[ onmousedown="md_script"]
[ onmouseenter="me_script"]
[ onmouseleave="ml_script"]
[ onmousemove="mm_script"][ onmouseout="mo_script"]
[ onmouseover="mov_script"][ onmouseup="mu_script"]
[ onpaste="p_script"][ onpropertychange="pc_script"]
[ onreadystatechange="rsc_script"]
[ onresizeend="ree_script"]
[ onresizestart="res_script"][ onselect="sl_script"]
[ onselectstart="ss_script"]
```

```
[ size="input_control_size"]
[ style="name_1: value_1"[; name_2: value_2"]
[...; name_n: value_n"]]
[ tabindex="position_number"][ title="title"]
[ type="checkbox"][ value="initial_value"]
[ width="width_pix"]{ />|</input>}
```

Syntax (File)

```
<input name="input_name"
  [ accept="MIME_type_1"[,MIME_type_2]
  [...,MIME_type_n]]][ accesskey="shortcut_key"]
  [ align="top"|"middle"|"bottom"|"left"|"right"]
  [ alt="alternate_name"][ class="class_name"]
  [ contenteditable="edit_string"]
  [ datafld="ds_col_name"][ datasrc="ds_identifier"]
  [ dir="ltr"|"rtl"][ disabled="disabled"]
  [ id="id_name"][ lang="lang_code"]
  [ language="javascript"|"jscript"|"vbs[cript]"]
  [ onbeforecut="bt_script"]
  [ onbeforeeditfocus="bef_script"]
  [ onbeforefocusenter="bfe_script"]
  [ onbeforefocusleave="bfl_script"]
  [ onbeforepaste="bp_script"][ onblur="bl_script"]
  [ onchange="ch_script"][ onclick="cl_script"]
  [ oncontextmenu="cm_script"]
  [ oncontrolselect="ctl_script"][ oncut="ct_script"]
  [ ondblclick="dc_script"][ ondrag="d_script"]
  [ ondragend="dd_script"][ ondragenter="de_script"]
  [ ondragleave="dl_script"][ ondragover="do_script"]
  [ ondragstart="ds_script"][ ondrop="dr_script"]
  [ onfilterchange="f_script"][ onfocus="fc_script"]
  [ onfocusenter="fe_script"]
  [ onfocusleave="fl_script"][ onhelp="hlp_script"]
  [ onkeydown="kd_script"][ onkeypress="kp_script"]
  [ onkeyup="ku_script"][ onlosecapture="lc_script"]
  [ onmousedown="md_script"]
  [ onmouseenter="me_script"]
  [ onmouseleave="ml_script"]
  [ onmousemove="mm_script"]
  [ onmouseout="mo_script"][ onmouseover="mov_script"]
  [ onmouseup="mu_script"][ onpaste="p_script"]
  [ onpropertychange="pc_script"]
  [ onreadystatechange="rsc_script"]
  [ onresize="rsz_script"][ onresizeend="ree_script"]
```

```
[ onresizestart="res_script"][ onselect="sl_script"]
[ onselectstart="ss_script"]
[ size="input_control_size"]
[ style="name_1: value_1"[; name_2: value_2"]
[...; name_n: value_n"]]
[ tabindex="position_number"][ title="title"]
[ type="FILE"][ value="initial_value"]
[ width="width_pix"]{ />|</input>}
```

Syntax (Hidden)

```
<input name="input_name"
  [ accept="MIME_type_1"[,MIME_type_2]
  [...,MIME_type_n]][ accesskey="shortcut_key"]
  [ align="top"|"middle"|"bottom"|"left"|"right"]
  [ alt="alternate_name"][ class="class_name"]
  [ datafld="ds_col_name"][ datasrc="ds_identifier"]
  [ dir="ltr"|"rtl"][ disabled="disabled"]
  [ id="id_name"][ lang="lang_code"]
  [ language="javascript"|"jscript"|"vbs[cript]"]
  [ onbeforeeditfocus="bef_script"]
  [ onbeforefocusenter="bfe_script"]
  [ onbeforefocusleave="bfl_script"]
  [ onblur="bl_script"][ onchange="ch_script"]
  [ onclick="cl_script"]
  [ oncontrolselect="ctl_script"]
  [ ondblclick="dc_script"][ onfocus="fc_script"]
  [ onfocusenter="fe_script"]
  [ onfocusleave="fl_script"][ onkeydown="kd_script"]
  [ onkeypress="kp_script"][ onkeyup="ku_script"]
  [ onlosecapture="lc_script"]
  [ onmousedown="md_script"][ onmousemove="mm_script"]
  [ onmouseout="mo_script"][ onmouseover="mov_script"]
  [ onmouseup="mu_script"]
  [ onpropertychange="pc_script"]
  [ onreadystatechange="rsc_script"]
  [ onresizeend="ree_script"]
  [ onresizestart="res_script"][ onselect="sl_script"]
  [ size="input_control_size"]
  [ style="name_1: value_1"[; name_2: value_2"]
  [...; name_n: value_n"]]
  [ tabindex="position_number"][ title="title"]
  [ type="hidden"][ value="initial_value"]
  [ width="width_pix"]{ />|</input>}
```

Syntax (Image)

```
<input name="input_name"[ accept="MIME_type_1"
  [,MIME_type_2][...,MIME_type_n]]
  [ accesskey="shortcut_key"]
  [ align="top"|"middle"|"bottom"|"left"|"right"
  |"absbottom"|"absmiddle"|"baseline"|"texttop"]
  [ alt="alternate_name"][ class="class_name"]
  [ contenteditable="edit_string"]
  [ datafld="ds_col_name"][ datasrc="ds_identifier"]
  [ dir="ltr"|"rtl"][ disabled="disabled"]
  [ id="id_name"][ ismap="ismap"][ lang="lang_code"]
  [ language="javascript"|"jscript"|"vbs[cript]"]
  [ lowsrc="low_res_uri"][ maxlength="max_length"]
  [ onbeforecut="bt_script"]
  [ onbeforeeditfocus="bef_script"]
  [ onbeforefocusenter="bfe_script"]
  [ onbeforefocusleave="bfl_script"]
  [ onbeforepaste="bp_script"][ onblur="bl_script"]
  [ onchange="ch_script"][ onclick="cl_script"]
  [ oncontextmenu="cm_script"]
  [ oncontrolselect="ctl_script"][ oncut="ct_script"]
  [ ondblclick="dc_script"][ ondrag="d_script"]
  [ ondragend="dd_script"][ ondragenter="de_script"]
  [ ondragleave="dl_script"][ ondragover="do_script"]
  [ ondragstart="ds_script"][ ondrop="dr_script"]
  [ onfilterchange="f_script"][ onfocus="fc_script"]
  [ onfocusenter="fe_script"]
  [ onfocusleave="fl_script"][ onhelp="hlp_script"]
  [ onkeydown="kd_script"][ onkeypress="kp_script"]
  [ onkeyup="ku_script"][ onlosecapture="lc_script"]
  [ onmousedown="md_script"]
  [ onmouseenter="me_script"]
  [ onmouseleave="ml_script"]
  [ onmousemove="mm_script"][ onmouseout="mo_script"]
  [ onmouseover="mov_script"][ onmouseup="mu_script"]
  [ onpaste="p_script"][ onpropertychange="pc_script"]
  [ onreadystatechange="rsc_script"]
  [ onresize="rsz_script"][ onresizeend="ree_script"]
  [ onresizestart="res_script"][ onselect="sl_script"]
  [ onselectstart="ss_script"]
  [ size="input_control_size"][ src="image_uri"]
  [ style="name_1: value_1"[; name_2: value_2"]
  [...; name_n: value_n"]]
```

```
[ tabindex="position_number"][ title="title"]
[ type="image"][ usemap="map_uri"]
[ value="initial_value"]
[ width="width_pix"]{ />|</input>}
```

Syntax (Password)

```
<input name="input_name"[ accept="MIME_type_1"
[,MIME_type_2][...,MIME_type_n]]
[ accesskey="shortcut_key"][ align="top"|"middle"
|"bottom"|"left"|"right"][ alt="alternate_name"]
[ autocomplete="off"|"on"][ class="class_name"]
[ contenteditable="edit_string"]
[ datafld="ds_col_name"][ datasrc="ds_identifier"]
[ dir="ltr"|"rtl"][ disabled="disabled"]
[ id="id_name"][ lang="lang_code"]
[ language="javascript"|"jscript"|"vbs[cript]"]
[ maxlength="max_length"][ onbeforecut="bt_script"]
[ onbeforeeditfocus="bef_script"]
[ onbeforefocusenter="bfe_script"]
[ onbeforefocusleave="bfl_script"]
[ onbeforepaste="bp_script"][ onblur="bl_script"]
[ onchange="ch_script"][ onclick="cl_script"]
[ oncontextmenu="cm_script"]
[ oncontrolselect="ctl_script"][ oncut="ct_script"]
[ ondblclick="dc_script"][ ondrag="d_script"]
[ ondragend="dd_script"][ ondragenter="de_script"]
[ ondragleave="dl_script"][ ondragover="do_script"]
[ ondragstart="ds_script"][ ondrop="dr_script"]
[ onfilterchange="f_script"][ onfocus="fc_script"]
[ onfocusenter="fe_script"]
[ onfocusleave="fl_script"][ onhelp="hlp_script"]
[ onkeydown="kd_script"][ onkeypress="kp_script"]
[ onkeyup="ku_script"][ onlosecapture="lc_script"]
[ onmousedown="md_script"]
[ onmouseenter="me_script"]
[ onmouseleave="ml_script"]
[ onmousemove="mm_script"][ onmouseout="mo_script"]
[ onmouseover="mov_script"][ onmouseup="mu_script"]
[ onpaste="p_script"][ onpropertychange="pc_script"]
[ onreadystatechange="rsc_script"]
[ onresize="rsz_script"][ onresizeend="ree_script"]
[ onresizestart="res_script"][ onselect="sl_script"]
[ onselectstart="ss_script"][ readonly="readonly"]
[ size="input_control_size"]
```

```
[ style="name_1: value_1"[; name_2: value_2"]
[...; name_n: value_n"]]
[ tabindex="position_number"][ title="title"]
[ type="password"][ value="initial_value"]
[ vcard_name="vCard_value"]
[ width="width_pix"]{ />|</input>}
```

Syntax (Radio Buttons)

```
<input name="input_name"[ accept="MIME_type_1"
[,MIME_type_2][...,MIME_type_n]]
[ accesskey="shortcut_key"]
[ align="top"|"middle"|"bottom"|"left"|"right"]
[ alt="alternate_name"][ checked="checked"]
[ class="class_name"]
[ contenteditable="edit_string"]
[ datafld="ds_col_name"][ datasrc="ds_identifier"]
[ dir="ltr"|"rtl"][ disabled="disabled"]
[ id="id_name"][ lang="lang_code"]
[ language="javascript"|"jscript"|"vbs[cript]"]
[ onbeforecut="bt_script"]
[ onbeforeeditfocus="bef_script"]
[ onbeforefocusenter="bfe_script"]
[ onbeforefocusleave="bfl_script"]
[ onbeforepaste="bp_script"][ onblur="bl_script"]
[ onchange="ch_script"][ onclick="cl_script"]
[ oncontextmenu="cm_script"]
[ oncontrolselect="ctl_script"][ oncut="ct_script"]
[ ondblclick="dc_script"][ ondrag="d_script"]
[ ondragend="dd_script"][ ondragenter="de_script"]
[ ondragleave="dl_script"][ ondragover="do_script"]
[ ondragstart="ds_script"][ ondrop="dr_script"]
[ onfilterchange="f_script"][ onfocus="fc_script"]
[ onfocusenter="fe_script"]
[ onfocusleave="fl_script"][ onhelp="hlp_script"]
[ onkeydown="kd_script"]
[ onkeypress="kp_script"][ onkeyup="ku_script"]
[ onlosecapture="lc_script"]
[ onmousedown="md_script"]
[ onmouseenter="me_script"]
[ onmouseleave="ml_script"]
[ onmousemove="mm_script"][ onmouseout="mo_script"]
[ onmouseover="mov_script"][ onmouseup="mu_script"]
[ onpaste="p_script"][ onpropertychange="pc_script"]
[ onreadystatechange="rsc_script"]
```

XHTML Syntax

```
[ onresizeend="ree_script"]
[ onresizestart="res_script"][ onselect="sl_script"]
[ onselectstart="ss_script"]
[ size="input_control_size"]
[ style="name_1: value_1"[; name_2: value_2"]
[...; name_n: value_n"]]
[ tabindex="position_number"][ title="title"]
[ type="radio"][ value="initial_value"]
[ width="width_pix"]{ />|</input>}
```

Syntax (Reset Button)

```
<input[ accept="MIME_type_1"[,MIME_type_2]
  [...,MIME_type_n]][ accesskey="shortcut_key"]
  [ align="top"|"middle"|"bottom"|"left"|"right"]
  [ alt="alternate_name"][ class="class_name"]
  [ contenteditable="edit_string"]
  [ datafld="ds_col_name"][ datasrc="ds_identifier"]
  [ dir="ltr"|"rtl"][ disabled="disabled"]
  [ id="id_name"][ lang="lang_code"]
  [ language="javascript"|"jscript"|"vbs[cript]"]
  [ name="input_name"][ onbeforecut="bt_script"]
  [ onbeforeeditfocus="bef_script"]
  [ onbeforefocusenter="bfe_script"]
  [ onbeforefocusleave="bfl_script"]
  [ onbeforepaste="bp_script"][ onblur="bl_script"]
  [ onchange="ch_script"][ onclick="cl_script"]
  [ oncontextmenu="cm_script"]
  [ oncontrolselect="ctl_script"][ oncut="ct_script"]
  [ ondblclick="dc_script"][ ondrag="d_script"]
  [ ondragend="dd_script"][ ondragenter="de_script"]
  [ ondragleave="dl_script"][ ondragover="do_script"]
  [ ondragstart="ds_script"][ ondrop="dr_script"]
  [ onfilterchange="f_script"][ onfocus="fc_script"]
  [ onfocusenter="fe_script"]
  [ onfocusleave="fl_script"][ onhelp="hlp_script"]
  [ onkeydown="kd_script"][ onkeypress="kp_script"]
  [ onkeyup="ku_script"][ onlosecapture="lc_script"]
  [ onmousedown="md_script"]
  [ onmouseenter="me_script"]
  [ onmouseleave="ml_script"]
  [ onmousemove="mm_script"][ onmouseout="mo_script"]
  [ onmouseover="mov_script"][ onmouseup="mu_script"]
  [ onpaste="p_script"][ onpropertychange="pc_script"]
  [ onreadystatechange="rsc_script"]
```

```
[ onresize="rsz_script"][ onresizeend="ree_script"]
[ onresizestart="res_script"][ onselect="sl_script"]
[ onselectstart="ss_script"]
[ size="input_control_size"]
[ style="name_1: value_1"[; name_2: value_2"]
[...; name_n: value_n"]]
[ tabindex="position_number"][ title="title"]
[ type="reset"][ value="initial_value"]
[ width="width_pix"]{ />|</input>}
```

Syntax *(Submit Button)*

```
<input[ accept="MIME_type_1"[,MIME_type_2]
    [...,MIME_type_n]][ accesskey="shortcut_key"]
[ align="top"|"middle"|"bottom"|"left"|"right"]
[ alt="alternate_name"][ class="class_name"]
[ contenteditable="edit_string"]
[ datafld="ds_col_name"][ datasrc="ds_identifier"]
[ dir="ltr"|"rtl"][ disabled="disabled"]
[ id="id_name"][ lang="lang_code"]
[ language="javascript"|"jscript"|"vbs[cript]"]
[ name="input_name"][ onbeforecut="bt_script"]
[ onbeforeeditfocus="bef_script"]
[ onbeforefocusenter="bfe_script"]
[ onbeforefocusleave="bfl_script"]
[ onbeforepaste="bp_script"][ onblur="bl_script"]
[ onchange="ch_script"][ onclick="cl_script"]
[ oncontextmenu="cm_script"]
[ oncontrolselect="ctl_script"][ oncut="ct_script"]
[ ondblclick="dc_script"][ ondrag="d_script"]
[ ondragend="dd_script"][ ondragenter="de_script"]
[ ondragleave="dl_script"][ ondragover="do_script"]
[ ondragstart="ds_script"][ ondrop="dr_script"]
[ onfilterchange="f_script"][ onfocus="fc_script"]
[ onfocusenter="fe_script"]
[ onfocusleave="fl_script"][ onhelp="hlp_script"]
[ onkeydown="kd_script"][ onkeypress="kp_script"]
[ onkeyup="ku_script"][ onlosecapture="lc_script"]
[ onmousedown="md_script"]
[ onmouseenter="me_script"]
[ onmouseleave="ml_script"]
[ onmousemove="mm_script"][ onmouseout="mo_script"]
[ onmouseover="mov_script"][ onmouseup="mu_script"]
[ onpaste="p_script"][ onpropertychange="pc_script"]
[ onreadystatechange="rsc_script"]
```

```
[ onresize="rsz_script"][ onresizeend="ree_script"]
[ onresizestart="res_script"][ onselect="sl_script"]
[ onselectstart="ss_script"]
[ size="input_control_size"]
[ style="name_1: value_1"[; name_2: value_2"]
[...; name_n: value_n"]]
[ tabindex="position_number"][ title="title"]
[ type="submit"][ usestyle][ value="initial_value"]
[ width="width_pix"]{ />|</input>}
```

Where

- **accept** (Web) is a list of one or more Internet Media Types (MIMETYPE) that this part of the form and the form-processing server will accept.
- **accesskey** (Web) assigns a shortcut key to the element in order to focus on it.
- **align** (Web) indicates the alignment of the input control. This attribute is deprecated; use a style sheet instead.
- **alt** (Web) describes an image for text-only browsers.
- ⊖ **autocomplete** (Web) suggests ("yes") or does not suggest ("no") values for a particular text field in a form.
- ⬚ **bgcolor** (Web) specifies the background color for the text box input control.
- **checked** (Web) sets the initial value of a check box or radio button to "on" (that is, checked or filled in).
- **class** (Web) specifies a class identification for the input control.
- ⊖ **contenteditable** (Web) specifies or obtains a value that indicates whether a user can edit the element content.
- ⬚ **cursor** (Web) specifies the cursor color for the text box input control.
- ⊖ **datafld** (Web) specifies the column name from the file that contains the data source object.
- ⊖ **datasrc** (Web) specifies the identifier of the data source object.
- **dir** (Web) specifies the direction in which the input control text is displayed: left-to-right or right-to-left.
- **disabled** (Web) prevents user input in the input control. This attribute is not available for use but may be in a future XHTML version.
- **id** (Web) provides a unique identifier name for the input control.
- **lang** (Web) specifies the code representing the language used for the input control text.
- ⊖ **language** (Web) declares the scripting language of the current script.
- ⊖ **lowsrc** (Web) specifies the URI of a low-resolution graphic to be loaded in the same location as the image named with the **src** attribute.
- **maxlengthth** (Web) sets a maximum number of characters for a text box or password text box on the current form.
- **name** (Web) labels the current input control.
- ⊖ **onafterupdate** (Web) names a script to run after data has been transferred from the element to the data resource.

- ☺ `onbeforecut` (Web) names a script to run when a user starts cutting a selection to the Clipboard but before any action actually takes place.
- ☺ `onbeforeeditfocus` (Web) names a script to run when a user starts activating an object but before the object actually becomes active.
- ☺ `onbeforefocusenter` (Web) names a script to run when a user starts focusing on an object but before the object actually gains focus.
- ☺ `onbeforefocusleave` (Web) names a script to run when a user starts leaving an object but before the object actually loses focus.
- ☺ `onbeforepaste` (Web) names a script to run when a user starts pasting an object but before any action actually takes place.
- ☺ `onbeforeupdate` (Web) names a script to run before data is transferred from the element to the data resource.
- `onblur` (Web) names a script to run when the input control loses focus.
- `onchange` (Web) names a script to run when an input control loses focus after it has gained focus and has had a value change.
- `onclick` (Web) names a script to run when a user moves the mouse pointer or other pointing device over the input control and clicks the device button.
- ☺ `oncontextmenu` (Web) names a script to run when a user right-clicks the mouse to open a shortcut menu.
- ☺ `oncontrolselect` (Web) names a script to run when a user selects a control.
- ☺ `oncut` (Web) names a script to run when a user cuts a selection to the Clipboard.
- `ondblclick` (Web) names a script to run when a user moves the mouse pointer or other pointing device over the input control and double-clicks the device button.
- ☺ `ondrag` (Web) names a script to run when a user drags a selection.
- ☺ `ondragend` (Web) names a script to run after a user completes a drag-and-drop operation.
- ☺ `ondragenter` (Web) names a script to run when a user drags a selection into an area in which it can be dropped.
- ☺ `ondragleave` (Web) names a script to run when a user drags a selection beyond an area in which it can be dropped.
- ☺ `ondragover` (Web) names a script to run when a user drags a selection over an area in which it can be dropped.
- ☺ `ondragstart` (Web) names a script to run when a user starts dragging a selection or element.
- ☺ `ondrop` (Web) names a script to run when a user releases the mouse button to drop a dragged selection.
- ☺ `onerrorupdate` (Web) names a script to run when an error occurs while data is updated in the data resource.
- ☺ `onfilterchange` (Web) names a script to run when a visual filter changes in any way.
- `onfocus` (Web) names a script to run when a user points the mouse pointer or other pointing device to focus on the current element.

- ☺ onfocusenter (Web) names a script to run when a user focuses on the current element in any way.
- ☺ onfocusleave (Web) names a script to run when a user inactivates the current element in any way.
- ☺ onhelp (Web) names a script to run when a user presses the F1 or Help key over the current element.
- onkeydown (Web) names a script to run when a user presses and holds down a key over the input control.
- onkeypress (Web) names a script to run when a user presses and releases a key over the input control.
- onkeyup (Web) names a script to run when a user releases a key that is currently held down over the input control.
- ☺ onlosecapture (Web) names a script to run when a user releases a selection that has been captured by the mouse.
- onmousedown (Web) names a script to run when a user moves the mouse pointer or other pointing device over the input control and presses and holds down the device button.
- ☺ onmouseenter (Web) names a script to run when a user moves the mouse pointer onto the object.
- ☺ onmouseleave (Web) names a script to run when the mouse pointer leaves the object.
- onmousemove (Web) names a script to run when a user moves the mouse pointer or other pointing device over the input control.
- onmouseout (Web) names a script to run when a user moves the mouse pointer or other pointing device away from the input control.
- onmouseover (Web) names a script to run the first time a user moves the mouse pointer or other pointing device over the input control.
- onmouseup (Web) names a script to run when a user moves the mouse pointer or other pointing device over the input control and releases a pressed-down device button.
- ☺ onpaste (Web) names a script to run when a user pastes the Clipboard contents onto the object.
- ☺ onpropertychange (Web) names a script to run when a property changes on the selected object in any way.
- ☺ onreadystatechange (Web) names a script to run when the status of an element has changed (for example, the element receives data).
- ☺ onresize (Web) names a script to run when a user resizes the selected object.
- ☺ onresizeend (Web) names a script to run after the object has been resized.
- ☺ onresizestart (Web) names a script to run as a user resizes the object.
- onselect (Web) names a script to run when a user selects some text in the input control.
- ☺ onselectstart (Web) names a script to run when a user starts selecting an object.

- `readonly` (Web) does not allow a user to change the current value of the input control.
- `size` (Web) is the maximum size of the current text box or password text box.
- `src` (Web) specifies an image file that is displayed on a graphical Submit button (that is, `type="image"`).
- `style` (Web) sets styles for the input control.
- `tabindex` (Web) defines the position of the input control in all the elements that a user can navigate to using a Tab or Shift + Tab key.
- `title` (Web) provides a title for the input control.
- `type` (Web) is the type of input control.
- `usemap` (Web) specifies a client-side image map that is displayed in a document or form.
- ⚙ `usestyle` (Web) indicates that the input-control text is the same style as other text on the page.
- `value` (Web) sets the initial value for the input control.
- ☉ `vcard_name` (Web) gets the vCard value of the object in conjunction with the `autocomplete` attribute.
- ⚙ `width` (Web) specifies the width, in pixels, of the input control.

Notes

- This inline element originated in HTML 2.0.
- `input` is an empty element.
- HTML automatically labels buttons created by `input`. Most browsers label input buttons using the value of the `value` attribute (Web).
- When you click an image, the browser acts as though you have clicked a Submit or Reset button.
- WebTV supports the following attributes for `input`: `accept`, `align`, `bgcolor`, `checked`, `cursor`, `disabled`, `id`, `maxlength`, `name`, `onblur`, `onchange`, `onclick`, `onfocus`, `onmouseover`, `onmouseup`, `onselect`, `readonly`, `size`, `src`, `type`, `usestyle`, `value`, and `width`.

Related Elements

`fieldset` (127), `form` (135), `isindex` (184), `label` (190), `legend` (195), `optgroup` (234), `option` (236), `select` (263), `textarea` (302)

For More Information

Learn more about the `input` element on page 609 in Chapter 7.

---

ins   Mark Insertions

Purpose

Marks document sections that have been inserted since the original document was created and posted.

Syntax

```
<ins[ accesskey="shortcut_key"][ cite="uri"]
  [ class="class_name"]
  [ contenteditable="edit_string"]
  [ datetime="datetime"][ dir="ltr"|"rtl"]
  [ disabled="disabled"][ id="id_name"]
  [ lang="lang_code"][ language="javascript"|"jscript"
  |"vbs[cript]"][ onbeforefocusenter="bfe_script"]
  [ onbeforefocusleave="bfl_script"]
  [ onblur="bl_script"][ onclick="cl_script"]
  [ oncontrolselect="ctl_script"]
  [ ondblclick="dc_script"][ onfocus="fc_script"]
  [ onfocusenter="fe_script"]
  [ onfocusleave="fl_script"][ onkeydown="kd_script"]
  [ onkeypress="kp_script"][ onkeyup="ku_script"]
  [ onmousedown="md_script"][ onmousemove="mm_script"]
  [ onmouseout="mo_script"][ onmouseover="mov_script"]
  [ onmouseup="mu_script"]
  [ onreadystatechange="rsc_script"]
  [ onresizeend="ree_script"]
  [ onresizestart="res_script"]
  [ style="name_1: value_1"[; "name_2: value_2"]
  [...; "name_n: value_n"]]
  [ tabindex="position_number"][ title="title"]>
inserted-section</ins>
```

Where

- ⊙ **accesskey** (Web) assigns a shortcut key to the object in order to focus on it.
- **cite** (Web) provides a URI for a document that contains the reason for a document change.
- **class** (Web) specifies a class identification for the text marked as inserted.
- ⊙ **contenteditable** (Web) specifies or obtains a value that indicates whether a user can edit the element content.
- **datetime** (Web) names the date and time at which a change in the document was made.
- **dir** (Web) specifies the direction in which the text marked as inserted is displayed: left-to-right or right-to-left.
- ⊙ **disabled** (Web) is a keyword that prevents a user from using the element.
- **id** (Web) provides a unique identifier name for the text marked as inserted.
- **lang** (Web) specifies the code for the language used for the text marked as inserted.

- ⊖ language (Web) declares the scripting language of the current script.
- ⊖ onbeforefocusenter (Web) names a script to run when a user starts focusing on an object but before the object actually gains focus.
- ⊖ onbeforefocusleave (Web) names a script to run when a user starts leaving an object but before the object actually loses focus.
- ⊖ onblur (Web) names a script to run when the object loses focus (that is, it is no longer the active element).
- onclick (Web) names a script to run when a user moves the mouse pointer or other pointing device over the text marked as inserted and clicks the button.
- ⊖ oncontrolselect (Web) names a script to run when a user selects a control.
- ondblclick (Web) names a script to run when a user moves the mouse pointer or other pointing device over the text marked as inserted and double-clicks the button.
- ⊖ onfocus (Web) names a script to run when a user points the mouse pointer or other pointing device to focus on the current element.
- ⊖ onfocusenter (Web) names a script to run when a user focuses on the current element in any way.
- ⊖ onfocusleave (Web) names a script to run when a user inactivates the current element in any way.
- onkeydown (Web) names a script to run when a user presses and holds down a key over the text marked as inserted.
- onkeypress (Web) names a script to run when a user presses and releases a key over the text marked as inserted.
- onkeyup (Web) names a script to run when a user releases a key that is currently held down over the text marked as inserted.
- onmousedown (Web) names a script to run when a user moves the mouse pointer or other pointing device over the text marked as inserted and presses and holds down the button.
- onmousemove (Web) names a script to run when a user moves the mouse pointer or other pointing device over the text marked as inserted.
- onmouseout (Web) names a script to run when a user moves the mouse pointer or other pointing device away from the text marked as inserted.
- onmouseover (Web) names a script to run the first time a user moves the mouse pointer or other pointing device over the text marked as inserted.
- onmouseup (Web) names a script to run when a user moves the mouse pointer or other pointing device over the text marked as inserted and releases a mouse button that is currently held down.
- ⊖ onreadystatechange (Web) names a script to run when the status of an element has changed (for example, the element receives data).
- ⊖ onresizeend (Web) names a script to run after the object has been resized.

- ⊖ onresizestart (Web) names a script to run as a user resizes the object.
- style (Web) sets styles for the text marked as inserted.
- ⊖ tabindex (Web) defines the position of the current element in all the elements that a user can navigate to using a Tab or Shift + Tab key.
- title (Web) provides a title for the text marked as inserted.
- *inserted-section* is the text marked as inserted.

Notes

- This element originated in HTML 4.0.
- Browsers may mark inserted text in various ways, such as changing the text to a special font or inserting revision marks.

Related Element

del (98)

isindex   Searchable Index

Purpose

Identifies the document as a searchable index with a single text input field.

Syntax

```
<isindex[ accesskey="shortcut_key"]
   [ action="submit_uri"][ class="class_name"]
   [ contenteditable="edit_string"]
   [ dir="ltr"|"rtl"][ disabled="disabled"]
   [ id="id_name"][ lang="lang_code"]
   [ language="javascript"|"jscript"|"vbs[cript]"]
   [ onbeforefocusenter="bfe_script"]
   [ onbeforefocusleave="bfl_script"]
   [ onblur="bl_script"][ oncontrolselect="ctl_script"]
   [ onfocus="fc_script"][ onfocusenter="fe_script"]
   [ onfocusleave="fl_script"]
   [ onreadystatechange="rsc_script"]
   [ onresize="rsz_script"][ onresizeend="ree_script"]
   [ onresizestart="res_script"][ prompt="prompt-text"]
   [ style="name_1: value_1"[; name_2: value_2"]
   [...; name_n: value_n"]]
   [ tabindex="position_number"]
   [ title="title"]{ />|</isindex>}
```

Where

- ⊖ `accesskey` (Web) assigns a shortcut key to the object in order to focus on it.
- ⊖ `action` (Web) sends the filled-in form to an HTTP or e-mail URI.
- `class` (Web) specifies a class identification for the index.
- ⊖ `contenteditable` (Web) specifies or obtains a value that indicates whether a user can edit the element content.
- `dir` (Web) specifies the direction in which the index text is displayed: left-to-right or right-to-left.
- ⊖ `disabled` (Web) is a keyword that prevents a user from using the element.
- `id` (Web) provides a unique identifier name for the index.
- `lang` (Web) specifies the code representing the language used for the index text.
- ⊖ `language` (Web) declares the scripting language of the current script.
- ⊖ `onbeforefocusenter` (Web) names a script to run when a user starts focusing on an object but before the object actually gains focus.
- ⊖ `onbeforefocusleave` (Web) names a script to run when a user starts leaving an object but before the object actually loses focus.
- ⊖ `onblur` (Web) names a script to run when the object loses focus (that is, it is no longer the active element).
- ⊖ `oncontrolselect` (Web) names a script to run when a user selects a control.
- ⊖ `onfocus` (Web) names a script to run when a user points the mouse pointer or other pointing device to focus on the current element.
- ⊖ `onfocusenter` (Web) names a script to run when a user focuses on the current element in any way.
- ⊖ `onfocusleave` (Web) names a script to run when a user inactivates the current element in any way.
- ⊖ `onreadystatechange` (Web) names a script to run when the status of an element has changed (for example, the element receives data).
- ⊖ `onresize` (Web) names a script to run when a user resizes the selected object.
- ⊖ `onresizeend` (Web) names a script to run after the object has been resized.
- ⊖ `onresizestart` (Web) names a script to run as a user resizes the object.
- `prompt` (Web) is a message that prompts the user for a one-line response with an unlimited number of characters.
- `style` (Web) sets styles for the index.
- ⊖ `tabindex` (Web) defines the position of the current element in all the elements that a user can navigate to using a Tab or Shift + Tab key.
- `title` (Web) provides a title for the index.

Notes

- This block-level element originated in HTML 2.0.
- isindex is deprecated and does not appear in the Strict DTD — only in the Transitional DTD. Because isindex will eventually be obsolete, it is best to use input instead.
- isindex is an empty element.
- Place isindex in the HEAD section of a document.
- isindex creates elementary HTML forms.
- Do not insert more than one isindex element in the HEAD section.
- If you don't supply prompt text, the default prompt is: "This is a searchable index. Enter search keywords:"
- The user response to the prompt should be from the Latin-1 character set only.

Related Elements

base (49), button (72), fieldset (127), form (135), head (148), input (167), label (190), legend (195), optgroup (234), option (236), select (263), textarea (302)

kbd   Keyboard Input

Purpose

Applies a keyboard-input (monospace) font to selected text.

Syntax

```
<kbd[ accesskey="shortcut_key"][ class="class_name"]
  [ contenteditable="edit_string"][ dir="ltr"|"rtl"]
  [ disabled="disabled"][ id="id_name"]
  [ lang="lang_code"][ language="javascript"|"jscript"
  |"vbs[cript]"][ onbeforecut="bt_script"]
  [ onbeforefocusenter="bfe_script"]
  [ onbeforefocusleave="bfl_script"]
  [ onbeforepaste="bp_script"][ onblur="bl_script"]
  [ onclick="cl_script"][ oncontextmenu="cm_script"]
  [ oncontrolselect="ctl_script"][ oncut="ct_script"]
  [ ondblclick="dc_script"][ ondrag="d_script"]
  [ ondragend="dd_script"][ ondragenter="de_script"]
  [ ondragleave="dl_script"][ ondragover="do_script"]
  [ ondragstart="ds_script"][ ondrop="dr_script"]
  [ onfocus="fc_script"][ onfocusenter="fe_script"]
  [ onfocusleave="fl_script"][ onhelp="hlp_script"]
  [ onkeydown="kd_script"][ onkeypress="kp_script"]
  [ onkeyup="ku_script"][ onlosecapture="lc_script"]
  [ onmousedown="md_script"]
```

```
[ onmouseenter="me_script"]
[ onmouseleave="ml_script"]
[ onmousemove="mm_script"][ onmouseout="mo_script"]
[ onmouseover="mov_script"][ onmouseup="mu_script"]
[ onpaste="p_script"][ onpropertychange="pc_script"]
[ onreadystatechange="rsc_script"]
[ onresize="rsz_script"][ onresizeend="ree_script"]
[ onresizestart="res_script"]
[ onselectstart="ss_script"]
[ style="name_1: value_1"[; "name_2: value_2"]
[...; "name_n: value_n"]]
[ tabindex="position_number"][ title="title"]>
text</kbd>
```

Where

- ⊖ **accesskey** (Web) assigns a shortcut key to the object in order to focus on it.
- **class** (Web) specifies a class identification for the keyboard input.
- ⊖ **contenteditable** (Web) specifies or obtains a value that indicates whether a user can edit the element content.
- **dir** (Web) specifies the direction in which the keyboard input is displayed: left-to-right or right-to-left.
- ⊖ **disabled** (Web) is a keyword that prevents a user from using the element.
- **id** (Web) provides a unique identifier name for the keyboard input.
- **lang** (Web) specifies the code for the language used for the keyboard input.
- ⊖ **language** (Web) declares the scripting language of the current script.
- ⊖ **onbeforecut** (Web) names a script to run when a user starts cutting a selection to the Clipboard but before any action actually takes place.
- ⊖ **onbeforefocusenter** (Web) names a script to run when a user starts focusing on an object but before the object actually gains focus.
- ⊖ **onbeforefocusleave** (Web) names a script to run when a user starts leaving an object but before the object actually loses focus.
- ⊖ **onbeforepaste** (Web) names a script to run when a user starts pasting an object but before any action actually takes place.
- ⊖ **onblur** (Web) names a script to run when the object loses focus (that is, it is no longer the active element).
- **onclick** (Web) names a script to run when a user moves the mouse pointer or other pointing device over the keyboard input and clicks the button.
- ⊖ **oncontextmenu** (Web) names a script to run when a user right-clicks the mouse to open a shortcut menu.
- ⊖ **oncontrolselect** (Web) names a script to run when a user selects a control.

- ⊖ `oncut` (Web) names a script to run when a user cuts a selection to the Clipboard.
- `ondblclick` (Web) names a script to run when a user moves the mouse pointer or other pointing device over the keyboard input and double-clicks the button.
- ⊖ `ondrag` (Web) names a script to run when a user drags a selection.
- ⊖ `ondragend` (Web) names a script to run after a user completes a drag-and-drop operation.
- ⊖ `ondragenter` (Web) names a script to run when a user drags a selection into an area in which it can be dropped.
- ⊖ `ondragleave` (Web) names a script to run when a user drags a selection beyond an area in which it can be dropped.
- ⊖ `ondragover` (Web) names a script to run when a user drags a selection over an area in which it can be dropped.
- ⊖ `ondragstart` (Web) names a script to run when a user starts dragging a selection or element.
- ⊖ `ondrop` (Web) names a script to run when a user releases the mouse button to drop a dragged selection.
- ⊖ `onfocus` (Web) names a script to run when a user points the mouse pointer or other pointing device to focus on the current element.
- ⊖ `onfocusenter` (Web) names a script to run when a user focuses on the current element in any way.
- ⊖ `onfocusleave` (Web) names a script to run when a user inactivates the current element in any way.
- ⊖ `onhelp` (Web) names a script to run when a user presses the F1 or Help key over the current element.
- `onkeydown` (Web) names a script to run when a user presses and holds down a key over the keyboard input.
- `onkeypress` (Web) names a script to run when a user presses and releases a key over the keyboard input.
- `onkeyup` (Web) names a script to run when a user releases a key that is currently held down over the keyboard input.
- ⊖ `onlosecapture` (Web) names a script to run when a user releases a selection that has been captured by the mouse.
- `onmousedown` (Web) names a script to run when a user moves the mouse pointer or other pointing device over the keyboard input and presses and holds down the button.
- ⊖ `onmouseenter` (Web) names a script to run when a user moves the mouse pointer onto the object.
- ⊖ `onmouseleave` (Web) names a script to run when the mouse pointer leaves the object.
- `onmousemove` (Web) names a script to run when a user moves the mouse pointer or other pointing device over the keyboard input.
- `onmouseout` (Web) names a script to run when a user moves the mouse pointer or other pointing device away from the keyboard input.

- onmouseover (Web) names a script to run the first time a user moves the mouse pointer or other pointing device over the keyboard input.
- onmouseup (Web) names a script to run when a user moves the mouse pointer or other pointing device over the keyboard input and releases a mouse button that is currently held down.
- ☺ onpaste (Web) names a script to run when a user pastes the Clipboard contents onto the object.
- ☺ onpropertychange (Web) names a script to run when a property changes on the selected object in any way.
- ☺ onreadystatechange (Web) names a script to run when the status of an element has changed (for example, the element receives data).
- ☺ onresize (Web) names a script to run when a user resizes the selected object.
- ☺ onresizeend (Web) names a script to run after the object has been resized.
- ☺ onresizestart (Web) names a script to run as a user resizes the object.
- ☺ onselectstart (Web) names a script to run when a user starts selecting an object.
- style (Web) sets styles for the keyboard input.
- ☺ tabindex (Web) defines the position of the current element in all the elements that a user can navigate to using a Tab or Shift + Tab key.
- title (Web) provides a title for the keyboard input.
- *text* represents one or more characters.

Notes

- This inline element originated in HTML 2.0.
- kbd is one of the elements in the %phrase entity. The other %phrase elements are abbr, acronym, cite, code, dfn, em, samp, strong, and var.
- kbd is a logical element, in which particular browsers are programmed to apply a certain style to the selected text. This is in contrast to a physical element in which you "code" the styles yourself.
- Many browsers use the same font for the following elements: code, kbd, pre, samp, and tt.
- To display two or more lines of preformatted text, use the PRE element.
- For the kbd element, WebTV supports the class and style attributes.

Related Elements

abbr (29), acronym (31), b (46), cite (83), code (87), dfn (101), em (120), i (154), pre (242), s (254), samp (258), strike (254), strong (276), tt (324), u (327), var (335)

N keygen   Generate Key

Purpose
Generates a public key in order to send a secure form.

Syntax
```
<keygen[ challenge="IA5STRONG"|"challenge_string"]
  [ name="pair_name"]>
```

Where
- N challenge (Web) specifies a string that users will enter to verify the submission of a secure form.
- N name (Web) labels the name-value pair to be sent via a secure form.

Notes
keygen is a child element of the form element.

A *public key* is one of the two keys in the type of encryption known as public key. A user makes this key available to other users, who can then encrypt messages to be sent to the original user. The other key is a private key, with which the original user decrypts encrypted messages.

Related Elements
fieldset (127), form (135), input (167), isindex (184), label (190), legend (195), optgroup (234), option (236), select (263), textarea (302)

label   Control Label

Purpose
Includes information with an input control.

Syntax
```
<label[ accesskey="shortcut_key"][ class="class_name"]
  [ contenteditable="edit_string"]
  [ datafld="ds_col_name"]
  [ dataformatas="html"|"text"]
  [ datasrc="ds_identifier"][ dir="ltr"|"rtl"]
  [ disabled="disabled"][ for="id_name"]
  [ id="id_name"][ lang="lang_code"]
  [ language="javascript"|"jscript"|"vbs[cript]"]
  [ onbeforecopy="bc_script"]
  [ onbeforecut="bt_script"]
  [ onbeforefocusenter="bfe_script"]
  [ onbeforefocusleave="bfl_script"]
```

```
[ onbeforepaste="bp_script"][ onblur="bl_script"]
[ onclick="cl_script"][ oncontextmenu="cm_script"]
[ oncontrolselect="ctl_script"][ oncut="ct_script"]
[ ondblclick="dc_script"][ ondrag="d_script"]
[ ondragend="dd_script"][ ondragenter="de_script"]
[ ondragleave="dl_script"][ ondragover="do_script"]
[ ondragstart="ds_script"][ ondrop="dr_script"]
[ onfocus="fc_script"][ onfocusenter="fe_script"]
[ onfocusleave="fl_script"][ onhelp="hlp_script"]
[ onkeydown="kd_script"][ onkeypress="kp_script"]
[ onkeyup="ku_script"][ onlosecapture="lc_script"]
[ onmousedown="md_script"][ onmousemove="mm_script"]
[ onmouseout="mo_script"][ onmouseover="mov_script"]
[ onmouseup="mu_script"][ onpaste="p_script"]
[ onpropertychange="pc_script"]
[ onreadystatechange="rsc_script"]
[ onresize="rsz_script"][ onresizeend="ree_script"]
[ onresizestart="res_script"]
[ onselectstart="ss_script"]
[ style="name_1: value_1"[; name_2: value_2"]
[...; name_n: value_n"]]
[ tabindex="position_number"][ title="title"]>
label_text</label>
```

Where

- **accesskey** (Web) assigns a shortcut key to the label in order to focus on it.
- **class** (Web) specifies a class identification for the label.
- ⊕ **contenteditable** (Web) specifies or obtains a value that indicates whether a user can edit the element content.
- ⊕ **datafld** (Web) specifies the column name from the file that contains the data source object.
- ⊕ **dataformatas** (Web) indicates whether the data for this element is formatted as plain text (that is, unformatted ASCII) or HTML.
- ⊕ **datasrc** (Web) specifies the identifier of the data source object.
- **dir** (Web) specifies the direction in which the label text is displayed: left-to-right or right-to-left.
- ⊕ **disabled** (Web) is a keyword that prevents a user from using the element.
- **for** (Web) names the control with which the current label is associated.
- **id** (Web) provides a unique identifier name for the label.
- **lang** (Web) specifies the code representing the language used for the label text.
- ⊕ **language** (Web) declares the scripting language of the current script.

- ⊖ `onbeforecopy` (Web) names a script to run when a user starts copying a selection to the Clipboard but before any action actually takes place.
- ⊖ `onbeforecut` (Web) names a script to run when a user starts cutting a selection to the Clipboard but before any action actually takes place.
- ⊖ `onbeforefocusenter` (Web) names a script to run when a user starts focusing on an object but before the object actually gains focus.
- ⊖ `onbeforefocusleave` (Web) names a script to run when a user starts leaving an object but before the object actually loses focus.
- ⊖ `onbeforepaste` (Web) names a script to run when a user starts pasting an object but before any action actually takes place.
- `onblur` (Web) names a script to run when the label loses focus.
- `onclick` (Web) names a script to run when a user moves the mouse pointer or other pointing device over the label and clicks the device button.
- ⊖ `oncontextmenu` (Web) names a script to run when a user right-clicks the mouse to open a shortcut menu.
- ⊖ `oncontrolselect` (Web) names a script to run when a user selects a control.
- ⊖ `oncut` (Web) names a script to run when a user cuts a selection to the Clipboard.
- `ondblclick` (Web) names a script to run when a user moves the mouse pointer or other pointing device over the label and double-clicks the device button.
- ⊖ `ondrag` (Web) names a script to run when a user drags a selection.
- ⊖ `ondragend` (Web) names a script to run after a user completes a drag-and-drop operation.
- ⊖ `ondragenter` (Web) names a script to run when a user drags a selection into an area in which it can be dropped.
- ⊖ `ondragleave` (Web) names a script to run when a user drags a selection beyond an area in which it can be dropped.
- ⊖ `ondragover` (Web) names a script to run when a user drags a selection over an area in which it can be dropped.
- ⊖ `ondragstart` (Web) names a script to run when a user starts dragging a selection or element.
- ⊖ `ondrop` (Web) names a script to run when a user releases the mouse button to drop a dragged selection.
- `onfocus` (Web) names a script to run when a user points the mouse pointer or other pointing device to focus on the current element.
- ⊖ `onfocusenter` (Web) names a script to run when a user focuses on the current element in any way.
- ⊖ `onfocusleave` (Web) names a script to run when a user inactivates the current element in any way.
- ⊖ `onhelp` (Web) names a script to run when a user presses the F1 or Help key over the current element.
- `onkeydown` (Web) names a script to run when a user presses and holds down a key over the label.

XHTML Syntax

- onkeypress (Web) names a script to run when a user presses and releases a key over the label.
- onkeyup (Web) names a script to run when a user releases a key that is currently held down over the label.
- ⊖ onlosecapture (Web) names a script to run when a user releases a selection that has been captured by the mouse.
- onmousedown (Web) names a script to run when a user moves the mouse pointer or other pointing device over the label and presses and holds down the device button.
- ⊖ onmouseenter (Web) names a script to run when a user moves the mouse pointer onto the object.
- ⊖ onmouseleave (Web) names a script to run when the mouse pointer leaves the object.
- onmousemove (Web) names a script to run when a user moves the mouse pointer or other pointing device over the label.
- onmouseout (Web) names a script to run when a user moves the mouse pointer or other pointing device away from the label.
- onmouseover (Web) names a script to run the first time a user moves the mouse pointer or other pointing device over the label.
- onmouseup (Web) names a script to run when a user moves the mouse pointer or other pointing device over the label and releases a pressed-down device button.
- ⊖ onpaste (Web) names a script to run when a user pastes the Clipboard contents onto the object.
- ⊖ onpropertychange (Web) names a script to run when a property changes on the selected object in any way.
- ⊖ onreadystatechange (Web) names a script to run when the status of an element has changed (for example, the element receives data).
- ⊖ onresize (Web) names a script to run when a user resizes the selected object.
- ⊖ onresizeend (Web) names a script to run after the object has been resized.
- ⊖ onresizestart (Web) names a script to run as a user resizes the object.
- ⊖ onselectstart (Web) names a script to run when a user starts selecting an object.
- style (Web) sets styles for the label.
- ⊖ tabindex (Web) defines the position of the current element in all the elements that a user can navigate to using a Tab or Shift + Tab key.
- title (Web) provides a title for the label.
- *label_text* is the label information.

Notes

- This inline element originated in HTML 4.0.
- When label is made active, it causes the input control with which it is associated to become active.
- In XHTML, a label element cannot contain another label element.

Related Elements

button (72), fieldset (127), form (135), input (167), isindex (184), legend (195), optgroup (234), option (236), select (263), textarea (302)

N layer   HTML Content Layer

Purpose

Defines opaque or transparent, positioned blocks of XHTML content that overlap other content in the current document.

Syntax

```
<layer[ above="top_layer_name"]
  [ background="picture_uri"]
  [ below="below_layer_name"]
  [ bgcolor="#rrggbb"|"color"]
  [ clip=[0|"l_pix,0|t_pix,]r_pix,b_pix"]
  [ height="height_pix"][ id="id_name"]
  [ left="left_pos_pix"][ name="layer_name"]
  [ onblur="bl_script"][ onfocus="fc_script"]
  [ onload="ol_script"][ onmouseout="mo_script"]
  [ onmouseover="mov_script"][ pagex="horz_pos_pix"]
  [ pagey="vert_pos_pix"][ src="source_uri"]
  [ top="top_pos_pix"][ visibility="inherit"|"show"
  |"hide"][ width="width_pix"][ z-index="order_num"]
  { />|</layer>}
```

Where

- N above (Web) names the top layer in the stack of layers.
- N background (Web) specifies an image file that is displayed in the background of the current layer.
- N below (Web) names the layer that is immediately below the newes. layer in the stack.
- N bgcolor (Web) specifies the background color for the layer.
- N clip (Web) specifies the dimensions of the layer window.
- N height (Web) specifies the height, in pixels, of the layer window.
- N id (Web) provides a unique identifier name for the layer.
- N left (Web) specifies the leftmost position, in pixels, of the left side of a layer window.
- N name (Web) provides a unique identifier name for the layer. In XHTML, name is deprecated; use id instead.
- N onblur (Web) names a script to run when the layer loses focus.
- N onfocus (Web) names a script to run when a user points the mouse pointer or other pointing device to focus on the current element.

- Ⓝ `onload` (Web) names a script to run after the active browser has finished loading a layer.
- Ⓝ `onmouseout` (Web) names a script to run when a user moves the mouse pointer or other pointing device away from the layer.
- Ⓝ `onmouseover` (Web) names a script to run the first time a user moves the mouse pointer or other pointing device over the layer.
- Ⓝ `pagex` (Web) specifies the horizontal position, in pixels, of the top left corner of the layer window within the current XHTML document.
- Ⓝ `pagey` (Web) specifies the vertical position, in pixels, of the top left corner of the layer window within the current XHTML document.
- Ⓝ `src` (Web) specifies a source file that contains the contents of the layer window.
- Ⓝ `top` (Web) specifies the topmost position, in pixels, of the top of a layer window.
- Ⓝ `visibility` (Web) specifies whether a layer is visible or hidden.
- Ⓝ `width` (Web) specifies the width, in pixels, of the layer window.
- Ⓝ `z-index` (Web) specifies the numerical order of the current layer.

Notes

- This is a Netscape extension, which is supported only within Netscape Navigator 4.0 or greater.
- `layer` is an empty element.
- `layer` specifies the absolute position of a layer.
- By default, a layer is transparent.
- You can use layers to animate a page or to modify a page almost instantly.
- You can stack multiple layers on a page, and you can nest layers.
- Use JavaScript to move, hide, expand, contract, rearrange, and change color and image characteristics of layers.

Related Elements

ilayer (160), nolayer (223)

---

legend	Fieldset Caption

Purpose

Adds a caption to a group of controls (that is, a `fieldset`).

Syntax

```
<legend[ accesskey="shortcut_key"]
  [ align="top"|"bottom"|"left"|"right"]
  [ class="class_name"]
  [ contenteditable="edit_string"][ dir="ltr"|"rtl"]
  [ disabled="disabled"][ id="id_name"]
  [ lang="lang_code"][ language="javascript"|"jscript"
  |"vbs[cript]"][ onbeforecopy="bc_script"]
```

```
[ onbeforecut="bt_script"]
[ onbeforefocusenter="bfe_script"]
[ onbeforefocusleave="bfl_script"]
[ onbeforepaste="bp_script"][ onblur="bl_script"]
[ onclick="cl_script"][ oncontextmenu="cm_script"]
[ oncontrolselect="ctl_script"][ oncopy="cp_script"]
[ oncut="ct_script"][ ondblclick="dc_script"]
[ onfocus="fc_script"][ onfocusenter="fe_script"]
[ onfocusleave="fl_script"][ onhelp="hlp_script"]
[ onkeydown="kd_script"][ onkeypress="kp_script"]
[ onkeyup="ku_script"][ onlosecapture="lc_script"]
[ onmousedown="md_script"]
[ onmouseenter="me_script"]
[ onmouseleave="ml_script"]
[ onmousemove="mm_script"][ onmouseout="mo_script"]
[ onmouseover="mov_script"][ onmouseup="mu_script"]
[ onpaste="p_script"][ onpropertychange="pc_script"]
[ onreadystatechange="rsc_script"]
[ onresize="rsz_script"][ onresizeend="ree_script"]
[ onresizestart="res_script"]
[ style="name_1: value_1"
[; name_2: value_2"][...; name_n: value_n"]]
[ tabindex="position_number"]
[ title="title"][ valign="top"|"bottom"]>
caption_text</legend>
```

Where

- accesskey (Web) assigns a shortcut key to the field set caption in order to focus on it.
- align (Web) aligns the caption with the current field set. This attribute is deprecated; use a style sheet instead.
- class (Web) specifies a class identification for the field set caption.
- ⊝ contenteditable (Web) specifies or obtains a value that indicates whether a user can edit the element content.
- dir (Web) specifies the direction in which the caption text is displayed: left-to-right or right-to-left.
- ⊝ disabled (Web) is a keyword that prevents a user from using the element.
- id (Web) provides a unique identifier name for the field set caption.
- lang (Web) specifies the code representing the language used for the field set caption.
- ⊝ language (Web) declares the scripting language of the current script.
- ⊝ onbeforecopy (Web) names a script to run when a user starts copying a selection to the Clipboard but before any action actually takes place.

- ⊖ `onbeforecut` (Web) names a script to run when a user starts cutting a selection to the Clipboard but before any action actually takes place.
- ⊖ `onbeforefocusenter` (Web) names a script to run when a user starts focusing on an object but before the object actually gains focus.
- ⊖ `onbeforefocusleave` (Web) names a script to run when a user starts leaving an object but before the object actually loses focus.
- ⊖ `onbeforepaste` (Web) names a script to run when a user starts pasting an object but before any action actually takes place.
- ⊖ `onblur` (Web) names a script to run when the object loses focus (that is, it is no longer the active element).
- `onclick` (Web) names a script to run when a user moves the mouse pointer or other pointing device over the caption and clicks the device button.
- ⊖ `oncontextmenu` (Web) names a script to run when a user right-clicks the mouse to open a shortcut menu.
- ⊖ `oncontrolselect` (Web) names a script to run when a user selects a control.
- ⊖ `oncopy` (Web) names a script to run when a user copies a selection to the Clipboard.
- ⊖ `oncut` (Web) names a script to run when a user cuts a selection to the Clipboard.
- `ondblclick` (Web) names a script to run when a user moves the mouse pointer or other pointing device over the caption and double-clicks the device button.
- ⊖ `onfocus` (Web) names a script to run when the current element receives focus (that is, is made active) by the mouse pointer or other pointing device.
- ⊖ `onfocusenter` (Web) names a script to run when a user focuses on the current element in any way.
- ⊖ `onfocusleave` (Web) names a script to run when a user inactivates the current element in any way.
- ⊖ `onhelp` (Web) names a script to run when a user presses the F1 or Help key over the current element.
- `onkeydown` (Web) names a script to run when a user presses and holds down a key over the caption.
- `onkeypress` (Web) names a script to run when a user presses and releases a key over the caption.
- `onkeyup` (Web) names a script to run when a user releases a key that is currently held down over the caption.
- ⊖ `onlosecapture` (Web) names a script to run when a user releases a selection that has been captured by the mouse.
- `onmousedown` (Web) names a script to run when a user moves the mouse pointer or other pointing device over the caption and presses and holds down the device button.
- ⊖ `onmouseenter` (Web) names a script to run when a user moves the mouse pointer onto the object.

- ⊖ onmouseleave (Web) names a script to run when the mouse pointer leaves the object.
- onmousemove (Web) names a script to run when a user moves the mouse pointer or other pointing device over the caption.
- onmouseout (Web) names a script to run when a user moves the mouse pointer or other pointing device away from the caption.
- onmouseover (Web) names a script to run the first time a user moves the mouse pointer or other pointing device over the caption.
- onmouseup (Web) names a script to run when a user moves the mouse pointer or other pointing device over the caption and releases a pressed-down device button.
- ⊖ onpaste (Web) names a script to run when a user pastes the Clipboard contents onto the object.
- ⊖ onpropertychange (Web) names a script to run when a property changes on the selected object in any way.
- ⊖ onreadystatechange (Web) names a script to run when the status of an element has changed (for example, the element receives data).
- ⊖ onresize (Web) names a script to run when a user resizes the selected object.
- ⊖ onresizeend (Web) names a script to run after the object has been resized.
- ⊖ onresizestart (Web) names a script to run as a user resizes the object.
- style (Web) sets styles for the caption.
- ⊖ tabindex (Web) defines the position of the current element in all the elements that a user can navigate to using a Tab or Shift + Tab key.
- title (Web) provides a title for the caption.
- ⊖ valign (Web) indicates the vertical alignment of the caption, above or below the table.
- *caption_text* represents one or more words.

Notes
This element originated in HTML 4.0.

Related Elements
button (72), fieldset (127), form (135), input (167), isindex (184), label (190), optgroup (234), option (236), select (263), textarea (302)

For More Information
Learn more about the legend element on page 616 in Chapter 7.

| **li** | **List Item** |

Purpose
Lists one item within an ordered, unordered, menu, or directory list.

Syntax

```
<li[ accesskey="shortcut_key"][ class="class_name"]
  [ contenteditable="edit_string"][ dir="ltr"|"rtl"]
  [ disabled="disabled"][ id="id_name"]
  [ lang="lang_code"][ language="javascript"|"jscript"
  |"vbs[cript]"][ onbeforecopy="bc_script"]
  [ onbeforecut="bt_script"]
  [ onbeforefocusenter="bfe_script"]
  [ onbeforefocusleave="bfl_script"]
  [ onbeforepaste="bp_script"][ onblur="bl_script"]
  [ onclick="cl_script"][ oncontextmenu="cm_script"]
  [ oncontrolselect="ctl_script"]
  [ oncopy="cp_script"][ oncut="ct_script"]
  [ ondblclick="dc_script"][ ondrag="d_script"]
  [ ondragend="dd_script"][ ondragenter="de_script"]
  [ ondragleave="dl_script"][ ondragover="do_script"]
  [ ondragstart="ds_script"][ ondrop="dr_script"]
  [ onfocus="fc_script"][ onfocusenter="fe_script"]
  [ onfocusleave="fl_script"][ onhelp="hlp_script"]
  [ onkeydown="kd_script"][ onkeypress="kp_script"]
  [ onkeyup="ku_script"]
  [ onlayoutcomplete="la_script"]
  [ onlosecapture="lc_script"]
  [ onmousedown="md_script"]
  [ onmouseenter="me_script"]
  [ onmouseleave="ml_script"]
  [ onmousemove="mm_script"][ onmouseout="mo_script"]
  [ onmouseover="mov_script"][ onmouseup="mu_script"]
  [ onpaste="p_script"][ onpropertychange="pc_script"]
  [ onreadystatechange="rsc_script"]
  [ onresize="rsz_script"][ onresizeend="ree_script"]
  [ onresizestart="res_script"]
  [ onselectstart="ss_script"]
  [ style="name_1: value_1"[; "name_2: value_2"]
  [...; "name_n: value_n"]]
  [ tabindex="position_number"][ title="title"]
  [ type="disk"|"square"|"circle"|"1"|"a"|"A"|"i"|"I"]
  [ value="cur_num"]>text</li>
```

Where

- ⊖ accesskey (Web) assigns a shortcut key to the object in order to focus on it.
- class (Web) specifies a class identification for the list item.

- ⊖ contenteditable (Web) specifies or obtains a value that indicates whether a user can edit the element content.
- dir (Web) specifies the direction in which the list-item text is displayed: left-to-right or right-to-left.
- ⊖ disabled (Web) is a keyword that prevents a user from using the element.
- id (Web) provides a unique identifier name for the list item.
- lang (Web) specifies the code for the language used for the list-item text.
- ⊖ language (Web) declares the scripting language of the current script.
- ⊖ onbeforecopy (Web) names a script to run when a user starts copying a selection to the Clipboard but before any action actually takes place.
- ⊖ onbeforecut (Web) names a script to run when a user starts cutting a selection to the Clipboard but before any action actually takes place.
- ⊖ onbeforefocusenter (Web) names a script to run when a user starts focusing on an object but before the object actually gains focus.
- ⊖ onbeforefocusleave (Web) names a script to run when a user starts leaving an object but before the object actually loses focus.
- ⊖ onbeforepaste (Web) names a script to run when a user starts pasting an object but before any action actually takes place.
- ⊖ onblur (Web) names a script to run when the object loses focus (that is, it is no longer the active element).
- onclick (Web) names a script to run when a user moves the mouse pointer or other pointing device over the list item and clicks the button.
- ⊖ oncontextmenu (Web) names a script to run when a user right-clicks the mouse to open a shortcut menu.
- ⊖ oncontrolselect (Web) names a script to run when a user selects a control.
- ⊖ oncopy (Web) names a script to run when a user copies a selection to the Clipboard.
- ⊖ oncut (Web) names a script to run when a user cuts a selection to the Clipboard.
- ondblclick (Web) names a script to run when a user moves the mouse pointer or other pointing device over the list item and double-clicks the button.
- ⊖ ondrag (Web) names a script to run when a user drags a selection.
- ⊖ ondragend (Web) names a script to run after a user completes a drag-and-drop operation.
- ⊖ ondragenter (Web) names a script to run when a user drags a selection into an area in which it can be dropped.
- ⊖ ondragleave (Web) names a script to run when a user drags a selection beyond an area in which it can be dropped.
- ⊖ ondragover (Web) names a script to run when a user drags a selection over an area in which it can be dropped.
- ⊖ ondragstart (Web) names a script to run when a user starts dragging a selection or element.
- ⊖ ondrop (Web) names a script to run when a user releases the mouse button to drop a dragged selection.

- ⊖ `onfocus` (Web) names a script to run when a user points the mouse pointer or other pointing device to focus on the current element.
- ⊖ `onfocusenter` (Web) names a script to run when a user focuses on the current element in any way.
- ⊖ `onfocusleave` (Web) names a script to run when a user inactivates the current element in any way.
- ⊖ `onhelp` (Web) names a script to run when a user presses the F1 or Help key over the current element.
- `onkeydown` (Web) names a script to run when a user presses and holds down a key over the list item.
- `onkeypress` (Web) names a script to run when a user presses and releases a key over the list item.
- `onkeyup` (Web) names a script to run when a user releases a key that is currently held down over the list item.
- ⊖ `onlayoutcomplete` (Web) names a script to run when a user lays out a selection using Print or Print Preview.
- `onmousedown` (Web) names a script to run when a user moves the mouse pointer or other pointing device over the list item and presses and holds down the button.
- ⊖ `onmouseenter` (Web) names a script to run when a user moves the mouse pointer onto the object.
- ⊖ `onmouseleave` (Web) names a script to run when the mouse pointer leaves the object.
- `onmousemove` (Web) names a script to run when a user moves the mouse pointer or other pointing device over the list item.
- `onmouseout` (Web) names a script to run when a user moves the mouse pointer or other pointing device away from the list item.
- `onmouseover` (Web) names a script to run the first time a user moves the mouse pointer or other pointing device over the list item.
- `onmouseup` (Web) names a script to run when a user moves the mouse pointer or other pointing device over the list item and releases a mouse button that is currently held down.
- ⊖ `onpaste` (Web) names a script to run when a user pastes the Clipboard contents onto the object.
- ⊖ `onpropertychange` (Web) names a script to run when a property changes on the selected object in any way.
- ⊖ `onreadystatechange` (Web) names a script to run when the status of an element has changed (for example, the element receives data).
- ⊖ `onresize` (Web) names a script to run when a user resizes the selected object.
- ⊖ `onresizeend` (Web) names a script to run after the object has been resized.
- ⊖ `onresizestart` (Web) names a script to run as a user resizes the object.
- ⊖ `onselectstart` (Web) names a script to run when a user starts selecting an object.
- `style` (Web) sets styles for the list item.

- ⊙ `tabindex` (Web) defines the position of the current element in all the elements that a user can navigate to using a Tab or Shift + Tab key.
- `title` (Web) provides a title for the list item.
- `type` (Web) sets a number or bullet format preceding a list item. This attribute is deprecated; consider using a style sheet instead.
- `value` (Web) sets the current number for a list item in an ordered list. This attribute is deprecated; consider using a style sheet instead.
- *text* represents one or more words.

Notes

- This element originated in HTML 2.0, and the `type` and `value` attributes (both of which are deprecated in HTML 4.0) are HTML 3.2 features.
- The `li` element lists one item within an ordered (`ol`), unordered (`ul`), menu (`menu`), or directory (`dir`) list. Note that both `dir` and `menu` are deprecated.
- `li` is a child element of the `dir`, `menu`, `ol`, and `ul` elements.
- A line break automatically occurs at the end of an `li` element and its contents. The size of the line break depends on whether or how you use cascading style sheets.
- Typically, list items are only separated by line breaks, but the `ul` and `ol` elements are followed by white space, just like paragraphs.
- The Netscape Editor inserts the pound sign (#) and other placeholders instead of numbers and bullets in ordered and unordered lists, respectively. To see the actual look of a list (that is, to view it as an actual document page), choose the Open Page command from the File menu.
- For the `li` element, WebTV supports the `class`, `style`, `type`, and `value` attributes.

Related Elements

`dir` (104), `menu` (212), `ol` (230), `ul` (331)

For More Information

Learn more about the `li` element on page 543 in Chapter 3.

link   Link

Purpose

Identifies a link from the current XHTML document to another document, primarily to provide internal documentation of the current document's URI.

Syntax

```
<link[ charset="ISO-8859-1"]["char_set"]
  [ class="class_name"][ dir="ltr"|"rtl"]
  [ disabled="disabled"][ href="link_uri"]
  [ hreflang="link_lang"][ id="id_name"]
  [ lang="lang_code"][ media=["screen"][,]["print"][,]
```

XHTML Syntax

```
["projection"][,]["braille"][,]["speech"][,]["all"]]
[ name="link_name"][ onclick="cl_script"]
[ ondblclick="dc_script"][ onkeydown="kd_script"]
[ onkeypress="kp_script"][ onkeyup="ku_script"]
[ onload="ol_script"][ onmousedown="md_script"]
[ onmousemove="mm_script"][ onmouseout="mo_script"]
[ onmouseover="mov_script"][ onmouseup="mu_script"]
[ onreadystatechange="rsc_script"]
[ rel="contents"|"index"|"glossary"|"copyright"
|"next"|"prev[ious]"|"start"|"help"|"bookmark"
|"stylesheet"|"alternate"|"chapter"|"section"
|"subsection"|"appendix"|"same"|"parent"
|"link_type_1"[ "link_type_2"[..."link_type_n"]]]
[ rev="contents"|"index"|"glossary"|"copyright"
|"next"|"prev[ious]"|"start"|"help"|"bookmark"
|"stylesheet"|"alternate"|"chapter"|"section"
|"subsection"|"appendix"|"same"|"parent"
|"link_type_3"[ "link_type_4"[..."link_type_m"]]]
[ src="source_uri"][ style="name_1: value_1"
[; "name_2: value_2"][...; "name_n: value_n"]]
[ target="window"|"_blank"|"_parent"|"_search"
|"_self"|"_top"][ title="title"]
[ type="content_type"]{ />|</link>}
```

Where

- charset (Web) specifies the character set for the hypertext link.
- class (Web) specifies a class identification for the link.
- dir (Web) specifies the direction in which the link text is displayed: left-to-right or right-to-left.
- ⊖ disabled (Web) prevents the link from receiving the focus.
- href (Web) specifies a URI for a link to another document.
- hreflang (Web) specifies the base language of the href link.
- id (Web) provides a unique identifier name for the link.
- lang (Web) specifies the code for the language used for the link text.
- media (Web) indicates the type of destination.
- ⊖ name (Web) names the image map.
- onclick (Web) names a script to run when a user moves the mouse pointer or other pointing device over the link and clicks the button.
- ondblclick (Web) names a script to run when a user moves the mouse pointer or other pointing device over the link and double-clicks the button.
- onkeydown (Web) names a script to run when a user presses and holds down a key over the link.
- onkeypress (Web) names a script to run when a user presses and releases a key over the link.

- onkeyup (Web) names a script to run when a user releases a key that is currently held down over the link.
- ⊖ onload (Web) names a script to run after the active browser has finished loading the applet.
- onmousedown (Web) names a script to run when a user moves the mouse pointer or other pointing device over the link and presses and holds down the button.
- onmousemove (Web) names a script to run when a user moves the mouse pointer or other pointing device over the link.
- onmouseout (Web) names a script to run when a user moves the mouse pointer or other pointing device away from the link.
- onmouseover (Web) names a script to run the first time a user moves the mouse pointer or other pointing device over the link.
- onmouseup (Web) names a script to run when a user moves the mouse pointer or other pointing device over the link and releases a mouse button that is currently held down.
- ⊖ onreadystatechange (Web) names a script to run when the status of an element has changed (for example, the element receives data).
- rel (Web) specifies a forward link type from the current link to the target anchor.
- rev (Web) specifies a backward link type from the target anchor to its originating link.
- Ⓝ src (Web) specifies a source file.
- style (Web) sets styles for the link.
- target (Web) loads a linked and named document in a particular window or frame. This attribute is deprecated; use the id attribute instead.
- title (Web) provides a title for the link.
- type (Web) specifies a type name of the link, for further documentation of the current document.

Notes

- This inline element originated in HTML 2.0. This is the preferred alternative to embed.
- Use the link element within the HEAD section of a document.
- You can use multiple link statements in the HEAD section. For example, businesses can use link to identify the author, the author's e-mail address, and the documents and types of documents that are linked to the current document.
- HTTP 1.1 does not include a Link header field. However, when other versions of HTTP include a Link header field, the link element and its attributes serve the same purposes as the Link header field.
- For the link element, WebTV supports the href and rel attributes.

Related Elements

base (49), head (148), isindex (184), meta (216), script (262), style (280), title (318)

For More Information

Learn more about the `link` element on page 625 in Chapter 8.

<table>
<tr><td>**map**</td><td>Map</td></tr>
</table>

Purpose

Names a client-side image map.

Syntax

```
<map name="map_name"[ class="class_name"]
   [ contenteditable="edit_string"][ dir="ltr"|"rtl"]
   [ disabled="disabled"][ id="id_name"]
   [ lang="lang_code"][ language="javascript"|"jscript"
   |"vbs[cript]"][ name="map_name"]
   [ onbeforecut="bt_script"]
   [ onbeforepaste="bp_script"][ onclick="cl_script"]
   [ oncut="ct_script"][ ondblclick="dc_script"]
   [ ondrag="d_script"][ ondragend="dd_script"]
   [ ondragenter="de_script"][ ondragleave="dl_script"]
   [ ondragover="do_script"][ ondragstart="ds_script"]
   [ ondrop="dr_script"][ onhelp="hlp_script"]
   [ onkeydown="kd_script"][ onkeypress="kp_script"]
   [ onkeyup="ku_script"][ onlosecapture="lc_script"]
   [ onmousedown="md_script"]
   [ onmouseenter="me_script"]
   [ onmouseleave="ml_script"]
   [ onmousemove="mm_script"][ onmouseout="mo_script"]
   [ onmouseover="mov_script"][ onmouseup="mu_script"]
   [ onpaste="p_script"][ onpropertychange="pc_script"]
   [ onreadystatechange="rsc_script"]
   [ onscroll="sc_script"][ onselectstart="ss_script"]
   [ style="name_1: value_1"[; "name_2: value_2"]
   [...; "name_n: value_n"]][ title="title"]>
   map_contents</map>
```

Where

- `name` (Web) names the image map. In XHTML, name is deprecated; use id again.
- `class` (Web) specifies a class identification for the image map.
- Ⓔ `contenteditable` (Web) specifies or obtains a value that indicates whether a user can edit the element content.
- `dir` (Web) specifies the direction in which the image map is displayed: left-to-right or right-to-left.
- Ⓔ `disabled` (Web) is a keyword that prevents a user from using the element.

- `id` (Web) provides a unique identifier name for the image map.
- `lang` (Web) specifies the code representing the language used for the element.
- ⊖ `language` (Web) declares the scripting language of the current script.
- ⊖ `onbeforecut` (Web) names a script to run when a user starts cutting a selection to the Clipboard but before any action actually takes place.
- ⊖ `onbeforepaste` (Web) names a script to run when a user starts pasting an object but before any action actually takes place.
- `onclick` (Web) names a script to run when a user moves the mouse pointer or other pointing device over the image map and clicks the device button.
- ⊖ `oncut` (Web) names a script to run when a user cuts a selection to the Clipboard.
- `ondblclick` (Web) names a script to run when a user moves the mouse pointer or other pointing device over the image map and double-clicks the device button.
- ⊖ `ondrag` (Web) names a script to run when a user drags a selection.
- ⊖ `ondragend` (Web) names a script to run after a user completes a drag-and-drop operation.
- ⊖ `ondragenter` (Web) names a script to run when a user drags a selection into an area in which it can be dropped.
- ⊖ `ondragleave` (Web) names a script to run when a user drags a selection beyond an area in which it can be dropped.
- ⊖ `ondragover` (Web) names a script to run when a user drags a selection over an area in which it can be dropped.
- ⊖ `ondragstart` (Web) names a script to run when a user starts dragging a selection or element.
- ⊖ `ondrop` (Web) names a script to run when a user releases the mouse button to drop a dragged selection.
- ⊖ `onhelp` (Web) names a script to run when a user presses the F1 or Help key over the current element.
- `onkeydown` (Web) names a script to run when a user presses and holds down a key over the image map.
- `onkeypress` (Web) names a script to run when a user presses and releases a key over the image map.
- `onkeyup` (Web) names a script to run when a user releases a key that is currently held down over the image map.
- ⊖ `onlosecapture` (Web) names a script to run when a user releases a selection that has been captured by the mouse.
- `onmousedown` (Web) names a script to run when a user moves the mouse pointer or other pointing device over the image map and presses and holds down the device button.
- ⊖ `onmouseenter` (Web) names a script to run when a user moves the mouse pointer onto the object.

XHTML Syntax

- ⊝ onmouseleave (Web) names a script to run when the mouse pointer leaves the object.
- onmousemove (Web) names a script to run when a user moves the mouse pointer or other pointing device over the image map.
- onmouseout (Web) names a script to run when a user moves the mouse pointer or other pointing device away from the image map.
- onmouseover (Web) names a script to run the first time a user moves the mouse pointer or other pointing device over the image map.
- onmouseup (Web) names a script to run when a user moves the mouse pointer or other pointing device over the image map and releases a pressed-down device button.
- ⊝ onpaste (Web) names a script to run when a user pastes the Clipboard contents onto the object.
- ⊝ onpropertychange (Web) names a script to run when a property changes on the selected object in any way.
- ⊝ onreadystatechange (Web) names a script to run when the status of an element has changed (for example, the element receives data).
- ⊝ onscroll (Web) names a script to run when a user moves the scroll box within the scroll bar.
- ⊝ onselectstart (Web) names a script to run when a user starts selecting an object.
- style (Web) sets styles for the image map.
- title (Web) provides a title for the image map.
- *map_contents* is the contents of the image map, defined by one or more **area** elements.

Notes

- This inline element originated in HTML 3.2.
- A client-side image map is stored in an XHTML document; a server-side image map is processed by a browser program. You can use both types in the same image map for browsers that do not support client-side image maps. Client-side image maps are rapidly taking the place of server-side image maps.
- You can mix the content of an **area** element with the content of block-level elements.
- The **area** element is a child element of the **map** element.
- For the **map** element, WebTV supports the **name** attribute.

Related Elements

area (41), img (162)

ⓔ 📺 marquee   Scrolling Marquee

Purpose

Creates a text marquee that scrolls within the current document.

Syntax

```
<marquee[ accesskey="shortcut_key"]
    [ align="left"|"center"|"right"|"top"|"bottom"]
    [ behavior=scroll|slide|alternate]
    [ bgcolor="#rrggbb"|"color"][ class="class_name"]
    [ contenteditable="edit_string"]
    [ datafld="ds_col_name"]
    [ dataformatas="html"|"text"]
    [ datasrc="ds_identifier"][ dir="ltr"|"rtl"]
    [ direction="down"|"left"|"right"|"up"]
    [ disabled="disabled"]
    [ height="height_pix"|height_%][ hspace="horiz_pix"]
    [ id="id_name"][ lang="lang_code"]
    [ language="javascript"|"jscript"|"vbs[cript]"]
    [ loop="number_of_plays"|"infinite"]
    [ onbeforecut="bt_script"]
    [ onbeforeeditfocus="bef_script"]
    [ onbeforefocusenter="bfe_script"]
    [ onbeforefocusleave="bfl_script"]
    [ onbeforepaste="bp_script"][ onblur="bl_script"]
    [ onbounce="bn_script"][ onclick="cl_script"]
    [ oncontextmenu="cm_script"]
    [ oncontrolselect="ctl_script"][ oncut="ct_script"]
    [ ondblclick="dc_script"][ ondrag="d_script"]
    [ ondragend="dd_script"][ ondragenter="de_script"]
    [ ondragleave="dl_script"][ ondragover="do_script"]
    [ ondragstart="ds_script"][ ondrop="dr_script"]
    [ onfilterchange="f_script"][ onfinish="fn_script"]
    [ onfocus="fc_script"][ onfocusenter="fe_script"]
    [ onfocusleave="fl_script"][ onhelp="hlp_script"]
    [ onkeydown="kd_script"][ onkeypress="kp_script"]
    [ onkeyup="ku_script"][ onlosecapture="lc_script"]
    [ onmousedown="md_script"]
    [ onmouseenter="me_script"]
    [ onmouseleave="ml_script"]
    [ onmousemove="mm_script"][ onmouseout="mo_script"]
    [ onmouseover="mov_script"][ onmouseup="mu_script"]
    [ onpaste="p_script"][ onpropertychange="pc_script"]
```

```
[ onreadystatechange="rsc_script"]
[ onresize="rsz_script"][ onresizeend="ree_script"]
[ onresizestart="res_script"][ onscroll="sc_script"]
[ onselectstart="ss_script"][ onstart="st_script"]
[ scrollamount="gap_pix"][ scrolldelay="millisecs"]
[ style="name_1: value_1"[; "name_2: value_2"]
[...; "name_n: value_n"]]
[ tabindex="position_number"][ title="title"]
[ transparency="trans_value"][ truespeed]
[ vspace="vert_pix"][ width="width_pix"|width_%]>
marquee_text</marquee>
```

Where

- ⊖ **accesskey** (Web) assigns a shortcut key to the object in order to focus on it.
- ⛶ **align** (Web) aligns the marquee with the margins.
- ⊖⛶ **behavior** (Web) specifies the way that the text within the marquee will scroll.
- ⊖⛶ **bgcolor** (Web) specifies the background color for the marquee.
- ⊖ **class** (Web) specifies a class identification for the element.
- ⊖ **contenteditable** (Web) specifies or obtains a value that indicates whether a user can edit the element content.
- ⊖ **dir** (Web) specifies the direction in which the marquee text is displayed: left-to-right or right-to-left.
- ⊖⛶ **direction** (Web) specifies the direction that the text scrolls within the marquee window.
- ⊖ **disabled** (Web) is a keyword that prevents a user from using the element.
- ⊖⛶ **height** (Web) specifies the height of the window in which the marquee will be placed.
- ⊖⛶ **hspace** (Web) is the horizontal area, in pixels, of the left and right sides of the marquee window and text, graphics, and links on the current page.
- ⊖ **id** (Web) provides a unique identifier name for the element.
- ⊖ **lang** (Web) specifies the code for the language used for the element.
- ⊖ **language** (Web) declares the scripting language of the current script.
- ⊖⛶ **loop** (Web) indicates the number of times that an embedded audio clip will play or the marquee will scroll.
- ⊖ **onbeforecut** (Web) names a script to run when a user starts cutting a selection to the Clipboard but before any action actually takes place.
- ⊖ **onbeforeeditfocus** (Web) names a script to run when a user starts activating an object but before the object actually becomes active.
- ⊖ **onbeforefocusenter** (Web) names a script to run when a user starts focusing on an object but before the object actually gains focus.

- ⊖ `onbeforefocusleave` (Web) names a script to run when a user starts leaving an object but before the object actually loses focus.
- ⊖ `onbeforepaste` (Web) names a script to run when a user starts pasting an object but before any action actually takes place.
- ⊖ `onblur` (Web) names a script to run when the marquee loses focus (that is, it is no longer the active element).
- ⊖ `onbounce` (Web) names a script to run when `behavior=` `"alternate"` (Web) and the marquee text reaches a side of the window in which it is scrolling.
- ⊖ `onclick` (Web) names a script to run when a user moves the mouse pointer or other pointing device over the emphasized text and clicks the device button.
- ⊖ `oncontextmenu` (Web) names a script to run when a user right-clicks the mouse to open a shortcut menu.
- ⊖ `oncontrolselect` (Web) names a script to run when a user selects a control.
- ⊖ `oncut` (Web) names a script to run when a user cuts a selection to the Clipboard.
- ⊖ `ondblclick` (Web) names a script to run when a user moves the mouse pointer or other pointing device over the emphasized text and double-clicks the device button.
- ⊖ `ondrag` (Web) names a script to run when a user drags a selection.
- ⊖ `ondragend` (Web) names a script to run after a user completes a drag-and-drop operation.
- ⊖ `ondragenter` (Web) names a script to run when a user drags a selection into an area in which it can be dropped.
- ⊖ `ondragleave` (Web) names a script to run when a user drags a selection beyond an area in which it can be dropped.
- ⊖ `ondragover` (Web) names a script to run when a user drags a selection over an area in which it can be dropped.
- ⊖ `ondragstart` (Web) names a script to run when a user starts dragging a selection or element.
- ⊖ `ondrop` (Web) names a script to run when a user releases the mouse button to drop a dragged selection.
- ⊖ `onfilterchange` (Web) names a script to run when a visual filter changes in any way.
- ⊖ `onfinish` (Web) names a script to run when the marquee text stops scrolling.
- ⊖ `onfocus` (Web) names a script to run when a user points the mouse pointer or other pointing device to focus on the current element.
- ⊖ `onfocusenter` (Web) names a script to run when a user focuses on the current element in any way.
- ⊖ `onfocusleave` (Web) names a script to run when a user inactivates the current element in any way.
- ⊖ `onhelp` (Web) names a script to run when a user presses the F1 or Help key over the current element.

- ⊝ `onkeydown` (Web) names a script to run when a user presses and holds down a key over the marquee.
- ⊝ `onkeypress` (Web) names a script to run when a user presses and releases a key over the marquee.
- ⊝ `onkeyup` (Web) names a script to run when a user releases a key that is currently held down over the marquee.
- ⊝ `onlosecapture` (Web) names a script to run when a user releases a selection that has been captured by the mouse.
- ⊝ `onmousedown` (Web) names a script to run when a user moves the mouse pointer or other pointing device over the marquee and presses and holds down the device button.
- ⊝ `onmouseenter` (Web) names a script to run when a user moves the mouse pointer onto the object.
- ⊝ `onmouseleave` (Web) names a script to run when the mouse pointer leaves the object.
- ⊝ `onmousemove` (Web) names a script to run when a user moves the mouse pointer or other pointing device over the marquee.
- ⊝ `onmouseout` (Web) names a script to run when a user moves the mouse pointer or other pointing device away from the marquee.
- ⊝ `onmouseover` (Web) names a script to run the first time a user moves the mouse pointer or other pointing device over the marquee.
- ⊝ `onmouseup` (Web) names a script to run when a user moves the mouse pointer or other pointing device over the marquee and releases a pressed-down device button.
- ⊝ `onpaste` (Web) names a script to run when a user pastes the Clipboard contents onto the object.
- ⊝ `onpropertychange` (Web) names a script to run when a property changes on the selected object in any way.
- ⊝ `onreadystatechange` (Web) names a script to run when the status of an element has changed (for example, the element receives data).
- ⊝ `onresize` (Web) names a script to run when a user resizes the selected object.
- ⊝ `onresizeend` (Web) names a script to run after the object has been resized.
- ⊝ `onresizestart` (Web) names a script to run as a user resizes the object.
- ⊝ `onscroll` (Web) names a script to run when a user moves the scroll box within the scroll bar.
- ⊝ `onselectstart` (Web) names a script to run when a user starts selecting an object.
- ⊝ `onstart` (Web) names a script to run when the loop starts.
- ⊝🖰 `scrollamount` (Web) specifies the gap, in pixels, from the end of the current marquee display and the beginning of the following display.
- ⊝🖰 `scrolldelay` (Web) specifies the time delay, in milliseconds, from the end of the current marquee display and the beginning of the following display.
- ⊝ `style` (Web) sets styles for the element.

- ☺ `tabindex` (Web) defines the position of the current element in all the elements that a user can navigate to using a Tab or Shift + Tab key.
- ☺ `title` (Web) provides a title for the element.
- 📺 `transparency` (Web) sets the level of transparency or opaqueness of the selected text.
- ☺ `truespeed` (Web) uses the `scrolldelay` value as the speed of the scrolling text.
- ☺📺 `vspace` (Web) is the vertical area, in pixels, of the top and bottom of the marquee window and other text, graphics, and links on the current page.
- ☺📺 `width` (Web) specifies the width of the window in which the marquee will be placed.
- *marquee_text* represents one or more characters.

Note

WebTV supports the following attributes for `marquee`: `align`, `behavior`, `bgcolor`, `direction`, `height`, `hspace`, `loop`, `scrollamount`, `scrolldelay`, `transparency`, `vspace`, and `width`.

menu	Menu List

Purpose

Displays a menu list of items.

Syntax

```
<menu[ accesskey="shortcut_key"]
  [ class="class_name"][ compact="compact"]
  [ contenteditable="edit_string"][ dir="ltr"|"rtl"]
  [ disabled="disabled"][ id="id_name"]
  [ lang="lang_code"][ onbeforecopy="bc_script"]
  [ onbeforecut="bt_script"]
  [ onbeforefocusenter="bfe_script"]
  [ onbeforefocusleave="bfl_script"]
  [ onbeforepaste="bp_script"][ onblur="bl_script"]
  [ onclick="cl_script"][ oncontextmenu="cm_script"]
  [ oncontrolselect="ctl_script"][ oncopy="cp_script"]
  [ oncut="ct_script"][ ondblclick="dc_script"]
  [ ondrag="d_script"][ ondragend="dd_script"]
  [ ondragenter="de_script"][ ondragleave="dl_script"]
  [ ondragover="do_script"][ ondragstart="ds_script"]
  [ ondrop="dr_script"][ onfocus="fc_script"]
  [ onfocusenter="fe_script"]
  [ onfocusleave="fl_script"][ onhelp="hlp_script"]
  [ onkeydown="kd_script"][ onkeypress="kp_script"]
```

```
[ onkeyup="ku_script"]
[ onlosecapture="lc_script"]
[ onmousedown="md_script"]
[ onmouseenter="me_script"]
[ onmouseleave="ml_script"]
[ onmousemove="mm_script"][ onmouseout="mo_script"]
[ onmouseover="mov_script"][ onmouseup="mu_script"]
[ onpaste="p_script"][ onpropertychange="pc_script"]
[ onreadystatechange="rsc_script"]
[ onresize="rsz_script"][ onresizeend="ree_script"]
[ onresizestart="res_script"]
[ onselectstart="ss_script"]
[ style="name_1: value_1"[; "name_2: value_2"]
[...; "name_n: value_n"]]
[ tabindex="position_number"][ title="title"]>
menu-list</menu>
```

Where

- ⊖ accesskey (Web) assigns a shortcut key to the object in order to focus on it.
- class (Web) specifies a class identification for the menu list.
- compact (Web) indicates that a browser might decrease the size of the space between a number or bullet and the list item.
- ⊖ contenteditable (Web) specifies or obtains a value that indicates whether a user can edit the element content.
- dir (Web) specifies the direction in which the menu list text is displayed: left-to-right or right-to-left.
- ⊖ disabled (Web) is a keyword that prevents a user from using the element.
- id (Web) provides a unique identifier name for the menu list.
- lang (Web) specifies the code for the language used for the menu list text.
- ⊖ onbeforecopy (Web) names a script to run when a user starts copying a selection to the Clipboard but before any action actually takes place.
- ⊖ onbeforecut (Web) names a script to run when a user starts cutting a selection to the Clipboard but before any action actually takes place.
- ⊖ onbeforefocusenter (Web) names a script to run when a user starts focusing on an object but before the object actually gains focus.
- ⊖ onbeforefocusleave (Web) names a script to run when a user starts leaving an object but before the object actually loses focus.
- ⊖ onbeforepaste (Web) names a script to run when a user starts pasting an object but before any action actually takes place.
- ⊖ onblur (Web) names a script to run when the object loses focus (that is, it is no longer the active element).
- onclick (Web) names a script to run when a user moves the mouse pointer or other pointing device over the menu list and clicks the button.

- ⊜ `oncontextmenu` (Web) names a script to run when a user right-clicks the mouse to open a shortcut menu.
- ⊜ `oncontrolselect` (Web) names a script to run when a user selects a control.
- ⊜ `oncopy` (Web) names a script to run when a user copies a selection to the Clipboard.
- ⊜ `oncut` (Web) names a script to run when a user cuts a selection to the Clipboard.
- `ondblclick` (Web) names a script to run when a user moves the mouse pointer or other pointing device over the menu list and double-clicks the button.
- ⊜ `ondrag` (Web) names a script to run when a user drags a selection.
- ⊜ `ondragend` (Web) names a script to run after a user completes a drag-and-drop operation.
- ⊜ `ondragenter` (Web) names a script to run when a user drags a selection into an area in which it can be dropped.
- ⊜ `ondragleave` (Web) names a script to run when a user drags a selection beyond an area in which it can be dropped.
- ⊜ `ondragover` (Web) names a script to run when a user drags a selection over an area in which it can be dropped.
- ⊜ `ondragstart` (Web) names a script to run when a user starts dragging a selection or element.
- ⊜ `ondrop` (Web) names a script to run when a user releases the mouse button to drop a dragged selection.
- ⊜ `onfocus` (Web) names a script to run when a user points the mouse pointer or other pointing device to focus on the current element.
- ⊜ `onfocusenter` (Web) names a script to run when a user focuses on the current element in any way.
- ⊜ `onfocusleave` (Web) names a script to run when a user inactivates the current element in any way.
- ⊜ `onhelp` (Web) names a script to run when a user presses the F1 or Help key over the current element.
- `onkeydown` (Web) names a script to run when a user presses and holds down a key over the menu list.
- `onkeypress` (Web) names a script to run when a user presses and releases a key over the menu list.
- `onkeyup` (Web) names a script to run when a user releases a key that is currently held down over the menu list.
- ⊜ `onlosecapture` (Web) names a script to run when a user releases a selection that has been captured by the mouse.
- `onmousedown` (Web) names a script to run when a user moves the mouse pointer or other pointing device over the menu list and presses and holds down the button.
- ⊜ `onmouseenter` (Web) names a script to run when a user moves the mouse pointer onto the object.

- ⊖ onmouseleave (Web) names a script to run when the mouse pointer leaves the object.
- onmousemove (Web) names a script to run when a user moves the mouse pointer or other pointing device over the menu list.
- onmouseout (Web) names a script to run when a user moves the mouse pointer or other pointing device away from the menu list.
- onmouseover (Web) names a script to run the first time a user moves the mouse pointer or other pointing device over the menu list.
- onmouseup (Web) names a script to run when a user moves the mouse pointer or other pointing device over the menu list and releases a mouse button that is currently held down.
- ⊖ onpaste (Web) names a script to run when a user pastes the Clipboard contents onto the object.
- ⊖ onpropertychange (Web) names a script to run when a property changes on the selected object in any way.
- ⊖ onreadystatechange (Web) names a script to run when the status of an element has changed (for example, the element receives data).
- ⊖ onresize (Web) names a script to run when a user resizes the selected object.
- ⊖ onresizeend (Web) names a script to run after the object has been resized.
- ⊖ onresizestart (Web) names a script to run as a user resizes the object.
- ⊖ onselectstart (Web) names a script to run when a user starts selecting an object.
- style (Web) sets styles for the menu list.
- ⊖ tabindex (Web) defines the position of the current element in all the elements that a user can navigate to using a Tab or Shift + Tab key.
- title (Web) provides a title for the menu list.
- *menu-list* represents one or more list items.

Notes

- This block-level element originated in HTML 2.0.
- Although menu is supported by HTML 4.0, it has been deprecated (that is, it will eventually be obsolete) and appears only in the Transitional DTD — not in the Strict DTD. Use other list elements (ol and ul) instead.
- Items on a menu list may or may not be preceded with bullets, depending on the browser.
- For the menu element, WebTV supports the class and style attributes.
- The HTML developers designed the menu element to list items in a single column.

Related Elements

dir (104), ol (230), ul (331)

meta
Meta

Purpose

Provides a description of the properties of the current document, including the author, an expiration date, and keywords, so that search engines can correctly identify it.

Syntax

```
<meta content="content-text"[ dir="ltr"|"rtl"]
   [ http-equiv="HTTP-header-field-name"]
   [ lang="lang_code"][ name="name-text"]
   [ onlayoutcomplete="la_script"]
   [ scheme="format_id"][ url="uri"]{ />|</meta>}
```

Where

- `content` (Web) provides text or character information.
- `dir` (Web) specifies the direction in which the meta text is displayed: left-to-right or right-to-left.
- `http-equiv` (Web) indicates that the meta-information will be bound to an HTTP response header.
- `lang` (Web) specifies the code for the language used for the meta text.
- `name` (Web) is the name, description, or identification of the contents of the current document.
- ⊖ `onlayoutcomplete` (Web) names a script to run when a user lays out a selection using Print or Print Preview.
- `scheme` (Web) identifies a particular format for the `content` attribute.
- 🖰 `url` (Web) specifies the URI of a Web page.

Notes

- This element originated in HTML 2.0.
- `meta` belongs in the HEAD section.
- `meta` is an empty element.
- You can consider the data associated with a `meta` statement as an index to the contents of the document. Search indexes use the `meta` attributes and keywords, along with the document title (the `title` element) and the first 250 or so words in the body of an XHTML document to identify and rank documents that match search keywords.
- `meta` can also provide information about document creation and modification information. For example, you can include the following information within a document's `meta` element: the author, the individual who maintains the document, the date the document was created, the last date the document was edited, and the document's expiration date.
- You can use multiple `meta` elements in an XHTML document.
- When using keywords within a `meta` statement, check spelling to ensure that search engines will use all your keywords properly.

- If you do not use the name attribute (Web), a server uses the http-equiv attribute (Web) as the name.
- HTTP servers use the meta information in various ways; there is no standard.
- For the meta element, WebTV supports the content, http-equiv, and url attributes.

Related Elements
base (49), head (148), isindex (184), link (202), script (262), style (280), title (318)

For More Information
Learn more about the meta element on page 527 in Chapter 2.

N multicol   Multiple Columns

Purpose
Applies a multiple-column format to a selected block of text, graphics, and/or links.

Syntax
```
<multicol cols="num_cols"[ gutter="gutter_pix"]
  [ width="width_pix"]>selected_area</multicol>
```

Where
- N cols (Web) specifies the number of columns in the selected area of the current document.
- N gutter (Web) specifies the white space, in pixels, between columns.
- N width (Web) specifies the width of all columns.
- N selected_area is a selected block.

Note
The multicol extension creates columns that are of equal width, separated by gutters of equal width.

e nextid   Unique Identifier

Purpose
Specifies a parameter that creates unique identifiers from within a text editor.

Syntax
```
<nextid[ onbeforecut="bt_script"]
  [ onbeforepaste="bp_script"][ onclick="cl_script"]
  [ oncontextmenu="cm_script"][ oncut="ct_script"]
  [ ondblclick="dc_script"][ ondragstart="ds_script"]
  [ onfilterchange="f_script"][ onhelp="hlp_script"]
```

[onkeydown="*kd_script*"][onkeypress="*kp_script*"]
[onkeyup="*ku_script*"][onmouseenter="*me_script*"]
[onmouseleave="*ml_script*"]
[onmousemove="*mm_script*"]
[onmouseover="*mov_script*"][onmouseup="*mu_script*"]
[onpaste="*p_script*"]
[onreadystatechange="*rsc_script*"]
[onselectstart="*ss_script*"]
parameter> </nextid>

Where

- ⊖ onbeforecut (Web) names a script to run when a user starts cutting a selection to the Clipboard but before any action actually takes place.
- ⊖ onbeforepaste (Web) names a script to run when a user starts pasting an object but before any action actually takes place.
- ⊖ onclick (Web) names a script to run when a user moves the mouse pointer or other pointing device over the no-frames content and clicks the device button.
- ⊖ oncontextmenu (Web) names a script to run when a user right-clicks the mouse to open a shortcut menu.
- ⊖ oncut (Web) names a script to run when a user cuts a selection to the Clipboard.
- ⊖ ondblclick (Web) names a script to run when a user moves the mouse pointer or other pointing device over the no-frames content and double-clicks the device button.
- ⊖ ondragstart (Web) names a script to run when a user starts dragging a selection or element.
- ⊖ onfilterchange (Web) names a script to run when a visual filter changes in any way.
- ⊖ onhelp (Web) names a script to run when a user presses the F1 or Help key over the current element.
- ⊖ onkeydown (Web) names a script to run when a user presses and holds down a key over the no-frames content.
- ⊖ onkeypress (Web) names a script to run when a user presses and releases a key over the no-frames content.
- ⊖ onkeyup (Web) names a script to run when a user releases a key that is currently held down over the no-frames content.
- ⊖ onmouseenter (Web) names a script to run when a user moves the mouse pointer onto the object.
- ⊖ onmouseleave (Web) names a script to run when the mouse pointer leaves the object.
- ⊖ onmousemove (Web) names a script to run when a user moves the mouse pointer or other pointing device over the no-frames content.
- ⊖ onmouseover (Web) names a script to run the first time a user moves the mouse pointer or other pointing device over the no-frames content.

XHTML Syntax

- ⊖ onmouseup (Web) names a script to run when a user moves the mouse pointer or other pointing device over the no-frames content and releases a pressed-down device button.
- ⊖ onpaste (Web) names a script to run when a user pastes the Clipboard contents onto the object.
- ⊖ onreadystatechange (Web) names a script to run when the status of an element has changed (for example, the element receives data).
- ⊖ onselectstart (Web) names a script to run when a user starts selecting an object.
- *parameter* represents the parameter that leads to the unique identifier.

Note

Use nextid within the HEAD section of a document.

⊖ Ⓝ 📺 nobr   No Break

Purpose

Turns off automatic word wrap and line breaks except for those caused by the following elements: br (70), p (238), or wbr (338).

Syntax

```
<nobr[ class="class_name"]
  [ contenteditable="edit_string"][ dir="ltr"|"rtl"]
  [ disabled="disabled"][ id="id_name"]
  [ lang="lang_code"][ language="javascript"|"jscript"
  |"vbs[cript]"][ onbeforecopy="bc_script"]
  [ onbeforecut="bt_script"]
  [ onbeforepaste="bp_script"][ onclick="cl_script"]
  [ oncontextmenu="cm_script"][ oncopy="cp_script"]
  [ oncut="ct_script"][ ondblclick="dc_script"]
  [ ondrag="d_script"][ ondragend="dd_script"]
  [ ondragenter="de_script"][ ondragleave="dl_script"]
  [ ondragover="do_script"][ ondragstart="ds_script"]
  [ ondrop="dr_script"][ onhelp="hlp_script"]
  [ onkeydown="kd_script"][ onkeypress="kp_script"]
  [ onkeyup="ku_script"][ onlosecapture="lc_script"]
  [ onmouseenter="me_script"]
  [ onmouseleave="ml_script"]
  [ onmouseover="mov_script"][ onmouseup="mu_script"]
  [ onpaste="p_script"][ onpropertychange="pc_script"]
  [ onreadystatechange="rsc_script"]
  [ onselectstart="ss_script"]
  [ style="name_1: value_1"[; "name_2: value_2"]
  [...; "name_n: value_n"]][ title="title"]>
text</nobr>
```

Where

- ⊕ `class` (Web) specifies a class identification for the element.
- ⊕ `contenteditable` (Web) specifies or obtains a value that indicates whether a user can edit the element content.
- ⊕ `dir` (Web) specifies the direction in which the element content is displayed: left-to-right or right-to-left.
- ⊕ `disabled` (Web) is a keyword that prevents a user from using the element.
- ⊕ `id` (Web) provides a unique identifier name for the element.
- ⊕ `lang` (Web) specifies the code representing the language used for the selected text.
- ⊕ `language` (Web) declares the scripting language of the current script.
- ⊕ `onbeforecopy` (Web) names a script to run when a user starts copying a selection to the Clipboard but before any action actually takes place.
- ⊕ `onbeforecut` (Web) names a script to run when a user starts cutting a selection to the Clipboard but before any action actually takes place.
- ⊕ `onbeforepaste` (Web) names a script to run when a user starts pasting an object but before any action actually takes place.
- ⊕ `onclick` (Web) names a script to run when a user moves the mouse pointer or other pointing device over the object and clicks the device button.
- ⊕ `oncontextmenu` (Web) names a script to run when a user right-clicks the mouse to open a shortcut menu.
- ⊕ `oncopy` (Web) names a script to run when a user copies a selection to the Clipboard.
- ⊕ `oncut` (Web) names a script to run when a user cuts a selection to the Clipboard.
- ⊕ `ondblclick` (Web) names a script to run when a user moves the mouse pointer or other pointing device over the object and double-clicks the device button.
- ⊕ `ondrag` (Web) names a script to run when a user drags a selection.
- ⊕ `ondragend` (Web) names a script to run after a user completes a drag-and-drop operation.
- ⊕ `ondragenter` (Web) names a script to run when a user drags a selection into an area in which it can be dropped.
- ⊕ `ondragleave` (Web) names a script to run when a user drags a selection beyond an area in which it can be dropped.
- ⊕ `ondragover` (Web) names a script to run when a user drags a selection over an area in which it can be dropped.
- ⊕ `ondragstart` (Web) names a script to run when a user starts dragging a selection or element.
- ⊕ `ondrop` (Web) names a script to run when a user releases the mouse button to drop a dragged selection.
- ⊕ `onhelp` (Web) names a script to run when a user presses the F1 or Help key over the current element.
- ⊕ `onkeydown` (Web) names a script to run when a user presses and holds down a key over the object.

- ☻ onkeypress (Web) names a script to run when a user presses and releases a key over the object.
- ☻ onkeyup (Web) names a script to run when a user releases a key that is currently held down over the object.
- ☻ onlosecapture (Web) names a script to run when a user releases a selection that has been captured by the mouse.
- ☻ onmouseenter (Web) names a script to run when a user moves the mouse pointer onto the object.
- ☻ onmouseleave (Web) names a script to run when the mouse pointer leaves the object.
- ☻ onmousemove (Web) names a script to run when a user moves the mouse pointer or other pointing device over the object.
- ☻ onmouseover (Web) names a script to run the first time a user moves the mouse pointer or other pointing device over the object.
- ☻ onmouseup (Web) names a script to run when a user moves the mouse pointer or other pointing device over the object and releases a pressed-down device button.
- ☻ onpaste (Web) names a script to run when a user pastes the Clipboard contents onto the object.
- ☻ onpropertychange (Web) names a script to run when a property changes on the selected object in any way.
- ☻ onreadystatechange (Web) names a script to run when the status of an element has changed (for example, the element receives data).
- ☻ onselectstart (Web) names a script to run when a user starts selecting an object.
- ☻ style (Web) sets styles for the element.
- ☻ title (Web) provides a title for the element.
- *text* represents one or more characters and spaces.

Related Elements

br (70), p (238), wbr (338)

Ⓝ 🖳 noembed   **Embed Alternate**

Purpose

Provides alternative content for browsers that do not support the use of the embed extension.

Syntax

```
<noembed>alternate_content</noembed>
```

Where

alternate_content represents characters, HTML elements, special characters, graphics, and/or links.

XHTML Syntax

Related Element

embed (123)

<table><tr><td>noframes</td><td>Frames Alternate</td></tr></table>

Purpose

Provides alternative content with no frames for browsers that do not support frames.

Syntax

```
<noframes[ class="class_name"]
   [ contenteditable="edit_string"][ dir="ltr"|"rtl"]
   [ disabled="disabled"][ id="id_name"]
   [ lang="lang_code"][ onclick="cl_script"]
   [ ondblclick="dc_script"][ onkeydown="kd_script"]
   [ onkeypress="kp_script"][ onkeyup="ku_script"]
   [ onmousedown="md_script"][ onmousemove="mm_script"]
   [ onmouseout="mo_script"][ onmouseover="mov_script"]
   [ onmouseup="mu_script"]
   [ onreadystatechange="rsc_script"]
   [ style="name_1: value_1"[; "name_2: value_2"]
   [; "name_n: value_n"]][ title="title"] >
   no_frame_content</noframes>
```

Where

- **class** (Web) specifies a class identification for the no-frames content.
- ⊖ **contenteditable** (Web) specifies or obtains a value that indicates whether a user can edit the element content.
- **dir** (Web) specifies the direction in which the no-frames content is displayed: left-to-right or right-to-left.
- ⊖ **disabled** (Web) is a keyword that prevents a user from using the element.
- **id** (Web) provides a unique identifier name for the no-frames content.
- **onclick** (Web) names a script to run when a user moves the mouse pointer or other pointing device over the no-frames content and clicks the device button.
- **ondblclick** (Web) names a script to run when a user moves the mouse pointer or other pointing device over the no-frames content and double-clicks the device button.
- **onkeydown** (Web) names a script to run when a user presses and holds down a key over the no-frames content.
- **onkeypress** (Web) names a script to run when a user presses and releases a key over the no-frames content.
- **onkeyup** (Web) names a script to run when a user releases a key that is currently held down over the no-frames content.

- onmousedown (Web) names a script to run when a user moves the mouse pointer or other pointing device over the no-frames content and presses and holds down the device button.
- onmousemove (Web) names a script to run when a user moves the mouse pointer or other pointing device over the no-frames content.
- onmouseout (Web) names a script to run when a user moves the mouse pointer or other pointing device away from the no-frames content.
- onmouseover (Web) names a script to run the first time a user moves the mouse pointer or other pointing device over the no-frames content.
- onmouseup (Web) names a script to run when a user moves the mouse pointer or other pointing device over the no-frames content and releases a pressed-down device button.
- ⊖ onreadystatechange (Web) names a script to run when the status of an element has changed (for example, the element receives data).
- style (Web) sets styles for the no-frames content.
- title (Web) provides a title for the no-frames content.
- *no_frame_content* represents characters, HTML elements, special characters, graphics, and/or links.

Notes

- This HTML 4.0 element was originally a Netscape extension and a Microsoft extension.
- You can insert the noframes element after a frame set or in the body of an XHTML document.

Related Elements

frame (139), frameset (141), iframe (158)

For More Information

Learn more about use the noframes element on page 589 in Chapter 5.

Ⓝnolayer   Layer Alternate

Purpose

Provides alternative content for browsers that do not support the use of the layer extension.

Syntax

```
<nolayer>alternate_content</nolayer>
```

Where

alternate_content represents characters, HTML elements, special characters, graphics, and/or links.

Note

This Netscape extension is supported only within Netscape Navigator 4.0 or greater.

XHTML Syntax

Related Elements

ilayer (160), layer (194)

---

noscript   Script Alternate

Purpose

Provides alternative content for browsers that do not support scripts.

Syntax

```
<noscript[ class="class_name"]
   [ contenteditable="edit_string"][ dir="ltr"|"rtl"]
   [ disabled="disabled"][ id="id_name"]
   [ lang="lang_code"][ onclick="cl_script"]
   [ ondblclick="dc_script"][ onkeydown="kd_script"]
   [ onkeypress="kp_script"][ onkeyup="ku_script"]
   [ onmousedown="md_script"][ onmousemove="mm_script"]
   [ onmouseout="mo_script"][ onmouseover="mov_script"]
   [ onmouseup="mu_script"]
   [ onreadystatechange="rsc_script"]
   [ style="name_1: value_1"[; "name_2: value_2"]
   [...; "name_n: value_n"]][ title="title"]>
alternate_content</noscript>
```

Where

- class (Web) specifies a class identification for the no-script content.
- ☺ contenteditable (Web) specifies or obtains a value that indicates whether a user can edit the element content.
- dir (Web) specifies the direction in which the no-script content is displayed: left-to-right or right-to-left.
- ☺ disabled (Web) is a keyword that prevents a user from using the element.
- id (Web) provides a unique identifier name for the no-script content.
- lang (Web) specifies the code representing the language used with text associated with the no-script content.
- onclick (Web) names a script to run when a user moves the mouse pointer or other pointing device over the no-script content and clicks the device button.
- ondblclick (Web) names a script to run when a user moves the mouse pointer or other pointing device over the no-script content and double-clicks the device button.
- onkeydown (Web) names a script to run when a user presses and holds down a key over the no-script content.
- onkeypress (Web) names a script to run when a user presses and releases a key over the no-script content.

- onkeyup (Web) names a script to run when a user releases a key that is currently held down over the no-script content.
- onmousedown (Web) names a script to run when a user moves the mouse pointer or other pointing device over the no-script content and presses and holds down the device button.
- onmousemove (Web) names a script to run when a user moves the mouse pointer or other pointing device over the no-script content.
- onmouseout (Web) names a script to run when a user moves the mouse pointer or other pointing device away from the no-script content.
- onmouseover (Web) names a script to run the first time a user moves the mouse pointer or other pointing device over the no-script content.
- onmouseup (Web) names a script to run when a user moves the mouse pointer or other pointing device over the no-script content and releases a pressed-down device button.
- ⊖ onreadystatechange (Web) names a script to run when the status of an element has changed (for example, the element receives data).
- style (Web) sets styles for the no-script content.
- title (Web) provides a title for the no-script content.
- *alternate_content* represents characters, HTML elements, special characters, graphics, and/or links.

Notes

- This block-level element originated in HTML 4.0.
- Use noscript to present alternate content for browsers that do not support or cannot run scripts.

Related Elements

script (262), server (267)

---

object   Embed Object

Purpose

Embeds a multimedia object, such as an image, video file, or sound file, within the current document.

Syntax

```
<object[ accesskey="shortcut_key"][ align="texttop"]
  |"middle"|"textmiddle"|"baseline"|"textbottom"
  |"left"|"center"|"right"|"absbottom"|"absmiddle"
  |"bottom"|"top"][ archive="a_uri_1"[ "a_uri_2"]
  [... "a_uri_n"][ border="border_pix"|"border_%"]
  [ class="class_name"][ classid="uri_id"]
  [ codebase="base_uri"]
```

```
[ codetype="Internet_Media_Type"]
[ contenteditable="edit_string"][ data="data_uri"]
[ datafld="ds_col_name"][ datasrc="ds_identifier"]
[ declare="declare"][ dir="ltr"|"rtl"]
[ disabled="disabled"][ height="height_pix"
|"height_%"][ hspace="horiz_pix"][ id="id_name"]
[ lang="lang_code"][ language="javascript"|"jscript"
|"vbs[cript]"][ name="input_name"]
[ onbeforeeditfocus="bef_script"]
[ onbeforefocusenter="bfe_script"]
[ onbeforefocusleave="bfl_script"]
[ onblur="bl_script"][ oncellchange="cc_script"]
[ onclick="cl_script"]
[ oncontrolselect="ctl_script"]
[ ondataavailable="da_script"]
[ ondatasetchanged="dsc_script"]
[ ondatasetcomplete="dsf_script"]
[ ondblclick="dc_script"][ ondrag="d_script"]
[ ondragend="dd_script"][ ondragenter="de_script"]
[ ondragleave="dl_script"][ ondragover="do_script"]
[ ondragstart="ds_script"][ ondrop="dr_script"]
[ onerror="e_script"][ onfocus="fc_script"]
[ onfocusenter="fe_script"]
[ onfocusleave="fl_script"][ onkeydown="kd_script"]
[ onkeypress="kp_script"][ onkeyup="ku_script"]
[ onlosecapture="lc_script"]
[ onmousedown="md_script"][ onmousemove="mm_script"]
[ onmouseout="mo_script"][ onmouseover="mov_script"]
[ onmouseup="mu_script"]
[ onpropertychange="pc_script"]
[ onreadystatechange="rsc_script"]
[ onresize="rsz_script"][ onresizeend="ree_script"]
[ onresizestart="res_script"]
[ onrowenter="re_script"][ onrowexit="rex_script"]
[ onrowsdelete="rd_script"]
[ onrowsinserted="rn_script"][ onscroll="sc_script"]
[ onselectstart="ss_script"]
[ STANDBY="message_text"][ style="name_1: value_1"
[; "name_2: value_2"]][...; "name_n: value_n"]
[ tabindex="position_number"][ title="title"]
[ type="Internet_Media_Type"][ usemap="map_uri"]
[ vspace="vert_pix"][ width="width_pix"|"width_%"]>
embedded_object</object>
```

Where

- ☺ `accesskey` (Web) assigns a shortcut key to the element in order to focus on it.
- `align` (Web) horizontally or vertically aligns the object within its page. The `absbottom`, `absmiddle`, `bottom`, and `top` values are Internet Explorer-only values. This is a deprecated attribute; use a style sheet instead.
- `archive` (Web) is a list of URIs in an archive related to the object.
- `border` (Web) turns on a border and sets the width, in pixels or as a percentage of the full-screen width, of the window surrounding the object. This is a deprecated attribute; use a style sheet instead.
- `class` (Web) specifies a class identification for the object.
- `classid` (Web) names an identifier for the object or class.
- `codebase` (Web) specifies the base URI of the object.
- `codetype` (Web) specifies a valid Internet Media Type (that is, MIME-TYPE) used by the program that will produce the object.
- ☺ `contenteditable` (Web) specifies or obtains a value that indicates whether a user can edit the element content.
- `data` (Web) specifies the URI of a document that includes object data to be embedded in the current document.
- ☺ `datafld` (Web) specifies the column name from the file that contains the data source object.
- ☺ `datasrc` (Web) specifies the identifier of the data source object.
- `declare` (Web) indicates that you are declaring, but not *instantiating* (that is, creating an object in memory and enabling it to be addressed), the object, usually for cross-reference purposes.
- `dir` (Web) specifies the direction in which the current text is displayed: left-to-right or right-to-left.
- ☺ `disabled` (Web) is a keyword that prevents a user from using the element.
- `height` (Web) specifies the height, in pixels or as a percentage of the full-screen, of the window in which the object will be placed.
- `hspace` (Web) is the horizontal area, in pixels, between the left margin of the page and the left margin of the applet window, image, or object. This attribute is deprecated; use a style sheet instead.
- `id` (Web) provides a unique identifier name for the current object.
- `lang` (Web) specifies the code representing the language used with the object's text.
- ☺ `language` (Web) declares the scripting language of the current script.
- `name` (Web) names the object if it will be submitted as part of a form.
- ☺ `onbeforeeditfocus` (Web) names a script to run when a user starts activating an object but before the object actually becomes active.
- ☺ `onbeforefocusenter` (Web) names a script to run when a user starts focusing on an object but before the object actually gains focus.
- ☺ `onbeforefocusleave` (Web) names a script to run when a user starts leaving an object but before the object actually loses focus.

- @ `onblur` (Web) names a script to run when the object loses focus (that is, it is no longer the active element).
- @ `oncellchange` (Web) names a script to run when data is modified in the data resource.
- `onclick` (Web) names a script to run when a user moves the mouse pointer or other pointing device over the object and clicks the device button.
- @ `oncontrolselect` (Web) names a script to run when a user selects a control.
- @ `ondataavailable` (Web) names a script to run sporadically when data is received from the data resource.
- @ `ondatasetchanged` (Web) names a script to run when a user changes a data set from the data resource.
- @ `ondatasetcomplete` (Web) names a script to run when all data has been received from the data resource.
- `ondblclick` (Web) names a script to run when a user moves the mouse pointer or other pointing device over the object and double-clicks the device button.
- @ `ondrag` (Web) names a script to run when a user drags a selection.
- @ `ondragend` (Web) names a script to run after a user completes a drag-and-drop operation.
- @ `ondragenter` (Web) names a script to run when a user drags a selection into an area in which it can be dropped.
- @ `ondragleave` (Web) names a script to run when a user drags a selection beyond an area in which it can be dropped.
- @ `ondragover` (Web) names a script to run when a user drags a selection over an area in which it can be dropped.
- @ `ondragstart` (Web) names a script to run when a user starts dragging a selection or element.
- @ `ondrop` (Web) names a script to run when a user releases the mouse button to drop a dragged selection.
- @ `onerror` (Web) specifies a script to run when the referred-to script experiences an error.
- @ `onfocus` (Web) names a script to run when a user points the mouse pointer or other pointing device to focus on the current element.
- @ `onfocusenter` (Web) names a script to run when a user focuses on the current element in any way.
- @ `onfocusleave` (Web) names a script to run when a user inactivates the current element in any way.
- `onkeydown` (Web) names a script to run when a user presses and holds down a key over the object.
- `onkeypress` (Web) names a script to run when a user presses and releases a key over the object.
- `onkeyup` (Web) names a script to run when a user releases a key that is currently held down over the object.
- @ `onlosecapture` (Web) names a script to run when a user releases a selection that has been captured by the mouse.

XHTML Syntax

- onmousedown (Web) names a script to run when a user moves the mouse pointer or other pointing device over the object and presses and holds down the device button.
- onmousemove (Web) names a script to run when a user moves the mouse pointer or other pointing device over the object.
- onmouseout (Web) names a script to run when a user moves the mouse pointer or other pointing device away from the object.
- onmouseover (Web) names a script to run the first time a user moves the mouse pointer or other pointing device over the object.
- onmouseup (Web) names a script to run when a user moves the mouse pointer or other pointing device over the object and releases a pressed-down device button.
- ⊕ onpropertychange (Web) names a script to run when a property changes on the selected object in any way.
- ⊕ onreadystatechange (Web) names a script to run when the status of an element has changed (for example, the element receives data).
- ⊕ onresize (Web) names a script to run when a user resizes the selected object.
- ⊕ onresizeend (Web) names a script to run after the object has been resized.
- ⊕ onresizestart (Web) names a script to run as a user resizes the object.
- ⊕ onrowenter (Web) names a script to run after the data in the current row has changed.
- ⊕ onrowexit (Web) names a script to run as a data source attempts to load data into the current row.
- ⊕ onrowsdelete (Web) names a script to run when a user starts to delete one or more rows from a set of records but before the deletion actually takes place.
- ⊕ onrowsinserted (Web) names a script to run when a user inserts one or more rows in the current set of records.
- ⊕ onscroll (Web) names a script to run when a user moves the scroll box within the scroll bar.
- ⊕ onselectstart (Web) names a script to run when a user starts selecting an object.
- standby (Web) displays a message while the object is loading onscreen.
- style (Web) sets styles for the object.
- tabindex (Web) defines the position of the object in all the elements that a user can navigate to using a Tab or Shift + Tab key.
- title (Web) provides a title for the object.
- type (Web) specifies a valid Internet Media Type (that is, MIMETYPE) of the data embedded in the current document.
- usemap (Web) specifies a client-side image map that is an embedded object within a document.

- vspace (Web) is the vertical area, in pixels, between the top margin of the page and the top margin of the applet window, image, or object. This attribute is deprecated; use a style sheet instead.
- width (Web) specifies the width, in pixels or as a percentage of the full screen, of the window in which the object will be placed.
- *embedded_object* represents an object that is embedded in the XHTML document.

Notes

- This inline element originated in HTML 4.0.
- The param element is a child element of object.
- It is preferable to use the param element instead of using both the data and classID attributes of object.
- object may replace the img and applet elements in future versions of HTML.
- If the value of the type attributes for the object element and a Content-Type HTTP header differ, the Content-Type HTTP header has priority.
- WebTV supports the following attributes for object: align, border, data, height, hspace, id, name, vspace, and width.

Related Elements

a (24), applet (37), img (162)

ol	Ordered List

Purpose

Starts and ends an ordered (numbered) list.

Syntax

```
<ol[ accesskey="shortcut_key"][ class="class_name"]
  [ compact="compact"][ contenteditable="edit_string"]
  [ dir="ltr"|"rtl"][ disabled="disabled"]
  [ id="id_name"][ lang="lang_code"]
  [ language="javascript"|"jscript"|"vbs[cript]"]
  [ onbeforecopy="bc_script"]
  [ onbeforecut="bt_script"]
  [ onbeforefocusenter="bfe_script"]
  [ onbeforefocusleave="bfl_script"]
  [ onbeforepaste="bp_script"][ onblur="bl_script"]
  [ onclick="cl_script"][ oncontextmenu="cm_script"]
  [ oncontrolselect="ctl_script"][ oncopy="cp_script"]
```

```
[ oncut="ct_script"][ ondblclick="dc_script"]
[ ondrag="d_script"][ ondragend="dd_script"]
[ ondragenter="de_script"][ ondragleave="dl_script"]
[ ondragover="do_script"][ ondragstart="ds_script"]
[ ondrop="dr_script"][ onfocus="fc_script"]
[ onfocusenter="fe_script"]
[ onfocusleave="fl_script"]
[ onhelp="hlp_script"][ onkeydown="kd_script"]
[ onkeypress="kp_script"][ onkeyup="ku_script"]
[ onlayoutcomplete="la_script"]
[ onlosecapture="lc_script"]
[ onmousedown="md_script"]
[ onmouseenter="me_script"]
[ onmouseleave="ml_script"]
[ onmousemove="mm_script"]
[ onmouseout="mo_script"][ onmouseover="mov_script"]
[ onmouseup="mu_script"][ onpaste="p_script"]
[ onpropertychange="pc_script"]
[ onreadystatechange="rsc_script"]
[ onresize="rsz_script"][ onresizeend="ree_script"]
[ onresizestart="res_script"]
[ onselectstart="ss_script"]
[ START="1"|"start_num"][ style="name_1: value_1"
[; "name_2: value_2"][...; "name_n: value_n"]]
[ tabindex="position_number"][ title="title"]
[ type="1"|"a"|"A"|"i"|"I"]>ordered-list-items</ol>
```

Where

- ☺ **accesskey** (Web) assigns a shortcut key to the object in order to focus on it.
- **class** (Web) specifies a class identification for the ordered list.
- **compact** (Web) indicates that a browser might decrease the size of the space between the number and the list item. This attribute is deprecated; use a style sheet instead.
- ☺ **contenteditable** (Web) specifies or obtains a value that indicates whether a user can edit the element content.
- **dir** (Web) specifies the direction in which the ordered list text is displayed: left-to-right or right-to-left.
- ☺ **disabled** (Web) is a keyword that prevents a user from using the element.
- **id** (Web) provides a unique identifier name for the ordered list.
- **lang** (Web) specifies the code for the language used for the ordered list text.
- ☺ **language** (Web) declares the scripting language of the current script.

XHTML Syntax

- ☻ `onbeforecopy` (Web) names a script to run when a user starts copying a selection to the Clipboard but before any action actually takes place.
- ☻ `onbeforecut` (Web) names a script to run when a user starts cutting a selection to the Clipboard but before any action actually takes place.
- ☻ `onbeforefocusenter` (Web) names a script to run when a user starts focusing on an object but before the object actually gains focus.
- ☻ `onbeforefocusleave` (Web) names a script to run when a user starts leaving an object but before the object actually loses focus.
- ☻ `onbeforepaste` (Web) names a script to run when a user starts pasting an object but before any action actually takes place.
- ☻ `onblur` (Web) names a script to run when the object loses focus (that is, it is no longer the active element).
- `onclick` (Web) names a script to run when a user moves the mouse pointer or other pointing device over the ordered list and clicks the button.
- ☻ `oncontextmenu` (Web) names a script to run when a user right-clicks the mouse to open a shortcut menu.
- ☻ `oncontrolselect` (Web) names a script to run when a user selects a control.
- ☻ `oncopy` (Web) names a script to run when a user copies a selection to the Clipboard.
- ☻ `oncut` (Web) names a script to run when a user cuts a selection to the Clipboard.
- `ondblclick` (Web) names a script to run when a user moves the mouse pointer or other pointing device over the ordered list and double-clicks the button.
- ☻ `ondrag` (Web) names a script to run when a user drags a selection.
- ☻ `ondragend` (Web) names a script to run after a user completes a drag-and-drop operation.
- ☻ `ondragenter` (Web) names a script to run when a user drags a selection into an area in which it can be dropped.
- ☻ `ondragleave` (Web) names a script to run when a user drags a selection beyond an area in which it can be dropped.
- ☻ `ondragover` (Web) names a script to run when a user drags a selection over an area in which it can be dropped.
- ☻ `ondragstart` (Web) names a script to run when a user starts dragging a selection or element.
- ☻ `ondrop` (Web) names a script to run when a user releases the mouse button to drop a dragged selection.
- ☻ `onfocus` (Web) names a script to run when a user points the mouse pointer or other pointing device to focus on the current element.
- ☻ `onfocusenter` (Web) names a script to run when a user focuses on the current element in any way.
- ☻ `onfocusleave` (Web) names a script to run when a user inactivates the current element in any way.
- ☻ `onhelp` (Web) names a script to run when a user presses the F1 or Help key over the current element.

- `onkeydown` (Web) names a script to run when a user presses and holds down a key over the ordered list.
- `onkeypress` (Web) names a script to run when a user presses and releases a key over the ordered list.
- `onkeyup` (Web) names a script to run when a user releases a key that is currently held down over the ordered list.
- ☺ `onlayoutcomplete` (Web) names a script to run when a user lays out a selection using Print or Print Preview.
- ☺ `onlosecapture` (Web) names a script to run when a user releases a selection that has been captured by the mouse.
- `onmousedown` (Web) names a script to run when a user moves the mouse pointer or other pointing device over the ordered list and presses and holds down the button.
- ☺ `onmouseenter` (Web) names a script to run when a user moves the mouse pointer onto the object.
- ☺ `onmouseleave` (Web) names a script to run when the mouse pointer leaves the object.
- `onmousemove` (Web) names a script to run when a user moves the mouse pointer or other pointing device over the ordered list.
- `onmouseout` (Web) names a script to run when a user moves the mouse pointer or other pointing device away from the ordered list.
- `onmouseover` (Web) names a script to run the first time a user moves the mouse pointer or other pointing device over the ordered list.
- `onmouseup` (Web) names a script to run when a user moves the mouse pointer or other pointing device over the ordered list and releases a mouse button that is currently held down.
- ☺ `onpaste` (Web) names a script to run when a user pastes the Clipboard contents onto the object.
- ☺ `onpropertychange` (Web) names a script to run when a property changes on the selected object in any way.
- ☺ `onreadystatechange` (Web) names a script to run when the status of an element has changed (for example, the element receives data).
- ☺ `onresize` (Web) names a script to run when a user resizes the selected object.
- ☺ `onresizeend` (Web) names a script to run after the object has been resized.
- ☺ `onresizestart` (Web) names a script to run as a user resizes the object.
- ☺ `onselectstart` (Web) names a script to run when a user starts selecting an object.
- `start` (Web) sets a numeric starting value for the current ordered list. This attribute is deprecated; consider using a style sheet instead.
- `style` (Web) sets styles for the ordered list.
- ☺ `tabindex` (Web) defines the position of the current element in all the elements that a user can navigate to using a Tab or Shift + Tab key.
- `title` (Web) provides a title for the ordered list.

- `type` (Web) sets a number format for an ordered list. This attribute is deprecated; consider using a style sheet instead.
- *ordered-list-items* represents one or more `li` items.

Notes

- This block-level element originated in HTML 2.0.
- Not all browsers recognize the `compact` attribute. `compact` has been deprecated (that is, it will eventually be obsolete) and appears only in the Transitional DTD — not in the Strict DTD.
- If you nest ordered lists, it's a good idea to indent each level of lists in the XHTML document to make it easier for you to ensure that each of the start and end elements are on the same level. However, you are not required to indent elements for various list levels.
- If you nest ordered lists, number types do not change automatically. To do so, use the `type` attribute. (See the example on page 548.)
- To continue numbering from a previous list, set the `value` attribute for the current list to the next higher number.
- `li` elements are embedded within `ol` elements.
- Typically, the `ul` and `ol` elements are followed by white space, just like paragraphs, but list items are only separated by line breaks.
- For the `ol` element, WebTV supports the `start` and `type` attributes.

Related Elements

dir (104), menu (212), ul (331)

For More Information

Learn more about the `ol` element on page 543 in Chapter 3.

---

optgroup   Option Group

Purpose

Groups and formats one or more options in a form.

Syntax

```
<optgroup label="label_name"
  [ accesskey="shortcut_key" ]
  [ class="class_name" ][ dir="ltr"|"rtl" ]
  [ disabled="disabled" ][ id="id_name" ]
  [ lang="lang_code" ][ onclick="cl_script" ]
  [ ondblclick="dc_script" ][ onkeydown="kd_script" ]
  [ onkeypress="kp_script" ][ onkeyup="ku_script" ]
  [ onmousedown="md_script" ][ onmousemove="mm_script" ]
  [ onmouseout="mo_script" ][ onmouseover="mov_script" ]
  [ onmouseup="mu_script" ][ style="name_1: value_1"
  [; "name_2: value_2" ][...; "name_n: value_n" ]]
  [ title="title" ]option-group-content</optgroup>
```

Where

- `label` (Web) labels the option group.
- `accesskey` (Web) assigns a shortcut key to the element in order to focus on it.
- `dir` (Web) specifies the direction in which the selection list text is displayed: left-to-right or right-to-left.
- `disabled` (Web) prevents user input associated with the option group. `disabled` is unavailable for this element but may be available in a future XHTML version.
- `id` (Web) provides a unique identifier name for the option group.
- `lang` (Web) specifies the code representing the language used for the option group text.
- `onclick` (Web) names a script to run when a user moves the mouse pointer or other pointing device over the option group and clicks the device button.
- `ondblclick` (Web) names a script to run when a user moves the mouse pointer or other pointing device over the option group and double-clicks the device button.
- `onkeydown` (Web) names a script to run when a user presses and holds down a key over the option group.
- `onkeypress` (Web) names a script to run when a user presses and releases a key over the option group.
- `onkeyup` (Web) names a script to run when a user releases a key that is currently held down over the option group.
- `onmousedown` (Web) names a script to run when a user moves the mouse pointer or other pointing device over the option group and presses and holds down the device button.
- `onmousemove` (Web) names a script to run when a user moves the mouse pointer or other pointing device over the option group.
- `onmouseout` (Web) names a script to run when a user moves the mouse pointer or other pointing device away from the option group.
- `onmouseover` (Web) names a script to run the first time a user moves the mouse pointer or other pointing device over the option group.
- `onmouseup` (Web) names a script to run when a user moves the mouse pointer or other pointing device over the option group and releases a pressed-down device button.
- `style` (Web) sets styles for the option group.
- `title` (Web) provides a title for the option group.
- *option-group-content* is the content of the option group.

Notes

- `optgroup` is a child element of `select`.
- Use the `select`, `optgroup`, and `option` elements to create a menu in a form.
- Specify each `optgroup` element in a `select` element.
- For the current version of HTML, do not nest `optgroups`. This may change in the future.
- The `option` element is a child of the `optgroup` element.

Related Elements
button (72), fieldset (127), form (135), input (167), isindex (184), label (190), option (236), select (263), textarea (302)

option	**List Option**

Purpose
Inserts a single option in a list box or drop-down list.

Syntax

```
<option[ class="class_name"][ dir="ltr"|"rtl"]
  [ disabled="disabled"][ id="id_name"]
  [ label="label_name"][ lang="lang_code"]
  [ language="javascript"|"jscript"|"vbs[cript]"]
  [ onbeforecopy="bc_script"]
  [ onbeforecut="bt_script"]
  [ onbeforefocusenter="bfe_script"]
  [ onbeforefocusleave="bfl_script"]
  [ onbeforepaste="bp_script"][ onblur="bl_script"]
  [ onclick="cl_script"][ oncontextmenu="cm_script"]
  [ oncontrolselect="ctl_script"][ oncopy="cp_script"]
  [ oncut="ct_script"][ ondblclick="dc_script"]
  [ ondrag="d_script"][ ondragend="dd_script"]
  [ ondragenter="de_script"][ ondragleave="dl_script"]
  [ ondragover="do_script"][ ondragstart="ds_script"]
  [ ondrop="dr_script"][ onfocus="fc_script"]
  [ onfocusenter="fe_script"]
  [ onfocusleave="fl_script"]
  [ onhelp="hlp_script"][ onkeydown="kd_script"]
  [ onkeypress="kp_script"][ onkeyup="ku_script"]
  [ onlayoutcomplete="la_script"]
  [ onlosecapture="lc_script"]
  [ onmousedown="md_script"][ onmousemove="mm_script"]
  [ onmouseout="mo_script"][ onmouseover="mov_script"]
  [ onmouseup="mu_script"]
  [ onpropertychange="pc_script"]
  [ onreadystatechange="rsc_script"]
  [ onselectstart="ss_script"]
  [ selected="selected"][ style="name_1: value_1"
  [; name_2: value_2"][...; name_n: value_n"]]
```

```
[ title="title"][ value="submitted_value"]>
text[</option>]
```

Where

- `class` (Web) specifies a class identification for the option.
- `dir` (Web) specifies the direction in which the option text is displayed: left-to-right or right-to-left.
- `disabled` (Web) prevents user input associated with the option. `disabled` is unavailable for this element but may be available in a future XHTML version.
- `id` (Web) provides a unique identifier name for the option.
- `label` (Web) labels the option.
- `lang` (Web) specifies the code representing the language used for the option text.
- ⊖ `language` (Web) declares the scripting language of the current script.
- `onclick` (Web) names a script to run when a user moves the mouse pointer or other pointing device over the option and clicks the device button.
- `ondblclick` (Web) names a script to run when a user moves the mouse pointer or other pointing device over the option and double-clicks the device button.
- `onkeydown` (Web) names a script to run when a user presses and holds down a key over the option.
- `onkeypress` (Web) names a script to run when a user presses and releases a key over the option.
- `onkeyup` (Web) names a script to run when a user releases a key that is currently held down over the option.
- ⊖ `onlayoutcomplete` (Web) names a script to run when a user lays out a selection using Print or Print Preview.
- ⊖ `onlosecapture` (Web) names a script to run when a user releases a selection that has been captured by the mouse.
- `onmousedown` (Web) names a script to run when a user moves the mouse pointer or other pointing device over the option and presses and holds down the device button.
- `onmousemove` (Web) names a script to run when a user moves the mouse pointer or other pointing device over the option.
- `onmouseout` (Web) names a script to run when a user moves the mouse pointer or other pointing device away from the option.
- `onmouseover` (Web) names a script to run the first time a user moves the mouse pointer or other pointing device over the option.
- `onmouseup` (Web) names a script to run when a user moves the mouse pointer or other pointing device over the option and releases a pressed-down device button.
- ⊖ `onpropertychange` (Web) names a script to run when a property changes on the selected object in any way.

- ☺ onreadystatechange (Web) names a script to run when the status of an element has changed (for example, the element receives data).
- ☺ onselectstart (Web) names a script to run when a user starts selecting an object.
- selected (Web) indicates that this option is highlighted when the menu opens and is the default.
- style (Web) sets styles for the option.
- title (Web) provides a title for the option.
- value (Web) specifies the submitted value for this option.
- *text* represents one or more words.

Notes

- This element originated in HTML 2.0.
- option is a child element of select and optgroup.
- Use the select, optgroup, and option elements to create a menu in a form.
- For the option element, WebTV supports the selected and value attributes.

Related Elements

button (72), fieldset (127), form (135), input (167), isindex (184), label (190), legend (195), optgroup (234), select (263), textarea (302)

For More Information

Learn more about the option element on page 616 in Chapter 7.

p	Paragraph

Purpose

Marks the start and end of a paragraph.

Syntax

```
<p[ accesskey="shortcut_key"]
   [ align="left"|"center"|"right"|"justify"]
   [ class="class_name"]
   [ contenteditable="edit_string"][ dir="ltr"|"rtl"]
   [ disabled="disabled"][ id="id_name"]
   [ lang="lang_code"][ language="javascript"|"jscript"
   |"vbs[cript]"][ onbeforecopy="bc_script"]
   [ onbeforecut="bt_script"]
   [ onbeforefocusenter="bfe_script"]
   [ onbeforefocusleave="bfl_script"]
   [ onbeforepaste="bp_script"][ onblur="bl_script"]
   [ onclick="cl_script"][ oncontextmenu="cm_script"]
```

```
[ oncontrolselect="ctl_script"][ oncopy="cp_script"]
[ oncut="ct_script"][ ondblclick="dc_script"]
[ ondrag="d_script"][ ondragend="dd_script"]
[ ondragenter="de_script"][ ondragleave="dl_script"]
[ ondragover="do_script"][ ondragstart="ds_script"]
[ ondrop="dr_script"][ onfocus="fc_script"]
[ onfocusenter="fe_script"]
[ onfocusleave="fl_script"]
[ onhelp="hlp_script"][ onkeydown="kd_script"]
[ onkeypress="kp_script"][ onkeyup="ku_script"]
[ onlayoutcomplete="la_script"]
[ onlosecapture="lc_script"]
[ onmousedown="md_script"]
[ onmouseenter="me_script"]
[ onmouseleave="ml_script"]
[ onmousemove="mm_script"][ onmouseout="mo_script"]
[ onmouseover="mov_script"][ onmouseup="mu_script"]
[ onpaste="p_script"][ onpropertychange="pc_script"]
[ onreadystatechange="rsc_script"]
[ onresize="rsz_script"][ onresizeend="ree_script"]
[ onresizestart="res_script"]
[ onselectstart="ss_script"]
[ style="name_1: value_1"[; "name_2: value_2"]
[...; "name_n: value_n"]]
[ tabindex="position_number"][ title="title"]>
text</p>
```

Where

- ⊕ **accesskey** (Web) assigns a shortcut key to the object in order to focus on it.
- **align** (Web) horizontally aligns the contents of a section of text. This attribute is deprecated; use a style sheet instead.
- **class** (Web) specifies a class identification for the paragraph break.
- ⊕ **contenteditable** (Web) specifies or obtains a value that indicates whether a user can edit the element content.
- **dir** (Web) specifies the direction in which the selected paragraph text is displayed: left-to-right or right-to-left.
- ⊕ **disabled** (Web) is a keyword that prevents a user from using the element.
- **id** (Web) provides a unique identifier name for the paragraph break.
- **lang** (Web) specifies the code for the language used for the text in the paragraph after the break.
- ⊕ **language** (Web) declares the scripting language of the current script.

- onclick (Web) names a script to run when a user moves the mouse pointer or other pointing device over the paragraph break and clicks the button.
- ondblclick (Web) names a script to run when a user moves the mouse pointer or other pointing device over the paragraph break and double-clicks the button.
- ⊝ onhelp (Web) names a script to run when a user presses the F1 or Help key over the current element.
- onkeydown (Web) names a script to run when a user presses and holds down a key over the paragraph break.
- onkeypress (Web) names a script to run when a user presses and releases a key over the paragraph break.
- onkeyup (Web) names a script to run when a user releases a key that is currently held down over the paragraph break.
- onmousedown (Web) names a script to run when a user moves the mouse pointer or other pointing device over the paragraph break and presses and holds down the button.
- onmousemove (Web) names a script to run when a user moves the mouse pointer or other pointing device over the paragraph break.
- onmouseout (Web) names a script to run when a user moves the mouse pointer or other pointing device away from the paragraph break.
- onmouseover (Web) names a script to run the first time a user moves the mouse pointer or other pointing device over the paragraph break.
- onmouseup (Web) names a script to run when a user moves the mouse pointer or other pointing device over the paragraph break and releases a mouse button that is currently held down.
- ⊝ onselectstart (Web) names a script to run when a user starts selecting an object.
- style (Web) sets styles for the paragraph after the break.
- ⊝ tabindex (Web) defines the position of the current element in all the elements that a user can navigate to using a Tab or Shift + Tab key.
- title (Web) provides a title for the paragraph break.
- text represents one or more characters, words, and/or sentences to be separated from the preceding paragraph.

Notes

- This block-level element originated in HTML 2.0.
- The align attribute is an HTML 3.2 feature. align is deprecated; it appears only in the Transitional DTD — not in the Strict DTD.
- A paragraph ends with a line break followed by another line break.
- The p element is a container for a paragraph.
- If you have changed the alignment of the current paragraph, the </p> end tag will turn off that alignment and return to left alignment (the default).
- For the p element, WebTV supports the align, class, and style attributes.

Related Element
br (70)

For More Information
Learn how to use the p element on page 521 in Chapter 2.

param	Parameter

Purpose
Specifies parameters and run-time values in order to *render* (that is, produce) an object onscreen.

Syntax
```
<param name="parm_name" [ datafld="ds_col_name" ]
  [ dataformatas="html"|"text" ][ id="id_name" ]
  [ datasrc="ds_identifier" ]
  [ type="Internet_Media_Type" ][ value="parm_value" ]
  [ valuetype="data"|"ref"|"object" ]{ />|</param>}
```

Where
- name (Web) names a run-time parameter.
- ⊖ datafld (Web) specifies the column name from the file that contains the data source object.
- ⊖ dataformatas (Web) indicates whether the data for this element is formatted as plain text (that is, unformatted ASCII) or HTML.
- ⊖ datasrc (Web) specifies the identifier of the data source object.
- id (Web) provides a unique identifier name for the element.
- type (Web) specifies a valid Internet Media Type (that is, MIMETYPE) of the parameter.
- value (Web) provides a value for the parameter defined by the name attribute.
- valuetype (Web) specifies the type of the value attribute: data string or URI.

Notes
- This element originated in HTML 3.2.
- param is an empty element.
- The param element is a child element of the object and applet elements.
- It is preferable to use the param element instead of using both the data and classid attributes of the object element.
- For the param element, WebTV supports the name and value attributes.

Related Element
applet (37)

pre   Preformatted Text

Purpose

Applies a monospace font to, and maintains the character-and-space formatting of, one or more lines of preformatted text.

Syntax

```
<pre[ accesskey="shortcut_key"][ class="class_name"]
   [ cols="num_cols"][ contenteditable="edit_string"]
   [ dir="ltr"|"rtl"][ disabled="disabled"]
   [ id="id_name"][ lang="lang_code"]
   [ language="javascript"|"jscript"|"vbs[cript]"]
   [ onbeforecopy="bc_script"]
   [ onbeforecut="bt_script"]
   [ onbeforefocusenter="bfe_script"]
   [ onbeforefocusleave="bfl_script"]
   [ onbeforepaste="bp_script"][ onblur="bl_script"]
   [ onclick="cl_script"][ oncontextmenu="cm_script"]
   [ oncontrolselect="ctl_script"][ oncopy="cp_script"]
   [ oncut="ct_script"][ ondblclick="dc_script"]
   [ ondrag="d_script"][ ondragend="dd_script"]
   [ ondragenter="de_script"][ ondragleave="dl_script"]
   [ ondragover="do_script"][ ondragstart="ds_script"]
   [ ondrop="dr_script"][ onfocus="fc_script"]
   [ onfocusenter="fe_script"]
   [ onfocusleave="fl_script"][ onhelp="hlp_script"]
   [ onkeydown="kd_script"][ onkeypress="kp_script"]
   [ onkeyup="ku_script"][ onlosecapture="lc_script"]
   [ onmousedown="md_script"]
   [ onmouseenter="me_script"]
   [ onmouseleave="ml_script"]
   [ onmousemove="mm_script"][ onmouseout="mo_script"]
   [ onmouseover="mov_script"][ onmouseup="mu_script"]
   [ onpaste="p_script"][ onpropertychange="pc_script"]
   [ onreadystatechange="rsc_script"]
   [ onresize="rsz_script"][ onresizeend="ree_script"]
   [ onresizestart="res_script"]
   [ onselectstart="ss_script"]
   [ style="name_1: value_1"[; "name_2: value_2"]
   [...; "name_n: value_n"]]
   [ tabindex="position_number"][ title="title"]
   [ width="text_block_width"][ wrap ]>text</pre>
```

Where

- ⊖ `accesskey` (Web) assigns a shortcut key to the object in order to focus on it.
- `class` (Web) specifies a class identification for the preformatted text.
- Ⓝ `cols` (Web) specifies the number of columns in the preformatted text.
- ⊖ `contenteditable` (Web) specifies or obtains a value that indicates whether a user can edit the element content.
- `dir` (Web) specifies the direction in which the current text is displayed: left-to-right or right-to-left.
- ⊖ `disabled` (Web) is a keyword that prevents a user from using the element.
- `id` (Web) provides a unique identifier name for the preformatted text.
- `lang` (Web) specifies the code for the language used for the preformatted text.
- ⊖ `language` (Web) declares the scripting language of the current script.
- ⊖ `onbeforecopy` (Web) names a script to run when a user starts copying a selection to the Clipboard but before any action actually takes place.
- ⊖ `onbeforecut` (Web) names a script to run when a user starts cutting a selection to the Clipboard but before any action actually takes place.
- ⊖ `onbeforefocusenter` (Web) names a script to run when a user starts focusing on an object but before the object actually gains focus.
- ⊖ `onbeforefocusleave` (Web) names a script to run when a user starts leaving an object but before the object actually loses focus.
- ⊖ `onbeforepaste` (Web) names a script to run when a user starts pasting an object but before any action actually takes place.
- ⊖ `onblur` (Web) names a script to run when the object loses focus (that is, it is no longer the active element).
- `onclick` (Web) names a script to run when a user moves the mouse pointer or other pointing device over the preformatted text and clicks the button.
- ⊖ `oncontextmenu` (Web) names a script to run when a user right-clicks the mouse to open a shortcut menu.
- ⊖ `oncontrolselect` (Web) names a script to run when a user selects a control.
- ⊖ `oncopy` (Web) names a script to run when a user copies a selection to the Clipboard.
- ⊖ `oncut` (Web) names a script to run when a user cuts a selection to the Clipboard.
- `ondblclick` (Web) names a script to run when a user moves the mouse pointer or other pointing device over the preformatted text and double-clicks the button.
- ⊖ `ondrag` (Web) names a script to run when a user drags a selection.
- ⊖ `ondragend` (Web) names a script to run after a user completes a drag-and-drop operation.

- ⊖ `ondragenter` (Web) names a script to run when a user drags a selection into an area in which it can be dropped.
- ⊖ `ondragleave` (Web) names a script to run when a user drags a selection beyond an area in which it can be dropped.
- ⊖ `ondragover` (Web) names a script to run when a user drags a selection over an area in which it can be dropped.
- ⊖ `ondragstart` (Web) names a script to run when a user starts dragging a selection or element.
- ⊖ `ondrop` (Web) names a script to run when a user releases the mouse button to drop a dragged selection.
- ⊖ `onfocus` (Web) names a script to run when a user points the mouse pointer or other pointing device to focus on the current element.
- ⊖ `onfocusenter` (Web) names a script to run when a user focuses on the current element in any way.
- ⊖ `onfocusleave` (Web) names a script to run when a user inactivates the current element in any way.
- ⊖ `onhelp` (Web) names a script to run when a user presses the F1 or Help key over the current element.
- `onkeydown` (Web) names a script to run when a user presses and holds down a key over the preformatted text.
- `onkeypress` (Web) names a script to run when a user presses and releases a key over the preformatted text.
- `onkeyup` (Web) names a script to run when a user releases a key that is currently held down over the preformatted text.
- ⊖ `onlosecapture` (Web) names a script to run when a user releases a selection that has been captured by the mouse.
- `onmousedown` (Web) names a script to run when a user moves the mouse pointer or other pointing device over the preformatted text and presses and holds down the button.
- ⊖ `onmouseenter` (Web) names a script to run when a user moves the mouse pointer onto the object.
- ⊖ `onmouseleave` (Web) names a script to run when the mouse pointer leaves the object.
- `onmousemove` (Web) names a script to run when a user moves the mouse pointer or other pointing device over the preformatted text.
- `onmouseout` (Web) names a script to run when a user moves the mouse pointer or other pointing device away from the preformatted text.
- `onmouseover` (Web) names a script to run the first time a user moves the mouse pointer or other pointing device over the preformatted text.
- `onmouseup` (Web) names a script to run when a user moves the mouse pointer or other pointing device over the preformatted text and releases a mouse button that is currently held down.
- ⊖ `onpaste` (Web) names a script to run when a user pastes the Clipboard contents onto the object.
- ⊖ `onpropertychange` (Web) names a script to run when a property changes on the selected object in any way.

- ⊖ onreadystatechange (Web) names a script to run when the status of an element has changed (for example, the element receives data).
- ⊖ onresize (Web) names a script to run when a user resizes the selected object.
- ⊖ onresizeend (Web) names a script to run after the object has been resized.
- ⊖ onresizestart (Web) names a script to run as a user resizes the object.
- ⊖ onselectstart (Web) names a script to run when a user starts selecting an object.
- style (Web) sets styles for the preformatted text.
- ⊖ tabindex (Web) defines the position of the current element in all the elements that a user can navigate to using a Tab or Shift + Tab key.
- title (Web) provides a title for the preformatted text.
- width (Web) sets a maximum line width for the preformatted text. This attribute is deprecated; use a style sheet instead.
- Ⓝ wrap (Web) is a keyword that indicates that the preformatted text wraps within the browser window.
- *text* represents one or more characters.

Notes

- This block-level element originated in HTML 2.0.
- Each instance of <pre> and </pre> causes a new paragraph.
- pre shows preformatted characters and spaces as typed.
- In XHTML, a pre element cannot contain nested big, img, object, small, sub, or sup elements.
- The width attribute is not accepted by all browsers. In fact, it is deprecated; it appears only in the Transitional DTD — not in the Strict DTD. Use style sheets to lay out documents.
- pre does not override text direction (the dir attribute).
- Do not use tabs within preformatted text — especially if you plan to use tabs in other parts of the document. The unwanted result may be clashing tab positions.
- Many browsers use the same font for the following elements: code, kbd, pre, samp, and tt.
- For the pre element, WebTV supports the class and style attributes.

Related Elements

acronym (31), b (46), cite (83), code (87), dfn (106), em (120), i (154), kbd (186), s (254), samp (258), strike (254), strong (276), tt (324), u (327), var (335)

| **q** | **Inline Quote** |

Purpose
Formats a short inline quotation.

Syntax

```
<q[ accesskey="shortcut_key"][ cite="uri"]
  [ class="class_name"]
  [ contenteditable="edit_string"][ dir="ltr"|"rtl"]
  [ disabled="disabled"][ id="id_name"]
  [ lang="lang_code"][ language="javascript"|"jscript"
  |"vbs[cript]"][ onbeforefocusenter="bfe_script"]
  [ onbeforefocusleave="bfl_script"]
  [ onblur="bl_script"][ onclick="cl_script"]
  [ oncontrolselect="ctl_script"]
  [ ondblclick="dc_script"][ ondrag="d_script"]
  [ ondragend="dd_script"][ ondragenter="de_script"]
  [ ondragleave="dl_script"][ ondragover="do_script"]
  [ ondragstart="ds_script"][ ondrop="dr_script"]
  [ onfocus="fc_script"][ onfocusenter="fe_script"]
  [ onfocusleave="fl_script"][ onkeydown="kd_script"]
  [ onkeypress="kp_script"][ onkeyup="ku_script"]
  [ onmousedown="md_script"]
  [ onmousemove="mm_script"][ onmouseout="mo_script"]
  [ onmouseover="mov_script"][ onmouseup="mu_script"]
  [ onreadystatechange="rsc_script"]
  [ onresizeend="ree_script"]
  [ onresizestart="res_script"]
  [ onselectstart="ss_script"]
  [ style="name_1: value_1"[; "name_2: value_2"]
  [...; "name_n: value_n"]]
  [ tabindex="position_number"][ title="title"]>
  text</q>
```

Where
- $\ominus$ accesskey (Web) assigns a shortcut key to the object in order to focus on it.
- cite (Web) provides a URI for a document or message that contains information about a quote.
- class (Web) specifies a class identification for the quote.
- $\ominus$ contenteditable (Web) specifies or obtains a value that indicates whether a user can edit the element content.
- dir (Web) specifies the direction in which the quote is displayed: left-to-right or right-to-left.

- ⊝ `disabled` (Web) is a keyword that prevents a user from using the element.
- `id` (Web) provides a unique identifier name for the quote.
- `lang` (Web) specifies the code for the language used for the quote.
- ⊝ `language` (Web) declares the scripting language of the current script.
- ⊝ `onbeforefocusenter` (Web) names a script to run when a user starts focusing on an object but before the object actually gains focus.
- ⊝ `onbeforefocusleave` (Web) names a script to run when a user starts leaving an object but before the object actually loses focus.
- ⊝ `onblur` (Web) names a script to run when the object loses focus (that is, it is no longer the active element).
- `onclick` (Web) names a script to run when a user moves the mouse pointer or other pointing device over the quote and clicks the button.
- ⊝ `oncontrolselect` (Web) names a script to run when a user selects a control.
- `ondblclick` (Web) names a script to run when a user moves the mouse pointer or other pointing device over the quote and double-clicks the button.
- ⊝ `ondrag` (Web) names a script to run when a user drags a selection.
- ⊝ `ondragend` (Web) names a script to run after a user completes a drag-and-drop operation.
- ⊝ `ondragenter` (Web) names a script to run when a user drags a selection into an area in which it can be dropped.
- ⊝ `ondragleave` (Web) names a script to run when a user drags a selection beyond an area in which it can be dropped.
- ⊝ `ondragover` (Web) names a script to run when a user drags a selection over an area in which it can be dropped.
- ⊝ `ondragstart` (Web) names a script to run when a user starts dragging a selection or element.
- ⊝ `ondrop` (Web) names a script to run when a user releases the mouse button to drop a dragged selection.
- ⊝ `onfocus` (Web) names a script to run when a user points the mouse pointer or other pointing device to focus on the current element.
- ⊝ `onfocusenter` (Web) names a script to run when a user focuses on the current element in any way.
- ⊝ `onfocusleave` (Web) names a script to run when a user inactivates the current element in any way.
- `onkeydown` (Web) names a script to run when a user presses and holds down a key over the quote.
- `onkeypress` (Web) names a script to run when a user presses and releases a key over the quote.
- `onkeyup` (Web) names a script to run when a user releases a key that is currently held down over the quote.
- `onmousedown` (Web) names a script to run when a user moves the mouse pointer or other pointing device over the quote and presses and holds down the button.

- onmousemove (Web) names a script to run when a user moves the mouse pointer or other pointing device over the quote.
- onmouseout (Web) names a script to run when a user moves the mouse pointer or other pointing device away from the quote.
- onmouseover (Web) names a script to run the first time a user moves the mouse pointer or other pointing device over the quote.
- onmouseup (Web) names a script to run when a user moves the mouse pointer or other pointing device over the quote and releases a mouse button that is currently held down.
- ⊝ onreadystatechange (Web) names a script to run when the status of an element has changed (for example, the element receives data).
- ⊝ onresizeend (Web) names a script to run after the object has been resized.
- ⊝ onresizestart (Web) names a script to run as a user resizes the object.
- ⊝ onselectstart (Web) names a script to run when a user starts selecting an object.
- style (Web) sets styles for the quote.
- ⊝ tabindex (Web) defines the position of the current element in all the elements that a user can navigate to using a Tab or Shift + Tab key.
- title (Web) provides a title for the quote.
- *text* represents one or more characters.

Notes

This inline element originated in HTML 4.0.

Related Elements

bdo (52), br (70), code (87), kbd (186), pre (242), samp (258), span (272), sub (281), sup (284), tt (324)

⊝ rt   Ruby Text

Purpose

Specifies annotation or pronunciation text, known as ruby text.

Syntax

```
<rt[ accesskey="shortcut_key"][ class="class_name"]
  [ contenteditable="edit_string"][ dir="ltr"|"rtl"]
  [ disabled="disabled"][ id="id_name"]
  [ lang="lang_code"][ language="javascript"|"jscript"
  |"vbs[cript]"][ name=" object_name"]
  [ onafterupdate="au_script"]
  [ onbeforecut="bt_script"]
```

```
[ onbeforefocusenter="bfe_script"]
[ onbeforefocusleave="bfl_script"]
[ onbeforepaste="bp_script"]
[ onbeforeupdate="bu_script"][ onblur="bl_script"]
[ onclick="cl_script"][ oncontextmenu="cm_script"]
[ oncontrolselect="ctl_script"][ oncut="ct_script"]
[ ondblclick="dc_script"][ ondragstart="ds_script"]
[ onerrorupdate="eu_script"]
[ onfilterchange="f_script"][ onfocus="fc_script"]
[ onfocusenter="fe_script"]
[ onfocusleave="fl_script"][ onhelp="hlp_script"]
[ onkeydown="kd_script"][ onkeypress="kp_script"]
[ onkeyup="ku_script"][ onmousedown="md_script"]
[ onmouseenter="me_script"]
[ onmouseleave="ml_script"] onmousemove="mm_script"]
[ onmouseout="mo_script"][ onmouseover="mov_script"]
[ onmouseup="mu_script"][ onpaste="p_script"]
[ onreadystatechange="rsc_script"]
[ onresizeend="ree_script"]
[ onresizestart="res_script"]
[ onselectstart="ss_script"]
[ style="name_1: value_1"[; name_2: value_2"]
[...; name_n: value_n"]]]
[ tabindex="position_number"][ title="title"]>
ruby-text</rt>
```

Where

- Ⓔ accesskey (Web) assigns a shortcut key to the element in order to focus on it.
- Ⓔ class (Web) specifies a class identification for the ruby text.
- Ⓔ contenteditable (Web) specifies or obtains a value that indicates whether a user can edit the element content.
- Ⓔ dir (Web) specifies the direction in which the ruby text is displayed: left-to-right or right-to-left.
- Ⓔ disabled (Web) is a keyword that prevents a user from using the element.
- Ⓔ id (Web) provides a unique identifier name for the ruby text.
- Ⓔ lang (Web) specifies the code for the language used for the ruby text.
- Ⓔ language (Web) declares the scripting language of the current script.
- Ⓔ name (Web) is the unique name of the ruby-text object.
- Ⓔ onafterupdate (Web) names a script to run after data has been transferred from the element to the data resource.
- Ⓔ onbeforecut (Web) names a script to run when a user starts cutting a selection to the Clipboard but before any action actually takes place.

- ⊕ onbeforefocusenter (Web) names a script to run when a user starts focusing on an object but before the object actually gains focus.
- ⊕ onbeforefocusleave (Web) names a script to run when a user starts leaving an object but before the object actually loses focus.
- ⊕ onbeforepaste (Web) names a script to run when a user starts pasting an object but before any action actually takes place.
- ⊕ onbeforeupdate (Web) names a script to run before data is transferred from the element to the data resource.
- ⊕ onblur (Web) names a script to run when the ruby text loses focus (that is, it is no longer the active element).
- ⊕ onclick (Web) names a script to run when a user moves the mouse pointer or other pointing device over the ruby text and clicks the button.
- ⊕ oncontextmenu (Web) names a script to run when a user right-clicks the mouse to open a shortcut menu.
- ⊕ oncontrolselect (Web) names a script to run when a user selects a control.
- ⊕ oncut (Web) names a script to run when a user cuts a selection to the Clipboard.
- ⊕ ondblclick (Web) names a script to run when a user moves the mouse pointer or other pointing device over the ruby text and double-clicks the button.
- ⊕ ondragstart (Web) names a script to run when a user starts dragging a selection or element.
- ⊕ onerrorupdate (Web) names a script to run when an error occurs while data is updated in the data resource.
- ⊕ onfilterchange (Web) names a script to run when a visual filter changes in any way.
- ⊕ onfocus (Web) names a script to run when a user points the mouse pointer or other pointing device to focus on the current element.
- ⊕ onfocusenter (Web) names a script to run when a user focuses on the current element in any way.
- ⊕ onfocusleave (Web) names a script to run when a user inactivates the current element in any way.
- ⊕ onhelp (Web) names a script to run when a user presses the F1 or Help key over the current element.
- ⊕ onkeydown (Web) names a script to run when a user presses and holds down a key over the ruby text.
- ⊕ onkeypress (Web) names a script to run when a user presses and releases a key over the ruby text.
- ⊕ onkeyup (Web) names a script to run when a user releases a key that is currently held down over the ruby text.
- ⊕ onmousedown (Web) names a script to run when a user moves the mouse pointer or other pointing device over the ruby text and presses and holds down the button.
- ⊕ onmouseenter (Web) names a script to run when a user moves the mouse pointer onto the object.

- Ⓔ onmouseleave (Web) names a script to run when the mouse pointer leaves the object.
- Ⓔ onmousemove (Web) names a script to run when a user moves the mouse pointer or other pointing device over the ruby text.
- Ⓔ onmouseout (Web) names a script to run when a user moves the mouse pointer or other pointing device away from the ruby text.
- Ⓔ onmouseover (Web) names a script to run the first time a user moves the mouse pointer or other pointing device over the ruby text.
- Ⓔ onmouseup (Web) names a script to run when a user moves the mouse pointer or other pointing device over the ruby text and releases a mouse button that is currently held down.
- Ⓔ onpaste (Web) names a script to run when a user pastes the Clipboard contents onto the object.
- Ⓔ onreadystatechange (Web) names a script to run when the status of an element has changed (for example, the element receives data).
- Ⓔ onresizeend (Web) names a script to run after the object has been resized.
- Ⓔ onresizestart (Web) names a script to run as a user resizes the object.
- Ⓔ onselectstart (Web) names a script to run when a user starts selecting an object.
- Ⓔ style (Web) sets styles for the ruby text.
- Ⓔ tabindex (Web) defines the position of the current element in all the elements that a user can navigate to using a Tab or Shift + Tab key.
- Ⓔ title (Web) provides a title for the ruby text.
- *ruby-text* is the text on which the ruby element is applied.

Notes
- rt is an inline element.
- rt is a child of the ruby element. rt and its contents are the only valid object within ruby.
- rt and ruby are supported by Internet Explorer 5.0 (and greater).

Related Element
ruby (251)

Ⓔ **ruby**   **Ruby Text Interpretation**

Purpose
Specifies the location and identity of annotation or pronunciation ruby text.

Syntax
```
<ruby[ accesskey="shortcut_key"][ class="class_name"]
   [ contenteditable="edit_string"][ dir="ltr"|"rtl"]
   [ disabled="disabled"][ id="id_name"]
   [ lang="lang_code"][ language="javascript"|"jscript"
```

XHTML Syntax

```
|"vbs[cript]"][ name=" object_name"]
[ onafterupdate="au_script"]
[ onbeforecut="bt_script"]
[ onbeforefocusenter="bfe_script"]
[ onbeforefocusleave="bfl_script"]
[ onbeforepaste="bp_script"]
[ onbeforeupdate="bu_script"][ onblur="bl_script"]
[ onclick="cl_script"][ oncontextmenu="cm_script"]
[ oncontrolselect="ctl_script"][ oncut="ct_script"]
[ ondblclick="dc_script"][ ondragstart="ds_script"]
[ onerrorupdate="eu_script"]
[ onfilterchange="f_script"][ onfocus="fc_script"]
[ onfocusenter="fe_script"]
[ onfocusleave="fl_script"][ onhelp="hlp_script"]
[ onkeydown="kd_script"][ onkeypress="kp_script"]
[ onkeyup="ku_script"][ onmousedown="md_script"]
[ onmouseenter="me_script"]
[ onmouseleave="ml_script"] onmousemove="mm_script"]
[ onmouseout="mo_script"][ onmouseover="mov_script"]
[ onmouseup="mu_script"][ onpaste="p_script"]
[ onreadystatechange="rsc_script"]
[ onresizeend="ree_script"]
[ onresizestart="res_script"]
[ onselectstart="ss_script"]
[ style="name_1: value_1"[; name_2: value_2"]
[...; name_n: value_n"]]]
[ tabindex="position_number"][ title="title"]>
rt-contents</ruby>
```

Where

- ⊖ **accesskey** (Web) assigns a shortcut key to the element in order to focus on it.
- ⊖ **class** (Web) specifies a class identification for the ruby text.
- ⊖ **contenteditable** (Web) specifies or obtains a value that indicates whether a user can edit the element content.
- ⊖ **dir** (Web) specifies the direction in which the ruby text is displayed: left-to-right or right-to-left.
- ⊖ **disabled** (Web) is a keyword that prevents a user from using the element.
- ⊖ **id** (Web) provides a unique identifier name for the ruby text.
- ⊖ **lang** (Web) specifies the code for the language used for the ruby text.
- ⊖ **language** (Web) declares the scripting language of the current script.
- ⊖ **name** (Web) is the unique name of the ruby-text object.
- ⊖ **onafterupdate** (Web) names a script to run after data has been transferred from the element to the data resource.

- ⊖ onbeforecut (Web) names a script to run when a user starts cutting a selection to the Clipboard but before any action actually takes place.
- ⊖ onbeforefocusenter (Web) names a script to run when a user starts focusing on an object but before the object actually gains focus.
- ⊖ onbeforefocusleave (Web) names a script to run when a user starts leaving an object but before the object actually loses focus.
- ⊖ onbeforepaste (Web) names a script to run when a user starts pasting an object but before any action actually takes place.
- ⊖ onbeforeupdate (Web) names a script to run before data is transferred from the element to the data resource.
- ⊖ onblur (Web) names a script to run when the element loses focus (that is, it is no longer the active element).
- ⊖ onclick (Web) names a script to run when a user moves the mouse pointer or other pointing device over the element and clicks the button.
- ⊖ oncontextmenu (Web) names a script to run when a user right-clicks the mouse to open a shortcut menu.
- ⊖ oncontrolselect (Web) names a script to run when a user selects a control.
- ⊖ oncut (Web) names a script to run when a user cuts a selection to the Clipboard.
- ⊖ ondblclick (Web) names a script to run when a user moves the mouse pointer or other pointing device over the element and double-clicks the button.
- ⊖ ondragstart (Web) names a script to run when a user starts dragging a selection or element.
- ⊖ onerrorupdate (Web) names a script to run when an error happens while data is updated in the data resource.
- ⊖ onfilterchange (Web) names a script to run when a visual filter changes in any way.
- ⊖ onfocus (Web) names a script to run when a user points the mouse pointer or other pointing device to focus on the current element.
- ⊖ onfocusenter (Web) names a script to run when a user focuses on the current element in any way.
- ⊖ onfocusleave (Web) names a script to run when a user inactivates the current element in any way.
- ⊖ onhelp (Web) names a script to run when a user presses the F1 or Help key over the current element.
- ⊖ onkeydown (Web) names a script to run when a user presses and holds down a key over the element.
- ⊖ onkeypress (Web) names a script to run when a user presses and releases a key over the element.
- ⊖ onkeyup (Web) names a script to run when a user releases a key that is currently held down over the element.
- ⊖ onmousedown (Web) names a script to run when a user moves the mouse pointer or other pointing device over the element and presses and holds down the button.

- ⊖ onmouseenter (Web) names a script to run when a user moves the mouse pointer onto the object.
- ⊖ onmouseleave (Web) names a script to run when the mouse pointer leaves the object.
- ⊖ onmousemove (Web) names a script to run when a user moves the mouse pointer or other pointing device over the element.
- ⊖ onmouseout (Web) names a script to run when a user moves the mouse pointer or other pointing device away from the element.
- ⊖ onmouseover (Web) names a script to run the first time a user moves the mouse pointer or other pointing device over the element.
- ⊖ onmouseup (Web) names a script to run when a user moves the mouse pointer or other pointing device over the element and releases a mouse button that is currently held down.
- ⊖ onpaste (Web) names a script to run when a user pastes the Clipboard contents onto the object.
- ⊖ onreadystatechange (Web) names a script to run when the status of an element has changed (for example, the element receives data).
- ⊖ onresizeend (Web) names a script to run after the object has been resized.
- ⊖ onresizestart (Web) names a script to run as a user resizes the object.
- ⊖ onselectstart (Web) names a script to run when a user starts selecting an object.
- ⊖ style (Web) sets styles for the element.
- ⊖ tabindex (Web) defines the position of the current element in all the elements that a user can navigate to using a Tab or Shift + Tab key.
- ⊖ title (Web) provides a title for the element.
- *rt-contents* is the rt element and its contents.

Notes

- ruby is an inline element.
- rt is a child of the ruby element. rt (and its contents) is the only valid object within ruby.
- rt and ruby are supported by Internet Explorer 5.0 (and greater).
- For more information about ruby, go to http://www.w3.org/TR/ruby.

Related Element

rt (248)

---

s|strike   Strikethrough

Purpose

Strikes through selected text.

Syntax

```
<s|strike[ accesskey="shortcut_key"]
  [ class="class_name"]
  [ contenteditable="edit_string"][ dir="ltr"|"rtl"]
  [ disabled="disabled"][ id="id_name"]
  [ lang="lang_code"][ language="javascript"|"jscript"
  |"vbs[cript]"][ onbeforecopy="bc_script"]
  [ onbeforecut="bt_script"]
  [ onbeforefocusenter="bfe_script"]
  [ onbeforefocusleave="bfl_script"]
  [ onbeforepaste="bp_script"][ onblur="bl_script"]
  [ onclick="cl_script"][ oncontextmenu="cm_script"]
  [ oncontrolselect="ctl_script"][ oncopy="cp_script"]
  [ oncut="ct_script"][ ondblclick="dc_script"]
  [ ondrag="d_script"][ ondragend="dd_script"]
  [ ondragenter="de_script"][ ondragleave="dl_script"]
  [ ondragover="do_script"][ ondragstart="ds_script"]
  [ ondrop="dr_script"][ onfocus="fc_script"]
  [ onfocusenter="fe_script"]
  [ onfocusleave="fl_script"][ onhelp="hlp_script"]
  [ onkeydown="kd_script"][ onkeypress="kp_script"]
  [ onkeyup="ku_script"][ onlosecapture="lc_script"]
  [ onmousedown="md_script"]
  [ onmouseenter="me_script"]
  [ onmouseleave="ml_script"]
  [ onmousemove="mm_script"][ onmouseout="mo_script"]
  [ onmouseover="mov_script"][ onmouseup="mu_script"]
  [ onpaste="p_script"][ onpropertychange="pc_script"]
  [ onreadystatechange="rsc_script"]
  [ onresize="rsz_script"][ onresizeend="ree_script"]
  [ onresizestart="res_script"]
  [ onselectstart="ss_script"]
  [ style="name_1: value_1"[; "name_2: value_2"]
  [...; "name_n: value_n"]]
  [ tabindex="position_number"][ title="title"]>
text</s|strike>
```

Where

- $\oplus$ **accesskey** (Web) assigns a shortcut key to the object in order to focus on it.
- **class** (Web) specifies a class identification for the strikethrough text.
- $\oplus$ **contenteditable** (Web) specifies or obtains a value that indicates whether a user can edit the element content.

- dir (Web) specifies the direction in which the strikethrough text is displayed: left-to-right or right-to-left.
- ⊜ disabled (Web) is a keyword that prevents a user from using the element.
- id (Web) provides a unique identifier name for the strikethrough text.
- lang (Web) specifies the code for the language used for the strikethrough text.
- ⊜ language (Web) declares the scripting language of the current script.
- ⊜ onbeforecopy (Web) names a script to run when a user starts copying a selection to the Clipboard but before any action actually takes place.
- ⊜ onbeforecut (Web) names a script to run when a user starts cutting a selection to the Clipboard but before any action actually takes place.
- ⊜ onbeforefocusenter (Web) names a script to run when a user starts focusing on an object but before the object actually gains focus.
- ⊜ onbeforefocusleave (Web) names a script to run when a user starts leaving an object but before the object actually loses focus.
- ⊜ onbeforepaste (Web) names a script to run when a user starts pasting an object but before any action actually takes place.
- ⊜ onblur (Web) names a script to run when the object loses focus (that is, it is no longer the active element).
- onclick (Web) names a script to run when a user moves the mouse pointer or other pointing device over the strikethrough text and clicks the button.
- ⊜ oncontextmenu (Web) names a script to run when a user right-clicks the mouse to open a shortcut menu.
- ⊜ oncontrolselect (Web) names a script to run when a user selects a control.
- ⊜ oncopy (Web) names a script to run when a user copies a selection to the Clipboard.
- ⊜ oncut (Web) names a script to run when a user cuts a selection to the Clipboard.
- ondblclick (Web) names a script to run when a user moves the mouse pointer or other pointing device over the strikethrough text and double-clicks the button.
- ⊜ ondrag (Web) names a script to run when a user drags a selection.
- ⊜ ondragend (Web) names a script to run after a user completes a drag-and-drop operation.
- ⊜ ondragenter (Web) names a script to run when a user drags a selection into an area in which it can be dropped.
- ⊜ ondragleave (Web) names a script to run when a user drags a selection beyond an area in which it can be dropped.
- ⊜ ondragover (Web) names a script to run when a user drags a selection over an area in which it can be dropped.
- ⊜ ondragstart (Web) names a script to run when a user starts dragging a selection or element.
- ⊜ ondrop (Web) names a script to run when a user releases the mouse button to drop a dragged selection.

- ⊖ onfocus (Web) names a script to run when a user points the mouse pointer or other pointing device to focus on the current element.
- ⊖ onfocusenter (Web) names a script to run when a user focuses on the current element in any way.
- ⊖ onfocusleave (Web) names a script to run when a user inactivates the current element in any way.
- ⊖ onhelp (Web) names a script to run when a user presses the F1 or Help key over the current element.
- onkeydown (Web) names a script to run when a user presses and holds down a key over the strikethrough text.
- onkeypress (Web) names a script to run when a user presses and releases a key over the strikethrough text.
- onkeyup (Web) names a script to run when a user releases a key that is currently held down over the strikethrough text.
- ⊖ onlosecapture (Web) names a script to run when a user releases a selection that has been captured by the mouse.
- onmousedown (Web) names a script to run when a user moves the mouse pointer or other pointing device over the strikethrough text and presses and holds down the button.
- ⊖ onmouseenter (Web) names a script to run when a user moves the mouse pointer onto the object.
- ⊖ onmouseleave (Web) names a script to run when the mouse pointer leaves the object.
- onmousemove (Web) names a script to run when a user moves the mouse pointer or other pointing device over the strikethrough text.
- onmouseout (Web) names a script to run when a user moves the mouse pointer or other pointing device away from the strikethrough text.
- onmouseover (Web) names a script to run the first time a user moves the mouse pointer or other pointing device over the strikethrough text.
- onmouseup (Web) names a script to run when a user moves the mouse pointer or other pointing device over the strikethrough text and releases a mouse button that is currently held down.
- ⊖ onpaste (Web) names a script to run when a user pastes the Clipboard contents onto the object.
- ⊖ onpropertychange (Web) names a script to run when a property changes on the selected object in any way.
- ⊖ onreadystatechange (Web) names a script to run when the status of an element has changed (for example, the element receives data).
- ⊖ onresize (Web) names a script to run when a user resizes the selected object.
- ⊖ onresizeend (Web) names a script to run after the object has been resized.
- ⊖ onresizestart (Web) names a script to run as a user resizes the object.
- ⊖ onselectstart (Web) names a script to run when a user starts selecting an object.
- style (Web) sets styles for the strikethrough text.

- ☺ `tabindex` (Web) defines the position of the current element in all the elements that a user can navigate to using a Tab or Shift + Tab key.
- `title` (Web) provides a title for the strikethrough text.
- *text* represents one or more characters.

Notes

- This inline element originated in HTML 2.0.
- s and `strike` are identical.
- Although s and `strike` are supported by HTML 4.0, they have been deprecated (that is, they will eventually be obsolete) and appear only in the Transitional DTD — not in the Strict DTD. Use style sheets to specify font attributes.
- s and `strike` are elements in the `%fontstyle` entity. The other `%fontstyle` elements are `big`, `i`, `small`, and `tt`. Another deprecated element in the `%fontstyle` entity is `U`.
- For the s and `strike` elements, WebTV supports the `class` and `style` attributes.

Related Elements

b (46), `big` (57), `em` (120), `font` (131), `i` (154), `small` (268), `strong` (276), `sub` (281), `sup` (284), `tt` (324), `u` (327)

---

samp	Sample Output

Purpose

Applies a sample program output (monospace) font to selected text.

Syntax

```
<samp[ accesskey="shortcut_key"][ class="class_name"]
   [ contenteditable="edit_string"]
   [ dir="ltr"|"rtl"][ disabled="disabled"]
   [ id="id_name"][ lang="lang_code"]
   [ language="javascript"|"jscript"|"vbs[cript]"]
   [ onbeforecopy="bc_script"]
   [ onbeforecut="bt_script"]
   [ onbeforefocusenter="bfe_script"]
   [ onbeforefocusleave="bfl_script"]
   [ onbeforepaste="bp_script"][ onclick="cl_script"]
   [ oncontextmenu="cm_script"]
   [ oncontrolselect="ctl_script"][ oncopy="cp_script"]
   [ oncut="ct_script"][ ondblclick="dc_script"]
   [ ondrag="d_script"][ ondragend="dd_script"]
   [ ondragenter="de_script"][ ondragleave="dl_script"]
```

XHTML Syntax

```
[ ondragover="do_script"][ ondragstart="ds_script"]
[ ondrop="dr_script"][ onfocus="fc_script"]
[ onfocusenter="fe_script"]
[ onfocusleave="fl_script"][ onhelp="hlp_script"]
[ onkeydown="kd_script"][ onkeypress="kp_script"]
[ onkeyup="ku_script"][ onlosecapture="lc_script"]
[ onmousedown="md_script"]
[ onmouseenter="me_script"]
[ onmouseleave="ml_script"]
[ onmousemove="mm_script"][ onmouseout="mo_script"]
[ onmouseover="mov_script"][ onmouseup="mu_script"]
[ onpaste="p_script"][ onpropertychange="pc_script"]
[ onreadystatechange="rsc_script"]
[ onresize="rsz_script"][ onresizeend="ree_script"]
[ onresizestart="res_script"]
[ onselectstart="ss_script"]
[ style="name_1: value_1"[; "name_2: value_2"]
[...; "name_n: value_n"]]
[ tabindex="position_number"][ title="title"]>
text</samp>
```

Where

- Ⓔ accesskey (Web) assigns a shortcut key to the object in order to focus on it.
- class (Web) specifies a class identification for the sample output.
- Ⓔ contenteditable (Web) specifies or obtains a value that indicates whether a user can edit the element content.
- dir (Web) specifies the direction in which the sample output text is displayed: left-to-right or right-to-left.
- Ⓔ disabled (Web) is a keyword that prevents a user from using the element.
- id (Web) provides a unique identifier name for the sample output.
- lang (Web) specifies the code for the language used for the sample output text.
- Ⓔ language (Web) declares the scripting language of the current script.
- Ⓔ onbeforecopy (Web) names a script to run when a user starts copying a selection to the Clipboard but before any action actually takes place.
- Ⓔ onbeforecut (Web) names a script to run when a user starts cutting a selection to the Clipboard but before any action actually takes place.
- Ⓔ onbeforefocusenter (Web) names a script to run when a user starts focusing on an object but before the object actually gains focus.
- Ⓔ onbeforefocusleave (Web) names a script to run when a user starts leaving an object but before the object actually loses focus.
- Ⓔ onbeforepaste (Web) names a script to run when a user starts pasting an object but before any action actually takes place.

- ⊖ `onblur` (Web) names a script to run when the object loses focus (that is, it is no longer the active element).
- `onclick` (Web) names a script to run when a user moves the mouse pointer or other pointing device over the sample output and clicks the button.
- ⊖ `oncontextmenu` (Web) names a script to run when a user right-clicks the mouse to open a shortcut menu.
- ⊖ `oncontrolselect` (Web) names a script to run when a user selects a control.
- ⊖ `oncopy` (Web) names a script to run when a user copies a selection to the Clipboard.
- ⊖ `oncut` (Web) names a script to run when a user cuts a selection to the Clipboard.
- `ondblclick` (Web) names a script to run when a user moves the mouse pointer or other pointing device over the sample output and double-clicks the button.
- ⊖ `ondrag` (Web) names a script to run when a user drags a selection.
- ⊖ `ondragend` (Web) names a script to run after a user completes a drag-and-drop operation.
- ⊖ `ondragenter` (Web) names a script to run when a user drags a selection into an area in which it can be dropped.
- ⊖ `ondragleave` (Web) names a script to run when a user drags a selection beyond an area in which it can be dropped.
- ⊖ `ondragover` (Web) names a script to run when a user drags a selection over an area in which it can be dropped.
- ⊖ `ondragstart` (Web) names a script to run when a user starts dragging a selection or element.
- ⊖ `ondrop` (Web) names a script to run when a user releases the mouse button to drop a dragged selection.
- ⊖ `onfocus` (Web) names a script to run when a user points the mouse pointer or other pointing device to focus on the current element.
- ⊖ `onfocusenter` (Web) names a script to run when a user focuses on the current element in any way.
- ⊖ `onfocusleave` (Web) names a script to run when a user inactivates the current element in any way.
- ⊖ `onhelp` (Web) names a script to run when a user presses the F1 or Help key over the current element.
- `onkeydown` (Web) names a script to run when a user presses and holds down a key over the sample output.
- `onkeypress` (Web) names a script to run when a user presses and releases a key over the sample output.
- `onkeyup` (Web) names a script to run when a user releases a key that is currently held down over the sample output.
- ⊖ `onlosecapture` (Web) names a script to run when a user releases a selection that has been captured by the mouse.

- `onmousedown` (Web) names a script to run when a user moves the mouse pointer or other pointing device over the sample output and presses and holds down the button.
- ⊖ `onmouseenter` (Web) names a script to run when a user moves the mouse pointer onto the object.
- ⊖ `onmouseleave` (Web) names a script to run when the mouse pointer leaves the object.
- `onmousemove` (Web) names a script to run when a user moves the mouse pointer or other pointing device over the sample output.
- `onmouseout` (Web) names a script to run when a user moves the mouse pointer or other pointing device away from the sample output.
- `onmouseover` (Web) names a script to run the first time a user moves the mouse pointer or other pointing device over the sample output.
- `onmouseup` (Web) names a script to run when a user moves the mouse pointer or other pointing device over the sample output and releases a mouse button that is currently held down.
- ⊖ `onpaste` (Web) names a script to run when a user pastes the Clipboard contents onto the object.
- ⊖ `onpropertychange` (Web) names a script to run when a property changes on the selected object in any way.
- ⊖ `onreadystatechange` (Web) names a script to run when the status of an element has changed (for example, the element receives data).
- ⊖ `onresize` (Web) names a script to run when a user resizes the selected object.
- ⊖ `onresizeend` (Web) names a script to run after the object has been resized.
- ⊖ `onresizestart` (Web) names a script to run as a user resizes the object.
- ⊖ `onselectstart` (Web) names a script to run when a user starts selecting an object.
- `style` (Web) sets styles for the sample output.
- ⊖ `tabindex` (Web) defines the position of the current element in all the elements that a user can navigate to using a Tab or Shift + Tab key.
- `title` (Web) provides a title for the sample output.
- *text* represents one or more characters.

Notes

- This inline element originated in HTML 2.0.
- `samp` is one of the elements in the `%phrase` entity. The other `%phrase` elements are `abbr`, `acronym`, `cite`, `code`, `dfn`, `em`, `kbd`, `strong`, and `var`.
- `samp` is a logical element, in which particular browsers are programmed to apply a certain style to the selected text. This is in contrast to a physical element in which you "code" the styles yourself.
- Many browsers use the same font for the following elements: `code`, `kbd`, `pre`, `samp`, and `tt`.
- To display two or more lines of preformatted text, use the `pre` element.

Related Elements

abbr (29), acronym (31), b (46), cite (83), code (87), dfn (101), em (120), kbd (186), pre (242), strong (276), tt (324), var (335)

---

script	Script

Purpose

Includes a script in a document.

Syntax

```
<script type="Internet_Media_Type"
  [ charset="ISO-8859-1"|"char_set"]
  [ class="class_name"][ defer="defer"]
  [ disabled="disabled"][ event="event_name"]
  [ for="element_name"][ id="id_name"]
  [ lang="lang_code"][ language="javascript"|"jscript"
  |"vbs[cript]"][ onload="ol_script"]
  [ onpropertychange="pc_script"]
  [ onreadystatechange="rsc_script"]
  [ src="ext_script_uri"][ title="title"]>script</script>
```

Where

- **type** (Web) specifies the scripting language, which must be a valid Internet Media Type (that is, MIMETYPE).
- **charset** (Web) names the source of the character set of the data referred to by the SRC attribute.
- ⊖ **class** (Web) specifies a class identification for the element.
- **defer** (Web) is a keyword that states that the browser or processor may defer the execution of the script.
- ⊖ **disabled** (Web) is a keyword that prevents a user from using the element.
- ⊖ **event** (Web) names the event related to the current script. **event** is unavailable for this element but may be available in the future.
- ⊖ **for** (Web) names the element with which the current script is associated. **for** is unavailable for this element but may be available in the future.
- ⊖ **id** (Web) provides a unique identifier name for the element.
- ⊖ **lang** (Web) provides the code representing the language used for the controls text.

- ⊖Ⓝ `language` (Web) declares the scripting language of the current script.
- ⊖ `onload` (Web) names a script to run after the active browser has finished loading the script.
- ⊖ `onpropertychange` (Web) names a script to run when a property changes on the selected object in any way.
- ⊖ `onreadystatechange` (Web) names a script to run when the status of an element has changed (for example, the element receives data).
- `src` (Web) specifies a URI in which an external script to run is stored.
- ⊖ `title` (Web) provides a title for the element.
- *script* is the current script.

Notes

- This inline element originated in HTML 3.2.
- `script` is a child element of the `blockquote`, `body`, and `form` elements.
- Insert `script` statements in the HEAD section of documents in which one or more scripts appear.
- Use the `type` attribute to specify a valid scripting language. The `language` attribute is deprecated.
- In XHTML, the `script` and `style` element declarations include `#PCDATA` content. This means that `script` and `style` can include both elements and character data. So, rather than including < and & characters as text (which XHTML processors may interpret as markup delimiters), insert `&lt;` and `&amp;`, respectively.
- For the `script` element, WebTV supports the `language` and `src` attributes.

Related Elements

`head` (148), `noscript` (224), `server` (267), `style` (280)

For More Information

Learn more about the `script` element on page 655 in Chapter 10.

---

select   Selection-List Menu

Purpose

Creates a selection-list menu in a form.

Syntax

```
<select name="element_name"[ accesskey="shortcut_key"]
   [ align="bottom"|"middle"|"top"|"left"|"right"
   |"absmiddle"|"absbottom"|"texttop"|"baseline"]
   [ autoactivate][ bgcolor="#rrggbb"|"color"]
   [ class="class_name"][ datafld="ds_col_name"]
   [ datasrc="ds_identifier"][ dir="ltr"|"rtl"]
```

```
[ disabled="disabled"][ id="id_name"]
[ lang="lang_code"][ language="javascript"|"jscript"
|"vbs[cript]"][ multiple="multiple"]
[name="element_name"][ onbeforecut="bt_script"]
[ onbeforeeditfocus="bef_script"]
[ onbeforefocusenter="bfe_script"]
[ onbeforefocusleave="bfl_script"]
[ onbeforepaste="bp_script"][ onblur="bl_script"]
[ onchange="ch_script"][ onclick="cl_script"]
[ oncontextmenu="cm_script"]
[ oncontrolselect="ctl_script"][ oncut="ct_script"]
[ ondblclick="dc_script"][ ondragenter="de_script"]
[ ondragleave="dl_script"][ ondragover="do_script"]
[ ondrop="dr_script"][ onfocus="fc_script"]
[ onfocusenter="fe_script"]
[ onfocusleave="fl_script"][ onhelp="hlp_script"]
[ onkeydown="kd_script"][ onkeypress="kp_script"]
[ onkeyup="ku_script"][ onlosecapture="lc_script"]
[ onmousedown="md_script"]
[ onmouseenter="me_script"]
[ onmouseleave="ml_script"]
[ onmousemove="mm_script"][ onmouseout="mo_script"]
[ onmouseover="mov_script"][ onmouseup="mu_script"]
[ onpaste="p_script"][ onpropertychange="pc_script"]
[ onreadystatechange="rsc_script"]
[ onresize="rsz_script"][ onresizeend="ree_script"]
[ onresizestart="res_script"][ onscroll="sc_script"]
[ onselectstart="ss_script"]
[ selcolor="#rrggbb"|"color"][ size="no_of_rows"]
[ style="name_1: value_1"[; name_2: value_2"]
[...; name_n: value_n"]]
[ tabindex="position_number"]
[ text="#rrggbb"|"color"][ title="title"]
[ type="select-multiple"|"select-one"][ usestyle]
>list-contents</select>
```

Where

- name (Web) names the current drop-down list or list box.
- ⊖ accesskey (Web) assigns a shortcut key to the element in order to focus on it.
- ⊖ align (Web) aligns the list box or drop-down list with the surrounding area of the XHTML document.
- ⌂ autoactivate (Web) automatically activates the selection list when a user focuses on it.

- 🖻 bgcolor (Web) specifies the background color for the selection list.
- class (Web) specifies a class identification for the selection list.
- ⊖ datafld (Web) specifies the column name from the file that contains the data source object.
- ⊖ datasrc (Web) specifies the identifier of the data source object.
- dir (Web) specifies the direction in which the selection list text is displayed: left-to-right or right-to-left.
- disabled (Web) prevents user input associated with the selection list. disabled is not available for this element but may be available in a future XHTML version.
- id (Web) provides a unique identifier name for the selection list.
- lang (Web) provides the code representing the language used for the selection list text.
- ⊖ language (Web) declares the scripting language of the current script.
- multiple (Web) is a keyword that indicates that a user is allowed to select more than one item from a selection list.
- ⊖ onbeforecut (Web) names a script to run when a user starts cutting a selection to the Clipboard but before any action actually takes place.
- ⊖ onbeforeeditfocus (Web) names a script to run when a user starts activating an object but before the object actually becomes active.
- ⊖ onbeforefocusenter (Web) names a script to run when a user starts focusing on an object but before the object actually gains focus.
- ⊖ onbeforefocusleave (Web) names a script to run when a user starts leaving an object but before the object actually loses focus.
- ⊖ onbeforepaste (Web) names a script to run when a user starts pasting an object but before any action actually takes place.
- onblur (Web) names a script to run when the selection list loses focus.
- onchange (Web) names a script to run when the selection list loses focus after it has gained focus and has had a value change.
- onclick (Web) names a script to run when a user moves the mouse pointer or other pointing device over the selection list and clicks the device button.
- ⊖ oncontextmenu (Web) names a script to run when a user right-clicks the mouse to open a shortcut menu.
- ⊖ oncontrolselect (Web) names a script to run when a user selects a control.
- ⊖ oncut (Web) names a script to run when a user cuts a selection to the Clipboard.
- ondblclick (Web) names a script to run when a user moves the mouse pointer or other pointing device over the selection list and double-clicks the device button.
- ⊖ ondragenter (Web) names a script to run when a user drags a selection into an area in which it can be dropped.
- ⊖ ondragleave (Web) names a script to run when a user drags a selection beyond an area in which it can be dropped.

XHTML Syntax

- ⊝ ondragover (Web) names a script to run when a user drags a selection over an area in which it can be dropped.
- ⊝ ondrop (Web) names a script to run when a user releases the mouse button to drop a dragged selection.
- onfocus (Web) names a script to run when a user points the mouse pointer or other pointing device to focus on the current element.
- ⊝ onfocusenter (Web) names a script to run when a user focuses on the current element in any way.
- ⊝ onfocusleave (Web) names a script to run when a user inactivates the current element in any way.
- ⊝ onhelp (Web) names a script to run when a user presses the F1 or Help key over the current element.
- onkeydown (Web) names a script to run when a user presses and holds down a key over the selection list.
- onkeypress (Web) names a script to run when a user presses and releases a key over the selection list.
- onkeyup (Web) names a script to run when a user releases a key that is currently held down over the selection list.
- ⊝ onlosecapture (Web) names a script to run when a user releases a selection that has been captured by the mouse.
- onmousedown (Web) names a script to run when a user moves the mouse pointer or other pointing device over the selection list and presses and holds down the device button.
- ⊝ onmouseenter (Web) names a script to run when a user moves the mouse pointer onto the object.
- ⊝ onmouseleave (Web) names a script to run when the mouse pointer leaves the object.
- onmousemove (Web) names a script to run when a user moves the mouse pointer or other pointing device over the selection list.
- onmouseout (Web) names a script to run when a user moves the mouse pointer or other pointing device away from the selection list.
- onmouseover (Web) names a script to run the first time a user moves the mouse pointer or other pointing device over the selection list.
- onmouseup (Web) names a script to run when a user moves the mouse pointer or other pointing device over the selection list and releases a pressed-down device button.
- ⊝ onpaste (Web) names a script to run when a user pastes the Clipboard contents onto the object.
- ⊝ onpropertychange (Web) names a script to run when a property changes on the selected object in any way.
- ⊝ onreadystatechange (Web) names a script to run when the status of an element has changed (for example, the element receives data).
- ⊝ onresize (Web) names a script to run when a user resizes the selected object.
- ⊝ onresizeend (Web) names a script to run after the object has been resized.

- ☺ onresizestart (Web) names a script to run as a user resizes the object.
- ☺ onscroll (Web) names a script to run when a user moves the scroll box within the scroll bar.
- ☺ onselectstart (Web) names a script to run when a user starts selecting an object.
- ⛶ selcolor (Web) specifies the background color of the selections in the selection list.
- size (Web) specifies the maximum number of rows (that is, items) in the selection list.
- style (Web) sets styles for the selection list.
- tabindex (Web) defines the position of the selection list in all the elements that a user can navigate to using a Tab or Shift + Tab key.
- ⛶ text (Web) specifies the text color of the selections in the selection list.
- title (Web) provides a title for the selection list.
- ☺ type (Web) specifies the type of list box: one from which the user can select several items or one from which the user can select one item.
- ⛶ usestyle (Web) indicates that the selection-list text is the same style as other text on the page.
- *list-contents* is the items on the list, each enclosed within the parent element, option.

Notes

- This inline element originated in HTML 2.0.
- Use the select, optgroup, and option elements to create a menu in a form.
- WebTV supports the following attributes for select: autoactivate, bgcolor, onblur, onchange, onclick, onfocus, multiple, name, setcolor, size, text, and usestyle.

Related Elements

fieldset (127), form (135), input (167), isindex (184), label (190), legend (195), optgroup (234), option (236), textarea (302)

For More Information

Learn more about the select element on page 616 in Chapter 7.

Ⓝ server   Server-Side Script

Purpose

Includes a JavaScript compiled by LiveWire in a document.

Syntax

```
<server>server_side_script</server>
```

Where

server_side_script is the current script.

Notes

• server is similar to the script element. However, it is interpreted at the server (server-side) rather than the browser (client-side). For example, `<server>write("Hello!")</server>` would be run by the Netscape server and appear as *Hello!* on the client computer desktop.
• Technologies such as ASP and PHP also enable you to use server-side scripts in your documents.

Related Elements

noscript (224), script (262)

---

small   Small Text

Purpose

Displays text in a smaller font than the default starting font.

Syntax

```
<small[ accesskey="shortcut_key"][ class="class_name"]
   [ contenteditable="edit_string"][ dir="ltr"|"rtl"]
   [ disabled="disabled"][ id="id_name"]
   [ lang="lang_code"][ language="javascript"|"jscript"
   |"vbs[cript]"][ onbeforecopy="bc_script"]
   [ onbeforecut="bt_script"]
   [ onbeforefocusenter="bfe_script"]
   [ onbeforefocusleave="bfl_script"]
   [ onbeforepaste="bp_script"][ onclick="cl_script"]
   [ oncontextmenu="cm_script"]
   [ oncontrolselect="ctl_script"][ oncopy="cp_script"]
   [ oncut="ct_script"][ ondblclick="dc_script"]
   [ ondrag="d_script"][ ondragend="dd_script"]
   [ ondragenter="de_script"][ ondragleave="dl_script"]
   [ ondragover="do_script"][ ondragstart="ds_script"]
   [ ondrop="dr_script"][ onfocus="fc_script"]
   [ onfocusenter="fe_script"]
   [ onfocusleave="fl_script"][ onhelp="hlp_script"]
   [ onkeydown="kd_script"][ onkeypress="kp_script"]
   [ onkeyup="ku_script"][ onlosecapture="lc_script"]
   [ onmousedown="md_script"]
   [ onmouseenter="me_script"]
   [ onmouseleave="ml_script"]
   [ onmousemove="mm_script"]
   [ onmouseout="mo_script"][ onmouseover="mov_script"]
   [ onmouseup="mu_script"][ onpaste="p_script"]
   [ onpropertychange="pc_script"]
```

```
[ onreadystatechange="rsc_script"]
[ onresize="rsz_script"][ onresizeend="ree_script"]
[ onresizestart="res_script"]
[ onselectstart="ss_script"]
[ style="name_1: value_1"[; "name_2: value_2"]
[...; "name_n: value_n"]]
[ tabindex="position_number"][ title="title"]>
text</small>
```

Where

- ⊖ `accesskey` (Web) assigns a shortcut key to the object in order to focus on it.
- `class` (Web) specifies a class identification for the small text.
- ⊖ `contenteditable` (Web) specifies or obtains a value that indicates whether a user can edit the element content.
- `dir` (Web) specifies the direction in which the small text is displayed: left-to-right or right-to-left.
- ⊖ `disabled` (Web) is a keyword that prevents a user from using the element.
- `id` (Web) provides a unique identifier name for the small text.
- `lang` (Web) specifies the code for the language used for the small text.
- ⊖ `language` (Web) declares the scripting language of the current script.
- ⊖ `onbeforecopy` (Web) names a script to run when a user starts copying a selection to the Clipboard but before any action actually takes place.
- ⊖ `onbeforecut` (Web) names a script to run when a user starts cutting a selection to the Clipboard but before any action actually takes place.
- ⊖ `onbeforefocusenter` (Web) names a script to run when a user starts focusing on an object but before the object actually gains focus.
- ⊖ `onbeforefocusleave` (Web) names a script to run when a user starts leaving an object but before the object actually loses focus.
- ⊖ `onbeforepaste` (Web) names a script to run when a user starts pasting an object but before any action actually takes place.
- ⊖ `onblur` (Web) names a script to run when the object loses focus (that is, it is no longer the active element).
- `onclick` (Web) names a script to run when a user moves the mouse pointer or other pointing device over the small text and clicks the button.
- ⊖ `oncontextmenu` (Web) names a script to run when a user right-clicks the mouse to open a shortcut menu.
- ⊖ `oncontrolselect` (Web) names a script to run when a user selects a control.
- ⊖ `oncopy` (Web) names a script to run when a user copies a selection to the Clipboard.
- ⊖ `oncut` (Web) names a script to run when a user cuts a selection to the Clipboard.

- **ondblclick** (Web) names a script to run when a user moves the mouse pointer or other pointing device over the small text and double-clicks the button.
- ⊖ **ondrag** (Web) names a script to run when a user drags a selection.
- ⊖ **ondragend** (Web) names a script to run after a user completes a drag-and-drop operation.
- ⊖ **ondragenter** (Web) names a script to run when a user drags a selection into an area in which it can be dropped.
- ⊖ **ondragleave** (Web) names a script to run when a user drags a selection beyond an area in which it can be dropped.
- ⊖ **ondragover** (Web) names a script to run when a user drags a selection over an area in which it can be dropped.
- ⊖ **ondragstart** (Web) names a script to run when a user starts dragging a selection or element.
- ⊖ **ondrop** (Web) names a script to run when a user releases the mouse button to drop a dragged selection.
- ⊖ **onfocus** (Web) names a script to run when a user points the mouse pointer or other pointing device to focus on the current element.
- ⊖ **onfocusenter** (Web) names a script to run when a user focuses on the current element in any way.
- ⊖ **onfocusleave** (Web) names a script to run when a user inactivates the current element in any way.
- ⊖ **onhelp** (Web) names a script to run when a user presses the F1 or Help key over the current element.
- **onkeydown** (Web) names a script to run when a user presses and holds down a key over the small text.
- **onkeypress** (Web) names a script to run when a user presses and releases a key over the small text.
- **onkeyup** (Web) names a script to run when a user releases a key that is currently held down over the small text.
- ⊖ **onlosecapture** (Web) names a script to run when a user releases a selection that has been captured by the mouse.
- **onmousedown** (Web) names a script to run when a user moves the mouse pointer or other pointing device over the small text and presses and holds down the button.
- ⊖ **onmouseenter** (Web) names a script to run when a user moves the mouse pointer onto the object.
- ⊖ **onmouseleave** (Web) names a script to run when the mouse pointer leaves the object.
- **onmousemove** (Web) names a script to run when a user moves the mouse pointer or other pointing device over the small text.
- **onmouseout** (Web) names a script to run when a user moves the mouse pointer or other pointing device away from the small text.
- **onmouseover** (Web) names a script to run the first time a user moves the mouse pointer or other pointing device over the small text.

- onmouseup (Web) names a script to run when a user moves the mouse pointer or other pointing device over the small text and releases a mouse button that is currently held down.
- ⊜ onpaste (Web) names a script to run when a user pastes the Clipboard contents onto the object.
- ⊜ onpropertychange (Web) names a script to run when a property changes on the selected object in any way.
- ⊜ onreadystatechange (Web) names a script to run when the status of an element has changed (for example, the element receives data).
- ⊜ onresize (Web) names a script to run when a user resizes the selected object.
- ⊜ onresizeend (Web) names a script to run after the object has been resized.
- ⊜ onresizestart (Web) names a script to run as a user resizes the object.
- ⊜ onselectstart (Web) names a script to run when a user starts selecting an object.
- style (Web) sets styles for the small text.
- ⊜ tabindex (Web) defines the position of the current element in all the elements that a user can navigate to using a Tab or Shift + Tab key.
- title (Web) provides a title for the small text.
- *text* represents one or more characters.

Notes

- This inline element originated in HTML 3.2.
- small is one of the elements in the %fontstyle entity. The other %fontstyle elements are b, big, i, and tt. Deprecated elements in the %fontstyle entity are s, strike, and u.
- Some HTML editors convert small to <font size=-1>text</font>, its equivalent.
- For the small element, WebTV supports the class and style attributes.

Related Elements

b (46), big (57), font (131), i (154), s (254), strike (254), tt (324), u (327)

N ⌖ spacer   White Space

Purpose

Formats horizontal and/or vertical white space in an XHTML document.

Syntax

```
<spacer[ align="left"|"right"|"top"|"absmiddle"
   |"absbottom"|"texttop"|"middle"|"baseline"
   |"bottom"][ height="height_pix"][ size="size_pix"]
   [ type="horizontal"|"vertical"|"block"]
   [ width="width_pix"]{ />|</spacer>}
```

Where

- ⊠📺 align (Web) aligns the white-space block with the surrounding text, graphics, and links.
- ⊠📺 height (Web) specifies the height of the white-space block (type="block").
- ⊠📺 size (Web) specifies the width or height of the white space (type="horizontal" or type="vertical").
- ⊠📺 type (Web) specifies the type of white-space area.
- ⊠📺 width (Web) specifies the width of the white-space block (type="block").

Notes

- spacer is an empty element.
- For the spacer element, WebTV supports the align, height, size, type, and width attributes.
- You can use style sheets to add white space to a document. This is preferable to using spacer because spacer is supported only by Netscape Navigator, WebTV, and compatible browsers.

---

span .... Spanned Section

Purpose

Marks the beginning of a new section in a document.

Syntax

```
<span[ accesskey="shortcut_key"][ class="class_name"]
   [ contenteditable="edit_string"]
   [ datafld="ds_col_name"]
   [ dataformatas="html"|"text"]
   [ datasrc="ds_identifier"][ dir="ltr"|"rtl"]
   [ disabled="disabled"][ id="id_name"]
   [ lang="lang_code"][ language="javascript"|"jscript"
   |"vbs[cript]"][ onbeforecopy="bc_script"]
   [ onbeforecut="bt_script"]
   [ onbeforeeditfocus="bef_script"]
   [ onbeforefocusenter="bfe_script"]
   [ onbeforefocusleave="bfl_script"]
   [ onbeforepaste="bp_script"][ onblur="bl_script"]
```

XHTML Syntax

```
[ onclick="cl_script"][ oncontextmenu="cm_script"]
[ oncontrolselect="ctl_script"][ oncopy="cp_script"]
[ oncut="ct_script"][ ondblclick="dc_script"]
[ ondrag="d_script"][ ondragend="dd_script"]
[ ondragenter="de_script"][ ondragleave="dl_script"]
[ ondragover="do_script"][ ondragstart="ds_script"]
[ ondrop="dr_script"][ onfilterchange="f_script"]
[ onfocus="fc_script"][ onfocusenter="fe_script"]
[ onfocusleave="fl_script"][ onhelp="hlp_script"]
[ onkeydown="kd_script"][ onkeypress="kp_script"]
[ onkeyup="ku_script"][ onlosecapture="lc_script"]
[ onmousedown="md_script"]
[ onmouseenter="me_script"]
[ onmouseleave="ml_script"]
[ onmousemove="mm_script"][ onmouseout="mo_script"]
[ onmouseover="mov_script"][ onmouseup="mu_script"]
[ onpaste="p_script"][ onpropertychange="pc_script"]
[ onreadystatechange="rsc_script"]
[ onresize="rsz_script"][ onresizeend="ree_script"]
[ onresizestart="res_script"]
[ onselectstart="ss_script"]
[ style="name_1: value_1"[; "name_2: value_2"]
[...; "name_n: value_n"]]
[ tabindex="position_number"][ title="title"]>
span-text</span>
```

Where

- ⊖ accesskey (Web) assigns a shortcut key to the object in order to focus on it.
- class (Web) specifies a class identification for the span section of the document.
- ⊖ contenteditable (Web) specifies or obtains a value that indicates whether a user can edit the element content.
- ⊖ datafld (Web) specifies the column name from the file that contains the data source object.
- ⊖ dataformatas (Web) indicates whether the data for this element is formatted as plain text (that is, unformatted ASCII) or HTML.
- ⊖ datasrc (Web) specifies the identifier of the data source object.
- dir (Web) specifies the direction in which the span section text is displayed: left-to-right or right-to-left.
- ⊖ disabled (Web) is a keyword that prevents a user from using the element.
- id (Web) provides a unique identifier name for the span section.
- lang (Web) specifies the code for the language used for the span text.
- ⊖ language (Web) declares the scripting language of the current script.

- ☺ onbeforecopy (Web) names a script to run when a user starts copying a selection to the Clipboard but before any action actually takes place.
- ☺ onbeforecut (Web) names a script to run when a user starts cutting a selection to the Clipboard but before any action actually takes place.
- ☺ onbeforeeditfocus (Web) names a script to run when a user starts activating an object but before the object actually becomes active.
- ☺ onbeforefocusenter (Web) names a script to run when a user starts focusing on an object but before the object actually gains focus.
- ☺ onbeforefocusleave (Web) names a script to run when a user starts leaving an object but before the object actually loses focus.
- ☺ onbeforepaste (Web) names a script to run when a user starts pasting an object but before any action actually takes place.
- ☺ onblur (Web) names a script to run when the object loses focus (that is, it is no longer the active element).
- onclick (Web) names a script to run when a user moves the mouse pointer or other pointing device over the span section and clicks the button.
- ☺ oncontextmenu (Web) names a script to run when a user right-clicks the mouse to open a shortcut menu.
- ☺ oncontrolselect (Web) names a script to run when a user selects a control.
- ☺ oncopy (Web) names a script to run when a user copies a selection to the Clipboard.
- ☺ oncut (Web) names a script to run when a user cuts a selection to the Clipboard.
- ondblclick (Web) names a script to run when a user moves the mouse pointer or other pointing device over the span section and double-clicks the button.
- ☺ ondrag (Web) names a script to run when a user drags a selection.
- ☺ ondragend (Web) names a script to run after a user completes a drag-and-drop operation.
- ☺ ondragenter (Web) names a script to run when a user drags a selection into an area in which it can be dropped.
- ☺ ondragleave (Web) names a script to run when a user drags a selection beyond an area in which it can be dropped.
- ☺ ondragover (Web) names a script to run when a user drags a selection over an area in which it can be dropped.
- ☺ ondragstart (Web) names a script to run when a user starts dragging a selection or element.
- ☺ ondrop (Web) names a script to run when a user releases the mouse button to drop a dragged selection.
- ☺ onfilterchange (Web) names a script to run when a visual filter changes in any way.
- ☺ onfocus (Web) names a script to run when a user points the mouse pointer or other pointing device to focus on the current element.
- ☺ onfocusenter (Web) names a script to run when a user focuses on the current element in any way.

- ☺ onfocusleave (Web) names a script to run when a user inactivates the current element in any way.
- ☺ onhelp (Web) names a script to run when a user presses the F1 or Help key over the current element.
- onkeydown (Web) names a script to run when a user presses and holds down a key over the span section.
- onkeypress (Web) names a script to run when a user presses and releases a key over the span section.
- onkeyup (Web) names a script to run when a user releases a key that is currently held down over the span section.
- ☺ onlosecapture (Web) names a script to run when a user releases a selection that has been captured by the mouse.
- onmousedown (Web) names a script to run when a user moves the mouse pointer or other pointing device over the span section and presses and holds down the button.
- ☺ onmouseenter (Web) names a script to run when a user moves the mouse pointer onto the object.
- ☺ onmouseleave (Web) names a script to run when the mouse pointer leaves the object.
- onmousemove (Web) names a script to run when a user moves the mouse pointer or other pointing device over the span section.
- onmouseout (Web) names a script to run when a user moves the mouse pointer or other pointing device away from the span section.
- onmouseover (Web) names a script to run the first time a user moves the mouse pointer or other pointing device over the span section.
- onmouseup (Web) names a script to run when a user moves the mouse pointer or other pointing device over the span section and releases a mouse button that is currently held down.
- ☺ onpaste (Web) names a script to run when a user pastes the Clipboard contents onto the object.
- ☺ onpropertychange (Web) names a script to run when a property changes on the selected object in any way.
- ☺ onreadystatechange (Web) names a script to run when the status of an element has changed (for example, the element receives data).
- ☺ onresize (Web) names a script to run when a user resizes the selected object.
- ☺ onresizeend (Web) names a script to run after the object has been resized.
- ☺ onresizestart (Web) names a script to run as a user resizes the object.
- ☺ onselectstart (Web) names a script to run when a user starts selecting an object.
- style (Web) sets styles for the span section.
- ☺ tabindex (Web) defines the position of the current element in all the elements that a user can navigate to using a Tab or Shift + Tab key.
- title (Web) provides a title for the span section.
- *span-text* represents the contents of the span section.

Notes

- This inline element originated in HTML 4.0.
- You can use span within other elements, such as paragraphs and list items.
- You can use span to apply styles and scripts to a particular section — even a single character or word — in a document. span is particularly useful with style sheets and dynamic HTML.
- For the span element, WebTV supports the class and style attributes.

Related Element

div (108)

strike   Strikethrough

See s|strike.

strong   Strong Emphasis

Purpose

Applies strong emphasis, usually boldface, to selected text.

Syntax

```
<strong[ accesskey="shortcut_key"]
  [ class="class_name"]
  [ contenteditable="edit_string"][ dir="ltr"|"rtl"]
  [ disabled="disabled"][ id="id_name"]
  [ lang="lang_code"][ language="javascript"|"jscript"
  |"vbs[cript]"][ onbeforecopy="bc_script"]
  [ onbeforecut="bt_script"]
  [ onbeforefocusenter="bfe_script"]
  [ onbeforefocusleave="bfl_script"]
  [ onbeforepaste="bp_script"][ onblur="bl_script"]
  [ onclick="cl_script"][ oncontextmenu="cm_script"]
  [ oncontrolselect="ctl_script"][ oncopy="cp_script"]
  [ oncut="ct_script"][ ondblclick="dc_script"]
  [ ondrag="d_script"][ ondragend="dd_script"]
  [ ondragenter="de_script"][ ondragleave="dl_script"]
  [ ondragover="do_script"][ ondragstart="ds_script"]
  [ ondrop="dr_script"][ onfocus="fc_script"]
  [ onfocusenter="fe_script"]
  [ onfocusleave="fl_script"][ onhelp="hlp_script"]
```

```
[ onkeydown="kd_script"][ onkeypress="kp_script"]
[ onkeyup="ku_script"][ onlosecapture="lc_script"]
[ onmousedown="md_script"]
[ onmouseenter="me_script"]
[ onmouseleave="ml_script"]
[ onmousemove="mm_script"][ onmouseout="mo_script"]
[ onmouseover="mov_script"][ onmouseup="mu_script"]
[ onpaste="p_script"][ onpropertychange="pc_script"]
[ onreadystatechange="rsc_script"]
[ onresize="rsz_script"][ onresizeend="ree_script"]
[ onresizestart="res_script"]
[ onselectstart="ss_script"]
[ style="name_1: value_1"[; "name_2: value_2"]
[...; "name_n: value_n"]]
[ tabindex="position_number"][ title="title"]>
text</strong>
```

Where

- ⊖ accesskey (Web) assigns a shortcut key to the object in order to focus on it.
- class (Web) specifies a class identification for the strongly emphasized text.
- ⊖ contenteditable (Web) specifies or obtains a value that indicates whether a user can edit the element content.
- dir (Web) specifies the direction in which the strongly emphasized text is displayed: left-to-right or right-to-left.
- ⊖ disabled (Web) is a keyword that prevents a user from using the element.
- id (Web) provides a unique identifier name for the strongly emphasized text.
- lang (Web) specifies the code for the language used for the strongly emphasized text.
- ⊖ language (Web) declares the scripting language of the current script.
- ⊖ onbeforecopy (Web) names a script to run when a user starts copying a selection to the Clipboard but before any action actually takes place.
- ⊖ onbeforecut (Web) names a script to run when a user starts cutting a selection to the Clipboard but before any action actually takes place.
- ⊖ onbeforefocusenter (Web) names a script to run when a user starts focusing on an object but before the object actually gains focus.
- ⊖ onbeforefocusleave (Web) names a script to run when a user starts leaving an object but before the object actually loses focus.
- ⊖ onbeforepaste (Web) names a script to run when a user starts pasting an object but before any action actually takes place.
- ⊖ onblur (Web) names a script to run when the object loses focus (that is, it is no longer the active element).

- onclick (Web) names a script to run when a user moves the mouse pointer or other pointing device over the strongly emphasized text and clicks the button.
- ⊖ oncontextmenu (Web) names a script to run when a user right-clicks the mouse to open a shortcut menu.
- ⊖ oncontrolselect (Web) names a script to run when a user selects a control.
- ⊖ oncopy (Web) names a script to run when a user copies a selection to the Clipboard.
- ⊖ oncut (Web) names a script to run when a user cuts a selection to the Clipboard.
- ondblclick (Web) names a script to run when a user moves the mouse pointer or other pointing device over the strongly emphasized text and double-clicks the button.
- ⊖ ondrag (Web) names a script to run when a user drags a selection.
- ⊖ ondragend (Web) names a script to run after a user completes a drag-and-drop operation.
- ⊖ ondragenter (Web) names a script to run when a user drags a selection into an area in which it can be dropped.
- ⊖ ondragleave (Web) names a script to run when a user drags a selection beyond an area in which it can be dropped.
- ⊖ ondragover (Web) names a script to run when a user drags a selection over an area in which it can be dropped.
- ⊖ ondragstart (Web) names a script to run when a user starts dragging a selection or element.
- ⊖ ondrop (Web) names a script to run when a user releases the mouse button to drop a dragged selection.
- ⊖ onfocus (Web) names a script to run when a user points the mouse pointer or other pointing device to focus on the current element.
- ⊖ onfocusenter (Web) names a script to run when a user focuses on the current element in any way.
- ⊖ onfocusleave (Web) names a script to run when a user inactivates the current element in any way.
- ⊖ onhelp (Web) names a script to run when a user presses the F1 or Help key over the current element.
- onkeydown (Web) names a script to run when a user presses and holds down a key over the strongly emphasized text.
- onkeypress (Web) names a script to run when a user presses and releases a key over the strongly emphasized text.
- onkeyup (Web) names a script to run when a user releases a key that is currently held down over the strongly emphasized text.
- ⊖ onlosecapture (Web) names a script to run when a user releases a selection that has been captured by the mouse.
- onmousedown (Web) names a script to run when a user moves the mouse pointer or other pointing device over the strongly emphasized text and presses and holds down the button.

- ⊖ onmouseenter (Web) names a script to run when a user moves the mouse pointer onto the object.
- ⊖ onmouseleave (Web) names a script to run when the mouse pointer leaves the object.
- onmousemove (Web) names a script to run when a user moves the mouse pointer or other pointing device over the strongly emphasized text.
- onmouseout (Web) names a script to run when a user moves the mouse pointer or other pointing device away from the strongly emphasized text.
- onmouseover (Web) names a script to run the first time a user moves the mouse pointer or other pointing device over the strongly emphasized text.
- onmouseup (Web) names a script to run when a user moves the mouse pointer or other pointing device over the strongly emphasized text and releases a mouse button that is currently held down.
- ⊖ onpaste (Web) names a script to run when a user pastes the Clipboard contents onto the object.
- ⊖ onpropertychange (Web) names a script to run when a property changes on the selected object in any way.
- ⊖ onreadystatechange (Web) names a script to run when the status of an element has changed (for example, the element receives data).
- ⊖ onresize (Web) names a script to run when a user resizes the selected object.
- ⊖ onresizeend (Web) names a script to run after the object has been resized.
- ⊖ onresizestart (Web) names a script to run as a user resizes the object.
- ⊖ onselectstart (Web) names a script to run when a user starts selecting an object.
- style (Web) sets styles for the strongly emphasized text.
- ⊖ tabindex (Web) defines the position of the current element in all the elements that a user can navigate to using a Tab or Shift + Tab key.
- title (Web) provides a title for the strongly emphasized text.
- *text* represents one or more characters.

Notes

- This inline element originated in HTML 2.0.
- strong is one of the elements in the %phrase entity. The other %phrase elements are abbr, acronym, cite, code, dfn, em, kbd, samp, and var.
- strong is a logical element, in which particular browsers are programmed to apply a certain style to the selected text. This is in contrast to a physical element (such as b), in which you "code" the styles yourself.
- For the strong element, WebTV supports the class and style attributes.

Related Elements

b (46), big (57), em (120), font (131), i (154), s (254), small (268), strike (254), sub (281), sup (284), u (327)

style   Style

Purpose

Provides style information and overrides a linked cascading style sheet.

Syntax

```
<style type="style_sheet_language"
  [ behavior:url(uri)][ dir="ltr"|"rtl"]
  [ disabled="disabled"][ lang="lang_code"]
  [ media=["screen"][,]["print"][,]["projection"]
  [,]["braille"][,]["speech"][,]["all"]]
  [ onerror="e_script"]
  [ onreadystatechange="rsc_script"]
  [ title="title"]>text</style>
```

Where

- type (Web) specifies a language (that is, the Internet Media Type) for the current style.
- ℮ behavior (Web) specifies a URI that sets dynamic HTML behavior.
- dir (Web) specifies the direction in which the current text is displayed: left-to-right or right-to-left.
- ℮ disabled (Web) prevents the element from receiving the focus.
- lang (Web) specifies the code for the language used for the style.
- media (Web) indicates the type of destination for the document.
- ℮ onerror (Web) specifies a script to run when the referred-to script experiences an error.
- ℮ onreadystatechange (Web) names a script to run when the status of an element has changed (for example, the element receives data).
- title (Web) provides a title for the style.
- text represents one or more words or lines of text.

Notes

- This element originated in HTML 3.2.
- The style element is closely related to the style attribute. For more information about the style attribute, refer to pages Web and Web.
- Embed style within the HEAD section.
- In XHTML, the script and style element declarations include #PCDATA content. This means that script and style can include both elements and character data. So, rather than including < and &

characters as text (which XHTML processors may interpret as markup delimiters), insert < and &, respectively.
- For detailed information about properties (that is, styles) and style sheets, see Section 2, *Cascading Style Sheet Syntax* (Web).

Related Elements
head (148), script (262)

For More Information
Learn more about the style element on page 626 in Chapter 8.

---

sub
Subscript

Purpose
Moves one or more selected characters below the base line on which other characters sit and applies a smaller font.

Syntax
```
<sub[ accesskey="shortcut_key"][ class="class_name"]
 [ contenteditable="edit_string"][ dir="ltr"|"rtl"]
 [ disabled="disabled"][ id="id_name"]
 [ lang="lang_code"][ language="javascript"|"jscript"
 |"vbs[cript]"][ onbeforecopy="bc_script"]
 [ onbeforecut="bt_script"]
 [ onbeforefocusenter="bfe_script"]
 [ onbeforefocusleave="bfl_script"]
 [ onbeforepaste="bp_script"][ onblur="bl_script"]
 [ onclick="cl_script"][ oncontextmenu="cm_script"]
 [ oncontrolselect="ctl_script"][ oncopy="cp_script"]
 [ oncut="ct_script"][ ondblclick="dc_script"]
 [ ondrag="d_script"][ ondragend="dd_script"]
 [ ondragenter="de_script"][ ondragleave="dl_script"]
 [ ondragover="do_script"][ ondragstart="ds_script"]
 [ ondrop="dr_script"][ onfocus="fc_script"]
 [ onfocusenter="fe_script"]
 [ onfocusleave="fl_script"][ onhelp="hlp_script"]
 [ onkeydown="kd_script"][ onkeypress="kp_script"]
 [ onkeyup="ku_script"][ onlosecapture="lc_script"]
 [ onmousedown="md_script"]
 [ onmouseenter="me_script"]
 [ onmouseleave="ml_script"]
 [ onmousemove="mm_script"][ onmouseout="mo_script"]
 [ onmouseover="mov_script"][ onmouseup="mu_script"]
 [ onpaste="p_script"]
```

```
[ onpropertychange="pc_script"]
[ onreadystatechange="rsc_script"]
[ onresize="rsz_script"][ onresizeend="ree_script"]
[ onresizestart="res_script"]
[ onselectstart="ss_script"]
[ style="name_1: value_1"[; "name_2: value_2"]
[...; "name_n: value_n"]]
[ tabindex="position_number"][ title="title"]>
characters</sub>
```

Where

- ⊖ **accesskey** (Web) assigns a shortcut key to the object in order to focus on it.
- **class** (Web) specifies a class identification for the subscript characters.
- ⊖ **contenteditable** (Web) specifies or obtains a value that indicates whether a user can edit the element content.
- **dir** (Web) specifies the direction in which the subscript characters are displayed: left-to-right or right-to-left.
- ⊖ **disabled** (Web) is a keyword that prevents a user from using the element.
- **id** (Web) provides a unique identifier name for the subscript characters.
- **lang** (Web) specifies the code for the language used for the subscript characters.
- ⊖ **language** (Web) declares the scripting language of the current script.
- ⊖ **onbeforecopy** (Web) names a script to run when a user starts copying a selection to the Clipboard but before any action actually takes place.
- ⊖ **onbeforecut** (Web) names a script to run when a user starts cutting a selection to the Clipboard but before any action actually takes place.
- ⊖ **onbeforefocusenter** (Web) names a script to run when a user starts focusing on an object but before the object actually gains focus.
- ⊖ **onbeforefocusleave** (Web) names a script to run when a user starts leaving an object but before the object actually loses focus.
- ⊖ **onbeforepaste** (Web) names a script to run when a user starts pasting an object but before any action actually takes place.
- ⊖ **onblur** (Web) names a script to run when the object loses focus (that is, it is no longer the active element).
- **onclick** (Web) names a script to run when a user moves the mouse pointer or other pointing device over the subscript characters and clicks the button.
- ⊖ **oncontextmenu** (Web) names a script to run when a user right-clicks the mouse to open a shortcut menu.
- ⊖ **oncontrolselect** (Web) names a script to run when a user selects a control.
- ⊖ **oncopy** (Web) names a script to run when a user copies a selection to the Clipboard.
- ⊖ **oncut** (Web) names a script to run when a user cuts a selection to the Clipboard.

- `ondblclick` (Web) names a script to run when a user moves the mouse pointer or other pointing device over the subscript characters and double-clicks the button.
- ⊝ `ondrag` (Web) names a script to run when a user drags a selection.
- ⊝ `ondragend` (Web) names a script to run after a user completes a drag-and-drop operation.
- ⊝ `ondragenter` (Web) names a script to run when a user drags a selection into an area in which it can be dropped.
- ⊝ `ondragleave` (Web) names a script to run when a user drags a selection beyond an area in which it can be dropped.
- ⊝ `ondragover` (Web) names a script to run when a user drags a selection over an area in which it can be dropped.
- ⊝ `ondragstart` (Web) names a script to run when a user starts dragging a selection or element.
- ⊝ `ondrop` (Web) names a script to run when a user releases the mouse button to drop a dragged selection.
- ⊝ `onfocus` (Web) names a script to run when a user points the mouse pointer or other pointing device to focus on the current element.
- ⊝ `onfocusenter` (Web) names a script to run when a user focuses on the current element in any way.
- ⊝ `onfocusleave` (Web) names a script to run when a user inactivates the current element in any way.
- ⊝ `onhelp` (Web) names a script to run when a user presses the F1 or Help key over the current element.
- `onkeydown` (Web) names a script to run when a user presses and holds down a key over the subscript characters.
- `onkeypress` (Web) names a script to run when a user presses and releases a key over the subscript characters.
- `onkeyup` (Web) names a script to run when a user releases a key that is currently held down over the subscript characters.
- ⊝ `onlosecapture` (Web) names a script to run when a user releases a selection that has been captured by the mouse.
- `onmousedown` (Web) names a script to run when a user moves the mouse pointer or other pointing device over the subscript characters and presses and holds down the button.
- ⊝ `onmouseenter` (Web) names a script to run when a user moves the mouse pointer onto the object.
- ⊝ `onmouseleave` (Web) names a script to run when the mouse pointer leaves the object.
- `onmousemove` (Web) names a script to run when a user moves the mouse pointer or other pointing device over the subscript characters.
- `onmouseout` (Web) names a script to run when a user moves the mouse pointer or other pointing device away from the subscript characters.
- `onmouseover` (Web) names a script to run the first time a user moves the mouse pointer or other pointing device over the subscript characters.

- onmouseup (Web) names a script to run when a user moves the mouse pointer or other pointing device over the subscript characters and releases a mouse button that is currently held down.
- ☺ onpaste (Web) names a script to run when a user pastes the Clipboard contents onto the object.
- ☺ onpropertychange (Web) names a script to run when a property changes on the selected object in any way.
- ☺ onreadystatechange (Web) names a script to run when the status of an element has changed (for example, the element receives data).
- ☺ onresize (Web) names a script to run when a user resizes the selected object.
- ☺ onresizeend (Web) names a script to run after the object has been resized.
- ☺ onresizestart (Web) names a script to run as a user resizes the object.
- ☺ onselectstart (Web) names a script to run when a user starts selecting an object.
- style (Web) sets styles for the subscript characters.
- ☺ tabindex (Web) defines the position of the current element in all the elements that a user can navigate to using a Tab or Shift + Tab key.
- title (Web) provides a title for the subscript characters.
- *characters* represents one or more characters.

Notes

- This inline element originated in HTML 3.2.
- For the sub element, WebTV supports the class and style attributes.

Related Elements

bdo (52), big (57), br (70), font (131), q (246), small (268), span (272), sup (284)

sup	Superscript

Purpose

Moves one or more selected characters above the baseline on which other characters sit and applies a smaller font.

Syntax

```
<sup[ accesskey="shortcut_key"][ class="class_name"]
  [ contenteditable="edit_string"][ dir="ltr"|"rtl"]
  [ disabled="disabled"][ id="id_name"]
  [ lang="lang_code"][ language="javascript"|"jscript"
  |"vbs[cript]"][ onbeforecopy="bc_script"]
```

```
[ onbeforecut="bt_script"]
[ onbeforefocusenter="bfe_script"]
[ onbeforefocusleave="bfl_script"]
[ onbeforepaste="bp_script"][ onblur="bl_script"]
[ onclick="cl_script"][ oncontextmenu="cm_script"]
[ oncontrolselect="ctl_script"][ oncopy="cp_script"]
[ oncut="ct_script"][ ondblclick="dc_script"]
[ ondrag="d_script"][ ondragend="dd_script"]
[ ondragenter="de_script"][ ondragleave="dl_script"]
[ ondragover="do_script"][ ondragstart="ds_script"]
[ ondrop="dr_script"][ onfocus="fc_script"]
[ onfocusenter="fe_script"]
[ onfocusleave="fl_script"][ onhelp="hlp_script"]
[ onkeydown="kd_script"][ onkeypress="kp_script"]
[ onkeyup="ku_script"][ onlosecapture="lc_script"]
[ onmousedown="md_script"]
[ onmouseenter="me_script"]
[ onmouseleave="ml_script"]
[ onmousemove="mm_script"][ onmouseout="mo_script"]
[ onmouseover="mov_script"][ onmouseup="mu_script"]
[ onpaste="p_script"][ onpropertychange="pc_script"]
[ onreadystatechange="rsc_script"]
[ onresize="rsz_script"][ onresizeend="ree_script"]
[ onresizestart="res_script"]
[ onselectstart="ss_script"]
[ style="name_1: value_1"[; "name_2: value_2"]
[...; "name_n: value_n"]]
[ tabindex="position_number"][ title="title"]>
characters</sup>
```

Where

- ☺ accesskey (Web) assigns a shortcut key to the object in order to focus on it.
- class (Web) specifies a class identification for the superscript characters.
- ☺ contenteditable (Web) specifies or obtains a value that indicates whether a user can edit the element content.
- dir (Web) specifies the direction in which the superscript characters are displayed: left-to-right or right-to-left.
- ☺ disabled (Web) is a keyword that prevents a user from using the element.
- id (Web) provides a unique identifier name for the superscript characters.
- lang (Web) specifies the code for the language used for the superscript characters.

- ⊝ `language` (Web) declares the scripting language of the current script.
- ⊝ `onbeforecopy` (Web) names a script to run when a user starts copying a selection to the Clipboard but before any action actually takes place.
- ⊝ `onbeforecut` (Web) names a script to run when a user starts cutting a selection to the Clipboard but before any action actually takes place.
- ⊝ `onbeforefocusenter` (Web) names a script to run when a user starts focusing on an object but before the object actually gains focus.
- ⊝ `onbeforefocusleave` (Web) names a script to run when a user starts leaving an object but before the object actually loses focus.
- ⊝ `onbeforepaste` (Web) names a script to run when a user starts pasting an object but before any action actually takes place.
- ⊝ `onblur` (Web) names a script to run when the object loses focus (that is, it is no longer the active element).
- `onclick` (Web) names a script to run when a user moves the mouse pointer or other pointing device over the superscript characters and clicks the button.
- ⊝ `oncontextmenu` (Web) names a script to run when a user right-clicks the mouse to open a shortcut menu.
- ⊝ `oncontrolselect` (Web) names a script to run when a user selects a control.
- ⊝ `oncopy` (Web) names a script to run when a user copies a selection to the Clipboard.
- ⊝ `oncut` (Web) names a script to run when a user cuts a selection to the Clipboard.
- `ondblclick` (Web) names a script to run when a user moves the mouse pointer or other pointing device over the superscript characters and double-clicks the button.
- ⊝ `ondrag` (Web) names a script to run when a user drags a selection.
- ⊝ `ondragend` (Web) names a script to run after a user completes a drag-and-drop operation.
- ⊝ `ondragenter` (Web) names a script to run when a user drags a selection into an area in which it can be dropped.
- ⊝ `ondragleave` (Web) names a script to run when a user drags a selection beyond an area in which it can be dropped.
- ⊝ `ondragover` (Web) names a script to run when a user drags a selection over an area in which it can be dropped.
- ⊝ `ondragstart` (Web) names a script to run when a user starts dragging a selection or element.
- ⊝ `ondrop` (Web) names a script to run when a user releases the mouse button to drop a dragged selection.
- ⊝ `onfocus` (Web) names a script to run when a user points the mouse pointer or other pointing device to focus on the current element.
- ⊝ `onfocusenter` (Web) names a script to run when a user focuses on the current element in any way.
- ⊝ `onfocusleave` (Web) names a script to run when a user inactivates the current element in any way.

- ☺ onhelp (Web) names a script to run when a user presses the F1 or Help key over the current element.
- onkeydown (Web) names a script to run when a user presses and holds down a key over the superscript characters.
- onkeypress (Web) names a script to run when a user presses and releases a key over the superscript characters.
- onkeyup (Web) names a script to run when a user releases a key that is currently held down over the superscript characters.
- ☺ onlosecapture (Web) names a script to run when a user releases a selection that has been captured by the mouse.
- onmousedown (Web) names a script to run when a user moves the mouse pointer or other pointing device over the superscript characters and presses and holds down the button.
- ☺ onmouseenter (Web) names a script to run when a user moves the mouse pointer onto the object.
- ☺ onmouseleave (Web) names a script to run when the mouse pointer leaves the object.
- onmousemove (Web) names a script to run when a user moves the mouse pointer or other pointing device over the superscript characters.
- onmouseout (Web) names a script to run when a user moves the mouse pointer or other pointing device away from the superscript characters.
- onmouseover (Web) names a script to run the first time a user moves the mouse pointer or other pointing device over the superscript characters.
- onmouseup (Web) names a script to run when a user moves the mouse pointer or other pointing device over the superscript characters and releases a mouse button that is currently held down.
- ☺ onpaste (Web) names a script to run when a user pastes the Clipboard contents onto the object.
- ☺ onpropertychange (Web) names a script to run when a property changes on the selected object in any way.
- ☺ onreadystatechange (Web) names a script to run when the status of an element has changed (for example, the element receives data).
- ☺ onresize (Web) names a script to run when a user resizes the selected object.
- ☺ onresizeend (Web) names a script to run after the object has been resized.
- ☺ onresizestart (Web) names a script to run as a user resizes the object.
- ☺ onselectstart (Web) names a script to run when a user starts selecting an object.
- style (Web) sets styles for the superscript characters.
- ☺ tabindex (Web) defines the position of the current element in all the elements that a user can navigate to using a Tab or Shift + Tab key.
- title (Web) provides a title for the superscript characters.
- *characters* represents one or more characters.

Notes
- This inline element originated in HTML 3.2.
- For the sup element, WebTV supports the `class` and `style` attributes.

Related Elements
bdo (52), big (57), br (70), font (136), q (246), small (268), span (272), sub (281)

table   Table

Purpose
Defines a table.

Syntax
```
<table[ accesskey="shortcut_key"]
  [ align="left"|"center"|"right"|"bleedleft"
  |"bleedright"|"justify"][ background="picture-uri"]
  [ bgcolor="#rrggbb"|"color"][ border="border_pix"]
  [ bordercolor="#rrggbb"|"color"]
  [ bordercolordark="#rrggbb"|"color"]
  [ bordercolorlight="#rrggbb"|"color"]
  [ cellpadding="cell_pad"][ cellspacing="cell_space"]
  [ class="class_name"][ cols="num_cols"]
  [ contenteditable="edit_string"]
  [ datapagesize="num_records"]
  [ datasrc="ds_identifier"][ dir="ltr"|"rtl"]
  [ disabled="disabled"][ FRAME="void"|"above"|"below"
  |"border"|"box"|"hsides"|"lhs"|"rhs"|"vsides"]
  [ gradangle="gradient_angle_value"]
  [ gradcolor="#rrggbb"|"color"]
  [ height=height pix"|height%][ hspace="horiz_pix"]
  [ id="id_name"][ lang="lang_code"]
  [ language="javascript"|"jscript"|"vbs[cript]"]
  [ nowrap="nowrap"][ onbeforecut="bt_script"]
  [ onbeforeeditfocus="bef_script"]
  [ onbeforefocusenter="bfe_script"]
  [ onbeforefocusleave="bfl_script"]
  [ onbeforepaste="bp_script"][ onblur="bl_script"]
  [ onclick="cl_script"][ oncontextmenu="cm_script"]
  [ oncontrolselect="ctl_script"][ oncut="ct_script"]
  [ ondblclick="dc_script"][ ondrag="d_script"]
  [ ondragend="dd_script"][ ondragenter="de_script"]
```

XHTML Syntax

```
[ ondragleave="dl_script" ][ ondragover="do_script" ]
[ ondragstart="ds_script" ][ ondrop="dr_script" ]
[ onfilterchange="f_script" ][ onfocus="fc_script" ]
[ onfocusenter="fe_script" ]
[ onfocusleave="fl_script" ][ onhelp="hlp_script" ]
[ onkeydown="kd_script" ][ onkeypress="kp_script" ]
[ onkeyup="ku_script" ][ onlosecapture="lc_script" ]
[ onmousedown="md_script" ]
[ onmouseenter="me_script" ]
[ onmouseleave="ml_script" ]
[ onmousemove="mm_script" ][ onmouseout="mo_script" ]
[ onmouseover="mov_script" ][ onmouseup="mu_script" ]
[ onpaste="p_script" ][ onpropertychange="pc_script" ]
[ onreadystatechange="rsc_script" ]
[ onresize="rsz_script" ][ onresizeend="ree_script" ]
[ onresizestart="res_script" ][ onscroll="sc_script" ]
[ onselectstart="ss_script" ][ rules="none"|"groups"
|"rows"|"cols"|"all" ][ style="name_1: value_1"
[; "name_2: value_2" ][...; "name_n: value_n" ]]
[ tabindex="position_number" ][ title="title" ]
[ transparency="trans_value" ][ vspace="vert_pix" ]
[ width="width_pix"|width_% ]>table-contents</table>
```

Where

- ⊖ accesskey (Web) assigns a shortcut key to the object in order to focus on it.
- align (Web) indicates the horizontal alignment of the text within the table: aligned with the left or right margin or centered between the left and right margins. bleedleft, bleedright, and justify are Microsoft-defined values. This attribute is deprecated; use a style sheet instead.
- ⊖⌖ background (Web) specifies an image file that is displayed in the background of the table.
- bgcolor (Web) specifies the background color for the table. This attribute is deprecated; use a style sheet instead.
- border (Web) turns on a table border and sets its width in pixels.
- ⊖ bordercolor (Web) is the color of the table border.
- ⊖ bordercolordark (Web) is the color of the table border shadow.
- ⊖ bordercolorlight (Web) is the color of the table border highlight.
- cellpadding (Web) sets spacing, in pixels or by percentage of the window width, between cell borders and the cell contents.
- cellspacing (Web) sets spacing, in pixels or by percentage of the window width, between the cells.
- class (Web) specifies a class identification for the table.
- ⊖Ⓝ cols (Web) specifies the number of columns in the current table.

- ⊖ contenteditable (Web) specifies or obtains a value that indicates whether a user can edit the element content.
- ⊖ datapagesize (Web) indicates the number of records included in a repeated table.
- ⊖ datasrc (Web) specifies the identifier of the data source object.
- dir (Web) specifies the direction in which the table contents are displayed: left-to-right or right-to-left.
- ⊖ disabled (Web) is a keyword that prevents a user from using the element.
- frame (Web) specifies the table borders that are displayed onscreen or are hidden.

●—NOTE

The frame attribute refers to the border of the table and is not related to the frame element (**139**).

- ⧄ gradangle (Web) specifies a gradient angle to gradually change the color in a table.
- ⧄ gradcolor (Web) specifies the end color for a gradient. Use this attribute in conjunction with the bgcolor attribute.
- ⊖ℕ⧄ height (Web) specifies the height of the table, in pixels or as a percentage of the entire height of the computer screen.
- ℕ⧄ hspace (Web) sets the vertical area, in pixels, in which the table will fit.
- id (Web) provides a unique identifier name for the table.
- lang (Web) specifies the code for the language used for the table contents.
- ⊖ language (Web) declares the scripting language of the current script.
- ⧄ nowrap (Web) disables word wrap within the table.
- ⊖ onbeforecut (Web) names a script to run when a user starts cutting a selection to the Clipboard but before any action actually takes place.
- ⊖ onbeforeeditfocus (Web) names a script to run when a user starts activating an object but before the object actually becomes active.
- ⊖ onbeforefocusenter (Web) names a script to run when a user starts focusing on an object but before the object actually gains focus.
- ⊖ onbeforefocusleave (Web) names a script to run when a user starts leaving an object but before the object actually loses focus.
- ⊖ onbeforepaste (Web) names a script to run when a user starts pasting an object but before any action actually takes place.
- ⊖ onblur (Web) names a script to run when the object loses focus (that is, it is no longer the active element).
- onclick (Web) names a script to run when a user moves the mouse pointer or other pointing device over the table and clicks the device button.
- ⊖ oncontextmenu (Web) names a script to run when a user right-clicks the mouse to open a shortcut menu.

- ⊖ oncontrolselect (Web) names a script to run when a user selects a control.
- ⊖ oncut (Web) names a script to run when a user cuts a selection to the Clipboard.
- ondblclick (Web) names a script to run when a user moves the mouse pointer or other pointing device over the table and double-clicks the device button.
- ⊖ ondrag (Web) names a script to run when a user drags a selection.
- ⊖ ondragend (Web) names a script to run after a user completes a drag-and-drop operation.
- ⊖ ondragenter (Web) names a script to run when a user drags a selection into an area in which it can be dropped.
- ⊖ ondragleave (Web) names a script to run when a user drags a selection beyond an area in which it can be dropped.
- ⊖ ondragover (Web) names a script to run when a user drags a selection over an area in which it can be dropped.
- ⊖ ondragstart (Web) names a script to run when a user starts dragging a selection or element.
- ⊖ ondrop (Web) names a script to run when a user releases the mouse button to drop a dragged selection.
- ⊖ onfilterchange (Web) names a script to run when a visual filter changes in any way.
- ⊖ onfocus (Web) names a script to run when a user points the mouse pointer or other pointing device to focus on the current element.
- ⊖ onfocusenter (Web) names a script to run when a user focuses on the current element in any way.
- ⊖ onfocusleave (Web) names a script to run when a user inactivates the current element in any way.
- ⊖ onhelp (Web) names a script to run when a user presses the F1 or Help key over the current element.
- onkeydown (Web) names a script to run when a user presses and holds down a key over the table.
- onkeypress (Web) names a script to run when a user presses and releases a key over the table.
- onkeyup (Web) names a script to run when a user releases a key that is currently held down over the table.
- ⊖ onlosecapture (Web) names a script to run when a user releases a selection that has been captured by the mouse.
- onmousedown (Web) names a script to run when a user moves the mouse pointer or other pointing device over the table and presses and holds down the device button.
- ⊖ onmouseenter (Web) names a script to run when a user moves the mouse pointer onto the object.
- ⊖ onmouseleave (Web) names a script to run when the mouse pointer leaves the object.
- onmousemove (Web) names a script to run when a user moves the mouse pointer or other pointing device over the table.

XHTML Syntax

- onmouseout (Web) names a script to run when a user moves the mouse pointer or other pointing device away from the table.
- onmouseover (Web) names a script to run the first time a user moves the mouse pointer or other pointing device over the table.
- onmouseup (Web) names a script to run when a user moves the mouse pointer or other pointing device over the table and releases a pressed-down device button.
- ⊖ onpaste (Web) names a script to run when a user pastes the Clipboard contents onto the object.
- ⊖ onpropertychange (Web) names a script to run when a property changes on the selected object in any way.
- ⊖ onreadystatechange (Web) names a script to run when the status of an element has changed (for example, the element receives data).
- ⊖ onresize (Web) names a script to run when a user resizes the selected object.
- ⊖ onresizeend (Web) names a script to run after the object has been resized.
- ⊖ onresizestart (Web) names a script to run as a user resizes the object.
- ⊖ onscroll (Web) names a script to run when a user moves the scroll box within the scroll bar.
- ⊖ onselectstart (Web) names a script to run when a user starts selecting an object.
- rules (Web) specifies the display of the inside table borders.
- style (Web) sets styles for the column group.
- ⊖ tabindex (Web) defines the position of the current element in all the elements that a user can navigate to using a Tab or Shift + Tab key.
- title (Web) provides a title for the table.
- ▯ transparency (Web) sets the level of transparency or opaqueness of the table.
- ⓝ vspace (Web) sets the vertical area, in pixels, in which the table will fit.
- width (Web) indicates the absolute width of the table, in pixels or as a percentage of the full-screen width.
- *table-contents* are the rows and columns; the table header (thead), table body (tbody), table footer (tfoot), and th (table headings) elements; and/or the td (table data) elements within the table.

Notes

- This block-level element originated in HTML 3.2.
- A table must contain at least one row.
- A tfoot element must precede the optional tbody element within a table so that the browser can calculate the dimensions and contents of the footer.

- The bgcolor value defined within table is overridden by the bgcolor defined for table rows (tr), which in turn is overridden by the bgcolor defined for table headings (th) and table data (td).
- border="0" removes a border.
- The border attribute must be specified in order for the frame or rules attribute to be used.
- Using percentages for the height and width attributes can cause unexpected results. Of course, specifying actual heights and widths in pixels means that you must spend time measuring and calculating.
- The rules attribute is valid only if you use the following elements: tbody, tfoot, and thead.
- The following elements are child elements of table: caption, col, colgroup, tbody, tfoot, and thead.
- WebTV supports the following attributes for table: align, background, bgcolor, border, cellpadding, cellspacing, class, gradangle, gradcolor, height, hspace, id, lang, nowrap, style, transparency, and width.

Related Elements
caption (76), col (90), colgroup (92), tbody (293), td (297), tfoot (307), th (310), thead (315), tr (319)

For More Information
Learn more about the table element on page 555 in Chapter 4.

tbody	Table Body

Purpose
Defines the body of a table and allows you to align the table body rows as a single unit.

Syntax

```
<tbody[ accesskey="shortcut_key"]
  [ align="left"|"center"|"right"|"justify"
  |"char"][ bgcolor="#rrggbb"|"color"]
  [ char="character"][ charoff="offset"]
  [ class="class_name"]
  [ contenteditable="edit_string"][ dir="ltr"|"rtl"]
  [ disabled="disabled"][ id="id_name"]
  [ lang="lang_code"][ language="javascript"|"jscript"
  |"vbs[cript]"][ onbeforecut="bt_script"]
  [ onbeforefocusenter="bfe_script"]
  [ onbeforefocusleave="bfl_script"]
  [ onbeforepaste="bp_script"][ onblur="bl_script"]
```

```
[ onclick="cl_script"][ oncontextmenu="cm_script"]
[ oncontrolselect="ctl_script"][ oncut="ct_script"]
[ ondblclick="dc_script"][ ondrag="d_script"]
[ ondragend="dd_script"][ ondragenter="de_script"]
[ ondragleave="dl_script"][ ondragover="do_script"]
[ ondragstart="ds_script"][ ondrop="dr_script"]
[ onfocus="fc_script"][ onfocusenter="fe_script"]
[ onfocusleave="fl_script"][ onhelp="hlp_script"]
[ onkeydown="kd_script"][ onkeypress="kp_script"]
[ onkeyup="ku_script"][ onlosecapture="lc_script"]
[ onmousedown="md_script"]
[ onmouseenter="me_script"]
[ onmouseleave="ml_script"]
[ onmousemove="mm_script"][ onmouseout="mo_script"]
[ onmouseover="mov_script"][ onmouseup="mu_script"]
[ onpaste="p_script"][ onpropertychange="pc_script"]
[ onreadystatechange="rsc_script"]
[ onresizeend="ree_script"]
[ onresizestart="res_script"]
[ onselectstart="ss_script"]
[ style="name_1: value_1"[; "name_2: value_2"]
[...; "name_n: value_n"]]
[ tabindex="position_number"][ title="title"]
[ valign="middle"|"top"|"bottom"|"baseline"]>
table-body</tbody>
```

Where

- ⊖ accesskey (Web) assigns a shortcut key to the object in order to focus on it.
- align (Web) indicates the horizontal alignment of the text within the table body: aligned with the left or right margin, centered between the left and right margins, or aligned with a particular character. This attribute is deprecated and does not appear in any HTML 4.0 DTD; use a style sheet instead.
- ⊖ bgcolor (Web) specifies the background color for the table body cells.
- char (Web) names a character from which text is aligned in both directions.
- charoff (Web) sets the horizontal distance between the left or right margin and the first occurrence of the char character.
- class (Web) specifies a class identification for the table body.
- ⊖ contenteditable (Web) specifies or obtains a value that indicates whether a user can edit the element content.
- dir (Web) specifies the direction in which the table body contents are displayed: left-to-right or right-to-left.

- ⊖ `disabled` (Web) is a keyword that prevents a user from using the element.
- `id` (Web) provides a unique identifier name for the table body.
- `lang` (Web) specifies the code for the language used within the table body.
- ⊖ `language` (Web) declares the scripting language of the current script.
- ⊖ `onbeforecut` (Web) names a script to run when a user starts cutting a selection to the Clipboard but before any action actually takes place.
- ⊖ `onbeforefocusenter` (Web) names a script to run when a user starts focusing on an object but before the object actually gains focus.
- ⊖ `onbeforefocusleave` (Web) names a script to run when a user starts leaving an object but before the object actually loses focus.
- ⊖ `onbeforepaste` (Web) names a script to run when a user starts pasting an object but before any action actually takes place.
- ⊖ `onblur` (Web) names a script to run when the object loses focus (that is, it is no longer the active element).
- `onclick` (Web) names a script to run when a user moves the mouse pointer or other pointing device over the table body and clicks the device button.
- ⊖ `oncontextmenu` (Web) names a script to run when a user right-clicks the mouse to open a shortcut menu.
- ⊖ `oncontrolselect` (Web) names a script to run when a user selects a control.
- ⊖ `oncut` (Web) names a script to run when a user cuts a selection to the Clipboard.
- `ondblclick` (Web) names a script to run when a user moves the mouse pointer or other pointing device over the table body and double-clicks the device button.
- ⊖ `ondrag` (Web) names a script to run when a user drags a selection.
- ⊖ `ondragend` (Web) names a script to run after a user completes a drag-and-drop operation.
- ⊖ `ondragenter` (Web) names a script to run when a user drags a selection into an area in which it can be dropped.
- ⊖ `ondragleave` (Web) names a script to run when a user drags a selection beyond an area in which it can be dropped.
- ⊖ `ondragover` (Web) names a script to run when a user drags a selection over an area in which it can be dropped.
- ⊖ `ondragstart` (Web) names a script to run when a user starts dragging a selection or element.
- ⊖ `ondrop` (Web) names a script to run when a user releases the mouse button to drop a dragged selection.
- ⊖ `onfocus` (Web) names a script to run when a user points the mouse pointer or other pointing device to focus on the current element.
- ⊖ `onfocusenter` (Web) names a script to run when a user focuses on the current element in any way.
- ⊖ `onfocusleave` (Web) names a script to run when a user inactivates the current element in any way.

- ⊖ onhelp (Web) names a script to run when a user presses the F1 or Help key over the current element.
- onkeydown (Web) names a script to run when a user presses and holds down a key over the table body.
- onkeypress (Web) names a script to run when a user presses and releases a key over the table body.
- onkeyup (Web) names a script to run when a user releases a key that is currently held down over the table body.
- ⊖ onlosecapture (Web) names a script to run when a user releases a selection that has been captured by the mouse.
- onmousedown (Web) names a script to run when a user moves the mouse pointer or other pointing device over the table body and presses and holds down the device button.
- ⊖ onmouseenter (Web) names a script to run when a user moves the mouse pointer onto the object.
- ⊖ onmouseleave (Web) names a script to run when the mouse pointer leaves the object.
- onmousemove (Web) names a script to run when a user moves the mouse pointer or other pointing device over the table body.
- onmouseout (Web) names a script to run when a user moves the mouse pointer or other pointing device away from the table body.
- onmouseover (Web) names a script to run the first time a user moves the mouse pointer or other pointing device over the table body.
- onmouseup (Web) names a script to run when a user moves the mouse pointer or other pointing device over the table body and releases a pressed-down device button.
- ⊖ onpaste (Web) names a script to run when a user pastes the Clipboard contents onto the object.
- ⊖ onpropertychange (Web) names a script to run when a property changes on the selected object in any way.
- ⊖ onreadystatechange (Web) names a script to run when the status of an element has changed (for example, the element receives data).
- ⊖ onresizeend (Web) names a script to run after the object has been resized.
- ⊖ onresizestart (Web) names a script to run as a user resizes the object.
- ⊖ onselectstart (Web) names a script to run when a user starts selecting an object.
- style (Web) sets styles for the table body.
- ⊖ tabindex (Web) defines the position of the current element in all the elements that a user can navigate to using a Tab or Shift + Tab key.
- title (Web) provides a title for the table body.
- valign (Web) indicates the vertical alignment of the table body, from the top to the bottom.
- *table-body* indicates the rows that make up the body of a table.

Notes

- This is an HTML 4.0 element. Previously, it was a Microsoft extension.
- A table can contain more than one table body.
- A table group (that is, tbody, tfoot, and/or thead) must contain one or more rows.
- A tfoot element must precede the optional tbody element within a table so that the browser can calculate the dimensions and contents of the foot.
- When a table contains a body without thead or tfoot sections, the tbody element is optional.

Related Elements

caption (76), col (90), colgroup (92), table (288), td (297), tfoot (307), th (310), thead (315), tr (315)

For More Information

Learn more about the tbody element on page 565 in Chapter 4.

td   Table Data

Purpose

Defines the data in a table cell.

Syntax

```
<td[ abbr=abbr_text][ accesskey="shortcut_key"]
  [ align="left"|"center"|"right"|"justify"|"char]
  [ axis="categ_name"[ ,categ_name[..., categ_name]
  [ background="picture_uri"]
  [ bgcolor="#rrggbb"|"color"]
  [ bordercolor="#rrggbb"|"color"]
  [ bordercolordark="#rrggbb"|"color"]
  [ bordercolorlight="#rrggbb"|"color"]
  [ char="character"][ charoff="offset"]
  [ class="class_name"][ colsPAN="num_cols"|"1"|"0"]
  [ contenteditable="edit_string"][ dir="ltr"|"rtl"]
  [ disabled="disabled"]
  [ gradangle="gradient_angle_value"]
  [ gradcolor="#rrggbb"|"color"]
  [ headers="id_name"[ id_name[...id_name]]
  [ height="height_pix"|"height_%"]
  [ id="id_name"][ lang="lang_code"]
  [ language="javascript"|"jscript"|"vbs[cript]"]
  [ nowrap="nowrap"][ onbeforecopy="bc_script"]
  [ onbeforecut="bt_script"]
```

```
[ onbeforeeditfocus="bef_script"]
[ onbeforefocusenter="bfe_script"]
[ onbeforefocusleave="bfl_script"]
[ onbeforepaste="bp_script"][ onblur="bl_script"]
[ onclick="cl_script"][ oncontextmenu="cm_script"]
[ oncontrolselect="ctl_script"][ oncopy="cp_script"]
[ oncut="ct_script"][ ondblclick="dc_script"]
[ ondrag="d_script"][ ondragend="dd_script"]
[ ondragenter="de_script"][ ondragleave="dl_script"]
[ ondragover="do_script"][ ondragstart="ds_script"]
[ ondrop="dr_script"][ onfilterchange="f_script"]
[ onfocus="fc_script"][ onfocusenter="fe_script"]
[ onfocusleave="fl_script"][ onhelp="hlp_script"]
[ onkeydown="kd_script"][ onkeypress="kp_script"]
[ onkeyup="ku_script"][ onlosecapture="lc_script"]
[ onmousedown="md_script"]
[ onmouseenter="me_script"]
[ onmouseleave="ml_script"]
[ onmousemove="mm_script"][ onmouseout="mo_script"]
[ onmouseover="mov_script"][ onmouseup="mu_script"]
[ onpaste="p_script"][ onpropertychange="pc_script"]
[ onreadystatechange="rsc_script"]
[ onresizeend="ree_script"]
[ onresizestart="res_script"]
[ onselectstart="ss_script"]
[ rowspan="num_rows"|"1"|"0"]
[ scope=row|col|rowgroup|colgroup]
[ style="name_1: value_1"[; "name_2: value_2"]
[...; "name_n: value_n"]]
[ tabindex="position_number"][ title="title"]
[ transparency="trans_value"]
[ valign="middle"|"top"|"bottom"|"baseline"]
[ width="width_pix"|"width_%"]>cell-contents</td>
```

Where

- abbr (Web) is an abbreviation for the content of the cell.
- Ⓔ accesskey (Web) assigns a shortcut key to the object in order to focus on it.
- align (Web) indicates the horizontal alignment of the text within the table cell: aligned with the left or right margin, centered between the left and right margins, or aligned with a particular character. This attribute is deprecated and does not appear in any HTML 4.0 DTD; use a style sheet instead.

- `axis` (Web) is a list of one or more axis names, separated by commas, that categorize related cells.
- ⊖📑 `background` (Web) specifies an image file that is displayed in the background of the cell.
- `bgcolor` (Web) specifies the background color for the cell. This attribute is deprecated; use a style sheet instead.
- ⊖ `bordercolor` (Web) is the color of the cell border.
- ⊖ `bordercolordark` (Web) is the color of the cell border shadow.
- ⊖ `bordercolorlight` (Web) is the color of the cell border highlight.
- `char` (Web) names a character from which text is aligned in both directions.
- `charoff` (Web) sets the horizontal distance (offset) between the left or right margin and the first occurrence of the `char` character.
- `class` (Web) specifies a class identification for the cell.
- `colspan` (Web) specifies the number of columns over which the current cell will extend.
- ⊖ `contenteditable` (Web) specifies or obtains a value that indicates whether a user can edit the element content.
- `dir` (Web) specifies the direction in which the cell contents are displayed: left-to-right or right-to-left.
- ⊖ `disabled` (Web) is a keyword that prevents a user from using the element.
- 📑 `gradangle` (Web) specifies a gradient angle to gradually change the color in a table.
- 📑 `gradcolor` (Web) specifies the end color for a gradient. Use this attribute in conjunction with the `bgcolor` attribute.
- `headers` (Web) lists one or more cell identifiers that provide information about the current cell.
- ⊖📑 `height` (Web) specifies the height of the cell, in pixels or as a percentage.
- `id` (Web) provides a unique identifier name for the cell.
- `lang` (Web) specifies the code for the language used within the cell.
- ⊖ `language` (Web) declares the scripting language of the current script.
- `nowrap` (Web) disables word wrap within the current cell. This attribute is deprecated; use a style sheet instead.
- ⊖ `onbeforecopy` (Web) names a script to run when a user starts copying a selection to the Clipboard but before any action actually takes place.
- ⊖ `onbeforecut` (Web) names a script to run when a user starts cutting a selection to the Clipboard but before any action actually takes place.
- ⊖ `onbeforeeditfocus` (Web) names a script to run when a user starts activating an object but before the object actually becomes active.
- ⊖ `onbeforefocusenter` (Web) names a script to run when a user starts focusing on an object but before the object actually gains focus.
- ⊖ `onbeforefocusleave` (Web) names a script to run when a user starts leaving an object but before the object actually loses focus.
- ⊖ `onbeforepaste` (Web) names a script to run when a user starts pasting an object but before any action actually takes place.

- ⊖ onblur (Web) names a script to run when the object loses focus (that is, it is no longer the active element).
- onclick (Web) names a script to run when a user moves the mouse pointer or other pointing device over the cell and clicks the device button.
- ⊖ oncontextmenu (Web) names a script to run when a user right-clicks the mouse to open a shortcut menu.
- ⊖ oncontrolselect (Web) names a script to run when a user selects a control.
- ⊖ oncopy (Web) names a script to run when a user copies a selection to the Clipboard.
- ⊖ oncut (Web) names a script to run when a user cuts a selection to the Clipboard.
- ondblclick (Web) names a script to run when a user moves the mouse pointer or other pointing device over the cell and double-clicks the device button.
- ⊖ ondrag (Web) names a script to run when a user drags a selection.
- ⊖ ondragend (Web) names a script to run after a user completes a drag-and-drop operation.
- ⊖ ondragenter (Web) names a script to run when a user drags a selection into an area in which it can be dropped.
- ⊖ ondragleave (Web) names a script to run when a user drags a selection beyond an area in which it can be dropped.
- ⊖ ondragover (Web) names a script to run when a user drags a selection over an area in which it can be dropped.
- ⊖ ondragstart (Web) names a script to run when a user starts dragging a selection or element.
- ⊖ ondrop (Web) names a script to run when a user releases the mouse button to drop a dragged selection.
- ⊖ onfilterchange (Web) names a script to run when a visual filter changes in any way.
- ⊖ onfocus (Web) names a script to run when a user points the mouse pointer or other pointing device to focus on the current element.
- ⊖ onfocusenter (Web) names a script to run when a user focuses on the current element in any way.
- ⊖ onfocusleave (Web) names a script to run when a user inactivates the current element in any way.
- ⊖ onhelp (Web) names a script to run when a user presses the F1 or Help key over the current element.
- onkeydown (Web) names a script to run when a user presses and holds down a key over the cell.
- onkeypress (Web) names a script to run when a user presses and releases a key over the cell.
- onkeyup (Web) names a script to run when a user releases a key that is currently held down over the cell.

- ⊖ `onlosecapture` (Web) names a script to run when a user releases a selection that has been captured by the mouse.
- `onmousedown` (Web) names a script to run when a user moves the mouse pointer or other pointing device over the cell and presses and holds down the device button.
- ⊖ `onmouseenter` (Web) names a script to run when a user moves the mouse pointer onto the object.
- ⊖ `onmouseleave` (Web) names a script to run when the mouse pointer leaves the object.
- `onmousemove` (Web) names a script to run when a user moves the mouse pointer or other pointing device over the cell.
- `onmouseout` (Web) names a script to run when a user moves the mouse pointer or other pointing device away from the cell.
- `onmouseover` (Web) names a script to run the first time a user moves the mouse pointer or other pointing device over the cell.
- `onmouseup` (Web) names a script to run when a user moves the mouse pointer or other pointing device over the cell and releases a pressed-down device button.
- ⊖ `onpaste` (Web) names a script to run when a user pastes the Clipboard contents onto the object.
- ⊖ `onpropertychange` (Web) names a script to run when a property changes on the selected object in any way.
- ⊖ `onreadystatechange` (Web) names a script to run when the status of an element has changed (for example, the element receives data).
- ⊖ `onresizeend` (Web) names a script to run after the object has been resized.
- ⊖ `onresizestart` (Web) names a script to run as a user resizes the object.
- ⊖ `onselectstart` (Web) names a script to run when a user starts selecting an object.
- `rowspan` (Web) specifies the number of rows down which the current cell will extend.
- `scope` (Web) uses the `row`, `col`, `rowgroup`, or `colgroup` keywords to specify one or more cells that provide information for the current cell.
- `style` (Web) sets styles for the cell.
- ⊖ `tabindex` (Web) defines the position of the current element in all the elements that a user can navigate to using a Tab or Shift + Tab key.
- `title` (Web) provides a title for the cell.
- 🗔 `transparency` (Web) sets the level of transparency or opaqueness of the cell.
- `valign` (Web) indicates the vertical alignment of the cell contents, from the top to the bottom.
- `width` (Web) specifies the width of the cell, in pixels or as a percentage (Internet Explorer only).
- `cell-contents` represents the data within the current cell.

Notes

- This element originated in HTML 3.2.
- When you create long and complicated tables, consider indenting the td and th elements under the tr elements in the XHTML document. This can help you to check for the accuracy of the elements and attributes that you select.
- If a browser does not support align="justify", it may revert to align="left". Note that the align attribute is deprecated; it is best to use a style sheet instead.
- The bgcolor value defined within td overrides the bgcolor defined for the row (tr) or the table (table).
- td is a child element of the tr element.
- WebTV supports the following attributes for td: align, background, bgcolor, class, colspan, gradangle, gradcolor, height, nowrap, rowspan, style, transparency, valign, and width.

Related Elements

caption (76), col (90), colgroup (92), table (288), tbody (293), tfoot (307), th (310), thead (315), tr (319)

For More Information

Learn more about the td element on page 561 in Chapter 4.

textarea   Multiline Text Input Area

Purpose

Inserts a multiline area for text input.

Syntax

```
<textarea cols="number_of_columns"
  rows="number_of_rows"[ accesskey="shortcut_key" ]
  [ bgcolor="#rrggbb"|"color"][ class="class_name" ]
  [ contenteditable="edit_string" ]
  [ cursor="#rrggbb"|"color"][ datafld="ds_col_name" ]
  [ datasrc="ds_identifier"][ dir="ltr"|"rtl" ]
  [ disabled="disabled"][ error="error_text" ]
  [ id="id_name"][ lang="lang_code" ]]
  [ language="javascript"|"jscript"|"vbs[cript]" ]
  [ name="element_name"][ onafterupdate="au_script" ]
  [ onbeforecopy="bc_script" ]
  [ onbeforecut="bt_script" ]
  [ onbeforeeditfocus="bef_script" ]
  [ onbeforefocusenter="bfe_script" ]
  [ onbeforefocusleave="bfl_script" ]
  [ onbeforepaste="bp_script" ]
```

```
[ onbeforeupdate="bu_script"][ onblur="bl_script"]
[ onchange="ch_script"][ onclick="cl_script"]
[ oncontextmenu="cm_script"]
[ oncontrolselect="ctl_script"][ oncut="ct_script"]
[ ondblclick="dc_script"][ ondrag="d_script"]
[ ondragend="dd_script"][ ondragenter="de_script"]
[ ondragleave="dl_script"][ ondragover="do_script"]
[ ondragstart="ds_script"][ ondrop="dr_script"]
[ onerrorupdate="eu_script"]
[ onfilterchange="f_script"][ onfocus="fc_script"]
[ onfocusenter="fe_script"]
[ onfocusleave="fl_script"][ onhelp="hlp_script"]
[ onkeydown="kd_script"][ onkeypress="kp_script"]
[ onkeyup="ku_script"][ onlosecapture="lc_script"]
[ onmousedown="md_script"]
[ onmouseenter="me_script"]
[ onmouseleave="ml_script"]
[ onmousemove="mm_script"][ onmouseout="mo_script"]
[ onmouseover="mov_script"][ onmouseup="mu_script"]
[ onpaste="p_script"][ onpropertychange="pc_script"]
[ onreadystatechange="rsc_script"]
[ onresize="rsz_script"][ onresizeend="ree_script"]
[ onresizestart="res_script"][ onscroll="sc_script"]
[ onselect="sl_script"][ onselectstart="ss_script"]
[ readonly="readonly"][ style="name_1: value_1"
[; name_2: value_2"][...; name_n: value_n"]]]
[ tabindex="position_number"][ title="title"]
[ type="textarea"][ usestyle][ wrap="off"
|"hard"|"soft"|"physical"|"virtual"]>
text-lines</textarea>
```

Where

- cols (Web) indicates the width of the text input area, by the number of columns, one per character.
- rows (Web) indicates the height of the text input area, by the number of text lines, one row per line of text.
- accesskey (Web) assigns a shortcut key to the element in order to focus on it.
- ⛁ bgcolor (Web) specifies the background color for the text area.
- class (Web) specifies a class identification for the input area.
- ⊖ contenteditable (Web) specifies or obtains a value that indicates whether a user can edit the element content.
- ⛁ cursor (Web) specifies the cursor color for the text area.
- ⊖ datafld (Web) specifies the column name from the file that contains the data source object.

- ⊖ `datasrc` (Web) specifies the identifier of the data source object.
- `dir` (Web) specifies the direction in which the input area text is displayed: left-to-right or right-to-left.
- `disabled` (Web) prevents user input in the text area. `disabled` is unavailable for this element but may be available in a future XHTML version.
- ⍩ `error` (Web) specifies error text for the text area.
- `id` (Web) provides a unique identifier name for the input area.
- `lang` (Web) provides the code representing the language used for the input area text.
- ⊖ `language` (Web) declares the scripting language of the current script.
- `name` (Web) specifies the name of this text input area.
- ⊖ `onafterupdate` (Web) names a script to run after data has been transferred from the element to the data resource.
- ⊖ `onbeforecopy` (Web) names a script to run when a user starts copying a selection to the Clipboard but before any action actually takes place.
- ⊖ `onbeforecut` (Web) names a script to run when a user starts cutting a selection to the Clipboard but before any action actually takes place.
- ⊖ `onbeforeeditfocus` (Web) names a script to run when a user starts activating an object but before the object actually becomes active.
- ⊖ `onbeforefocusenter` (Web) names a script to run when a user starts focusing on an object but before the object actually gains focus.
- ⊖ `onbeforefocusleave` (Web) names a script to run when a user starts leaving an object but before the object actually loses focus.
- ⊖ `onbeforepaste` (Web) names a script to run when a user starts pasting an object but before any action actually takes place.
- ⊖ `onbeforeupdate` (Web) names a script to run before data is transferred from the element to the data resource.
- `onblur` (Web) names a script to run when the input area loses focus.
- `onchange` (Web) names a script to run when an input area loses focus after it has gained focus and has had a value change.
- `onclick` (Web) names a script to run when a user moves the mouse pointer or other pointing device over the input area and clicks the device button.
- ⊖ `oncontextmenu` (Web) names a script to run when a user right-clicks the mouse to open a shortcut menu.
- ⊖ `oncontrolselect` (Web) names a script to run when a user selects a control.
- ⊖ `oncut` (Web) names a script to run when a user cuts a selection to the Clipboard.
- `ondblclick` (Web) names a script to run when a user moves the mouse pointer or other pointing device over the input area and double-clicks the device button.
- ⊖ `ondrag` (Web) names a script to run when a user drags a selection.
- ⊖ `ondragend` (Web) names a script to run after a user completes a drag-and-drop operation.

- Ⓔ `ondragenter` (Web) names a script to run when a user drags a selection into an area in which it can be dropped.
- Ⓔ `ondragleave` (Web) names a script to run when a user drags a selection beyond an area in which it can be dropped.
- Ⓔ `ondragover` (Web) names a script to run when a user drags a selection over an area in which it can be dropped.
- Ⓔ `ondragstart` (Web) names a script to run when a user starts dragging a selection or element.
- Ⓔ `ondrop` (Web) names a script to run when a user releases the mouse button to drop a dragged selection.
- Ⓔ `onerrorupdate` (Web) names a script to run when an error occurs while data is updated in the data resource.
- Ⓔ `onfilterchange` (Web) names a script to run when a visual filter changes in any way.
- `onfocus` (Web) names a script to run when a user points the mouse pointer or other pointing device to focus on the current element.
- Ⓔ `onfocusenter` (Web) names a script to run when a user focuses on the current element in any way.
- Ⓔ `onfocusleave` (Web) names a script to run when a user inactivates the current element in any way.
- Ⓔ `onhelp` (Web) names a script to run when a user presses the F1 or Help key over the current element.
- `onkeydown` (Web) names a script to run when a user presses and holds down a key over the input area.
- `onkeypress` (Web) names a script to run when a user presses and releases a key over the input area.
- `onkeyup` (Web) names a script to run when a user releases a key that is currently held down over the input area.
- Ⓔ `onlosecapture` (Web) names a script to run when a user releases a selection that has been captured by the mouse.
- `onmousedown` (Web) names a script to run when a user moves the mouse pointer or other pointing device over the input area and presses and holds down the device button.
- Ⓔ `onmouseenter` (Web) names a script to run when a user moves the mouse pointer onto the object.
- Ⓔ `onmouseleave` (Web) names a script to run when the mouse pointer leaves the object.
- `onmousemove` (Web) names a script to run when a user moves the mouse pointer or other pointing device over the input area.
- `onmouseout` (Web) names a script to run when a user moves the mouse pointer or other pointing device away from the input area.
- `onmouseover` (Web) names a script to run the first time a user moves the mouse pointer or other pointing device over the input area.
- `onmouseup` (Web) names a script to run when a user moves the mouse pointer or other pointing device over the input area and releases a pressed-down device button.

- ⊜ onpaste (Web) names a script to run when a user pastes the Clipboard contents onto the object.
- ⊜ onpropertychange (Web) names a script to run when a property changes on the selected object in any way.
- ⊜ onreadystatechange (Web) names a script to run when the status of an element has changed (for example, the element receives data).
- ⊜ onresize (Web) names a script to run when a user resizes the selected object.
- ⊜ onresizeend (Web) names a script to run after the object has been resized.
- ⊜ onresizestart (Web) names a script to run as a user resizes the object.
- ⊜ onscroll (Web) names a script to run when a user moves the scroll box within the scroll bar.
- onselect (Web) names a script to run when a user selects some text in the input area.
- ⊜ onselectstart (Web) names a script to run when a user starts selecting an object.
- readonly (Web) does not allow a user to change the current value of the input area.
- style (Web) sets styles for the input area.
- tabindex (Web) defines the position of the input area in all the elements that a user can navigate to using a Tab or Shift + Tab key.
- title (Web) provides a title for the input area.
- ⊜ type (Web) specifies the type of control: a multiline text area.
- ⊘ usestyle (Web) indicates that the text area text is the same style as other text on the page.
- ⊜◻ wrap (Web) indicates whether the text wraps when it reaches the right margin of the text box.
- *text-lines* is the default text in the text input area.

Notes

- This inline element originated in HTML 2.0.
- In a text input area, you can type more characters than will be displayed at any time. You can use the vertical and horizontal scroll bars to scroll around the text in a text input area.
- WebTV supports the following attributes for textarea: bgcolor, cols, cursor, disabled, error, id, name, onblur, onchange, onfocus, onselectstart, readonly, rows, and usestyle.

Related Elements

button (72), fieldset (127), form (135), input (167), isindex (184), label (190), legend (195), optgroup (234), option (236), select (263)

For More Information

Learn more about the textarea element on page 610 in Chapter 7.

tfoot	**Table Footer**

Purpose

Defines the footer rows at the bottom of a table and enables you to align the table footer rows as a single unit.

Syntax

```
<tfoot[ accesskey="shortcut_key"]
    [ align="left"|"center"|"right"|"justify"
    |"char"][ bgcolor="#rrggbb"|"color"]
    [ char="character"][ charoff="offset"]
    [ class="class_name"]
    [ contenteditable="edit_string"][ dir="ltr"|"rtl"]
    [ disabled="disabled"][ id="id_name"]
    [ lang="lang_code"][ language="javascript"|"jscript"
    |"vbs[cript]"][ onbeforecut="bt_script"]
    [ onbeforefocusenter="bfe_script"]
    [ onbeforefocusleave="bfl_script"]
    [ onbeforepaste="bp_script"][ onblur="bl_script"]
    [ onclick="cl_script"][ oncontextmenu="cm_script"]
    [ oncontrolselect="ctl_script"][ oncut="ct_script"]
    [ ondblclick="dc_script"][ ondragenter="de_script"]
    [ ondragstart="ds_script"][ onfocus="fc_script"]
    [ onfocusenter="fe_script"]
    [ onfocusleave="fl_script"][ onhelp="hlp_script"]
    [ onkeydown="kd_script"][ onkeypress="kp_script"]
    [ onkeyup="ku_script"][ onlosecapture="lc_script"]
    [ onmousedown="md_script"]
    [ onmouseenter="me_script"]
    [ onmouseleave="ml_script"]
    [ onmousemove="mm_script"][ onmouseout="mo_script"]
    [ onmouseover="mov_script"][ onmouseup="mu_script"]
    [ onpaste="p_script"][ onpropertychange="pc_script"]
    [ onreadystatechange="rsc_script"]
    [ onresizeend="ree_script"]
    [ onresizestart="res_script"]
    [ onselectstart="ss_script"]
    [ style="name_1: value_1"[; "name_2: value_2"]
    [...; "name_n: value_n"]]
    [ tabindex="position_number"][ title="title"]
    [ valign="middle"|"top"|"bottom"|"baseline"]>
    table-footer-contents[</tfoot>]
```

Where

- ⊖ `accesskey` (Web) assigns a shortcut key to the object in order to focus on it.
- `align` (Web) indicates the horizontal alignment of the text within the table footer: aligned with the left or right margin, centered between the left and right margins, or aligned with a particular character. This attribute is deprecated and does not appear in any HTML 4.0 DTD; use a style sheet instead.
- ⊖ `bgcolor` (Web) specifies the background color for the table footer cells.
- `char` (Web) names a character from which text is aligned in both directions.
- `charoff` (Web) sets the horizontal distance between the left or right margin and the first occurrence of the `char` character.
- `class` (Web) specifies a class identification for the table footer.
- ⊖ `contenteditable` (Web) specifies or obtains a value that indicates whether a user can edit the element content.
- `dir` (Web) specifies the direction in which the table footer contents are displayed: left-to-right or right-to-left.
- ⊖ `disabled` (Web) is a keyword that prevents a user from using the element.
- `id` (Web) provides a unique identifier name for the table footer.
- `lang` (Web) specifies the code for the language used within the table footer.
- ⊖ `language` (Web) declares the scripting language of the current script.
- ⊖ `onbeforecut` (Web) names a script to run when a user starts cutting a selection to the Clipboard but before any action actually takes place.
- ⊖ `onbeforefocusenter` (Web) names a script to run when a user starts focusing on an object but before the object actually gains focus.
- ⊖ `onbeforefocusleave` (Web) names a script to run when a user starts leaving an object but before the object actually loses focus.
- ⊖ `onbeforepaste` (Web) names a script to run when a user starts pasting an object but before any action actually takes place.
- ⊖ `onblur` (Web) names a script to run when the object loses focus (that is, it is no longer the active element).
- `onclick` (Web) names a script to run when a user moves the mouse pointer or other pointing device over the table footer and clicks the button.
- ⊖ `oncontextmenu` (Web) names a script to run when a user right-clicks the mouse to open a shortcut menu.
- ⊖ `oncontrolselect` (Web) names a script to run when a user selects a control.
- ⊖ `oncut` (Web) names a script to run when a user cuts a selection to the Clipboard.
- `ondblclick` (Web) names a script to run when a user moves the mouse pointer or other pointing device over the table footer and double-clicks the button.

- ⊕ `ondragenter` (Web) names a script to run when a user drags a selection into an area in which it can be dropped.
- ⊕ `ondragstart` (Web) names a script to run when a user starts dragging a selection or element.
- ⊕ `onfocus` (Web) names a script to run when a user points the mouse pointer or other pointing device to focus on the current element.
- ⊕ `onfocusenter` (Web) names a script to run when a user focuses on the current element in any way.
- ⊕ `onfocusleave` (Web) names a script to run when a user inactivates the current element in any way.
- ⊕ `onhelp` (Web) names a script to run when a user presses the F1 or Help key over the current element.
- `onkeydown` (Web) names a script to run when a user presses and holds down a key over the table footer.
- `onkeypress` (Web) names a script to run when a user presses and releases a key over the table footer.
- `onkeyup` (Web) names a script to run when a user releases a key that is currently held down over the table footer.
- ⊕ `onlosecapture` (Web) names a script to run when a user releases a selection that has been captured by the mouse.
- `onmousedown` (Web) names a script to run when a user moves the mouse pointer or other pointing device over the table footer and presses and holds down the button.
- ⊕ `onmouseenter` (Web) names a script to run when a user moves the mouse pointer onto the object.
- ⊕ `onmouseleave` (Web) names a script to run when the mouse pointer leaves the object.
- `onmousemove` (Web) names a script to run when a user moves the mouse pointer or other pointing device over the table footer.
- `onmouseout` (Web) names a script to run when a user moves the mouse pointer or other pointing device away from the table footer.
- `onmouseover` (Web) names a script to run the first time a user moves the mouse pointer or other pointing device over the table footer.
- `onmouseup` (Web) names a script to run when a user moves the mouse pointer or other pointing device over the table footer and releases a mouse button that is currently held down.
- ⊕ `onpaste` (Web) names a script to run when a user pastes the Clipboard contents onto the object.
- ⊕ `onpropertychange` (Web) names a script to run when a property changes on the selected object in any way.
- ⊕ `onreadystatechange` (Web) names a script to run when the status of an element has changed (for example, the element receives data).
- ⊕ `onresizeend` (Web) names a script to run after the object has been resized.
- ⊕ `onresizestart` (Web) names a script to run as a user resizes the object.

XHTML Syntax

- ⊝ onselectstart (Web) names a script to run when a user starts selecting an object.
- style (Web) sets styles for the table footer.
- ⊝ tabindex (Web) defines the position of the current element in all the elements that a user can navigate to using a Tab or Shift + Tab key.
- title (Web) provides a title for the table footer.
- valign (Web) indicates the vertical alignment of the table footer, from the top to the bottom.
- *table-footer* is the rows that make up the bottom of a table.

Notes

- This is an HTML 4.0 element. Previously, it was a Microsoft extension.
- A table group (that is, tbody, tfoot, and/or thead) must contain one or more rows.
- tfoot must precede the optional tbody element within a table so that the browser can calculate the dimensions and contents of the footer.

Related Elements

caption (76), col (90), colgroup (92), table (288), tbody (293), td (297), th (310), thead (315), tr (319)

For More Information

Learn more about the tfoot element on page 565 in Chapter 4.

th	Table Heading

Purpose

Defines a heading in a table cell and applies emphasis, such as boldface, to it.

Syntax

```
<th[ abbr=abbr_text] [ accesskey="shortcut_key"]
   [ align="left"|"center"|"right"|"justify"|"char]
   [ axis="categ_name"[ ,categ_name[..., categ_name]]
   [ background="picture-uri"]
   [ bgcolor="#rrggbb"|"color"]
   [ bordercolor="#rrggbb"|"color"]
   [ char="character"][ charoff="offset"]
   [ class="class_name"][ colspan="num_cols"|"1"|"0"]
   [ contenteditable="edit_string"][ dir="ltr"|"rtl"]
   [ disabled="disabled"]
   [ gradangle="gradient_angle_value"]
   [ gradcolor="#rrggbb"|"color"]
   [ headers="id_name"[ id_name[...id_name]]
   [ height="height_pix"|"height_%"]
```

```
[ id="id_name"][ lang="lang_code"]
[ language="javascript"|"jscript"|"vbs[cript]"]
[ nowrap="nowrap"][ onbeforecopy="bc_script"]
[ onbeforecut="bt_script"]
[ onbeforefocusenter="bfe_script"]
[ onbeforefocusleave="bfl_script"]
[ onbeforepaste="bp_script"][ onblur="bl_script"]
[ onclick="cl_script"][ oncontextmenu="cm_script"]
[ oncontrolselect="ctl_script"][ oncopy="cp_script"]
[ oncut="ct_script"][ ondblclick="dc_script"]
[ ondragenter="de_script"][ ondragstart="ds_script"]
[ onfilterchange="f_script"][ onfocus="fc_script"]
[ onfocusenter="fe_script"]
[ onfocusleave="fl_script"][ onhelp="hlp_script"]
[ onkeydown="kd_script"][ onkeypress="kp_script"]
[ onkeyup="ku_script"][ onlosecapture="lc_script"]
[ onmousedown="md_script"]
[ onmouseenter="me_script"]
[ onmouseleave="ml_script"]
[ onmousemove="mm_script"][ onmouseout="mo_script"]
[ onmouseover="mov_script"][ onmouseup="mu_script"]
[ onpaste="p_script"][ onpropertychange="pc_script"]
[ onreadystatechange="rsc_script"]
[ onresizeend="ree_script"]
[ onresizestart="res_script"]
[ onselectstart="ss_script"]
[ rowspan="num_rows"|"1"|"0"]
[ scope=row|col|rowgroup|colgroup]
[ style="name_1: value_1"[; "name_2: value_2"]
[...; "name_n: value_n"]]
[ tabindex="position_number"][ title="title"]
[ transparency="trans_value"]
[ valign="middle"|"top"|"bottom"|"baseline"]
[ width="width_pix"|"width_%"]>cell-contents</th>
```

Where

- abbr (Web) is an abbreviation for the content of the cell.
- ☺ accesskey (Web) assigns a shortcut key to the object in order to focus on it.
- align (Web) indicates the horizontal alignment of the text within the heading cell: aligned with the left or right margin, centered between the left and right margins, or aligned with a particular character. This attribute is deprecated and does not appear in any HTML 4.0 DTD; use a style sheet instead.

- `axis` (Web) is a list of one or more axis names, separated by commas, that categorize related cells.
- ⊖ `background` (Web) specifies an image file that is displayed in the background of the cell.
- `bgcolor` (Web) specifies the background color for the cell. This attribute is deprecated; use a style sheet instead.
- ⊖ `bordercolor` (Web) is the color of the cell border.
- `char` (Web) names a character from which text is aligned in both directions.
- `charoff` (Web) sets the horizontal distance between the left or right margin and the first occurrence of the `char` character.
- `class` (Web) specifies a class identification for the cell.
- `colspan` (Web) specifies the number of columns over which the current cell will extend.
- ⊖ `contenteditable` (Web) specifies or obtains a value that indicates whether a user can edit the element content.
- `dir` (Web) specifies the direction in which the cell contents are displayed: left-to-right or right-to-left.
- ⊖ `disabled` (Web) is a keyword that prevents a user from using the element.
- ⫸ `gradangle` (Web) specifies a gradient angle to gradually change the color in a table.
- ⫸ `gradcolor` (Web) specifies the end color for a gradient. Use this attribute in conjunction with the `bgcolor` attribute.
- `headers` (Web) lists one or more identifiers for cells that provide information about the current cell.
- ⊖ `height` (Web) specifies the height of the cell, in pixels or as a percentage.
- `id` (Web) provides a unique identifier name for the cell.
- `lang` (Web) specifies the code for the language used within the cell.
- ⊖ `language` (Web) declares the scripting language of the current script.
- `nowrap` (Web) disables word wrap within the current cell.
- ⊖ `onbeforecopy` (Web) names a script to run when a user starts copying a selection to the Clipboard but before any action actually takes place.
- ⊖ `onbeforecut` (Web) names a script to run when a user starts cutting a selection to the Clipboard but before any action actually takes place.
- ⊖ `onbeforefocusenter` (Web) names a script to run when a user starts focusing on an object but before the object actually gains focus.
- ⊖ `onbeforefocusleave` (Web) names a script to run when a user starts leaving an object but before the object actually loses focus.
- ⊖ `onbeforepaste` (Web) names a script to run when a user starts pasting an object but before any action actually takes place.
- ⊖ `onblur` (Web) names a script to run when the object loses focus (that is, it is no longer the active element).
- `onclick` (Web) names a script to run when a user moves the mouse pointer or other pointing device over the cell and clicks the button.

- ⊖ `oncontextmenu` (Web) names a script to run when a user right-clicks the mouse to open a shortcut menu.
- ⊖ `oncontrolselect` (Web) names a script to run when a user selects a control.
- ⊖ `oncopy` (Web) names a script to run when a user copies a selection to the Clipboard.
- ⊖ `oncut` (Web) names a script to run when a user cuts a selection to the Clipboard.
- `ondblclick` (Web) names a script to run when a user moves the mouse pointer or other pointing device over the cell and double-clicks the button.
- ⊖ `ondragenter` (Web) names a script to run when a user drags a selection into an area in which it can be dropped.
- ⊖ `ondragstart` (Web) names a script to run when a user starts dragging a selection or element.
- ⊖ `onfilterchange` (Web) names a script to run when a visual filter changes in any way.
- ⊖ `onfocus` (Web) names a script to run when a user points the mouse pointer or other pointing device to focus on the current element.
- ⊖ `onfocusenter` (Web) names a script to run when a user focuses on the current element in any way.
- ⊖ `onfocusleave` (Web) names a script to run when a user inactivates the current element in any way.
- ⊖ `onhelp` (Web) names a script to run when a user presses the F1 or Help key over the current element.
- `onkeydown` (Web) names a script to run when a user presses and holds down a key over the cell.
- `onkeypress` (Web) names a script to run when a user presses and releases a key over the cell.
- `onkeyup` (Web) names a script to run when a user releases a key that is currently held down over the cell.
- ⊖ `onlosecapture` (Web) names a script to run when a user releases a selection that has been captured by the mouse.
- `onmousedown` (Web) names a script to run when a user moves the mouse pointer or other pointing device over the cell and presses and holds down the button.
- ⊖ `onmouseenter` (Web) names a script to run when a user moves the mouse pointer onto the object.
- ⊖ `onmouseleave` (Web) names a script to run when the mouse pointer leaves the object.
- `onmousemove` (Web) names a script to run when a user moves the mouse pointer or other pointing device over the cell.
- `onmouseout` (Web) names a script to run when a user moves the mouse pointer or other pointing device away from the cell.
- `onmouseover` (Web) names a script to run the first time a user moves the mouse pointer or other pointing device over the cell.

- onmouseup (Web) names a script to run when a user moves the mouse pointer or other pointing device over the cell and releases a mouse button that is currently held down.
- ⊝ onpaste (Web) names a script to run when a user pastes the Clipboard contents onto the object.
- ⊝ onpropertychange (Web) names a script to run when a property changes on the selected object in any way.
- ⊝ onreadystatechange (Web) names a script to run when the status of an element has changed (for example, the element receives data).
- ⊝ onresizeend (Web) names a script to run after the object has been resized.
- ⊝ onresizestart (Web) names a script to run as a user resizes the object.
- ⊝ onselectstart (Web) names a script to run when a user starts selecting an object.
- rowspan (Web) specifies the number of rows down which the current cell will extend.
- style (Web) sets styles for the cell.
- ⊝ tabindex (Web) defines the position of the current element in all the elements that a user can navigate to using a Tab or Shift + Tab key.
- title (Web) provides a title for the cell.
- ⍟ transparency (Web) sets the level of transparency or opaqueness of the cell.
- valign (Web) indicates the vertical alignment of the cell contents, from the top to the bottom.
- width (Web) specifies the width of the cell, in pixels or as a percentage (Internet Explorer only).
- *cell-contents* is the data within the current cell.

Notes

- This element originated in HTML 3.2.
- When you create long and complicated tables, consider indenting the td and th elements under tr elements. This can help you to check for the accuracy of the elements and attributes that you select.
- If a browser does not support align="justify", it may revert to align="left". Note that the align attribute is deprecated and does not appear in any HTML 4.0 DTD — use a style sheet to lay out pages.
- The bgcolor attribute value defined within th overrides the bgcolor defined for the row (tr) or the table (table).
- th is a child element of the tr element.
- WebTV supports the following attributes for th: align, bgcolor, class, colspan, gradangle, gradcolor, height, nowrap, rowspan, style, transparency, valign, and width.

Related Elements

caption (76), col (90), colgroup (92), table (288), tbody (293), td (297), tfoot (307), thead (315), tr (319)

XHTML Syntax

For More Information
Learn more about the th element on page 560 in Chapter 4.

thead	Table Header

Purpose
Defines the header rows at the top of a table and enables you to align the table header rows as a single unit.

Syntax

```
<thead[ accesskey="shortcut_key"]
  [ align="left"|"center"|"right"|"justify"
  |"char"][ bgcolor="#rrggbb"|"color"]
  [ char="character"][ charoff="offset"]
  [ class="class_name"]
  [ contenteditable="edit_string"][ dir="ltr"|"rtl"]
  [ disabled="disabled"][ id="id_name"]
  [ lang="lang_code"][ language="javascript"|"jscript"
  |"vbs[cript]"][ onbeforecut="bt_script"]
  [ onbeforefocusenter="bfe_script"]
  [ onbeforefocusleave="bfl_script"]
  [ onbeforepaste="bp_script"][ onblur="bl_script"]
  [ onclick="cl_script"][ oncontextmenu="cm_script"]
  [ oncontrolselect="ctl_script"][ oncut="ct_script"]
  [ ondblclick="dc_script"][ ondragenter="de_script"]
  [ ondragstart="ds_script"][ onhelp="hlp_script"]
  [ onkeydown="kd_script"][ onkeypress="kp_script"]
  [ onkeyup="ku_script"][ onlosecapture="lc_script"]
  [ onmousedown="md_script"]
  [ onmouseenter="me_script"]
  [ onmouseleave="ml_script"]
  [ onmousemove="mm_script"][ onmouseout="mo_script"]
  [ onmouseover="mov_script"][ onmouseup="mu_script"]
  [ onpaste="p_script"][ onpropertychange="pc_script"]
  [ onreadystatechange="rsc_script"]
  [ onresizeend="ree_script"]
  [ onresizestart="res_script"]
  [ onselectstart="ss_script"]
  [ style="name_1: value_1"[; "name_2: value_2"]
  [...; "name_n: value_n"]]
  [ tabindex="position_number"][ title="title"]
  [ valign="middle"|"top"|"bottom"|"baseline"]>
table-header</thead>
```

Where

- ⊕ `accesskey` (Web) assigns a shortcut key to the object in order to focus on it.
- `align` (Web) indicates the horizontal alignment of the text within the table header: aligned with the left or right margin, centered between the left and right margins, or aligned with a particular character. This attribute is deprecated and does not appear in any HTML 4.0 DTD; use a style sheet instead.
- ⊕ `bgcolor` (Web) specifies the background color for the table header.
- `char` (Web) names a character from which text is aligned in both directions.
- `charoff` (Web) sets the horizontal distance between the left or right margin and the first occurrence of the `char` character.
- `class` (Web) specifies a class identification for the table header.
- ⊕ `contenteditable` (Web) specifies or obtains a value that indicates whether a user can edit the element content.
- `dir` (Web) specifies the direction in which the table header contents are displayed: left-to-right or right-to-left.
- ⊕ `disabled` (Web) is a keyword that prevents a user from using the element.
- `id` (Web) provides a unique identifier name for the table header.
- `lang` (Web) specifies the code for the language used within the table header.
- ⊕ `language` (Web) declares the scripting language of the current script.
- ⊕ `onbeforecut` (Web) names a script to run when a user starts cutting a selection to the Clipboard but before any action actually takes place.
- ⊕ `onbeforefocusenter` (Web) names a script to run when a user starts focusing on an object but before the object actually gains focus.
- ⊕ `onbeforefocusleave` (Web) names a script to run when a user starts leaving an object but before the object actually loses focus.
- ⊕ `onbeforepaste` (Web) names a script to run when a user starts pasting an object but before any action actually takes place.
- ⊕ `onblur` (Web) names a script to run when the object loses focus (that is, it is no longer the active element).
- `onclick` (Web) names a script to run when a user moves the mouse pointer or other pointing device over the table header and clicks the button.
- ⊕ `oncontextmenu` (Web) names a script to run when a user right-clicks the mouse to open a shortcut menu.
- ⊕ `oncontrolselect` (Web) names a script to run when a user selects a control.
- ⊕ `oncut` (Web) names a script to run when a user cuts a selection to the Clipboard.

- `ondblclick` (Web) names a script to run when a user moves the mouse pointer or other pointing device over the table header and double-clicks the button.
- ⊖ `ondragenter` (Web) names a script to run when a user drags a selection into an area in which it can be dropped.
- ⊖ `ondragstart` (Web) names a script to run when a user starts dragging a selection or element.
- ⊖ `onfocus` (Web) names a script to run when a user points the mouse pointer or other pointing device to focus on the current element.
- ⊖ `onfocusenter` (Web) names a script to run when a user focuses on the current element in any way.
- ⊖ `onfocusleave` (Web) names a script to run when a user inactivates the current element in any way.
- ⊖ `onhelp` (Web) names a script to run when a user presses the F1 or Help key over the current element.
- `onkeydown` (Web) names a script to run when a user presses and holds down a key over the table header.
- `onkeypress` (Web) names a script to run when a user presses and releases a key over the table header.
- `onkeyup` (Web) names a script to run when a user releases a key that is currently held down over the table header.
- ⊖ `onlosecapture` (Web) names a script to run when a user releases a selection that has been captured by the mouse.
- `onmousedown` (Web) names a script to run when a user moves the mouse pointer or other pointing device over the table header and presses and holds down the button.
- ⊖ `onmouseenter` (Web) names a script to run when a user moves the mouse pointer onto the object.
- ⊖ `onmouseleave` (Web) names a script to run when the mouse pointer leaves the object.
- `onmousemove` (Web) names a script to run when a user moves the mouse pointer or other pointing device over the table header.
- `onmouseout` (Web) names a script to run when a user moves the mouse pointer or other pointing device away from the table header.
- `onmouseover` (Web) names a script to run the first time a user moves the mouse pointer or other pointing device over the table header.
- `onmouseup` (Web) names a script to run when a user moves the mouse pointer or other pointing device over the table header and releases a mouse button that is currently held down.
- ⊖ `onpaste` (Web) names a script to run when a user pastes the Clipboard contents onto the object.
- ⊖ `onpropertychange` (Web) names a script to run when a property changes on the selected object in any way.
- ⊖ `onreadystatechange` (Web) names a script to run when the status of an element has changed (for example, the element receives data).
- ⊖ `onresizeend` (Web) names a script to run after the object has been resized.

- ⊖ onresizestart (Web) names a script to run as a user resizes the object.
- ⊖ onselectstart (Web) names a script to run when a user starts selecting an object.
- style (Web) sets styles for the table header.
- ⊖ tabindex (Web) defines the position of the current element in all the elements that a user can navigate to using a Tab or Shift + Tab key.
- title (Web) provides a title for the table header.
- valign (Web) indicates the vertical alignment of the table header, from the top to the bottom.
- *table-header* represents the rows that make up the top of a table.

Notes

- This is an HTML 4.0 element. Previously, it was a Microsoft extension.
- A table group (that is, tbody, tfoot, and/or thead) must contain one or more rows.
- When you include a header in a table, you must use thead.
- If a tbody or tfoot element follows a table header, you can omit the </thead> end tag.

Related Elements

caption (76), col (90), colgroup (92), table (288), tbody (293), td (297), tfoot (307), th (310), tr (319)

For More Information

Learn more about the thead element on page 565 in Chapter 4.

title	Document Title

Purpose

Specifies a title for the current XHTML document.

Syntax

```
<title[ dir="ltr"|"rtl"][ disabled="disabled"]
[ id="id_name"][ lang="lang_code"]
[ onlayoutcomplete="la_script"]
[ onreadystatechange="rsc_script"]>
title-text</title>
```

Where

- dir (Web) specifies the direction in which the title text is displayed: left-to-right or right-to-left.
- ⊖ disabled (Web) is a keyword that prevents a user from using the element.
- ⊖ id (Web) provides a unique identifier name for the text.
- lang (Web) specifies the code for the language used for the title.

- ⊖ onlayoutcomplete (Web) names a script to run when a user lays out a selection using Print or Print Preview.
- ⊖ onreadystatechange (Web) names a script to run when the status of an element has changed (for example, the element receives data).
- *title-text* represents one or more characters that make up the title.

Notes

- This element originated in HTML 2.0.
- There can be only one title in an XHTML document.
- Titles can contain characters but not HTML elements or tags (that is, markup).
- title is valid only within the HEAD section.
- Limit a title to 64 characters and spaces, so that it fits within a browser's title bar.
- Use a meaningful title to describe the content of the document.
- The title attribute is related to the title element. The title element refers to an entire document; the title attribute refers to a particular element.
- Many browsers and computers also display their names on the title bar.

Related Element

head (148)

For More Information

Learn more about the title element on page 520 in Chapter 2.

tr	Table Row

Purpose

Defines a table row.

Syntax

```
<tr[ accesskey="shortcut_key"]
  [ align="left"|"center"|"right"|"justify"|"char]
  [ bgcolor="#rrggbb"|"color"]
  [ bordercolor="#rrggbb"|"color"]
  [ bordercolordark="#rrggbb"|"color"]
  [ bordercolorlight="#rrggbb"|"color"]
  [ char="character"][ charoff="offset"]
  [ class="class_name"]
  [ contenteditable="edit_string"][ dir="ltr"|"rtl"]
  [ disabled="disabled"][ height="height_pix"
  |"height_%"][ id="id_name"][ lang="lang_code"]
  [ language="javascript"|"jscript"|"vbs[cript]"]
  [ nowrap="nowrap"][ onbeforecopy="bc_script"]
```

XHTML Syntax

```
[ onbeforecut="bt_script"]
[ onbeforeeditfocus="bef_script"]
[ onbeforefocusenter="bfe_script"]
[ onbeforefocusleave="bfl_script"]
[ onbeforepaste="bp_script"][ onblur="bl_script"]
[ onclick="cl_script"][ oncontextmenu="cm_script"]
[ oncontrolselect="ctl_script"][ oncopy="cp_script"]
[ oncut="ct_script"][ ondblclick="dc_script"]
[ ondrag="d_script"][ ondragend="dd_script"]
[ ondragenter="de_script"][ ondragleave="dl_script"]
[ ondragover="do_script"][ ondragstart="ds_script"]
[ ondrop="dr_script"][ onfilterchange="f_script"]
[ onfocus="fc_script"][ onfocusenter="fe_script"]
[ onfocusleave="fl_script"][ onhelp="hlp_script"]
[ onkeydown="kd_script"][ onkeypress="kp_script"]
[ onkeyup="ku_script"][ onlosecapture="lc_script"]
[ onmousedown="md_script"]
[ onmouseenter="me_script"]
[ onmouseleave="ml_script"]
[ onmousemove="mm_script"][ onmouseout="mo_script"]
[ onmouseover="mov_script"][ onmouseup="mu_script"]
[ onpaste="p_script"]
[ onpropertychange="pc_script"]
[ onreadystatechange="rsc_script"]
[ onresizeend="ree_script"]
[ onresizestart="res_script"]
[ onselectstart="ss_script"]
[ style="name_1: value_1"[; "name_2: value_2"]
[...; "name_n: value_n"]]
[ tabindex="position_number"][ title="title"]
[ transparency="trans_value"]
[ valign="middle"|"top"|"bottom"|"baseline"]
[ width="width_pix"|"width_%"]>row-contents</tr>
```

Where

- ⊖ accesskey (Web) assigns a shortcut key to the object in order to focus on it.
- align (Web) indicates the horizontal alignment of the text within the table row: aligned with the left or right margin, centered between the left and right margins, or aligned with a particular character. This attribute is deprecated; use a style sheet instead.
- bgcolor (Web) specifies the background color for the row. This attribute is deprecated; use a style sheet instead.

- ℮ `bordercolor` (Web) is the color of the border around all the cells in the row.
- ℮ `bordercolordark` (Web) is the color of the row border shadow.
- ℮ `bordercolorlight` (Web) is the color of the row border highlight.
- `char` (Web) names a character from which text is aligned in both directions.
- `charoff` (Web) sets the horizontal distance between the left or right margin and the first occurrence of the `char` character.
- `class` (Web) specifies a class identification for the row.
- ℮ `contenteditable` (Web) specifies or obtains a value that indicates whether a user can edit the element content.
- `dir` (Web) specifies the direction in which the row contents are displayed: left-to-right or right-to-left.
- ℮ `disabled` (Web) is a keyword that prevents a user from using the element.
- ℮ `height` (Web) specifies the height of the row, in pixels or as a percentage.
- `id` (Web) provides a unique identifier name for the row.
- `lang` (Web) specifies the code for the language used within the row.
- ℮ `language` (Web) declares the scripting language of the current script.
- ℮ `onbeforecopy` (Web) names a script to run when a user starts copying a selection to the Clipboard but before any action actually takes place.
- ℮ `onbeforecut` (Web) names a script to run when a user starts cutting a selection to the Clipboard but before any action actually takes place.
- ℮ `onbeforeeditfocus` (Web) names a script to run when a user starts activating an object but before the object actually becomes active.
- ℮ `onbeforefocusenter` (Web) names a script to run when a user starts focusing on an object but before the object actually gains focus.
- ℮ `onbeforefocusleave` (Web) names a script to run when a user starts leaving an object but before the object actually loses focus.
- ℮ `onbeforepaste` (Web) names a script to run when a user starts pasting an object but before any action actually takes place.
- ℮ `onblur` (Web) names a script to run when the object loses focus (that is, it is no longer the active element).
- `onclick` (Web) names a script to run when a user moves the mouse pointer or other pointing device over the row and clicks the button.
- ℮ `oncontextmenu` (Web) names a script to run when a user right-clicks the mouse to open a shortcut menu.
- ℮ `oncontrolselect` (Web) names a script to run when a user selects a control.
- ℮ `oncopy` (Web) names a script to run when a user copies a selection to the Clipboard.
- ℮ `oncut` (Web) names a script to run when a user cuts a selection to the Clipboard.
- `ondblclick` (Web) names a script to run when a user moves the mouse pointer or other pointing device over the row and double-clicks the button.

- ⊖ `ondrag` (Web) names a script to run when a user drags a selection.
- ⊖ `ondragend` (Web) names a script to run after a user completes a drag-and-drop operation.
- ⊖ `ondragenter` (Web) names a script to run when a user drags a selection into an area in which it can be dropped.
- ⊖ `ondragleave` (Web) names a script to run when a user drags a selection beyond an area in which it can be dropped.
- ⊖ `ondragover` (Web) names a script to run when a user drags a selection over an area in which it can be dropped.
- ⊖ `ondragstart` (Web) names a script to run when a user starts dragging a selection or element.
- ⊖ `ondrop` (Web) names a script to run when a user releases the mouse button to drop a dragged selection.
- ⊖ `onfilterchange` (Web) names a script to run when a visual filter changes in any way.
- ⊖ `onfocus` (Web) names a script to run when a user points the mouse pointer or other pointing device to focus on the current element.
- ⊖ `onfocusenter` (Web) names a script to run when a user focuses on the current element in any way.
- ⊖ `onfocusleave` (Web) names a script to run when a user inactivates the current element in any way.
- ⊖ `onhelp` (Web) names a script to run when a user presses the F1 or Help key over the current element.
- `onkeydown` (Web) names a script to run when a user presses and holds down a key over the row.
- `onkeypress` (Web) names a script to run when a user presses and releases a key over the row.
- `onkeyup` (Web) names a script to run when a user releases a key that is currently held down over the row.
- ⊖ `onlosecapture` (Web) names a script to run when a user releases a selection that has been captured by the mouse.
- `onmousedown` (Web) names a script to run when a user moves the mouse pointer or other pointing device over the row and presses and holds down the button.
- ⊖ `onmouseenter` (Web) names a script to run when a user moves the mouse pointer onto the object.
- ⊖ `onmouseleave` (Web) names a script to run when the mouse pointer leaves the object.
- `onmousemove` (Web) names a script to run when a user moves the mouse pointer or other pointing device over the row.
- `onmouseout` (Web) names a script to run when a user moves the mouse pointer or other pointing device away from the row.
- `onmouseover` (Web) names a script to run the first time a user moves the mouse pointer or other pointing device over the row.
- `onmouseup` (Web) names a script to run when a user moves the mouse pointer or other pointing device over the row and releases a mouse button that is currently held down.

- ⊖ `onpaste` (Web) names a script to run when a user pastes the Clipboard contents onto the object.
- ⊖ `onpropertychange` (Web) names a script to run when a property changes on the selected object in any way.
- ⊖ `onreadystatechange` (Web) names a script to run when the status of an element has changed (for example, the element receives data).
- ⊖ `onresizeend` (Web) names a script to run after the object has been resized.
- ⊖ `onresizestart` (Web) names a script to run as a user resizes the object.
- ⊖ `onselectstart` (Web) names a script to run when a user starts selecting an object.
- `style` (Web) sets styles for the row.
- ⊖ `tabindex` (Web) defines the position of the current element in all the elements that a user can navigate to using a Tab or Shift + Tab key.
- `title` (Web) provides a title for the row.
- ⍚ `transparency` (Web) sets the level of transparency or opaqueness of the row.
- `valign` (Web) indicates the vertical alignment of the row contents, from the top to the bottom.
- `width` (Web) specifies the width of the row, in pixels or as a percentage (Internet Explorer only).
- `row-contents` comprise contents, `th` (table headings) elements, and `td` (table data) elements of the current row.

Notes

- This element originated in HTML 3.2.
- When you create long and complicated tables, consider indenting the `td` and `th` elements under the `tr` elements in the XHTML document. This can help you to check for the accuracy of the elements and attributes that you select.
- The `bgcolor` value defined within `tr` overrides the `bgcolor` defined for the table (`table`) but is overridden by the `bgcolor` defined for table headings (`th`) and table data (`td`).
- The `td` and `th` elements are child elements of the `tr` element, which in turn is a child of the `table` element.
- WebTV supports the following attributes for `tr`: `align`, `bgcolor`, `class`, `nowrap`, `style`, `transparency`, and `valign`.

Related Elements

`caption` (76), `col` (90), `colgroup` (92), `table` (288), `tbody` (293), `td` (297), `tfoot` (307), `th` (310), `thead` (315)

For More Information

Learn more about the `tr` element on page 560 in Chapter 4.

tt	Teletype Text

Purpose

Applies a teletype (monospace) font to selected text.

Syntax

```
<tt[ accesskey="shortcut_key"][ class="class_name"]
  [ contenteditable="edit_string"][ dir="ltr"|"rtl"]
  [ disabled="disabled"][ id="id_name"]
  [ lang="lang_code"][ language="javascript"|"jscript"
  |"vbs[cript]"][ onbeforecopy="bc_script"]
  [ onbeforecut="bt_script"]
  [ onbeforefocusenter="bfe_script"]
  [ onbeforefocusleave="bfl_script"]
  [ onbeforepaste="bp_script"][ onblur="bl_script"]
  [ onclick="cl_script"][ oncontextmenu="cm_script"]
  [ oncontrolselect="ctl_script"][ oncopy="cp_script"]
  [ oncut="ct_script"][ ondblclick="dc_script"]
  [ ondrag="d_script"][ ondragend="dd_script"]
  [ ondragenter="de_script"][ ondragleave="dl_script"]
  [ ondragover="do_script"][ ondragstart="ds_script"]
  [ ondrop="dr_script"][ onfocus="fc_script"]
  [ onfocusenter="fe_script"]
  [ onfocusleave="fl_script"][ onhelp="hlp_script"]
  [ onkeydown="kd_script"][ onkeypress="kp_script"]
  [ onkeyup="ku_script"][ onlosecapture="lc_script"]
  [ onmousedown="md_script"]
  [ onmouseenter="me_script"]
  [ onmouseleave="ml_script"]
  [ onmousemove="mm_script"][ onmouseout="mo_script"]
  [ onmouseover="mov_script"][ onmouseup="mu_script"]
  [ onpaste="p_script"][ onpropertychange="pc_script"]
  [ onreadystatechange="rsc_script"]
  [ onresize="rsz_script"][ onresizeend="ree_script"]
  [ onresizestart="res_script"]
  [ onselectstart="ss_script"]
  [ style="name_1: value_1"[; "name_2: value_2"]
  [...; "name_n: value_n"]]
  [ tabindex="position_number"][ title="title"]>
  text</tt>
```

Where

- ⊕ accesskey (Web) assigns a shortcut key to the object in order to focus on it.

- `class` (Web) specifies a class identification for the teletype text.
- ⊜ `contenteditable` (Web) specifies or obtains a value that indicates whether a user can edit the element content.
- `dir` (Web) specifies the direction in which the teletype text is displayed: left-to-right or right-to-left.
- ⊜ `disabled` (Web) is a keyword that prevents a user from using the element.
- `id` (Web) provides a unique identifier name for the teletype text.
- `lang` (Web) specifies the code for the language used for the teletype text.
- ⊜ `language` (Web) declares the scripting language of the current script.
- ⊜ `onbeforecopy` (Web) names a script to run when a user starts copying a selection to the Clipboard but before any action actually takes place.
- ⊜ `onbeforecut` (Web) names a script to run when a user starts cutting a selection to the Clipboard but before any action actually takes place.
- ⊜ `onbeforefocusenter` (Web) names a script to run when a user starts focusing on an object but before the object actually gains focus.
- ⊜ `onbeforefocusleave` (Web) names a script to run when a user starts leaving an object but before the object actually loses focus.
- ⊜ `onbeforepaste` (Web) names a script to run when a user starts pasting an object but before any action actually takes place.
- ⊜ `onblur` (Web) names a script to run when the object loses focus (that is, it is no longer the active element).
- `onclick` (Web) names a script to run when a user moves the mouse pointer or other pointing device over the teletype text and clicks the button.
- ⊜ `oncontextmenu` (Web) names a script to run when a user right-clicks the mouse to open a shortcut menu.
- ⊜ `oncontrolselect` (Web) names a script to run when a user selects a control.
- ⊜ `oncopy` (Web) names a script to run when a user copies a selection to the Clipboard.
- ⊜ `oncut` (Web) names a script to run when a user cuts a selection to the Clipboard.
- `ondblclick` (Web) names a script to run when a user moves the mouse pointer or other pointing device over the teletype text and double-clicks the button.
- ⊜ `ondrag` (Web) names a script to run when a user drags a selection.
- ⊜ `ondragend` (Web) names a script to run after a user completes a drag-and-drop operation.
- ⊜ `ondragenter` (Web) names a script to run when a user drags a selection into an area in which it can be dropped.
- ⊜ `ondragleave` (Web) names a script to run when a user drags a selection beyond an area in which it can be dropped.
- ⊜ `ondragover` (Web) names a script to run when a user drags a selection over an area in which it can be dropped.
- ⊜ `ondragstart` (Web) names a script to run when a user starts dragging a selection or element.

- ⊝ ondrop (Web) names a script to run when a user releases the mouse button to drop a dragged selection.
- ⊝ onfocus (Web) names a script to run when a user points the mouse pointer or other pointing device to focus on the current element.
- ⊝ onfocusenter (Web) names a script to run when a user focuses on the current element in any way.
- ⊝ onfocusleave (Web) names a script to run when a user inactivates the current element in any way.
- ⊝ onhelp (Web) names a script to run when a user presses the F1 or Help key over the current element.
- onkeydown (Web) names a script to run when a user presses and holds down a key over the teletype text.
- onkeypress (Web) names a script to run when a user presses and releases a key over the teletype text.
- onkeyup (Web) names a script to run when a user releases a key that is currently held down over the teletype text.
- ⊝ onlosecapture (Web) names a script to run when a user releases a selection that has been captured by the mouse.
- onmousedown (Web) names a script to run when a user moves the mouse pointer or other pointing device over the teletype text and presses and holds down the button.
- ⊝ onmouseenter (Web) names a script to run when a user moves the mouse pointer onto the object.
- ⊝ onmouseleave (Web) names a script to run when the mouse pointer leaves the object.
- onmousemove (Web) names a script to run when a user moves the mouse pointer or other pointing device over the teletype text.
- onmouseout (Web) names a script to run when a user moves the mouse pointer or other pointing device away from the teletype text.
- onmouseover (Web) names a script to run the first time a user moves the mouse pointer or other pointing device over the teletype text.
- onmouseup (Web) names a script to run when a user moves the mouse pointer or other pointing device over the teletype text and releases a mouse button that is currently held down.
- ⊝ onpaste (Web) names a script to run when a user pastes the Clipboard contents onto the object.
- ⊝ onpropertychange (Web) names a script to run when a property changes on the selected object in any way.
- ⊝ onreadystatechange (Web) names a script to run when the status of an element has changed (for example, the element receives data).
- ⊝ onresize (Web) names a script to run when a user resizes the selected object.
- ⊝ onresizeend (Web) names a script to run after the object has been resized.
- ⊝ onresizestart (Web) names a script to run as a user resizes the object.

- ⊙ onselectstart (Web) names a script to run when a user starts selecting an object.
- style (Web) sets styles for the teletype text.
- ⊙ tabindex (Web) defines the position of the current element in all the elements that a user can navigate to using a Tab or Shift + Tab key.
- title (Web) provides a title for the teletype text.
- *text* represents one or more characters.

Notes

- This inline element originated in HTML 2.0.
- tt is one of the elements in the %fontstyle entity. The other %fontstyle elements are b, big, i, and small. Deprecated elements in the %fontstyle entity are s, strike, and u.
- tt is a physical element in which you "code" the styles yourself, as opposed to logical elements, in which particular browsers are programmed to apply a certain style to the selected text.
- Many browsers use the same font for the following elements: code, kbd, pre, samp, and tt.
- To display two or more lines of preformatted text, use the pre element.
- For the tt element, WebTV supports the class and style attributes.

Related Elements

b (46), big (57), code (87), font (131), i (154), kbd (186), pre (242), s (254), samp (258), strike (254), u (327)

---

u **Underlined**

Purpose

Underlines selected text.

Syntax

```
<u[ accesskey="shortcut_key"][ class="class_name"]
  [ contenteditable="edit_string"][ dir="ltr"|"rtl"]
  [ disabled="disabled"][ id="id_name"]
  [ lang="lang_code"][ language="javascript"|"jscript"
  |"vbs[cript]"][ onbeforecopy="bc_script"]
  [ onbeforecut="bt_script"]
  [ onbeforefocusenter="bfe_script"]
  [ onbeforefocusleave="bfl_script"]
  [ onbeforepaste="bp_script"][ onblur="bl_script"]
  [ onclick="cl_script"][ oncontextmenu="cm_script"]
  [ oncontrolselect="ctl_script"][ oncopy="cp_script"]
  [ oncut="ct_script"][ ondblclick="dc_script"]
```

```
[ ondrag="d_script"][ ondragend="dd_script" ]
[ ondragenter="de_script"][ ondragleave="dl_script" ]
[ ondragover="do_script"][ ondragstart="ds_script" ]
[ ondrop="dr_script"][ onfocus="fc_script" ]
[ onfocusenter="fe_script" ]
[ onfocusleave="fl_script"][ onhelp="hlp_script" ]
[ onkeydown="kd_script"][ onkeypress="kp_script" ]
[ onkeyup="ku_script"][ onlosecapture="lc_script" ]
[ onmousedown="md_script" ]
[ onmouseenter="me_script" ]
[ onmouseleave="ml_script" ]
[ onmousemove="mm_script"][ onmouseout="mo_script" ]
[ onmouseover="mov_script"][ onmouseup="mu_script" ]
[ onpaste="p_script"][ onpropertychange="pc_script" ]
[ onreadystatechange="rsc_script" ]
[ onresize="rsz_script"][ onresizeend="ree_script" ]
[ onresizestart="res_script" ]
[ onselectstart="ss_script" ]
[ style="name_1: value_1"[; "name_2: value_2" ]
[...; "name_n: value_n"]]
[ tabindex="position_number"][ title="title" ]>
text</u>
```

Where

- ⊖ `accesskey` (Web) assigns a shortcut key to the object in order to focus on it.
- `class` (Web) specifies a class identification for the underlined text.
- ⊖ `contenteditable` (Web) specifies or obtains a value that indicates whether a user can edit the element content.
- `dir` (Web) specifies the direction in which the underlined text is displayed: left-to-right or right-to-left.
- ⊖ `disabled` (Web) is a keyword that prevents a user from using the element.
- `id` (Web) provides a unique identifier name for the underlined text.
- `lang` (Web) specifies the code for the language used for the underlined text.
- ⊖ `language` (Web) declares the scripting language of the current script.
- ⊖ `onbeforecopy` (Web) names a script to run when a user starts copying a selection to the Clipboard but before any action actually takes place.
- ⊖ `onbeforecut` (Web) names a script to run when a user starts cutting a selection to the Clipboard but before any action actually takes place.

- ⊖ `onbeforefocusenter` (Web) names a script to run when a user starts focusing on an object but before the object actually gains focus.
- ⊖ `onbeforefocusleave` (Web) names a script to run when a user starts leaving an object but before the object actually loses focus.
- ⊖ `onbeforepaste` (Web) names a script to run when a user starts pasting an object but before any action actually takes place.
- ⊖ `onblur` (Web) names a script to run when the object loses focus (that is, it is no longer the active element).
- `onclick` (Web) names a script to run when a user moves the mouse pointer or other pointing device over the underlined text and clicks the button.
- ⊖ `oncontextmenu` (Web) names a script to run when a user right-clicks the mouse to open a shortcut menu.
- ⊖ `oncontrolselect` (Web) names a script to run when a user selects a control.
- ⊖ `oncopy` (Web) names a script to run when a user copies a selection to the Clipboard.
- ⊖ `oncut` (Web) names a script to run when a user cuts a selection to the Clipboard.
- `ondblclick` (Web) names a script to run when a user moves the mouse pointer or other pointing device over the underlined text and double-clicks the button.
- ⊖ `ondrag` (Web) names a script to run when a user drags a selection.
- ⊖ `ondragend` (Web) names a script to run after a user completes a drag-and-drop operation.
- ⊖ `ondragenter` (Web) names a script to run when a user drags a selection into an area in which it can be dropped.
- ⊖ `ondragleave` (Web) names a script to run when a user drags a selection beyond an area in which it can be dropped.
- ⊖ `ondragover` (Web) names a script to run when a user drags a selection over an area in which it can be dropped.
- ⊖ `ondragstart` (Web) names a script to run when a user starts dragging a selection or element.
- ⊖ `ondrop` (Web) names a script to run when a user releases the mouse button to drop a dragged selection.
- ⊖ `onfocus` (Web) names a script to run when a user points the mouse pointer or other pointing device to focus on the current element.
- ⊖ `onfocusenter` (Web) names a script to run when a user focuses on the current element in any way.
- ⊖ `onfocusleave` (Web) names a script to run when a user inactivates the current element in any way.
- ⊖ `onhelp` (Web) names a script to run when a user presses the F1 or Help key over the current element.
- `onkeydown` (Web) names a script to run when a user presses and holds down a key over the underlined text.
- `onkeypress` (Web) names a script to run when a user presses and releases a key over the underlined text.

- onkeyup (Web) names a script to run when a user releases a key that is currently held down over the underlined text.
- ⊝ onlosecapture (Web) names a script to run when a user releases a selection that has been captured by the mouse.
- onmousedown (Web) names a script to run when a user moves the mouse pointer or other pointing device over the underlined text and presses and holds down the button.
- ⊝ onmouseenter (Web) names a script to run when a user moves the mouse pointer onto the object.
- ⊝ onmouseleave (Web) names a script to run when the mouse pointer leaves the object.
- onmousemove (Web) names a script to run when a user moves the mouse pointer or other pointing device over the underlined text.
- onmouseout (Web) names a script to run when a user moves the mouse pointer or other pointing device away from the underlined text.
- onmouseover (Web) names a script to run the first time a user moves the mouse pointer or other pointing device over the underlined text.
- onmouseup (Web) names a script to run when a user moves the mouse pointer or other pointing device over the underlined text and releases a mouse button that is currently held down.
- ⊝ onpaste (Web) names a script to run when a user pastes the Clipboard contents onto the object.
- ⊝ onpropertychange (Web) names a script to run when a property changes on the selected object in any way.
- ⊝ onreadystatechange (Web) names a script to run when the status of an element has changed (for example, the element receives data).
- ⊝ onresize (Web) names a script to run when a user resizes the selected object.
- ⊝ onresizeend (Web) names a script to run after the object has been resized.
- ⊝ onresizestart (Web) names a script to run as a user resizes the object.
- ⊝ onselectstart (Web) names a script to run when a user starts selecting an object.
- style (Web) sets styles for the underlined text.
- ⊝ tabindex (Web) defines the position of the current element in all the elements that a user can navigate to using a Tab or Shift + Tab key.
- title (Web) provides a title for the underlined text.
- text represents one or more characters.

Notes

- This inline element originated in HTML 2.0.
- Although u is supported by HTML 4.0, it has been deprecated (that is, it will eventually be obsolete) and appears only in the Transitional DTD — not in the Strict DTD. Use style sheets to specify font attributes.

- u is a deprecated element in the %fontstyle entity. The other %fontstyle elements are b, big, i, small, and tt. Other deprecated elements in the %fontstyle entity are s and strike.
- It's best not to use underlined text because users may confuse it with links.
- For the u element, WebTV supports the class and style attributes.

Related Elements

b (46), big (57), em (120), font (131), i (154), s (254), small (268), strike (254), strong (276), sub (281), sup (284), tt (324)

ul	Unordered List

Purpose

Starts an unordered (bulleted) list.

Syntax

```
<ul[ accesskey="shortcut_key"][ class="class_name"]
  [ compact="compact"][ contenteditable="edit_string"]
  [ dir="ltr"|"rtl"][ disabled="disabled"]
  [ id="id_name"][ lang="lang_code"]
  [ language="javascript"|"jscript"|"vbs[cript]"]
  [ onbeforecopy="bc_script"]
  [ onbeforecut="bt_script"]
  [ onbeforefocusenter="bfe_script"]
  [ onbeforefocusleave="bfl_script"]
  [ onbeforepaste="bp_script"][ onblur="bl_script"]
  [ onclick="cl_script"][ oncontextmenu="cm_script"]
  [ oncontrolselect="ctl_script"][ oncopy="cp_script"]
  [ oncut="ct_script"][ ondblclick="dc_script"]
  [ ondrag="d_script"][ ondragend="dd_script"]
  [ ondragenter="de_script"][ ondragleave="dl_script"]
  [ ondragover="do_script"][ ondragstart="ds_script"]
  [ ondrop="dr_script"][ onfocus="fc_script"]
  [ onfocusenter="fe_script"]
  [ onfocusleave="fl_script"][ onhelp="hlp_script"]
  [ onkeydown="kd_script"][ onkeypress="kp_script"]
  [ onkeyup="ku_script"]
  [ onlayoutcomplete="la_script"]
  [ onlosecapture="lc_script"]
  [ onmousedown="md_script"]
  [ onmouseenter="me_script"]
  [ onmouseleave="ml_script"]
```

```
[ onmousemove="mm_script"][ onmouseout="mo_script"]
[ onmouseover="mov_script"][ onmouseup="mu_script"]
[ onpaste="p_script"][ onpropertychange="pc_script"]
[ onreadystatechange="rsc_script"]
[ onresize="rsz_script"][ onresizeend="ree_script"]
[ onresizestart="res_script"]
[ onselectstart="ss_script"]
[ style="name_1: value_1"[; "name_2: value_2"]
[...; "name_n: value_n"]]
[ tabindex="position_number"][ title="title"]
[ type="disc"|"square"|"circle"]>
unordered-list-items</ul>
```

Where

- ⊖ accesskey (Web) assigns a shortcut key to the object in order to focus on it.
- class (Web) specifies a class identification for the unordered list.
- compact (Web) indicates that a browser might decrease the size of the space between the bullet and the list item. This attribute is deprecated; use a style sheet instead.
- ⊖ contenteditable (Web) specifies or obtains a value that indicates whether a user can edit the element content.
- dir (Web) specifies the direction in which the unordered list text is displayed: left-to-right or right-to-left.
- ⊖ disabled (Web) is a keyword that prevents a user from using the element.
- id (Web) provides a unique identifier name for the unordered list.
- lang (Web) specifies the code for the language used for the unordered list text.
- ⊖ language (Web) declares the scripting language of the current script.
- ⊖ onbeforecopy (Web) names a script to run when a user starts copying a selection to the Clipboard but before any action actually takes place.
- ⊖ onbeforecut (Web) names a script to run when a user starts cutting a selection to the Clipboard but before any action actually takes place.
- ⊖ onbeforefocusenter (Web) names a script to run when a user starts focusing on an object but before the object actually gains focus.
- ⊖ onbeforefocusleave (Web) names a script to run when a user starts leaving an object but before the object actually loses focus.
- ⊖ onbeforepaste (Web) names a script to run when a user starts pasting an object but before any action actually takes place.
- ⊖ onblur (Web) names a script to run when the object loses focus (that is, it is no longer the active element).
- onclick (Web) names a script to run when a user moves the mouse pointer or other pointing device over the unordered list and clicks the button.

- ⊖ `oncontextmenu` (Web) names a script to run when a user right-clicks the mouse to open a shortcut menu.
- ⊖ `oncontrolselect` (Web) names a script to run when a user selects a control.
- ⊖ `oncopy` (Web) names a script to run when a user copies a selection to the Clipboard.
- ⊖ `oncut` (Web) names a script to run when a user cuts a selection to the Clipboard.
- `ondblclick` (Web) names a script to run when a user moves the mouse pointer or other pointing device over the unordered list and double-clicks the button.
- ⊖ `ondrag` (Web) names a script to run when a user drags a selection.
- ⊖ `ondragend` (Web) names a script to run after a user completes a drag-and-drop operation.
- ⊖ `ondragenter` (Web) names a script to run when a user drags a selection into an area in which it can be dropped.
- ⊖ `ondragleave` (Web) names a script to run when a user drags a selection beyond an area in which it can be dropped.
- ⊖ `ondragover` (Web) names a script to run when a user drags a selection over an area in which it can be dropped.
- ⊖ `ondragstart` (Web) names a script to run when a user starts dragging a selection or element.
- ⊖ `ondrop` (Web) names a script to run when a user releases the mouse button to drop a dragged selection.
- ⊖ `onfocus` (Web) names a script to run when a user points the mouse pointer or other pointing device to focus on the current element.
- ⊖ `onfocusenter` (Web) names a script to run when a user focuses on the current element in any way.
- ⊖ `onfocusleave` (Web) names a script to run when a user inactivates the current element in any way.
- ⊖ `onhelp` (Web) names a script to run when a user presses the F1 or Help key over the current element.
- `onkeydown` (Web) names a script to run when a user presses and holds down a key over the unordered list.
- `onkeypress` (Web) names a script to run when a user presses and releases a key over the unordered list.
- `onkeyup` (Web) names a script to run when a user releases a key that is currently held down over the unordered list.
- ⊖ `onlayoutcomplete` (Web) names a script to run when a user lays out a selection using Print or Print Preview.
- ⊖ `onlosecapture` (Web) names a script to run when a user releases a selection that has been captured by the mouse.
- `onmousedown` (Web) names a script to run when a user moves the mouse pointer or other pointing device over the unordered list and presses and holds down the button.
- ⊖ `onmouseenter` (Web) names a script to run when a user moves the mouse pointer onto the object.

- ⊖ onmouseleave (Web) names a script to run when the mouse pointer leaves the object.
- onmousemove (Web) names a script to run when a user moves the mouse pointer or other pointing device over the unordered list.
- onmouseout (Web) names a script to run when a user moves the mouse pointer or other pointing device away from the unordered list.
- onmouseover (Web) names a script to run the first time a user moves the mouse pointer or other pointing device over the unordered list.
- onmouseup (Web) names a script to run when a user moves the mouse pointer or other pointing device over the unordered list and releases a mouse button that is currently held down.
- ⊖ onpaste (Web) names a script to run when a user pastes the Clipboard contents onto the object.
- ⊖ onpropertychange (Web) names a script to run when a property changes on the selected object in any way.
- ⊖ onreadystatechange (Web) names a script to run when the status of an element has changed (for example, the element receives data).
- ⊖ onresize (Web) names a script to run when a user resizes the selected object.
- ⊖ onresizeend (Web) names a script to run after the object has been resized.
- ⊖ onresizestart (Web) names a script to run as a user resizes the object.
- ⊖ onselectstart (Web) names a script to run when a user starts selecting an object.
- style (Web) sets styles for the unordered list.
- ⊖ tabindex (Web) defines the position of the current element in all the elements that a user can navigate to using a Tab or Shift + Tab key.
- title (Web) provides a title for the unordered list.
- type (Web) sets a bullet style. This attribute is deprecated.
- *unordered-list-items* represents one or more entries for the list.

Notes

- This block-level element originated in HTML 2.0, and the type attribute is an HTML 3.2 feature.
- Not all browsers recognize the compact attribute. compact has been deprecated (that is, it will eventually be obsolete) and appears only in the Transitional DTD — not in the Strict DTD.
- If you nest an unordered list, it's a good idea to indent each level of lists in the XHTML document to ensure that each of the start and end tags is on the same level. Indenting levels is not required.
- When you nest unordered lists, there are three automatic levels of bullets: solid disk (the highest), circle, and square (the lowest). However, different browsers display different symbols for bullets at certain levels.
- The li element is a child element of ul.

- Typically, the ul and ol elements are followed by white space, just like paragraphs, but list items are only separated by line breaks.
- For the ul element, WebTV supports the type attribute.

Related Elements
dir (104), li (198), menu (212), ol (230)

For More Information
Learn more about the ul element on page 545 in Chapter 3.

---

var   **Variable**

XHTML Syntax

Purpose
Indicates variable text by emphasizing it, usually with italics.

Syntax
```
<var[ accesskey="shortcut_key"][ class="class_name"]
  [ contenteditable="edit_string"][ dir="ltr"|"rtl"]
  [ disabled="disabled"][ id="id_name"]
  [ lang="lang_code"][ language="javascript"|"jscript"
  |"vbs[cript]"][ onbeforecut="bt_script"]
  [ onbeforefocusenter="bfe_script"]
  [ onbeforefocusleave="bfl_script"]
  [ onbeforepaste="bp_script"][ onblur="bl_script"]
  [ onclick="cl_script"][ oncontextmenu="cm_script"]
  [ oncontrolselect="ctl_script"][ oncut="ct_script"]
  [ ondblclick="dc_script"][ ondrag="d_script"]
  [ ondragend="dd_script"][ ondragenter="de_script"]
  [ ondragleave="dl_script"][ ondragover="do_script"]
  [ ondragstart="ds_script"][ ondrop="dr_script"]
  [ onfocus="fc_script"][ onfocusenter="fe_script"]
  [ onfocusleave="fl_script"][ onhelp="hlp_script"]
  [ onkeydown="kd_script"][ onkeypress="kp_script"]
  [ onkeyup="ku_script"][ onlosecapture="lc_script"]
  [ onmousedown="md_script"]
  [ onmouseenter="me_script"]
  [ onmouseleave="ml_script"]
  [ onmousemove="mm_script"][ onmouseout="mo_script"]
  [ onmouseover="mov_script"][ onmouseup="mu_script"]
  [ onpaste="p_script"][ onpropertychange="pc_script"]
  [ onreadystatechange="rsc_script"]
  [ onresize="rsz_script"][ onresizeend="ree_script"]
```

```
[ onresizestart="res_script"]
[ onselectstart="ss_script"]
[ style="name_1: value_1"[; "name_2: value_2"]
[...; "name_n: value_n"]]
[ tabindex="position_number"][ title="title"]>
text</var>
```

Where

- ⊖ accesskey (Web) assigns a shortcut key to the object in order to focus on it.
- class (Web) specifies a class identification for the variable.
- ⊖ contenteditable (Web) specifies or obtains a value that indicates whether a user can edit the element content.
- dir (Web) specifies the direction in which the variable text is displayed: left-to-right or right-to-left.
- ⊖ disabled (Web) is a keyword that prevents a user from using the element.
- id (Web) provides a unique identifier name for the variable.
- lang (Web) specifies the code for the language used for the variable text.
- ⊖ language (Web) declares the scripting language of the current script.
- ⊖ onbeforecut (Web) names a script to run when a user starts cutting a selection to the Clipboard but before any action actually takes place.
- ⊖ onbeforefocusenter (Web) names a script to run when a user starts focusing on an object but before the object actually gains focus.
- ⊖ onbeforefocusleave (Web) names a script to run when a user starts leaving an object but before the object actually loses focus.
- ⊖ onbeforepaste (Web) names a script to run when a user starts pasting an object but before any action actually takes place.
- ⊖ onblur (Web) names a script to run when the object loses focus (that is, it is no longer the active element).
- onclick (Web) names a script to run when a user moves the mouse pointer or other pointing device over the variable and clicks the button.
- ⊖ oncontextmenu (Web) names a script to run when a user right-clicks the mouse to open a shortcut menu.
- ⊖ oncontrolselect (Web) names a script to run when a user selects a control.
- ⊖ oncut (Web) names a script to run when a user cuts a selection to the Clipboard.
- ondblclick (Web) names a script to run when a user moves the mouse pointer or other pointing device over the variable and double-clicks the button.
- ⊖ ondrag (Web) names a script to run when a user drags a selection.
- ⊖ ondragend (Web) names a script to run after a user completes a drag-and-drop operation.
- ⊖ ondragenter (Web) names a script to run when a user drags a selection into an area in which it can be dropped.

- ⊖ `ondragleave` (Web) names a script to run when a user drags a selection beyond an area in which it can be dropped.
- ⊖ `ondragover` (Web) names a script to run when a user drags a selection over an area in which it can be dropped.
- ⊖ `ondragstart` (Web) names a script to run when a user starts dragging a selection or element.
- ⊖ `ondrop` (Web) names a script to run when a user releases the mouse button to drop a dragged selection.
- ⊖ `onfocus` (Web) names a script to run when a user points the mouse pointer or other pointing device to focus on the current element.
- ⊖ `onfocusenter` (Web) names a script to run when a user focuses on the current element in any way.
- ⊖ `onfocusleave` (Web) names a script to run when a user inactivates the current element in any way.
- ⊖ `onhelp` (Web) names a script to run when a user presses the F1 or Help key over the current element.
- `onkeydown` (Web) names a script to run when a user presses and holds down a key over the variable.
- `onkeypress` (Web) names a script to run when a user presses and releases a key over the variable.
- `onkeyup` (Web) names a script to run when a user releases a key that is currently held down over the variable.
- ⊖ `onlosecapture` (Web) names a script to run when a user releases a selection that has been captured by the mouse.
- `onmousedown` (Web) names a script to run when a user moves the mouse pointer or other pointing device over the variable and presses and holds down the button.
- ⊖ `onmouseenter` (Web) names a script to run when a user moves the mouse pointer onto the object.
- ⊖ `onmouseleave` (Web) names a script to run when the mouse pointer leaves the object.
- `onmousemove` (Web) names a script to run when a user moves the mouse pointer or other pointing device over the variable.
- `onmouseout` (Web) names a script to run when a user moves the mouse pointer or other pointing device away from the variable.
- `onmouseover` (Web) names a script to run the first time a user moves the mouse pointer or other pointing device over the variable.
- `onmouseup` (Web) names a script to run when a user moves the mouse pointer or other pointing device over the variable and releases a mouse button that is currently held down.
- ⊖ `onpaste` (Web) names a script to run when a user pastes the Clipboard contents onto the object.
- ⊖ `onpropertychange` (Web) names a script to run when a property changes on the selected object in any way.
- ⊖ `onreadystatechange` (Web) names a script to run when the status of an element has changed (for example, the element receives data).

- ⊖ onresize (Web) names a script to run when a user resizes the selected object.
- ⊖ onresizeend (Web) names a script to run after the object has been resized.
- ⊖ onresizestart (Web) names a script to run as a user resizes the object.
- ⊖ onselectstart (Web) names a script to run when a user starts selecting an object.
- style (Web) sets styles for the variable.
- ⊖ tabindex (Web) defines the position of the current element in all the elements that a user can navigate to using a Tab or Shift + Tab key.
- title (Web) provides a title for the variable.
- *text* represents one or more characters.

Notes

- This inline element originated in HTML 2.0.
- var is one of the elements in the %phrase entity. The other %phrase elements are abbr, acronym, cite, code, dfn, em, kbd, samp, and strong.
- var is a logical element, in which particular browsers are programmed to apply a certain style to the selected text. This is in contrast to a physical element, in which you "code" the styles yourself.
- Many browsers use italics for the following elements: i, cite, em, and var.
- For the var element, WebTV supports the class and style attributes.

Related Elements

b (46), big (57), cite (83), em (120), font (131), i (154), small (268), strong (276), sub (281), sup (284), tt (324), u (327)

---

 wbr   **Word Break**

Purpose

Inserts a line break, if needed, within a no-break (nobr) line.

Syntax

```
<nobr[ contenteditable="edit_string"]
  [ disabled="disabled"][ id="id_name"]>
text<wbr>text</nobr>
```

Where

- ⊖ contenteditable (Web) specifies or obtains a value that indicates whether a user can edit the element content.
- ⊖ disabled (Web) is a keyword that prevents a user from using the element.

- ⊖ id (Web) provides a unique identifier name for the word break.
- *text* represents one or more characters.

Note

Embed wbr within the nobr element.

Related Elements

br (70), nobr (219), p (238)

⊖xml	XML Content

Purpose

Indicates XML content in an XHTML document.

Syntax

```
<xml[ contenteditable="edit_string"]
   [ disabled="disabled"][ id="id_name"]
   [ ns="namespace"]
   [ ondataavailable="da_script"]
   [ ondatasetchanged="dsc_script"]
   [ ondatasetcomplete="dsf_script"]
   [ onreadystatechange="rsc_script"]
   [ onrowenter="re_script"][ onrowexit="rex_script"]
   [ onrowsdelete="rd_script"]
   [ onrowsinserted="rn_script"]
   [ src="xml_uri"]{ />|</xml>
```

Where

- ⊖ contenteditable (Web) specifies or obtains a value that indicates whether a user can edit the element content.
- ⊖ disabled (Web) is a keyword that prevents a user from using the element.
- ⊖ id (Web) provides a unique identifier name for the element.
- ⊖ ns (Web) specifies an XML namespace.
- ⊖ ondataavailable (Web) names a script to run sporadically when data is received from the data resource.
- ⊖ ondatasetchanged (Web) names a script to run when a user changes a data set from the data resource.
- ⊖ ondatasetcomplete (Web) names a script to run when all data has been received from the data resource.
- ⊖ onreadystatechange (Web) names a script to run when the status of an element has changed (for example, the element receives data).
- ⊖ onrowenter (Web) names a script to run after the data in the current row has changed.
- ⊖ onrowexit (Web) names a script to run as a data source attempts to load data into the current row.

XHTML Syntax

- ⊖ onrowsdelete (Web) names a script to run when a user starts to delete one or more rows from a set of records but before the deletion actually takes place.
- ⊖ onrowsinserted (Web) names a script to run when a user inserts one or more rows in the current set of records.
- ⊖ src (Web) specifies the URI of an external XML document.

Note

xml is an empty element.

in plain english in pla
sh in plain english in
glish in plain english
in plain english in pla
sh in plain english in
glish in plain english
in plain english in pla
glish in plain english
in plain english in pla
sh in plain english in
glish in plain english
in plain english in pla
sh in plain english in
glish in plain english
in plain english in pla
lish in plain english
in plain english in pla
sh in plain english in
glish in plain english
in plain english in pla
sh in plain english in
lish in plain english
in plain english in pla
glish in plain english

Cascading Style Sheets in Plain English

This section of the book is for those of you who know how you want to style an XHTML document but may not remember the name of a particular property. The following table is composed of four columns:

- The first column contains alphabetically arranged, *italicized* keywords that represent styling tasks to be performed.

- The second column identifies the name of the property with which you'll accomplish the specified task.

- The third column lists the page number in Part I, "XHTML Reference" where you'll find a complete description of the property, its syntax, its attributes, and more.

- The last column lists the page number in Part II, "XHTML Tutorial" where you can learn how to use a particular property.

If you want to . . .	Use this property	Located on this reference page	Located on this tutorial page
apply styles to an element when a user *activates* it	:active	373	
automatically insert content *after* the content of an element	:after	373	
specify the *azimuth* location (in a 360-degree left-to-right arc) of a sound file	azimuth	374	
automatically insert content *before* the content of an element	:before	383	
set all *border properties*	border	383	
set the *bottom-border color* of a box	border-bottom-color	385	
set *bottom-border properties*	border-bottom	384	
set the *bottom-border style* of a box	border-bottom-style	387	
set the *bottom-border width*	border-bottom-width	388	631
set all *border colors*	border-color	389	631
set all *border styles*	border-style	400	632
control all *border widths*	border-width	405	
control or size the *bottom margin*	margin-bottom	448	630
control an element's *bottom offset position*	bottom	406	
control or size the *bottom padding*	padding-bottom	465	
specify *character set* characteristics	@charset	408	
specify *character spacing*	letter-spacing	441	633
float an element after a margin is *clear*	clear	408	

If you want to . . .	Use this property	Located on this reference page	Located on this tutorial page
decorate or blink text lines	text-decoration	488	635
define the *clipping area* of a box	clip	409	
start a *comment*	*/	372	
end a *comment*	/*	372	
generate *content* before or after the current element	content	411	
increment one or more named *counters*	counter-increment	412	
reset one or more named *counters*	counter-reset	412	
set *crop marks* for a page box	marks	454	
sound an auditory *cue* before and/or after an element	cue	413	
sound an auditory *cue after* an element	cue-after	414	
sound an auditory *cue before* an element	cue-before	414	
specify the *cursor type* for the mouse pointer or other pointing device	cursor	415	
display the current element in a particular way onscreen or printed	display	417	
specify the *elevation* (from top-to-bottom) of a sound file	elevation	419	
show or hide borders for *empty table-cells*	empty-cells	419	
apply styles to a *first-child element*	:first-child	420	
style the *first letter* of a paragraph	first-letter	421	

Continued

If you want to . . .	Use this property	Located on this reference page	Located on this tutorial page
style the *first line* of a paragraph	:first-line	422	
set the *first-page-box style* of a document	:first	420	
float an element right or left	float	422	632
apply styles to an element when it is the *focused-on* element	:focus	423	
adjust the *font aspect value*	font-size-adjust	432	
specify up to six *font descriptor* values	@font-face	425	
select a *font family* or name	font-family	429	635
set all *font properties*	font	424	624, 629, 635
set the *font size*	font-size	430	635
set all *font styles*	font-style	434	635
set bold or light *font weight*	font-weight	435	635
specify element *height*	height	436	
set *horizontal alignment* of text	text-align	487	629
apply styles to an element when a user *hovers* over it	:hover	437	
import styles from an external style sheet	@import	438	
identify an *important statement*	!important	438	
indent the first line	text-indent	488	
apply styles to an element that matches a particular *language*	:lang	439	
set the *left-border color* of a box	border-left-color	392	
set *left-border properties*	border-left	391	

If you want to . . .	Use this property	Located on this reference page	Located on this tutorial page
set the *left-border style* of a box	`border-left-style`	**393**	
set *left-border width*	`border-left-width`	**394**	**631**
control or size the *left margin*	`margin-left`	**449**	**629, 630**
control an element's *left offset position*	`left`	**440**	
set the *left-page-box style* of a document	`:left`	**440**	
control or size the *left padding*	`padding-left`	**466**	
set a *list item image type*	`list-style-image`	**444**	**544, 546, 641**
set a *list number or bullet type*	`list-style-type`	**445**	**544, 546, 641**
control all *list properties*	`list-style`	**443**	**544, 546, 641**
specify a *list's position*	`list-style-position`	**444**	**544, 546, 641**
control or size all *margins*	`margin`	**446**	**630**
create and specify the dimensions of a *marker box*	`marker-offset`	**453**	
indicate the *media type* in which a styled document is to be output	`@media`	**456**	
control or size all *padding*	`padding`	**464**	
attach or scroll the *page-background image*	`background-attachment`	**377**	**628**
specify the *page-background color*	`background-color`	**378**	**628**
specify a *page-background image*	`background-image`	**380**	**628**

Continued

If you want to . . .	Use this property	Located on this reference page	Located on this tutorial page
set the *page-background image position*	background-position	381	629
specify one or more *page-background properties*	background	375	
specify the *page-foreground (text) color*	color	410	
repeat a *page-background image*	background-repeat	382	629
specify the *maximum height* of the selected element	max-height	454	
specify the *maximum width* of the selected element	max-width	455	
specify the *minimum height* of the selected element	min-height	457	
specify the *minimum width* of the selected element	min-width	458	
specify the minimum number of *orphan* paragraph lines left at the bottom of a page	orphans	458	
set all *outline colors*	outline-color	460	
set all *outline properties*	outline	459	
set all *outline styles*	outline-style	461	
control all *outline widths*	outline-width	462	
specify whether and how the contents of a box *overflow*	overflow	463	
set *page-box* characteristics	@page	468	

If you want to . . .	Use this property	Located on this reference page	Located on this tutorial page
set *page-box* dimensions and orientation	`size`	**481**	
insert a *page break* *after* the current page box	`page-break-after`	**470**	
insert a *page break* *before* the current page box	`page-break-before`	**471**	
insert a *page break* *inside* the current page box	`page-break-inside`	**472**	
name a *page type*	`page`	**470**	
pause before and/or after an element is spoken	`pause`	**473**	
pause after an element is spoken	`pause-after`	**474**	
pause before an element is spoken	`pause-before`	**475**	
set the *pitch* of a speaking-voice	`pitch`	**476**	
vary the *pitch range*	`pitch-range`	**476**	
play a background sound as an element's content is spoken	`play-during`	**477**	
position the current element	`position`	**478**	**574, 580**
specify pairs of *quotation marks* that open and close a quotation	`quotes`	**478**	
specify the *richness* of a voice	`richness`	**480**	
set the *right-border color* of a box	`border-right-color`	**396**	
set *right-border properties*	`border-right`	**395**	

Continued

If you want to . . .	Use this property	Located on this reference page	Located on this tutorial page
set the *right-border style* of a box	border-right-style	397	
set *right-border width*	border-right-width	398	631
control or size the *right margin*	margin-right	450	629, 630, 632
control an element's *right offset position*	right	481	
set the *right-page-box style* of a document	:right	480	
control or size the *right padding*	padding-right	466	
set a *small-cap font variant*	font-variant	435	635
set *"speak" table-cell header characteristics*	speak-header	483	
control the *speaking rate*	speech-rate	485	
specify whether text is *spoken*	speak	482	
set the *stack level* of the current box in a stack of elements	z-index	500	
set *spoken numerals* in a document	speak-numeral	484	
set *spoken punctuation* in a document	speak-punctuation	484	
specify the highest *stress* (inflection) level in a voice	stress	486	
select a *stretched or condensed font*	font-stretch	433	
specify the *table caption* position and alignment	caption-side	407	
set a *table-cell border collapse* or separation	border-collapse	389	

If you want to . . .	Use this property	Located on this reference page	Located on this tutorial page
specify *table-cell border spacing* from adjacent cells	border-spacing	399	
specify a *table layout*	table-layout	486	
change the *text case*	text-transform	491	635
specify *text direction*	direction	416	
apply one or more *text shadow effects*	text-shadow	489	
set the *top-border color* of a box	border-top-color	402	
set *top-border properties*	border-top	401	
set the *top-border style* of a box	border-top-style	403	
set *top-border width*	border-top-width	404	631
control or size the *top margin*	margin-top	452	629, 630
control an element's *top offset position*	top	492	
control or size the *top padding*	padding-top	467	
embed or override the *Unicode bidirectional algorithm* for the current element	unicode-bidi	492	
apply styles to an *unvisited link*	:link	442	
set the *vertical alignment*	vertical-align	493	633
specify whether a box in which an element resides is *visible* or invisible	visibility	494	
apply styles to a *visited link*	:visited	495	

Continued

If you want to . . .	Use this property	Located on this reference page	Located on this tutorial page
select a *voice family* or name	voice-family	**495**	
specify the median *volume* of a waveform file	volume	**496**	
control *white space*	white-space	**497**	
specify the minimum number of *widow* paragraph lines left at the top of a page	widows	**498**	
set an element's *width*	width	**498**	
set *spacing* between words	word-spacing	**499**	**635**

in plain english in pla
sh in plain english in
glish in plain english
in plain english in pla
sh in plain english in
glish in plain english
in plain english in pla
glish in plain english
in plain english in pla
sh in plain english in
glish in plain english
in plain english in pla
sh in plain english in
glish in plain english
in plain english in pla
lish in plain english
in plain english in pla
sh in plain english in
glish in plain english
in plain english in pla
sh in plain english in
lish in plain english
n plain english in pla
glish in plain english

Cascading Style Sheets A to Z

This reference is a comprehensive table of all the CSS2 properties covered in this book. The following table is composed of three columns:

- The first column contains alphabetically arranged element names.
- The second column lists the page number in Section 2, *Cascading Style Sheet Syntax*, in the reference.
- The third column lists the page number in Chapter 8, *Styling Documents with CSS*, in the tutorial.

Continued

Continued

Cascading Style Sheets by Category

CSS1 and CSS2 properties can be divided into four categories:

- *At-rules.* The elements in this category enable you to set overall default characteristics for a document.
- *Properties.* This is the largest category. It enables you to assign properties to XHTML elements.
- *Pseudo-elements.* The elements in this category enable you to specify particular styles for the first line or first letter of a paragraph and document content that occurs before and/or after the current document.
- *Pseudo-classes.* This category enables you to categorize elements by hierarchy or by their current status.

Tables CAT-1 through CAT-4 list the CSS1 and CSS2 properties covered in this book, according to category. To learn more about a particular property, refer to the page numbers shown in the third column of each table.

●—NOTE

Cascading style sheets are covered in detail in "Cascading Style Sheet Syntax" (page **371**) and in Chapter 8, "Styling Documents with CSS2" (page **623**).

Table CAT-1   *CSS Elements in the At-Rules Category*

Element	Page Number
@charset	408
@font-face	425
@import	438
@media	456
@page	468

Table CAT-2   *CSS Elements in the Properties Category*

Element	Page Number
*/	372
/*	372
azimuth	374
background	375
background-attachment	377
background-color	378
background-image	380
background-position	381
background-repeat	382
border	383
border-bottom	384
border-bottom-color	385
border-bottom-style	387
border-bottom-width	388
border-collapse	389
border-color	389
border-left	391
border-left-color	392

Continued

Table CAT-2 *Continued*

Element	Page Number
font-size-adjust	432
font-stretch	433
font-style	434
font-variant	435
font-weight	435
height	436
!important	438
left	440
letter-spacing	441
line-height	442
list-style	443
list-style-image	444
list-style-position	444
list-style-type	445
margin	446
margin-bottom	448
margin-left	449
margin-right	450
margin-top	452
marker-offset	453
marks	454
max-height	454
max-width	455
min-height	457
min-width	458
orphans	458
outline	459
outline-color	460
outline-style	461
outline-width	462
overflow	463
padding	464
padding-bottom	465

Continued

Table CAT-2 *Continued*

Element	Page Number
visibility	494
voice-family	495
volume	496
white-space	497
widows	498
width	498
word-spacing	499
z-index	500

Table CAT-3 *CSS Elements in the Pseudo-Classes Category*

Element	Page Number
:active	373
:first	420
:first-child	420
:focus	423
:hover	437
:lang	439
:left	440
:link	442
:right	480
:visited	495

Table CAT-4 *CSS Elements in the Pseudo-Elements Category*

Element	Page Number
:after	373
:before	383
:first-letter	421
:first-line	422

in plain english in pl
sh in plain english in
glish in plain english
in plain english in pl
sh in plain english in
glish in plain english
in plain english in pl
glish in plain english
in plain english in pl
sh in plain english in
glish in plain english
in plain english in pl
sh in plain english in
glish in plain english
in plain english in pl
lish in plain english
in plain english in pl
sh in plain english in
glish in plain english
in plain english in pl
sh in plain english in
lish in plain english
in plain english in pl
glish in plain english

Cascading Style Sheet Syntax

In May of 1996, the World Wide Web Consortium (W3C) announced the development of cascading style sheets (CSS), which are sets of document style sheets that enable Web page developers to change a document's format and look — just as they would change a word-processing document.

The era of cascading style sheets is still at its very beginning. Two cascading style sheet standards exist: CSS1 and CSS2. CSS1 was the first standard for cascading style sheets — a simple set of rules to format and enhance text, paragraphs, and entire documents. CSS2, the current standard, adds to the CSS1 base a set of styles for visual browsers, aural devices, printers, Braille devices, and so on, as well as table layout styles, internationalization features, and more. CSS is relatively stable, although neither version — CSS1 and especially CSS2 — is completely supported by Web browsers.

Cascading style sheets (CSS) are made up of sets of rules that are applied to elements. A style sheet rule is composed of two parts: The *selector* is the XHTML to which the rule applies, and the *declaration* consists of the property (similar to an attribute) and the value — both within brackets.

CSS1 and CSS2 properties fall into four categories:

- *Properties*, the largest category, enable you to assign properties to XHTML elements.
- *Pseudo-elements* enable you to specify particular styles for the first line or first letter of a paragraph and document content that occurs before and/or after the current document.
- *Pseudo-classes* enable you to categorize elements by hierarchy or by their current status.
- *At-rules* enable you to set overall default characteristics for a document.

To keep up-to-date with CSS, be sure to periodically visit the style sheet home page at http://www.w3.org/style/.

Style Sheet Properties

This section is comprised of properties for cascading style sheets (CSS2) based on the Cascading Style Sheets, Level 2 CSS2 Specification. The properties are listed alphabetically, and each listing includes a brief description, the syntax, and notes.

/ I /   Comment

Purpose

Places a comment in the document.

Syntax

```
*/ comment-text /*
```

Where

comment text is the text comprising the comment.

Notes

- Use a comment to document a line or part of a style or style sheet. For example, you can state the reason for using a particular property rather than another. Or, for someone who will maintain this document, you can describe how you created a complex style sheet.
- You can see the comment in the source file but not in the published document.
- */ and /* are comparable to HTML's and XML's <!- and->.

:active   Activate

Purpose
Applies styles to an element when a user activates it.

Syntax
```
element-type:active {property}
```

Where
- *element-type* is the name of the element being activated.
- *property* represents one or more style-sheet properties.

Notes
- This pseudo-class originated in CSS2.
- The :active pseudo-class enables you to apply styles to an element when it is active.
- The :active pseudo-class is related to the XHTML alink attribute.
- In CSS1, :active, :link, and :visited were mutually exclusive. Now, you can :active, :link, and :visit a particular element.

Related Pseudo-Classes
:focus (423), :hover (437)

:after   After Content

Purpose
Automatically inserts content *after* the content of an element.

Syntax
```
<element-type:after>content
</element-type:before>
```

Where
- *element-type* is the name of the current element.
- *content* represents the after-element content being styled.

Notes
- This pseudo-element originated in CSS2.
- You can combine :after with :first-letter and/or :first-line to affect the first letter and/or first line of a paragraph.

Related Pseudo-Element
:before (383)

Related Property
content (793)

azimuth

Spatial Azimuth

Purpose

Specifies the left-to-right stereo speaker location of a sound file.

Syntax

```
azimuth: range_angle|((left-side|far-left|left
    |center-left|center|center-right|right|far-right
    |right-side)|behind)|leftwards|rightwards|inherit
```

Where

- *range_angle* is a specific angle in the arc in which stereo speakers are arranged. Valid values range from −360deg (degrees) to 360deg.
- left-side is a keyword that indicates that the sound is on the left side of the arc — at 270deg. If azimuth: left-side behind, the sound is at 270deg.
- far-left is a keyword that indicates that the sound is on the far left side of the arc — at 300deg. If azimuth: far-left behind, the sound is at 240deg.
- left is a keyword that indicates that the sound is on the left side — at 320deg. If azimuth: left behind, the sound is at 220deg.
- center-left is a keyword that indicates that the sound is to the left of center — at 340deg. If azimuth: center-left behind, the sound is at 200deg.
- center is a keyword that indicates that the sound is straight ahead — at 0deg. This is the default. If azimuth: center behind, the sound is straight behind — at 180deg.
- center-right is a keyword that indicates that the sound is to the right of center — at 20deg. If azimuth: center-right behind, the sound is at 160deg.
- right is a keyword that indicates that the sound is farther right on the arc — at 40deg. If azimuth: right behind, the sound is at 140deg.
- far-right is a keyword that indicates that the sound is on the far right side of the arc — at 60deg. If azimuth: far-right behind, the sound is at 120deg.
- right-side is a keyword that indicates that the sound is on the right side of the arc — at 90deg. If azimuth: right-side behind, the sound is at 90deg.
- behind is a keyword that indicates that the sound is moved 90 degrees — in conjunction with the left-side, far-left, left, center-left, center, center-right, right, far-right, and right-side keywords.
- leftwards is a keyword that indicates that the sound is moved 20 degrees to the left, or counterclockwise from the current position.
- rightwards is a keyword that indicates that the sound is moved 20 degrees to the right, or clockwise from the current position.
- inherit is a keyword that indicates that this property takes the same computed value as its parent.

Cascading Style Sheet Syntax

Notes

- This property, which originated in CSS2, applies to all elements.
- As defined in the *Random House Dictionary of the English Language*, an *azimuth* is "the arc of the horizon measured clockwise from the south point, in astronomy, or from the north point, in navigation, to the point where a vertical circle through a given heavenly body intersects with the horizon." In surveying, the azimuth is "the angle of horizontal deviation, measured clockwise, of a bearing from a standard direction, as from north or south."
- The arc of the azimuth is like a clock face with 0 degrees (and 360) at the 12, 90 degrees (and –270) at the 3, 180 degrees (and –180) at the 6, and 270 degrees (and –90) at the 9.
- By default, the characteristics of this property are inherited.

Related Properties

cue (413), cue-after (414), cue-before (414), elevation (419), pause (473), pause-after (474), pause-before (475), pitch (476), pitch-range (476), play-during (477), richness (480), speak (482), speak-numeral (484), speak-punctuation (489), speech-rate (485), stress (486), voice-family (495), volume (496)

---

background   Background Properties

Purpose

Specifies one, two, three, four, or five properties for the page background.

Syntax

```
background: [background-color_value]
  | [background-image_value]
  | [background-repeat_value]
  | [background-attachment_value]
  | [background-position_value]|inherit
```

Where

- *background-color_value* specifies the background color. For more information, see the background-color property (378).
- *background-image_value* specifies the background image. For more information, see the background-image property (380).
- *background-repeat_value* repeats a background image. For more information, see the background-repeat property (382).
- *background-attachment_value* specifies whether the background image is fixed or scrolls. For more information, see the background-attachment property (377).
- *background-position_value* specifies a starting position for a background image. For more information, see the background-position property (381).

- inherit is a keyword that indicates that this property takes the same computed value as its parent.

Notes

- This property originated in CSS1.
- background specifies multiple properties for page backgrounds in the same way that you can individually set rules for the following properties: background-attachment, background-color, background-image, background-position, and background-repeat.
- You do not need to specify the property name. The browser should interpret the unique values for each property.
- By default, the characteristics of this property are not inherited.
- Table R2-1 contains selected hexadecimal color values.

Related Properties

background-attachment (377), background-color (378), background-image (380), background-position (381), background-repeat (382)

Table R2-1 *Selected Colors and Their Hexadecimal Values*

Color	Hexadecimal Value
black	#000000
bright cyan	#00FFFF
bright fuchsia	#FF00FF
bright medium yellow	#FFFF00
dark blue	#0000AA
dark blue-green	#006666
dark gray	#808080
dark lime green	#00AA00
dark purple	#880088
dark red	#AA0000
gray-white	#DDDDDD
light rose	#FFB6C1
medium blue	#0000CC
medium cyan	#00CCCC
medium dull green	#22AA22
medium fuchsia	#CC00CC

Cascading Style Sheet Syntax

Color	Hexadecimal Value
medium fuchsia	#CC00CC
medium gold	#FFFFAA
medium gold-green	#CCCC00
medium gray	#999999
medium lime green	#00CC00
medium peach	#FAAAAC
medium red	#CC0000
medium rose	#FFADDA
navy blue	#0000FF
off-white 1	#F0F7F7
off-white 2	#FFFFF2
off-white 3	#F0F0F0
orange-red	#FF6347
pale blue	#AAADEA
pale cyan	#C0FFEE
pale gold	#FFFFCC
pale green	#ADEADA
pale green-gray	#AADEAD
pale purple	#ADAADA
pumpkin	#FF8127
reddish brown	#550000
strong blue	#0000FF
strong lime green	#00FF00
strong red	#FF0000
white	#FFFFFF

---

background-attachment — Attach Background Image

Purpose

Specifies whether the background image is fixed or scrolls in the background of the page.

Syntax

```
background-attachment: scroll|fixed|inherit
```

Where

- scroll scrolls a background image as a user scrolls up or down the current page.
- fixed freezes the background image in place on the current page.
- inherit is a keyword that indicates that this property takes the same computed value as its parent.

Notes

- This property, which originated in CSS1, applies to all elements.
- By default, the characteristics of this property are not inherited.

Related Properties

background (375), background-color (378), background-image (380), background-position (381), background-repeat (382)

For More Information

Learn about the background-attachment property on page 628 in Chapter 8, "Styling Documents with CSS2."

---

background-color   Background Color

Purpose

Specifies a background color for the current document or document part.

Syntax

```
background-color:
  (color-name|#rgb|#rrggbb|rgb(rrr,ggg,bbb)
  |rgb(rrr%,ggg%,bbb%))|transparent|inherit
```

Where

- *color-name* represents a foreground color by valid name (that is, Red (#FF0000), Maroon (#800000), Yellow (#FFFF00), Green (#008000), Lime (#00FF00), Teal (#008080), Olive (#808000), Aqua (#00FFFF), Blue (#0000FF), Navy (#000080), Purple (#800080), Fuchsia (#FF00FF), Black (#000000), Gray (#808080), White (#FFFFFF), and the default, Silver (#C0C0C0)). CSS2 adds the following color keywords: ActiveBorder, ActiveCaption, AppWorkspace, Background, ButtonFace, ButtonHighlight, ButtonShadow, ButtonText, CaptionText, GrayText, Highlight, Highlight Text, InactiveBorder, InactiveCaption, InactiveCaption Text, InfoBackground, InfoText, Menu, MenuText, Scrollbar, ThreeDDarkShadow, ThreeDFace, ThreeDHighlight, ThreeD LightShadow, ThreeDShadow, Window, WindowFrame, and WindowText. All color names are case-insensitive. Table R2-2 (379) names the color keywords and lists the affected object for each.
- *#rgb* is a three-digit hexadecimal color code, where *r* represents the red attributes, from 0 to F; *g* represents the green attributes, from 0 to F; and *b* represents the blue attributes, from 0 to F.

- **#*rrggbb*** is a six-digit hexadecimal color code, where *rr* represents the red attributes, from 00 to FF; *gg* represents the green attributes, from 00 to FF; and *bb* represents the blue attributes, from 00 to FF.
- **rgb(*rrr,ggg,bbb*)** represents absolute red-green-blue values, each ranging from 000 to 255.
- **rgb(*rrr.d%*, *ggg.e%*, *bbb.f%*)** represents the relative red-green-blue values, each ranging from 0.0% to 100.0%, where 0.0% is equivalent to an absolute value of 000, and 100.0% is equivalent to 255.
- **transparent** represents no background color. This is the default.
- **inherit** is a keyword that indicates that this property takes the same computed value as its parent.

Notes

- This property, which originated in CSS1, applies to all elements.
- The initial color value is set within the user's browser.
- By default, the characteristics of this property are not inherited.
- Table R2-1 (376) contains selected hexadecimal color values.

Related Properties

background (375), **background-attachment** (377), **background-image** (380), **background-position** (381), **background-repeat** (382), **color** (410)

For More Information

Learn about the **background-color** property on page 628 in Chapter 8, "Styling Documents with CSS2."

Table R2-2 *CSS2 Color Names*

Name	Affected Object
ActiveBorder	Border of the active window
ActiveCaption	Caption of the active window
AppWorkspace	Background of the multiple-document interface
Background	Background of the desktop
ButtonFace	Face of three-dimensional buttons
ButtonHighlight	Highlight on three-dimensional buttons
ButtonShadow	Shadow on three-dimensional buttons
ButtonText	Text on three-dimensional buttons
CaptionText	Text of captions, size boxes, and scroll bar arrow boxes
GrayText	Disabled text
Highlight	Selected items in a control

Continued

Table R2-2   *Continued*

Name	Affected Object
HighlightText	Selected text in a control
InactiveBorder	Border of an inactive window
InactiveCaption	Caption object of an inactive window
InactiveCaptionText	Caption text in an inactive window
InfoBackground	Background of Tooltip (bubble help and so on) controls
InfoText	Text of Tooltips
Menu	Background of menus
MenuText	Text of menus
Scrollbar	Background of scroll bars
ThreeDDarkShadow	Dark shadow of three-dimensional objects
ThreeDFace	Face of three-dimensional objects
ThreeDHighlight	Highlight of three-dimensional objects
ThreeDLightShadow	Light shadow of three-dimensional objects
ThreeDShadow	Shadow of three-dimensional objects
Window	Background of windows
WindowFrame	Frame of windows
WindowText	Text in windows

background-image   **Background Image**

Purpose

Specifies a background image for the current document or document part.

Syntax

```
background-image: uri(uri_name)|none|inherit
```

Where

- uri is a reserved keyword that indicates that a URI will follow.
- *uri_name* names the URI of the image to be used for the background.
- none indicates no background image.
- inherit is a keyword that indicates that this property takes the same computed value as its parent.

Notes

- This property, which originated in CSS1, applies to all elements.
- By default, the characteristics of this property are not inherited.

Related Properties

background (375), background-attachment (377), background-color (378), background-position (381), background-repeat (382)

For More Information

Learn about the background-image property on page 628 in Chapter 8, "Styling Documents with CSS2."

background-position | Background Image Position

Purpose

Specifies a starting position for a background image.

Syntax

```
background-position: (([+|-]h_percent%
  [[+|-]v_percent%])|([+|-] h_length
  [[+|-]v_length])|((top|center|bottom)
  |(left|center|right)))|inherit
```

Where

- *h_percent* is a positive or negative value that is relative to the left-to-right position of the image. Follow each *h_percent* with a percentage sign (%).
- *v_percent* is a positive or negative value that is relative to the top-to-bottom position of the image. The default is 50%. Follow each *v_percent* with a percentage sign (%).
- *h_length* is a positive or negative value of the left-to-right position of the image away from the top-left corner. Follow each value with a two-letter abbreviation representing the unit of measure.
- *v_length* is a positive or negative value of the left-to-right position of the image away from the top-left corner. Follow each value with a two-letter abbreviation representing the unit of measure.
- top is a keyword that positions the background image in the top-to-bottom plane at the top of the current box's padding edge.
- center is a keyword that positions the background image in the top-to-bottom plane in the center of the current box.
- bottom is a keyword that positions the background image in the top-to-bottom plane at the bottom of the current box's padding edge.
- left is a keyword that positions the background image in the left-to-right plane at the left of the current box's padding edge.
- center is a keyword that positions the background image in the left-to-right plane in the center of the current box.
- right is a keyword that positions the background image in the left-to-right plane at the right of the current box's padding edge.
- inherit is a keyword that indicates that this property takes the same computed value as its parent.

Notes

- This property originated in CSS1.
- Valid relative units of measure are em (the height of the current font), ex (the height of the letter x in the current font), and px (pixels, relative to the size of the window). Valid absolute units of measure are in (inches), cm (centimeters), mm (millimeters), pt (points), and pc (picas).
- If you specify one percentage or length, that value determines the horizontal position of the image.
- You can combine percentages and lengths. However, do not combine percentages or lengths with keywords.
- The default value of 0% 0% is equivalent to the values of background position: top left and background position: left top.
- The value of 0% 50% is equivalent to background position: left, background position: left center and background position: center left.
- The value of 50% 0% is equivalent to background position: top, background position: top center and background position: center top.
- The value of 100% 0% is equivalent to background position: right top and background position: top right.
- The value of 0% 100% is equivalent to background position: left bottom and background position: bottom left.
- The value of 100% 100% is equivalent to background position: bottom right and background position: right bottom.
- By default, the characteristics of this property are not inherited.

Related Properties

background (375), background-attachment (377), background-color (378), background-image (380), background-repeat (382)

For More Information

Learn about the background-position property on page 629 in Chapter 8, "Styling Documents with CSS2."

---

background-repeat	**Background Repeat**

Purpose

Repeats a background image onscreen a specified number of times.

Syntax

```
background-repeat: repeat|repeat-x|repeat-y
  |no-repeat|inherit
```

Where

- repeat fills the page completely with the image.
- repeat-x fills the page horizontally from the left edge to the right edge.

- `repeat-y` fills the page vertically from top to bottom.
- `no-repeat` does not repeat the image.
- `inherit` is a keyword that indicates that this property takes the same computed value as its parent.

Notes

- This property, which originated in CSS1, applies to all elements.
- By default, the characteristics of this property are not inherited.

Related Properties

background (375), background-attachment (377), background-color (378), background-image (380), background-position (381)

For More Information

Learn about the `background-repeat` property on page 629 in Chapter 8, "Styling Documents with CSS2."

:before   Before Content

Purpose

Automatically inserts content *before* the content of an element.

Syntax

```
<element-type:before>content
</element-type:before>
```

Where

- `element-type` is the name of the current element.
- `content` represents the before-element content being styled.

Notes

- This pseudo-element originated in CSS2.
- You can combine `:after` with `:first-letter` and/or `:first-line` to affect the first letter and/or first line of a paragraph.

Related Property

content (793)

Related Pseudo-Element

:after (373)

border   Border Properties

Purpose

Specifies the color, style, and/or width of all four borders of a box.

Syntax

```
border: ([border-width_value][ border-style_value]
[ border-color_value])|inherit
```

Where

- *border-width_value* specifies the width of all four borders. For more information, see the `border-width` property (405).
- *border-style_value* specifies the style of all four borders. For more information, see the `border-style` property (400).
- *border-color_value* specifies the color of all four borders. For more information, see the `border-color` property (389).
- `inherit` is a keyword that indicates that this property takes the same computed value as its parent.

Notes

- This property originated in CSS1.
- This shortcut property specifies multiple properties for the four borders in the same way that you can individually set rules for the following properties: `border-color`, `border-style`, and `border-width`.
- You do not need to specify the property name. The browser should interpret the unique values for each property.
- There is no initial value for this property.
- By default, the characteristics of this property are not inherited.
- A border is outside the content of the page but within the page edges and the margins.
- Table R2-1 (376) contains selected hexadecimal color values.

Related Properties

`border-bottom` (384), `border-collapse` (389), `border-color` (389), `border-left` (391), `border-right` (395), `border-spacing` (399), `border-style` (400), `border-top` (401), `border-width` (405)

---

border-bottom   Bottom Border Properties

Purpose

Specifies the color, style, and/or width of the bottom border of a box.

Syntax

```
border-bottom: ([border-bottom-width_value]
[border-style_value] [border-color_value])
|inherit
```

Where

- *border-bottom-width_value* specifies the border width. For more information, see the `border-width` property (405).
- *border-style_value* specifies the border style. For more information, see the `border-style` property (400).
- *border-color_value* specifies the border color. For more information, see the `border-color` property (389).
- `inherit` is a keyword that indicates that this property takes the same computed value as its parent.

Notes

- This property originated in CSS1.
- This property specifies multiple properties for a bottom border in the same way that you can individually set rules for the following properties: `border-bottom-color`, `border-bottom-style`, and `border-bottom-width`.
- You do not need to specify the property name. The browser should interpret the unique values for each property.
- There is no initial value for this property.
- By default, the characteristics of this property are not inherited.
- `border-bottom` accepts only one style, in contrast to `border-style` (400), which accepts as many as four.
- A border is outside the content of the page but within the page edges and the margins.
- Table R2-1 (376) contains selected hexadecimal color values.

Related Properties

`border` (383), `border-bottom-color` (385), `border-bottom-style` (387), `border-bottom-width` (388), `border-collapse` (389), `border-left` (391), `border-right` (395), `border-spacing` (399), `border-top` (401)

border-bottom-color | Bottom Border Color

Purpose

Sets the color of the bottom border of a box.

Syntax

```
border-bottom-color: (color-name_b|#rgb_b|#rrggbb_b
 |rgb (rrr_b,ggg_b,bbb_b)|rgb(rrr_b%,ggg_b%,bbb_b%))
 |transparent|inherit
```

Where

- *color-name_b* represents the bottom-border color by valid name (that is, Red (#FF0000), Maroon (#800000), Yellow (#FFFF00), Green (#008000), Lime (#00FF00), Teal (#008080), Olive (#808000), Aqua (#00FFFF), Blue (#0000FF), Navy (#000080), Purple (#800080), Fuchsia (#FF00FF), Black (#000000), Gray (#808080), White (#FFFFFF), and the default, Silver (#C0C0C0)). CSS2 adds the following color keywords: ActiveBorder, ActiveCaption, AppWorkspace, Background, ButtonFace, ButtonHighlight, ButtonShadow, ButtonText, CaptionText, GrayText, Highlight, Highlight Text, InactiveBorder, InactiveCaption, InactiveCaption Text, InfoBackground, InfoText, Menu, MenuText, Scrollbar, ThreeDDarkShadow, ThreeDFace, ThreeDHighlight, Three DLightShadow, ThreeDShadow, Window, WindowFrame, and WindowText. All color names are case-insensitive. Table R2-2 (379) names the color keywords and lists the affect object for each.
- *#rgb_b* represents a three-digit hexadecimal bottom-border color code, where *r* represents the red attributes, from 0 to F; *g* represents the green attributes, from 0 to F; and *b* represents the blue attributes, from 0 to F.
- *#rrggbb_b* represents a six-digit hexadecimal bottom-border color code, where *rr* represents the red attributes, from 00 to FF; *gg* represents the green attributes, from 00 to FF; and *bb* represents the blue attributes, from 00 to FF.
- rgb(*rrr_b*,*ggg_b*,*bbb_b*) represents absolute red-green-blue values for the bottom border. Each of the values ranges from 000 to 255.
- rgb(*rrr.d_b%*, *ggg.e_b%*, *bbb.f_b%*) represents the relative red-green-blue values for the bottom border, ranging from 0.0% to 100.0%, where 0.0% is equivalent to an absolute value of 000, and 100.0% is equivalent to 255.
- transparent is a keyword that indicates that the background is transparent.
- inherit is a keyword that indicates that this property takes the same computed value as its parent.

Notes

- This property, which originated in CSS2, applies to all elements.
- A border is outside the content of the page but within the page edges and the margins.
- The initial border color value is set within the user's browser.
- By default, the characteristics of this property are not inherited.
- Table R2-1 (376) contains selected hexadecimal color values.

Related Properties

border-collapse (389), border-color (389), border-left-color (392), border-right-color (396), border-spacing (399), border-top-color (402)

border-bottom-style   Bottom Border Style

Purpose

Formats the bottom border of a box.

Syntax

```
border-bottom-style:
  none|hidden|dotted|dashed|solid|double|groove
  |ridge|inset|outset|inherit
```

Where

- none omits a border. This overrides any border-width (405) value.
- hidden omits a border and takes precedence over any other value for this border.
- dotted draws a dotted-line border over the element background.
- dashed draws a dashed-line border over the element background.
- solid draws a solid-line border over the element background.
- double draws a double-solid-line border over the element background.
- groove draws a three-dimensional grooved border over the element background using the border-color or border-top-color value.
- ridge draws a three-dimensional ridged border over the element background using the border-color or border-top-color value.
- inset draws a three-dimensional inset over the element background using the border-color or border-top-color value.
- outset draws a three-dimensional outset over the element background using the border-color or border-top-color value.
- inherit is a keyword that indicates that this property takes the same computed value as its parent.

Notes

- This property originated in CSS2.
- A border is outside the content of the page but within the page edges and the margins.
- Some browsers cannot interpret the border-bottom-style values and will draw a solid line instead.
- By default, the characteristics of this property are not inherited.

Related Properties

border-collapse (389), border-left-style (393), border-right-style (397), border-spacing (399), border-style (400), border-top-style (403), empty-cells (419)

border-bottom-width	Bottom Border Width

Purpose

Sets the width of the bottom border of a box.

Syntax

border-bottom-width: thin | medium | thick | length
    | inherit

Where

- thin is a narrower width than medium or thick.
- medium is wider than thin but narrower than thick.
- thick is wider than thin or medium.
- length is a positive value followed by a two-letter abbreviation representing the unit of measure.
- inherit is a keyword that indicates that this property takes the same computed value as its parent.

Notes

- This property, which originated in CSS1, applies to all elements.
- A border is outside the content of the page but within the page edges and the margins.
- The width of borders varies from browser to browser.
- Valid relative units of measure are em (the height of the current font), ex (the height of the letter x in the current font), and px (pixels, relative to the size of the window). Valid absolute units of measure are in (inches), cm (centimeters), mm (millimeters), pt (points), and pc (picas).
- By default, the characteristics of this property are not inherited.

Related Properties

border-collapse (389), border-left-width (394), border-right-width (398), border-spacing (399), border-top-width (404), border-width (405)

For More Information

Learn about the border-bottom-width property on page 631 in Chapter 8, "Styling Documents with CSS2."

border-collapse — Cell Border Collapse?

Purpose
Collapses (hides) or separates a table-cell border.

Syntax
```
border-collapse: collapse|separate|inherit
```

Where
- **collapse** is a keyword that indicates that a row or column is hidden within a table. This is the default.
- **separate** is a keyword that indicates that a cell has its own separate border.
- **inherit** is a keyword that indicates that this property takes the same computed value as its parent.

Notes
- This property, which originated in CSS2, applies to table and inline-table elements (such as the XHTML **table** element).
- Collapsed columns and rows still affect table layout.
- By default, the characteristics of this property are inherited.

Related Properties
border-spacing (399), display (417), empty-cells (419), speak-header (483), table-layout (486), visibility (494)

For More Information
- For more information about table cells and table-cell borders, refer to "Section 17.6" in the *Cascading Style Sheets, Level 2 CSS Specification* (http://www.w3.org/TR/REC-CSS2/).

border-color — Border Color

Purpose
Sets colors of one, two, three, or four borders of a box.

Syntax
```
border-color: (color-name_t|#rgb_t|#rrggbb_t
   |rgb(rrr_t,ggg_t,bbb_t)|rgb(rrr_t%,ggg_t%,bbb_t%))
   (color-name_rt|#rgb_rt|#rrggbb_rt
   |rgb(rrr_r,ggg_r,bbb_r)|rgb(rrr_r%,ggg_r%,bbb_r%))
   (color-name_b|#rgb_b|#rrggbb_b
   |rgb(rrr_b,ggg_b,bbb_b) |rgb(rrr_b%,ggg_b%,bbb_b%))
```

```
(color-name_l | #rgb_l | #rrggbb_l
| rgb(rrr_l,ggg_l,bbb_l) | rgb(rrr_l%,ggg_l%,bbb_l%))
| inherit
```

Where

- *color-name_t*, *color-name_r*, *color-name_b*, and *color-name_l* specify border colors for the top, right, bottom, and left borders by valid name (that is, Red (#FF0000), Maroon (#800000), Yellow (#FFFF00), Green (#008000), Lime (#00FF00), Teal (#008080), Olive (#808000), Aqua (#00FFFF), Blue (#0000FF), Navy (#000080), Purple (#800080), Fuchsia (#FF00FF), Black (#000000), Gray (#808080), White (#FFFFFF), and the default, Silver (#C0C0C0)). CSS2 adds the following color keywords: ActiveBorder, ActiveCaption, AppWorkspace, Background, ButtonFace, ButtonHighlight, ButtonShadow, ButtonText, CaptionText, GrayText, Highlight, Highlight Text, InactiveBorder, InactiveCaption, InactiveCaption Text, InfoBackground, InfoText, Menu, MenuText, Scrollbar, ThreeDDarkShadow, ThreeDFace, ThreeDHighlight, Three DLightShadow, ThreeDShadow, Window, WindowFrame, and WindowText. All color names are case-insensitive. Table R2.2 (379) names the color keywords and lists the affected object for each.
- *#rgb_t*, *#rgb_r*, *#rgb_b*, and *#rgb_l* each represent a three-digit hexadecimal color code for the top, right, bottom, and left borders, where *r* represents the red attributes, from 0 to F; *g* represents the green attributes, from 0 to F; and *b* represents the blue attributes, from 0 to F.
- *#rrggbb_t*, *#rrggbb_r*, *#rrggbb_b*, and *#rrggbb_l* each represent a six-digit hexadecimal color code for the top, right, bottom, and left borders, where *rr* represents the red attributes, from 00 to FF; *gg* represents the green attributes, from 00 to FF; and *bb* represents the blue attributes, from 00 to FF.
- rgb(*rrr_t,ggg_t,bbb_t*), rgb(*rrr_rt,ggg_rt,bbb_r*), rgb(*rrr_b,ggg_b,bbb_b*), and rgb(*rrr_l,ggg_l,bbb_l*) each represent absolute red-green-blue values for the top, right, bottom, and left borders. Each of the values ranges from 000 to 255.
- rgb(*rrr.d_t%, ggg.e_t%, bbb.f_t%*), rgb(*rrr.d_r%, ggg.e_r%, bbb.f_r%*), rgb(*rrr.d_b%, ggg.e_b%, bbb.f_b%*), and rgb(*rrr.d_l%, ggg.e_l%, bbb.f_l%*) each represent the relative red-green-blue values for the top, right, bottom, and left borders, each ranging from 0.0% to 100.0%, where 0.0% is equivalent to an absolute value of 000, and 100.0% is equivalent to 255.
- inherit is a keyword that indicates that this property takes the same computed value as its parent.

Notes

- This shortcut property, which originated in CSS1, applies to all elements.
- A border is outside the content of the page but within the page edges and the margins.
- The initial border color value is set within the user's browser.

- By default, the characteristics of this property are not inherited.
- Table R2-1 (376) contains selected hexadecimal color values.

Related Properties

border-bottom-color (385), border-collapse (389), border-left-color (392), border-right-color (396), border-spacing (399), border-top-color (402)

For More Information

Learn about the border-color property on page 631 in Chapter 8, "Styling Documents with CSS2."

border-left   Left Border Properties

Purpose

Specifies the color, style, and/or width of the left border of a box.

Syntax

```
border-left: [ border-left-width_value]
  [ border-style_value] [ border-color_value]
  |inherit
```

Where

- *border-left-width_value* specifies the border width. For more information, see the border-width property (405).
- *border-style_value* specifies the border style. For more information, see the border-style property (400).
- *border-color_value* specifies the border color. For more information, see the border-color property (389).
- inherit is a keyword that indicates that this property takes the same computed value as its parent.

Notes

- This property originated in CSS1.
- This property specifies multiple properties for left borders in the same way that you can individually set rules for the following properties: border-left-color, border-left-style, and border-left-width.
- You do not need to specify the property name. The browser should interpret the unique values for each property.
- There is no initial value for this property.
- By default, the characteristics of this property are not inherited.
- border-left accepts only one style, in contrast to border-style, which accepts as many as four.
- A border is outside the content of the page but within the page edges and the margins.
- Table R2-1 (376) contains selected hexadecimal color values.

Related Properties

border (383), border-bottom (384), border-collapse (389), border-left-color (392), border-left-style (393), border-left-width (394), border-right (395), border-spacing (399), border-top (401)

border-left-color   Left Border Color

Purpose

Sets the color of the left border of a box.

Syntax

```
border-left-color: color-name_l | #rgb_l | #rrggbb_l
  | rgb(rrr_l,ggg_l,bbb_l)  | rgb(rrr_l%,ggg_l%,bbb_l%)
  | inherit
```

Where

- *color-name_l* specifies the left-border color by valid name (that is, Red (#FF0000), Maroon (#800000), Yellow (#FFFF00), Green (#008000), Lime (#00FF00), Teal (#008080), Olive (#808000), Aqua (#00FFFF), Blue (#0000FF), Navy (#000080), Purple (#800080), Fuchsia (#FF00FF), Black (#000000), Gray (#808080), White (#FFFFFF), and the default, Silver (#C0C0C0)). CSS2 adds the following case-insensitive color keywords: ActiveBorder, ActiveCaption, AppWorkspace, Background, ButtonFace, ButtonHighlight, ButtonShadow, ButtonText, CaptionText, GrayText, Highlight, HighlightText, Inactive Border, InactiveCaption, InactiveCaptionText, Info Background, InfoText, Menu, MenuText, Scrollbar, ThreeDDark Shadow, ThreeDFace, ThreeDHighlight, ThreeDLightShadow, ThreeDShadow, Window, WindowFrame, and WindowText. Table R2.2 (379) names the color keywords and lists the affected object for each.
- *#rgb_l* represents a three-digit hexadecimal left-border color code, where *r* represents the red attributes, from 0 to F; *g* represents the green attributes, from 0 to F; and *b* represents the blue attributes, from 0 to F.
- *#rrggbb_l* represents a six-digit hexadecimal left-border color code, where *rr* represents the red attributes, from 00 to FF; *gg* represents the green attributes, from 00 to FF; and *bb* represents the blue attributes, from 00 to FF.
- rgb(*rrr_l,ggg_l,bbb_l*) represents absolute red-green-blue values for the left border. Each of the values ranges from 000 to 255.

- `rgb(`*rrr.d_l*`%,` *ggg.e_l*`%,` *bbb.f_l*`%)` represents the relative red-green-blue values for the left border, ranging from 0.0% to 100.0%, where 0.0% is equivalent to an absolute value of 000, and 100.0% is equivalent to 255.
- `inherit` is a keyword that indicates that this property takes the same computed value as its parent.

Notes

- This property, which originated in CSS2, applies to all elements.
- A border is outside the content of the page but within the page edges and the margins.
- The initial border color value is set within the user's browser.
- By default, the characteristics of this property are not inherited.
- Table R2-1 (376) contains selected hexadecimal color values.

Related Properties

`border-bottom-color` (385), `border-collapse` (389), `border-color` (389), `border-right-color` (396), `border-spacing` (399), `border-top-color` (402)

border-left-style	Left Border Style

Purpose

Formats the left border of a box.

Syntax

```
border-left-style:
    none|hidden|dotted|dashed|solid|double|groove
    |ridge|inset|outset|inherit
```

Where

- `none` omits a border. This overrides any `border-width` (405) value.
- `hidden` omits a border and takes precedence over any other value for this border.
- `dotted` draws a dotted-line border over the element background.
- `dashed` draws a dashed-line border over the element background.
- `solid` draws a solid-line border over the element background.
- `double` draws a double-solid-line border over the element background.
- `groove` draws a three-dimensional grooved border over the element background using the `border-color` or `border-top-color` value.
- `ridge` draws a three-dimensional ridged border over the element background using the `border-color` or `border-top-color` value.

- inset draws a three-dimensional inset over the element background using the border-color or border-top-color value.
- outset draws a three-dimensional outset over the element background using the border-color or border-top-color value.
- inherit is a keyword that indicates that this property takes the same computed value as its parent.

Notes

- This property originated in CSS2.
- A border is outside the content of the page but within the page edges and the margins.
- Some browsers cannot interpret the border-left-style values and draw a solid line instead.
- By default, the characteristics of this property are not inherited.

Related Properties

border-bottom-style (387), border-collapse (389), border-right-style (397), border-spacing (399), border-style (400), border-top-style (403), empty-cells (419)

---

border-left-width	Left Border Width

Purpose

Sets the width of the left border of a box.

Syntax

border-left-width: thin | medium | thick | length | inherit

Where

- thin is a narrower width than medium or thick.
- medium is wider than thin but narrower than thick.
- thick is wider than thin or medium.
- length is a positive value followed by a two-letter abbreviation representing the unit of measure.
- inherit is a keyword that indicates that this property takes the same computed value as its parent.

Notes

- This property, which originated in CSS1, applies to all elements.
- A border is outside the content of the page but within the page edges and the margins.
- The width of borders varies from browser to browser.

- Valid relative units of measure are em (the height of the current font), ex (the height of the letter x in the current font), and px (pixels, relative to the size of the window). Valid absolute units of measure are in (inches), cm (centimeters), mm (millimeters), pt (points), and pc (picas).
- By default, the characteristics of this property are not inherited.

Related Properties

border-bottom-width (388), border-collapse (389), border-right-width (398), border-spacing (399), border-top-width (404), border-width (405)

For More Information

Learn about the border-left-width property on page 631 in Chapter 8, "Styling Documents with CSS2."

border-right	Right Border Properties

Purpose

Specifies the color, style, and/or width of the right border of a box.

Syntax

```
border-right: [ border-right-width_value]
  [ border-style_value] [ border-color_value]
  |inherit
```

Where

- *border-right-width_value* specifies the border width. For more information, see the border-width property (405).
- *border-style_value* specifies the border style. For more information, see the border-style property (400).
- *border-color_value* specifies the border color. For more information, see the border-color property (389).
- inherit is a keyword that indicates that this property takes the same computed value as its parent.

Notes

- This property originated in CSS1.
- This property specifies multiple properties for right borders in the same way that you can individually set rules for the following properties: border-right-color, border-right-style, and border-right-width.
- You do not need to specify the property name. The browser should interpret the unique values for each property.
- There is no initial value for this property.
- By default, the characteristics of this property are not inherited.
- border-right accepts only one style, in contrast to border-style, which accepts as many as four.

- A border is outside the content of the page but within the page edges and the margins.
- Table R2-1 (376) contains selected hexadecimal color values.

Related Properties

border (383), border-bottom (384), border-collapse (389), border-left (391), border-right-color (396), border-right-style (397), border-right-width (398), border-spacing (399), border-top (401)

---

border-right-color | Right Border Color

Purpose

Sets the color of the right border of a box.

Syntax

```
border-right-color: color-name_r|#rgb_r|#rrggbb_r
    |rgb(rrr_r,ggg_r,bbb_r)|rgb(rrr_r%,ggg_r%,bbb_r%)
    |inherit
```

Where

- *color-name_r* specifies the right-border color by valid name (that is, Red (#FF0000), Maroon (#800000), Yellow (#FFFF00), Green (#008000), Lime (#00FF00), Teal (#008080), Olive (#808000), Aqua (#00FFFF), Blue (#0000FF), Navy (#000080), Purple (#800080), Fuchsia (#FF00FF), Black (#000000), Gray (#808080), White (#FFFFFF), and the default, Silver (#C0C0C0)). CSS2 adds the following case-insensitive color keywords: ActiveBorder, ActiveCaption, AppWorkspace, Background, ButtonFace, ButtonHighlight, ButtonShadow, ButtonText, CaptionText, GrayText, Highlight, HighlightText, Inactive Border, InactiveCaption, InactiveCaptionText, Info Background, InfoText, Menu, MenuText, Scrollbar, ThreeDDark Shadow, ThreeDFace, ThreeDHighlight, ThreeDLightShadow, ThreeDShadow, Window, WindowFrame, and WindowText. Table R2.2 (379) names the color keywords and lists the affected object for each.
- *#rgb_r* represents a three-digit hexadecimal right-border color code, where *r* represents the red attributes, from 0 to F; *g* represents the green attributes, from 0 to F; and *b* represents the blue attributes, from 0 to F.
- *#rrggbb_r* represents a six-digit hexadecimal right-border color code, where *rr* represents the red attributes, from 00 to FF; *gg* represents the green attributes, from 00 to FF; and *bb* represents the blue attributes, from 00 to FF.
- rgb(*rrr_r,ggg_r,bbb_r*) represents absolute red-green-blue values for the right border. Each of the values ranges from 000 to 255.

- rgb(*rrr.d_r%*, *ggg.e_r%*, *bbb.f_r%*) represents the relative red-green-blue values for the right border, ranging from 0.0% to 100.0%, where 0.0% is equivalent to an absolute value of 000, and 100.0% is equivalent to 255.
- inherit is a keyword that indicates that this property takes the same computed value as its parent.

Notes

- This property, which originated in CSS2, applies to all elements.
- A border is outside the content of the page but within the page edges and the margins.
- The initial border color value is set within the user's browser.
- By default, the characteristics of this property are not inherited.
- Table R2-1 (376) contains selected hexadecimal color values.

Related Properties

border-bottom-color (385), border-collapse (389), border-color (389), border-left-color (392), border-spacing (399), border-top-color (402)

border-right-style — Right Border Style

Purpose

Formats the right border of a box.

Syntax

```
border-right-style:
  none | hidden | dotted | dashed | solid | double | groove
  | ridge | inset | outset | inherit
```

Where

- none omits a border. This overrides any border-width (405) value.
- hidden omits a border and takes precedence over any other value for this border.
- dotted draws a dotted-line border over the element background.
- dashed draws a dashed-line border over the element background.
- solid draws a solid-line border over the element background.
- double draws a double-solid-line border over the element background.
- groove draws a three-dimensional grooved border over the element background using the border-color or border-right-color value.
- ridge draws a three-dimensional ridged border over the element background using the border-color or border-right-color value.

Cascading Style Sheet Syntax

- inset draws a three-dimensional inset over the element background using the border-color or border-right-color value.
- outset draws a three-dimensional outset over the element background using the border-color or border-right-color value.
- inherit is a keyword that indicates that this property takes the same computed value as its parent.

Notes

- This property originated in CSS2.
- A border is outside the content of the page but within the page edges and the margins.
- Some browsers cannot interpret the border-right-style values and draw a solid line instead.
- By default, the characteristics of this property are not inherited.

Related Properties

border-bottom-style (387), border-collapse (389), border-left-style (393), border-spacing (399), border-style (400), border-top-style (403), empty-cells (419)

border-right-width	Right Border Width

Purpose

Sets the width of the right border.

Syntax

border-right-width: thin | medium | thick | length | inherit

Where

- thin is a narrower width than medium or thick.
- medium is wider than thin but narrower than thick.
- thick is wider than thin or medium.
- length is a positive value followed by a two-letter abbreviation representing the unit of measure.
- inherit is a keyword that indicates that this property takes the same computed value as its parent.

Notes

- This property, which originated in CSS1, applies to all elements.
- A border is outside the content of the page but within the page edges and the margins.
- The width of borders varies from browser to browser.

- Valid relative units of measure are **em** (the height of the current font), **ex** (the height of the letter x in the current font), and **px** (pixels, relative to the size of the window). Valid absolute units of measure are **in** (inches), **cm** (centimeters), **mm** (millimeters), **pt** (points), and **pc** (picas).
- By default, the characteristics of this property are not inherited.

Related Properties
border-bottom-width (388), border-collapse (389), border-left-width (394), border-spacing (399), border-top-width (404), border-width (405)

For More Information
Learn about the **border-right-width** property on page 631 in Chapter 8, "Styling Documents with CSS2."

border-spacing   Cell Border Spacing

Purpose
Separates a cell border from adjacent borders.

Syntax
    border-spacing: [h_length] [v_length]|inherit

Where
- **h_length** and **v_length** are positive horizontal-length and vertical-length cell-separation values followed by a two-letter abbreviation representing the unit of measure.
- **inherit** is a keyword that indicates that this property takes the same computed value as its parent.

Notes
- This property, which originated in CSS2, applies to table and inline-table elements (such as the XHTML **table** element).
- This property is related to the XHTML **cellspacing** attribute.
- Valid relative units of measure are **em** (the height of the current font), **ex** (the height of the letter x in the current font), and **px** (pixels, relative to the size of the window). Valid absolute units of measure are **in** (inches), **cm** (centimeters), **mm** (millimeters), **pt** (points), and **pc** (picas).
- By default, the characteristics of this element are inherited.

Related Properties
border-collapse (389), display (417), empty-cells (419), speak-header (483), table-layout (486), visibility (494)

For More Information
- For more information about table cells and table-cell borders, refer to "Section 17.6" in the *Cascading Style Sheets, Level 2 CSS Specification* (http://www.w3.org/TR/REC-CSS2/).

Cascading Style Sheet Syntax

border-style — Border Style

Purpose

Formats one, two, three, or four borders of a box.

Syntax

```
border-style:
  ([none|hidden|dotted|dashed|solid|double|groove
  |ridge|inset|outset]
  [none|hidden|dotted|dashed|solid|double|groove
  |ridge|inset|outset]
  [none|hidden|dotted|dashed|solid|double|groove
  |ridge|inset|outset]
  [none|hidden|dotted|dashed|solid|double|groove
  |ridge|inset|outset])|inherit
```

Where

- none omits a border. This overrides any **border-width** (405) value. This is the default.
- hidden omits a border and takes precedence over any other value for this border.
- dotted draws a dotted-line border over the element background.
- dashed draws a dashed-line border over the element background.
- solid draws a solid-line border over the element background.
- double draws a double-solid-line border over the element background.
- groove draws a three-dimensional grooved border over the element background using the **border-color** value.
- ridge draws a three-dimensional ridged border over the element background using the **border-color** value.
- inset draws a three-dimensional inset over the element background using the **border-color** value.
- outset draws a three-dimensional outset over the element background using the **border-color** (389) value.
- inherit is a keyword that indicates that this property takes the same computed value as its parent.

Notes

- This property, which originated in CSS1, applies to all elements.
- A border is outside the content of the page but within the page edges and the margins.
- Some browsers cannot interpret most **border-style** values and draw a solid line instead.
- By default, the characteristics of this property are not inherited.
- If you supply one style, all borders are set to that style.

- If you supply two or three styles, the browser supplies styles from the opposite side of the element. Elements are paired as follows: top and bottom, left and right.

Related Properties

border-bottom-style (387), border-collapse (389), border-left-style (393), border-right-style (397), border-spacing (399), border-top-style (403), empty-cells (419)

Reference

Learn about the border-style property on page 632 in Chapter 8, "Styling Documents with CSS2."

---

border-top   Top Border Properties

Purpose

Specifies the color, style, and/or width of the top border of a box.

Syntax

```
border-top: [ border-top-width_value ]
  [ border-style_value ] [ border-color_value ]
  | inherit
```

Where

- *border-top-width_value* specifies the border width. For more information, see the border-top-width property (404).
- *border-style_value* specifies the border style. For more information, see the border-style property (400).
- *border-color_value* specifies the border color. For more information, see the border-color property (389).
- inherit is a keyword that indicates that this property takes the same computed value as its parent.

Notes

- This property originated in CSS1.
- This property specifies multiple properties for borders in the same way that you can individually set rules for the following properties: border-top-color, border-top-style, and border-top-width.
- You do not need to specify the property name. The browser should interpret the unique values for each property.
- There is no initial value for this property.
- By default, the characteristics of this property are not inherited.
- border-top accepts only one style, in contrast to border-style, which accepts as many as four.

- A border is outside the content of the page but within the page edges and the margins.
- Table R2-1 (376) contains selected hexadecimal color values.

Related Properties

border (383), border-bottom (384), border-collapse (389), border-left (391), border-right (395), border-spacing (399), border-top-color (402), border-top-style (403), border-top-width (404)

border-top-color	**Top Border Color**

Purpose

Sets the color of the top border of a box.

Syntax

```
border-top-color: color-name_t|#rgb_t|#rrggbb_t
|rgb(rrr_t,ggg_t,bbb_t)|rgb(rrr_t%,ggg_t%,bbb_t%)
|inherit
```

Where

- *color-name_t* specifies the top-border color by valid name (that is, Red (#FF0000), Maroon (#800000), Yellow (#FFFF00), Green (#008000), Lime (#00FF00), Teal (#008080), Olive (#808000), Aqua (#00FFFF), Blue (#0000FF), Navy (#000080), Purple (#800080), Fuchsia (#FF00FF), Black (#000000), Gray (#808080), White (#FFFFFF), and the default, Silver (#C0C0C0)). CSS2 adds the following case-insensitive color keywords: ActiveBorder, ActiveCaption, AppWorkspace, Background, ButtonFace, ButtonHighlight, ButtonShadow, ButtonText, CaptionText, GrayText, Highlight, HighlightText, InactiveBorder, InactiveCaption, Inactive CaptionText, InfoBackground, InfoText, Menu, MenuText, Scrollbar, ThreeDDarkShadow, ThreeDFace, ThreeDHighlight, ThreeDLightShadow, ThreeDShadow, Window, WindowFrame, and WindowText. Table R2.2 (379) names the color keywords and lists the affected object for each.
- *#rgb_t* represents a three-digit hexadecimal top-border color code, where *r* represents the red attributes, from 0 to F; *g* represents the green attributes, from 0 to F; and *b* represents the blue attributes, from 0 to F.
- *#rrggbb_t* represents a six-digit hexadecimal top-border color code, where *rr* represents the red attributes, from 00 to FF; *gg* represents the green attributes, from 00 to FF; and *bb* represents the blue attributes, from 00 to FF.

- `rgb(`*rrr_t,ggg_t,bbb_t* `)` represents absolute red-green-blue values for the top border. Each of the values ranges from 000 to 255.
- `rgb(`*rrr.d_t%, ggg.e_t%, bbb.f_t%* `)` represents the relative red-green-blue values for the top border, ranging from 0.0% to 100.0%, where 0.0% is equivalent to an absolute value of 000, and 100.0% is equivalent to 255.
- `inherit` is a keyword that indicates that this property takes the same computed value as its parent.

Notes

- This property, which originated in CSS2, applies to all elements.
- A border is outside the content of the page but within the page edges and the margins.
- The initial border color value is set within the user's browser.
- By default, the characteristics of this property are not inherited.
- Table R2-1 (376) contains selected hexadecimal color values.

Related Properties

`border-bottom-color` (385), `border-collapse` (389), `border-color` (389), `border-left-color` (392), `border-right-color` (396), `border-spacing` (399)

---

border-top-style   Top Border Style

Purpose

Formats the top border of a box.

Syntax

```
border-top-style:
   none|hidden|dotted|dashed|solid|double|groove
   |ridge|inset|outset|inherit
```

Where

- `none` omits a border. This overrides any `border-width` (405) value.
- `hidden` omits a border and takes precedence over any other value for this border.
- `dotted` draws a dotted-line border over the element background.
- `dashed` draws a dashed-line border over the element background.
- `solid` draws a solid-line border over the element background.
- `double` draws a double-solid-line border over the element background.
- `groove` draws a three-dimensional grooved border over the element background using the `border-color` or `border-top-color` value.
- `ridge` draws a three-dimensional ridged border over the element background using the `border-color` or `border-top-color` value.

- inset draws a three-dimensional inset over the element background using the border-color or border-top-color value.
- outset draws a three-dimensional outset over the element background using the border-color or border-top-color value.
- inherit is a keyword that indicates that this property takes the same computed value as its parent.

Notes

- This property originated in CSS2.
- A border is outside the content of the page but within the page edges and the margins.
- Some browsers cannot interpret the border-top-style values and draw a solid line instead.
- By default, the characteristics of this property are not inherited.

Related Properties

border-bottom-style (387), border-collapse (389), border-left-style (393), border-right-style (397), border-spacing (399), border-style (400), empty-cells (419)

border-top-width	Top Border Width

Purpose

Sets the width of the top border of a box.

Syntax

border-top-width: thin | medium | thick | length | inherit

Where

- thin is a narrower width than medium or thick.
- medium is wider than thin but narrower than thick.
- thick is wider than thin or medium.
- length is a positive value followed by a two-letter abbreviation representing the unit of measure.
- inherit is a keyword that indicates that this property takes the same computed value as its parent.

Notes

- This property, which originated in CSS1, applies to all elements.
- A border is outside the content of the page but within the page edges and the margins.
- The width of borders varies from browser to browser.

- Valid relative units of measure are em (the height of the current font), ex (the height of the letter x in the current font), and px (pixels, relative to the size of the window). Valid absolute units of measure are in (inches), cm (centimeters), mm (millimeters), pt (points), and pc (picas).
- By default, the characteristics of this property are not inherited.

Related Properties

border-bottom-width (388), border-collapse (389), border-left-width (394), border-right-width (398), border-spacing (399), border-width (405)

For More Information

Learn about the border-top-width property on page 631 in Chapter 8, "Styling Documents with CSS2."

---

border-width   Border Width

Purpose

Sets the width of one, two, three, or four borders of a box.

Syntax

```
border-width: [thin|medium|thick|length]
    [thin|medium|thick|length][thin|medium|thick|length]
    [thin|medium|thick|length]|inherit
```

Where

- thin is a narrower width than medium or thick.
- medium is wider than thin but narrower than thick. This is the default.
- thick is wider than thin or medium.
- length is a positive value followed by a two-letter abbreviation representing the unit of measure.
- inherit is a keyword that indicates that this property takes the same computed value as its parent.

Notes

- This property, which originated in CSS1, applies to all elements.
- A border is outside the content of the page but within the page edges and the margins.
- The shorthand property, border-width, is the equivalent of border-top-width, border-right-width, border-bottom-width, and/or border-left-width, in that order.
- If you supply one width, all borders are set to that width.

- If you supply two or three widths, the browser supplies widths from the opposite side of the element. Elements are paired as follows: top and bottom, left and right.
- The width of borders varies from browser to browser.
- Valid relative units of measure are em (the height of the current font), ex (the height of the letter x in the current font), and px (pixels, relative to the size of the window). Valid absolute units of measure are in (inches), cm (centimeters), mm (millimeters), pt (points), and pc (picas).
- By default, the characteristics of this property are not inherited.

Related Properties

border-bottom-width (388), border-collapse (389), border-left-width (394), border-right-width (398), border-spacing (399), border-top-width (404)

bottom	Bottom Offset

Purpose

Controls the location of the bottom edge of a box from the bottom edge of the block that contains the box.

Syntax

bottom: *length* | *percent%* | auto | inherit

Where

- *length* is a positive or negative value followed by a two-letter abbreviation representing the unit of measure.
- *percent* is a positive or negative value that is relative to the size of the image. Follow *percent* with a percentage sign (%).
- auto is a keyword that represents a value automatically calculated by the user's browser. This is the default.
- inherit is a keyword that indicates that this property takes the same computed value as its parent.

Notes

- This property originated in CSS2.
- This property sets the absolute position of the current box, in pixels, as a percentage of the original size, or by calculating its width automatically, in respect to the block that contains the box.
- Valid relative units of measure are em (the height of the current font), ex (the height of the letter x in the current font), and px (pixels, relative to the size of the window). Valid absolute units of measure are in (inches), cm (centimeters), mm (millimeters), pt (points), and pc (picas).

- This property applies to elements that are positioned.
- By default, the characteristics of this property are not inherited.

Related Properties
left (440), position (478), right (481), top (492)

---

caption-side   Table Caption Position

Purpose
Specifies the position and alignment of a table caption.

Syntax
caption-side: <u>top</u>|bottom|left|right|inherit

Where
- top is a keyword that indicates that the caption box is placed above the table box. This is the default.
- bottom is a keyword that indicates that the caption box is placed below the table box.
- left is a keyword that indicates that the caption box is placed to the left of the table box.
- right is a keyword that indicates that the caption box is placed to the right of the table box.
- inherit is a keyword that indicates that this property takes the same computed value as its parent.

Notes
- This property, which originated in CSS2, applies to table-caption elements.
- Captions that are above or below a table behave like block-level elements; captions that are left or right of the table may behave like inline elements.
- A caption may inherit certain properties from the table with which it is associated.
- To align a caption within its caption box, use the text-align property.
- If a left-aligned or right-aligned caption has a width value of auto, a browser may compute a width that is too narrow. It is best to set an explicit width.
- By default, the characteristics of this property are inherited.

Related Properties
display (417), empty-cells (419), speak-header (483), table-layout (486), text-align (487), width (498)

@charset — Character-Set Rule

Purpose

Specifies a character set in an external style sheet.

Syntax

```
@charset character_encoding;
```

Where

`character_encoding` represents a character encoding from the Universal Character Set (ISO/IEC 10646).

Notes

- This at-rule originated in CSS2.
- If you use @charset in an external style sheet, it must appear at the beginning.
- XML and XHTML require that processors support the UTF-8 (the default) and UTF-16 character codes. Processors can also support additional character codes.
- UTF-8 includes ASCII as a subset.
- The precedence order of various character-encoding declarations is as follows:
  1. An HTTP Content-Type = *charset*
  2. The @charset at-rule
  3. Character set elements and attributes in XHTML or XML documents
- If a style or style sheet is embedded within a document, it uses the character set declared for that document.

Related XML Productions

EncName , EncodingDecl

Related Attributes

charset (Web)

clear — Clear Element

Purpose

Displays a floating element after the prior element is clear.

Syntax

```
clear: none|left|right|both|inherit
```

Where

- none does not wait for the margins to be clear; the element floats at the current alignment setting. This is the default.
- left floats an element below the bottom edge of left-floating boxes.
- right floats an element below the bottom edge of right-floating boxes.
- both floats an element below the bottom edges of all floating boxes.
- inherit is a keyword that indicates that this property takes the same computed value as its parent.

Notes

- This property, which originated in CSS1, applies only to block-level elements.
- By default, the characteristics of this property are not inherited.

Related Properties

float (422), position (478)

---

clip   Clipping Region

Purpose

Defines the clipping (visible) area of a box.

Syntax

clip: *shape* | auto | inherit

Where

- *shape* is used for the top, right, bottom, and left box offsets. For more information, see bottom, left, right, and top.
- auto is a keyword that represents the size and location of the box. This is the default.
- inherit is a keyword that indicates that this property takes the same computed value as its parent.

Notes

- This property, which originated in CSS2, applies to block-level and replaced elements.
- By default, this property is not inherited.

Related Properties

bottom (406), left (440), overflow (463), right (481), top (492)

color	Foreground Text Color

Purpose
Specifies a color for the current element's document text.

Syntax
```
color: color-name | #rgb | #rrggbb | rgb(rrr,ggg,bbb)
     | rgb(rrr%,ggg%,bbb%) | inherit
```

Where
- *color-name* specifies a foreground color by valid name (that is, Red (#FF0000), Maroon (#800000), Yellow (#FFFF00), Green (#008000), Lime (#00FF00), Teal (#008080), Olive (#808000), Aqua (#00FFFF), Blue (#0000FF), Navy (#000080), Purple (#800080), Fuchsia (#FF00FF), Black (#000000), Gray (#808080), White (#FFFFFF), and the default, Silver (#C0C0C0)). CSS2 adds the following case-insensitive color keywords: ActiveBorder, ActiveCaption, AppWorkspace, Background, ButtonFace, ButtonHighlight, ButtonShadow, ButtonText, CaptionText, GrayText, Highlight, HighlightText, InactiveBorder, InactiveCaption, InactiveCaptionText, InfoBackground, InfoText, Menu, MenuText, Scrollbar, ThreeDDarkShadow, ThreeDFace, ThreeDHighlight, Three DLightShadow, ThreeDShadow, Window, WindowFrame, and WindowText. Table R2.2 (379) names the color keywords and lists the affected object for each.
- *#rgb* is a three-digit hexadecimal color code, where *r* represents the red attributes, from 0 to F; *g* represents the green attributes, from 0 to F; and *b* represents the blue attributes, from 0 to F.
- *#rrggbb* is a six-digit hexadecimal color code, where *rr* represents the red attributes, from 00 to FF; *gg* represents the green attributes, from 00 to FF; and *bb* represents the blue attributes, from 00 to FF.
- rgb(*rrr,ggg,bbb*) represents absolute red-green-blue values, each ranging from 000 to 255.
- rgb(*rrr.d%*, *ggg.e%*, *bbb.f%*) represents the relative red-green-blue values, each ranging from 0.0% to 100.0%, where 0.0% is equivalent to an absolute value of 000, and 100.0% is equivalent to 255.
- inherit is a keyword that indicates that this property takes the same computed value as its parent.

Notes
- This property, which originated in CSS1, applies to all elements.
- The initial color value is set within the user's browser.
- By default, the characteristics of this property are inherited.
- Table R2-1 (376) contains selected hexadecimal color values.

Related Property
background-color (378)

content   Generate Content

Purpose

Generates content before or after the current element.

Syntax

```
content: (string|uri(uri)|counter|attr(att)|open-quote
    |close-quote|no-open-quote|no-close-quote)
    [string|uri(uri)|counter|attr(att)|open-quote
    |close-quote|no-open-quote|no-close-quote]
    [...string|uri(uri)|counter|attr(att)|open-quote
    |close-quote|no-open-quote|no-close-quote]
    |inherit
```

Where

- *string* is one or more textual characters.
- uri(*uri*) represents the URI of an external document (for example, uri("bullet.gif").
- *counter* is a named counter in one of the following formats: counter(*name*), counter(*name,style*), counter(*name,string*), or counter(*name,string,style*).
- attr is a keyword that indicates that an attribute follows.
- *att* represents the name of an attribute for an element.
- open-quote is a keyword that represents an open-quote string specified in the quotes property.
- close-quote is a keyword that represents a close-quote string specified in the quotes property.
- no-open-quote is a keyword that represents an empty string for an open quote, but either increments or decrements the level of quotes nesting.
- no-close-quote is a keyword that represents an empty string for a close quote, but either increments or decrements the level of quotes nesting.
- inherit is a keyword that indicates that this property takes the same computed value as its parent.

Notes

- This property originated in CSS2.
- Some browsers may not import an external document if it is a foreign media type.
- By default, this property is not inherited.

Related Property

quotes (478)

Related Pseudo-Elements

:after (373), :before (383)

counter-increment   Increment Counter

Purpose

Increments one or more named counters.

Syntax

```
counter-increment: (identifier [integer])
@@ [ identifier [integer]]
@@ [ ...identifier [integer]]|none|[inherit]
```

Where

- *identifier* represents the name of a counter.
- *integer* indicates the positive, zero, or negative value to which the counter is incremented each time the element occurs.
- none is a keyword that indicates that the counter is not displayed. This is the default.
- inherit is a keyword that indicates that this property takes the same computed value as its parent.

Notes

- This property, which originated in CSS2, applies to all elements.
- By default, the characteristics of this property are not inherited.
- Every time you use a counter for a child element, a new instance of the counter is created.
- You can apply list-style-type styles to counters.

Related Property

counter-reset (412)

counter-reset   Reset Counter

Purpose

Resets (initializes) one or more named counters.

Syntax

```
counter-reset: (identifier [integer])
[ identifier [integer]]
[ ...identifier [integer]]|none|inherit
```

Where

- *identifier* represents the name of a counter.
- *integer* indicates the positive, zero, or negative value to which the counter is set each time the element occurs.
- none is a keyword that indicates that the counter is not displayed. This is the default.
- inherit is a keyword that indicates that this property takes the same computed value as its parent.

Notes

- This property, which originated in CSS2, applies to all elements.
- By default, the characteristics of this property are not inherited.
- Every time you use a counter for a child element, a new instance of the counter is created.
- You can apply list-style-type styles to counters.

Related Property

counter-increment (412)

---

cue   Cue Element

Purpose

Sounds an auditory cue before and/or after an element.

Syntax

cue: (uri(*b_uri_name*)|none)(uri(*a_uri_name*)|none)
|inherit

Where

- uri is a keyword that indicates that a URI name will follow.
- *b-uri_name* names the URI of the sound cue file that is sounded before the element.
- *a-uri_name* names the URI of the sound cue file that is sounded after the element.
- none indicates no sound cue.
- inherit is a keyword that indicates that this property takes the same computed value as its parent.

Notes

- This property, which originated in CSS2, applies to all elements.
- If you provide the URI of a file that is not a sound file, the browser should ignore the file as if cue: none.
- If you provide two values (such as two URIs or none none), the first value is cue-before, and the second value is cue-after. If you provide one value, that value is used for both cue-before and cue-after.
- By default, the characteristics of this property are not inherited.

Related Properties

azimuth (374), cue-after (414), cue-before (414), elevation (419),
pause (473), pause-after (474), pause-before (475), pitch (476),
pitch-range (476), play-during (477), richness (480), speak (482),
speak-numeral (484), speak-punctuation (484), speech-rate (485),
stress (486), voice-family (495), volume (496)

cue-after   Cue After Element

Purpose

Sounds an auditory cue after an element.

Syntax

cue-after: uri(*uri_name*)|<u>none</u>|inherit

Where

- uri is a keyword that indicates that a URI name will follow.
- *uri_name* names the URI of the sound cue file.
- none indicates no sound cue. This is the default.
- inherit is a keyword that indicates that this property takes the same
  computed value as its parent.

Notes

- This property, which originated in CSS2, applies to all elements.
- If you provide the URI of a file that is not a sound file, the browser
  should ignore the file as if cue-after: none.
- By default, the characteristics of this property are not inherited.

Related Properties

azimuth (374), cue (413), cue-before (414), elevation (419), pause (473),
pause-after (479), pause-before (475), pitch (476), pitch-range (476),
play-during (477), richness (480), speak (482), speak-numeral (484),
speak-punctuation (484), speech-rate (485), stress (485), voice-
family (495), volume (496)

cue-before   Cue Before Element

Purpose

Sounds an auditory cue before an element.

Syntax

cue-before: uri(*uri_name*)|<u>none</u>|inherit

Where

- uri is a keyword that indicates that a URI name will follow.
- *uri_name* names the URI of the sound cue file.

- none indicates no sound cue. This is the default.
- inherit is a keyword that indicates that this property takes the same computed value as its parent.

Notes

- This property, which originated in CSS2, applies to all elements.
- If you provide the URI of a file that is not a sound file, the browser should ignore the file as if cue-before: none.
- By default, the characteristics of this property are not inherited.

Related Properties

azimuth (374), cue (413), cue-after (414), elevation (419), pause (473), pause-after (474), pause-before (475), pitch (476), pitch-range (476), play-during (477), richness (480), speak (482), speak-numeral (484), speak-punctuation (484), speech-rate (485), stress (486), voice-family (495), volume (496)

---

cursor   Cursor Type

Purpose

Specifies the cursor type for the mouse pointer or other pointing device.

Syntax

```
cursor: ([uri(uri_name), ][uri(uri_name), ]
    [...uri(uri_name), ](@@auto|crosshair|default|pointer
    |move|e-resize|ne-resize|nw-resize|n-resize
    |se-resize|sw-resize|s-resize|w-resize|text|wait
    |help))|inherit
```

Where

- uri is a keyword that indicates that a URI name will follow.
- *uri_name* names the URI of the image to be used for the pointer.
- auto is a keyword that indicates that the browser determines the device-pointer image. This is the default.
- crosshair is a keyword that displays a small crosshair device-pointer.
- default is a keyword that indicates that the computer platform determines the device-pointer image.
- pointer is a keyword that displays a device-pointer image indicating a link.
- move is a keyword that displays a device-pointer image indicating that a move can take place.
- e-resize is a keyword that displays a device-pointer image indicating a resize of the eastern edge of the element.
- ne-resize is a keyword that displays a device-pointer image indicating a resize of the northeastern edge of the element.

- nw-resize is a keyword that displays a device-pointer image indicating a resize of the northwestern edge of the element.
- n-resize is a keyword that displays a device-pointer image indicating a resize of the northern edge of the element.
- se-resize is a keyword that displays a device-pointer image indicating a resize of the southeastern edge of the element.
- sw-resize is a keyword that displays a device-pointer image indicating a resize of the southwestern edge of the element.
- s-resize is a keyword that displays a device-pointer image indicating a resize of the southern edge of the element.
- w-resize is a keyword that displays a device-pointer image indicating a resize of the western edge of the element.
- text is a keyword that displays a device-pointer image indicating that text can be selected.
- wait is a keyword that displays a device-pointer image indicating that the program is busy and action cannot currently be taken.
- help is a keyword that displays a device-pointer image indicating that help information is available for the pointed-to object.
- inherit is a keyword that indicates that this property takes the same computed value as its parent.

Notes

- This property, which originated in CSS2, applies to all elements.
- By default, the characteristics of this property are inherited.

direction	Text Direction

Purpose

Specifies the direction in which text is displayed or printed.

Syntax

direction: ltr | rtl | inherit

Where

- ltr indicates that text is printed or displayed in a left-to-right direction. This is the default.
- rtl indicates that text is printed or displayed in a right-to-left direction.
- inherit is a keyword that indicates that this property takes the same computed value as its parent.

Notes

- This property originated in CSS1.
- This property controls the base direction for the unicode-bidi property.

- This property sets the direction of blocks. If `direction` is to control inline-level elements, the value of `unicode-bidi` must be `embed` or `override`.
- When `direction` controls table columns, cells within the columns do not inherit `direction`.
- Browsers may ignore the `direction` property in user and author style sheets.
- By default, the characteristics of this property are inherited.

Related Property

`unicode-bidi` (492)

display   Display Element

Purpose

Displays the current element in a particular way onscreen or in a printed format.

Syntax

```
display: inline|block|list-item|run-in|compact
    |marker|table|inline-table|table-row-group
    |table-header-group|table-footer-group
    |table-row|table-column-group|table-column
    |table-cell|table-caption|none|inherit
```

Where

- `inline` displays one or more inline boxes on the same line as the element that was most recently displayed. This is the default.
- `block` creates a *principal box*, in which the current element is displayed.
- `list-item` creates a principal box and adds a list-item marker.
- `run-in` creates a block or inline box, depending on the current element.
- `compact` creates a block or inline *compact box* (formatted like a one-line inline box), depending on the current element.
- `marker` creates a box that is used in conjunction with the `:after` (373) or `:before` (383) pseudo-elements with block-level elements. However, sometimes `marker` can be inline.
- `table` causes the current element to act as if it were a table (the XHTML `table` element). Browsers may ignore this CSS2 value.
- `inline-table` causes the current element to act as if it were an inline table (the XHTML `table` element). Browsers may ignore this CSS2 value.

- `table-row-group` causes the current element to act as if it were a group of table rows (the XHTML `tbody` element). Browsers may ignore this CSS2 value.
- `table-header-group` causes the current element to act as if it were a group of table header rows (the XHTML `thead` element). Browsers may ignore this CSS2 value.
- `table-footer-group` causes the current element to act as if it were a group of table footer rows (the XHTML `tfoot` element). Browsers may ignore this CSS2 value.
- `table-row` causes the current element to act as if it were a table row (the XHTML `tr` element). Browsers may ignore this CSS2 value.
- `table-column-group` causes the current element to act as if it were a group of table columns (the XHTML `colgroup` element). Browsers may ignore this CSS2 value.
- `table-column` causes the current element to act as if it were a table column (the XHTML `col` element). Browsers may ignore this CSS2 value.
- `table-cell` causes the current element to act as if it were a table cell (the XHTML `td` and `th` elements). Browsers may ignore this CSS2 value.
- `table-caption` causes the current element to act as if it were a table caption (the XHTML `caption` element). Browsers may ignore this CSS2 value.
- `none` does not display the element, its child elements, or the box.
- `inherit` is a keyword that indicates that this property takes the same computed value as its parent.

Notes

- This property originated in CSS1.
- An inline box is large enough to hold the content of the element. If the content is longer than one line, a new box is created for each line.
- The `background`, `border`, `visibility`, and `width` properties apply to `table-column` and `table-column-group` elements.
- Although table cells have content, padding, and borders, they do not have margins.
- Netscape 6 and Opera 4 both support this property.
- By default, the characteristics of this property are not inherited.

Related Properties

`background` (375), `border` (383), `caption-side` (407), `empty-cells` (419), `speak-header` (483), `table-layout` (486), `visibility` (494), `width` (498)

elevation

Spatial Elevation

Purpose
Specifies the top-to-bottom stereo speaker location of a sound file.

Syntax
    elevation: range_angle|below|level|above|higher|lower|inherit

Where
- *range_angle* is a specific angle in the elevation in which stereo speakers are arranged. Valid values range from –90deg (degrees) to 90deg.
- below is a keyword that indicates that the sound is below the level elevation — at -90deg.
- level is a keyword that indicates that the sound is approximately at the same level as the user — at 0deg.
- above is a keyword that indicates that the sound is above the level elevation — at 90deg.
- higher is a keyword that indicates that the sound is 10 degrees higher than the previous elevation.
- lower is a keyword that indicates that the sound is 10 degrees lower than the previous elevation.
- inherit is a keyword that indicates that this property takes the same computed value as its parent.

Notes
- This property, which originated in CSS2, applies to all elements.
- By default, the characteristics of this property are inherited.

Related Properties
azimuth (374), cue (413), cue-after (414), cue-before (414), pause (473), pause-after (474), pause-before (475), pitch (476), pitch-range (476), play-during (477), richness (480), speak (482), speak-numeral (484), speak-punctuation (484), speech-rate (485), stress (486), voice-family (495), volume (496)

empty-cells

Empty-Cell Borders

Purpose
Shows or hides borders around empty table cells.

Syntax
    empty-cells: show|hide|inherit

Where
- show is a keyword that indicates that empty cells have borders.
- hide is a keyword that indicates that empty cells do not have borders.

Cascading Style Sheet Syntax

- inherit is a keyword that indicates that this property takes the same computed value as its parent.

Notes

- This property, which originated in CSS2, applies to table-cell elements.
- If all the empty cells in a row have a value of empty-cells: hide and visibility: hidden, the implicit result is display: none.
- By default, the characteristics of this property are inherited.

Related Properties

border-collapse (389), border-spacing (399), caption-side (407), display (417), speak-header (483), table-layout (486), visibility (494)

For More Information

For more information about table cells and table-cell borders, refer to "Section 17.6" in the *Cascading Style Sheets, Level 2 CSS Specification* (http://www.w3.org/TR/REC-CSS2/).

:first   First Page

Purpose

Sets a unique style for the first-page box of a document.

Syntax

```
@page :first { properties }
```

Where

- @page indicates that page-box characteristics will follow.
- properties are CSS2 properties.

Note

This pseudo-class originated in CSS2.

Related Pseudo-Classes

:left (440), :right (480)

:first-child   First Child Element

Purpose

Applies styles to an element that is the first child of a parent element.

Syntax

```
element-type:first-child {property}
```

Where

- *element-type* is the name of a first-child element.
- *property* represents one or more style-sheet properties.

Note

- This pseudo-class originated in CSS2.
- The :first-child pseudo-class enables you to apply styles to a particular class of an element type.

:first-letter   First Letter

Purpose

Styles the first letter of a paragraph.

Syntax

```
<element-type:first-letter>first_character
</element-type:first-letter>
```

Where

- *element-type* is the name of the element being styled.
- *first_character* represents the first character in a paragraph.

Notes

- This pseudo-element, which originated in CSS1, applies to block-level elements.
- Use :first-letter for dropped caps and initial caps.
- For :first-letter, you can use the following properties: background-attachment (377), background-color (378), background-image (380), background-position (381), background-repeat (382), border (383), border-bottom (384), border-bottom-width (388), border-color (389), border-left (391), border-left-width (394), border-right (395), border-right-width (398), border-style (400), border-top (401), border-top-width (404), border-width (405), clear (408), color (410), float (422), font (424), font-family (429), font-size (430), font-style (434), font-variant (435), font-weight (435), line-height (442), margin (446), margin-bottom (448), margin-left (449), margin-right (450), margin-top (452), padding (464), padding-bottom (465), padding-left (466), padding-right (466), padding-top (467), text-decoration (488), text-transform (491), vertical-align (493) (if the value of float is none), and word-spacing (499).
- You can use the class attribute to specify :first-letter rules for all paragraphs in a particular class.
- The :first-letter pseudo-element is similar to a floated element (see the float property on page 422).

Related Pseudo-Element

:first-line (422)

:first-line   First Line

Purpose

Styles the first line of a paragraph.

Syntax

```
<element-type:first-line>first_line_text
</element-type:first-line>
```

Where

- *element-type* is the name of the element being styled.
- *first_line_text* represents the contents of the first line.

Notes

- This pseudo-element, which originated in CSS1, applies to block-level elements.
- For :first-line, you can use the following properties: background-attachment (377), background-color (378), background-image (380), background-position (381), background-repeat (382), clear (408), color (410), font (424), font-family (429), font-size (430), font-style (434), font-variant (435), font-weight (435), letter-spacing (441), line-height (442), text-decoration (488), text-transform (491), vertical-align (493), and word-spacing (499).
- You can use the class attribute (786) to specify :first-line rules for all paragraphs in a particular class.

Related Pseudo-Element

:first-letter (421)

float   Float Element

Purpose

Floats or inserts the element in the document.

Syntax

```
float: left|right|none|inherit
```

Where

- `left` floats the element on the left side and wraps text on its right side.
- `right` floats the element on the right side and wraps text on its left side.
- `none` displays the element as inserted on the page. This is the default.
- `inherit` is a keyword that indicates that this property takes the same computed value as its parent.

Notes

- This property, which originated in CSS1, applies to all elements but those that have been placed in the document. The `float` property also does not apply to generated content.
- By default, the characteristics of this property are not inherited.

Related Properties

`clear` (408), `position` (478)

For More Information

- Learn about the `float` property on page 632 in Chapter 8, "Styling Documents with CSS2."
- For more information about the `float` property, see "Section 9.5.1" in the *Cascading Style Sheets, Level 2 CSS Specification* (`http://www.w3.org/TR/REC-CSS2/`).

:focus   Focus

Purpose

Applies styles to an element when it is the active element.

Syntax

`element-type:focus {property}`

Where

- `element-type` is the name of the element being focused on.
- `property` represents one or more style-sheet properties.

Notes

- This pseudo-class originated in CSS2.
- The `:focus` pseudo-class enables you to apply styles to an element when a user has activated it.
- The `:focus` pseudo-class is related to the XHTML `alink` attribute.

Related Pseudo-Classes

`:active` (373), `:hover` (437)

font | Font Properties

Purpose

Specifies up to six properties for fonts.

Syntax

```
font: [[font-style_value]|[ font-variant_value]
   |[ font-weight_value ]| font-size_value
   [ /line-height_value ]
   | font-family_value]|caption|icon|menu
   |message-box|small-caption|status-bar|inherit
```

Where

- *font-style_value* specifies the font style. For more information, see the font-style property (434).
- *font-variant_value* specifies the font variant. For more information, see the font-variant property (435).
- *font-weight_value* specifies the font weight. For more information, see the font-weight property (435).
- *font-size_value* specifies the font size. For more information, see the font-size property (430).
- *line-height_value* specifies the line height. Be sure to precede the line-height_value with a slash (/). For more information, see the line-height property (442).
- *font-family_value* specifies the font family. For more information, see the font-family property (429).
- caption is a keyword that represents the font used for control captions. Typical *controls* are objects in forms and dialog boxes.
- icon is a keyword that represents the font used in icon labels.
- menu is a keyword that represents the font used in menus and menu lists.
- message-box is a keyword that represents the font used in dialog boxes.
- small-caption is a keyword that represents the font used to label smaller controls.
- status-bar is a keyword that represents the font used in the status bars at the bottom of windows.
- inherit is a keyword that indicates that this property takes the same computed value as its parent.

Notes

- This property originated in CSS1.
- This property specifies multiple properties for fonts in the same way that you can individually set rules for the following properties: font-size, font-style, font-variant, font-weight, and line-height.
- You do not need to specify the property name. The browser should interpret the unique values for each property.

- If you do not specify a particular value, the browser uses the initial value.
- By default, the value of line-height is the height of one line of text.
- All values for individual font properties are set to their default values.
- You can set percentage values for font-size and line-height only.
- By default, the characteristics of this property are inherited.

Related Properties

font-family (429), font-size (438), font-size-adjust (432), font-stretch (433), font-style (434), font-variant (435), font-weight (435), line-height (442)

Related At-Rule

@font-face (425)

For More Information

Learn about the font property on page 424 in Chapter 8, "Styling Documents with CSS2."

@font-face   Font-Face Rule

Purpose

Specifies a value for each font descriptor.

Syntax

```
@font-face { [font-family: font-family_value;]
   [ font-size: font-size_value]
   [ font-stretch: font-stretch_value]
   [ font-style: font-style_value]
   [ font-variant: font-variant_value]
   [ font-weight: font-weight_value]
   [ units-per-em: units-per-em_value]
   [ unicode-range: unicode-range_value]
   [ src: src_value][ panose-1: panose-1_list]
   [ stemv: stemv_width][ stemh_width: stemh_width]
   [ slope: slope_angle][ cap-height: cap-height_value]
   [ x-height: x-height_value][ascent: ascent_value]
   [ descent: descent_value][ widths: widths_value]
   [ bbox: bbox_value]
   [ definition-src: definition src_value]
   [ baseline: baseline_value]
   [ centerline: centerline_value]
   [ mathline: mathline_value][ topline: topline_value]
```

Where

- font-family is a CSS2 descriptor keyword that indicates that one or more font families will follow. Note that font-family has the same name as its CSS font property counterpart. For more information, see font-family (429).
- *font-family_value* has the same values as its CSS2 font property counterpart, except that inherit is omitted.
- font-size is a CSS2 descriptor keyword that has the same name as its CSS font property counterpart. For more information, see font-size (430).
- *font-size_value*, which enables the same absolute values as its CSS font property counterpart, can be composed of one value or a list of values, separated by commas. Relative values and the inherit value are omitted, and a new value, all, enables all sizes.
- font-stretch is a CSS2 descriptor keyword that has the same name as its CSS font property counterpart. For more information, see font-stretch (433).
- *font-stretch_value* has the same values as its CSS font property counterpart, except that inherit, wider, and narrower are omitted. A new value, all, enables all styles. *font-stretch_value* can be composed of one value or a list of values, separated by commas.
- font-style is a CSS2 descriptor keyword that has the same name as its CSS font property counterpart. For more information, see font-style (434).
- *font-style_value* has the same values as its CSS font property counterpart, except for a new value, all, which enables all styles, and the omission of inherit. *font-style_value* can be composed of one value or a list of values, separated by commas.
- font-variant is a CSS2 descriptor keyword that has the same name as its CSS font property counterpart. For more information, see font-variant (435).
- *font-variant_value* has the same values as its CSS font property counterpart, except that inherit is omitted.
- font-weight is a CSS2 descriptor keyword that has the same name as its CSS font property counterpart. For more information, see font-weight (435).
- *font-weight_value* has the same values as its CSS font property counterpart, except that inherit, bolder, and lighter are omitted. A new value, all, enables all styles. *font-weight_value* can be composed of one value or a list of values, separated by commas.
- units-per-em is a CSS2 descriptor keyword that indicates that a *units-per-em* value will follow.
- *units-per-em_value* is a numeric value that specifies the number of units on a square on which a particular glyph is designed. Syntax: units-per-em: *number*.
- unicode-range is a CSS2 descriptor keyword that indicates that a Unicode-range value will follow.

Cascading Style Sheet Syntax

- *unicode-range* represents an explicit range of Unicode characters that you might want to use in a document. Syntax: `unicode-range:` `(U+nnnn [,U+nnnn][..., U+nnnn])|` `(U+nnnn [-U+nnnn])`.
- `src:` is a CSS2 descriptor keyword that indicates that font-face-name information will follow.
- *src_value* represents one or more external font resources or the names of one or more locally installed font face names. Syntax: src: ([uri(*uri_string*) [format([*format_string*[, *format_string*) [..., *format_string*)]]]]|*font-face-name*] [uri(*uri_string*)[format([*format_string* [, *format_string*)[..., *format_string*)]]] |*font-face-name*]) ([uri(*uri_string*) [format([*format_string*[, *format_string*) [..., *format_string*)]]]]|*font-face-name*] [uri(*uri_string*)[format([*format_string* [, *format_string*)[..., *format_string*)]]] |*font-face-name*]) (...[uri(*uri_string*) [format([*format_string*[, *format_string*) [..., *format_string*)]]]]|*font-face-name*] [uri(*uri_string*)[format([*format_string* [, *format_string*)[..., *format_string*)]]] |*font-face-name*]).
- `panose-1` is a CSS2 descriptor keyword that indicates that Panose-1 information will follow.
- *panose-1_list* represents a list of ten decimal Panose-1 integers, each separated from the other by white space. Syntax: `panose-1:` `integer_0 integer_1 integer_2 integer_3 integer_4` `integer_5 integer_6 integer_7 integer_8 integer_9`.
- `stemv` is a CSS2 descriptor keyword that indicates that a vertical-stem width will follow.
- *stemv_width* represents the vertical stem width of the named font. If you use this descriptor, you must also use the `units-per-em` descriptor. Syntax: stemv: *integer*.
- `stemh` is a CSS2 descriptor keyword that indicates that a horizontal-stem width will follow.
- *stemh_width* represents the horizontal stem width of the named font. If you use this descriptor, you must also use the `units-per-em` descriptor. Syntax: stemh: *integer*.
- `slope` is a CSS2 descriptor keyword that indicates that a vertical-slope angle will follow.
- *slope-angle* represents the vertical slope angle of the named font. The default value is 0. Syntax: slope: *integer*.
- `cap-height` is a CSS2 descriptor keyword that indicates that an upper-case-characters height will follow.
- *cap-height_value* represents the height number of uppercase characters. If you use this descriptor, you must also use the `units-per-em` descriptor. Syntax: cap-height: *integer*.
- `x-height` is a CSS2 descriptor keyword that indicates that the height number of lowercase characters will follow.
- *x-height_value* represents the height number of lowercase characters. If you use this descriptor, you must also use the `units-per-em` descriptor. Syntax: x-height: *integer*.
- `ascent` is a CSS2 descriptor keyword that indicates that an above-baseline height will follow.

- *ascent_value* represents the maximum height of the font above the baseline. If you specify an ascent, you must also use the units-per-em descriptor. Syntax: `ascent:` *integer*.
- `descent` is a CSS2 descriptor keyword that indicates that a below-baseline depth will follow.
- *descent_value* represents the maximum depth of the font below the baseline. If you specify a descent, you must also use the units-per-em descriptor. Syntax: `descent:` *integer*.
- `widths` is a CSS2 descriptor keyword that indicates that widths of characters in the named font will follow.
- *widths_value* represents font-width values. Syntax: `widths:` `([U+nnnn [U+nnnn [...U+nnnn ]]]`*width_number* `[`*width_number* `[`*width_number* `]])[, ([U+nnnn [U+nnnn` `[...U+nnnn ]]]`*width_number* `[`*width_number* `[`*width_number* `]]).`
- `bbox` is a CSS2 descriptor keyword that indicates that information about the font's bounding box will follow.
- *bbox_value* specifies lower-left x, lower-left y, upper-right x, and upper-right y bounding-box values — in that order. `Syntax: bbox:` *llx_num*, *lly_num*, *urx_num*, *ury_num*.
- `definition-src` is a CSS2 descriptor keyword that indicates that the URI of an external font-definition resource will follow.
- *definition-src_value* is the URI of an external font-definition resource. Syntax: `definition-src: uri(`*uri_string*`)`.
- `baseline` is a CSS2 descriptor keyword that indicates that the font's lower baseline information will follow.
- *baseline_value* represents the em-square location of the lower baseline. If you use this descriptor, you must also use the units-per-em descriptor. Syntax: `baseline:` *baseline-value*.
- `centerline` is a CSS2 descriptor keyword that indicates that the font's central baseline information will follow.
- *centerline_value* represents the em-square location of the central baseline. If you use this descriptor, you must also use the units-per-em descriptor. Syntax: `centerline:` *centerline-value*.
- `mathline` is a CSS2 descriptor keyword that indicates that the font's mathematical baseline information will follow.
- *mathline_value* represents the em-square location of the mathematical baseline. If you use this descriptor, you must also use the units-per-em descriptor. Syntax: `mathline:` *mathline-value*.
- `topline` is a CSS2 descriptor keyword that indicates that the font's top baseline information will follow.
- *topline_value* represents the em-square location of the top baseline. If you use this descriptor, you must also use the units-per-em descriptor. Syntax: `topline:` *topline-value*.

Notes

- This at-rule originated in CSS2.
- If you omit a font descriptor, a particular font property's default value is used.
- Because fonts and font types of the same declared size actually differ in height and weight, `units-per-em` is a way to standardize the sizes of unlike fonts.
- The `unicode-range` descriptor, which originated in CSS2, enables you to select one or more Unicode characters to use in a document. The default is the entire ISO 10646 character set, whether or not those characters occur in the character set for the named font family. You can specify single characters as follows: `unicode-range: U+nnnn`. You can use single-character wildcards as follows: `unicode-range: U+nnn?`, `unicode-range: U+n??n`, `unicode-range: U+n???`, and so on. You can specify ranges of characters as follows: `unicode-range:U+nnnn-U+nnnn`, where a dash indicates that the end of the range follows. You can specify combinations of single characters and ranges of characters by entering commas.
- The `widths` descriptor uses the same Unicode-character and Unicode-character range formats and wildcards as the `unicode-range` descriptor.
- Font formats supported by the `src` descriptor are Embedded OpenType (.eot), Intellifont, OpenType (.ttf), PostScript Type 1 (.pfa, .pfb), Speedo, TrueDoc Portable Font Resource (.pfr), TrueType (.ttf), and TrueType with GX extensions.
- The `panose-1` descriptor describes Latin TrueType fonts in ten ways: family, serif style, weight, proportion, contrast, stroke variation, arm style, letterform, midline, and x-height.

Related Properties

`font` (424), `font-family` (429), `font-size` (430), `font-size-adjust` (432), `font-stretch` (433), `font-style` (434), `font-variant` (435), `font-weight` (435)

For More Information

For more information on `panose-1`, refer to "Section 15.3.6 in the *Cascading Style Sheets, Level 2 CSS Specification* (`http://www.w3.org/TR/REC-CSS2/`).

font-family   Font Family

Purpose

Specifies one or more fonts by name, font family, or both.

Syntax

```
font-family:
  [["]family_name_1|serif
```

Cascading Style Sheet Syntax

```
|sans-serif|cursive|fantasy|monospace]
[, ["]family_name_2["]]|serif
|sans-serif|cursive|fantasy|monospace]
[..., ["]family_name_n["]|serif
|sans-serif|cursive|fantasy|monospace])|inherit
```

Where

- `family-name` is the name of a specific typeface.
- `serif`, `sans-serif`, `cursive`, `fantasy`, and `monospace` are the names of generic typefaces that might match one or more font-family names on a particular computer.
- `inherit` is a keyword that indicates that this property takes the same computed value as its parent.

Notes

- This property, which originated in CSS1, applies to all elements.
- This CSS property has a counterpart CSS descriptor.
- This property specifies a font by name and/or font family.
- You can specify multiple font families.
- It is a good idea to end a list of font families with at least one generic typeface. This ensures that a font family will be defined.
- The initial `font-family` value is set by the user's browser.
- Use quotation marks to enclose family names of two or more words separated by spaces (for example, "Courier New" or "Bookman Old Style").
- By default, the characteristics of this property are inherited.

Related Properties

`font` (424), `font-size` (438), `font-size-adjust` (432), `font-stretch` (433), `font-style` (434), `font-variant` (435), `font-weight` (435)

Related At-Rule

`@font-face` (425)

For More Information

Learn about the `font-family` property on page 635 in Chapter 8, "Styling Documents with CSS2."

font-size   Font Size

Purpose

Specifies an absolute or relative font size.

Syntax

```
font-size: length|percent%|(xx-small|x-small
   |small|medium|large|x-large|xx-large)
   |(larger|smaller)|inherit
```

Where

- *length* is a positive value followed by a two-letter abbreviation representing the unit of measure.
- *percent* is a positive value that is relative to the font size of the element immediately above the current element. Follow *percent* with a percentage sign (%).
- xx-small is a keyword that represents a font size that is 1.2 times smaller than x-small.
- x-small is a keyword that represents a font size that is 1.2 times larger than xx-small and 1.2 times smaller than small.
- small is a keyword that indicates a font size that is 1.2 times larger than x-small and 1.2 times smaller than medium.
- medium is a keyword that indicates a font size that is 1.2 times larger than xx-small and 1.2 times smaller than large.
- large is a keyword that indicates a font size that is 1.2 times larger than medium and 1.2 times smaller than x-large.
- x-large is a keyword that indicates a font size that is 1.2 times larger than large and 1.2 times smaller than xx-large.
- xx-large is a keyword that indicates a font size that is 1.2 times larger than x-large.
- larger is one size larger than the font of the parent element.
- smaller is one size smaller than the font of the parent element.
- inherit is a keyword that indicates that this property takes the same computed value as its parent.

Notes

- This property, which originated in CSS1, applies to all elements.
- This CSS property has a counterpart CSS descriptor.
- Valid relative units of measure are em (the height of the current font), ex (the height of the letter x in the current font), and px (pixels, relative to the size of the window). Valid absolute units of measure are in (inches), cm (centimeters), mm (millimeters), pt (points), and pc (picas).
- By default, the computed value of this property is inherited.

Related Properties

font (424), font-family (429), font-size-adjust (432), font-stretch (433), font-style (434), font-variant (435), font-weight (435)

Related At-Rule

@font-face (425)

For More Information

Learn about the font-size property on page 635 in Chapter 8, "Styling Documents with CSS2."

font-size-adjust   Font Size Adjust

Purpose
Adjusts a font's aspect value.

Syntax
```
font-size-adjust: number | none | inherit
```

Where
- *number* represents an absolute numeric value of the aspect ratio.
- none is a keyword that indicates that the font's x-height is not pre-served; it changes when the font size changes. This is the default.
- inherit is a keyword that indicates that this property takes the same computed value as its parent.

Notes
- This property, which originated in CSS2, applies to all elements.
- This property applies to the aspect value of the first font in a list of fonts. It will scale subsequent fonts using the following formula:

  font_size_1(font_aspect_value_1/font_aspect_value_2)
  = font_size_2

  where:
  - *font_size_1* represents the font size of the first font on the font-family list.
  - *font_aspect_value_1* represents the aspect value of the first font on the list.
  - *font_aspect_value_2* represents the aspect value of subsequent fonts.
  - *font_size_2* represents the font size of subsequent fonts on the list.
- The *aspect value* is the font size divided by the x-height. The higher the aspect value of a font, the more readable it will be at a small font size.
- The *x-height* is the measurement of the body of a lowercase character from the top of the character down to the baseline.
- The x-height descriptor in the @font-face at-rule indicates that the height number of lowercase characters will follow. If you use the x-height descriptor, you can specify both the font size and the x-height.
- By default, the computed value of this property is inherited.

Related Properties
font (424), font-family (429), font-size (430), font-stretch (433), font-style (434), font-variant (435), font-weight (435)

Related At-Rule
@font-face (425)

font-stretch   Stretched Font

Purpose
Selects a condensed or expanded version of a font.

Syntax
```
font-stretch: normal|wider|narrower
   |ultra-condensed|extra-condensed|condensed
   |semi-condensed|semi-expanded|expanded
   |extra-expanded|ultra-expanded|inherit
```

Where
- normal is a keyword that represents any variation that is not condensed and not expanded. This is the default.
- wider is a keyword that represents a variation that is the next wider stretch value from the current stretch.
- narrower is a keyword that represents a variation that is the next narrower stretch value from the current stretch.
- ultra-condensed is a keyword that represents the most condensed variation.
- extra-condensed is a keyword that represents a variation that is more condensed than condensed but less condensed than ultra-condensed.
- condensed is a keyword that represents a variation that is more condensed than semi-condensed but less condensed than extra-condensed.
- semi-condensed is a keyword that represents a variation that is more condensed than normal but less condensed than condensed.
- semi-expanded is a keyword that represents a variation that is more expanded than normal but less expanded than expanded.
- expanded is a keyword that represents a variation that is more expanded than semi-expanded but less expanded than extra-expanded.
- extra-expanded is a keyword that represents a variation that is more expanded than expanded but less expanded than ultra-expanded.
- ultra-expanded is a keyword that represents the most expanded variation.
- inherit is a keyword that indicates that this property takes the same computed value as its parent.

Notes
- This property, which originated in CSS2, applies to all elements.
- This CSS property has a counterpart CSS descriptor.
- By default, the characteristics of this property are inherited.

Related Properties

font (424), font-family (429), font-size (430), font-size-adjust (432), font-style (434), font-variant (435), font-weight (435)

Related At-Rule

@font-face (425)

---

font-style   Font Style

Purpose

Specifies one or more text enhancements.

Syntax

font-style: <u>normal</u> | italic | oblique | inherit

Where

- normal is a keyword that indicates text that is not italicized. This is the default.
- italic is a keyword that indicates italicized text.
- oblique is a keyword that usually indicates slightly italicized text.
- inherit is a keyword that indicates that this property takes the same computed value as its parent.

Notes

- This property, which originated in CSS1, applies to all elements.
- This CSS property has a counterpart CSS descriptor.
- This property specifies the degree of slant for text.
- If you choose italic and the current typeface does not offer italics, text may be oblique instead.
- Synonyms for *oblique* include *slanted* and *incline*. A synonym for *italic* is *cursive*.
- By default, the characteristics of this property are inherited.

Related Properties

font (424), font-family (429), font-size (438), font-size-adjust (432), font-stretch (433), font-variant (435), font-weight (435)

Related At-Rule

@font-face (425)

For More Information

Learn about the font-style property on page 635 in Chapter 8, "Styling Documents with CSS2."

font-variant   Font Variations

Purpose
Specifies one or more font variations.

Syntax
font-variant: <u>normal</u> | small-caps | inherit

Where
- normal is a keyword that represents any variation that is not small caps. This is the default.
- small-caps is a keyword that represents a variation that is all uppercase characters that are smaller than the usual uppercase characters in a typeface.
- inherit is a keyword that indicates that this property takes the same computed value as its parent.

Notes
- This property, which originated in CSS1, applies to all elements.
- This CSS property has a counterpart CSS descriptor.
- This property specifies the case of text.
- If a typeface does not include smaller uppercase characters, standard uppercase characters may be scaled down or may replace small caps.
- By default, the characteristics of this property are inherited.

Related Properties
font (424), font-family (429), font-size (438), font-size-adjust (432), font-stretch (433), font-style (434), font-weight (435)

Related At-Rule
@font-face (425)

For More Information
Learn about the font-variant property on page 635 in Chapter 8, "Styling Documents with CSS2."

font-weight   Bold or Light Font

Purpose
Specifies the degree of boldness or lightness of a font.

Syntax
font-weight: <u>normal</u> | bold | bolder | lighter
  | 100 | 200 | 300 | 400 | 500 | 600 | 700 | 800 | 900 | inherit

Where
- normal is a keyword that indicates the standard non-bold, non-light weight text. This is the default.
- bold is a keyword that indicates the standard boldface text.
- bolder is a keyword that indicates bolder than standard boldface. It can be the equivalent of ultra bold or heavy text. This is a relative value.
- lighter is a keyword that indicates the equivalent of light text. This is a relative value.
- 100 is a keyword that indicates the lightest weight.
- 200 and 300 are keywords that indicate somewhere between light and normal weight.
- 400 is a keyword that is the equivalent of normal weight.
- 500 and 600 are keywords that indicate somewhere between normal and bold weight. 500 is the equivalent of a medium weight.
- 700 is a keyword that indicates the equivalent of bold weight.
- 800 and 900 are keywords that indicate bolder than bold weight.
- inherit is a keyword that indicates that this property takes the same computed value as its parent.

Notes
- This property, which originated in CSS1, applies to all elements.
- This CSS property has a counterpart CSS descriptor.
- This property specifies the boldness or lightness of the font, in an absolute or relative value.
- By default, the characteristics of this property are inherited.

Related Properties
font (424), font-family (429), font-size (430), font-size-adjust (432), font-stretch (433), font-style (434), font-variant (435)

Related At-Rule
@font-face (425)

For More Information
Learn about the font-weight property on page 635 in Chapter 8, "Styling Documents with CSS2."

---

height   Element Height

Purpose
Specifies the height of the selected element.

Syntax
height: *length* | *percent*% | <u>auto</u> | inherit

Where

- *length* is a positive value followed by a two-letter abbreviation representing the unit of measure.
- *percent* is a positive value that is relative to the size of the image. Follow *percent* with a percentage sign (%).
- auto is a keyword that represents a value automatically calculated by the user's browser.
- inherit is a keyword that indicates that this property takes the same computed value as its parent.

Notes

- This property, which originated in CSS1, applies to all elements except selected inline elements and individual or grouped table columns.
- This property sets the height of the selected element, in pixels, or by calculating its height automatically, scaled proportionately with the width.
- Valid relative units of measure are em (the height of the current font), ex (the height of the letter x in the current font), and px (pixels, relative to the size of the window). Valid absolute units of measure are in (inches), cm (centimeters), mm (millimeters), pt (points), and pc (picas).
- If the element is higher than the specified height, the browser will scale the element.
- If the height of the element is equal to auto, the aspect ratio (that is, the current proportions of the element) is maintained.
- If both the height and width of the element are equal to auto, the browser does not change the element's dimensions.
- By default, the characteristics of this property are not inherited.

Related Properties

max-height (454), max-width (455), min-height (457), min-width (458), width (498)

:hover   Hover

Purpose

Applies styles to an element when a user moves over it.

Syntax

```
element-type:hover {property}
```

Where

- *element-type* is the name of the element being hovered over.
- *property* represents one or more style-sheet properties.

Notes

- This pseudo-class originated in CSS2.
- The :hover pseudo-class enables you to apply styles to an element when a user moves over it with a pointing device.
- The :hover pseudo-class is related to the XHTML alink attribute.
- Browsers that do not support interactive behaviors may not support :hover.

Related Pseudo-Classes

:active (373), :focus (423)

@import   Import Styles Rule

Purpose

Imports styles from an external style sheet.

Syntax

```
@import [uri(]"stylesheet.css"[)]
    [media-type[,media-type[...,media-type]]];
```

Where

- uri indicates that the URI of an external style sheet will follow.
- stylesheet.css is the name of an external style sheet.
- media-type represents types of styled media. For more information, see @media (456).

Notes

- This at-rule originated in CSS2.
- The @import rule must be located before any internal rules in a style sheet.

!important   Important Declaration

Purpose

States that the current declaration is more important than others.

Syntax

```
! important;
```

Notes

- This declaration originated in CSS1.
- Add ! important; to the end of a declaration to specify that the declaration overrides other declarations.
- Both users and document authors can create their own style sheets. For example, a user who needs help in viewing documents can attach a style sheet that enlarges a font, changes to an easy-to-read font, or both.

- In CSS1, an author-defined important declaration overrode a user-defined important declaration. In CSS2, a user-defined important declaration overrides an author-defined important declaration.

:lang   Language

Purpose
Applies styles to an element that matches a particular language.

Syntax
```
element-type:lang(code)
```

Where
- *element-type* is the name of the element styled.
- *code* represents the two-character language code.

Notes
- This pseudo-class originated in CSS2.
- The `:lang` pseudo-class enables you to apply language-related styles to a particular element.
- The `:lang` pseudo-class is related to the `IanaCode`, `ISO639Code`, `Langcode`, `LanguageID`, `Subcode`, and `UserCode` XML productions and the `xml:lang` processing instruction. (An *XML production* is an instruction or a component that is part of an instruction.) In XHTML, `:lang` is related to the `lang` attribute and the `meta` element. To learn more about XML, refer to *XML in Plain English*, also written by Sandra E. Eddy and published by IDG Books Worldwide.
- Because of Internet internationalization, declaring a language can be very important.
- You can use the `xml:lang` attribute with any XML production to declare a language used as character data and attribute values in an XML document.
- Language codes and country codes are case-insensitive. Although not required, the language code is usually in lowercase, and the country code is usually in uppercase.

For More Information
- For a list of language codes, see Appendix C, Internationization: Language Codes and Country Codes (743).
- For a list of XML-supported `xml:lang` attribute values, see IETF_RFC_1766 (`ftp://ftp.isi.edu/in-notes/rfc1766.txt`).

:left
Left Page

Purpose
Sets a unique style for the left-page boxes of a document.

Syntax
```
@page :left { properties }
```

Where
- @page indicates that page-box characteristics will follow.
- *properties* are CSS2 properties.

Notes
- This pseudo-class originated in CSS2.
- The :left and :right pseudo-classes enable a page designer to specify separate styles for left and right pages.
- Browsers automatically grade pages as left or right.

Related Pseudo-Classes
:first (420), :right (480)

left
Left Offset

Purpose
Controls the location of the left edge of a box from the left edge of the block that contains the box.

Syntax
```
left: length | percent% | auto | inherit
```

Where
- *length* is a positive or negative value followed by a two-letter abbreviation representing the unit of measure.
- *percent* is a positive or negative value that is relative to the size of the image. Follow *percent* with a percentage sign (%).
- auto is a keyword that represents a value automatically calculated by the user's browser. This is the default.
- inherit is a keyword that indicates that this property takes the same computed value as its parent.

Notes
- This property, which originated in CSS2, applies to elements that are positioned.
- This property sets the absolute position of the current box, in pixels, as a percentage of the original size, or by calculating its width automatically, in respect to the block that contains the box.

- Valid relative units of measure are em (the height of the current font), ex (the height of the letter x in the current font), and px (pixels, relative to the size of the window). Valid absolute units of measure are in (inches), cm (centimeters), mm (millimeters), pt (points), and pc (picas).
- By default, the characteristics of this property are not inherited.

Related Properties

bottom (406), position (478), right (481), top (492)

---

letter-spacing   Character Spacing

Purpose

Sets spacing between characters.

Syntax

letter-spacing: <u>normal</u> | [+ | -] *length* | inherit

Where

- normal is a keyword that represents the normal spacing between characters. This is the default.
- *length* is a positive or negative value followed by a two-letter abbreviation representing the unit of measure. *length* is usually an increase in the spacing between characters. When the *length* value is negative, spacing may decrease — depending on the browser.
- inherit is a keyword that indicates that this property takes the same computed value as its parent.

Notes

- This property, which originated in CSS1, applies to all elements.
- If you select normal, a browser can justify the selected text.
- Valid relative units of measure are em (the height of the current font), ex (the height of the letter x in the current font), and px (pixels, relative to the size of the window). Valid absolute units of measure are in (inches), cm (centimeters), mm (millimeters), pt (points), and pc (picas).
- By default, the characteristics of this property are inherited.

Related Properties

text-align (487), text-decoration (488), text-indent (488), text-shadow (489), text-transform (491), white-space (497), word-spacing (499)

For More Information

Learn about the letter-spacing property on page 633 in Chapter 8, "Styling Documents with CSS2."

line-height   Baseline Height

Purpose
Specifies the height of the text line from baseline to baseline.

Syntax
line-height: <u>normal</u> | *number* | *length* | *percent%* | inherit

Where
- normal is a keyword that indicates the parent element's line height. The numeric value for normal should range between 1.0 and 1.2.
- *number* is a number by which the current font size is multiplied to result in a new line height.
- *length* is a positive value followed by a two-letter abbreviation representing the unit of measure.
- *percent* is a positive value that is relative to the size of the line height. Follow *percent* with a percentage sign (%).
- inherit is a keyword that indicates that this property takes the same computed value as its parent.

Notes
- This property originated in CSS1.
- This property specifies the height from baseline to baseline, in a number multiplied by the present font size, the length (in the default unit of measure), or a percentage of the present font size.
- Valid relative units of measure are em (the height of the current font), ex (the height of the letter x in the current font), and px (pixels, relative to the size of the window). Valid absolute units of measure are in (inches), cm (centimeters), mm (millimeters), pt (points), and pc (picas).
- Negative values are not valid.
- The initial line-height value is set by the user's browser.
- By default, the characteristics of this property are inherited.

Related Property
vertical-align (493)

:link   Unvisited Link

Purpose
Applies styles to a link that has not been visited by a user.

Syntax
anchor:link {*property*}

Where

- *anchor* represents the name of a hyperlink anchor.
- *property* represents one or more style-sheet properties.

Notes

- This pseudo-class originated in CSS2.
- The :link pseudo-class enables you to apply styles to an unvisited link.
- The :link pseudo-class is related to the XHTML link attribute.
- In CSS1, :active, :link, and :visited were mutually exclusive. Now, you can :active, :link, and :visit a particular element.

Related Pseudo-Classes

:active (373), :visited (495)

---

list-style   List Style Properties

Purpose

Specifies up to three properties for lists.

Syntax

```
list-style: ([ list-style-type_value]
  |[ list-style-position_value]
  |[ list-style-image_value])
  |inherit
```

Where

- *list-style-type_value* specifies the list-style type. For more information, see the list-style-type property (445).
- *list-style-position_value* specifies the list-item position. For more information, see the list-style-position property (444).
- *list-style-image_value* specifies the list-item image. For more information, see the list-style-image property (444).
- inherit is a keyword that indicates that this property takes the same computed value as its parent.

Notes

- This property originated in CSS1.
- This shortcut property specifies multiple properties for list-item markers in the same way that you can individually set rules for the following properties: list-style-image, list-style-position, and list-style-type.

- You do not need to specify the property name. The browser should interpret the unique values for each property.
- By default, the characteristics of this property are inherited.

Related Properties

list-style-image (444), list-style-position (444), list-style-type (445)

For More Information

Learn about the list-style property on page 544, 546, and 641 in Chapter 8, "Styling Documents with CSS2."

list-style-image   List-Style Image

Purpose

Specifies the image preceding items on an ordered or unordered list.

Syntax

    list-style-image: uri(uri_name)|none|inherit

Where

- uri is a keyword that indicates that a URI name will follow.
- uri_name names the URI of the image to be used for the list-item marker.
- none indicates no list-item marker image. This is the default.
- inherit is a keyword that indicates that this property takes the same computed value as its parent.

Notes

- This property, which originated in CSS1, applies to list-item elements.
- By default, the characteristics of this property are inherited.

Related Properties

list-style (443), list-style-position (444), list-style-type (445)

For More Information

Learn about the list-style-image property on page 544, 546, and 641 in Chapter 8, "Styling Documents with CSS2."

list-style-position   List-Style Position

Purpose

Specifies the position of the marker box inside or outside the principal box.

Syntax

    list-style-position: inside|outside|inherit

Where

- inside places the marker box inside the principal box.
- outside places the marker box outside the principal box.
- inherit is a keyword that indicates that this property takes the same computed value as its parent.

Notes

- This property, which originated in CSS1, applies to list-item elements.
- By default, the characteristics of this property are inherited.

Related Properties

list-style (443), list-style-image (444), list-style-type (445)

For More Information

Learn about the list-style-position property on page 544, 546, and 641 in Chapter 8, "Styling Documents with CSS2."

---

list-style-type   List-Style Type

Purpose

Specifies the number or bullet type preceding items on an ordered or unordered list.

Syntax

    list-style-type: disc|circle|square|decimal
      |decimal-leading zero|lower-roman|upper-roman
      |lower-greek|lower-alpha|lower-latin
      |upper-alpha|hebrew|armenian|georgian
      |cjk-ideographic|hiragana|katakana|hiragana-iroha
      |katakana-iroha|none|inherit

Where

- disc uses filled bullets. This is the default.
- circle uses unfilled circles.
- square uses filled square bullets.
- decimal uses Arabic numerals (1, 2, 3, etc.).
- decimal-leading-zero uses Arabic numerals with leading zeroes (01,02, 03, etc.).
- lower-roman uses small Roman numerals (i, ii, iii, etc.).
- upper-roman uses large Roman numerals (I, II, III, etc.).
- lower-greek uses the classical lowercase Greek alphabet (alpha, beta, gamma, etc.).

- lower-alpha uses lowercase alphabetic letters (a, b, c, etc.).
- lower-latin uses lowercase ASCII characters (a, b, c, etc.).
- upper-alpha uses uppercase alphabetic letters (A, B, C, etc.).
- hebrew uses numbering from the Hebrew character set.
- armenian uses numbering from the Armenian character set.
- georgian uses numbering from the Georgian character set.
- cjk-ideographic uses ideographic numbering.
- hiragana uses numbering from the Armenian character set.
- katakana uses numbering from the Hiragana character set.
- hiragana-iroha uses numbering from the Hiragana-Iroha character set.
- katakana-iroha uses numbering from the Katakana-Iroha character set.
- none uses no bullets or numbers.
- inherit is a keyword that indicates that this property takes the same computed value as its parent.

Notes

- This property, which originated in CSS1, applies to list-item elements.
- By default, the characteristics of this property are inherited.

Related Properties

list-style (443), list-style-image (444), list-style-position (444)

For More Information

Learn about the list-style-type property on page 544, 546, and 641 in Chapter 8, "Styling Documents with CSS2."

Learn about the list-style-type property on page 544, 546, and 641 in Chapter 8, "Styling Documents with CSS2."

margin	Margin Characteristics

Purpose

Turns on or off one, two, three, or four margins, or sets margin size of a box.

Syntax

```
margin: ([length_top|percent_top%|auto]
    [length_right|percent_right%|auto]
    [length_bottom|percent_bottom%|auto]
    [length_left|percent_left%|auto])|inherit
```

Where

- *length_top*, *length_right*, *length_bottom*, and *length_left* are positive or negative fixed values followed by a two-letter abbreviation representing the unit of measure.
- *percent_top*, *percent_right*, *percent_bottom*, and *percent_left* are positive values that are relative to the parent element's selected margins. Follow *percent* with a percentage sign (%).

- `auto` represents top-margin, right-margin, bottom-margin, and left-margin values automatically calculated by the user's browser.
- `inherit` is a keyword that indicates that this property takes the same computed value as its parent.

Notes

- This property, which originated in CSS1, applies to all elements.
- This shortcut property for `margin-top`, `margin-right`, `margin-bottom`, and `margin-left` (in that order) turns one, two, three, or four margins on or off, or sets margin size (in the default unit of measure) as a percentage of the current width, or automatically by calculating a minimum amount.
- Valid relative units of measure are `em` (the height of the current font), `ex` (the height of the letter x in the current font), and `px` (pixels, relative to the size of the window). Valid absolute units of measure are `in` (inches), `cm` (centimeters), `mm` (millimeters), `pt` (points), and `pc` (picas).
- If you supply one value, all margins are set to that value.
- Margins are always transparent.
- If you supply two or three values, the browser supplies values from the opposite side of the element. Elements are paired as follows: top and bottom, left and right.
- A margin is above the content of the page, borders, and padding but within the page edges.
- Horizontal margins — each in its own box — do not collapse. When two vertical margins are adjacent, they may collapse, or form one box. Vertical margins collapse when document flow is normal. A positive margin width of the new box is no greater than the maximum margin width for one of the prior boxes. A negative margin width of the new box is the result of subtracting the negative measurement from the positive measurement of the prior boxes or subtracting only negative measurements from zero. Vertical margins do not collapse when one of the boxes floats or the boxes are absolutely and relatively located on the page.
- By default, the characteristics of this property are not inherited.

Related Properties

`margin-bottom` (448), `margin-left` (449), `margin-right` (450), `margin-top` (452), `marks` (454), `orphans` (458), `page` (470), `page-break-after` (470), `page-break-before` (471), `page-break-inside` (472), `size` (481), `widows` (498)

Related At-Rule

`@page` (468)

Related Pseudo-Classes

`:first` (420), `:left` (440), `:right` (480)

For More Information

Learn about the `margin` property on page 630 in Chapter 8, "Styling Documents with CSS2."

margin-bottom   Bottom Margin

Purpose

Turns on or off the bottom margin and/or specifies the bottom-margin size of a box.

Syntax

margin-bottom: <u>0</u> | *length* | *percent%* | auto | inherit

Where

- 0 represents the parent element's current bottom margin. This is the default.
- *length* is a positive or negative value followed by a two-letter abbreviation representing the unit of measure.
- *percent* is a positive value that is relative to the parent element's bottom margin. Follow *percent* with a percentage sign (%).
- auto is a keyword that represents a value automatically calculated by the user's browser.
- inherit is a keyword that indicates that this property takes the same computed value as its parent.

Notes

- This property, which originated in CSS1, applies to all elements.
- This property turns bottom margins on or off, or sets a margin size (in the default unit of measure) as a percentage of the current height, or automatically by calculating a minimum amount.
- margin-bottom is a visual media type.
- Valid relative units of measure are em (the height of the current font), ex (the height of the letter x in the current font), and px (pixels, relative to the size of the window). Valid absolute units of measure are in (inches), cm (centimeters), mm (millimeters), pt (points), and pc (picas). margin-bottom can have a negative value.
- A margin is above the content of the page, borders, and padding but within the page edges.
- Margins are always transparent.
- Horizontal margins — each in its own box — do not collapse. When two vertical margins are adjacent, they may collapse, or form one box. Vertical margins collapse when document flow is normal. A positive margin width of the new box is no greater than the maximum margin width for one of the prior boxes. A negative margin width of the new box is the result of subtracting the negative measurement from the positive measurement of the prior boxes or subtracting only negative measurements from zero. Vertical margins do not collapse when one of the boxes floats or the boxes are absolutely and relatively located on the page.
- By default, the characteristics of this property are not inherited.

Related Properties

margin (446), margin-bottom (448), margin-right (458), margin-top (452), marks (454), orphans (458), page (470), page-break-after (470), page-break-before (471), page-break-inside (472), size (481), widows (498)

Related At-Rule

@page (468)

Related Pseudo-Classes

:first (420), :left (440), :right (480)

For More Information

Learn about the margin-bottom property on page 630 in Chapter 8, "Styling Documents with CSS2."

---

margin-left   Left Margin

Purpose

Turns on or off the left margin or sets the left-margin size of a box.

Syntax

margin-left: <u>0</u> | *length* | *percent*% | auto | inherit

Where

- 0 represents the parent element's current left margin.
- *percent* is a positive value that is relative to the parent element's left margin. Follow *percent* with a percentage sign (%).
- *length* is a positive or negative value followed by a two-letter abbreviation representing the unit of measure.
- auto is a keyword that represents a value automatically calculated by the user's browser.
- inherit is a keyword that indicates that this property takes the same computed value as its parent.

Notes

- This property, which originated in CSS1, applies to all elements.
- This property turns the left margin on or off and/or sets the left margin size (in the default unit of measure) as a percentage of the current width, or automatically by calculating a minimum amount.
- margin-left is a visual media type.
- Valid relative units of measure are em (the height of the current font), ex (the height of the letter x in the current font), and px (pixels, relative to the size of the window). Valid absolute units of measure are in (inches), cm (centimeters), mm (millimeters), pt (points), and pc (picas).
- margin-top can have a negative value.

Cascading Style Sheet Syntax

- A margin is above the content of the page, borders, and padding but within the page edges.
- Margins are always transparent.
- Horizontal margins — each in its own box — do not collapse. When two vertical margins are adjacent, they may collapse, or form one box. Vertical margins collapse when document flow is normal. A positive margin width of the new box is no greater than the maximum margin width for one of the prior boxes. A negative margin width of the new box is the result of subtracting the negative measurement from the positive measurement of the prior boxes or subtracting only negative measurements from zero. Vertical margins do not collapse when one of the boxes floats or the boxes are absolutely and relatively located on the page.
- By default, the characteristics of this property are not inherited.

Related Properties

margin (446), margin-bottom (448), margin-right (450), margin-top (452), marks (454), orphans (458), page (470), page-break-after (470), page-break-before (471), page-break-inside (472), size (481), widows (498)

Related At-Rule

@page (468)

Related Pseudo-Classes

:first (420), :left (440), :right (480)

For More Information

Learn how to use the margin-left property on page 629 and 630 in Chapter 8, "Styling Documents with CSS2."

margin-right	Right Margin

Purpose

Turns on or off the right margin and/or sets the right-margin size of a box.

Syntax

margin-right: 0 | length | percent% | auto | inherit

Where

- 0 represents the parent element's current right margin. This is the default.
- percent is a positive value that is relative to the parent element's right margin. Follow percent with a percentage sign (%).
- length is a positive or negative value followed by a two-letter abbreviation representing the unit of measure.

- `auto` is a keyword that represents a value automatically calculated by the user's browser.
- `inherit` is a keyword that indicates that this property takes the same computed value as its parent.

Notes

- This property, which originated in CSS1, applies to all elements.
- This property turns right margins on or off, or sets the margin size (in the default unit of measure) as a percentage of the current width, or automatically by calculating a minimum amount.
- `margin-right` is a visual media type.
- Valid relative units of measure are `em` (the height of the current font), `ex` (the height of the letter x in the current font), and `px` (pixels, relative to the size of the window). Valid absolute units of measure are `in` (inches), `cm` (centimeters), `mm` (millimeters), `pt` (points), and `pc` (picas). `margin-right` can have a negative value.
- A margin is above the content of the page, borders, and padding but within the page edges.
- Margins are always transparent.
- Horizontal margins — each in its own box — do not collapse. When two vertical margins are adjacent, they may collapse, or form one box. Vertical margins collapse when document flow is normal. A positive margin width of the new box is no greater than the maximum margin width for one of the prior boxes. A negative margin width of the new box is the result of subtracting the negative measurement from the positive measurement of the prior boxes or subtracting only negative measurements from zero. Vertical margins do not collapse when one of the boxes floats or the boxes are absolutely and relatively located on the page.
- By default, the characteristics of this property are not inherited.

Related Properties

`margin` (446), `margin-bottom` (448), `margin-left` (449), `margin-top` (452), `marks` (454), `orphans` (458), `page` (470), `page-break-after` (470), `page-break-before` (471), `page-break-inside` (472), `size` (481), `widows` (498)

Related At-Rule

`@page` (468)

Related Pseudo-Classes

`:first` (420), `:left` (440), `:right` (480)

For More Information

Learn how to use the `margin-right` property on page 629, 630, and 632 in Chapter 8, "Styling Documents with CSS2."

margin-top	Top Margin

Purpose

Turns on or off the top margin or sets the top-margin size of a box.

Syntax

margin-top: <u>0</u>│*length*│*percent*%│auto│inherit

Where

- 0 represents the parent element's current top margin. This is the default.
- *percent* is a positive value that is relative to the parent element's top margin. Follow *percent* with a percentage sign (%).
- *length* is a positive or negative value followed by a two-letter abbreviation representing the unit of measure.
- auto is a keyword that represents a value automatically calculated by the user's browser.
- inherit is a keyword that indicates that this property takes the same computed value as its parent.

Notes

- This property, which originated in CSS1, applies to all elements.
- This property turns top margins on or off, or sets a margin size (in the default unit of measure) as a percentage of the current height, or automatically by calculating a minimum amount.
- margin-top is a visual media type.
- Valid relative units of measure are em (the height of the current font), ex (the height of the letter x in the current font), and px (pixels, relative to the size of the window). Valid absolute units of measure are in (inches), cm (centimeters), mm (millimeters), pt (points), and pc (picas). margin-top can have a negative value.
- A margin is above the content of the page, borders, and padding but within the page edges.
- Margins are always transparent.
- Horizontal margins — each in its own box — do not collapse. When two vertical margins are adjacent, they may collapse, or form one box. Vertical margins collapse when document flow is normal. A positive margin width of the new box is no greater than the maximum margin width for one of the prior boxes. A negative margin width of the new box is the result of subtracting the negative measurement from the positive measurement of the prior boxes or subtracting only negative measurements from zero. Vertical margins do not collapse when one of the boxes floats or the boxes are absolutely and relatively located on the page.
- By default, the characteristics of this property are not inherited.

Related Properties

margin (446), margin-bottom (448), margin-left (449), margin-right (450), marks (454), orphans (458), page (470), page-break-after (470), page-break-before (471), page-break-inside (472), size (481), widows (498)

Related At-Rule

@page (468)

Related Pseudo-Classes

:first (420), :left (440), :right (480)

For More Information

Learn how to use the margin-top property on page 629 and 630 in Chapter 8, "Styling Documents with CSS2."

---

marker-offset	Marker Offset

Purpose

Creates and specifies the dimensions of a marker box.

Syntax

```
marker-offset: length | auto | inherit
```

Where

- length is a positive value followed by a two-letter abbreviation representing the unit of measure.
- auto is a keyword that represents a value automatically calculated by the user's browser. This is the default.
- inherit is a keyword that indicates that this property takes the same computed value as its parent.

Notes

- This property, which originated in CSS2, applies to elements with a characteristic of display: marker.
- Use a marker box to control marker content and location. A *marker box* is a one-line box used for text decoration and lists. In fact, marker boxes are often created automatically for lists.
- Valid relative units of measure are em (the height of the current font), ex (the height of the letter x in the current font), and px (pixels, relative to the size of the window). Valid absolute units of measure are in (inches), cm (centimeters), mm (millimeters), pt (points), and pc (picas).
- By default, the characteristics of this property are not inherited.

Related Properties

display (417), line-height (442), overflow (463), text-align (487), vertical-align (493), width (498)

Related Pseudo-Elements

:after (373), :before (383)

marks — Crop Marks

Purpose

Sets crop marks for a page box.

Syntax

marks: (crop|cross)|none|inherit

Where

- **crop** indicates the printing of *crop marks*, which are the edges of the final bound page.
- **cross** indicates the printing of *register marks*, which enable the alignment of a set of printed pages.
- **none** is a keyword that indicates that there are no crop marks. This is the default.
- **inherit** is a keyword that indicates that this property takes the same computed value as its parent.

Note

This property originated in CSS2.

Related Properties

margin (446), margin-bottom (448), margin-left (449), margin-right (450), margin-top (452), orphans (458), page (470), page-break-after (470), page-break-before (471), page-break-inside (472), size (481), widows (498)

Related At-Rule

@page (468)

Related Pseudo-Classes

:first (420), :left (440), :right (480)

max-height — Maximum Element Height

Purpose

Specifies the maximum height of the selected element.

Syntax

max-height: *length*|*percent%*|none|inherit

Where

- *length* is a positive value followed by a two-letter abbreviation representing the unit of measure.
- *percent* is a positive value that is relative to the size of the image. Follow *percent* with a percentage sign (%).
- none is a keyword that indicates that there is no maximum height. This is the default.
- inherit is a keyword that indicates that this property takes the same computed value as its parent.

Notes

- This property originated in CSS2.
- This property sets the maximum height of the selected element, in pixels, as a percentage of the original size, or by calculating its width automatically, scaled proportionately with the height.
- Valid relative units of measure are em (the height of the current font), ex (the height of the letter x in the current font), and px (pixels, relative to the size of the window). Valid absolute units of measure are in (inches), cm (centimeters), mm (millimeters), pt (points), and pc (picas).
- By default, the characteristics of this property are not inherited.

Related Properties

height (436), max-width (455), min-height (457), min-width (458), width (498)

max-width   Maximum Element Width

Purpose

Specifies the maximum width of the selected element.

Syntax

max-width: *length* | *percent*% | none | inherit

Where

- *length* is a positive value followed by a two-letter abbreviation representing the unit of measure.
- *percent* is a positive value that is relative to the size of the image. Follow *percent* with a percentage sign (%).
- none is a keyword that indicates that there is no maximum width. This is the default.
- inherit is a keyword that indicates that this property takes the same computed value as its parent.

Notes

- This property originated in CSS2.

- This property sets the maximum width of the selected element, in pixels, as a percentage of the original size, or by calculating its width automatically, scaled proportionately with the height.
- Valid relative units of measure are em (the height of the current font), ex (the height of the letter x in the current font), and px (pixels, relative to the size of the window). Valid absolute units of measure are in (inches), cm (centimeters), mm (millimeters), pt (points), and pc (picas).
- By default, the characteristics of this property are not inherited.

Related Properties

height (436), max-height (454), min-height (457), min-width (458), width (498)

@media	Media Type Rule

Purpose

Indicates the media type in which a styled document is to be output.

Syntax

```
@media [all][,aural][,braille][,embossed][,handheld]
  [,print][,projection][,screen][,tty][,tv]
```

Where

- all is a keyword representing all media devices. This is the default.
- aural is a keyword representing speech synthesizing devices.
- braille is a keyword representing Braille tactile feedback devices.
- embossed is a keyword representing paged Braille printing devices.
- handheld is a keyword representing handheld devices.
- print is a keyword representing printing devices and print-preview modes.
- projection is a keyword representing projection devices and transparencies.
- screen is a keyword representing color computer monitors.
- tty is a keyword representing fixed-pitch teletypes, terminals, and some portable devices.
- tv is a keyword representing television-type devices.

Notes

- This at-rule originated in CSS2.
- Media-type names are case-insensitive.
- Media types can encompass several properties: continuous or paged; visual, aural, or tactile; grid or bitmap; interactive or static; or all, which includes all types.
- The aural media type is continuous (not paged) and can be both interactive and static.

- The `braille` media type is continuous (not paged), tactile (not visual or aural), grid (not bitmap), and both interactive and static.
- The `embossed` media type is paged (not continuous), tactile (not visual or aural), grid (not bitmap), and both interactive and static.
- The `handheld` media type is both continuous and paged, visual (not tactile or aural), grid (not bitmap), and both interactive and static.
- The `print` media type is paged (not continuous), visual (not tactile or aural), bitmap (not grid), and static (not interactive).
- The `projection` media type is paged (not continuous), visual (not tactile or aural), bitmap (not grid), and static (not interactive).
- The `screen` media type is continuous (not paged), visual (not tactile or aural), bitmap (not grid), and both static and interactive.
- The `tty` media type is both continuous and paged, visual (not aural or tactile), grid (not bitmap), and both static and interactive.
- The `tv` media type is both continuous and paged, both visual and aural (but not tactile), bitmap (not grid), and both static and interactive.

min-height — Minimum Element Height

Purpose

Specifies the minimum height of the selected element.

Syntax

```
min-width: length | percent% | inherit
```

Where

- *length* is a positive value followed by a two-letter abbreviation representing the unit of measure.
- *percent* is a positive value that is relative to the size of the image. Follow *percent* with a percentage sign (%).
- *inherit* is a keyword that indicates that this property takes the same computed value as its parent.

Notes

- This property originated in CSS2.
- This property sets the minimum height of the selected element, in pixels, as a percentage of the original size, or by calculating its width automatically, scaled proportionally with the height.
- The default value of this property is 0.
- Valid relative units of measure are `em` (the height of the current font), `ex` (the height of the letter x in the current font), and `px` (pixels, relative to the size of the window). Valid absolute units of measure are `in` (inches), `cm` (centimeters), `mm` (millimeters), `pt` (points), and `pc` (picas).
- By default, the characteristics of this property are not inherited.

Related Properties

height (436), max-height (454), max-width (455), min-width (458), width (498)

min-width   Minimum Element Width

Purpose

Specifies the minimum width of the selected element.

Syntax

```
min-width: length | percent% | inherit
```

Where

- *length* is a positive value followed by a two-letter abbreviation representing the unit of measure.
- *percent* is a positive value that is relative to the size of the image. Follow *percent* with a percentage sign (%).
- inherit is a keyword that indicates that this property takes the same computed value as its parent.

Notes

- This property originated in CSS2.
- This property sets the minimum width of the selected element, in pixels, as a percentage of the original size, or by calculating its width automatically, scaled proportionately with the height.
- Valid relative units of measure are em (the height of the current font), ex (the height of the letter x in the current font), and px (pixels, relative to the size of the window). Valid absolute units of measure are in (inches), cm (centimeters), mm (millimeters), pt (points), and pc (picas).
- By default, the characteristics of this property are not inherited.

Related Properties

height (436), max-height (454), max-width (455), min-height (457), width (498)

orphans   Orphans Paragraph Breaks

Purpose

Specifies the minimum number of paragraph-lines left at the bottom of a page.

Syntax

```
orphans: integer | inherit
```

Where

- *integer* indicates the minimum paragraph-lines that must remain at the bottom of a page when a page break is inserted within the last paragraph on a page. The default setting is 2 lines.
- inherit is a keyword that indicates that this property takes the same computed value as its parent.

Notes

- This property, which originated in CSS2, applies to block-level elements.
- By default, the characteristics of this property are inherited.

Related Properties

margin (446), margin-bottom (448), margin-left (449), margin-right (450), margin-top (452), marks (459), page (470), page-break-after (470), page-break-before (471), page-break-inside (472), size (481), widows (498)

Related At-Rule

@page (468)

Related Pseudo-Classes

:first (420), :left (440), :right (480)

---

outline   Outline Properties

Purpose

Specifies the color, style, and/or width of the outline around an object.

Syntax

outline: ([*outline-color_value*][*outline-style_value*]
   [*outline-width_value*]) | inherit

Where

- *outline-color_value* specifies the color of the outline. For more information, see the outline-color property (460).
- *outline-style_value* specifies the style of the outline. For more information, see the outline-style property (461).
- *outline-width_value* specifies the width of the outline. For more information, see the outline-width property (462).
- inherit is a keyword that indicates that this property takes the same computed value as its parent.

Notes

- This property, which originated in CSS2, applies to all elements.

- This shortcut property specifies multiple properties for the outline in the same way that you can individually set rules for the following properties: `outline-color`, `outline-style`, and `outline-width`.
- According to the *Cascading Style Sheets, Level 2 CSS Specification* (http://www.w3.org/TR/REC-CSS2/), outlines do not take up space, and outlines may be non-rectangular.
- There is no initial value for this property.
- By default, the characteristics of this property are not inherited.
- Table R2-1 (376) contains selected hexadecimal color values.

Related Properties

`border` (383), `border-bottom` (384), `border-bottom-color` (385), `border-bottom-style` (387), `border-bottom-width` (388), `border-color` (389), `border-left` (391), `border-left-color` (392), `border-left-style` (393), `border-left-width` (394), `border-right` (395), `border-right-color` (396), `border-right-style` (397), `border-right-width` (398), `border-style` (400), `border-top` (401), `border-top-color` (402), `border-top-style` (403), `border-top-width` (404), `border-width` (405), `outline-color` (460), `outline-style` (461), `outline-width` (462)

outline-color	**Outline Color**

Purpose

Sets colors of the outline around an object.

Syntax

```
outline-color: color-name|#rgb|#rrggbb
  |rgb(rrr,ggg,bbb)|rgb(rrr%,ggg%,bbb%)|invert|inherit
```

Where

- *color-name* specifies an outline color by valid name (that is, Red (#FF0000), Maroon (#800000), Yellow (#FFFF00), Green (#008000), Lime (#00FF00), Teal (#008080), Olive (#808000), Aqua (#00FFFF), Blue (#0000FF), Navy (#000080), Purple (#800080), Fuchsia (#FF00FF), Black (#000000), Gray (#808080), White (#FFFFFF), and the default, Silver (#C0C0C0)). CSS2 adds the following case-insensitive color keywords: ActiveBorder, ActiveCaption, AppWorkspace, Background, ButtonFace, ButtonHighlight, ButtonShadow, ButtonText, CaptionText, GrayText, Highlight, Highlight Text, InactiveBorder, InactiveCaption, InactiveCaption Text, InfoBackground, InfoText, Menu, MenuText, Scrollbar, ThreeDDarkShadow, ThreeDFace, ThreeDHighlight, ThreeDLight Shadow, ThreeDShadow, Window, WindowFrame, and WindowText. Table R2.2 (379) names the color keywords and lists the affected object for each.

- #*rgb* is a three-digit hexadecimal color code, where *r* represents the red attributes, from 0 to F; *g* represents the green attributes, from 0 to F; and *b* represents the blue attributes, from 0 to F.
- #*rrggbb* is a six-digit hexadecimal color code, where *rr* represents the red attributes, from 00 to FF; *gg* represents the green attributes, from 00 to FF; and *bb* represents the blue attributes, from 00 to FF.
- rgb(*rrr*,*ggg*,*bbb*) represents absolute red-green-blue values, each ranging from 000 to 255.
- rgb(*rrr.d%*, *ggg.e%*, *bbb.f%*) represents the relative red-green-blue values, each ranging from 0.0% to 100.0%, where 0.0% is equivalent to an absolute value of 000, and 100.0% is equivalent to 255.
- invert is a keyword that indicates that the default outline colors are inverted (for example, blue becomes yellow, black becomes white, green becomes purple, red becomes aqua, and so on). This is the default.
- inherit is a keyword that indicates that this property takes the same computed value as its parent.

Notes

- This property, which originated in CSS2, applies to all elements.
- An outline is a layer drawn on top of a box.
- An outline is outside the edge of a border.
- You can use this property in conjunction with pseudo-classes to outline particular objects.
- By default, the characteristics of this property are not inherited.
- Table R2-1 (376) contains selected hexadecimal color values.

Related Properties

border (383), border-bottom (384), border-bottom-color (385), border-color (389), border-left (391), border-left-color (392), border-right (395), border-right-color (396), border-top (401), border-top-color (402), outline (459), outline-style (461), outline-width (462)

| outline-style | Outline Style |

Purpose

Formats the outline of an object.

Syntax

outline-style: ([none|hidden|dotted|dashed|solid
|double|groove|ridge|inset|outset]) |inherit

Where

- none omits a border. This overrides any outline-width (462) value. This is the default.

- hidden omits a border and takes precedence over any other value for this border.
- dotted draws a dotted-line border over the element background.
- dashed draws a dashed-line border over the element background.
- solid draws a solid-line border over the element background.
- double draws a double-solid-line border over the element background.
- groove draws a three-dimensional grooved border over the element background using the border-color (389) value.
- ridge draws a three-dimensional ridged border over the element background using the border-color value.
- inset draws a three-dimensional inset over the element background using the border-color value.
- outset draws a three-dimensional outset over the element background using the border-color value.
- inherit is a keyword that indicates that this property takes the same computed value as its parent.

Notes

- This property, which originated in CSS2, applies to all elements.
- Some browsers, which cannot interpret most outline-style values, will draw a solid line instead.
- You can use this property in conjunction with pseudo-classes to outline particular objects.
- By default, the characteristics of this property are not inherited.

Related Properties

border (383), border-bottom (384), border-bottom-style (387), border-left (391), border-left-style (393), border-right (395), border-right-style (397), border-style (400), border-top (401), border-top-style (403), outline (459), outline-color (460), outline-width (462)

outline-width	Outline Width

Purpose

Sets the width of the outline of an object.

Syntax

outline-width: [thin|medium|thick|*length*]|inherit

Where

- thin is a narrower width than medium or thick.
- medium is wider than thin but narrower than thick. This is the default.
- thick is wider than thin or medium.
- *length* is a positive value followed by a two-letter abbreviation representing the unit of measure.

- `inherit` is a keyword that indicates that this property takes the same computed value as its parent.

Notes

- This property, which originated in CSS2, applies to all elements.
- Valid relative units of measure are `em` (the height of the current font), `ex` (the height of the letter x in the current font), and `px` (pixels, relative to the size of the window). Valid absolute units of measure are `in` (inches), `cm` (centimeters), `mm` (millimeters), `pt` (points), and `pc` (picas).
- You can use this property in conjunction with pseudo-classes to outline particular objects.
- By default, the characteristics of this property are not inherited.

Related Properties

`border` (383), `border-bottom` (384), `border-bottom-width` (388), `border-color` (389), `border-left` (391), `border-left-width` (394), `border-right` (395), `border-right-width` (398), `border-top` (401), `border-top-width` (404), `border-width` (405), `outline` (459), `outline-color` (460), `outline-style` (461)

overflow   Box Overflow?

Purpose

Specifies whether and how the contents of a box overflow.

Syntax

`overflow:` <u>`visible`</u>`|hidden|scroll|auto|inherit`

Where

- `visible` is a keyword that indicates that content can overflow its box. This is the default.
- `hidden` is a keyword that indicates that content cannot overflow its box; it is clipped. No scroll bar ever appears in the box.
- `scroll` is a keyword that indicates that content cannot overflow its box; it is clipped. A scroll bar always appears in the box.
- `auto` is a keyword that represents a value automatically calculated by the user's browser.
- `inherit` is a keyword that indicates that this property takes the same computed value as its parent.

Notes

- This property originated in CSS2.
- Some browsers clip content even though `overflow: visible`.
- By default, this property is not inherited.

Related Property

`clip` (409)

padding	**Padding Characteristics**

Purpose

Turns on or off one, two, three, or four paddings, or sets the padding size of a box.

Syntax

```
padding: [ length_top | percent_top% ]
   [ length_right | percent_right% ]
   [ length_bottom | percent_bottom% ]
   [ length_left | percent_left% ] | inherit
```

Where

- *length_top*, *length_right*, *length_bottom*, and *length_left* are positive fixed values followed by a two-letter abbreviation representing the unit of measure.
- *percent_top*, *percent_right*, *percent_bottom*, and *percent_left* are positive values that are relative to the parent element's selected paddings. Follow *percent* with a percentage sign (%).
- inherit is a keyword that indicates that this property takes the same computed value as its parent.

Notes

- This property, which originated in CSS1, applies to all elements.
- This shortcut property for padding-top, padding-right, padding-bottom, and padding-left (in that order) turns one, two, three, or four paddings on or off, or sets padding size (in the default unit of measure) as a percentage of the current width, or automatically by calculating a minimum amount.
- Valid relative units of measure are em (the height of the current font), ex (the height of the letter x in the current font), and px (pixels, relative to the size of the window). Valid absolute units of measure are in (inches), cm (centimeters), mm (millimeters), pt (points), and pc (picas).
- If you supply one value, all paddings are set to that value.
- If you supply two or three values, the browser supplies values from the opposite side of the element. Elements are paired as follows: top and bottom, left and right.
- Padding is outside the content of the page, within the page edges, and below margins and borders.
- By default, the characteristics of this property are not inherited.

Related Properties

padding-bottom (465), padding-left (466), padding-right (466),
padding-top (467)

padding-bottom   Bottom Padding

Purpose

Turns on or off bottom padding and/or specifies the bottom-padding size of
a box.

Syntax

padding-bottom: *0* | *length* | *percent%* | inherit

Where

- 0 represents the parent element's current bottom padding. This is the
  default.
- *percent* is a positive value that is relative to the parent element's bottom padding. Follow *percent* with a percentage sign (%).
- *length* is a positive value followed by a two-letter abbreviation representing the unit of measure.
- inherit is a keyword that indicates that this property takes the same
  computed value as its parent.

Notes

- This property, which originated in CSS1, applies to all elements.
- This property turns bottom padding on or off, or sets a padding size (in
  the default unit of measure) as a percentage of the current height, or
  automatically by calculating a minimum amount.
- Valid relative units of measure are em (the height of the current font),
  ex (the height of the letter x in the current font), and px (pixels, relative
  to the size of the window). Valid absolute units of measure are in
  (inches), cm (centimeters), mm (millimeters), pt (points), and pc (picas).
- Padding is outside the content of the page, within the page edges, and
  below margins and borders.
- By default, the characteristics of this property are not inherited.

Related Properties

padding (464), padding-left (466), padding-right (466), padding-
top (467)

padding-left   Left Padding

Purpose
Turns on or off left padding or sets the left-padding size of a box.

Syntax
padding-left: <u>0</u> | *length* | *percent%* | inherit

Where
- 0 represents the parent element's current left padding.
- *percent* is a positive value that is relative to the parent element's left padding. Follow *percent* with a percentage sign (%).
- *length* is a positive value followed by a two-letter abbreviation representing the unit of measure.
- inherit is a keyword that indicates that this property takes the same computed value as its parent.

Notes
- This property, which originated in CSS1, applies to all elements.
- This property turns the left padding on or off and/or sets the left-padding size (in the default unit of measure) as a percentage of the current width, or automatically by calculating a minimum amount.
- Valid relative units of measure are em (the height of the current font), ex (the height of the letter x in the current font), and px (pixels, relative to the size of the window). Valid absolute units of measure are in (inches), cm (centimeters), mm (millimeters), pt (points), and pc (picas).
- Padding is outside the content of the page, within the page edges, and below margins and borders.
- By default, the characteristics of this property are not inherited.

Related Properties
padding (464), padding-bottom (465), padding-right (466), padding-top (467)

padding-right   Right Padding

Purpose
Turns on or off the right padding and/or sets the right-padding size of a box.

Syntax
padding-right: <u>0</u> | *length* | *percent%* | inherit

Where

- 0 represents the parent element's current right padding.
- *percent* is a positive value that is relative to the parent element's right padding. Follow *percent* with a percentage sign (%).
- *length* is a positive value followed by a two-letter abbreviation representing the unit of measure.
- *inherit* is a keyword that indicates that this property takes the same computed value as its parent.

Notes

- This property, which originated in CSS1, applies to all elements.
- This property turns right padding on or off, or sets the padding size (in the default unit of measure) as a percentage of the current width, or automatically by calculating a minimum amount.
- Valid relative units of measure are em (the height of the current font), ex (the height of the letter x in the current font), and px (pixels, relative to the size of the window). Valid absolute units of measure are in (inches), cm (centimeters), mm (millimeters), pt (points), and pc (picas).
- Padding is outside the content of the page, within the page edges, and below margins and borders.
- By default, the characteristics of this property are not inherited.

Related Properties

padding (464), padding-bottom (465), padding-left (466), padding-top (467)

padding-top   Top Padding

Purpose

Turns on or off top padding or sets the top-padding size of a box.

Syntax

padding-top: 0 | *length* | *percent*% | inherit

Where

- 0 represents the parent element's current top padding.
- *percent* is a positive value that is relative to the parent element's top padding. Follow *percent* with a percentage sign (%).
- *length* is a positive value followed by a two-letter abbreviation representing the unit of measure.
- *inherit* is a keyword that indicates that this property takes the same computed value as its parent.

Notes

- This property, which originated in CSS1, applies to all elements.
- This property turns top padding on or off, or sets a padding size (in the default unit of measure) as a percentage of the current height, or automatically by calculating a minimum amount.
- Valid relative units of measure are em (the height of the current font), ex (the height of the letter x in the current font), and px (pixels, relative to the size of the window). Valid absolute units of measure are in (inches), cm (centimeters), mm (millimeters), pt (points), and pc (picas).
- Padding is outside the content of the page, within the page edges, and below margins and borders.
- By default, the characteristics of this property are not inherited.

Related Properties

padding (464), padding-bottom (465), padding-left (466), padding-right (466)

@page   **Page Rule**

Purpose

Sets the characteristics of a page box.

Syntax

```
@page [:left|:right|:first] {
  [margin: margin_settings;]
  ([margin-bottom: margin_bottom_settings;]
  [margin-left: margin_left_settings;]
  [margin-right: margin_right_settings;]
  [margin-top: margin_top_settings;])
  [marks: marks_settings;]
  [orphans: orphans_settings;]
  [page: page_settings;]
  [page-break-after: page_break_after_settings;]
  [page-break-before: page_break_before_settings;]
  [page-break-inside: page_break_inside_settings;]
  [size: size_settings;]
  [widows: widows_settings;]
}
```

Where

- :left sets a unique style for the left-page boxes of a document. For more information, see the :left pseudo-class (440).

- :right sets a unique style for the right-page boxes of a document. For more information, see the :right pseudo-class (480).
- :first sets a unique style for the first-page box of a document. For more information, see the :first pseudo-class (420).
- margin sets the margin size of one, two, three, or four margins in a page box. For more information, see the margin property (446).
- margin-bottom sets the bottom-margin size of the page box. For more information, see the margin-bottom property (448).
- margin-left sets the left-margin size of the page box. For more information, see the margin-left property (449).
- margin-right sets the right-margin size of the page box. For more information, see the margin-right property (450).
- margin-top sets the top-margin size of the page box. For more information, see the margin-top property (452).
- marks sets crop marks for a page box. For more information, see the marks property (454).
- orphans specifies the number of paragraph-lines left at the bottom of a page. For more information, see the orphans property (458).
- page names a page type. For more information, see the page property (470).
- page-break-after inserts a page break after the current page box. For more information, see the page-break-after property (470).
- page-break-before inserts a page break before the current page box. For more information, see the page-break-before property (471).
- page-break-inside inserts a page break inside the current page box. For more information, see the page-break-inside property (472).
- size sets the dimensions and orientation of the page box.
- widows specifies the number of paragraph-lines left at the top of a page. For more information, see the widows property (498).

Notes

- This at-rule originated in CSS2.
- This at-rule sets the dimensions, orientation, and margins (margin-top, margin-right, margin-bottom, and margin-left) of the page box.
- A page box contains the boxes on a particular page and the margins in which the page content is enclosed.

Related Properties

margin (446), margin-bottom (448), margin-left (449), margin-right (450), margin-top (452), marks (454), orphans (458), page (470), page-break-after (470), page-break-before (471), page-break-inside (472), size (481), widows (498)

Cascading Style Sheet Syntax

For More Information

For more information about paged media, refer to "Section 13: Paged Media" in the *Cascading Style Sheets, Level 2 CSS Specification* (`http://www.w3.org/TR/REC-CSS2/`).

page	Page-Type Name

Purpose

Names a page type.

Syntax

```
page: page_type_identifier | auto
```

Where

- *page_type_identifier* is the name of the page type.
- `auto` is a keyword that represents a page-type name automatically calculated by the user's browser. This is the default.

Notes

- This property, which originated in CSS2, applies to block-level elements.
- When a style sheet processor encounters a page that is different from the previous page, it inserts one or two page breaks (depending on other page properties, such as forced printing on a left or right page) and produces a new page box. The page-box settings remain the same until the processor encounters the next page with different properties.
- By default, the characteristics of this property are inherited.

Related Properties

`margin` (446), `margin-bottom` (448), `margin-left` (449), `margin-right` (450), `margin-top` (452), `marks` (454), `orphans` (458), `page-break-after` (470), `page-break-before` (471), `page-break-inside` (472), `size` (481), `widows` (498)

Related At-Rule

`@page` (468)

Related Pseudo-Classes

`:first` (420), `:left` (440), `:right` (480)

page-break-after	Page Break After

Purpose

Inserts a page break after the current page box.

Syntax

page-break-after: <u>auto</u> | always | avoid | left | right | inherit

Where

- auto is a keyword that indicates that a page break is not forced or prevented after the page box is produced. This is the default.
- always is a keyword that indicates that a page break always is inserted after the page box is produced.
- avoid is a keyword that indicates that a page break is prevented after the page box is produced.
- left is a keyword that indicates that after a page break occurs, the next page will be a left page.
- right is a keyword that indicates that after a page break occurs, the next page will be a left page.
- inherit is a keyword that indicates that this property takes the same computed value as its parent.

Notes

- This property, which originated in CSS2, applies to block-level elements.
- The current page break is affected by the parent element's page-break-inside settings, the page-break-after settings of the prior element, and the page-break-before settings of the next element. The always, left, and right values have precedence over avoid when these page-break-inside, page-break-after, and page-break-before settings are not equal to auto.
- By default, this property is inherited.

Related Properties

margin (446), margin-bottom (448), margin-left (449), margin-right (450), margin-top (452), marks (454), orphans (458), page (470), page-break-before (471), page-break-inside (472), size (481), widows (498)

Related At-Rule

@page (468)

Related Pseudo-Classes

:first (420), :left (440), :right (480)

page-break-before   Page Break Before

Purpose

Inserts a page break before the current page box.

Syntax

```
page-break-before:  auto | always | avoid | left | right
    | inherit
```

Where

- auto is a keyword that indicates that a page break is not forced or prevented after the page box is produced. This is the default.
- always is a keyword that indicates that a page break always is inserted after the page box is produced.
- avoid is a keyword that indicates that a page break is prevented after the page box is produced.
- left is a keyword that indicates that after a page break occurs, the next page will be a left page.
- right is a keyword that indicates that after a page break occurs, the next page will be a left page.
- inherit is a keyword that indicates that this property takes the same computed value as its parent.

Notes

- This property, which originated in CSS2, applies to block-level elements.
- The current page break is affected by the parent element's **page-break-inside** settings, the **page-break-after** settings of the prior element, and the **page-break-before** settings of the next element. The **always**, **left**, and **right** values have precedence over **avoid** when these **page-break-inside**, **page-break-after**, and **page-break-before** settings are not equal to **auto**.
- By default, this property is inherited.

Related Properties

margin (446), margin-bottom (448), margin-left (449), margin-right (450), margin-top (452), marks (454), orphans (458), page (470), page-break-after (470), page-break-inside (472), size (481), widows (498)

Related At-Rule

@page (468)

Related Pseudo-Classes

:first (420), :left (440), :right (480)

---

page-break-inside   Page Break Inside

Purpose

Inserts a page break inside the current page box.

Syntax

```
page-break-inside:  avoid | auto | inherit
```

Where

- avoid is a keyword that indicates that a page break is prevented after the page box is produced.
- auto is a keyword that indicates that a page break is not forced or prevented after the page box is produced. This is the default.
- inherit is a keyword that indicates that this property takes the same computed value as its parent.

Notes

- This property, which originated in CSS2, applies to block-level elements.
- The current page break is affected by the parent element's page-break-inside settings, the page-break-after settings of the prior element, and the page-break-before settings of the next element. The always, left, and right values have precedence over avoid when these page-break-inside, page-break-after, and page-break-before settings are not equal to auto.
- By default, this property is inherited.

Related Properties

margin (446), margin-bottom (448), margin-left (449), margin-right (450), margin-top (452), marks (454), orphans (458), page (470), page-break-after (470), page-break-before (471), size (473), widows (498)

Related At-Rule

@page (468)

Related Pseudo-Classes

:first (420), :left (440), :right (480)

---

pause   Pause Speaking

Purpose

Pauses after and/or before an element is spoken.

Syntax

```
pause: [b_time| b_percentage][a_time| b_percentage]
    |inherit
```

Where

- *b_time* specifies the absolute pause, in seconds and milliseconds, before the element is spoken.
- *b_percentage* specifies the inverse percentage of the value of speech-rate (481) before the element is spoken.
- *a_time* specifies the absolute pause, in seconds and milliseconds, after the element is spoken.

- *a_percentage* specifies the inverse percentage of the value of speech-rate after the element is spoken.
- inherit is a keyword that indicates that this property takes the same computed value as its parent.

Notes

- This property, which originated in CSS2, applies to all elements.
- The *b_percentage* and *a_percentage* values are the inverse of the speech-rate value. So, if the speech-rate is 60 words per minute (1,000 milliseconds), a pause of 100% is also 1,000 milliseconds, and a pause of 50% is 500 milliseconds.
- Pauses are inserted between the content of the element and the content of the cue-before or cue-after property.
- By default, the characteristics of this property are not inherited.

Related Properties

azimuth (374), cue (413), cue-after (414), cue-before (414), elevation (419), pause-after (474), pause-before (475), pitch (476), pitch-range (476), play-during (477), richness (480), speak (482), speak-numeral (484), speak-punctuation (484), speech-rate (485), stress (486), voice-family (495), volume (496)

pause-after	**Pause After**

Cascading Style Sheet Syntax

Purpose

Pauses after an element is spoken.

Syntax

pause-after: [*time* | *percentage* | inherit]

Where

- *time* specifies the absolute pause, in seconds and milliseconds, after the element is spoken.
- *percentage* specifies the inverse percentage of the value of speech-rate (485) after the element is spoken.
- inherit is a keyword that indicates that this property takes the same computed value as its parent.

Notes

- This property, which originated in CSS2, applies to all elements.
- The *percentage* value is the inverse of the speech-rate value. So, if the speech-rate is 60 words per minute (1,000 milliseconds), a pause of 100% is also 1,000 milliseconds, and a pause of 50% is 500 milliseconds.

- Pauses are inserted between the content of the element and the content of the cue-before or cue-after property.
- By default, the characteristics of this property are not inherited.

Related Properties

azimuth (374), cue (413), cue-after (414), cue-before (414), elevation (419), pause (473), pause-before (475), pitch (476), pitch-range (476), play-during (477), richness (480), speak (482), speak-numeral (484), speak-punctuation (484), speech-rate (485), stress (486), voice-family (495), volume (496)

pause-before	Pause Before

Purpose

Pauses before an element is spoken.

Syntax

pause-before: [*time* | *percentage* | inherit

Where

- *time* specifies the absolute pause, in seconds and milliseconds, after the element is spoken.
- *percentage* specifies the inverse percentage of the value of speech-rate (485) after the element is spoken.
- inherit is a keyword that indicates that this property takes the same computed value as its parent.

Notes

- This property, which originated in CSS2, applies to all elements.
- The *percentage* value is the inverse of the speech-rate value. So, if the speech-rate is 60 words per minute (1,000 milliseconds), a pause of 100% is also 1,000 milliseconds, and a pause of 50% is a pause of 500 milliseconds.
- Any pauses are inserted between the content of the element and the content of the cue-before or cue-after property.
- By default, the characteristics of this property are not inherited.

Related Properties

azimuth (374), cue (413), cue-after (414), cue-before (414), elevation (419), pause (473), pause-after (474), pitch (476), pitch-range (476), play-during (477), richness (480), speak (482), speak-numeral (484), speak-punctuation (484), speech-rate (485), stress (486), voice-family (495), volume (496)

pitch — Pitch

Purpose
Sets the pitch of a speaking voice.

Syntax
pitch: *frequency* | x-low | low | <u>medium</u> | high | x-high | inherit

Where
- *frequency* represents an absolute pitch measured in hertz (Hz).
- x-low is a keyword that represents a pitch that is lower than low.
- low is a keyword that represents a pitch that is lower than medium but higher than x-low.
- medium is a keyword that represents a pitch that is lower than high but higher than low. This is the default.
- high is a keyword that represents a pitch that is lower than x-high but higher than medium.
- x-high is a keyword that represents a pitch that is higher than high.
- inherit is a keyword that indicates that this property takes the same computed value as its parent.

Notes
- This property, which originated in CSS2, applies to all elements.
- The *pitch*, or frequency, sets the tone of a speaking voice — from the highest soprano to the lowest bass.
- The pitch of the x-low, low, medium, high, and x-high keywords do not have absolute values in Hz. The selected voice family determines the starting pitch value.
- By default, the characteristics of this property are inherited.

Related Properties
azimuth (374), cue (413), cue-after (414), cue-before (414), elevation (419), pause (473), pause-after (474), pause-before (475), pitch-range (476), play-during (477), richness (480), speak (482), speak-numeral (484), speak-punctuation (484), speech-rate (485), stress (486), voice-family (495), volume (496)

pitch-range — Pitch Range

Purpose
Varies the range of pitch for a voice.

Syntax
pitch-range: *number* | inherit

Where

- *number* represents a pitch variation. Valid values range from 0 (a relatively monotone voice) to 100 (a relatively animated voice). The value of 50 represents a standard voice.
- inherit is a keyword that indicates that this property takes the same computed value as its parent.

Notes

- This property, which originated in CSS2, applies to all elements.
- By default, the characteristics of this property are inherited.

Related Properties

azimuth (374), cue (413), cue-after (414), cue-before (414), elevation (419), pause (473), pause-after (474), pause-before (475), pitch (476), play-during (477), richness (480), speak (482), speak-numeral (484), speak-punctuation (484), speech-rate (485), stress (486), voice-family (495), volume (496)

play-during   Play Background Sound

Purpose

Plays a sound while an element's content is spoken.

Syntax

```
play-during: uri(uri_name) [mix] [repeat]|auto|none
   |inherit
```

Where

- uri is a keyword that indicates that a URI name will follow.
- *uri_name* names the URI of the sound file.
- mix is a keyword that indicates that the parent element's sound continues to play and is mixed with the current element's sound.
- repeat is a keyword that indicates that the sound is repeated while the element is spoken. If repeat is absent, the sound file plays once and is clipped if it is longer than the element's "speak" characteristics.
- auto is a keyword that represents a sound that has continued to play from the parent element. This is the default.
- none indicates that no sound is played.
- inherit is a keyword that indicates that this property takes the same computed value as its parent. The sound is restarted when the current element is spoken.

Notes

- This property, which originated in CSS2, applies to all elements.
- By default, the characteristics of this property are not inherited.

Related Properties

azimuth (374), cue (413), cue-after (414), cue-before (414),
elevation (419), pause (473), pause-after (474), pause-before (475),
pitch (476), pitch-range (476), richness (480), speak (482), speak-
numeral (484), speak-punctuation (484), speech-rate (485), stress
(486), voice-family (495), volume (496)

position	Position Element

Purpose

Positions the current element in a particular way onscreen or in a printed
format.

Syntax

position: <u>static</u>|relative|absolute|fixed|inherit

Where

- static places the box inline or block, depending on the current element. The CSS processor ignores left and top properties. This is the
  default.
- relative places the box inline or block, depending on the current element. Then, the CSS processor offsets the box relative to the position
  that it would normally hold.
- absolute places the box according to its left, right, top, and bottom
  properties. An absolute box's margins cannot collapse, and the layout of its
  sibling boxes is not affected.
- fixed places the box according to its left, right, top, and bottom
  properties and is fixed in reference to its page or *viewport* (a viewing
  area).
- inherit is a keyword that indicates that this property takes the same
  computed value as its parent.

Note

This property, which originated in CSS2, applies to all elements but not generated content (for example, :after and :before pseudo-elements).

Related Properties

bottom (406), clear (408), float (422), left (440), right (481), top (492)

quotes	Quotation Marks

Purpose

Specifies pairs of quotation marks that open and close a quotation.

Cascading Style Sheet Syntax

Syntax

quotes: (*s_quote e_quote*) [*s_quote e_quote*]
[... *s_quote e_quote*] | none | @@inherit

Where

- *s_quote* represents the starting quotation mark.
- *e_quote* represents the ending quotation mark.
- none is a keyword that indicates that no quotation marks will be displayed.
- inherit is a keyword that indicates that this property takes the same computed value as its parent.

Notes

- This property, which originated in CSS2, applies to all elements.
- By default, the characteristics of this property are inherited.
- Supported quotation marks are listed in Table R2-3.

Related Property

content (411)

Related Pseudo-Elements

:after (373), :before (383)

Table R2-3 *Quotation Marks Supported by the Quotes Property*

Image	Mark	Hexadecimal Code
"	Quotation mark, straight quote, or double prime	#x0022
'	Apostrophe or single prime	#x0027
«	Left-pointing double angle quotation mark	#x00AB
»	Right-pointing double angle quotation mark	#x00BB
`	Left-pointing single quotation mark	#x2018
´	Right-pointing single quotation mark	#x2019
"	Left double quotation mark or smart quote	#x201C
"	Right double quotation mark or smart quote	#x201D
„	Double low-9 quotation mark	#x201E
<	Single-left-pointing angle quotation mark	#x2039
>	Single-right-pointing angle quotation mark	#x203A

richness
Voice Richness

Purpose

Specifies the richness of a voice.

Syntax

```
richness: number | inherit
```

Where

- *number* represents a richness level. Valid values range from 0 (a softer, smoother voice) to 100 (a louder, harsher voice). The default value of 50 represents a standard richness level.
- inherit is a keyword that indicates that this property takes the same computed value as its parent.

Notes

- This property, which originated in CSS2, applies to all elements.
- A richer voice carries well in a larger room.
- By default, the characteristics of this property are inherited.

Related Properties

azimuth (374), cue (413), cue-after (414), cue-before (414), elevation (419), pause (473), pause-after (474), pause-before (475), pitch (476), pitch-range (476), play-during (477), speak (482), speak-numeral (484), speak-punctuation (484), speech-rate (485), stress (486), voice-family (495), volume (496)

:right
Right Page

Purpose

Sets a unique style for the right-page boxes of a document.

Syntax

```
@page :right { properties }
```

Where

- @page indicates that page-box characteristics will follow.
- *properties* are CSS2 properties.

Notes

- This pseudo-class originated in CSS2.
- The :left and :right pseudo-classes enable a page designer to specify separate styles for left and right pages.
- Browsers automatically grade pages as left or right.

right
Right Offset

Purpose

Controls the location of the right edge of a box from the right edge of the block that contains the box.

Syntax

right: *length* | *percent*% | auto | inherit

Where

- *length* is a positive or negative value followed by a two-letter abbreviation representing the unit of measure.
- *percent* is a positive or negative value that is relative to the size of the image. Follow *percent* with a percentage sign (%).
- auto is a keyword that represents a value automatically calculated by the user's browser. This is the default.
- inherit is a keyword that indicates that this property takes the same computed value as its parent.

Notes

- This property, which originated in CSS2, applies to elements that are positioned.
- This property sets the absolute position of the current box, in pixels, as a percentage of the original size, or by calculating its width automatically, in respect to the block that contains the box.
- Valid relative units of measure are em (the height of the current font), ex (the height of the letter x in the current font), and px (pixels, relative to the size of the window). Valid absolute units of measure are in (inches), cm (centimeters), mm (millimeters), pt (points), and pc (picas).
- By default, the characteristics of this property are not inherited.

Related Properties

bottom (406), left (440), position (478), top (492)

size
Page-Box Size

Purpose

Sets the dimensions and orientation of a page box.

Syntax

size: *w_length* | *h_length* | auto | portrait | landscape | inherit

Where

- `w_length` is a positive, absolute page-box-width value followed by a two-letter abbreviation representing the unit of measure.
- `h_length` is a positive, absolute page-box-height value followed by a two-letter abbreviation representing the unit of measure.
- `auto` is a keyword that represents a value that automatically matches the sheet on which the page box resides. This relative size is the default.
- `portrait` is a keyword that makes the page-box long and narrow — with the same proportions as a standard letter. This is a relative page-box size.
- `landscape` is a keyword that makes the page-box short and wide — with the same proportions as a standard spreadsheet. This is a relative page-box size.
- `inherit` is a keyword that indicates that this property takes the same computed value as its parent.

Note

- This property originated in CSS2.
- Valid relative units of measure are `em` (the height of the current font), `ex` (the height of the letter x in the current font), and `px` (pixels, relative to the size of the window). Valid absolute units of measure are `in` (inches), `cm` (centimeters), `mm` (millimeters), `pt` (points), and `pc` (picas).

Related Properties

`margin` (446), `margin-bottom` (448), `margin-left` (449), `margin-right` (450), `margin-top` (452), `marks` (454), `orphans` (458), `page` (470), `page-break-after` (470), `page-break-before` (471), `page-break-inside` (472), `widows` (498)

Related At-Rule

`@page` (468)

Related Pseudo-Classes

`:first` (420), `:left` (440), `:right` (480)

speak   Speak?

Purpose

Specifies whether text is spoken.

Syntax

speak: <u>normal</u>|none|spell-out|inherit

Where

- `normal` is a keyword that indicates that the aural browser uses a set of rules to *speak* an element and its child elements.

- `none` is a keyword that indicates that no speaking takes place.
- `spell-out` is a keyword that indicates that the text is spelled out one letter at a time.
- `inherit` is a keyword that indicates that this property takes the same computed value as its parent.

Notes

- This property, which originated in CSS2, applies to all elements.
- By default, the characteristics of this property are inherited. So, if you do not want the current element to be spoken, be sure to turn off any speak characteristics of the parent element.

Related Properties

`azimuth` (374), `cue` (413), `cue-after` (414), `cue-before` (414), `display` (417), `elevation` (419), `pause` (473), `pause-after` (474), `pause-before` (475), `pitch` (476), `pitch-range` (476), `play-during` (477), `richness` (480), `speak-numeral` (484), `speak-punctuation` (484), `speech-rate` (485), `stress` (486), `voice-family` (495), `volume` (496)

speak-header   Speak Table Header

Purpose

Sets table-cell header "speak" characteristics.

Syntax

`speak-header: once|always|inherit`

Where

- `once` is a keyword that indicates that a table header (identified by a table header element such as the XHTML `th` element) is spoken the first time a cell in a particular set of cells is selected.
- `always` is a keyword that indicates that a table header is spoken every time a particular cell is selected.
- `inherit` is a keyword that indicates that this property takes the same computed value as its parent.

Notes

- This property, which originated in CSS2, applies to elements that contain table header information.
- By default, the characteristics of this property are inherited.

Related Properties

`caption-side` (407), `display` (417), `table-layout` (486)

speak-numeral   Speak-Numeral

Purpose
Controls how numerals are spoken in a document.

Syntax
```
speak-numeral: digits | continuous | inherit
```

Where
- `digits` is a keyword that indicates that numerals are spoken one digit at a time (for example, 561 is spoken as *Five Six One*).
- `continuous` is a keyword that indicates that numerals are spoken as a whole(for example, 561 is spoken as *Five Hundred and Sixty-One*). This is the default.
- `inherit` is a keyword that indicates that this property takes the same computed value as its parent.

Notes
- This property, which originated in CSS2, applies to all elements.
- By default, the characteristics of this property are inherited.

Related Properties
`azimuth` (374), `cue` (413), `cue-after` (414), `cue-before` (414), `elevation` (419), `pause` (473), `pause-after` (474), `pause-before` (475), `pitch` (476), `pitch-range` (476), `play-during` (477), `richness` (480), `speak` (482), `speak-punctuation` (484), `speech-rate` (485), `stress` (486), `voice-family` (495), `volume` (496)

speak-punctuation   Speak Punctuation

Purpose
Controls how punctuation is spoken in a document.

Syntax
```
speak-punctuation: code | none | inherit
```

Where
- `code` is a keyword that indicates that punctuation is to be spoken.
- `none` is a keyword that indicates no spoken punctuation but the insertion of pauses to indicate particular types of punctuation. This is the default.
- `inherit` is a keyword that indicates that this property takes the same computed value as its parent.

Notes
- This property, which originated in CSS2, applies to all elements.

Cascading Style Sheet Syntax

- By default, the characteristics of this property are inherited.

Related Properties

azimuth (374), cue (413), cue-after (414), cue-before (414),
elevation (419), pause (473), pause-after (474), pause-before (475),
pitch (476), pitch-range (476), play-during (477), richness (480),
speak (482), speak-numeral (484), speech-rate (485), stress (486),
voice-family (495), volume (496)

speech-rate   Speech Rate

Purpose
Controls the speaking rate.

Syntax

speech-rate: *number* | x-slow | slow | medium | fast | x-fast | faster |
slower | inherit

Where

- *number* represents an absolute rate of speech measured in words per minute.
- x-slow is a keyword that represents a speech rate of 80 words per minute.
- slow is a keyword that represents a speech rate of 120 words per minute.
- medium is a keyword that represents a speech rate of 180 to 200 words per minute. This is the default.
- fast is a keyword that represents a speech rate of 300 words per minute.
- x-fast is a keyword that represents a speech rate of 500 words per minute.
- faster is a keyword that increases the current speech rate by 40 words per minute.
- slower is a keyword that decreases the current speech rate by 40 words per minute.
- inherit is a keyword that indicates that this property takes the same computed value as its parent.

Notes
- This property, which originated in CSS2, applies to all elements.
- By default, the characteristics of this property are inherited.

Related Properties
azimuth (374), cue (413), cue-after (414), cue-before (414),
elevation (419), pause (473), pause-after (474), pause-before (475),
pitch (476), pitch-range (476), play-during (477), richness (480),
speak (482), speak-numeral (484), speak-punctuation (484), stress
(486), voice-family (495), volume (496)

Cascading Style Sheet Syntax

stress
Voice Stress

Purpose

Specifies the highest level of inflection in a voice.

Syntax

```
stress: number | inherit
```

Where

- *number* represents an inflection level. Valid values range from 0 (a low level of inflection) to 100 (a high level). The default value of 50 represents a standard stress level.
- inherit is a keyword that indicates that this property takes the same computed value as its parent.

Notes

- This property, which originated in CSS2, applies to all elements.
- The value of stress varies depending on the selected voice.
- By default, the characteristics of this property are inherited.

Related Properties

azimuth (374), cue (413), cue-after (414), cue-before (414), elevation (419), pause (473), pause-after (474), pause-before (475), pitch (476), pitch-range (476), play-during (477), richness (480), speak (482), speak-numeral (484), speak-punctuation (484), speech-rate (485), voice-family (495), volume (496)

table-layout
Table Width Layout

Purpose

Specifies a layout for the cells, rows, and columns that make up a table.

Syntax

```
table-layout: auto | fixed | inherit
```

Where

- auto is a keyword that represents a value automatically calculated by the user's browser. This is the default.
- fixed is a keyword that indicates that the fixed table layout algorithm is used.
- inherit is a keyword that indicates that this property takes the same computed value as its parent.

Notes

- This property, which originated in CSS2, applies to table and inline-table elements (such as the XHTML table element).

- The `fixed` value usually results in a quickly rendered table.
- By default, the characteristics of this property are not inherited.

Related Properties

`border-collapse` (389), `border-spacing` (399), `caption-side` (407), `display` (417), `empty-cells` (419), `height` (436), `speak-header` (483), `text-align` (487), `vertical-align` (493), `visibility` (494), `width` (498)

text-align   Horizontal Text Alignment

Purpose

Sets the horizontal alignment of selected text.

Syntax

`text-align:` <u>`left`</u>`|right|center|justify|`*`align_string`*
`|inherit`

Where

- `left` aligns text within the element with the left margin.
- `right` aligns text within the element with the right margin.
- `center` centers text within the element between the left and right margins.
- `justify` aligns text within the element with both the left and right margins.
- *align_string* is a string with which table-column cells will align.
- `inherit` is a keyword that indicates that this property takes the same computed value as its parent.

Notes

- This property, which originated in CSS1, applies to block-level elements.
- This property specifies the alignment of text: with the left or right margin, with both left and right margins, or centered between the margins in a block of text.
- If you align elements other than table-column cells with *align_string*, the text direction (`rtl` or `ltr`) determines the alignment.
- The initial alignment value depends on the user's browser and the direction in which the language is displayed.
- By default, the characteristics of this property are inherited.

Related Properties

`letter-spacing` (441), `text-align` (487), `text-decoration` (488), `text-indent` (488), `text-shadow` (489), `text-transform` (491), `vertical-align` (493), `white-space` (497), `word-spacing` (499)

For More Information

Learn about the `text-align` property on page 629 in Chapter 8, "Styling Documents with CSS2."

text-decoration	**Enhance Text**

Purpose

Enhances text with lines or blinking.

Syntax

```
text-decoration: none| ([underline][overline]
  [line-through][blink]) |inherit
```

Where

- none does not decorate the selected text. This is the default.
- underline underlines the selected text.
- overline draws a line over the selected text.
- line-through strikes through the selected text.
- blink turns the display of selected text on and off.
- inherit is a keyword that indicates that this property takes the same computed value as its parent.

Notes

- This property, which originated in CSS1, applies to all elements.
- By default, the characteristics of this property are not inherited. However, the children of the current elements should have the same text-decoration properties.
- Browsers are not required to support the blink value.

Related Properties

letter-spacing (441), text-align (487), text-indent (488), text-shadow (489), text-transform (491), white-space (497), word-spacing (449)

For More Information

Learn about the text-decoration property on page 635 in Chapter 8, "Styling Documents with CSS2."

text-indent	**First-Line Indention**

Purpose

Indents the first line of text.

Syntax

```
text-indent: length|percent%|inherit
```

Cascading Style Sheet Syntax

Where

- *length* is a positive or negative value followed by a two-letter abbreviation representing the unit of measure.
- *percent* is a positive or negative value that is relative to the width of the parent element. Follow *percent* with a percentage sign (%).
- inherit is a keyword that indicates that this property takes the same computed value as its parent.

Notes

- This property, which originated in CSS1, applies to block-level elements.
- This property specifies the first-line indention of the text, measured from the left margin (in the default unit of measure) or as a percentage of change from the original indent.
- The default value of text-indent is 0.
- Valid relative units of measure are em (the height of the current font), ex (the height of the letter x in the current font), and px (pixels, relative to the size of the window). Valid absolute units of measure are in (inches), cm (centimeters), mm (millimeters), pt (points), and pc (picas).
- By default, the characteristics of this property are inherited.

Related Properties

letter-spacing (441), text-align (487), text-decoration (488), text-shadow (489), text-transform (491), white-space (497), word-spacing (449)

text-shadow   Text Shadow

Purpose

Applies one or more shadow effects to text.

Syntax

```
text-shadow: none|([ color-name|#rgb|#rrggbb
|rgb(rrr,ggg,bbb)|rgb(rrr%,ggg%,bbb%)][ h_length]
[ v_length][ blur_length],)
([ color-name|#rgb|#rrggbb|rgb(rrr,ggg,bbb)
|rgb(rrr%,ggg%,bbb%)][ h_length][ v_length]
[ blur_length])]|inherit
```

Where

- none is a keyword that indicates no text shadow. This is the default.

- *color-name* specifies a shadow color by valid name (that is, Red (#FF0000), Maroon (#800000), Yellow (#FFFF00), Green (#008000), Lime (#00FF00), Teal (#008080), Olive (#808000), Aqua (#00FFFF), Blue (#0000FF), Navy (#000080), Purple (#800080), Fuchsia (#FF00FF), Black (#000000), Gray (#808080), White (#FFFFFF), and the default, Silver (#C0C0C0)). CSS2 adds the following case-insensitive color keywords: ActiveBorder, ActiveCaption, AppWorkspace, Background, ButtonFace, ButtonHighlight, ButtonShadow, ButtonText, CaptionText, GrayText, Highlight, Highlight Text, InactiveBorder, InactiveCaption, InactiveCaption Text, InfoBackground, InfoText, Menu, MenuText, Scrollbar, ThreeDDarkShadow, ThreeDFace, ThreeDHighlight, Three DLightShadow, ThreeDShadow, Window, WindowFrame, and WindowText. Table R2.2 (379) names the color keywords and lists the affected object for each. You can specify a color before or after length values.
- *#rgb* is a three-digit hexadecimal color code, where *r* represents the red attributes, from 0 to F; *g* represents the green attributes, from 0 to F; and *b* represents the blue attributes, from 0 to F. You can specify a color before or after length values.
- *#rrggbb* is a six-digit hexadecimal color code, where *rr* represents the red attributes, from 00 to FF; *gg* represents the green attributes, from 00 to FF; and *bb* represents the blue attributes, from 00 to FF. You can specify a color before or after length values.
- rgb(*rrr,ggg,bbb*) represents absolute red-green-blue values, each ranging from 000 to 255. You can specify a color before or after length values.
- rgb(*rrr.d%, ggg.e%, bbb.f%*) represents the relative red-green-blue values, each ranging from 0.0% to 100.0%, where 0.0% is equivalent to an absolute value of 000, and 100.0% is equivalent to 255. You can specify a color before or after length values.
- *h_length* is a positive or negative value for the horizontal distance between the shadow and the text. A positive value puts the shadow to the right of the text, and a negative value puts the shadow to the left of the text. Follow the *h_length* value with a two-letter abbreviation representing the unit of measure.
- *v_length* is a positive or negative value for the vertical distance between the shadow and the text. A positive value puts the shadow below the text, and a negative value puts the shadow above the text. Follow the *v_length* value with a two-letter abbreviation representing the unit of measure.
- *blur_length* is a positive or negative value of a blur effect on the shadow. Follow the *blur_length* value with a two-letter abbreviation representing the unit of measure.
- inherit is a keyword that indicates that this property takes the same computed value as its parent.

Notes

- This property, which originated in CSS2, applies to all elements.
- Valid relative units of measure are em (the height of the current font), ex (the height of the letter x in the current font), and px (pixels, relative to the size of the window). Valid absolute units of measure are in (inches), cm (centimeters), mm (millimeters), pt (points), and pc (picas).
- The initial color value is set within the user's browser.
- Consider using text-shadow with the :first-letter and :first-line pseudo-elements.
- By default, the characteristics of this property are not inherited.
- Table R2-1 (376) contains selected hexadecimal color values.

Related Properties

letter-spacing (441), text-align (487), text-decoration (488),
text-indent (488), text-transform (491), white-space (497),
word-spacing (499)

text-transform   Change Case

Purpose

Changes case of the selected text.

Syntax

text-transform: capitalize | uppercase | lowercase
   | none | inherit

Where

- capitalize applies initial uppercase to the selected text.
- uppercase applies all uppercase to the selected text.
- lowercase applies all lowercase to the selected text.
- none turns off the value inherited from the parent. This is the default.
- inherit is a keyword that indicates that this property takes the same computed value as its parent.

Notes

- This property, which originated in CSS1, applies to all elements.
- This property transforms text to initial uppercase, all uppercase, all lowercase, or unchanged for its current case.
- By default, the characteristics of this property are inherited.

Related Properties

letter-spacing (441), text-align (487), text-decoration (488),
text-indent (488), text-shadow (489), white-space (497),
word-spacing (499)

For More Information

Learn about the `text-transform` property on page 635 in Chapter 8, "Styling Documents with CSS2."

top	Top Offset

Purpose

Controls the location of the top edge of a box within the block that contains it.

Syntax

`top: length | percent% | auto | inherit`

Where

- *length* is a positive or negative value followed by a two-letter abbreviation representing the unit of measure.
- *percent* is a positive or negative value that is relative to the size of the image. Follow *percent* with a percentage sign (%).
- `auto` is a keyword that represents a value automatically calculated by the user's browser. This is the default.
- `inherit` is a keyword that indicates that this property takes the same computed value as its parent.

Notes

- This property, which originated in CSS2, applies to elements that are positioned.
- This property sets the absolute position of the current box, in pixels, as a percentage of the original size, or by calculating its width automatically, with respect to the block that contains the box.
- Valid relative units of measure are `em` (the height of the current font), `ex` (the height of the letter x in the current font), and `px` (pixels, relative to the size of the window). Valid absolute units of measure are `in` (inches), `cm` (centimeters), `mm` (millimeters), `pt` (points), and `pc` (picas).
- By default, the characteristics of this property are not inherited.

Related Properties

bottom (406), left (440), position (478), right (481)

unicode-bidi	Unicode Bidirectional

Purpose

Instructs the Unicode bidirectional algorithm to open an additional level of embedding or to create an override for the current element.

Syntax

unicode-bidi: <u>normal</u> | embed | bidi-override | inherit

Where

- **normal** is a keyword that does not open a new embedding level. This is the default.
- **embed** is a keyword that opens a new embedding level for an inline-level element following the value of the **direction** property.
- **bidi-override** is a keyword that overrides reordering for an inline-level element, or an inline-level element nested within a block-level element, following the value of the **direction** property.
- **inherit** is a keyword that indicates that this property takes the same computed value as its parent. Be careful about how you use this keyword for **unicode-bidi**.

Notes

- This property originated in CSS2.
- The **direction** property controls the base direction for the **unicode-bidi** property.
- The **direction** property sets the direction of blocks. If **direction** is to control inline-level elements, the value of **unicode-bidi** must be **embed** or **override**.
- The Unicode algorithm enables 15 levels of embedding.
- By default, the characteristics of this property are not inherited.

Related Property

direction (416)

vertical-align   Vertical Alignment

Purpose

Sets the vertical alignment of the element.

Syntax

vertical-align: <u>baseline</u> | sub | super | top
| text-top | middle | bottom
| text-bottom | *percent%* | *length* | inherit

Where

- **baseline** vertically aligns the element with the baseline of the current element, or the parent element if the current element has no baseline. This is the default.
- **sub** makes the element a subscript.
- **super** makes the element a superscript.
- **top** vertically aligns the top of the element with the top of the highest element on the current line.

- `text-top` vertically aligns the element with the top of the parent element's typeface.
- `middle` vertically aligns the element with the middle of the parent element, computed by starting with the baseline and adding half the x-height of the parent element's typeface.
- `bottom` vertically aligns the bottom of the element with the bottom of the lowest element on the current line.
- `text-bottom` vertically aligns the bottom of the element with the bottom of the parent element's typeface.
- *percent* is a positive value that is relative to the element's height. Follow *percent* with a percentage sign (%).
- *length* is a positive value followed by a two-letter abbreviation representing the unit of measure.
- `inherit` is a keyword that indicates that this property takes the same computed value as its parent.

Notes

- This property, which originated in CSS1, applies to inline-level and table-cell elements.
- This property specifies the vertical alignment of text with the baseline or font, or as a percentage above or below the baseline.
- Using the top or bottom values may result in an inadvertent loop in the display of the element.
- A vertical alignment of a cell aligns that cell within a table row. Values of `sub`, `super`, `text-bottom`, and `text-top` do not apply to the alignment of the contents of table cells.
- Valid relative units of measure are `em` (the height of the current font), `ex` (the height of the letter x in the current font), and `px` (pixels, relative to the size of the window). Valid absolute units of measure are `in` (inches), `cm` (centimeters), `mm` (millimeters), `pt` (points), and `pc` (picas).
- By default, the characteristics of this property are not inherited.

Related Properties

`text-align` (487)

For More Information

Learn about the `vertical-align` property on page 633 in Chapter 8, "Styling Documents with CSS2."

visibility | Visible Box?

Purpose

Specifies whether a box in which an element resides is visible or invisible.

Syntax

`visibility: visible|hidden|collapse|inherit`

Where

- visible is a keyword that indicates that the box is visible.
- hidden is a keyword that indicates that the box is invisible.
- collapse is a keyword that indicates that the box is invisible and may be collapsed.
- inherit is a keyword that indicates that this property takes the same computed value as its parent. This is the default.

Notes

- This property, which originated in CSS2, applies to all elements.
- By default, this property is not inherited.
- There is probably not a way to make visible the child elements of an invisible parent element.

Related Properties

border-collapse (389), border-spacing (399), display (417), empty-cells (419)

:visited   Visited Link

Purpose

Applies styles to a link that has been visited by a user.

Syntax

```
anchor:visited {property}
```

Where

- *anchor* represents the name of a hyperlink anchor.
- *property* represents one or more style-sheet properties.

Notes

- This pseudo-class originated in CSS2.
- The :visited pseudo-class enables you to apply styles to a visited link.
- The :visited pseudo-class is related to the XHTML vlink attribute.
- In CSS1, :active, :link, and :visited were mutually exclusive. Now, you can :active, :link, and :visit a particular element.

Related Pseudo-Classes

:link (442)

voice-family   Voice Family

Purpose

Specifies one or more voices by name, family, or both.

Syntax

```
voice-family: [voice_name_1|male|female|child]
    [,voice_name_2|male|female|child]
    [...,voice_name_n|male|female|child]|inherit
```

Where

- *voice_name* is the name of a specific voice.
- male is a keyword that indicates that a generic male voice will be used.
- female is a keyword that indicates that a generic female voice will be used.
- child is a keyword that indicates that a generic child voice will be used.
- inherit is a keyword that indicates that this property takes the same computed value as its parent.

Notes

- This property, which originated in CSS2, applies to all elements.
- You can choose whether to enclose a specific voice name in quotation marks.
- It is a good idea to end a list of voice families with at least one generic voice. This ensures that a voice family will be defined.
- By default, the characteristics of this property are inherited.

Related Properties

azimuth (374), cue (413), cue-after (414), cue-before (414), elevation (419), pause (473), pause-after (474), pause-before (475), pitch (476), pitch-range (476), play-during (477), richness (480), speak (482), speak-numeral (484), speak-punctuation (484), speech-rate (485), stress (486), volume (496)

volume   Median Waveform Volume

Purpose

Specifies the median volume of a waveform file.

Syntax

```
volume: number|percentage|silent|x-soft|soft|medium
    |loud|x-loud|inherit
```

Where

- *number* represents an audible volume level. Valid values range from 0 (the minimum level) to 100 (the maximum level).
- *percentage* is an audible volume level that is relative to the level inherited from the parent element. Follow *percent* with a percentage sign (%).
- silent is a keyword that represents no volume at all.
- x-soft is a keyword that represents an audible volume level of 0.

- `soft` is a keyword that represents an audible volume level of 25.
- `medium` is a keyword that represents an audible volume level of 50.
- `loud` is a keyword that represents an audible volume level of 75.
- `x-loud` is a keyword that represents an audible volume level of 100.
- `inherit` is a keyword that indicates that this property takes the same computed value as its parent.

Notes

- This property, which originated in CSS2, applies to all elements.
- Because this property specifies the median volume, some volume levels will be either higher or lower than the specified volume.
- Listeners should be able to set volume levels.
- This property adjusts the dynamic range of a waveform file.
- By default, the characteristics of this property are inherited.

Related Properties

`azimuth` (374), `cue` (413), `cue-after` (414), `cue-before` (414), `elevation` (419), `pause` (473), `pause-after` (474), `pause-before` (475), `pitch` (476), `pitch-range` (476), `play-during` (477), `richness` (480), `speak` (482), `speak-numeral` (484), `speak-punctuation` (484), `speech-rate` (485), `stress` (486), `voice-family` (495)

white-space   White Space

Purpose

Turns on or off white space.

Syntax

`white-space:` <u>`normal`</u>`|pre|nowrap|inherit`

Where

- `normal` is a keyword that indicates no addition of white space to an element. This is the default.
- `pre` is a keyword that indicates that the element is treated as preformatted content in the same way that the XHTML `pre` element works.
- `nowrap` is a keyword that indicates no addition of white space and no wrapping of text unless it is controlled by a line-break element (such as XHTML's `br`).
- `inherit` is a keyword that indicates that this property takes the same computed value as its parent.

Notes

- This property, which originated in CSS1, applies to block-level elements.
- This property specifies whether white space is eliminated as in normal XHTML documents or preformatted as in the `pre` element.
- By default, the characteristics of this property are inherited.

Related Properties

letter-spacing (441), text-align (487), text-decoration (488), text-indent (488), text-shadow (489), text-transform (491), word-spacing (499)

For More Information

Learn about the white-space property on page 635 in Chapter 8, "Styling Documents with CSS2."

widows   Widows Paragraph Breaks

Purpose

Specifies the minimum number of paragraph-lines left at the top of a page.

Syntax

widows: *integer* | inherit

Where

- *integer* indicates the minimum paragraph-lines that must remain at the top of a page when a page break is inserted within the first paragraph on a page. The default setting is 2 lines.
- inherit is a keyword that indicates that this property takes the same computed value as its parent.

Notes

- This property, which originated in CSS2, applies to block-level elements.
- By default, the characteristics of this property are inherited.

Related Properties

margin (446), margin-bottom (448), margin-left (449), margin-right (450), margin-top (452), marks (454), orphans (458), page (470), page-break-after (470), page-break-before (471), page-break-inside (472), size (481)

Related At-Rule

@page (468)

Related Pseudo-Classes

:first (420), :left (440), :right (480)

width   Element Width

Purpose

Specifies the width of the selected element.

Syntax

width: *length*│*percent%*│<u>auto</u>│inherit

Where

- *length* is a positive value followed by a two-letter abbreviation representing the unit of measure.
- *percent* is a positive value that is relative to the size of the image. Follow *percent* with a percentage sign (%).
- auto is a keyword that represents a value automatically calculated by the user's browser.
- inherit is a keyword that indicates that this property takes the same computed value as its parent.

Notes

- This property, which originated in CSS1, applies to all elements except selected inline elements and individual or grouped table rows.
- This property sets the width of the selected element, in pixels, as a percentage of the original size, or by calculating its width automatically, scaled proportionately with the height.
- Valid relative units of measure are em (the height of the current font), ex (the height of the letter x in the current font), and px (pixels, relative to the size of the window). Valid absolute units of measure are in (inches), cm (centimeters), mm (millimeters), pt (points), and pc (picas).
- If the element is wider than the width value, the browser will scale the element.
- If the height of the element is equal to auto, the aspect ratio (proportions of the element) is maintained.
- If both the height and width of the element are equal to auto, the browser does not change the element's dimensions.
- By default, the characteristics of this property are not inherited.

Related Properties

height (436), max-height (454), max-width (455), min-height (457), min-width (458)

---

word-spacing   Word Spacing

Purpose

Sets spacing between words.

Syntax

word-spacing: <u>normal</u>│@@ [+│-]*length*│inherit

Where

- normal is a keyword that represents the normal spacing between words.

Cascading Style Sheet Syntax

- *length* is a positive value followed by a two-letter abbreviation representing the unit of measure. *length* is usually an increase in the spacing between words but can be a decrease (a negative value) — depending on the browser.
- inherit is a keyword that indicates that this property takes the same computed value as its parent.

Notes

- This property, which originated in CSS1, applies to all elements.
- Valid relative units of measure are em (the height of the current font), ex (the height of the letter x in the current font), and px (pixels, relative to the size of the window). Valid absolute units of measure are in (inches), cm (centimeters), mm (millimeters), pt (points), and pc (picas).
- By default, the characteristics of this property are inherited.

Related Properties

letter-spacing (441), text-align (487), text-decoration (488), text-indent (488), text-shadow (489), text-transform (491), white-space (497)

For More Information

Learn how to use the word-spacing property on page 499 in Chapter 8, "Styling Documents with CSS2."

z-index   Stack Level

Purpose

Sets the level of the current box in a stack of elements.

Syntax

z-index: <u>auto</u> | *integer* | inherit

Where

- auto is a keyword that represents a value automatically calculated by the user's browser. This is the default.
- *integer* indicates the number of the current box in the stack. If there is no stack for the current box, the value of *integer* is 0.
- inherit is a keyword that indicates that this property takes the same computed value as its parent.

Notes

- This property, which originated in CSS2, applies to elements that are positioned.
- By default, the characteristics of this property are not inherited.

XHTML Tutorial

Part Two introduces XHTML — from the basics to advanced topics. The chapters in this part provide all the information you'll need to design and create robust XHTML documents. You will learn about document structure (elements and extensions, tags, attributes, and entities), content (text, graphics, and links), formats (lists, tables, frames, forms), and styling properties. In addition, you'll find out how to check your documents and declare new XHTML elements and attributes. If you are completely new to XHTML, be sure to read through every chapter and test each example. If you are familiar with XHTML, you can browse the subjects you know to brush up and focus on the topics you want to learn.

IN THIS PART

in plain english in pl
sh in plain english in
glish in plain english
in plain english in pl
sh in plain english in
glish in plain english
in plain english in pl
glish in plain english
in plain english in pl
sh in plain english in
glish in plain english
in plain english in pl
sh in plain english in
glish in plain english
in plain english in pl
lish in plain english
in plain english in pl
sh in plain english in
glish in plain english
in plain english in pl
sh in plain english in
lish in plain english
in plain english in pl
glish in plain english

Introducing XHTML

What is XHTML and how did it come into existence? XHTML, the next generation of HTML, is a markup language used to combine text, graphics, and other multimedia links to parts of the current document, to other documents, and to other objects. *Markup* simply refers to the marks that editors make on manuscripts to be revised. Markup in XHTML documents consists of *elements*, which define chunks of an XHTML document; *attributes*, which format or enhance those chunks; *entities*, which are one or more characters that represent a special character not found usually on your keyboard or are shortcuts to a chunk of text or even an entire document; and *notation*, which are sets of symbols or the characters that make up an alphabet. The non-markup part of an XHTML document is each element's contents — primarily text but also images. To summarize, markup is the instructions to the programs that process and build documents, and character data is everything else in the document.

1

XHTML is a hypertext language. *Hypertext*, which distinguishes XHTML documents from other types of documents, allows a user to connect disconnected chunks of text and multimedia — graphics, animation, audio, and video — into an informal arrangement of information. In essence, using hypertext the user builds a temporary document tailored to his or her own needs.

This chapter provides a brief history of hypertext and places XHTML within the context of its parent markup languages — SGML, HTML, and XML.

The History of Hypertext

The concept of hypertext is more than 50 years old. In July 1945, Vannevar Bush wrote an article for Atlantic Monthly. In "As We May Think," he described a machine for "browsing and making notes in an extensive online text and graphics system."

Theodor Holm Nelson coined the terms hypertext and *hypermedia* (which encompasses both text and multimedia) in 1960. He wrote the book *Computer Lib/Dream Machines* (originally published by Mindful Press in 1974 and reprinted in 1987 by Microsoft Press), which influenced the introduction of the World Wide Web. In the late 1970s, Nelson introduced Project Xanadu, which produced digital library and hypertext publishing systems — another pioneering effort, but unfortunately one that did not reach fruition.

Although universities and other institutions experimented with hypertext during the '60s and '70s, it generally faded into the background until Apple introduced Hypercard in 1987 and Apple and Microsoft developed their Mac and Windows help systems, with which users can click hypertext terms to jump from one topic to another or to open a description box.

The World Wide Web

The World Wide Web demonstrates the true and best nature of hypertext. You can link to most pages on the Web by clicking on hyperlinks on Web pages or by typing in their URLs, or addresses, regardless of the server on which they reside — anywhere in the world. For example, you can start a session on the Web by viewing a document in California, clicking on a link to jump to a document in Australia or Japan, going to the next one in France or Sweden, and so on, until you weave your way around the world several times in just a few minutes. Hypertext, the feature that differentiates the Web from all other Internet resources, allows you to leave the traditional way of reading a series of printed or online pages sequentially, line by line, from top to bottom, and page by page until you reach the end of the document or the end of your attention span, whichever happens first.

The Web is a relatively new part of the Internet. In the late 1980s, researchers at the European Laboratory for Particle Physics (CERN) in Switzerland developed the Web to make their jobs easier; they wanted easy access to research documents networked at their laboratory. Note that these researchers included Tim Berners-Lee, who is regarded as the father of the Web. By 1990, they introduced a text-only browser and developed HTML, and in 1991, they implemented the Web at CERN. They introduced the Web to the Internet community in 1992. Thus started the revolution.

A Short History of Markup Languages

XHTML is just the latest in a series of closely related markup languages, starting with SGML, extending through several generations of HTML and its extensions, and continuing through XML.

SGML

Standard Generalized Markup Language (SGML), the granddaddy of HTML, XML, and XHTML, was made an ISO (International Organization for Standardization) standard in 1986. Because it is a standard, commercial organizations worldwide use SGML for document publishing and distribution. SGML documents can contain text and multimedia elements and can also include headings of all levels, paragraphs, and a few formatted elements. Unlike HTML documents, those written in SGML do not contain formats or enhancements, such as boldface, center alignment, and so on. Each SGML document has an associated *document type definition* (DTD), which defines rules for document contents. DTDs can stand by themselves; for example, each version of HTML has been defined in a DTD.

1

Introducing DTDs

Document type definitions (DTDs) define elements and their characteristics, values, entities, and notation. As the foundation of SGML-related documents, DTDs enable a markup-language developer to create elements that set the structure, content, and format of a document or set of documents. SGML and XML developers either produce new DTDs or use existing DTDs for documents and document sets. Creators of HTML and XHTML documents associate their documents with one of three HTML DTDs (strict, transitional, and frameset), which define all the elements and attributes for a particular version of HTML. You'll learn more about the three XHTML DTDs in the "Reading and Interpreting the XHTML DTD" sidebar (533) in Chapter 2, *Constructing a Basic Document*.

DTDs permit individuals, companies, and departments to set the structure, appearance, and content of various types of documents, ranging from memoranda, letters, and reports to end-user and technical manuals. For example, you can define custom elements to specify a rigid structure (such as an introduction, five chapters, and two appendices for a technical manual) or a more flexible structure (such as a letter's fixed name/address/date and its completely open body section). DTDs also allow the creation of custom markup languages (that is, sets of custom elements) for particular industries and occupations.

To learn more about DTDs, refer to Chapter 2, *Constructing a Basic Document* (515), and Chapter 11, *Customizing XHTML* (673).

HTML

HTML, HyperText Markup Language, has been designed to handle the World Wide Web's hypermedia functionality. Within a simple text document, an HTML writer inserts a predefined element, or command, that describes the document to browsers, search indexes, computers, networks, and people; defines the look of the document; and links one site on the Internet to another. HTML provides elements with which you can define, format, or enhance pages for the Web in the following ways:

- You can select text and change its typeface or font size, or enhance it with boldface, italics, underlines, or strikethroughs.

- You can decorate a document with graphics of all shapes and sizes or use them as image maps a user can click to link to other pages. You can also embed *GIF animations*, which are series of several graphic files incorporated into a single file.

- You can construct fill-out forms, which allow the user to send you mail, answer questionnaires, and even order from your online catalog.

- You can create tables, which allow you to have more control over a document's formats and arrange data in easy-to-understand columns.

- You can specify background colors for an HTML document, entire table, table row, or even a particular table cell.

- You can insert links to other sections of the current document, documents at other sites, audio files, and video files.

- Instead of single pages onscreen, you can use *frames*, which are multiple panes, each of which can display its own HTML document. For example, you can display two small static frames with a site title and table of contents linking to individual pages displayed one at a time in a larger third frame.

●─NOTE───────────────────────────

HTML includes elements and attributes for enhancing and formatting documents. For example, use the FONT element to specify the typeface and font size for selected text or the ALIGN attribute to align selected text or an object on a page. Although styling elements and attributes are still supported in the current HTML standard, new versions of HTML *deprecate* (eventually make obsolete) these elements and attributes in favor of cascading style sheets. For more information about using cascading style sheets, refer to Chapter 8, *Styling Documents with CSS2* (623). In *Part 1: XHTML Reference*, refer to *Cascading Style Sheets in Plain English* (343), *Cascading Style Sheets A to Z* (355), and Section 2, *Cascading Style Sheet Syntax* (371).

HTML has gone through several iterations during its brief lifetime. The first version of HTML, 1.0, appeared in 1990, and an unofficial version, HTML+, was introduced in late 1993. HTML+ features included fill-out forms, tables, and captioned figures, but did not include paragraph formatting or text enhancements. HTML+ contained 78 elements, many of which no longer remain in HTML. Many of the obsolete elements defined document components such as abstracts, notes, and bylines. HTML 2.0, released in 1994, was the first version to have a formal specification and be an official standard (see RFC 1866). This version contained 49 elements. In March 1995, HTML 3.0 appeared. New features included tables, the capability to have text flow around images, the FIG element for inline figures, and mathematical elements. Also included were formatting features, such as horizontal tabs and banners, which remained in place as a user scrolled down or up a page. The NOTE element, which was a feature of HTML+ but had disappeared from HTML 2.0, reappeared. Attributes for the FORM element appeared in this version. HTML 3.0 (and a number of its elements) has expired and is no longer supported.

Introduced in May 1996, HTML 3.2 was regarded as the true successor to HTML 2.0 (in other words, bypassing HTML 3.0). HTML 3.2, which added 19 new elements, kept the tables and text flow attributes from HTML 3.0 and incorporated many Netscape extensions (see the following section).

The 4.0 version of HTML, which was code-named Cougar during its development, has added support for the OBJECT element (225), a powerful image and multimedia embedding element. In addition, HTML 4.0 supports cascading style sheets (see the note earlier in this section), enhancements to fill-out forms and tables, client-side scripting, *internationalization* (that is, recognition of languages made up of special-character alphabets that may be readable in the right-to-left direction), and additional special characters for mathematics and advanced publishing.

●—NOTE————————————————————————

If you are familiar with computer programs, you know that versions are numbered: The first version of a program is 1.0, and the next major versions are usually 2.0, 3.0, and so on. Program developers also use numbers on the right side of the decimal point to indicate minor releases. For example, a version that corrects program errors might be called 2.1 or even 2.01 — if few corrections are necessary. A version that includes a few new features as well as corrections might be called 2.5. At the time of this writing, the current version of HTML is actually 4.01; the developers have made minor corrections (.01) to the major version, HTML 4.0.

Microsoft, Netscape, and WebTV Extensions and Attributes

Starting in HTML 2.0 and continuing to this day, the Microsoft Corporation and the Netscape Communications Corporation (now a subsidiary of America Online) have developed proprietary elements that have been supported by their browsers, Microsoft Internet Explorer and Netscape Navigator. These are known as Microsoft and Netscape extensions. Microsoft developers originated the OBJECT multimedia element (225), frames, and some table elements. Netscape created the FONT (131), CENTER (79), BIG (57), SMALL (268), SUB (281), and SUP (284) elements; frames; and client-side image maps. All of these extensions have been added to HTML. In addition, both Microsoft and Netscape have added new attributes to existing elements.

WebTV Network service is a television-based browser with which you can browse the Internet, access e-mail services, and optionally interact with certain television channels and programs. The WebTV browser supports the elements and attributes of HTML 3.2; the BGSOUND (56), EMBED (123), and MARQUEE (208) Microsoft extensions; and the EMBED, NOBR (219), and NOEMBED (221) Netscape extensions. In addition, WebTV developers have created two unique WebTV extensions: AUDIOSCOPE (45) and BLACKFACE (61).

●—NOTE

It is very important to note that Microsoft, Netscape, WebTV, and other proprietary extensions are not supported by most Web browsers. So, if you want your Web pages to be read by the widest audience, do not incorporate extensions into your documents; just use HTML elements and attributes.

In Section 1, XHTML Syntax (21), Microsoft, Netscape, and WebTV extensions are identified by the ⊖, N, and ⛶ icons preceding the extension name. In addition, you'll find a complete list of extensions in Appendix A, Elements by HTML Version and Activity (689).

XML

The Extensible Markup Language (XML) is a subset of SGML, which means that you can write DTDs to create your own markup languages — with elements and attributes customized for your business, industry, or science. As a subset, XML is composed of many SGML productions, but is much less complex than SGML. After you write a custom language, you can use XML — in the same way that you use HTML — to create documents. Unlike HTML, XML is case-sensitive: A lowercase version of an XML element is completely different from an uppercase version.

You can display XML data within an HTML document and use HTML elements and attributes within an XML document. In fact, XML and HTML documents look very much alike, so you probably will find it easy to make a transition from HTML to XML.

XHTML

XHTML is a hybrid that combines the best of HTML and XML. According to the XHTML 1.0 recommendation, XHTML is "a reformulation of HTML 4 as an XML 1.0 application, and three DTDs corresponding to the ones defined by HTML 4." This means that you can use the well-tested HTML 4.0 language to write your Web documents but can also create custom elements when a document or document set requires it. So, XHTML extends and expands upon HTML. Note that XHTML follows the XML model in that it is case-sensitive.

Comparing HTML, XML, and XHTML Documents

Because HTML, XML, and XHTML are so closely related, there are bound to be ways in which the languages are identical and other ways in which they differ.

The Similarities

HTML, XML, and XHTML documents essentially use the same structure of markup and character data. Once you have learned one of these languages, you are well on your way to understanding another.

HTML, XML, and XHTML all support the Unicode Consortium's Universal Character Set (UCS), which not only includes special characters, including punctuation and mathematical symbols, but also adds foreign-language characters and alphabets, to make all three languages international standards. Note that many browsers and operating systems do not fully support the use of the entire Unicode character set. For more information about using special characters in your XHTML documents, see "Inserting Entities" (526) in Chapter 2, *Constructing a Basic Document*. For a list of supported characters, refer to Appendix B, *Unicode Characters and Character Sets* (697).

HTML, XML, and XHTML support the use of *cascading style sheets*, which help you to define the structure and appearance of an entire large, complex document. However, whereas HTML and XHTML style their own outputs in many ways, XML requires styles for formatted and enhanced output. In addition, XML — as a subset of SGML — goes beyond HTML by supporting the full version of Document Style Semantics and Specification Language (DSSSL). The future style sheet standard for XML will be XML Stylesheet Language (XSL), which is based on DSSSL Online, a subset of DSSSL created specifically for electronic documents. For more information about using cascading style sheets, refer to Chapter 8, *Styling Documents with CSS2* (623). In *Part 1: XHTML Reference*, refer to *Cascading Style Sheets in Plain English* (343), *Cascading Style Sheets A to Z* (355), and *Cascading Style Sheet Syntax* (371).

The Differences

HTML, XML, and XHTML document processing differ. In general, HTML documents are processed by Web browsers, and XML documents are processed by XML parsers. Web browsers are designed to ignore many small errors, such as missing punctuation or invalid construction of statements. Even if an HTML document contains improperly coded markup, the browser will manage to create output — although it might not be formatted correctly. On the other hand, XML documents must follow XML standards stringently. If an XML document is coded badly, the errors may result in an end to processing and a flow of error messages. XHTML documents are processed by up-to-date Web browsers that support XHTML. Because XHTML follows XML rules, you have to be more careful about using correct syntax and proper case. There is a major benefit to this: Your documents will be more likely to endure future maintenance, ranging from major changes to minor edits. As you read through the rest of this tutorial, you'll learn about the specifics of creating stable and accurate XHTML documents.

in plain english in pl
sh in plain english in
glish in plain english
in plain english in pl
sh in plain english in
glish in plain english
in plain english in pl
glish in plain english
in plain english in pl
sh in plain english in
glish in plain english
in plain english in pl
sh in plain english in
glish in plain english
in plain english in pl
lish in plain english
in plain english in pl
sh in plain english in
glish in plain english
in plain english in pl
sh in plain english in
lish in plain english
in plain english in pl
glish in plain english

Constructing a
Basic Document

2

An XHTML document combines character data — text and optional graphics — with markup — elements, attributes, entities, and so on. You can construct an XHTML document any way you wish. Some people write the document first, editing and polishing it as they would any word-processing document. Then they insert the markup to prepare the document for publishing on the Web. Others insert elements and attributes as they write the document. Some authors use word processors to create all types of documents, including XHTML pages. Others prefer to use editors specifically developed to create XHTML documents.

Constructing a page using a word processor or text editor is as simple as creating any other document. Launch the program and start typing elements, attributes, and text. Don't worry about spaces or setting margins, as browsers do not interpret carriage returns and other control characters. When you save the XHTML document, name it, give it a file type of text or ASCII, and make sure that it has an **HTM** or **HTML** extension.

Starting a Document

Because XHTML documents must conform to XML standards, they must meet certain rules set by the XML declaration, the DOCTYPE declaration, and the declaration of the root element. Although the XML declaration isn't required, authors are strongly encouraged to use it. However, the declaration is required if you plan to use character sets other than the default UTF-8 or UTF-16. The XML declaration tells browsers that this is an XML document, and the supported XML version is 1.0. This means that the XML document follows the rules in the XML 1.0 recommendation.

```
<?xml version="1.0"?>
```

The <? and ?> characters simply mark the beginning and end of the statement. XML requires that processors support the UTF-8 and UTF-16 character codes; these are the defaults, so they need not be declared. However, if you want to make active another encoding, you can declare it (for example, the Latin-1 encoding, ISO-8859-1, within the XML declaration):

```
<?xml version="1.0" encoding="ISO-8859-1"?>
```

Although the XML declaration is not required, it is a good idea to include it in all your XHTML documents.

The following statement in the document must declare the document type and refer to one of three DTDs, either at the World Wide Web Consortium (W3C), as in this example, or stored on your own computer:

```
<!DOCTYPE html
   PUBLIC "-//W3C//DTD XHTML 1.0 Strict//EN"
   "DTD/xhtml1-strict.dtd">

<!DOCTYPE html
   PUBLIC "-//W3C//DTD XHTML 1.0 Transitional//EN"
   "DTD/xhtml1-transitional.dtd">

<!DOCTYPE html
   PUBLIC "-//W3C//DTD XHTML 1.0 Frameset//EN"
   "DTD/xhtml1-frameset.dtd">
```

Each of these statements is an XML document type declaration. After the <! delimiter, the statement declares that the document type (DOCTYPE) is html. The keyword PUBLIC indicates that the following file (within the quotation marks) is freely available to the public. W3C represents the World Wide Web Consortium; DTD is the file type; XHTML 1.0 is the current version name and number; Strict, Transitional,

and `Frameset` state the type of DTD; and `EN` represents the language, English. `DTD/xhtml1-name.dtd` refers to the actual DTD. `Strict` refers to a strict version of HTML 4.0: Elements and attributes that have been deprecated and frameset elements are not included. `Transitional` includes all elements and attributes, including those that have been deprecated. As you might guess, the `Frameset` DTD is devoted to framed documents. Each document type declaration ends with the > delimiter.

2

●—**NOTE** ───

Unless you are committed to using framesets, your document type declarations should refer to the Strict DTD. Then, as XHTML evolves, you won't have to worry about editing out the once-deprecated elements that have now been eliminated from new versions of the XHTML standard.

The *root element* is the parent of all other elements — the element within which all other elements are nested. In other words, all non-root elements are child elements of the root. The `html` element is the root element of all XHTML documents. So, the first element in a document must be `<html>`, and the last line must be `</html>`. All other elements — that is, the child elements — are enclosed within `<html>` and `</html>`.

A *namespace* is a collection of valid names usually defined by an organization that oversees a particular computing specialty — although anyone can write a namespace. The `<html>` *start tag* (a start tag indicates the start of an element and its contents) must include the `xmlns` keyword attribute, state the URI of the XHTML namespace, and refer to the default language — in this case, en (which represents English):

```
<html xmlns="http://www.w3.org/1999/xhtml"
    xml:lang="en" lang="en">
```

Note that the use of both the `xml:lang` and `lang` attributes is the *only* valid way of specifying a language code. For a list of language codes and country codes, refer to Appendix C, *Internationalization: Language Codes and Country Codes* (743).

So, the first part of an XHTML document should look something like this:

```
<?xml version="1.0"?>
<!DOCTYPE html
    PUBLIC "-//W3C//DTD XHTML 1.0 Strict//EN"
    "DTD/xhtml1-strict.dtd">
<html xmlns="http://www.w3.org/1999/xhtml"
    xml:lang="en" lang="en">
```

XHTML is a work in progress. Although XHTML 1.0 is an official W3C recommendation, new versions are bound to appear. You'll find the latest version of the XHTML recommendation at `http://www.w3.org/TR/xhtml1`.

2

●─NOTE

XHTML documents that are completely compatible with XML either use the XHTML specification or the XML Document Object Model (DOM) to set the rules for document development. In this case, the Internet media type is either `text/xml` or `application/xml`, which are not supported by older Web browsers. If you wish to gradually evolve from HTML to XML, you can use the HTML specification or DOM as your guide. So, your documents' Internet media type should be `text/html`. This means that HTML browsers — even older ones — can still process your existing documents, although XHTML processors may not — at least without potential errors and warning messages. If you go this route, keep in mind that the W3C has determined that HTML will not advance further, so change your HTML documents to XHTML.

● Word Processors and Text Editors versus XHTML Editors

You can create a document by using a word processor or text editor or by using an XHTML editor. Both have advantages and disadvantages.

- If you use a word processor or text editor, which produces documents of all kinds, you have to remember to include some of the boilerplate statements that XHTML editors automatically include in the HEAD section at the top of an HTML document. However, you are not required to include most boilerplate statements — no matter how you create a document. It's a good idea to include `meta` (216) elements that identify character encodings.

- An XHTML editor, which is tailored to produce XHTML documents, automatically inserts an **HTM** or **HTML** extension when you save a document; a word processor may add a **DOC** extension, and a text editor may add a **TXT** extension. Then you will have to rename the document as an **HTM** or **HTML** document before uploading it to a server.

- A word processor adds hidden formatting codes as you work on a document. When you save a document as a word-processing file, the codes remain. Browsers viewing this file may display some of the formatting codes — an undesirable result. However, saving a document as a text or HTML file automatically strips out the formatting codes.

- If you use an XHTML editor, you can't always easily view the markup in the underlying XHTML code, especially in the HEAD section at the top of the document. So, if you need to edit your document, you might have to make a greater effort to select attributes (such as filling in one or two dialog boxes) rather than overtyping a number or a color name or code in the document itself.

- An XHTML editor will construct statements using the appropriate syntax and the attributes that you have selected. If you use a word processor or text editor, you have to understand how to use the syntax and enter it using XML rules and standards.

- The software publishers that develop XHTML editors want you to upgrade whenever they release a new version. So, they add many functions that make document creation easier. They often provide templates and graphics, spell checkers, thesauruses, and dictionaries.

- For a variety of reasons, many XHTML documents must be edited at the XHTML code level — regardless of the way in which they were originally created. For example, to tailor a page for a particular browser, a page writer could add nonstandard XHTML statements not currently supported by the XHTML editor with which he or she is working. Or, a writer who wants to search for and replace all second-level headings with third-level headings in a document could use a full-featured word processor to perform a one-step search-and-replace-all operation rather than using an XHTML editor, which might allow only a search-and-replace for text shown on-screen.

If you are tempted to use an older HTML editor, be careful. Some legacy HTML editors produce output that looks very little like XHTML.

Building Document Structure

Elements are the basic building blocks of your XHTML document. So, as you build a document, you select elements as declared and directed from one of the three XHTML DTDs. Elements are just the beginning of the markup that you use in your documents. As you add elements, you also add attributes, set attribute values, and insert entities.

Inserting Elements, Start Tags, and End Tags

All XHTML documents contain the root element, html (153), and its child elements (and their child elements) nested within. Child elements must be completely nested within their parent elements; elements should never overlap. When you start a non-empty element, XML rules require that you finish it — each non-empty element must have both a start tag and an end tag. (You'll learn about empty elements in the following section.)

Following is a simple example of element usage. There is a start tag, followed by content, and completed with an end tag.

```
<p>This is one sentence and one paragraph.</p>
```

In the example, `<p>` (238) is a start tag indicating the beginning of a paragraph, and `</p>` is an end tag marking the end of that paragraph. An XHTML paragraph is a block-level element, which starts and ends with a line break.

Browsers and XHTML editors are programmed to know that the less-than (<) symbol marks the beginning of a start or end tag and the greater-than (>) symbol marks the end. In addition, browsers and XHTML editors recognize the slash (/), which distinguishes between a start tag and an end tag. The text within the two symbols (for example, p) is the actual element and attributes on which the browser acts.

●—NOTE

HTML is case-insensitive, which means that you can enter element names using either uppercase or lowercase. However, XML is case-sensitive: A lowercase version of an element (p) is completely different from an uppercase version (P). The XHTML recommendation states that "XHTML documents must use lowercase for all HTML element and attribute names."

So, XHTML elements have both a start tag and an end tag. Non-empty elements use the following format:

```
<start-tag>element-contents</end-tag>
```

In the following example:

```
<title>Chocolate Chip Cookies</title>
```

where:

- < marks the beginning of the start tag
- title (318) is the XHTML element enclosed within the start tag, the command that the browser will interpret
- > marks the completion of the start tag
- *Chocolate Chip Cookies* is the text that will appear in the browser title bar when the page is loaded

- < marks the beginning of the end tag
- /title marks the end of the element, the required end of a title element (the slash (/) symbol is included in all end tags)
- > marks the completion of the end tag.

NOTE

Some HTML and XHTML references and tutorials refer to non-empty elements with required start tags and end tags as containers. In the prior example, the end tag states very clearly that the title text is complete; it is contained within the start tag and end tag. Without the </title> end tag, an HTML browser would treat all following text as part of the title, until it encountered any start tag. An XHTML browser would probably issue a warning message. An XML parser would report an error and stop processing.

Almost all XHTML documents are composed of several generations of elements. One way of ensuring an error-free document is to take care of how parent and child elements are nested. Obviously, this becomes complicated every time you add another layer of elements. Look at the following example of nesting three generations of elements:

```
<p>This is <b>one</b> sentence and <b><i>one</i></b>
paragraph.</p>
```

The / (bold)(46) start and end tags are completely nested within the <p>/</p> (paragraph)(238) tags, and the <i>/</i> (italics)(154) tags are entirely within the second instance of / using the following symmetrical structure:

```
<p>              </p>
   <b>         </b>
      <i>   <i>
```

Headings and Paragraphs

When you create an XHTML document, chances are that you will start it with a heading followed by one or more paragraphs and probably insert another heading and more paragraphs, and so on, until you reach the end of the document. (Of course, you probably will insert images, links, and other page components on the page, too.) Typically, the first heading in a document uses the top-level h1 element:

```
<h1>My Home Page</h1>
<p>Welcome to my home page. Feel free to browse around my
site.</p>
```

Most experienced Web developers would urge you to have just one h1 heading per page. The next heading usually is one level below h1:

```
<h2>About This Site</h2>
<p>This site is made up of four pages: this home page, my
biography, a photo album, and my favorite links.</p>
```

Note that each heading start tag must have a matching end tag. Without the end tag, the heading formats would continue indefinitely. Because XHTML demands start tags and end tags for all non-empty elements, each paragraph must have its own start tag and end tag.

Introducing Extended Backus-Naur Form (EBNF) Notation

The XML 1.0 Recommendation uses Extended Backus-Naur Form (EBNF) notation to define the syntax for declaring element types, lists of attributes, entities, and so on. EBNF defines the standard syntax for DTDs and document markup. DTD notation enables you to specify components, valid values and ranges of values, and the location of particular elements in the hierarchy of declared elements. DTD syntax uses special characters to delimit or connect components. For example, the less-than symbol (<), which also delimits the beginning of start and end tags, marks the beginning of components, such as declarations, start tags, and end tags. Quotation marks (") and single-quote marks (') indicate the beginning and end of strings, and sets of parentheses (( )) group parts of expressions. Sets of brackets ([ ]) group optional ranges of characters or other components. Other characters connect components in various ways. For example, the pipe (|) or comma (,) connects components from which you can choose or specifies the order in which elements can be used. The not symbol (^) precedes grouped characters that are not allowed in a particular instance (for example, to state that certain characters are not permitted as values).

Later in this chapter, you'll learn more about DTDs in the sidebar *Reading and Interpreting the XHTML DTD* (533). In addition, refer to the section "A DTD Primer" (675) in Chapter 11, *Customizing XHTML*. For a complete EBNF reference, which is needed if you want to explore the XML 1.0 specification, see Appendix D, *EBNF Reference* (753).

Using Empty Elements

Empty elements contain no text content; they typically represent future content, such as images, image maps, line breaks, and so forth. It is important to note that empty elements can include attributes, which might mark a particular location in a document or point to a file (such as a picture or a sound file) to be placed in the document.

You can specify empty elements in two ways: You can use start tags and end tags as you would with non-empty elements, or you can use a shortcut form that combines start tags and end tags into a single tag:

```
<br />
```

This empty element consists of a single tag with no attributes. The br element (70) inserts a line break. (Note the space between the element name and the slash.)

In the following example, `<img>`(image) (162) is an empty element with separate start tags and end tags:

```
<img src="goldens.gif">
</img>
```

The `<img>` start tag includes an attribute that refers to a source image file, `goldens.gif`. You can also express this statement in the following shorthand form, which combines the start tag and the end tag:

```
<img src="goldens.gif" />
```

Simply insert the slash (/) immediately before the > delimiter to indicate an end tag. The shorthand version provides an extra advantage: People looking at the document source code will be able to tell immediately that an element is empty.

XHTML contains the following empty elements: area (41), base (49), basefont (51), br (70), col (90), frame (139), hr (149), img (162), input (167), isindex (184), meta (216), param (241), and spacer (271). Empty Microsoft and WebTV extensions are bgsound (56) and embed (123). The empty Netscape extension is embed. The ilayer (160) and layer (194) extensions can be empty but are usually not.

Adding Attributes and Attribute Values

Elements — both non-empty and empty — may add attributes, usually using the following syntax (the first for non-empty elements and the second for empty ones):

```
<start-tag option1="value1"
   option2="value2"></end-tag>
```

or

```
<start-tag option1="value1"
   option2="value2" />
```

The start tag, within the less-than and greater-than symbols, includes all the attributes. The following statement includes two attributes and their values enclosed within quotation marks:

```
<table border width="120" height="80">
```

where:

- `<` marks the beginning of the start tag
- `table` (288) is the element name, which marks the beginning of a table
- `border` (Web) is an attribute that turns on a table border
- `width="120"` (Web) is an attribute that sets the table width to 120 pixels
- `height="80"` (Web) is an attribute that sets the table height to 80 pixels
- `>` marks the completion of the start tag.

NOTE

The required end tag, which completes the definition of the table, is several table rows below the start tag and does not appear in this example.

The prior example demonstrates that attributes are pairs of names (for example, `width`) and values (for example, `"120"`) associated with an element. An attribute adds important information that refines its element. For example, an attribute can format or enhance an element, identify an element to make it unique among other same-name elements, or even name a script to be used when a particular event takes place. As you have learned, you can find attributes in two places in your documents — within start tags and within empty-element tags. Specific attributes work with particular elements, so it's always a good idea to refer to *XHTML Syntax* (21), in Part I when you are using an element and its attributes for the first time.

●—**NOTE** —————————————————————————————

In XHTML, every attribute value must be surrounded by quotation marks or single quotes of the same type. A value that starts with a quotation mark must end with a quotation mark, and a value that starts with a single quote must end with a single quote. When you test a new document and see warning messages or missing attribute values, look for mismatched or absent quotes first.

The following code demonstrates the empty `meta` element (216), which describes properties such as keywords that search engines can use to find the current document, author, creation date, and so on.

```
<meta name="keywords" content="html, html reference,
publishing, computer books, internet books" />
```

The example also shows that you can include so many attributes and attribute values that content is not easily seen, which means that you might want to reformat your code to make the XHTML document easier to read. For example:

```
<meta
    name="keywords"
    content="html, html reference, publishing,
        computer books, internet books" />
```

The above example shows how an element might be formatted. The start tag begins in the one column; each of the attributes is on one or more lines and indented. It is important to note that attribute values must always be enclosed within quotation marks or single quote marks.

For detailed information about XHTML attributes, refer to Appendix E, *Attributes in Depth* (Web).

●—**NOTE** —————————————————————————————

Most HTML browsers ignore elements and attributes that they don't recognize. For example, when you use Microsoft extensions and Netscape extensions that are not included in the HTML 4.0 element set, Microsoft Internet Explorer or Netscape Navigator can interpret the elements and their attributes, but many other browsers can't. Future XHTML browsers probably will not ignore elements and attributes that they don't recognize. So, it is important to test your documents before you post them to your Web site. To learn more about testing documents, refer to Chapter 9, *Testing and Maintaining Documents* (645).

Using Attributes to Style a Document

You have already seen examples of elements (b and i) that apply formatting and enhancement styles to selected text. You can also apply styles using attributes. For example, the deprecated align attribute enables you to align selected text with the left margin or right margin, center the selection within the left and right margins, or justify the selection between the left and right margins. Or, the deprecated bgcolor attribute (for the body (65), table (288), td (297), th (310), and tr (319) elements) sets the background color. Remember that deprecated attributes appear in the Transitional DTD — not the Strict DTD.

You'll notice a trend here. XHTML deprecates most "styling" elements and attributes in favor of cascading style sheets. For more information about using cascading style sheets, refer to Chapter 8, *Styling Documents with CSS2* (623). In *Part 1: XHTML Reference*, refer to *Cascading Style Sheets in Plain English* (343), *Cascading Style Sheets A to Z* (355), and *Cascading Style Sheet Syntax* (371).

Inserting Entities

In Chapter 1, you learned that entities are storage containers for information, ranging from a single character to an entire file. In HTML and XHTML based on one of the predefined HTML DTDs, entities are primarily nicknames for special characters. In XML, these types of entities are known as *general entities*. Use an entity reference to refer to an entity. The syntax for a general entity starts with an ampersand and ends with a semicolon.

In addition to supporting the full set of HTML entities, XHTML supports four reserved entity references: & (which inserts an ampersand (&)), < (for a less-than symbol (<)), > (for a greater-than symbol (>)), and " (which inserts a quotation mark (")). Since all these symbols are used in markup, use the entities — rather than typing the actual characters — to insert the symbols in document text. This prevents errors in document processing.

The following code lists the reserved entity references, each in a separate paragraph:

```
<p>&amp; is an ampersand.</p>
<p>&lt; is a less-than symbol.</p>
<p>&gt; is a greater-than symbol.</p>
<p>&quot; is a quotation mark.</p>
```

Entities are sets of characters from the International Standard ISO 10646-1, or Unicode Standard. So, you can use entities to insert characters that you won't find on your keyboard. For example, you can place accents over letters, as in *résumé*, by using the following code:

```
r&eacute;sum&eacute;
```

The `&eacute;` entity name, which is from the Latin 1 Supplementary character set, inserts an accented *e* into text. Entity names are predefined shortcuts to commonly used characters. Many characters are referred to by entity codes. For example:

```
&#233;
```

is another way of displaying the accented e, *ê*.

To look up particular entity names or codes, refer to Appendix B, *Unicode Characters and Character Sets* (697).

● **NOTE** ─────────────────────────────────────

Parameter entities, a different category of entity, place information into the DTD, at the location of an entity reference. When you write XML DTDs for XML documents and document sets, or to extend the XHTML language, you use parameter entities to insert long names, technical terms, and even separate files into your documents. For example, you can use a three- or four-character word to refer to a long company name or difficult-to-type phrase. Or, in a computer manual or employee handbook, you can use a set of entity references to insert the chapters that make up the book. You can learn more about entities in DTDs in the sidebar *Reading and Interpreting the XHTML DTD* (533), later in this chapter. To learn how to declare entities in DTDs, refer to "Declaring Entities" (684) in Chapter 11, *Customizing XHTML.*

The Contents of an XHTML Document

An XHTML document contains two parts: the HEAD section and the BODY section. This means that the head and body elements are children of the `html` element (153).

The HEAD Section

The HEAD section of an XHTML document, started and ended with the optional `<head>` (148) start tag and `</head>` end tag, describes the document to programs, such as browsers, search indexes, and XHTML validators; to other XHTML documents; and to those who edit the document. HEAD section elements are `title` (318), `isindex` (184), `base` (49), `style` (280), `script` (262), `meta` (216), and `link` (202).

Use the meta element to provide the name of the author, the date on which the document was created, and the last date it was edited. It is important to mention that the meta element can also include a list of keywords that search indexes will use to match keywords that people have entered and to rank your document with other documents on a list (see the example on page 525). Search indexes also use the title element as a document identifier. Some browsers use styles within the style elements (and style attributes within most XHTML elements) to specify document formats. For more information about styling documents, refer to Chapter 8, *Styling Documents with CSS2* (623). In *Part 1: XHTML Reference,* refer to *Cascading Style Sheets in Plain English* (343), *Cascading Style Sheets A to Z* (355), and *Cascading Style Sheet Syntax* (371).

Except for the title, the contents of the HEAD section do not appear when the Web page is loaded. Some detail-oriented people will argue accurately that the title is not on the page; it's above the page in the browser's title bar.

Except for the title, about the only way to see the contents of the HEAD section is to view the document in an XHTML editor, word processor, or text editor. In a typical browser, viewing the source code only shows you the BODY section of the document — not the HEAD section.

The BODY Section

The BODY section of an XHTML document, started and ended with the optional <body> (65) start tag and </body> end tag, contains all the parts of the document that visitors can see, including text, links, and multimedia. It's easy to identify BODY section elements: Simply subtract the HEAD elements (title, isindex, base, style, script, meta, and link) from the rest of the HTML 4.0 or XHTML 1.0 element set, and there you have it.

Commenting a Document

Comments are an important part of HTML, XHTML, and XML documents. Without comments, you, or those maintaining Web pages, might have problems understanding particular lines of code. To insert a comment in an HTML, XHTML, and XML document, enter the <!-- (23) delimiter, type the comment, and end with the --> delimiter:

```
<!-- This comment overflows to a second line, but that's OK
with me and with the browser. -->
```

When a browser displays the body of the document, the comment will not be displayed onscreen. Because double hyphens (--) are reserved in comment delimiters, do not place them within the comment text. This means that comments should never be embedded within other comments. Embedded double hyphens may cause a Web browser or processor to misinterpret the remaining part of a comment.

You can insert comments almost anywhere in a document. However, there are important exceptions. Do not place comments at the very top of the document; the XML declaration must always be the first line in a document. In addition, do not embed comments within tags.

● **NOTE** ──────────────────────────────

As you read through the examples in this book, you'll notice a complete lack of comments. This is not a case of "do as I say, not as I do." It's simply a space-saving maneuver; I'd like to show you as many lines of code as possible.

Adding Links to a Document

Hypertext links mark the major difference between Web documents and plain text files or word-processing documents. In documents without links, readers start at the top of the first page and finish at the bottom of the last page. If they need to look up a word or term, they consult a dictionary or another book. However, when readers browse through Web documents, they learn about some words or terms by clicking them (if they are set up as links). The click activates the link and displays new information from the same document or an entirely different document in the browser window.

Whether a link goes to a spot in the current document or a separate document, its most important attribute is the URI, which gives the absolute or relative address of the target of the link. An *absolute URI* starts with the name of an Internet protocol, such as http:, ftp:, gopher:, file:, mailto:, and so forth, continues with the name of the computer on which the resource is located, and concludes with the file name and extension of the resource. A *relative URI* is a less-than-complete name. For example, if the file is located on your computer, there is no need to furnish the computer name. Instead, the URI may contain a combination of the folder name (if it differs from the current one), the file name and extension (if they differ), and the name of a location within the file. It doesn't matter whether you write an absolute or relative URI: If the link works properly, the URI is valid.

Use the a element to construct an HTML link. A typical HTML link is as follows:

```
<p>Click on <a href="http://www.example.com/">
Example</a> tolink to our home page.</p>
```

In the output document, the link will look something like this:

Click on Example to link to our home page.

You'll find out how to create a link using a graphic in the following section, "Decorating a Document with Multimedia." To learn all about links in HTML, XHTML, and XML, read through Chapter 6, *Linking to Other Resources* (597).

Decorating a Document with Multimedia

Use the a (24), img (162), or object (225) element to insert graphics or multimedia files in an XHTML document. Note the following:

- Always remember that many users access the Web with a slow (14.4 or 28.8) modem or connection to their Internet Service Providers (ISPs). Loading speed is critically important; most users are not willing to wait more than a minute or two.

- To accelerate graphic loading, use the img tag's height (Web) and width (Web) attributes to specify height and width, respectively. Then, the browser knows how much space to reserve for the graphic, and can go ahead and load other parts of the page on-screen. You can also use height and width to scale a graphic as it loads.

- For Microsoft Internet Explorer and Netscape Navigator users only, you can load a low-resolution and high-resolution version of a JPEG graphic file using the img element and the lowsrc (Web) and src (Web) attributes. To load a low-resolution, faster-loading version of a graphic file, use the lowsrc attribute, unique to Internet Explorer and Netscape Navigator. Then load the high-resolution version using the src attribute. The low-resolution version gives the user a chance to get a first look before deciding to stay at your page.

- JPEG files are usually smaller than GIF files, which makes them faster to load.

- One way of getting around having a large graphic in a document is to use a thumbnail version instead. Then, the user can either see the large graphic by clicking a link or can ignore the graphic altogether.

- You can reduce loading time for a graphic file by reducing its number of colors.

- You can reduce loading time for audio and video files by setting a lower sampling frequency.

- The newest browsers have built-in audio and video players. However, users with older browsers must download special audio players or video players, install them, and perhaps configure them before they will operate.

- Downloading or accessing a large multimedia file should be the user's choice. So, either insert a text or graphic link.

- It's a good idea to show the size of a large file before a user commits to loading it or downloading it.

- If you are writing an XHTML document for Microsoft Internet Explorer users only, you can use the bgsound element (56) to play an audio file when a user first visits your site. Choose the sound file carefully; some users will be annoyed by certain tunes, and others will not be willing to wait extra time for the sound file to load.

Supported Multimedia Formats

This section lists supported formats for graphics, audio, and video files.

Graphics Formats

The most used graphics formats are GIF and JPEG. In addition, you can use PNG (Portable Network Graphics), XBM bitmaps (a UNIX graphics standard), and Adobe's Portable Document Format (PDF), which requires the Adobe Acrobat reader.

Chances are you will use graphics in your documents much more than other types of multimedia files. To insert a graphics file into a document, use the img element. For example:

```
<img src="scene.gif">
```

displays the scene.gif file in the Web browser window.

Figure 2-1 shows both graphics as part of a Web document.

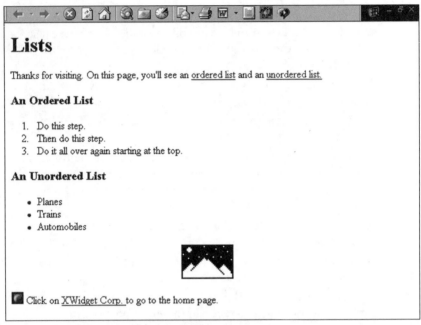

Lists

Thanks for visiting. On this page, you'll see an <u>ordered list</u> and an <u>unordered list.</u>

An Ordered List

1. Do this step.
2. Then do this step.
3. Do it all over again starting at the top.

An Unordered List

- Planes
- Trains
- Automobiles

Click on <u>XWidget Corp.</u> to go to the home page.

Figure 2-1   *Sample XHTML document as viewed in a browser program.*

You can use a graphic file as a link. For example:

```
<a href="http://www.xw.com/">
<img src="button.gif"></a>
Click on <a href="http://www.xw.com/"> XWidget Corp. </a> to
go to the home page.
```

In the example, there are two instances of the a element: one that turns the graphic into a link and another that makes the company name a link.

●─NOTE

Use the `mailto` URI to send a message. For example:

```
<p>Send me a message at <a href="mailto:eddygrp@sover.net">
eddygrp@sover.net</a>.</p>
```

Learning About JPEG and GIF Graphic Formats

The most popular graphic formats for Web pages are JPEG and GIF. Developed by the Joint Photographic Experts Group, JPEG is the best format for photographic 24-bit images, with over 16 million colors possible. JPEG files compress very efficiently and lose very little image quality. However, every time you compress a JPEG file, it loses some of its quality.

GIF files are 8-bit files, which means that they are limited to 256 colors. However, GIFs have some definite advantages. You can make parts of GIF files transparent, so you are not limited to rectangular images. GIF files can be *interlaced*: An image can load onto a page in stages. You can also animate GIF files.

2

Audio Formats   AU is the most commonly used audio format because it has both Windows and Macintosh support. Macintosh supports the AIFF format, and Windows supports both MID (MIDI) and WAV (waveform) files. MPEG (Motion Pictures Expert Group) audio is another valid format.

Video Formats   Popular video formats include MPEG (Motion Pictures Expert Group), QuickTime, and AVI, which is a Windows-only format.

Reading and Interpreting the XHTML DTD

To get the most from XHTML, you should become familiar with its DTDs. In order to do that, you should understand the statements and symbols that make up a DTD. At first, this might seem to be a difficult task, but you'll change your mind once you pick up a few basics. As you know, a DTD contains statements that specify rules for a markup language. The statements declare all the elements, attributes, entities, and so forth that make up the language.

Perhaps the most important piece of a language is the element. An element declaration looks something like the XHTML table element and its child elements, caption, thead, tfoot, tbody, colgroup, col, tr, th, and td:

```
<!ELEMENT table
      (caption?, (col*|colgroup*), thead?, tfoot?,
(tbody+|tr+))>
<!ELEMENT caption  %Inline;>
```

Continued

```
<!ELEMENT thead    (tr)+>
<!ELEMENT tfoot    (tr)+>
<!ELEMENT tbody    (tr)+>
<!ELEMENT colgroup (col)*>
<!ELEMENT col      EMPTY>
<!ELEMENT tr       (th|td)+>
<!ELEMENT th       %Flow;>
<!ELEMENT td       %Flow;>
```

Notice that each element declaration begins with the `<!` delimiter and the `ELEMENT` keyword. Following that is a list of child elements, within parentheses. You'll also find child elements under the `thead`, `tfoot`, `tbody`, `colgroup`, and `tr` elements. Most of these children represent table rows (`tr`) and cells (`th` and `td`).

The EBNF notation uses certain characters to indicate how often an element can be used and in what order: A comma indicates that the listed components must be used in the order in which they appear. This means that the child element used immediately after the `table` element is `caption`. However, a question mark following an element (for example, `caption`) indicates that it is optional and can be used one time only. An asterisk indicates that an element, such as `col` and `colgroup`, can occur an unlimited number of times in a document. A plus sign, such as that following `tbody`, indicates that an element, such as `tbody`, *must* occur one or more times. However, the `tbody` and `tr` elements are divided by a `|`, which indicates that you must choose one of the two.

In the caption declaration, `%Inline;` is a parameter entity (PE), which is a specific entity that occurs in DTDs. Remember that entities are shortcuts. The XHTML DTD is loaded with PEs; without them, the DTD would be hundreds of pages long. The `%Inline;` PE:

```
<!-- %Inline; covers inline or "text-level" elements -->
<!ENTITY % Inline "(#PCDATA | %inline; | %misc;)*">
```

states that inline elements (those that do not cause line breaks before or after) contain either *parsed character data* (`#PCDATA`), which can include characters, other elements, or other entities or four miscellaneous elements (`ins`, `del`, `script`, and `noscript`), which can be either inline or block-level.

Many declarations have associated comments, which start with `--` and end with `-->`. An element declaration ends with the `>` delimiter (see the comment above the example `% Inline` declaration).

Every element in the HTML DTD has a list of attributes. The table element's attributes are as follows:

```
<!ATTLIST table
  %attrs;
  summary     %Text;        #IMPLIED
  width       %Length;      #IMPLIED
  border      %Pixels;      #IMPLIED
  frame       %TFrame;      #IMPLIED
  rules       %TRules;      #IMPLIED
  cellspacing %Length;      #IMPLIED
  cellpadding %Length;      #IMPLIED
  >
```

An attribute list, which begins with the `<!` delimiter and the keyword `ATTLIST` and ends with the `>` delimiter, names the element again. Notice the number of PEs (`%attrs;`, `%Text;`, and so forth). All these PEs are shortcuts that prevent the rapid expansion of the DTD. The `#IMPLIED` keyword indicates that an attribute is optional; you are not required to use it with the element. When you see the `#REQUIRED` keyword next to a particular attribute, you must use that attribute whenever you use the element.

This sidebar just brushes the surface of DTD viewing and development. To learn more, refer to "A DTD Primer" (675) in Chapter 11, *Customizing XHTML*.

Converting an HTML Document to XHTML

An XHTML document is somewhere between HTML and XML. It uses the HTML DTD for its elements, attributes, and other markup objects, but it follows XML rules. Because XHTML follows XML rules, you have to be more careful about using correct syntax, and you have to start an XHTML document differently than the normal HTML document.

A typical HTML document can start with the `<html>` start tag and nothing more, although you are encouraged to include the following document type declaration:

```
<!DOCTYPE HTML PUBLIC "-//W3C//DTD HTML 4.0//EN">
```

However, an XHTML document starts with an XML declaration and document type declaration, and the <html> start tag must include the xmlns keyword attribute, state the URI of the XHTML namespace, and, using both the xml:lang and lang attributes, refer to the default language in which the document is written. (For an example, see the "Starting a Document" section (516) in this chapter.)

Then, go through each line of the document, checking for the following:

- Make sure that each element name and attribute name is changed to all lowercase characters. XML is case-sensitive, so a name expressed in uppercase characters is not the same as the identical name in lowercase.

- In XHTML documents, every start tag for a non-empty element must have a matching end tag. This is not the case in HTML documents.

- HTML empty elements are formatted in the same way as other elements: You do not have the option of combining the start tag and end tag into one. Empty-element tags in XHTML can use the following syntax: <br />. Remember to insert a space immediately before the slash (for example, <img src= "image.gif" />).

- All attribute values must be enclosed within quotation marks or single quotes.

- Do not include line breaks within attribute values.

- All attributes and attribute values must be entered completely; keywords, such as compact or checked, are no longer valid as single keywords. Change the values to compact="compact" and checked="checked", respectively. Other affected attributes are: declare, defer, disabled, ismap, multiple, noresize, noshade, nowrap, readonly, and selected.

- Make sure that the start tags and end tags for every nested element are completely within the parent element's start tags and end tags.

- The name attribute is deprecated in XHTML and will be obsolete in a future version. So, whenever you find an instance of name, make every effort to change to the id attribute, which serves the same purpose in XHTML. Note that the values of both the name and id attributes must be unique in the document in which they are located.

- The script and style elements have a declared content of
#PCDATA, which means that they can include child elements,
other markup, and character data. So, do not enter characters
that indicate markup (for example, <, >,]]>, --, or &) within
the <script>/</script> and <style>/</style> tags. Use entities (such as <, >, or &) instead, use external script
and style documents, or edit the contents of the elements.

- Do not insert more than one isindex (184) element in a HEAD
section. Remember that isindex is deprecated; use the input
(167) element in the BODY section instead.

- If you declare a character encoding in the XML declaration
(for example, encoding= ISO-8859-8), then in the HEAD
section, you should add a meta statement that duplicates
the encoding:

```
<meta http-equiv="Content-type" content='text/xml;
charset="ISO-8859-8"' />
```

After editing the document, test it with an XHTML browser
or processor. Then clean up any errors found and reported during
processing.

A Sample XHTML Document

This section contains a short XHTML document (see Figure 2-1),
which demonstrates the insertion of two lists, a graphic, and two
links — one graphical and one textual.

```
<?xml version="1.0"?>
<!DOCTYPE html
   PUBLIC "-//W3C//DTD XHTML 1.0 Strict//EN"
   "DTD/xhtml1-strict.dtd">
<html xmlns="http://www.w3.org/1999/xhtml"
   xml:lang="EN" lang="EN">
<head>
<title>A Sample XHTML Document</title>
</head>
<body bgcolor="white">
<h1>Lists</h1>
Thanks for visiting. On this page, you'll see an
<a href="http://www.xxx.com/ol">ordered list</a>
and an
<a href="http://www.xxx.com/ul">unordered list.</A>
<h3>An Ordered List</h3>
<ol>
```

```
<li>Do this step.</li>
<li>Then do this step.</li>
<li>Do it all over again starting at the top.</li>
</ol>
<h3>An Unordered List</h3>
<ul>
<li>Planes</li>
<li>Trains</li>
<li>Automobiles</li>
</ul>
<center><img src="scene.gif"></center>
<p><a href="http://www.xw.com/">
<img src="button.gif"></a>
Click on <a href="http://www.xw.com/"> XWidget Corp. </a> to
go to the home page.</p>
</body>
</html>
```

in plain english in pl
sh in plain english in
glish in plain english
in plain english in pl
sh in plain english in
glish in plain english
in plain english in pl
glish in plain english
in plain english in pl
sh in plain english in
glish in plain english
in plain english in pl
sh in plain english in
glish in plain english
in plain english in pl
lish in plain english
in plain english in pl
sh in plain english in
glish in plain english
in plain english in pl
sh in plain english in
lish in plain english
in plain english in pl
glish in plain english

Using Lists in Documents

This chapter discusses the structure and presentation of lists in XHTML documents. The HTML DTD defines four types of lists: ordered (numbered) and unordered (bulleted), which are the most common; definition (glossaries); and simple. The most commonly used lists in XHTML documents are ordered and unordered.

- Each entry in an *ordered list* appears in a specific order and is preceded by a number. Typically, the first item in an ordered list is preceded by the number 1, the second item is preceded by 2, and so on. A good example of an ordered list is a set of instructions, where each step depends on the step prior to it. You can use attributes or style sheet properties to change the number type or the starting number for a particular list. Use style sheet properties to format a list. For more information about ordered lists, refer to the "Constructing an Ordered List" section (543) in this chapter.

- An *unordered list* is a collection of list items that don't have any particular sequence; each entry typically starts with a bullet, which implies that the list items don't have to be read or performed in a particular order. Use attributes or style sheet properties to format a list or to change the bullet type of one item or all the items in a list. For more information about unordered lists, refer to the "Constructing an Unordered List" section (545) in this chapter.

- Instead of the single list items found in ordered and unordered lists, *definition lists* are made up of pairs of items: terms and definitions. The most common type of definition list is a glossary. To learn more about definition lists, see the "Creating a Glossary" section (549) in this chapter.

- *Simple lists*, whose elements (dir (104) and menu (212) are now deprecated, are made up of entries that are not preceded by numbers or bullets. The reason for the deprecation is that you can use style sheets to format simple lists without having to select specific list elements. Simple lists are not covered in this book.

Essentially, any list has the following structure: The beginning of the list is marked with a start tag followed by a number of single or paired list items and, at the conclusion of the list, an end tag. The element that starts and ends the list is a parent element that contains one or more repeating nested single or paired child elements.

Why Use Lists?

The main reason for inserting lists in documents is the predefined and preformatted nature of the list elements and attributes in the XHTML 1.0 DTD. List elements and attributes automatically apply particular formats to individual entries and entire lists. This distinguishes list text from the text in paragraphs before and after the list. So, numbered lists of instructions or product features are conspicuous on a Web page.

A specific list's bullets, numbers, text enhancements, and alignments have been defined for the page developer, which saves planning and design time and effort. For example, in a definition list, the developer doesn't have to left-align each term and indent each definition in a particular way; the dt and dd elements include alignment and indention, respectively.

Ordered Lists Versus Unordered Lists

The most commonly used lists — ordered and unordered — contain list items enclosed within start tags and end tags: The document developer enters one list item, followed by the next one, and so forth, in the order in which he or she wants them to appear onscreen or on the page. The true difference between ordered and unordered lists is whether the order of list items really matters. For example, if you are setting up a program or installing a computer peripheral, order can be quite important: You must insert a CD before you can access its contents or execute the installation program, or you probably have to install and set up software before attaching the device to your computer. On the other hand, if you are shopping for groceries or writing a list of Saturday chores, the first item on your list could just as well be your last.

Constructing an Ordered List

To mark an ordered list in an HTML document, use the ol (230) element: Begin with the <ol> start tag and end with the </ol> end tag. Use the li (198) element to specify individual list items: Begin each entry on the list with the <li> start tag and complete it with the </li> end tag.

Create a standard ordered list as follows:

```
<ol>
    <li>Open garage door.</li>
    <li>Clean garage.</li>
    <li>Paint garage floor.</li>
    <li>Wait for paint to dry.</li>
    <li>Drive car into garage.</li>
    <li>Close garage door.</li>
</ol>
```

When the browser processes the list, it precedes each list item with a number, as shown in Figure 3-1.

You can either use an attribute or style sheet property to change the type of the number that precedes all items on a list or individual list items. The deprecated type (Web) attribute sets the type for the list (under the ol element) or list item (the li element). The type attribute enables you to select a number type of 1, a, A, i, or I. For example:

```
<ol type="A">
```

or

```
<ol type="1">
```

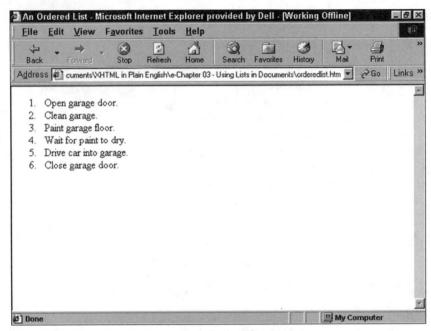

Figure 3-1 *An ordered list composed of six list items.*

The default is 1, which represents the standard (1, 2, 3, and so forth) numbering system. The a and A values assign lowercase or uppercase alphabetic characters, respectively. The i and I values assign lowercase or uppercase Roman numerals, respectively.

You can explicitly state the starting number for a particular item by using the start (Web) attribute, which is also deprecated:

```
<ol start="5">
```

Obviously, the default starting number is 1 (or the starting number of its number type counterpart). But, think of a numbered list that is interrupted by a paragraph of narrative. You may have had to close the list with an end tag, but when you resume the list, you want to have the latitude of setting the starting number yourself. You also can set the sequence number for a list item using the value (Web) attribute.

Note that you can use the list-style (443), list-style-image (444), list-style-position (444), and list-style-type (445) cascading-style-sheet properties to style a list. However, these properties are not supported by all browsers. For more information about using cascading style sheets, refer to Chapter 8, *Styling Documents with CSS2* (623).

In HTML, you can use the value of attributes — such as class (Web) and id (Web) — to identify one or several elements for special treatment. For example, you can format a class of ordered lists or an ordered list with a particular identifier in a different way from all the other ordered lists in a document. The class attribute specifies one or more classifications for its element, and id gives a unique name that identifies its element.

Constructing an Unordered List

To mark the beginning and end of an unordered list in an HTML document, use the ul (331) element: Start with the <ul> start tag, use the <li> and </li> tags to start and end individual list items, and conclude with the </ul> end tag.

Code a typical unordered list as follows:

```
<ul>
    <li>Clean dining room.</li>
    <li>Fix kitchen sink.</li>
    <li>Prepare three casseroles.</li>
    <li>Bake a cake.</li>
    <li>Clean garage.</li>
    <li>Sweep basement floor.</li>
    <li>Buy candles.</li>
    <li>Replace bathroom faucet gasket.</li>
</ul>
```

When the browser processes the list, it precedes each list item with a bullet (see Figure 3-2).

The ul element has its own version of the type attribute. However, instead of specifying the number type as it does for the ol element, the type attribute under the ul element determines the bullet style: disc, square, or circle. To use the type attribute for an unordered list, include the attribute in the start tag:

```
<ul type="disc">
```

The disc type is a filled circle, the square type is a filled square, and the circle type is an unfilled circle. For information about replacing bullets with small graphics, refer to the "Formatting Lists" section (551) at the end of this chapter.

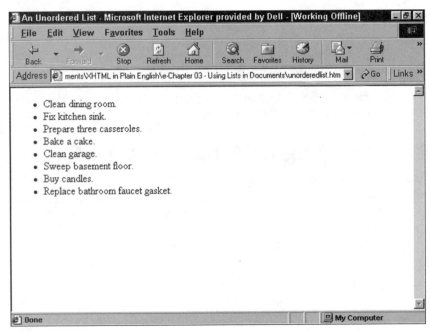

Figure 3-2 *An unordered list.*

Since items on an unordered list are preceded by bullets, there is no need for a `start` attribute for the `ul` element.

Remember that the preferred method of styling lists is to use the `list-style` (443), `list-style-image` (444), `list-style-position` (444), and `list-style-type` (445) cascading-style-sheet properties. For more information about using cascading style sheets, refer to Chapter 8, *Styling Documents with CSS2* (623).

Nesting Lists

You can embed one list within another: ordered within ordered or unordered, and unordered within unordered or ordered. In fact, you can nest several layers of ordered lists and unordered lists in any imaginable combination.

Nesting a list in HTML is easy to do. Simply place an entire list *completely* within the start tags and end tags of another list. (It is important to reiterate that you cannot overlap elements in XHTML documents, so one entire list must be completely embedded within another.)

●—NOTE———————————————————————————

A definition list (dl) is actually a type of nested list with two child elements: the term (dt) and the description (dd). Within each definition list are one or more pairs of terms and descriptions. For more information about definition lists, refer to the following section, "Creating a Glossary" (549).

Note the following ordered list, which contains an unordered list:

```
<ol>
    <li>Unwrap the CD-ROM.</li>
    <li>Insert the CD-ROM into the carousel.</li>
    <ul>
        <li>Your player must be turned on.</li>
        <li>Preset the volume to 3.</li>
    </ul>
    <li>Press the Play button.</li>
    <li>Sit back and listen.</li>
</ol>
```

In this example (see Figure 3-3), the bullets emphasize important points that can be performed at any time. Note that the unordered list is completely enclosed within the ordered list.

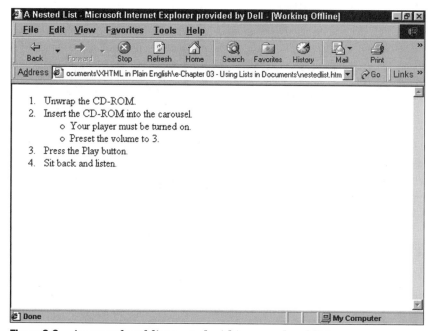

Figure 3-3 *An unordered list nested within an ordered list.*

You can use nested lists to create the outline of a document (see Figure 3-4) using different number types (such as A, 1, a, and so forth) for each level of the outline. For example, look at the following outlined version of Chapter 2 of this book (note that some headings have been shortened so that certain long lines can be indented and not wrap to the next line):

```
<h3>Chapter 2: Constructing a Basic Document</h3>
<ol type="A">
  <li>Starting a Document</li>
  <li>Building Document Structure</li>
    <ol type="1">
      <li>Inserting Elements and Tags</li>
      <li>Using Empty Elements</li>
      <li>Adding Attributes and Attribute Values</li>
        <ol type="a">
          <li>Using Attributes</li>
        </ol>
      <li>Inserting Entities</li>
    </ol>
  <li>The Contents of an XHTML Document</li>
    <ol type="1">
      <li>The HEAD Section</li>
      <li>The BODY Section</li>
    </ol>
  <li>Commenting a Document</li>
  <li>Adding Links to a Document</li>
  <li>Decorating a Document with Multimedia</li>
    <ol type="1">
      <li>Supported Multimedia Formats</li>
        <ol type="a">
          <li>Graphics Formats</li>
          <li>Audio Formats</li>
          <li>Video Formats</li>
        </ol>
    </ol>
  <li>Converting an HTML Document to XHTML</li>
  <li>A Sample XHTML Document</li>
</ol>
```

This segment of the book outline includes several nested lists — in three levels.

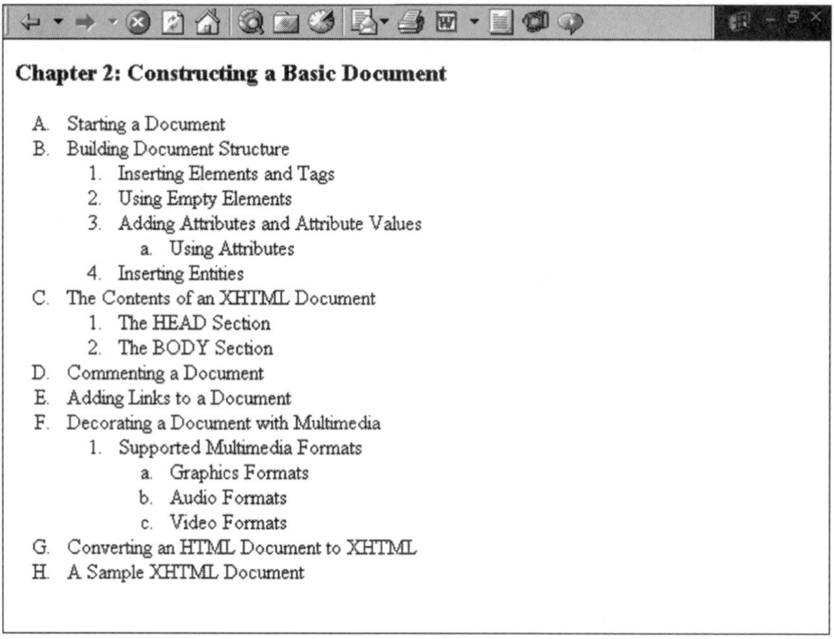

Chapter 2: Constructing a Basic Document

A. Starting a Document
B. Building Document Structure
    1. Inserting Elements and Tags
    2. Using Empty Elements
    3. Adding Attributes and Attribute Values
        a. Using Attributes
    4. Inserting Entities
C. The Contents of an XHTML Document
    1. The HEAD Section
    2. The BODY Section
D. Commenting a Document
E. Adding Links to a Document
F. Decorating a Document with Multimedia
    1. Supported Multimedia Formats
        a. Graphics Formats
        b. Audio Formats
        c. Video Formats
G. Converting an HTML Document to XHTML
H. A Sample XHTML Document

Figure 3-4   *An outline of this book's Chapter 2.*

● **NOTE** ───────────────────────────

The best way to format complicated XHTML statements, such as those that embed child elements within parent elements, is to indent lines in order to show the nesting. Indenting can show you whether your code will be correct and can save you from error messages. The prior example shows three levels of nesting with list items (<li>/</li>) slightly indented under <ol>/</ol> tags.

Creating a Glossary

Definition lists contain pairs of nested list items: terms and definitions embedded within definition-list start tags and end tags. To mark a definition list in an HTML document, begin with the <dl> start tag and end with the </dl> end tag. Use the <dt> and </dt> tags to start and end individual definition terms, and the <dd> and </dd> tags to start and end individual definition descriptions. The dt element left-aligns each definition term, and the dd element indents each definition description from the left margin. Note that each definition term *must* be paired with a definition description. Finally, close the list with the `</dl>` end tag. A glossary, such as the one (759) in this book, is the most common example of a definition list.

A typical definition list looks something like this:

```
<dl>
<dt>acquaintance</dt>
<dd>a person whom we know well enough to borrow from but not
well enough to lend to. A degree of friendship called slight
when the object is poor or obscure, and intimate when he is
rich or famous.</dd>
<dt>alliance</dt>
<dd>in international politics, the union of two thieves who
have their hands so deeply inserted into each other's pocket
that they cannot safely plunder a third.</dd>
<dt>bore</dt>
<dd>a person who talks when you wish him to listen.</dd>
<dt>destiny</dt>
<dd>a tyrant's excuse for crime and a fool's excuse for
failure.</dd>
</dl>
```

The example contains four definitions from *The Devil's Dictionary*, by Ambrose Bierce. Figure 3-5 shows the definition list.

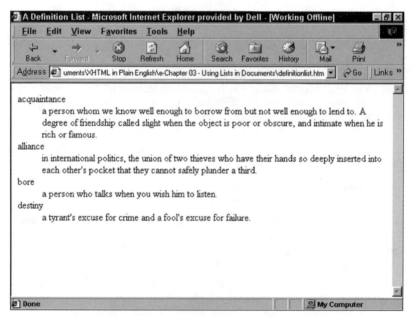

Figure 3-5 *A definition list from Ambrose Bierce's* **The Devil's Dictionary.**

The actual appearance of a definition list depends on the browser that processes the document.

Formatting Lists

The visual difference between XHTML lists and standard paragraph text essentially comes down to that of formatting: Items on ordered lists are preceded by numbers, those on unordered lists are preceded by bullets, and definition lists contain definition terms in boldface and definition descriptions indented from the left margin.

Because of the predefined DTD, you cannot easily modify lists in HTML. For example, items on ordered lists are preceded by a number or a letter chosen from five types, and unordered list items are headed by one of three bullet types. The structure of each type of list — including the sizes of breaks before and after each item, distances between numbers or bullets and list-item text, and alignments — is set by default. However, remember that you can change some formats and enhancements by using style sheets, which you will learn about in Chapter 8, *Styling Documents with CSS2* (623).

On the other hand, if you extend XHTML by declaring new list items, the structure and look of your lists can vary, depending on the DTD developer. You can use the basic structure of HTML lists as a guide for XML list elements and attributes. Or, you can declare several sets of list elements that are dedicated to various list formats and designs. For more information about extending XHTML, refer to Chapter 11, *Customizing XHTML* (673).

If you want to insert small graphics in place of unordered list bullets, you can do so. Just be prepared to spend some time and effort on the task. The trick is to simulate a list and to combine graphics and relatively short list items. If list items overflow to multiple lines, you may have an alignment problem. However, you can solve this by attaching a style sheet to set alignment and to add white space between the graphic and the text.

To code an unordered list and to change the bullets to graphics, find or create a bullet graphic and then enter lines similar to the following:

```
<p><img src="blue.gif" /> Do this.</p>
<p><img src="blue.gif" /> Do that before or after.</p>
<p><img src="blue.gif" /> Do this any time.</p>
<p><img src="blue.gif" /> Do this in any order.</p>
```

Figure 3-6 shows the results.

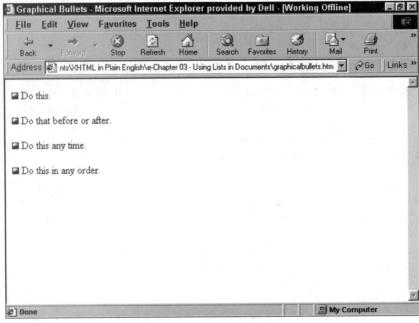

Figure 3-6   *An unordered list with custom bullet graphics.*

By default, images are left-aligned. Make sure that graphics are sized properly — typically no more than about ten pixels square. When you simulate unordered lists and work with custom bullets, be prepared to fine-tune the list, the graphics, and your formats a few times.

in plain english in pl
sh in plain english in
glish in plain english
in plain english in pl
sh in plain english in
glish in plain english
in plain english in pl
glish in plain english
in plain english in pl
sh in plain english in
glish in plain english
in plain english in pl
sh in plain english in
glish in plain english
in plain english in pl
lish in plain english
in plain english in pl
sh in plain english in
glish in plain english
in plain english in pl
sh in plain english in
lish in plain english
in plain english in pl
glish in plain english

Adding Tables to Documents

A table is composed of horizontal rows and vertical columns. The *cells*, which are the intersections of rows and columns, contain the actual data. The spreadsheet is probably the most commonly used table in the computer world. Most spreadsheets are made up of the following components:

- A heading, which is usually bold and a larger point size than the other text in the sheet, usually spreads horizontally across several cells near or at the top row.

- The *column labels*, which are usually boldface or bold-italicized text in a slightly smaller point size than the heading, are the subheadings spread across one or two rows under the heading. Column labels identify the contents of the columns below them.

- The *row labels*, which are usually formatted the same way as the column labels, are the subheadings in one or two leftmost columns. Row labels identify the contents of the rows to their right.

- The actual data is placed in the remaining cells in the sheet — below the column labels and to the right of the row labels.

XHTML tables usually contain the same four components. Use tables to organize and display information, such as monthly or quarterly income and expenses or a set of names and addresses. As you will find out in the "Using Tables for Page Layout" section (574) at the end of the chapter, you can also use tables to lay out your Web pages in a series of invisible grids.

Why Use Tables?

4

The main reason for using tables in documents is to present sets of related information in a concise way. Rather than repeatedly displaying heading and label information in separate paragraphs, as shown below:

```
In the first quarter, the income was $14,000 and the expenses
were $5,000.

In the second quarter, the income was $17,350 and the
expenses were $6,200.

In the third quarter, the income was $18,800 and the expenses
were $7,500.

In the fourth quarter, the income was $21,750 and the
expenses were $8,925.
```

you can display that information once and organize the data within a table, like this:

	Quarter 1	Quarter 2	Quarter 3	Quarter 4
Income	$14,000	$17,350	$18,800	$21,750
Expenses	$5,000	$6,200	$7,500	$8,925

Or like this:

	Income	Expenses
Quarter 1	$14,000	$5,000
Quarter 2	$17,350	$6,200
Quarter 3	$18,800	$7,500
Quarter 4	$21,750	$8,925

The XHTML 1.0 DTD has predefined elements and attributes for tables, table sections, heading cells, and data cells. Table elements and attributes automatically apply particular formats to tables, table rows, and individual cells. This distinguishes tables and their contents from other text on the page.

You can use table-element attributes to format a table and its contents. This means that you don't have to devote time and energy to creating your own designs and formats. For example, in any table, you can change alignments, apply background color, insert padding between cells or between data. And of course, you can style tables and table components using cascading style sheets. For more information about using cascading style sheets, refer to Chapter 8, *Styling Documents with CSS2* (623).

Building Simple Tables

The HTML specification contains five main elements with which you can specify the components of a table. (You'll learn about other table-related elements as this chapter continues.) HTML table elements are *row-centric*: A table is constructed row by row.

- table (288), which defines the entire table, is the root table-creation element; the other four main elements, which are child elements of table, are embedded within the <table> start tag and the </table> end tag.

- The caption (76) element specifies the title of a table — above, below, to the left, or to the right of the table. If you use a caption, which is optional, it must be the first element after the <table> start tag.

- The tr (table row) (319) element defines a single row in the table. So, the contents of a particular row are completely embedded within the <tr> start tag and the </tr> end tag.

- The th (table heading) (310) element defines a single heading cell within a defined row. So, it follows that th is a child element of tr. By default, the contents of a table heading are formatted in boldface. A table-heading cell can appear anywhere in a table.

- The td (table data) (297) element, the non-heading counterpart of th and the other child element of tr, defines a single data cell nested within a table row. Except for the boldface, td is identical to th.

So, a typical XHTML table is coded like this:

```
<table>
  <caption>caption text</caption>
  <tr>
```

```
<th>first header cell contents</th>
<th>second header cell contents</th>
<th>third header cell contents</th>
<th>fourth header cell contents</th>
</tr>
<tr>
<td>first data cell text</td>
<td>second data cell text</td>
<td>third data cell text</td>
<td>fourth data cell text</td>
</tr>
</table>
```

This example contains two rows made up of four columns each. Of course, most tables will be larger than this.

●—**NOTE**—

In your XHTML documents, you can format statements any way you want. For example, you can indent any number of characters from the left margin, omit indentions altogether and start each line at the left margin, place the elements side by side, or start a new line with each start tag or end tag. Simply use a formatting scheme that enables you and future developers to read your table accurately.

Remember that you insert attributes and attribute values within start tags. In XHTML documents, use attributes to change the appearance of an entire table, one or more rows, one or more cells, cell contents, or any combination thereof. As you continue working through this chapter, you'll see many examples of the use of table attributes.

Inserting a Table Caption

As you learned earlier in this chapter, the caption element (76), which is a child of the table element (288), enables you to add a caption above, below, to the left, or to the right of a table. A table caption is not required, but it's a good idea to use a caption to identify the table and its contents. Then, if you wish, you can use the captions to create a table of tables that you can include in your site map. Remember that if you wish to add a caption to a table, the <caption> start tag, its contents, and the </caption> end tag must occur immediately after the <table> start tag. For most browsers, the default position of a caption is above the table. The following table (see the top table in Figure 4-1) allows the browser to set the location of the caption:

```
<table border>
  <caption>A sample caption</caption>
  <tr>
    <th>Word Processing</th>
    <th>Spreadsheets</th>
    <th>Databases</th>
  </tr>
  <tr>
    <td>125</td>
    <td>8</td>
    <td>6</td>
  </tr>
</table>
```

●─NOTE───────────────────────────────

Without the `border` attribute, the borders around a table and its cells are invisible. Sometimes this is necessary (for example, when you use a table as a grid for page layout). However, to indicate the dividing lines between rows and columns, be sure to include `border` with the `<table>` start tag:

```
<table border="1">
```

When you add the `align` attribute (Web) to the `<caption>` start tag, you can set a particular caption location. For example:

```
<table>
  <caption align="bottom">A sample caption</caption>
  <tr>
    <th>Word Processing</th>
    <th>Spreadsheets</th>
    <th>Databases</th>
  </tr>
  <tr>
    <td>125</td>
    <td>8</td>
    <td>6</td>
  </tr>
</table>
```

Notice what happens when you omit the `border` attribute (Web) from the table (see the second table in Figure 4-1).

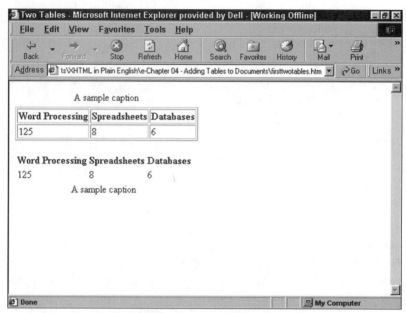

Figure 4-1   *Two tables showing the default caption location and a specified caption position.*

Adding Table Rows

After you start a table and optionally define a table caption, the natural thing is to start adding rows and to define the cells within the rows. Figure 4-1 shows two examples of a table composed of two rows, each with three cells. In other words, the table contains two rows and three columns.

To insert a row, start with the table-row (<tr>) start tag (319), specify individual cells, and complete the row with the </tr> end tag. For example:

```
<tr>
    <th>Word Processing</th>
    <th>Spreadsheets</th>
    <th>Databases</th>
</tr>
```

is one row with three cells.

Creating Table Heading Cells

Within each row, you have the option of inserting table heading cells and table data cells. You can use heading cells to contain heading information such as column labels and row labels. Any cell in a table can be a table-heading cell.

To define a table-heading cell in a row, start with the table-heading (<th>) start tag (310), insert cell contents, and conclude with the </th> end tag. In Figure 4-1, **Word Processing**, **Spreadsheets**, and **Databases**, which are the contents of table-heading cells, are column labels for the table data in the following row.

Setting Table Data Cells

Most XHTML tables contain many more table-data cells than table-heading cells. The following example (see the top table in Figure 4-2) shows the XHTML version of the first table in this chapter.

```
<table border="4">
  <caption>Your first table</caption>
  <tr>
    <td></td>
    <th>Quarter 1</th>
    <th>Quarter 2</th>
    <th>Quarter 3</th>
    <th>Quarter 4</th>
  </tr>
  <tr>
    <th>Income</th>
    <td>$14,000</td>
    <td>$17,350</td>
    <td>$18,800</td>
    <td>$21,750</td>
  </tr>
  <tr>
    <th>Expenses</th>
    <td>$5,000</td>
    <td>$6,200</td>
    <td>$7,500</td>
    <td>$8,925</td>
  </tr>
</table>
```

The <th> and </th> tags mark the cells that contain column and row labels, and the <td> and </td> tags mark the cells that hold the data. Notice that the <table> start tag contains a 4-pixel wide border definition.

```
<table border width="260" height="120">
  <tr>
    <td></td>
```

```
      <th>Quarter 1</th>
      <th>Quarter 2</th>
      <th>Quarter 3</th>
      <th>Quarter 4</th>
    </tr>
    <tr>
      <th>Income</th>
      <td>$14,000</td>
      <td>$17,350</td>
      <td>$18,800</td>
      <td>$21,750</td>
    </tr>
    <tr>
      <th>Expenses</th>
      <td>$5,000</td>
      <td>$6,200</td>
      <td>$7,500</td>
      <td>$8,925</td>
    </tr>
  </table>
```

Now, the <table> start tag includes specific measurements for width and height. (See the bottom table in Figure 4-2.)

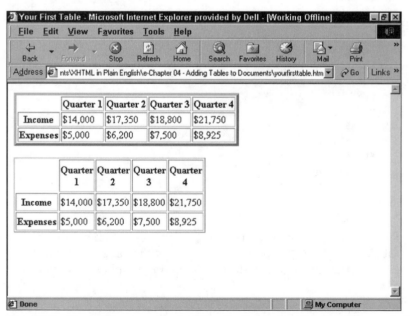

Figure 4-2 *Two tables composed of identical data but having different looks.*

Spanning Rows and Columns

As you create more complex tables, use the colspan (Web) and rowspan (Web) attributes to combine selected table-header cells or table-data cells by columns and rows, respectively. As cells are joined, borders between the cells are erased and cell contents are extended from the left margin toward the right margin column-wise, or from the top margin toward the bottom margin row-wise.

The value given to each of these attributes specifies the number of cells to be united; the default value is 1. For example, if colspan="3", the current cell is consolidated with the two cells immediately to the right. And, if rowspan="4", the current cell is consolidated with the four cells below it. If colspan="0", the span extends through the remaining columns in the table; if rowspan="0", the span extends through the remaining rows in the table.

The main reason for using the colspan and rowspan attributes is to improve the look of a table. In the following example (see Figure 4-3), which is based on an example in the HTML 4.0 specification, the heading *Average* applies to both the subheadings: *height* and *weight*. Because the heading is comprised of a main heading (*Average*) and two subheadings (*height* and *weight*), it takes up two rows. So, the left-most empty area must explicitly encompass two rows. Then, rather than have *Average* appear twice — over *height* and *weight* — you can use a single instance of the term, which spans two columns. To balance the table further, the final heading, *Red eyes*, breaks into two one-word lines (that is, rows).

```
<table border="1">
  <caption align="bottom">
    <em>A test table with merged cells</em>
  </caption>
  <tr>
    <th rowspan="2"></th>
    <th colspan="2">Average</th>
    <th rowspan="2">Red<br>eyes</th>
  </tr>
  <tr>
    <th>height</th>
    <th>weight</th>
  </tr>
  <tr>
    <th>Males</th>
    <td>1.9</td>
    <td>0.003</td>
    <td>40%</td>
```

```
    </tr>
    <tr>
      <th>Females</th>
      <td>1.7</td>
      <td>0.002</td>
      <td>43%</td>
    </tr>
</table>
```

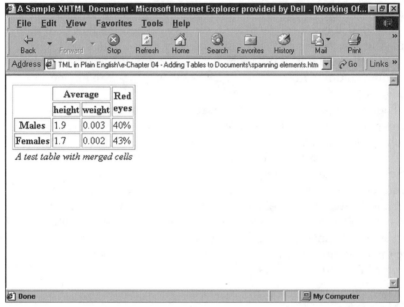

Figure 4-3 *A table that demonstrates the use of the rowspan and colspan attributes.*

● **NOTE** ─────────────────────────────────

If you forget to remove cell contents from rows and columns affected by rowspan and colspan settings, you may inadvertently change the dimensions of the table. You'll probably increase the row width or column height because you have forgotten to remove extra `<td>/</td>` or `<th>/</th>` tag pairs. One way to handle this is to change your table one step at a time, viewing the effects after each modification and correcting mistakes before you continue to the next change. Another solution is to format the statements making up the table: Place each table cell in a row on a separate line, with the entire set indented within its `<tr>` start tag and `</tr>` end tag. Then it is easy to count each cell in a set and discover any discrepancies in the count with other rows. Yet another fix is to draw the table with pencil and paper and either check the existing code or recode the table.

Constructing Table Sections

Earlier in this chapter, you learned that tables are made up of rows with embedded cells. Typically, the contents of each cell in the top row label the columns, and the contents of the cells in the leftmost column label the rows. To divide a table into heading cells and data cells, use the th and td elements, respectively.

You can break a table into sections in other ways — in a table head, table foot, and one or more table bodies, using the thead (315), tfoot (307), and tbody (293) elements respectively. Simply mark the beginning of a table section with a start tag and conclude the section with an end tag.

You can also separate a table into individual columns and column groups, or both using the col (90) and colgroup (92) elements. The col element groups attributes for one or more columns but does not set a column group. Note that the col element is empty, which means that it has no content. However, empty elements such as col can have attributes. In fact, this is the sole purpose of col. The colgroup element defines an explicit column group. If a table does not include one or more explicitly defined column groups, the entire table is a single column group. Note that many browsers do not support the colgroup element.

The following table, as shown in Figure 4-4, demonstrates the thead, tbody, tfoot, col, and colgroup elements.

```
<table border="1" bgcolor="white" width="550">
  <thead valign="middle" bgcolor="yellow">
    <tr>
      <th></th>
      <th>Income</th>
      <th>Expenses</th>
    </tr>
  </thead>
  <tbody valign="bottom">
    <colgroup align="left" />
    <colgroup span="2" align="right" />
    <tr>
      <th>Quarter 1</th>
      <td>800</td>
      <td>784</td>
    </tr>
    <tr>
      <th>Quarter 2</th>
      <td>1000</td>
      <td>1150</td>
    </tr>
```

```
       <tr>
         <th>Quarter 3</th>
         <td>1200</td>
         <td>975</td>
       </tr>
       <tr>
         <th>Quarter 4</th>
         <td>1300</td>
         <td>1230</td>
       </tr>
     </tbody>
   <tfoot valign="baseline">
       <col>
       <tr>
         <td></td>
         <td colspan="2" align="center">
           <font size="2">
             <i>These are preliminary figures.</i>
           </font>
         </td>
       </tr>
     </col>
   </tfoot>
 </table>
```

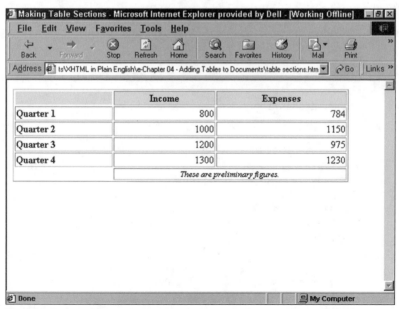

Figure 4-4   *A table with thead, tbody, and tfoot rows and thead, tfoot, and tbody sections.*

Decorating a Table

XHTML provides many ways to enhance the look of a table — including the alignment of cell contents; inserting or omitting table and cell borders; adding space between cell borders and cell contents; using colors for entire tables, borders, and cells; and much more. This section demonstrates the use of attributes to change the appearance of tables and their contents.

●─NOTE

> Keep in mind that many styling attributes have been deprecated in favor of style-sheet properties. For example, most alignment attributes have been deprecated in the HTML 4.0 recommendation. So, rather than use an alignment attribute, seriously consider using a style-sheet property to align a table or its contents. For more information about using cascading style sheets in your XHTML documents, refer to Chapter 8, Styling Documents with CSS2 (623).

Aligning Table Contents

You can align cell contents horizontally or vertically. Use the `align` attribute (Web) for left-to-right alignment, and use `valign` (Web) for top-to-bottom alignment. The following table (see the top table in Figure 4-5) illustrates left, center, and right alignment. (The `width` attribute (Web) ensures that the table is wide enough to display these alignments properly.)

```
<table border width="120" height="120">
  <tr>
    <th colspan="3">Files</th>
  </tr>
  <tr>
    <th>Word Processing</th>
    <th>Spreadsheets</th>
    <th>Databases</th>
  </tr>
  <tr>
    <td align="left">125</td>
    <td align="center">8</td>
    <td align="right">6</td>
  </tr>
</table>
```

The following table (see the bottom table in Figure 4-5) demonstrates top, middle, bottom, and baseline alignment. Use the height attribute (Web) to increase table height and exaggerate vertical alignment.

```
<table border height="180">
  <tr>
    <th>Word Processing</th>
    <th>Spreadsheets</th>
    <th>Databases</th>
    <th>Presentations</th>
  </tr>
  <tr>
    <td valign="top">125</td>
    <td valign="middle">8</td>
    <td valign="bottom">6</td>
    <td valign="baseline">12</td>
  </tr>
</table>
```

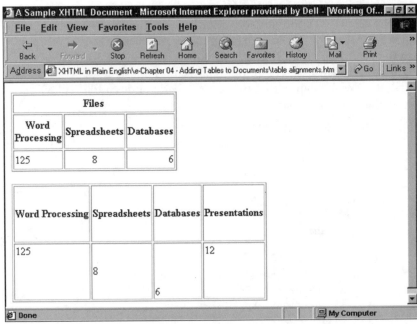

Figure 4-5 *Examples of horizontal and vertical alignment.*

Using Cell Spacing and Cell Padding

The cellspacing attribute (Web) sets spacing, in pixels or as a percentage, between all the cells in the table, including those adjacent to the table frame. Setting cellspacing usually makes the cell and table borders wider than the default. It's a good idea to set the cellpadding value before specifying the table or column width. The following table (see the top table in Figure 4-6) shows the results of setting cellspacing to 8 pixels.

```
<table border cellspacing="8">
  <tr>
    <th>Word Processing</th>
    <th>Spreadsheets</th>
    <th>Databases</th>
  </tr>
  <tr>
    <td>125</td>
    <td>8</td>
    <td>6</td>
  </tr>
</table>
```

The cellpadding attribute (Web) sets spacing, in pixels or as a percentage, between cell borders and the cell contents. So, cellpadding usually surrounds cell contents with additional white space. It's a good idea to set cellpadding (Web) values before specifying the table or column width. The following table (see the bottom table in Figure 4-6) demonstrates a cellpadding value of 10 pixels. Notice that the column labels and data are further away from the left margin of the cells, and the labels are indented from the right margin.

```
<table border cellpadding="10">
  <tr>
    <th>Word Processing</th>
    <th>Spreadsheets</th>
    <th>Databases</th>
  </tr>
  <tr>
    <td>125</td>
    <td>8</td>
    <td>6</td>
  </tr>
</table>
```

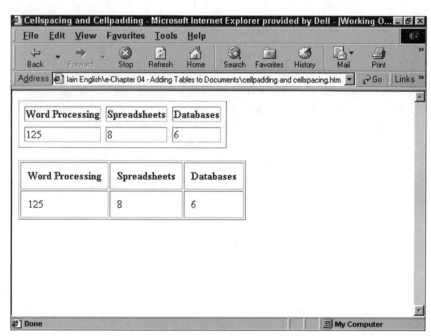

Figure 4-6   *Examples of cell spacing and cell padding.*

Bringing Color to a Table

Using the bgcolor attribute (Web), you can add color to the background of an entire table, one or more table rows, individual cells in a table, or any combination. Use bgcolor to decorate a table or to emphasize certain parts of a table.

How does an XHTML processor decide on the color to use if you have set bgcolor values for the table, several rows, and a number of cells? The color that you specify for a cell overrides that of the row or table in which it is located, and the color of a row overrides that of its table (see Figure 4-7).

The following table includes bgcolor settings for the table, one table-heading cell, and one table-data cell.

```
<table bgcolor="#aaadea" border>
  <tr bgcolor=#ffffcc">
    <th >Word Processing</th>
    <th>Spreadsheets</th>
    <th>Databases</th>
```

```
        </tr>
        <tr>
            <td bgcolor="#ff8127" align="right">125</td>
            <td align="right">8</td>
            <td align="right">6</td>
        </tr>
    </table>
```

The background color of the table is pale blue (#aaadea), the background color of the first row is pale gold (#ffffcc), and the background color of the first cell in the second row is pumpkin (#ff8127).

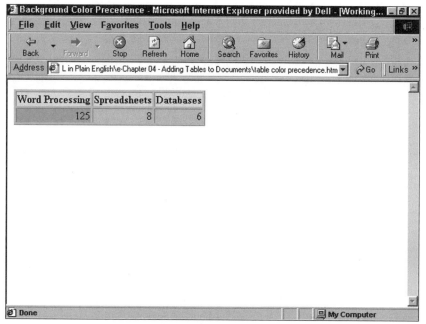

Figure 4-7   *The hierarchy of the bgcolor attribute for the table, th, and td elements.*

To emphasize the importance of column and row labels, they should look different from the rest of the table contents. To format selected cells or rows, you can apply combinations of boldface, italics, and other emphasis using b, i, strong, em, font, and other HTML elements. The following table (see the top table in Figure 4-8) uses the th element to apply boldface, the font element to increase point size, the i element to italicize column and row labels, and the bgcolor attribute to highlight the heading and labels.

```
<table border="4" bgcolor="white">
  <caption>Color in tables</caption>
  <tr>
    <th bgcolor="teal" font size="5" colspan="5"
      align="center">
    Quarterly Results
    </th>
  </tr>
  <tr>
    <td></td>
    <th bgcolor="silver" font size="4"><i>
      Quarter 1</i></font></th>
    <th bgcolor="silver" font size="4"><i>
      Quarter 2</i></font></th>
    <th bgcolor="silver" font size="4"><i>
      Quarter 3</i></font></th>
    <th bgcolor="silver" font size="4"><i>
      Quarter 4</i></font></th>
  </tr>
  <tr>
    <th bgcolor="silver"
      font size="4"><i>Income</font></i></th>
    <td align="right" >$14,000</td>
    <td align="right" >$17,350</td>
    <td align="right" >$18,800</td>
    <td align="right" >$21,750</td>
  </tr>
  <tr>
    <th bgcolor="silver"
      font size="4"><i>Expenses</font></i></th>
    <td align="right" >$5,000</td>
    <td align="right" >$6,200</td>
    <td align="right" >$7,500</td>
    <td align="right" >$8,925</td>
  </tr>
</table>
```

The following table (see the bottom table in Figure 4-8) uses color to emphasize cells that include the colspan attribute:

```
<table border>
  <tr>
    <td bgcolor="#0000ff">#0000ff</td>
    <td bgcolor="#ffffff" colspan="5">
    <td bgcolor="#00ff00">#00ff00</td>
  </tr>
  <tr>
    <td bgcolor="#00868b">#00868b</td>
    <td bgcolor="#00c5cd">#00c5cd</td>
    <td bgcolor="#ffffff" colspan="3"></td>
    <td bgcolor="#fff68f">#fff68f</td>
    <td bgcolor="#fff8dc">#fff8dc</td>
  </tr>
  <tr>
    <td bgcolor="#00757a">#004269</td>
    <td bgcolor="#00a3ab">#88a3ab</td>
    <td bgcolor="#ffdddd">#ffdddd</td>
    <td bgcolor="#ffffff"></td>
    <td bgcolor="#ffd46d">#ffd46d</td>
    <td bgcolor="#ffc46d">#ffc46d</td>
    <td bgcolor="#ffb46d">#ffb46d</td>
  </tr>
  <tr>
    <td bgcolor="#006460">#002047</td>
    <td bgcolor="#008190">#008190</td>
    <td bgcolor="#ffffff" colspan="3"></td>
    <td bgcolor="#ffb24b">#ffb24b</td>
    <td bgcolor="#ffa24b">#ffa24b</td>
  </tr>
  <tr>
    <td bgcolor="#005359">#000825</td>
    <td bgcolor="#ffffff" colspan="5">
    <td bgcolor="#ff9029">#ff9029</td>
  </tr>
</table>
```

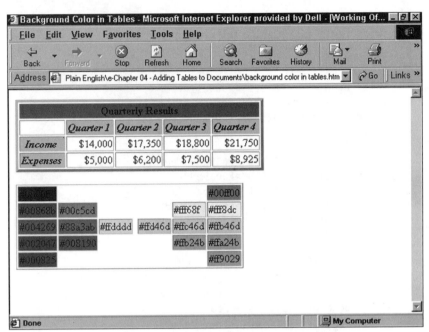

Figure 4-8 *Using background color to emphasize table cells.*

Using Tables for Page Layout

The typical way to lay out a Web document is to style it with a style sheet — in particular, with the cascading-style-sheet position (478) property. However, there is an alternate method: Create a table in which you set up an invisible grid of cells. With this approach, you use tables to format and organize page elements within the borders of cells. You can use the rowspan and colspan attributes (see the "Spanning Rows and Columns" section (563) earlier in this chapter) to change the dimensions of particular cells, or you can just let the amount of body text in a cell control the location of the following row. For example, you can break a page into two columns. The right column might contain several cells with headings-and-text pairs on a white background. The left column could be made up of one long cell with a list of links or highlights of your site on a red or blue background. Or you can ensure that a corporate logo is located in the upper-right corner of a page and that a link to corporate information stretches across the bottom of the page.

The following example (see Figure 4-9) uses three columns. The leftmost column contains all the headings except for the main heading at the top of the page. These headings are left-aligned and vertically aligned with the top of the cells in which they are located. The middle column simply inserts a vertical space to separate the contents of the leftmost and rightmost columns. The rightmost column, which represents the remaining width of the page, holds all the body text. Each text block is left-aligned and aligned with the top of its cells.

```html
<table width=95%>
  <tr>
    <td width="240" valign="top">
    <b>First Things</b><br />
    <font size="2">
      <i>Get this done first.</i>
    </font>
    </td>
    <td width="40"></td>
    <td>
      This page provides instructions for installing a
      program. Before installing the program, you
      should have installed an operating system. Your
      computer should also have a mouse, printer, and
      a modem. If you have installed from a CD-ROM,
      make sure that you have stored it in a place
      from which you can retrieve it later.
    </td>
  </tr>
  <tr>
    <td width="240" valign="top">
    <b>Requirements</b></td>
    <td></td>
    <td valign="top">
    Minimum requirements for installing the program
    are:
    </td>
  </tr>
  <tr>
    <td valign="top">
    <font size="2">
    <i>
      You'll need this hardware and software to run
      the program.
    </i>
    </font>
    </td>
    <td></td>
    <td>
      <ul>
```

```
            <li>An IBM or 100% compatible PC with an 80486
               (or greater) microprocessor.</li>
            <li>Windows 95 or 98 (or greater)</li>
            <li>At least 16 megabytes of RAM</li>
            <li>A CD-ROM drive for installation</li>
          </ul>
        </td>
      </tr>
    </table>
```

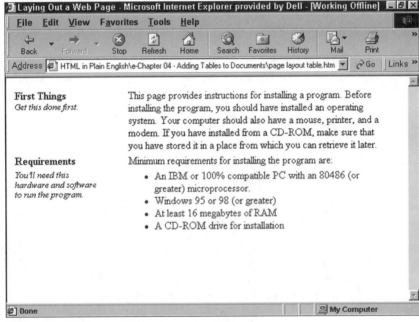

Figure 4-9 *Using a table to lay out a Web page.*

in plain english in pl
sh in plain english in
glish in plain english
in plain english in pl
sh in plain english in
glish in plain english
in plain english in pl
glish in plain english
in plain english in pl
sh in plain english in
glish in plain english
in plain english in pl
sh in plain english in
glish in plain english
in plain english in pl
lish in plain english
in plain english in pl
sh in plain english in
glish in plain english
in plain english in pl
sh in plain english in
lish in plain english
in plain english in pl
glish in plain english

Framing Documents

X HTML provides four elements with which you can divide a browser window into a set of smaller windows, each displaying all or part of a Web document. These small windows are called *frames*, and structures in which sets of frames are placed are known as *framesets*. The two central framing elements are frameset (141) and frame (139). Using frameset, you can define the number of frames in a frameset, set the percentage of the window devoted to each frame, and specify certain characteristics for the frameset. Then, using the frame element, specify individual frames and their attributes. The frame element, which is empty, is a placeholder for content; it simply names the URI of the document to be loaded into the frame during processing. The third element, iframe (158), which is closely related to the frame element, inserts a frame within a block of text in the same way that you would insert a graphic. The iframe element does not require the definition of a frameset. Note that some Web browsers do not support frames. So, whenever you design a set of frames-based Web documents, you should always include a "no-frames" section using the fourth framing element: noframes (222).

Why Use Frames?

The major reason to use frames and framesets in Web pages is to combine fixed and dynamic information in a single window. For example, a "framed" Web site can display your company name in a small, fixed frame and varying pages in a large frame: As visitors view page after page, the company name remains on display. Another common use for a frameset is to display a table of links to all the site's pages (similar to the table of contents for a book) in a small frame and the current page in a larger frame. Whenever a visitor clicks on a link in the small frame, a new page fills the large frame.

●─NOTE

In the future, the W3C may replace frames with cascading-style-sheet positioning. For more information, see the `position` property (478).

Planning for Effective Frames

Design framesets with great care. Many users, particularly those with small-screen monitors, dislike frames — especially if the frames in the framesets are improperly sized, or if there is no way to escape the frameset into a nonframes page.

All the frames in a frameset should usually contain material that is related in some way. For example, a large, main frame may include a document that displays company information, a product factsheet, or a chapter. The rest of the frames may include a variety of subsidiary information, such as the site title at the top of the window, a table of links on the left, and, at the bottom, buttons linking to the home page, the pages before and after the current page, copyright or corporate information, and so forth.

It's easy for frames to annoy rather than inform. For example, you should carefully size a frame that contains a heading, table of contents, or set of buttons. If a subsidiary frame is too large, it will take valuable space from the main frame, which should hold the most significant document. However, if the frame is too small, some of its contents may be hidden and not available for the user's action. (Imagine what can happen if a link to an important page is not visible or usable.) In general, the best frameset design is to have one frame dominate the browser window.

Occasionally, after visiting a framed site, you'll find that a frame remains onscreen when you move on to a nonframes site, and the nonframes pages that you visit are inserted into the frame. The only way to escape is to click the Back button repeatedly until you reach the page preceding the frames site. When you set up a frames site, you should always have a nonframes page at the top of the site. Then, on every page, provide an escape route to the nonframes page.

The main way to avoid problems with a frameset site is to test it using a variety of computers, monitors, and Web browsers.

Building a Frameset

Use the frameset element to divide a browser window into two or more smaller windows in which separate parts of one document or a few individual documents appear. The frameset element controls the structure of frames onscreen, the percentage of the entire screen set for each frame, and the overall appearance of the frameset.

As you know, a typical HTML document includes three main sets of start tags and end tags: <html></html> (153), <head></head> (148), and <body></body> (65), all of which set the main structure of the document. However, when you use frames, the basic document structure changes. According to the HTML 4.0 standard, the document is called a *frameset document*. A frameset document uses the following sets of start tags and end tags to determine the main document structure: <html></html>, <head></head>, and <frameset> and </frameset>.

XHTML and HTML framesets are arranged in rows and columns. The upper left corner of the first defined frame is located at the top left corner of the browser window. The rows (Web) and cols (Web) attributes divide the frameset into virtual rows and columns, respectively, as absolute measurements or percentages of the browser window. As a percentage value, an entire window measures 100% from top to bottom (row-wise) and 100% from side to side (columnwise). The following example defines a frameset composed of three rows that divide the screen into 25%, 25%, and 50% horizontally aligned segments:

```
<frameset rows=25%,*,50% cols=50%,*>
```

Notice that percentages are not enclosed within sets of quotation marks or single quote marks. The sum of the three rows named in the rows attribute is 100%. The vertical dimension of the screen is divided into two columns: the first 50% and the second the remaining amount of space, which adds up to 100% again. The asterisk (*)

tells the browser to calculate the rest of the value. You actually could have coded the frameset as follows:

```
<frameset rows=25%,*%,50% cols=50%,50%>
```

but the asterisk prevents human calculation errors that result in a value under or over 100% of a particular horizontal or vertical dimension. The asterisk can be placed in any position.

You can also specify the dimensions of frames in a frameset in absolute measurements, in pixels. For example:

```
<frameset rows="300",*,"300" cols="600",*>
```

The first and last row (that is, the first and last frame) are 300 pixels from top to bottom. The middle row (the second frame) encompasses the remaining part of the screen. The width of the first frame is 600 pixels, and the remaining frame takes up the remainder. Notice that XHTML supports the use of asterisks with absolute measurements.

You can also combine absolute numbers with asterisks. For example:

```
<frameset rows=1*,2*,3*>
```

In this case, the second row is twice the length of the first, and the third row is three times the length of the first.

Figure 5-1 shows the result of the following segment:

```
<frameset cols=20%,60%,*>
    <frame src="frame1.htm">
    <frame src="frame2.htm">
    <frame src="frame3.htm">
</frameset>
```

●─NOTE─────────────────────────

The HTML 4.0 and the XHTML 1.0 specifications contain the Frameset DTD, which contains an entity reference to the entire Transitional DTD and is essentially another version of the Transitional DTD. (The only difference is that the `frameset` element replaces the body element.) In fact, the Transitional DTD includes the four framing elements. Because the Frameset DTD and Transitional DTD are almost identical, they both contain declarations for deprecated elements and attributes that do not appear in the Strict DTD.

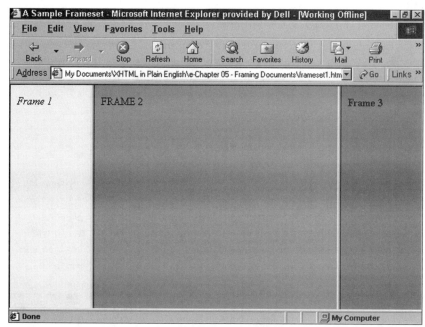

Figure 5-1 *A frameset that contains three frames.*

The following document type declaration "calls" the Frameset DTD:

```
<!DOCTYPE html PUBLIC "-//W3C//DTD XHTML 1.0
   Frameset//EN"
   "DTD/xhtml1-frameset.dtd">
```

The way that you code the frameset statements in the document determines whether a frameset is row-wise or columnwise. If you place the value of the rows attribute first:

```
<frameset rows=15%,*,15%>
```

frames are placed row by row until the last defined row is onscreen. On the other hand, if you set the cols value first:

```
<frameset cols=30%,*>
```

frames are inserted column by column until the last value is completed.

Specifying Frames

Use the `frame` element to control the content and appearance of a specific frame in the frameset. The `frame` element is empty: It's a placeholder for future content. In its most simple form, `frame` refers to a source file (using the `src` attribute (Web)). For example:

```
<frameset rows=20%,*>
   <frame src="title.htm" />
   <frame src="intro.htm" />
</frameset>
```

`frameset`'s rows attribute sets one frame at 20% of the screen row-wise; the other frame encompasses the remaining 80%. Because the `<frameset>` and `<frame>` start tags in the example contain no other attributes, the browser displays and formats the frameset using the default settings. Figure 5-2 shows this segment with `title.htm` in the 20% frame on the top and `intro.htm` in the remaining 80% frame.

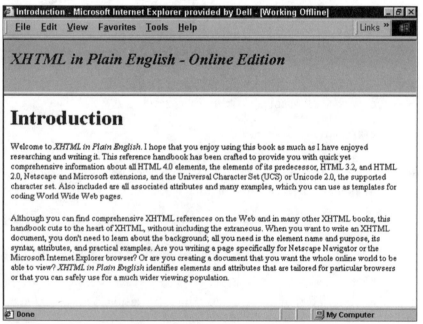

Figure 5-2   *A frameset with two filled row-wise frames.*

The `frame` element provides several attributes that control the look and behavior of a specific frame. For example, you can display or omit a border for a particular frame using the frameborder attribute. You can choose from two possible values for frameborder: frameborder="1" turns on a three-dimensional border, and frameborder="0" omits the border. By eliminating the border, you can produce framesets that look like nonframe documents.

The marginwidth and marginheight attributes control the size of the space between the margin borders and the contents of the frame. The marginwidth attribute specifies the size (in pixels) of the left and right margins, and marginheight sets the size (in pixels) of the top and bottom margins.

For example:

```
<frameset rows=20%,*>
    <frame src="title.htm" frameborder="0" />
    <frame src="intro.htm" marginwidth="30"
        marginheight="5" />
</frameset>
```

Figure 5-3 shows the results of using the frameborder, marginwidth, and marginheight attributes.

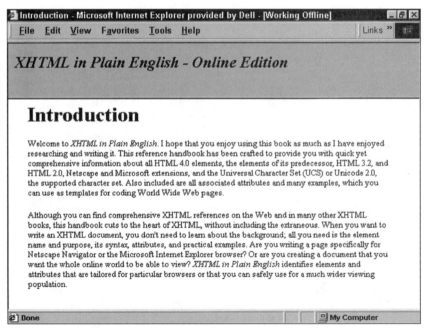

Figure 5-3 *The same frameset with changed frameborder, marginwidth, and marginheight settings.*

You can embed framesets within other framesets. The statements that set up the following four-frame frameset (see Figure 5-4) might look something like this:

```
<frameset cols=25%,*>
  <frame src="toc.htm"></frame>
  <frameset rows=15%,*,15%>
    <frame src="title.htm" />
    <frame src="intro.htm" />
    <frame src="mailto.htm" />
  </frameset>
</frameset>
```

The parent frameset contains an embedded child frameset. The parent defines the two columns, the leftmost of which contains the toc.htm document. The embedded frameset controls the dimensions of the three remaining frames, which are all located in the second column. You would probably include other attributes to control the appearance and behavior of individual frames within the parent and child framesets. When one frameset is nested within another, the browser processes the frames in the child frameset before it works on the parent frameset.

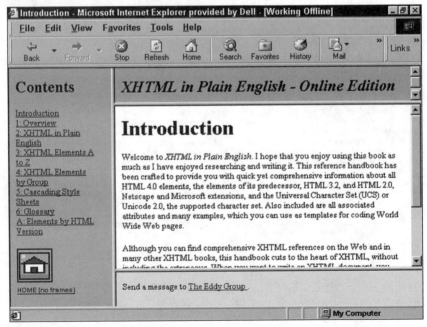

Figure 5-4 *A page with four frames.*

Adding Content to a Frame

The most important part of a frame is its content — a source document that is composed of any combination of text, graphics, links, and other objects. XHTML enables you to place specific content in a particular window or frame. In earlier versions of HTML, you would have used the target attribute, which is now deprecated, for this task. Now, it's best to use the name attribute to target a named frame.

The value of the name attribute determines whether a document appears in a new, blank frame, or in a particular frame based on the hierarchy of frames that a user has browsed since the start of his or her visit to your site. The value of name can either be a valid XHTML name, which must begin with an uppercase or lowercase character from the current alphabet, or one of the following reserved keywords:

- _blank, which loads the contents into a blank frame
- _parent, which loads the contents into the frame that is one level above the current frame
- _self, which replaces the contents of the current frame with the new document
- _top, which loads the content into the top frame in the frameset

Look at the following line containing a frame element:

```
<frame src="toc.htm" name="toc">
```

The URI refers to the toc.htm document, which loads a table of contents into the frame. The name of the frame is toc, which also refers to the document.

The following lines all make the window (or frame) named main the target:

```
<a href="intr.htm" name="main">Introduction
</a>
<a href="ch1.htm" name="main">An Overview of Markup
  Languages</a>
<a href="ch2.htm" name="main">Learning about XHTML</a>
```

The frame element also has attributes with which you can determine whether frames are resizeable and can be scrolled. You can prevent individuals from resizing frames by entering the noresize attribute. Because individual frames are part of a frameset, in some cases, the effect of setting noresize on a frame prevents other frames in the frameset from being resized, too. For example, let's say that you have a frameset consisting of three frames and taking 100% of the space onscreen. If frames one and two do not include the noresize attribute, you may be able to resize the common border between frames one and two. If frame three is set to noresize, any common borders between frame three and the other two frames cannot be resized.

Scrolling enables a user to move the content within a frame using a horizontal or vertical scrollbar. The value of the scrolling attribute either displays or hides scrollbars on a frame's right or bottom border. So, scrolling="yes" indicates that the current frame always has scrollbars (whether or not it needs it), and scrolling= "no" states that the current frame doesn't have scrollbars. When scrolling="auto", the size of the content determines whether the scrollbar is displayed or hidden.

```
<frameset cols=30%,*>
  <frame src="toc.htm" name="toc" scrolling="yes">
  <frame src="intro.htm" name="main" scrolling="auto">
</frameset>
```

Figure 5-5 shows a frameset with two frames. The small frame on the left always has a scrollbar; the large frame on the right has an optional scrollbar; the content determines the presence or absence of the scrollbar.

Floating an Inline Frame

Some Web browsers support earlier versions of HTML, which regard framesets and frames as Microsoft and Netscape extensions that are not to be recognized. Although HTML 4.0 and XHTML support the use of frames, some browsers may not. When a particular browser does not support frames, it is not programmed to understand the frameset and frame elements and their attributes. If a browser supports the iframe (158) element, you can place an inline, fixed-size frame and its source content (using the src attribute) within a document without defining a frameset. This enables you to simulate frames for browsers that do not support frames.

The following example from the HTML 4.01 specification shows how to code iframe lines:

```
<IFRAME src="foo.html" width="400" height="500"
        scrolling="auto" frameborder="1">
[Your user agent does not support frames or is currently
configured not to display frames. However, you may visit
  <A href="foo.html">the related document.</A>]
</IFRAME>
```

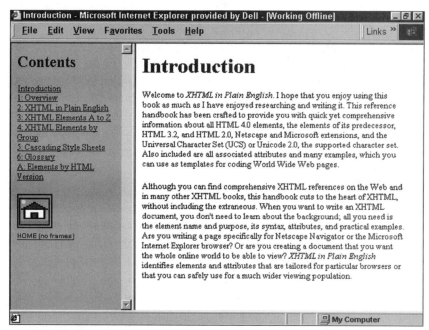

Figure 5-5   *Two frames — one with a required scrollbar and one with a scrollbar that is displayed when needed.*

Specifying a No-Frame Alternative

Another method for allowing for alternate nonframes content is to use the noframes element, which marks the beginning and end of nonframes content. So, define framesets and frames first and then complete your frameset document by adding a section starting with the <noframes> start tag and ending with the </noframes> end tag. Use the following structure:

```
<frameset attributes>
   <frame attributes></frame>
   <frame attributes></frame>
</frameset>
<noframes>
   content
</noframes>
```

When a nonframes browser encounters frameset and frame tags, the browser drops through the frameset and frame statements. When it reaches the noframes section, the browser displays the content of this noframes section.

Frames are not always easy to use — especially for users who have small-screen monitors and low graphic-resolution settings. Plus, some people just don't like frames. So, developers of frame documents should offer their users the choice between frames and nonframes. In the following example, the top four lines set up a frameset and load two documents into two frames. The remaining lines are the no-frames alternate content for browsers that do not support frames.

```
<frameset rows=50%,*>
   <frame src="intro.xml" />
   <frame src="doc01.xml" />
</frameset>
<noframes>
<h2>You Should Be Looking at Two Frames!</h2>
<p>If you are reading this message, you are using an
   XHTML browser that does not support frames. Try
   again with a different browser.
</p>
<img href="/pics/sadface.gif" />
</noframes>
```

A Sample Frameset

This and the next three examples make a no-frames home page and a frameset comprised of a table of contents (in the leftmost "nonresizable" frame) and a main frame, which holds various parts of an online book (see Figure 5-6). At the bottom of the table of contents and each document, you can click the home image or text to move back to the home page and end the frames.

```
<?xml version="1.0"?>
<!DOCTYPE html
   PUBLIC "-//W3C//DTD XHTML 1.0 Transitional//EN"
   "DTD/xhtml1-transitional.dtd">
<html>
<head>
   <title>The Eddy Group, Inc.</title>
   <meta name="keywords" content="html, html
   reference, publishing, computer books, internet
   books">
</head>
<body>
<font face="Letter Gothic" size="3">
<center>Welcome to The Eddy Group, Inc., home page.</center>
</font>
<p><font face="Letter Gothic" size="1">
```

Sandra E. Eddy, co-founder of The Eddy Group, has written
many books, including reference and tutorial books about
computer applications, Windows, and the Internet.
</font></p>
<p><font face="Letter Gothic" size="2">
Some of the resources at our site--</p>
<a href="fr_on1.htm" name="_self">
<h5 align="center"><i>XHTML in Plain English</i> - Online
Edition</h5></a>
<a href="fr_on2.htm" name="_self">
<h5 align="center">Attributes in Depth - Reference
Pages</h5></a>
<a href="fr_on3.htm" name="_self">
<h5 align="center"><i>The GIF Animator's Guide</i> - Online
Edition</h5></a>
<a href="fr_on4.htm" name="_self">
<h5 align="center">GIF Animation and Downloads Page</h5></a>
</font>
<font face="Letter Gothic" size="2">
<p>To learn more about our company, visit our
<a href=about.htm>corporate information</a> page.</p>
</font>
<font face="Letter Gothic" size="1">
<p>Copyright ©2000 by The Eddy Group, Inc.

<a href="mailto:eddygrp@sover.net">eddygrp@sover.net
</a></p></font>
</body>
</html>

The following example shows the frames page with two named
frames (Figure 5-7). On the left side is the table of contents, toc.htm,
which never changes. On the right side is the introduction or the file
linked to an entry in the table of contents. Other pages can then use
the name attribute (Web) to target the appropriate name to fill the
frame whenever a user wants to view a new document.

```
<?xml version="1.0"?>
<!DOCTYPE html
    PUBLIC "-//W3C//DTD XHTML 1.0 Frameset//EN"
    "DTD/xhtml1-frameset.dtd">
<html>
<head>
<title>XHTML in Plain English - Online Edition</title>
</head>
<frameset cols=30%,*>
<frame src="toc.htm" frameborder="0"
```

```
      noresize="noresize" name="toc" />
<frame src="intro.htm" frameborder="0" name="main" />
</frameset>
</html>
```

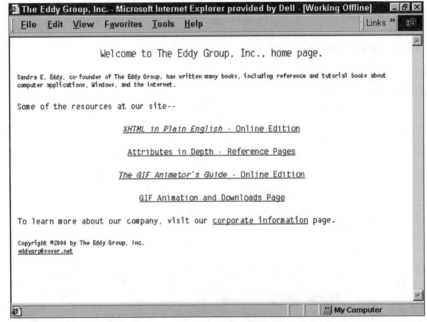

Figure 5-6 *A no-frames home page from which you can link to frames pages.*

The following document is the table of contents, toc.htm. Notice that each part (intro.htm through appc.htm) of the book is targeted to the frame named main. So, a user can click on a part of the book to display it in the rightmost frame. At the bottom of the table-of-contents document is a house image that, when clicked, jumps to the top ("_top") page at the site, the home page. This action closes the frames.

```
<!DOCTYPE html
  PUBLIC "-//W3C//DTD XHTML 1.0 Transitional//EN"
  "DTD/xhtml1-transitional.dtd">
<html>
<head>
   <title>Sample Document</title>
</head>
<body bgcolor="aqua">
<h2>Contents</h2>
```

```
<font face="book antigua" size="2">
<a href="intro.htm" name="main">Introduction</a>
<br /><a href="pt01.htm" name="main">1: Overview
<br /><a href="pt02.htm" name="main">2: XHTML in Plain
English</a>
<br /><a href="pt03.htm" name="main">3: XHTML Elements
A to Z</a>
<br /><a href="pt04.htm" name="main">4: XHTML Elements
by Group</a>
<br /><a href="pt05.htm" name="main">5: Cascading Style
Sheets</a>
<br /><a href="pt06.htm" name="main">6: Glossary</a>
<br /><a href="appa.htm" name="main">A: Elements by HTML
Version</a>
<br /><a href="appb.htm" name="main">B: Attributes in Depth</a>
<br /><a href="appc.htm" name="main">C: HTML Editors
</font></a>
<p><a href="home.htm" name="_top"><img src="crazhome.gif"
/></a></p>
<br />HOME (no frames)
</body>
</html>
```

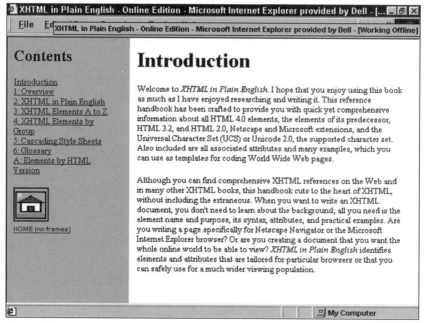

Figure 5-7   *The site's two frames.*

You can add a third frame to the document to hold the title (Figure 5-8). Create a short new title document to hold a <h2> heading:

```
<?xml version="1.0"?>
<!DOCTYPE html
    PUBLIC "-//W3C//DTD XHTML 1.0 Transitional//EN"
    "DTD/xhtml1-transitional.dtd">
<html>
<head>
<title>XHTML in Plain English - Online Edition</title>
</head>
<body bgcolor="aqua">
<h2><i>XHTML in Plain English - Online Edition</i></h2>
</body>
</html>
```

Then, change the frames document, making sure that a user cannot resize the new frame and that the only adjustable frame has a border.

```
<?xml version="1.0"?>
<!DOCTYPE html PUBLIC "-//W3C//DTD XHTML 1.0Frameset//EN">
"DTD/xhtml1-Frameset.dtd">
<html>
<head>
<title>XHTML in Plain English - Online Edition</title>
</head>
<frameset cols=30%,70%>
<frame src="toc.htm" frameborder="0"
    noresize="noresize" name="toc" scrolling="no" />
<frameset rows=17%,*>
<frame src="title.htm" frameborder="0"
    noresize="noresize" scrolling="no" />
<frame src="intro.htm" frameborder="1" name="main" />
</frameset></frameset>
</html>
```

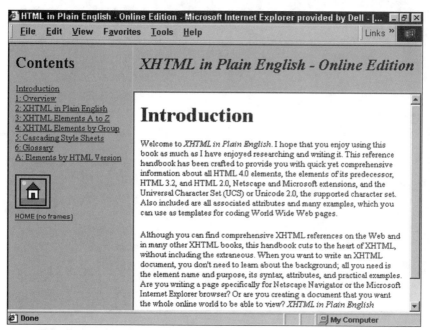

Figure 5-8   *The third frame holds the title.*

Linking to Other Resources

As you learned in Chapter 2, hypertext links mark the major difference between Web documents and plain text files or word-processing documents. Without links, a reader of a standard printed document, such as a book or a report, probably views content in order — from the first page to the last. By clicking a link, a visitor to a Web site can jump to a location within the current page, to another page at the site, or to a completely different site anywhere in the world. Someone who reads a hypertext document can either read pages sequentially or click links to read an author's biography, go to particular areas of interest, or explore the pages of a document cited in a footnote.

The centerpiece of a link is the URI, which states the absolute or relative address of the resource that is the target of the link. The a element (24) specifies a link, its attributes, and attribute values.

Why Use Links?

Hyperlinks distinguish Web documents from all other text-based documents. Links permit users to perform detailed research without accumulating piles of papers and books on their desks or document writers to attach many subsidiary pages to a paper document. In fact, links enable users to travel around the world — for research or enjoyment — while sitting in front of their computers. For example, an East Coast candidate for a California job can check out a company, its products and services, its history, and even its financials through its Web site before the first job interview occurs. Or, someone planning a trip to Europe can plan a complete itinerary before arranging for airline tickets and making hotel reservations — all through Web travel sites.

Absolute Versus Relative URIs

When you write links, you can use absolute URIs or relative URIs. An *absolute URI* starts with the name of an Internet protocol, such as `http:`, `ftp:`, `gopher:`, `file:`, `mailto:`, and so on. The next part of the syntax represents the *host name*, the actual address of the resource (such as `www.example.com`), which specifies (from left to right) the computer on which the server software is located, the registered name of the company or institution that owns the computer, and the domain of the computer. The URI usually concludes with a filename (such as `sample.xml`, `index.htm`, or `site.html`). Typically, you use absolute URIs to refer to pages away from your own Web site. An absolute URI looks something like this:

```
http://www.example.org/docs/phony01.html
```

A *relative URI* does not contain the complete Internet address. For example, if the current document and the document to which it links are located on the same computer, you don't need to enter an absolute URI. For example, you can use a folder name if the two documents are stored on the same drive in separate folders:

```
/docs/phony01.html
```

You can use the filename alone if the two documents share the same folder:

```
phony01.html
```

The simple fact is the only links that work properly include all the information that enables a browser to display the linked-to page — wherever it is located.

●—NOTE

In addition to other URIs, other schemes, such as UUIDs and OIDs, provide unique string identifiers, not link resources such as documents, files, or mailboxes.

Learning About the Structure of Links

The a element indicates a link in an XHTML document. For example:

```
<a title="Dog Quotations"
   href="http://www.twain.com/dog.htm">
Dog Quotations</a>
```

The <a> start tag marks the beginning of a link and includes the link attributes. In the example, the title attribute (Web) is the title of the link (in the same way that the title element (318) provides the title of the document). Some browsers display titles as tool tips, which are similar to balloon help messages. Browsers that support audio may "speak" the title. The href attribute (Web) names the URI of the link — in this case, an absolute URI. After the > delimiter that ends the start tag, is the text that either appears on the page (see Figure 6-1) or causes a new page to open onscreen. A user clicks the link (for example, Dog Quotations) to open the linked-to page (for example, http://www.twain. com/dog.htm). Finally, the </a> end tag concludes the link.

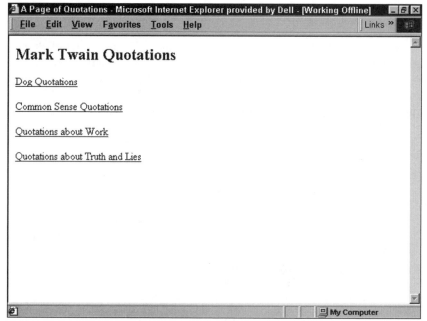

Figure 6-1   *Links to pages of Mark Twain quotations.*

●—NOTE————————————————————————————

The link (202), applet (37), embed (123), img (162), and object (225) elements are other linking elements — although a user cannot click any of these elements to go to a target resource. The link element, which occurs in the HEAD section, links to other documents such as external style sheets. The applet, embed, img, and object elements all "call" other files to use them in the current document.

Linking to Another Part of a Document

In XHTML, both absolute and relative URIs of both types can include a *fragment identifier* (which is indicated by a pound-sign symbol (#)) and a name that matches the value of the name attribute of the target section's a element. For example, a table of contents for a page might include the following entry:

```
<a href="#a">GIF Files</a>
```

The #a fragment identifier points to a section heading later in the document:

```
<a name="a"><h2>GIF Files</h2></a>
```

at another location in the current document. Visitors who click a jump to the *A heading* elsewhere on the page. The following code (see Figure 6-2) shows a more complete version of the table of contents and linked-to sections. (In real life, the text under each heading would be much longer, and the page would extend below the bottom margin.)

```
<font size="2">
<h4>Graphic Types</h4>
<p><a href="#a">GIF Files</a><br />
<p><a href="#b">JPG Files</a><br />
<p><a href="#c">BMP Files</a><br />
<a name="a"><h5>GIF Files</h5></a>
GIF (Graphics Interchange Format) are 8-bit files; GIF images
are limited to 256 colors. Because GIF files are small, they
load quickly. Because you can make GIFs transparent, they
lend themselves to animation.
<a name="b"><h5>JPG Files</h5></a>
Developed by the Joint Photographic Experts Group, JPG or
JPG, is the best format for photographic or near-photographic
24-bit images (that is, images that can use up to 16,777,216
different colors. JPEG files compress very efficiently and
lose very little image quality. However, whenever you save
(and compress) a JPEG file, it loses slightly more quality.
```

```
<a name="c"><h5>BMP Files</h5></a>
The BMP extension represents bitmap files. Bitmaps are made
up of pixels, which are dots on the computer screen. Create
bitmaps by using Paint or any other drawing package that
works with Windows. Windows wallpaper and icons are bitmaps.
</font>
```

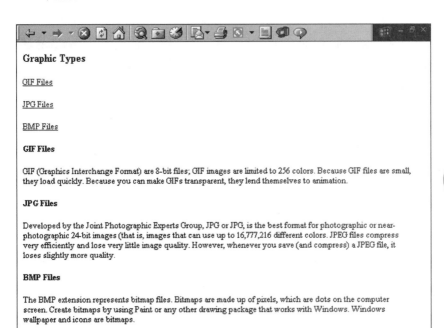

Figure 6-2   *Table-of-contents links to sections of a document.*

Linking to Another Document

The prior blockquote example (and its absolute URI) demonstrates how you can link to a document on a completely different computer. As you have learned, you can also link to documents on the same computer. Let's say that you want to expand the table of contents in the prior section. Perhaps you'd like to lengthen the descriptions of each graphics-type file and add links to technical information as well as to galleries of free image files. You would probably edit the Web page to look something like this (Figure 6-3):

```
<h4>Graphic Types</h4>
<p><a href="/gifdoc.htm">GIF Files</a></p>
<p><a href="/jpgdoc.htm">JPG Files</a></p>
<p><a href="/bmpdoc.htm">BMP Files</a></p>
```

You'd create a new document (`gifdoc.htm`, `jpgdoc.htm`, and `bmpdoc.htm`) to hold the descriptions and the links. When a visitor clicks a link, a new document replaces the old. After perusing the page, the visitor can click a link to go on to a page of technical information or a gallery. Or, he or she could click the Back button to return to the original table-of-contents page.

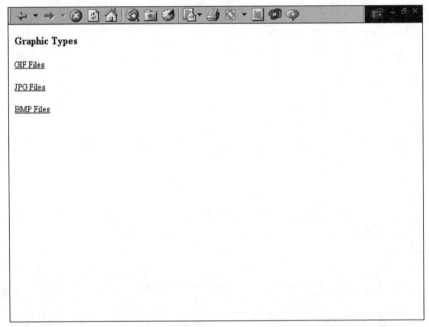

Figure 6-3 *Table-of-contents links to three external documents.*

●—NOTE

A special type of link enables visitors to send someone an e-mail message. For example, the following code creates a link to my e-mail address:

```
<p>Send me a message at
<a href="mailto:eddygrp@sover.net">eddygrp@sover.net
</a>.
</p>
```

When a visitor clicks a mailto: link, the browser opens an e-mail window in which he or she can write and send me a message.

Linking with Graphic Images

You can create a graphic link or a link that combines graphics and text. For example, you can insert a graphic link to the right of a text link:

```
<p>Click <a href="http://www.yahoo.com">Yahoo
<img src="button.gif"/></a> - a popular master directory and
search engine.</p>
```

or to the left of a text link:

```
<p>Click <a href="http://www.yahoo.com">
<img src="button.gif">Yahoo</a> - a popular master directory
and search engine.</p>
```

The following code creates a graphic link preceding a line that includes a text link:

```
<p><a href="http://www.yahoo.com">
<img src="button.gif"></a>
Click <a href="http://www.yahoo.com">Yahoo</a>
 - a popular master directory and search engine.
</p>
```

Figure 6-4 shows all three examples in a browser window.

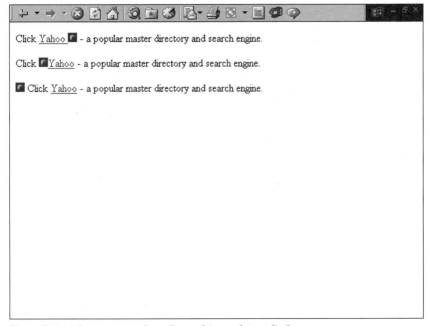

Figure 6-4   *Three examples of graphic and text links.*

The Future of Linking

As you have learned, XHTML provides one element, a, for text and graphic links. The XML language, through its XLinks and XPointers technologies, enables five types of hyperlinks: simple, extended, group, locator, and document.

- *Simple links* ("simple") are analogous to XHTML a links: Insert a simple link in a document to be able to jump from its location in the source document to a destination in either the same document or another document. As in HTML, simple links in XML always move in one direction, from the source location to the target location.

- *Extended links* (extended) enable you to define many links in one or more XML documents. When you use extended links, you can jump from any link in any document to a link resource in any document. You can identify the content associated with a particular link so that if the content changes but the identifier remains the same, you can still access the link.

- *Extended link groups* (group) are a particular type of extended link. Whatever their location — in the current document or in an external document — inline links and out-of-line links follow the same syntax.

- The locator and document keywords indicate types of extended links. The locator keyword specifies that a URI — and no other attributes — follows. The document keyword signals that an extended link that is an entire document follows.

For more information about XML links, refer to the W3C XLink working draft (http://www.w3.org/TR/xlink/). To learn about extended pointers, refer to the W3C XPointer working draft (http://www.w3.org/TR/WD-xptr/). Both the XLink and XPointer technologies are still at the working draft stage. According to W3C, a working draft is "a draft document and may be updated, replaced, or obsoleted by other documents at any time." You can infer from this statement that XML links are not well tested. So before you convert your documents and links to XML, check the W3C XML home page (http://www.w3.org/XML/) for the status of XML, XLink, XPointer, and other XML-related technologies.

Using Interactive Forms

I n its initial years, the World Wide Web was most important to educational and research institutions. In the last
few years of its development, the Web has become more busi-
ness-oriented. More and more corporations are using the Web
for marketing, advertising, and selling to online customers.

As the Internet has become more important to business
enterprises, software companies have developed Internet-ready
programs and added Internet features to their existing applications. For example, standard database programs now enable the
import of information from interactive forms into customer and
other records.

●—**NOTE**

Forms use both the client computer and server computer to enable communication between the visitor to a Web site and the site itself. A *client* computer, on which the Internet browser is installed and from which the visitor browses the Web, makes requests of a *server* program or *server* computer on which the Web pages are set up. Various Web technologies, such as form handlers and scripts, use the client, the server, or both to efficiently present Web pages. For example, many simple HTML documents are processed and displayed using the browser program and never use the server for processing. But HTML documents using new technologies, such as ASP (Active Server Pages) and PHP (originally named Personal Home Page and now PHP: Hypertext Preprocessor)—both of which are based on the server—show pages with some dynamic features. To sum up, *client-side* applications run on the client computer, and *server-side* applications run on the server. Some HTML pages run completely on the client, while others combine client- and server-side processing.

A well-designed form should gather information from a visitor to your site and process it in some way (preferably to send data to a selected database). So, you should design easy-to-use forms that will attract visitors and encourage them to give you information. A form handler can send the supplied information to a server for further processing using CGI scripts and the HTTP protocol or ASP, PHP, or other server-side technologies.

●—**NOTE**

A *protocol* is a set of rules and regulations that control communications between two computers that may or may not run under the same operating system or have the same microprocessor. A protocol enables the connection and transfer of information between the computers.

Why Use Forms?

It's easy to use an interactive form for businesses and organizations to collect information from prospective customers and clients. When the visitor sends a filled-in form to the site, the information is placed in a database for later use — to send merchandise, e-mail messages, or ground mail to the visitor. Any commercial site at which goods are offered and sold should have one or more underlying databases, which include both customer information and inventory information. The customer database produces lists of contacts for catalog mailings and e-mail contacts, and the inventory database allows for instantaneous checking for the availability of merchandise and ordering when quantities drop to a certain level. Often, Web-based marketing sites ask prospective customers to enter information into fill-in forms. Then that information is exported into databases for later processing as mailing lists or contact lists.

● — NOTE ───

Databases are typically made up of records, which are in turn composed of fields. A *field*, which is the smallest unit of information in a record, contains one piece of information, such as a city or telephone number. A *record* is composed of a group of related fields. For example, a record can contain all the appropriate information about a customer, an employee, or an inventory item. Use *forms*, or input forms, to enter information into the records in a database program.

Learning About Controls

Well-designed input forms enable individuals to efficiently enter information in a variety of ways — by typing into text boxes, by selecting items from lists, clicking option buttons, checking or clearing check boxes, and so forth. After inserting information into a form, the individual either clicks an OK button or presses the Enter key. At that point, the database program adds the record to the database. Input forms on the Web provide the same types of input choices, and an underlying program processes information in the same way as any other database application.

XHTML forms are composed of *controls*, which are individual components supported by combinations of elements and attributes. XHTML provides the following control types:

- The check box control type is a small square box that represents an on or off status. Specify a check box by using the input (Web) element and the type="checkbox" (Web) attribute and value.

- The file select control type is a file-uploading control. Specify the file select control type by using the input element and the type="file" attribute and value.

- The hidden control type is a field that is not displayed on the form. It is usually used to transfer information between the client and the server. Specify the hidden control type by using the input element and the type="hidden" attribute and value.

- The menu control type is a list box or, sometimes, a pull-down menu. Specify the menu control type by using the select element and either the optgroup (234) or option (236) element.

- The object control type is any type of multimedia object (image, video file, or sound file) within a form. Specify the object control type by using the object (225) element. A multimedia object can also be located outside a form.

- The radio button control type is a small round button in a group of buttons from which you can select only one at a time. Specify a radio button by using the input element and the type="radio" attribute and value. Radio buttons are also known as option buttons.

- The reset button control type is a command (push) button that you click to clear a form. Specify a reset button by using the button (72) element or the input element and the type= "reset" attribute and value.

●—NOTE

The button element, which is new to HTML 4.0, is designed specifically to create command buttons. In contrast, input is an all-purpose element with which you can create a variety of controls, including buttons. According to the HTML 4.0 recommendation, the button element "offers richer rendering capabilities than the input element."

- The submit button control type is a command button that you click to submit a form. Specify a submit button by using the button element or the input element and the type="submit" attribute and value.

- A multiple-line text box control type has a defined height and width. Specify a multiple-line text box control type by using the textarea (302) element.

- A single-line text box control type has just one line with no height or width settings. Specify a single-line text box control type by using the input element and the type="text" attribute and value.

Many forms — even in a single database — are designed to include some, but not all, fields in a record. For example, some fields contain the results of a calculation performed after the data are entered into a record. Other forms enable only some parts of a record (such as an employee name and telephone extension for a telephone list, or the name and personal address and telephone number for an address book) to be entered.

You can use a scripting language such as JavaScript or VBScript to create scripts that cause forms to become dynamic. For example, declarations for the XHTML forms elements (and most other XHTML elements) include scripting attributes that can be triggered when a certain event takes place: for example, a user activates a control (onfocus (Web)), inactivates an element by activating another (onblur (Web)), submits a form (onsubmit (Web)), resets a form (onreset (Web)), selects text (onselect (Web)), or changes the value of an element (onchange (Web)).

Creating a Form and Its Controls

Before you start developing any Web document, you should spend a sufficient amount of time to plan and design it. You should definitely use the same philosophy when creating a form. Laying out a form is similar to laying out the pages for a Web document. However, you should think about factors that are unique to form design: Forms should be easy to use and attractive to the user's eye (Figure 7-1). Keep the following points in mind:

- Users entering information should be able to move from control to control in a logical order.

- Make sure that the purpose of each control is completely clear to users entering data.

- Controls should not be too far apart, nor too close to each other, for easier data entry.

- Select easy-to-read fonts for the labels (displayed names of controls) as well as for the data being entered and displayed.

- Don't vary point sizes too much. Labels should be slightly larger or the same size as data.

Use the form (135) element to mark the start (<form>) and end (</form>) of a form. Then, insert controls and optional labels for those controls using the child elements of form. The empty input element sets most types of user input: characters that are typed, buttons that are clicked, and boxes and buttons that are selected. For example:

```
<form action="cgi-bin/form-example" method="post">
Type your name:<br />
<input type="text" name="name" size="40" /><br />
Type your email address:<br />
<input type="text" name="email" size="30" />
<br />
Type your street address:<br />
```

```
<textarea name="address" rows="3" cols="35">
</textarea>
<p>Type your password:<br />
<input type="password" name="pswd" size="10" maxlength="8"
/></p>
<p><input type="submit" />
<input type="reset" /></p>
</form>
```

The <form> start tag includes the action (the action attribute (Web)) and method of action (the method attribute (Web)) of form-handling processing. An input type of text indicates a one-line text box, submit specifies a submit command button, and reset denotes a reset command button. The textarea element defines a multi-line text box. Finally, complete the form with a </form> end tag.

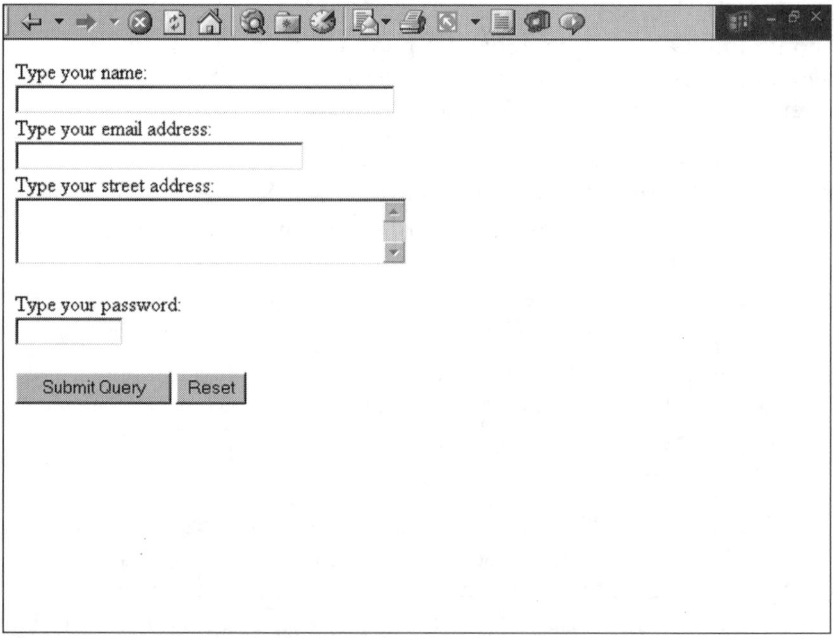

Figure 7-1 *A small form composed of four text boxes and two buttons.*

Using Text Controls

Text controls enable visitors to enter text into forms. Visitors can type names, addresses, telephone numbers, and so forth into one-line boxes. Using multi-line boxes, they can write messages or comments.

In Figure 7-1 opposite, the name, e-mail address, street address, and password boxes are text controls.

Using Check Boxes and Radio Buttons

Check boxes and radio buttons enable you to offer a choice of answers and, at the same time, control the input. Both types of controls enable you to offer multiple-choice answers. Your visitors can check any number of check boxes but are limited to one radio button choice. You can use the checked attribute (Web) to select a default check box or radio button. The following code (see Figure 7-2) sets up four check boxes, one of which is checked:

```
<form action="/cgi-bin/form-example" method="post">
<input type="checkbox" name="chb01"
  checked="checked" />WWW<br />
<input type="checkbox" name="chb02" />Gopher<br />
<input type="checkbox" name="chb03" />FTP<br />
<input type="checkbox" name="chb04" />Telnet<br />
<input type="submit" /><input type="reset" />
</form>
```

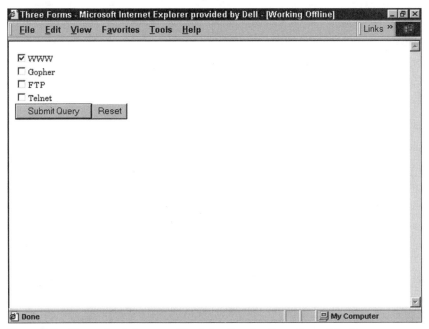

Figure 7-2   *Four check boxes with default submit and reset buttons.*

The following example (Figure 7-3) is a form with radio buttons (one of which is filled in or has a value of checked), an image for a submit button, and a standard reset button:

```
<form action="/cgi-bin/form-example" method="post">
<label for="rbuttons" id="rbuttons">
<b><i>Choose a path:</i></b></label>
<p><input type="radio" name="radio1" />
<b>Nature Path<br />
<input type="radio" name="radio2"
  checked="checked" />Railroad Bed<br />
<input type="radio" name="radio3" />
  Lakeside Path<br />
<input type="radio" name="radio4" />
  Hillcrest Path</font></b></p>
<input type="image" name="submit"
  src="submit_cube.gif" />
<p><input type="reset" /></p>
</form>
```

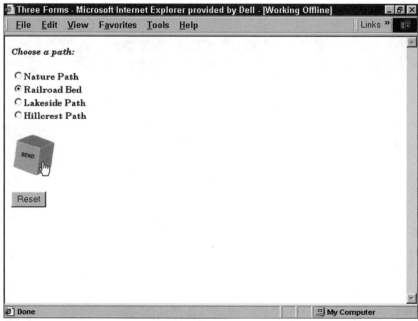

Figure 7-3 *A form with radio buttons and a graphical submit button.*

The final code (Figure 7-4) is a variation on the prior example. The primary change is that the values of the submit and reset buttons are set to *Send Data* and *Clear*, respectively:

```
<form action="/cgi-bin/form-example" method="post">
<label for="rbuttons" id="rbuttons">
<b><i>Choose a path:</i></b></label>
<p><b><input type="radio" name="radio1" />Nature Path
<br />
<input type="radio" name="radio2" />Railroad Bed
<br />
<input type="radio" name="radio3" />Lakeside Path
<br />
<input type="radio" name="radio4" checked="checked"
/>Hillcrest Path
</b>
</p><p>
<input type="submit" value="Send Data" />
<input type="reset" value="Clear" />
</p>
</form>
```

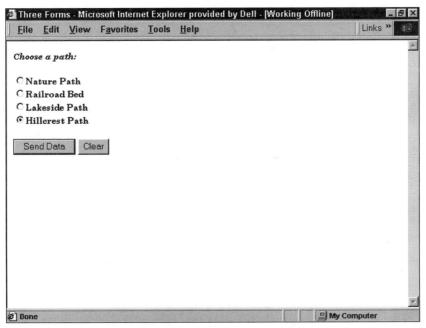

Figure 7-4 *A more textual radio button form.*

Inserting List Boxes

The list-box component of a form is controlled by the select (263), optgroup (234), and option (236) elements. Use the select element to mark the beginning (<select>) and end (</select>) of the box. Then, specify each item in the list using the option element. You can also group items with the optgroup element. The following statements create a form (see Figure 7-5) that enables a visitor to vote for the most intelligent breed of dog:

```
<h2>Vote for the Most Intelligent</h2>
<font="2">
<form action="cgi-bin/form-example" method="post">
<select name="dogs" size="8">
<option >Afghan Hound</option>
<option >Beagle</option>
<option >Doberman Pinscher</option>
<option selected>Golden Retriever</option>
<option>Labrador Retriever</option>
<option >Newfoundland</option>
<option >Standard Poodle</option>
<option >None of the above</option>
</select>
<p>If you selected <i>None of the above</i>, enter your
choice:
<input type="text" size="30" />
</p>
<input type="submit" value="Vote Now" />
<input type="reset" value="Try Again" />
</form>
</font>
```

Sectioning and Labeling a Form

You can enhance a form by giving it a label and dividing it into sections. Use the legend element (195) to create a form label, and use the fieldset element (127) to split a form into sets of fields, ideally related ones. The following example (Figure 7-6) shows a form with a label and field sets:

```
<form action="/cgi-bin/form-example" method="post">
<fieldset>
  <legend align="top"><b><font size="+1">
  Name Information</font></b></legend>
  First Name:<input type="text" name="name1"
  size="28" />  
  Last Name:<input type="text" name="name2"
  size="29" /><br />
```

```
</fieldset>
<p>
<fieldset>
  <legend align="top"><b><font size="+1">
  Address Information</font></b></legend>
  Address:<input type="text" name="address1"
  size="72" ><br />
          
      
  <input type="text" name="address2" size="72" />
  <br />
  City:    
  <input type="text" name="city" size="40" />
  State:<input type="text" name="state" size="2" />
  Zip:<input type="text" name="zip" size="9" /><br />
</fieldset>
</p>
<p>
  <input type="submit" >
  <input type="reset" >
</p>
</form>
```

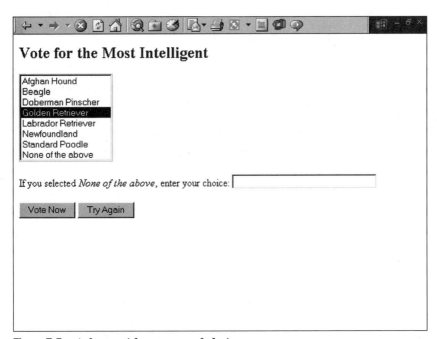

Figure 7-5 *A form with a menu of choices.*

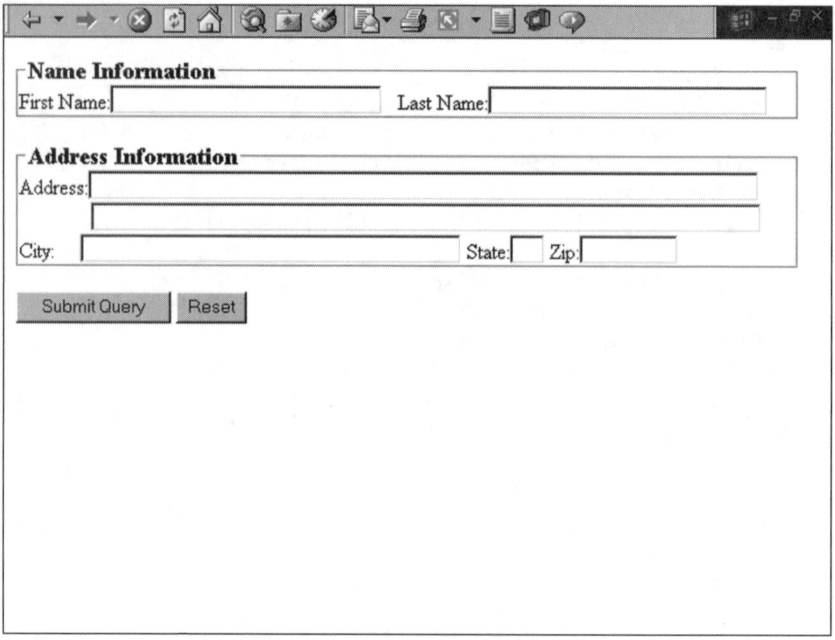

Figure 7-6   *A labeled form separated into field sets.*

Testing Your Forms

Once you have completed a fill-in form, you should test it by entering information into each text box, clicking the buttons in the form, and evaluating each of the remaining controls. Each control should work as planned and appear as designed. Also, test the form using as many Web browsers as possible. (Some browsers will work a little differently than others, but all should behave within your design parameters.) Go through many series of tests and edits until the form meets all your design and processing requirements.

Check completed forms by answering the following questions:

- Is each of the text boxes the proper dimensions? In your judgment, can you see enough of the text that you enter for a user to understand the contents in the text boxes? Have you allowed for the greatest amount of information that will ever be entered in the text boxes? Are all the typefaces and point sizes in text boxes easy to read on the monitor screen?

- Do check boxes alternately clear and check with each click under every browser with which you test a form?

- How many radio buttons can you select in any of the browsers with which you test? No more than one button in a group should be filled at any particular time.

- Are preselected options the proper choices? Are they highlighted properly?

- Are labels spelled correctly? Do labels appear in the selected font and point size? Consider emphasizing all labels with boldface, so that they will properly contrast with input information.

The measure of a control is whether it can be submitted to an application and be processed properly.

NOTE

The next generation of forms for the Web will be XForms (http://www. w3.org/MarkUp/Forms/). XForms will enable users to view forms using browsers and other devices without the developers having to design a special form for each. XForms will split forms into three pieces: the presentation; the logic with which field results are processed, calculated, and restricted; and different types of data. In addition, XForms will work with other Web technologies including the CSS and XSL style sheet languages.

7

Processing Forms

Without a means of transferring completed form information, a form just decorates your document. Information from a completed form must be moved in some way to an application that will process it. When a user clicks a submit button or submit graphic, a program or script should be activated. One of the browser program's many jobs is to transfer the information from the client computer to the URI specified in the action attribute (Web). Then, the form-handling program takes over, loads it into a database, sends it as an e-mail message, or reformats it so that it can be displayed onscreen — or some combination of all three.

In every version of HTML — including the current Version 4.0 — forms developers have used the method attribute to specify the Hypertext Transfer Protocol (HTTP) or CGI script by which the form is submitted to a server, which contains a program that processes the form. *HTTP* is a protocol for both clients and servers. *CGI*, or Common Gateway Interface, is a communications specification. To get an overview of CGI, see the following section, "Learning about CGI" (620). For more information about HTTP, refer to "Learning about HTTP" (621) at the end of the chapter.

Look at the following statement:

```
<form action="/cgi-bin/form-alpha" method="post">
```

The action attribute specifies a relative URI for the location of a *cgi-bin* (CGI binaries) folder that contains the script or program (form-alpha) that processes the form information. Once the connection is made to the server, the server takes over and searches for the form-alpha script or program. The script or program then processes the information and sends a message back to the server.

The basic rules controlling the action attribute are:

- The form-handling program must support the type of data in the submitted form.
- The URI for the processing program is either absolute or relative.
- When you send the form to an HTTP URI, the form is submitted to a program, which can be processed by a cgi-bin program or an HTTP script, a server-side form handler.

The method attribute can have two values: get and post. method="get" appends the submitted form information to a newly-created URI named by the action attribute using an *environment variable*, which is stored information about a particular program that other programs, including browsers, can use. The HTML 4.0 recommendation states that method="get" (Web) is deprecated, so plan to use method="post" most of the time. Note that some browsers and servers cannot handle the long query strings the get method produces. method="post" specifies the form to be sent to a server for processing. Although this method is recommended, it is difficult to use in some situations. For example, it requires more parsing if you are writing Perl from scratch. However, you can find well-tested libraries of code to use if you develop in ASP, JSP, or Perl with cgi-lib.

The following example simply shows that you can also use absolute URIs to specify the cgi-bin folder:

```
<form action="http://example.com/cgi-bin/pgm123"
   method="post">
```

In this case, the processing script or program is named pgm123.

Learning about CGI

The Common Gateway Interface (CGI) is a protocol that creates HTML in response to a user request in the form of a URI. CGI and HTTP work together to service requests from client computers. This task provides an overview of these protocols. CGI is a platform-independent interface (a gateway) between a client and server, which is sometimes known as the HTTP server. A gateway can be written in any language (C, C++, Perl, Python, and so on) that results in an executable file.

A CGI program runs when it is requested — in real time. This means that you can use the program to output up-to-date information immediately. CGI is executed on the server, so the client computer's resources are not used (as opposed to Java, which is executed on the client). A CGI program cannot make requests of users. The best that a user can do is to let XHTML provide the instructions for using a form, enter valid information in the form, click a submit button, and let submission instructions trigger the CGI program.

In the prior examples, you learned that cgi-bin is a folder. cgi-bin is also a reserved word for a folder that stores one or more cgi-bin programs.

Learning about HTTP

HTTP is a protocol that allows client computers and server computers to communicate. (Note that if you use certain technologies — such as ASP or PHP, for example — you won't have to learn much about HTTP.) Thus, if a browser program on a client computer requests a document from a program on the server, HTTP allows both events to occur. The markup language that you use to create the document is an important factor. Tim Berners-Lee, who is credited with developing the World Wide Web, also created HTTP.

in plain english in pla
sh in plain english in
glish in plain english
in plain english in pl
sh in plain english in
glish in plain english
in plain english in pl
glish in plain english
in plain english in pl
sh in plain english in
glish in plain english
in plain english in pl
sh in plain english in
glish in plain english
in plain english in pl
lish in plain english
in plain english in pl
sh in plain english in
glish in plain english
in plain english in pl
sh in plain english in
lish in plain english
in plain english in pl
glish in plain english

Styling Documents with CSS2

In the preceding chapters, you learned how to use HTML elements to control the structure, content, and some formats of your documents. When you associate a style sheet with a document, you can more closely govern the appearance of the document. Remember that HTML includes elements and attributes that enable you to format and enhance your documents. However, those who develop HTML recommendations encourage the evolution from elements and attributes that style to style sheets whose properties apply formats and enhancements to selections. In fact, HTML documents actually improve when you apply style sheet properties rather than styling attributes.

A style sheet enables a document developer to specify universal formats for all identical elements, thereby assisting in the development of organization-wide Web document standards. For example, all top-level headings (the h1 element) in a document set should always look the same, and each of the lower-level headings (h2, h3, h4, h5, and h6) should vary so that each descending level has a gradually reduced point size and different enhancements (through changing combinations of boldface, italics, bold italics, and so forth). Using a style sheet, a writer can change the font, font size, and color of all level-one headings by using a single styling rule. Without a style sheet, a writer would have to accept the default styles or redefine the look of every level-one heading. The standard style sheets that are used to style HTML documents are known as cascading style sheets (CSS).

● **NOTE**

> CSS is now in its second version (CSS2), so it is relatively stable, although neither version — CSS1 and especially CSS2 — is completely supported by Web browsers.

Cascading style sheets are made up of sets of rules that are applied to elements. A style sheet rule is composed of two parts: The *selector* is the HTML or XML element to which the rule applies, and the *declaration* consists of the property (similar to an attribute) and the value — both within brackets. Look at the following example:

```
p { font: 12pt "Century Schoolbook",
    "Times New Roman", serif;}
```

In the example, the p element (238) is the selector, font (424) is the CSS property, 12pt is the point size, "Century Schoolbook" and "Times New Roman" are specific typefaces, and serif is a generic typeface type. The font size value of 12pt (12 points) is an approximation. The font size probably depends on the editor with which you create the document, the browser with which you view the paragraph, or the printer with which you print it. The browser tries to use the first typeface in the list. If that is not available on the client computer, the browser attempts to use the second typeface. If that typeface is also unavailable, the browser finds a serif typeface with which to display the selected text.

Note that this chapter is a brief overview of cascading style sheets. For example, you can use style sheets to position objects on a page, and certain style-sheet properties enable disabled users to actually hear spoken page components. For detailed information about specific CSS1 and CSS2 properties, refer to *Cascading Style Sheet Syntax* (371). *Cascading Style Sheets in Plain English* (343) lists style sheet properties alphabetically, and *Cascading Style Sheets A to Z* (355) lists properties by function.

The W3C offers several style sheet resources — mostly oriented to HTML writers but also informative for XML developers. The home page is located at http://www.w3.org/style/. The W3C Core Styles site (http://www.w3.org/Style sheets/Core/) offers several predefined style sheets. Use them in your documents or, at the very least, use them as aids when you construct your own style sheets. You can validate your style sheet by downloading the W3C CSS Validation Service (http://jigsaw.w3.org/css-validator/).

Why Use Style Sheets?

If you have any experience with word-processing programs, you know that each document is automatically associated with a default style sheet or a style sheet that you or someone else created. A word-processing style sheet applies standard formats (such as left alignment, the Times New Roman font, and a point size of 10) to each paragraph of body text in a document, and applies a font such as Helvetica, a boldface enhancement, and a higher point size to headings. Just select the style, and all the properties are applied to the selected paragraph. With style sheets, you can develop well-formatted Web documents using a set of predefined standards, thereby controlling the look of each type of document — for example, home page, site map, and so forth. Style sheets also enable users to apply several styles at once to one or more paragraphs, which saves a great deal of time in document creation. For example, a style sheet can use the same fonts and point sizes for the headings and body text of all corporate press releases, and different sets of fonts and point sizes for employee manuals — assuming that the people who create and edit the documents follow the style sheet standards. Style sheets for HTML documents work in the same way as word-processing style sheets.

Associating Styles with a Document

You can associate styles with the elements in an HTML document in several ways: by linking an external style sheet, by inserting styles in a document or overriding an attached external style sheet, or by defining an attribute for a particular element. The W3C recommends using external style sheets.

To specify styles for an entire document, you can attach one or more external style sheet documents using the link element (202) in the HEAD section. For example:

```
<link href="styler.css" rel="style sheet"
   type="text/css">
```

The href attribute (Web) names a specific style sheet, and the type attribute names an Internet Media Type. The rel attribute (Web), which specifies the type of relationship of the link from the current document to the style sheet, uses a variety of keywords (such as style sheet) to identify the type of link. You can specify an alternate style sheet by using the keyword alternate. For example:

```
<link href="alt_styl.css" rel="alternate style sheet"
    type="text/css">
```

In both examples, the type attribute (Web) specifies the Internet Media Type (MIME) of text/css — in this case, text and cascading style sheet.

● **NOTE**

You also can associate style sheets using XML components. For the time being, use the link element instead.

Learning About the style Element

To embed styles within the current document or to override an attached external style sheet, use one or more style elements (280) in the HEAD section of a document. For example:

```
<style type="text/css">
body { margin: .75in;
        font: 12pt "Century Schoolbook",
        "Times New Roman", serif; }
</style>
```

The example shows that the boundaries of a style section are marked by a <style> start tag and a </style> end tag. To specify a particular style, name the element (for example, body (65)). Enter the { delimiter, name a property (margin: or font:), and type values (0.75in, 12pt, or "Century Schoolbook"). Divide property values with commas, and separate property/value sets with semicolons. Finally, close with the } delimiter. The properties in the example set margin and font style properties for the entire body of the HTML document.

● **NOTE**

You can end every property/value set with a semicolon (see the prior example). Then, in the future, if you add other properties and values, you will avoid having "missing semicolon" errors.

You can apply styles to a named class within an element. In the HEAD section, insert the style element:

```
<style type="text/css">
    p.stress { font: 14pt "Albertus Extra Bold",
            "Arial Black", sans-serif; }
</style>
```

Signal a class such as stress by preceding it with a pound sign (#). Then, apply the style in the BODY section (see the top example in Figure 8-1) using the class attribute (Web):

```
<p class="stress"> Watch out for the truck!</p>
<p>This stress-free paragraph is not affected.</p>
```

Use the style element and the id attribute (Web) to limit styles, too. Start by coding a style element in the HEAD section:

```
<style type="text/css">
   #exid {border-width: 1; border: solid;
          font-weight: bold;
          text-align: center;
          }
</style>
```

Then, add text and markup to the BODY section (see the bottom example in Figure 8-1):

```
<p class="stress">This paragraph is not affected.</p>
<p id="exid">See the #exid styles here.</p>
<p>Not affected at all.</p>
```

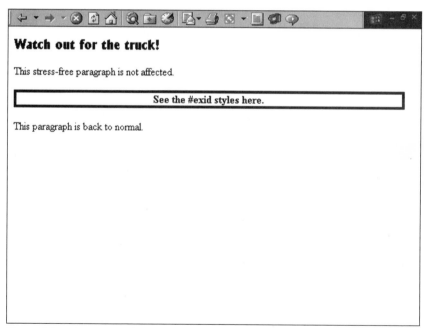

Figure 8-1 *Two examples of style element use.*

Learning About the style Attribute

To override style sheet properties for an occurrence of an element, you can use the style attribute, which uses the same values as the style element. The following example (Figure 8-2) applies font characteristics to the blockquote (61) element and a quotation from Iris Murdoch:

```
<blockquote style="font-size: 14pt; color: olive">
Dogs are very different from cats in that they can be images
of human virtue. They are like us.
</blockquote>
```

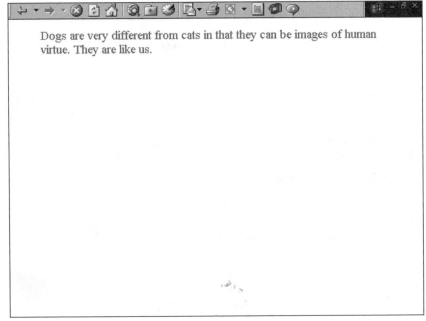

Figure 8-2 *Using the style attribute on a block quote.*

Laying Out Pages

Cascading style sheets provide several properties for the background of all the pages in a document. For example, you can choose from five individual background properties (background-image (380), background-color (378), background-attachment (377), background-position (381), and background-repeat (382)) or select one property (background (375)) that combines the five properties (see Figure 8-3). For example:

```
body { background-image: url(backg.gif);
       background-attachment: fixed;
       background-position: 0% 0%;
       background-repeat: repeat; }
```

The example also applies the text-align (487), margin-left (449), margin-right (450), margin-top (452), and font (424) properties to the pre element (242), which contains the quotation.

You don't need to explicitly include each of the background properties shown in the example. The following statement uses the background property to combine most of the prior background properties into a single property:

```
body {background: url(backg.gif)
      repeat fixed; }
```

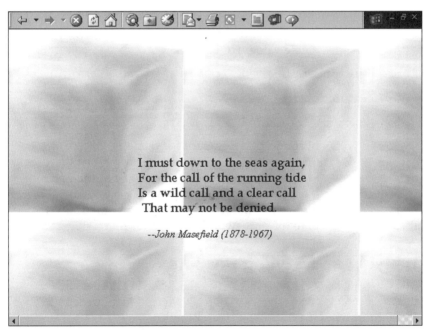

I must down to the seas again,
For the call of the running tide
Is a wild call and a clear call
That may not be denied.

--John Masefield (1878-1967)

Figure 8-3   *A variety of page background styles.*

Setting Margins and Padding

Using style properties, you can control two components at the edges of pages: the margin and padding. A *margin* is the outermost part of a page measured from the edge; *padding* is between the margin but outside the text, graphic content, and any borders. The margin and padding properties work in much the same way as the background properties. You can set margins and padding using four specific properties — one each for the bottom, left, right, and top margin or padding — or you can combine some or all properties. You can turn on or off individual margins and padding or set specific margin or padding widths.

For example, you can use the `margin` property (446) to combine the individual margin properties: `margin-top` (452), `margin-right` (450), `margin-bottom` (448), and `margin-left` (449) — in that order. If you supply one value for the `margin` property, all margins are set to that value. If you supply two values, the browser supplies values from the opposite sides of the element: top and bottom, right and left. Three values set the top, right, and bottom margins. The left margin obtains its value from its opposite, the right margin.

If you want to set all four margins to the same width, all you need to do is provide a single value. For example:

```
body {margin: 0.5in;}
```

is equivalent to:

```
body {margin: 0.5in 0.5in 0.5in 0.5in; }
```

To specify an absolute measurement for one, two, three, or four margins, specify a value followed by a two-letter abbreviation representing the unit of measure. To specify a percentage of the parent element's margins, enter a value followed by the percent sign. You can enter the `auto` keyword to have the browser automatically calculate a minimum value for one, two, three, or four margins.

Applying and Styling Borders

By styling the body element (65), you can add styled borders to every page. You can also add borders to objects affected by a particular element throughout a document. For example:

```
body {margin: 0.5in 0.5in 0.5in 0.5in;
     border-color: red;
     border-style: groove;
     border-width: 0.5in; }
```

applies half-inch margins and a red and black, groove, half-inch border to all four borders of every page (see Figure 8-4).

Figure 8-4   *A page with half-inch margins and a black and red, solid border.*

The border-bottom-width (388), border-left-width (394), border-right-width (398), and border-top-width (404) properties set the width of the bottom, left, right, and top borders — in that order. You can set each of the border-width properties with a keyword — thin, medium (the default), or thick — or with an absolute positive measurement followed by a two-letter abbreviation representing the unit of measure. If you supply one width, all borders are set to that width. If you supply two or three widths, the browser supplies widths from the opposite sides of the element. Elements are paired as follows: top and bottom, left and right.

The border-color (389) property sets colors of one, two, three, or four borders with a choice of five color-identifying options: the color name, two types of hexadecimal color codes, and the keyword rgb, followed by an absolute (decimal) red-green-blue value or a relative (percentage) red-green-blue value.

The border-style (400) property enables you to select the look of one, two, three, or four border lines from nine styles: dotted, dashed, solid, double, groove, ridge, inset, outset, or none. For example:

```
img { border-color: navy ;
   border-style: solid; border-width: thick;
   margin-right: 24pt; float: left; }
```

You can combine border properties by using the border property. The following example, which creates a thin, black, solid-line border, combines the border properties shown in the first example in this task and specifies margin-right (450) and float (422) properties for all img elements (162) in the document:

```
img { border: navy solid thick;
   margin-right: 24pt; float: left; }

<img src="puppy.jpg" alt="A Golden Puppy">
</img>
```

In the example, the border property creates a thin, black, double-line border around the image shown in Figure 8-5.

Figure 8-5 *An image surrounded by a thin, black, solid border.*

Maneuvering Paragraphs and Lines

Use the vertical-align property (493) to set the up-and-down alignment of the element with which it is associated. You can choose from
several keywords, or you can enter a percentage value (followed by a
percent symbol). To align the element vertically with the baseline of
the current element, enter the baseline keyword, which is the
default, or with the baseline of the parent element if the current element has no baseline. Remember that the *baseline* is the invisible line
on which a non-subscript or non-superscript character sits in a line
of text. In the following example, subscript text is always red and is
vertically aligned with the bottom of the parent element's typeface.

```
sub { vertical-align: text-bottom; color: red; }
```

The line-height property specifies the height of the text line
from baseline to baseline. You can either use a keyword or enter a
value. For example:

```
span { line-height: 110%; font-size: 12pt; }
```

In the example, the line height of a spanned selection is 110%
greater than the current line height, and the span's initial point size
is 12 points.

Placing Words and Characters on the Page

Kern is a printing term that indicates the adjustment of space between
two adjacent letters. Typically, the larger the size of a particular typeface (for example, those used for headings), the farther apart some
characters appear onscreen or on the printed page. Sometimes, this
results in words actually looking like separate letters, which readers
are less likely to recognize as words. The letter-spacing property
(441) sets spacing between characters using a keyword or measurement. The following example (see Figure 8-6) demonstrates letter
spacing by setting the six headings to the same typeface, point size,
and level of boldness:

```
h1 { letter-spacing: 4mm;
   font-family: Cornerstone;
   font-size: 18pt;
   font-weight: 800; }
h2 { letter-spacing: 3mm;
   font-family: Cornerstone;
   font-size: 18pt;
```

```
        font-weight: 800; }
h3 { letter-spacing: 2mm;
     font-family: Cornerstone;
     font-size: 18pt;
     font-weight: 800; }
h4 { letter-spacing: 1mm;
     font-family: Cornerstone;
     font-size: 18pt;
     font-weight: 800; }
h5 { letter-spacing: 0.5mm;
     font-family: Cornerstone;
     font-size: 18pt;
     font-weight: 800; }
h6 { letter-spacing: 0.1mm;
     font-family: Cornerstone;
     font-size: 18pt;
     font-weight: 800; }


<h1>AWAY FROM A WAVE</h1>
<h2>AWAY FROM A WAVE</h2>
<h3>AWAY FROM A WAVE</h3>
<h4>AWAY FROM A WAVE</h4>
<h5>AWAY FROM A WAVE</h5>
<h6>AWAY FROM A WAVE</h6>
```

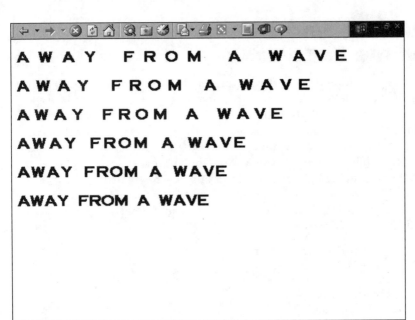

Figure 8-6 *An example of changing letter spacing.*

You can also compress and expand spacing between words. This enables you to fit more words on a single line (for example, to force the last word of a heading to join all the other words on a single line), to space out the words on a line (for example, to have text take up more room on a page), or to simulate justification — if you are prepared to spend a great deal of time on the task. You can also combine word spacing and line spacing to control the position of every character in a paragraph. The word-spacing (499) property works in the same way as letter-spacing: Use the normal keyword (the default) to represent the normal spacing between words, or specify positive or negative values to increase or decrease spacing. The following example sets word spacing within the six heading levels:

```
<h1 style="font-size: 14pt; word-spacing: 12pt>AWAY FROM A
WAVE</h1>
<h2 style="font-size: 14pt; word-spacing: 10pt>AWAY FROM A
WAVE</h2>
<h3 style="font-size: 14pt; word-spacing: 8pt>AWAY FROM A
WAVE</h3>
<h4 style="font-size: 14pt; word-spacing: 6pt>AWAY FROM A
WAVE</h4>
<h5 style="font-size: 14pt; word-spacing: 4pt>AWAY FROM A
WAVE</h5>
<h6 style="font-size: 14pt; word-spacing: normal>AWAY FROM A
WAVE</h6>
```

Specifying Text Characteristics

As you may guess, the font properties control the appearance of selected text. The six font properties work in the same way as most of the other properties covered in this chapter: You can specify five individual font properties (font-family (429), font-size (430), font-style (434), font-variant (435), and font-weight (435)) or combine each of these properties under one (font (424)). Other properties that affect text are text-transform (491), white-space (497), and text-decoration (488).

Selecting a Font Family

The font-family property specifies a typeface by one or more particular names (such as "Times New Roman" or "Arial"), a generic family
name (such as serif, sans-serif, cursive, fantasy, and monospace),
or a combination of both. Use quotation marks to enclose family
names comprised of two or more words that are separated by spaces
(for example, "Times New Roman" or "Bookman Old Style"). When
you use the font-family property, it is best to list more than one
typeface name. This approach ensures that you can define a font
family even if a specific font is not available on your computer.
The following example sets the typeface for the BODY section of
a document to Times New Roman. If that typeface isn't available,
the browser tries Book Antigua. If all else fails, the browser uses
one of the serif typefaces installed on the client computer.

```
body { font-family: "Times New Roman",
  "Book Antigua", serif; }
```

Setting the Font Size

The font-size property specifies an absolute or relative point size
using a value or a keyword. You can enter an absolute measurement,
followed by a two-letter abbreviation for the unit of measure, you can
specify a percentage of the parent element's point size, followed by
the percentage sign, or you can type a keyword that represents a size
relative to the current point size. The following example sets various
absolute point sizes for four levels of headings (see Figure 8-7):

```
h1   { font-family: Braggadocio, Impact,
       sans-serif;
       font-size: 60pt;
       font-weight: 900; }
h2   { font-family: Braggadocio, Impact,
       sans-serif;
       font-size: 48pt;
       font-weight: 800; }
h3   { font-family: Braggadocio, Impact,
       sans-serif;
       font-size: 36pt;
       font-weight: 700; }
h4   { font-family: Braggadocio, Impact,
```

8

```
        sans-serif;
        font-size: 24pt;
        font-weight: 600; }

<h1>Level-1 Heading</h1>
<h2>Level-2 Heading</h2>
<h3>Level-3 Heading</h3>
<h4>Level-4 Heading</h4>
```

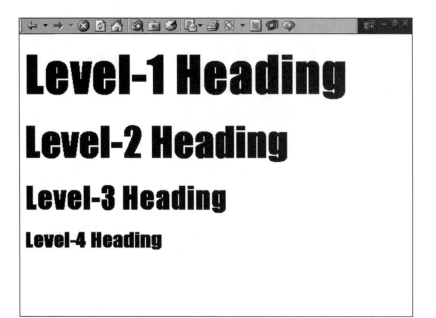

Figure 8-7 *Four levels of headings with varying point sizes.*

Enhancing Text

The font-style property enables you to enter a keyword to specify
the degree to which the text "leans." Be aware that most typefaces do
not offer two levels of italics. If you choose italic and the current typeface does not offer italics, text may be oblique instead, or the reverse.

```
h2 { font-style: italic;
     font-weight: bold;}
h3 { font-style: oblique;
     font-weight: bold;}
```

```
<h2>Italic text leans.</h2>
<h3>Oblique text leans, too.</h3>
```

Use the font-variant property to specify normal text (in this case, a mix of uppercase and lowercase characters that you typed) or *small caps*, which are uppercase characters that are smaller in size than standard uppercase characters. The following example contrasts HTML's default font characteristics with a small-caps quotation (see Figure 8-8):

```
blockquote { font-variant: small-caps; }

<p>Upon resigning as Secretary of State, Dean Acheson
said:</p>
<blockquote>A memorandum is written not to inform the reader
but to protect the writer.</blockquote>
<p>This shows the same quotation in regular uppercase
characters.</p>
<p>A MEMORANDUM IS WRITTEN NOT TO INFORM THE READER BUT TO
PROTECT THE WRITER.
</p>
```

In the example, paragraphs other than the block quotation use the HTML default font characteristics.

The weight of a font is the degree of boldness or lightness. You can set the weight of selected text by using the font-weight property and a keyword or number. The quotation in Figure 8-8 has a font-weight of 500 — somewhat bolder than normal text but less bold than the standard bold text.

Combining Font Characteristics

The font property combines multiple font properties in the same way that margin and border combine multiple margin and border properties. The font property specifies rules for the font-style, font-variant, font-weight, font-size, line-height, and font-family properties — in that order. For example:

```
p {font: small-caps/90%
  "times new roman", serif; }
```

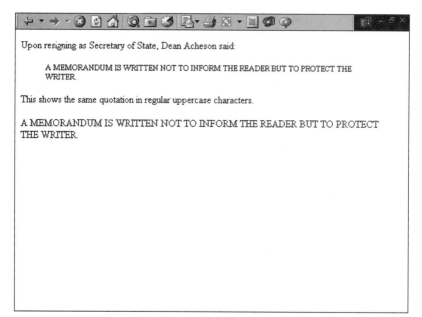

Upon resigning as Secretary of State, Dean Acheson said:

A MEMORANDUM IS WRITTEN NOT TO INFORM THE READER BUT TO PROTECT THE WRITER.

This shows the same quotation in regular uppercase characters.

A MEMORANDUM IS WRITTEN NOT TO INFORM THE READER BUT TO PROTECT THE WRITER.

Figure 8-8   *An example of the font-variant property.*

Changing Case

Use the `text-transform` property to change the case of selected text. The example shown in Figure 8-9 shows how `text-transform` modifies the heading, *A mix Of CASE.*

```
p.upper { text-transform: uppercase;
          font-size: 18pt;
          font-weight: bold; }
p.caps { text-transform: capitalize;
          font-size: 18pt;
          font-weight: bold; }
p.lower { text-transform: lowercase;
          font-size: 18pt;
          font-weight: bold; }
p.normal { font-size: 18pt;
            font-weight: bold; }

<p class="upper">The mix Of CASE</p>
<p class="caps">The mix Of CASE</p>
<p class="lower">The mix Of CASE</p>
<p class="normal">The mix Of CASE</p>
```

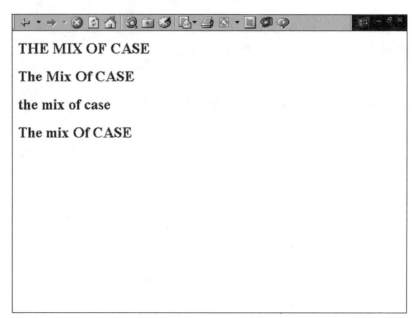

Figure 8-9 *Examples of how the text-transform property changes case.*

Decorating Text

The text-decoration property enables you to decorate text with lines over, under, and through selected text. You can also use text-decoration to "blink" a selection. The following example (see Figure 8-10) applies lines over and under the note class of the p element.

```
body { font-family: "Century Schoolbook",
       "Book Antigua", serif;
     font-size: 12pt; }
p.one { text-decoration: underline;
      font-weight: bold;
      font-family: sans-serif;
      font-size: 14pt;
      color: red; }

<p>To install this program, double-click the setup icon.</p>
<p class="one">
To be able to click, you must have a mouse and proper
software installed on your computer.
</p>
<p>Then, let the installation program take over. Follow the
instructions in each message box.</p>
```

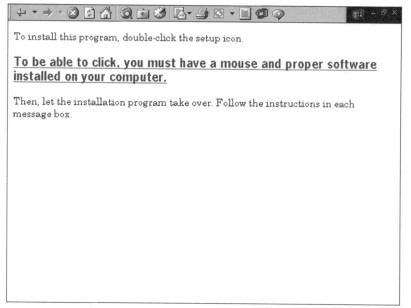

To install this program, double-click the setup icon.

To be able to click, you must have a mouse and proper software installed on your computer.

Then, let the installation program take over. Follow the instructions in each message box.

Figure 8-10 *Using text-decoration to emphasize the text in a note.*

Styling Lists

To style lists, you can specify four specific list-style properties, or use one property that combines one to four list-style properties.

The list-style-image property (444) specifies a list-item marker, which is the image preceding items on an ordered or unordered list. To import an image, specify the URI of the image file. If you enter the none keyword, no image will be imported, and the list will be preceded by the default black disc or Arabic numeral (1, 2, and so forth).

The list-style-position property (444) specifies the alignment of the items on an ordered or unordered list. List items can be aligned with a block indent or hanging indent.

The list-style-type (445) property specifies the number or bullet type preceding items on an ordered (numbered) or unordered (bulleted) list with the same choices as the type attribute (Web).

Use the list-style property (443) to combine the individual list-style properties: list-style-image, list-style-position, and list-style-type — in that order. Simply choose the keywords supported by the individual list-style property. You do not need to specify the property name; the browser should interpret the unique values for each property.

The following example (Figure 8-11) shows how you can use an image to precede the items in an unordered list.

```
ul { list-style-image: url("button.gif"); }

<h4>Graphic Types</h4>
<p>Click on one of the following links to learn about popular
graphic file types.
<ul>
<li><a href="/gifdoc.htm">GIF Files</a></li>
<li><a href="/jpgdoc.htm">JPEG Files</a></li>
<li><a href="/bmpdoc.htm">BMP Files</a></li>
<li><a href="/wmfdoc.htm">WMF Files</a></li>
<li><a href="/tifdoc.htm">TIFF Files</a></li>
</ul>
```

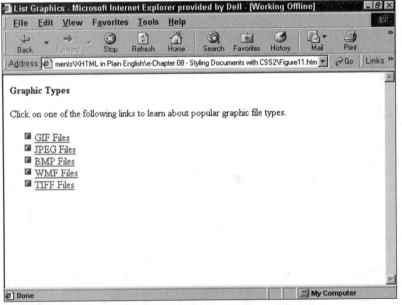

Figure 8-11 *An example of the list-style-image property.*

Testing and Maintaining Documents

An XHTML processor is a program that analyzes a document, determining what is markup and what is content. The processor can be a standalone program, devoted only to analyzing a document, or it can be part of another program, such as an XHTML editor or a browser. When you create a document with an XHTML editor, that editor usually checks for appropriate syntax, supported elements and attributes, and properly named URIs and files as you create and develop a document. The first time you look at a finished page with a browser, you will know if the document contains errors; it may be incomplete or the results are not as you planned.

Whether you test a document using a dedicated processor, XHTML editor, or browser, the program reduces the document to its smallest parts, examining each character for its meaning. For example, when the processor reads a less-than symbol (<), it is programmed to know the beginning of some markup — such as a start tag or end tag. And when the processor recognizes a greater-than symbol (>), it knows that it has reached the end of that markup. The processor notes the presence or absence of certain markup characters or words, too. For example, if a start tag is not followed in due time by a matching end tag, the processor may be programmed to ignore or observe the missing markup. Or, if an attribute value is not enclosed within a pair of quotation marks, the processor may produce strange results.

In the past, HTML-processing programs — namely browsers — were very forgiving: They tried very hard to process and send poorly coded documents to users' computer screens. On the other hand, XML documents are processed by XML parsers and must follow XML standards to the letter. XHTML falls somewhere in the middle. It follows XML rules, so you have to be more careful about using correct syntax and proper case. However, because XHTML is the next generation of HTML and is processed by many HTML browsers, you can probably make a few mistakes.

Why Test a Document?

Before posting a page, it is imperative to test it to make sure that you have used appropriate markup syntax, chosen HTML elements and attributes supported by the latest HTML specification, and properly named the URLs for links and graphics. Other than finding errors in markup, you should also see how your page looks under various browsers that support XHTML. If you don't properly test each of your Web documents and look at your pages as visitors will see them, your organization may lose credibility with potential clients.

Using a Browser for Testing

The easiest way to test a document is to open it in a browser window and look at the results (see Figure 9-1). However, most browsers that support XHTML also support HTML. HTML browsers excuse many errors, such as mismatched or missing quotation marks and missing end tags.

The following XHTML code contains several mistakes:

- The HEAD section ends with a start tag rather than an end tag.
- The alink attribute value is not enclosed in quotation marks.
- The first <dd> start tag has no end tag.
- The document does not include a </body> end tag.

```
<?xml version="1.0"?>
<!DOCTYPE html
    PUBLIC "-//W3C//DTD XHTML 1.0 Strict//EN"
```

```
"DTD/xhtml1-strict.dtd">
<html xmlns="http://www.w3.org/1999/xhtml"
  xml:lang="EN" lang="EN">
<head>
<title>Bad Code</title>
<head>
<body text="black" link="teal" vlink="maroon" alink=yellow>
<dl>
<dt>file</dt>
<dd>A set of organized and related information stored with a
unique filename.
<dt>menu</dt>
<dd>A list of commands available from a horizontal bar
immediately below the title bar.</dd>
</dl>
</html>
```

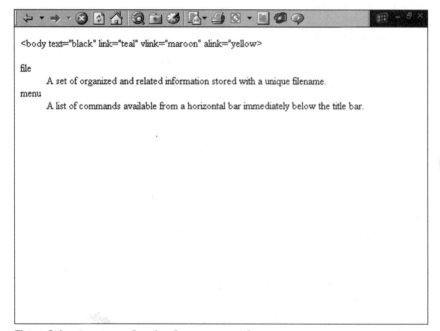

Figure 9-1 *An example of a document with errors.*

The figure shows that the browser has given up on processing the
<body> start tag because of the missing quotation marks. The browser
ignores the other errors.

The following is a corrected version of the code:

```
<?xml version="1.0"?>
<!DOCTYPE html
   PUBLIC "-//W3C//DTD XHTML 1.0 Strict//EN"
   "DTD/xhtml1-strict.dtd">
<html xmlns="http://www.w3.org/1999/xhtml"
   xml:lang="EN" lang="EN">
<head>
<title>A Sample XHTML Document</title>
</head>
<body text="black" link="teal"
   vlink="maroon" alink="yellow">
<dl>
<dt>file</dt>
<dd>A set of organized and related information stored with a
unique filename.</dd>
<dt>Menu</dt>
<dd>A list of commands available from a horizontal bar
immediately below the title bar.</dd>
</dl>
</body>
</html>
```

Figure 9-2 shows the document after it has been corrected. When you compare the two figures, you can see one glaring difference between the good and bad code. However, the browser barely reacts to the other problems. If you don't know what an error-free document should look like, you may never know that you should edit a few lines.

Using a Validator for Testing

XHTML validators, available as online services or as programs installed on your computer, check syntax, elements, and URLs using built-in or user-specified criteria. You also can use a validating XML parser to check Strictly Conforming XHTML documents. To use a validator, simply fill in a form with the URI of the document to be tested, click a button, and receive the results. Then, correct your XHTML document and run the validator again until the document is error-free and loads in a reasonable time. After validation is clean, look at your document using as many browsers as possible.

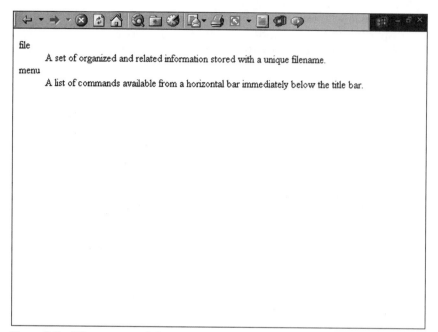

file
  A set of organized and related information stored with a unique filename.
menu
  A list of commands available from a horizontal bar immediately below the title bar.

Figure 9-2   *The corrected document.*

● **NOTE**

Running XHTML validators can be frustrating. Depending on the program, you need to spend some time interpreting and analyzing warning and error messages. An easier approach is to use an XHTML editor. Most editors enable you to create Web documents and check syntax simultaneously.

One of the best sources of validators is the World Wide Web Consortium (W3C), which is the parent organization of HTML, XHTML, XML, and many other Web technologies. The HTML home page (http://www.w3.org/MarkUp/) contains links to its validation service (http://validator.w3.org/) and HTML Tidy (http://www.w3.org/People/Raggett/tidy/), which was written by Dave Raggett. Tidy is a tool for evaluating, correcting, and reformatting HTML and converting HTML to XML. The Tidy home page includes documentation and links from which you can download various versions of Tidy.

Tidy is a downloadable command-line utility. After downloading Tidy, open an MS-DOS window, change to the folder in which you have placed Tidy and the file to be analyzed, enter the following, and press Enter:

```
tidy —m filename.ext
```

filename.ext is the name of the file and its extension (for example, codethis.htm). To produce a named log of the errors in the file, add the following option to the command line:

```
—f errors.txt
```

where errors.txt is the name of a text file that lists the errors. When Tidy evaluated the example of bad coding (646-647), the errors file contained the following comments:

```
Tidy (vers 13th January 2000) Parsing "badcode.htm"
line 5 column 1 - Warning: <html> has XML attribute
"xml:lang"
line 9 column 1 - Warning: <head> isn't allowed in <body>
elements
line 17 column 8 - Warning: end of file while parsing
attributes
line 17 column 8 - Error: missing quotemark for attribute
value
line 17 column 8 - Warning: <body> isn't allowed in <body>
elements
line 17 column 8 - Warning: expected "html PUBLIC" or "html
SYSTEM"

"badcode.htm" appears to be HTML proprietary
6 warnings/errors were found!

This document has errors that must be fixed before
using HTML Tidy to generate a tidied up version.
```

The file was too badly coded for Tidy to modify.

On the other hand, after Tidy evaluates the second example (648), the error file shows the following:

```
Tidy (vers 13th January 2000) Parsing "goodcode.htm"
line 4 column 1 - Warning: <html> has XML attribute
"xml:lang"

"goodcode.htm" appears to be HTML proprietary
1 warnings/errors were found!
```

You can ignore the comment about line 4, column 1 because Tidy is an HTML validator. You have learned that XHTML documents should contain the xml:lang attribute in their <html> start tags.

After evaluating the file, Tidy "tidies" it and leaves its mark by adding a properly formatted <meta> statement:

```
<?xml version="1.0"?>
<!DOCTYPE html PUBLIC "-//W3C//DTD XHTML 1.0 Strict//EN"
"DTD/xhtml1-strict.dtd">
<html xmlns="http://www.w3.org/1999/xhtml" xml:lang="EN"
lang="EN">
<head>
<meta name="generator" content="HTML Tidy, see www.w3.org" />
<title>A Sample XHTML Document</title>
</head>
<body text="black" link="teal" vlink="maroon" alink="yellow">
<dl>
<dt>file</dt>

<dd>A set of organized and related information stored with a
unique
filename.</dd>

<dt>Menu</dt>

<dd>A list of commands available from a horizontal bar
immediately
below the title bar.</dd>
</dl>
</body>
</html>
```

Maintaining Your Documents

It is an understatement to say that there are many HTML documents posted on the Web. As Web developers start to replace their HTML pages with XHTML, they should establish conversion checklists. As you know, current HTML browsers do not require strict adherence to HTML syntax, but browsers that support XHTML will force developers to meet coding standards more rigorously. Converting a typical HTML document to an XHTML document involves line-by-line editing — whether the initial document was created by hand or by an editing program.

When editing XHTML documents, check elements and attributes — particularly those that have been deprecated — against the latest HTML or XHTML standard. Using elements and attributes supported by the HTML specification is preferable to using Microsoft, Netscape, WebTV (and other) extensions, which are not supported by many browsers. In most cases, a browser will ignore syntax that it can't interpret. However, sometimes a browser will misinterpret XHTML statements with unpredictable results.

Whenever you edit an XHTML document, think about converting styling elements and attributes to CSS styling properties. As you know, most styling elements and attributes are deprecated in favor of stylesheets. As you review a particular document, consider adding comments throughout. Then, future editors evaluating and editing the document will work much more efficiently and easily.

For a list of other important topics related to the conversion of HTML documents to XHTML, refer to the "Converting an HTML Document to XHTML" section (535) in Chapter 2.

9

10

Creating Dynamic Documents

M any HTML documents are composed completely of HTML statements. In most cases, the appearance of these types of documents does not change. When you add *scripts*, which are small sections of programming code, to your documents, they become dynamic and interactive. So, if a user moves the mouse pointer over an area of the document, text colors might change or an image might be revealed. Or if he or she clicks, double-clicks, or presses a key on the keyboard, a message might appear onscreen.

As you learned in Chapter 7, many simple HTML documents are processed and displayed completely using the browser program, which runs on the client computer. Other documents — with or without scripts — use the client, server, or both. The scripts are written in scripting languages, such as JavaScript, JScript, and VBScript. These languages are officially known as HTML extensions: They *extend* the HTML language into new areas.

●—**NOTE**

This chapter is a brief overview of the features of the VBScript and JScript scripting languages. For more information about each language, refer to *Teach Yourself ASP*, which is co-authored by Sandra E. Eddy and published by IDG Books Worldwide. Another IDG Worldwide book, *JavaScript Bible*, by Danny Goodman, covers JavaScript comprehensively.

Why Use Scripts?

In Chapter 7, you learned about interactive forms, which users fill in and send to a computer serving a Web site. Scripts can enhance forms by making them interactive. So, when a user submits a form, the receiving Web site can send a thank-you message to the person at the other end. Or, a script can go even further: If the user submits certain information (such as a zip code), a script can check the entry against a database of zip codes. If the zip code and street address and/or city match, a thank-you message is sent. However, if the zip code seems to be inaccurate, the user can be prompted to correct the form and resubmit. Another example is missing information. If the user leaves a required field empty, the script can send a message to the user and redisplay the form.

As you can see, scripts automate a great deal of page production and interaction with users. Scripts also make pages much more interesting to view, thereby attracting more visitors than ever to your site.

●—**NOTE**

A document that includes a script requires special handling: It must be processed by an application that understands the scripting language. For example, Internet Explorer 4 (or greater) includes a VBScript processor that can interpret HTML documents with VBScript scripts; Netscape Navigator does not. If you have the PWS or IIS server installed on your computer, be aware that JScript and an interpreter are bundled with each.

10

Learning About Scripting Languages

The most popular scripting languages are related to an earlier technology. Visual Basic Scripting (VBScript) is a subset of Microsoft's Visual Basic, which in turn is an updated and sophisticated version of the BASIC programming language. JScript, JavaScript, and ECMAScript are nearly identical scripting languages that are distant relatives of the Java programming language. JScript, JavaScript, and ECMAScript are languages that experienced programmers will find easy to learn and to use. If you are a Java, C, or C++ programmer, you will definitely know the underlying structure and logic of these scripting languages. Although JScript, JavaScript, and ECMAScript are virtually the same language, you may have to make minor changes in your code if you move from one of these languages to another.

VBScript

VBScript, which is both easy to learn and to use, is probably the most popular scripting language for novice to advanced programmers. If you become familiar with VBScript, you can easily move up to Visual Basic in order to develop a variety of applications. VBScript is completely case-insensitive. Unlike JScript, you do not need to end each VBScript line with a semicolon (;).VBScript is available only on Internet Explorer and compatible browsers as a client-side scripting language.

JScript

After the inception of JavaScript, Microsoft developed JScript, which is virtually identical to JavaScript. JScript was able to run on the Microsoft Internet Explorer and read programs and applets written for Internet Explorer. JScript is case-sensitive. You should end every JScript line with a semicolon (;), which is not the case with VBScript.

JavaScript

JavaScript was developed by Netscape Communications and Sun Microsystems and is the original Java-related scripting language. JavaScript was originally designed to be incorporated into Web pages read by the Netscape Navigator browser. JavaScript allows Web developers to produce dynamic documents, and enables programmers to call routines written in Java, C, and C++.

10

ECMAScript

Until recently, the only central JavaScript standard had been maintained by Netscape. In 1997, the European Computer Manufacturers Association (ECMA), a standards organization (http://www.ecma.ch/), released the first standard, which is known as ECMA-262 or ECMA Script. ECMAScript incorporates most — but not all — JavaScript features. On the other hand, JScript fully conforms to the ECMAScript standard. Although ECMAScript is a standard, Web browsers do not fully support it at this point. You can download ECMAScript manuals from ftp://ftp.ecma.ch/ecma-st/e262-doc.exe (Microsoft Word format) or `ftp://ftp.ecma.ch/ecma-st/e262-pdf.pdf` (Adobe Acrobat Reader format), or order a free CD-ROM (which is updated every six months).

Introducing XHTML Events

HTML 4.0 supports a set of built-in *intrinsic events* that trigger a script when there is an action such as the click of a mouse button, the movement of the mouse pointer, the press of a keyboard key, the loading of a window, the click of a form button, and so forth. Intrinsic events are attributes (Web) of HTML elements; you can use many events with most elements, but others are limited to one or two. The most common intrinsic events are listed and described in Table 10-1.

Table 10-1 *HTML 4.0's Common Intrinsic Events*

Event	Page Number in Appendix E	The Script Runs When:
onblur	840	The current object is no longer the active object.
onclick	842	A user clicks an object.
ondblclick	845	A user double-clicks an object.
onfocus	850	The current object becomes active through some user action.
onkeydown	852	A user presses and holds down a key over an object.
onkeypress	853	A user presses and releases a key over an object.
onkeyup	853	A user releases a key.
onmousedown	855	A user presses and holds down a mouse button.
onmousemove	857	The mouse moves over an object.
onmouseout	858	The mouse moves away from an object.
onmouseover	858	A user moves the mouse over an object for the first time.
onmouseup	859	A pressed-down mouse button is released.
onselect	865	A user selects text in a form's text box.

10

Note that Microsoft and Netscape have defined additional events that may become part of a future HTML version.

Including Scripts in Your Documents

Whether you use VBScript, JScript, JavaScript, or ECMAScript, the beginning and end of a script in an HTML document are marked by the <script> start tag and the </script> end tag. In the following example (see Figure 10-1), the language attribute names the language, and Now is the function that issues the date and time. The <!-- and //--> delimiters are comments. Comments that enclose scripts prevent older browsers, which do not support scripting, from displaying the script as document text. Newer browsers recognize and ignore the comments. Note also that the words that start the sentence and the period that ends the sentence are both outside the script.

```
<?xml version="1.0"?>
<!DOCTYPE html
    PUBLIC "-//W3C//DTD XHTML 1.0 Strict//EN"
    "DTD/xhtml1-strict.dtd">
<html xmlns="http://www.w3.org/1999/xhtml"
    xml:lang="EN" lang="EN">
<head>
<title>Display the Date and Time</title>
</head>
<body>
<h2>Display the Date and Time</h2>
<p>The date and time are
<script language="VBSCRIPT">
<!--
document.write(Now)
//-->
</script>
.</p>
</body>
</html>
```

10

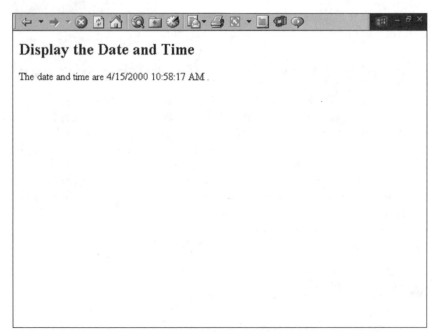

Figure 10-1 *A document with a short VBScript script.*

A counterpart script in JScript looks like this (see Figure 10-2):

```
<?xml version="1.0"?>
<!DOCTYPE html
  PUBLIC "-//W3C//DTD XHTML 1.0 Strict//EN"
  "DTD/xhtml1-strict.dtd">
<html xmlns="http://www.w3.org/1999/xhtml"
  xml:lang="EN" lang="EN">
<head>
<title>Display the Date and Time</title>
</head>
<body>
<h2>Display the Date and Time</h2>
<script language="JSCRIPT">
<!--
datetest=new Date();
//-->
</script>
<p>The date and time are
<script language="JSCRIPT">
<!--
document.write(datetest);
//-->
```

```
    </script>
    .</p>
    </body>
    </html>
```

In VBScript, you entered the <script> and </script> tags once: to call and write the Now function. In JScript, you need to use the script element twice: once to call the Date() function and once to write the results. You'll find differences like these as you learn both VBScript and JScript — and as you learn other scripting languages.

Figure 10-2   *A document with a short JScript script.*

Using Variables

As you probably know, a *variable* is a user-defined name that represents varying data of all types — characters, digits, character strings, and so forth. So, when you use a variable in your scripts, you don't have to enter the actual data itself; when the script is processed, the client or server program does it for you. Variables enable you to use "nicknames" or shortcuts to represent data, to allow a script to calculate value changes, and to enable you to replace one value with another quickly, rather than "hard-coding" each instance of a value. VBScript and JScript provide different ways of using variables.

Using Variables in VBScript

VBScript provides three statements — Dim, Private, and Public — with which you can declare one or more variables.

The Dim statement declares an *array* (a list of one or more data values in one or more *dimensions*). Think of an array as a table of rows and columns of values. For example, a two-dimensional array has two columns of values.

```
Dim Terms(4)

Dim Terms()

Dim date01
```

The first example declares an array of five terms, starting at 0 and ending at 4. The second example declares a dynamic array, which is a list that can contain any number of values and dimensions. The third example declares a single element. Use the ReDim (resize *dim*ensions) statement each time you want to change the number of values and dimensions. For example, the first ReDim statement for a particular value can specify an array of 6 rows and 4 columns, and the second can declare 8 rows and 3 columns.

```
ReDim Terms(5, 3)
ReDim Preserve Terms (7, 2)
```

●—NOTE

You should only declare a variable one time in a Web document — even one that incorporates several scripts.

The optional Preserve keyword retains the original values of the array.

The Private statement declares a list of variables that are available only in the script in which it is coded. In the following example, the PrivNum number is declared:

```
Private PrivNum
```

The Public statement declares one or more variables that are available to all scripting procedures in a document. It is very important to note that you must declare Public statements outside specific procedures — for example, before any procedures are declared.

Names of variables, such as Terms, PrivNum, and so forth, must follow certain rules. A name must start with an alphabetic character, must not be longer than 255 characters, cannot contain a period (.),

and must be unique. After you declare a variable, you should give
it a value.

The following example (see Figure 10-3) gives a string value to
each variable. Then, the strings are joined by using ampersands (&)
and spaces enclosed within quotation marks ("). Finally, StrName
is written.

```
<?xml version="1.0"?>
<!DOCTYPE html
    PUBLIC "-//W3C//DTD XHTML 1.0 Strict//EN"
    "DTD/xhtml1-strict.dtd">
<html xmlns="http://www.w3.org/1999/xhtml"
    xml:lang="EN" lang="EN">
<head>
<title>Examples of Strings</title>
</head>
<body>
<script language="VBSCRIPT">
<!--
Dim StrFirst, StrMiddle, StrLast, StrName
StrFirst = "Sandra"
StrMiddle = "E."
StrLast = "Eddy"
StrName = StrFirst & StrMiddle & StrLast
document.write StrName
//-->
</script>
<p>
<script language="VBSCRIPT">
<!--
 StrName = StrFirst & " " & _
    StrMiddle & " " & StrLast
document.write StrName
//-->
</script>
</p>
</body>
</html>
```

10

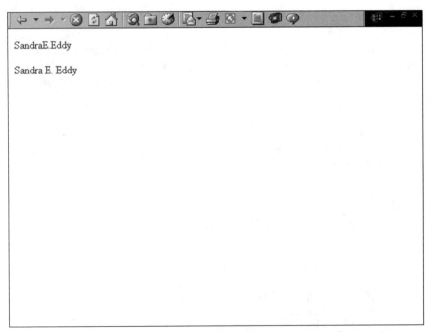

SandraE.Eddy

Sandra E. Eddy

Figure 10-3 *A document that uses a VBScript script to combine strings and write the result.*

Using Variables in JScript

The JScript developers have decided that the Dim statement is not necessary: When you give a variable a value, you state implicitly that the variable exists. For example:

```
ColorIt = "Red";
```

The name of the variable is on the left side of the equal sign, and its value is on the right.

You can use an array to declare multiple values for a variable. For example:

```
ColorIt = new Array(6);
ColorIt[0] = "Red";
ColorIt[2] = "Blue";
ColorIt[3] = "Green";
ColorIt[5] = "Cyan";
```

The first line of the example declares an array of seven variables, starting at 0 and ending at 6. Then four of the seven variables are given values. Be sure that you enclose the item number within brackets ([ ]), which are the characters that represent the array-index operator. And, as always, end each line with a semicolon.

What if you want to declare a variable without giving it a value until later in the Web document? Simply precede the variable declaration with the var keyword:

```
var ColorIt;
```

Of course, you can precede every variable with the var keyword. For example:

```
var ColorIt = "Red";
```

This example ensures that everyone knows that you are declaring a variable. Variables also take multiple values:

```
var several = "Red", "Celtics", "Knicks";
```

Variables can even include a formula to be calculated as well as subvariables:

```
var ComputeThis = 50, count, frammis = 6;
```

So, you can see that a single variable can include numbers, text, and even other variables with their own values.

Names of JScript variables must follow certain rules: A name cannot be a reserved JScript keyword, cannot contain spaces, and must be unique. In fact, the more unique a name is, the less likely you will have to change it if JScript developers add another reserved keyword to the list.

The following example (see Figure 10-4) is a counterpart to the prior VBScript example:

```
<?xml version="1.0"?>
<!DOCTYPE html
  PUBLIC "-//W3C//DTD XHTML 1.0 Strict//EN"
  "DTD/xhtml1-strict.dtd">
<html xmlns="http://www.w3.org/1999/xhtml"
  xml:lang="EN" lang="EN">
<head>
<title>Examples of Strings</title>
</head>
<body>
<script language="JSCRIPT">
<!--
StrFirst = "Sandra";
StrMiddle = "E.";
StrLast = "Eddy";
StrName = StrFirst += StrMiddle += StrLast;
```

```
document.write(StrName);
//-->
</script>
<p>
<script language="JSCRIPT">
<!--
NameArray = new Array("Sandra", "E.", "Eddy");
JndString = NameArray.join(" ")
document.write(JndString);
//-->
</script>
</p>
</body>
</html>
```

SandraE.Eddy

Sandra E. Eddy

Figure 10-4 *Using a JScript script to combine strings and write the result.*

Using Control Structures

In Web documents, processing normally flows from the top line of code to the bottom line. *Conditional statements*, or *control structures*, include two or more branches to different sections of a script, thereby breaking the top-to-bottom flow. If a certain condition is met, one section of the script is processed; if an alternate condition is met, another section is processed. For example, a script could branch to one section and process it if a value is greater than 5 or to another section if that value is less than 5. As you might imagine, control structures vary in VBScript and JScript.

Using Control Structures in VBScript

A simple conditional statement looks something like the following If... Then conditional example from Microsoft's VBScript Tutorial:

```
Sub FixDate()
    Dim myDate
    myDate = #2/13/95#
    If myDate < Now Then myDate = Now
End Sub
```

In the first line, Sub is a keyword that indicates the beginning of a *subroutine*, a section of script that is processed as a unit. The second line of the example declares a variable named myDate, and the following line gives myDate a date value. The fourth line sets the conditions for processing: If myDate is less than the current system date and time, the script changes myDate to the current system date and time. Otherwise, the script goes to the following line, End Sub, which is the end of the subroutine. At this point, processing continues — at the line following the line from which the subroutine was called. Another VBScript conditional statement is Select Case.

You can write a script that tests several instances of If... Then... Else statements (see Figure 10-5). Simply replace the Else that normally starts the last branching formula with an ElseIf, which ends the current If statement and starts another.

```
<?xml version="1.0"?>
<!DOCTYPE html
    PUBLIC "-//W3C//DTD XHTML 1.0 Strict//EN"
    "DTD/xhtml1-strict.dtd">
<html xmlns="http://www.w3.org/1999/xhtml"
    xml:lang="EN" lang="EN">
<head>
<title>How's the Weather?</title>
</head>
<body>
<script language="VBSCRIPT">
Dim Exclaim, Temp
Temp = 30
If Temp <= 32 Then
    document.write "It's freezing out here!"
ElseIf Temp > 32 Then
```

10

```
      document.write "It's warming up."
End If
</script>
</body>
</html>
```

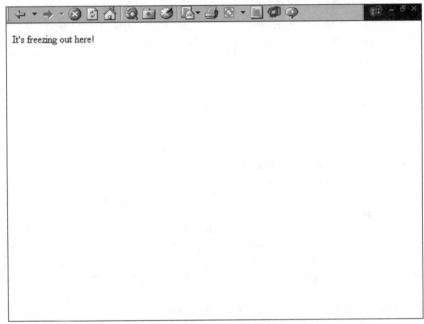

Figure 10-5   *Using a VBScript script conditional statement.*

10

To test the example, change the temperature to 33 or above.

Looping statements enable a Web processor to calculate a formula nested within the loop repeatedly until a particular value is reached or a condition remains or becomes true. VBScript supports four types of looping statements: Do... Loop, While... Wend, For... Next, and For Each... Next.

Do... Loop keeps looping as long as a condition is true or when a false condition becomes true. For example:

```
Sub IterateIt()
  Dim ItNum
  ItNum = 0
  Do Until ItNum = 10
    ItNum = ItNum + 1
  Loop
  MsgBox "ItNum is finally " & ItNum"
End Sub
```

The initial value (0) of ItNum is set in the third line of the example. The fourth line, which starts the Do... Loop, states that the loop is active until ItNum equals 10. The fifth line contains a formula that adds 1 to the value of ItNum, so ItNum will have succeeding values of 1, 2, 3, 4, and so forth, until it reaches the ultimate value of 10 and the loop ends. The sixth line displays the current value of ItNum in a message box, and the seventh line, Loop, marks the end of the loop lines. As long as ItNum is not equal to 10 (that is, ItNum is false), the lines within the loop are processed repeatedly. A While... Wend statement keeps looping as long as a condition is true. Microsoft recommends that you use Do... Loop instead.

The For... Next and For Each... Next statements also use counters to automate processing. The For... Next counterpart to the prior Do... Loop is:

```
For k = 0 To 10 Step 1
  ItNum = ItNum + k
  MsgBox "ItNum is now " & ItNum & "
Next
```

The Step keyword enables you to specify a value by which the variable is increased or decreased. For Each... Next enables you to write individual statements for multiple items in an array.

Using Control Structures in JScript

Conditional statements in JScript vary from those in VBScript. For example:

```
function FixDate() {
    var myDate = "2/13/95";
    if (myDate < Date())
    myDate = Date();
}
```

In the first line, function is a keyword that indicates the beginning of a section of script that is processed as a unit. (Remember that in VBScript, the keyword was Sub, for subroutine.) Most of the remaining part of the function looks almost the same as the VBScript subroutine: The second line declares a variable named myDate and gives it a date value. The following two lines set the conditions for processing: If myDate is less than the current system date and time, change myDate to the current system date and time. Otherwise, end the function. At this point, processing continues — at the line following the line from which the subroutine was called. Notice the presence of braces ({ }),

10

which enclose the entire function. When a variable is declared within a function, it only applies to the function.

The following code (see Figure 10-6), with the exception of the changed temperature, is the counterpart to the VBScript code shown in Figure 10-5:

```
<html>
<head>
<title>How's the Weather?</title>
</head>
<body>
<script language="JSCRIPT">
var Temp = 34;
if (Temp <= 32)
  document.write("It's freezing!");
else
if (Temp > 32)
  document.write("It's warming up.");
</script>
</body>
</html>
```

You can check this code by changing the temperature to below freezing.

JScript supports three versions of looping statements: for, while, and for... in. The for statement keeps looping as long as a condition is true. Look at this example from the Microsoft JScript Language Reference:

```
for (i = 0; i < 10; i++)
{
    j *= i;
}
```

In the first line of the statement, the initial value of i is set to 0, i is tested to find out if it is less than 10, and i is added (++) by 1. In the third line (within the braces), i is multiplied by itself (*=) to result in j. As long as i is less than 10, the lines within the loop are processed repeatedly.

The while statement is almost the opposite of the for statement. In contrast to the for statement, which keeps looping as long as a condition is true, while loops until a condition is false. So, if a condition starts out false, processing within the while loop will never occur. Unlike the for statement, in which an expression is initialized and incremented, while tests an expression and runs a statement only while the condition is true.

The for... in statement displays properties for objects named within. So, you can show characteristics of graphics, windows, and so forth to demonstrate familiarity with a visitor's Desktop or to repair a broken script.

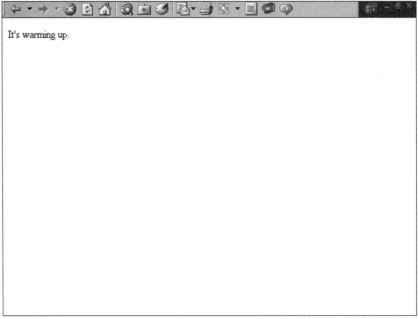

Figure 10-6 *The JScript counterpart to the example shown in Figure 10-5.*

Customizing XHTML

One of the most exciting differences between HTML and XHTML is the fact that you can use non-HTML elements and attributes in your documents. For example, if you want to express and display mathematical formulas, you no longer have to combine keyboard characters with a long series of subscripts (using the sub element) and superscripts (using the sup element), larger and smaller fonts (with the font, big, or small elements or font style-sheet properties), and special non-keyboard characters — or take further measures such as scanning or creating graphics. Now, you can associate the Mathematical Markup Language (MathML) recommendation in order to use its custom mathematical elements and attributes.

In Chapter 2, you learned that XHTML 1.0 is associated with the XML namespace using the xmlns attribute. So, remember that you express the <html> start tag as follows:

```
<html xmlns="http://www.w3.org/1999/xhtml"
  xml:lang="en" lang="en">
```

The xmlns attribute names the XML namespace URI: http://www.w3.org/1999/xhtml. This is the default for standard XHTML documents. The *X* in XHTML indicates that the language is *extensible*. In other words, you can extend XHTML beyond the standard XHTML namespace. The XHTML 1.0 recommendation (http://www.w3.org/TR/xhtml1) shows how to associate the MathML recommendation. The example (see Section 3.1.2, "Using XHTML with Other Namespaces") looks like this:

```
<html xmlns="http://www.w3.org/1999/xhtml"
    xml:lang="en" lang="en">
<head>
<title>A Math Example</title>
</head>
<body>
   <p>The following is MathML markup:</p>
   <math xmlns="http://www.w3.org/1998/Math/MathML">
     <apply> <log />
       <logbase>
         <cn> 3 </cn>
       </logbase>
       <ci> x </ci>
     </apply>
   </math>
</body>
</html>
```

Up to the </p> end tag, the document is composed of familiar elements — html, head, title, body, and p. However, look at the <math> start tag, which contains a URI for the MathML recommendation. You won't find the math element in any HTML 4.0 reference. Neither are the child elements enclosed within the $start tag and the$ end tag. However, you'll find these custom tags declared in the MathML recommendation. As you might have guessed, math is the root element of MathML documents; all other elements (apply, log, logbase, cn, and ci) are its child elements.

Why Declare New Elements and Attributes?

With a background in planning and developing DTDs, you can create your own custom XML-based language and use it to enhance your XHTML documents. For example, if you're part of an industry with a unique vocabulary (such as the mathematicians in the prior example), you can declare elements and attributes that use industry terms and display them properly. At the same time, you can also specify entities as shortcuts to long technical terms or even company names.

Or, you can make it easier to insert proper fields — all defined as custom elements — into database records.

Using one custom XML DTD, you can even set standards for classes of documents within your organization. This means that all site maps or departmental home pages, for instance, will have the same look — regardless of the author.

You can specify the order in which elements are used, thereby having greater control over your documents. For example, in filling a database, you can compel a Web page developer to request the first name first (with a `firstname` element, for example), followed by the middle initial (for example, `initial`), and then the last name (for example, `lastname`), the street address, the city, the state, and postal code — in that order. Then, the database designer makes sure that the receiving database record is set up in a parallel way, to accept the fields as they have been declared and as entered by the users of that page.

By setting default attribute values, you can make it easier for users to enter information into interactive forms. Predefining attribute values enables you to exert greater control over document (and possibly future database) content.

A DTD Primer

In the "Introducing DTDs" sidebar (508) in Chapter 1, you learned that *document type definitions* (DTDs) define elements and their attributes and attribute values, entities, and notation. A DTD determines the document structure, the type of content, and even the appearance of the document onscreen. The "Reading and Interpreting the XHTML DTD" sidebar (533) in Chapter 2 demonstrates how elements and attributes are declared using Extended Backus-Naur Form (EBNF) notation. You were introduced to EBNF in the "Introducing Extended Backus-Naur Form (EBNF) Notation" sidebar (522) in Chapter 2. You will learn more about EBNF in the "Coding a DTD with EBNF" (678) section later in this chapter.

Planning a DTD

Before you declare your first custom element, you should plan the DTD. To outline the construction and substance of the DTD, ask yourself the following questions:

- What is the purpose of the new elements and their attributes? Will they be used to display documents on the computer screen, print them on paper, or insert them in another application?

- What information will the XHTML browser or processor need to successfully process the documents?
- How many generations of elements will be required? How should the child elements relate to other children, to their descendants, or to their parent elements?
- How much will the elements and attributes contribute to page layout, paragraph alignment, and character formats?
- Will the elements or style-sheet properties define styles and formats?
- How should each declared attribute behave? Will you declare default attribute values?
- What elements will be required? Which elements will be optional?
- Will you require that certain elements be entered in a particular order?
- What types of entities will you define? Will some entities be used to specify shortcuts for technical terms, company names, or regularly used terms? Will you use other entities to refer to particular non-keyboard characters (such as accented letters, and so on)?

Setting Generations of Elements

After planning a DTD, the next step is to outline it, deciding on the structure of elements — from the root (the highest level), to the first generation of child elements, to all their descendants. Look at the following database components:

```
Name
Address
ID Number
```

Should any of these components be broken down further? For the sake of efficiency, the answer probably should be *yes*. For example, if you want to sort records by a customer's or employee's last name, by city, or by zip code, you should expand on the Name and Address fields as follows:

```
Name
     Title
     First Name
     Middle Initial
     Last Name
```

```
Suffix
```

```
Address
     Street Address
     Second Address
     City
     State
     Postal Code
     Country
     E-Mail Address
```

```
ID Number
```

Using this structure, you can address a person informally (by first name) or formally (by title — Mr., Mrs., or Ms.). You can differentiate between a father (a Sr. suffix) and son (Jr.) living at the same address. Because you can sort the record by many fields, you can target messages and mail to specific groups of people.

The best way to outline a DTD is to enter the highest-level components first. Then, fill in components for the next level down, the level below that, and so on. For example, in the database example, the Name, Address, and ID Number are all at the highest level. The second-level elements are indented under the highest-level components.

To decide if a component is indeed a top-level component, ask yourself whether any other component is at a higher level. For example, in most books, the book itself is the top-level element or the root. The chapter is at the next highest level: No other component comes between a chapter and the entire book. However, some larger books consist of parts under which sets of chapters are organized. When you insert a new top-level element, you may have to move other elements down a level.

After you place the highest-level components, decide whether they belong at their current level or even belong at all. For instance, in the database example, you might decide to eliminate the Name component altogether and move Title, First Name, Middle Initial, Last Name, and Suffix up to the next higher generation.

To synchronize the fields with the fields in their associated database, how many of these items should occur in a particular order? That requires your deciding how users should enter information and understanding how the database is organized.

Should you further enhance the database? For example, if you wish to insert photographs in certain records (for example, employees in a human resources database), where should you place the photo element? Should it be under the Last Name (where there may be several records with the same last name) or ID Number element

11

(which should be unique)? Should it be another high-level element? Obviously, the final answer is up to you.

Coding a DTD with EBNF

Extended Backus-Naur Form (EBNF) is the standard syntax that comprises the HTML DTDs, the XML DTD, and DTDs for custom markup languages. You use EBNF syntax to define the elements, attributes, entities, and other components that comprise any DTD. EBNF enables you to specify ranges of values, valid values, valid elements and entities, the location of particular elements in the hierarchy of elements, and much more. Before you declare your first element or write your first entity, take the time to learn EBNF, which is the International Standard ISO/IEC 14977: 1996 of the International Standardization Organization (ISO) and the International Electrotechnical Commission (IEC).

EBNF syntax is the "official" standard used by developers of SGML- and XML-based markup languages and for individuals learning about the components of markup languages such as XML, its parent SGML, and their close relative HTML.

Among EBNF's unique vocabulary are three terms: rule, production, and grammar. A *rule* is a statement that defines a *production*, the definition of a single component of a language. An entire set of productions is a *grammar*, which contains every rule for the language. Because it is a technical syntax, EBNF uses programming and mathematical terms, such as symbol, expression, operator, and operand.

EBNF uses special characters to delimit or connect components in XML documents. Each character has a unique meaning. In XHTML markup, you have already seen that the less-than symbol (<) marks the beginning of components and that the greater-than symbol (>) marks the end of components, such as start tags and end tags. Quotation marks (") and single-quote marks (') indicate the beginning and end of strings.

In DTDs, the less-than symbol (<) and greater-than symbol (>) also mark the beginning and end of element and attribute declarations. Sets of parentheses (( )) group parts of expressions, and sets of brackets ([ ]) group optional ranges of characters or other components. Within statements, other characters connect components. For example, the pipe (|) connects components from which you can, but are not required to, choose — in any particular order. And the comma (,) indicates that elements must be chosen in the order in which they are listed.

The plus sign, asterisk, and question mark are very important symbols in EBNF. An expression or component followed by a plus sign (+) indicates that the expression *must* appear one or more times. An expression or component followed by an asterisk (*) indicates that the expression *may* appear one or more times. An expression or component followed by a question mark (?) indicates that the expression is optional. Even the absence of a character indicates something: An expression or component without a succeeding symbol can be selected one time only.

EBNF also enables a custom-language developer to specify whether certain characters are permitted as element values. Simply use the not symbol (^) to precede characters that are not allowed. Using EBNF syntax, you can impose a great deal of control over document creation. For example, you can require the use of specific elements, define attributes for those elements, limit the attribute values that can be entered, and specify default attribute values.

For more information about EBNF symbols and usage, refer to Appendix D, *EBNF Reference* (753).

Adding Custom Elements to XHTML

Once you have decided on the generations of elements, attributes, and entities that will make up a DTD, you can start creating your DTD.

Since XHTML is an XML-based language, an XHTML DTD starts with the lines that start an XML document:

```
<?xml version="1.0"?>
<!DOCTYPE root_element [
```

As you know, the first line states that the document uses the XML Version 1.0 grammar. The document type (!DOCTYPE) declaration names the root element. The left bracket ([) indicates that all the element, attribute, entity, and notation declarations are included in the document. (To mark the end of a DTD, enter the]> delimiter.)

●—NOTE ─────────────────────────

In both XML and XHTML documents, the DOCTYPE declaration calls an external DTD subset, an internal DTD subset, or both. An *external DTD subset* is stored completely outside the document in which it is referenced, and an *internal DTD subset* is entirely within the document. For example, the three HTML DTDs are external DTDs, which are publicly available (the PUBLIC keyword) in the DTD folder at the W3C:

```
<!DOCTYPE html
    PUBLIC "-//W3C//DTD XHTML 1.0 Strict//EN"
    "DTD/xhtml1-strict.dtd">
```

Declaring Root and Child Elements

11

In the "Reading and Interpreting the XHTML DTD" sidebar (508) in Chapter 2, you saw the element declarations for the table element (288) and all its children — caption (76), col (90), colgroup (92), thead (315), tfoot (307), tbody (293), tr (319), th (310), and td (297). In fact, table is the root table-making element; caption, col, colgroup, thead, tfoot, and tbody are the child elements of table; tr is a child of thead, tfoot, and tbody; and th and td are children of tr. That's a relatively complex four generations of elements.

Most element declarations are more simple than that of table. For example, to declare the root element and the first generation of child elements of a simple employee database, enter the following:

```
<!DOCTYPE employee [
<!ELEMENT employee (first_name, last_name, address_1,
    address_2, city, state, zip, telephone, email,
    emp_id)>
```

The employee element is the root, and the elements listed within the parentheses are the first generation. The comma separating each child element indicates that each element is to be used in the order in which it appears on the list. If you separate all or some elements with pipe (|) symbols, you allow more latitude: Each element may occur one or more times and can appear in any order. You can use a combination of commas and pipes to control strictly the use of some elements and allow relaxation in the use of others. You can also place lists of elements, separated by pipes or commas, within parentheses. Parentheses group like elements in the same way that you can group mathematical expressions to move them up in the order of calculating precedence. Notice that the < symbol starts the statement, and the > symbol ends it.

Other special characters control each element or group of elements. Close the name of a child element with a ? (elementname?) to indicate that it may appear; follow the element with * (elementname*) to indicate that it may not appear at all, or may appear any number of times; or follow the element with a + to indicate that it must appear at least once or any number of times. If the element name is not followed by one of these three characters, it must appear just once. For example:

```
<!ELEMENT employee (first_name, last_name, address_1,
    address_2?, city, state, zip, telephone+, email*,
    emp_id)>
```

The question mark following `address_2` indicates that a second address may appear but is not required, the plus sign following `telephone` indicates that at least one telephone number must be supplied, and the asterisk following `email` requires one or more e-mail addresses.

After declaring the root element and listing the child elements, declare the individual child elements:

```
<!ELEMENT first_name    (#PCDATA)>
<!ELEMENT last_name     (#PCDATA)>
<!ELEMENT address_1     (#PCDATA)>
<!ELEMENT address_2     (#PCDATA)>
<!ELEMENT city          (#PCDATA)>
<!ELEMENT state         (#PCDATA)>
<!ELEMENT zip           (#PCDATA)>
<!ELEMENT telephone     (#PCDATA)>
<!ELEMENT email         (#PCDATA)>
<!ELEMENT emp_id        (#PCDATA)>
```

The keyword `#PCDATA` represents Parsed Character Data, which is any non-markup data (for example, a string, variable, entity, and so forth) or child elements that a developer or user can enter for this element. You could also list child elements for a particular child element and not allow the use of parsed character data. For example:

```
<!ELEMENT telephone    (voice|fax|cell)>
```

breaks the `telephone` element into child elements for three types of telephone numbers. Then, you would have to declare these elements later in the DTD:

```
<!ELEMENT voice    (#PCDATA)>
<!ELEMENT fax      (#PCDATA)>
<!ELEMENT cell     (#PCDATA)>
```

What if you want to declare an empty element? Simply add the `EMPTY` keyword to the element declaration:

```
<!ELEMENT linebreak EMPTY>
```

or

```
<!ELEMENT image     EMPTY>
```

●—**NOTE**————————————————————————————

If you think that a particular line of a DTD will be difficult for future developers to understand, it's easy to insert a comment. You can also use comments to separate parts of a DTD from others.

Declaring Lists of Attributes

When you declare an attribute list for an element, you provide additional information that will upgrade the element in some way. For example, you can format or enhance an element by aligning it, changing its color, adding a border, and so on. In a DTD, the ATTLIST keyword signals an attribute-list declaration — a list of attributes and their values for a particular element. Typically, each element in a DTD has an associated list of several attributes — all contributing in their own way to the element. An attribute list is located under the element with which it is associated. The following attribute lists declare the attributes and values for an empty horizontal rule element:

```
<!ELEMENT hrule EMPTY>
<!ATTLIST hrule
    id        id                  #REQUIRED
    align     (left|right|center) #IMPLIED
    noshade   (noshade)           #IMPLIED
    size      CDATA               #IMPLIED
    width     CDATA               #IMPLIED
>
```

or

```
<!ELEMENT hrule EMPTY>
<!ATTLIST hrule id      ID                  #REQUIRED>
<!ATTLIST hrule align (left|right|center) #IMPLIED>
<!ATTLIST hrule noshade  (noshade)         #IMPLIED>
<!ATTLIST hrule size       CDATA           #IMPLIED>
<!ATTLIST hrule width      CDATA           #IMPLIED>
```

Note that these examples, which show the two valid ways of declaring attributes, are based on the horizontal rule (hr) element declaration in the HTML 4.0 DTD. Either type of attribute list is valid. The id attribute requires that an identifier (the ID type) be used with the element. (For more information about XML attribute types, refer to *XML in Plain English* or *Teach Yourself XML*, both by Sandra E. Eddy and published by IDG Books Worldwide.) The optional align attribute provides a choice of left-, right-, or centered alignment. The optional noshade attribute gives a default value of no shading for the rule. The optional size and width attributes control the top-to-bottom depth and side-to-side width of the rule.

●—**NOTE**————————————————————————————

The align, noshade, size, and width attributes are deprecated and found only in the Transitional DTD. The HTML 4.0 specification recommends that you use style sheet properties instead.

Setting Attribute Types and Values

When you assign an attribute type to a particular attribute in the attribute-list declaration, you control both the attribute value and the type of value that is allowed. For example, CDATA, the most common attribute type, enables you to limit the attribute value of a string to character data only. So, by giving an attribute a CDATA attribute type, you are actually stating that the attribute value is both a string and character data. The default declaration, which is at the end of an attribute-list declaration, enables you to make an attribute's use required or optional. You can also fix one valid value, set a default value that can be changed, or list a set of valid values.

You can set a default attribute value in two ways: You can suggest the value or insist on it. The difference is the #FIXED keyword. Look at the following two examples:

```
<!ATTLIST  info  company  CDATA   "Acme">
<!ATTLIST  info  company  CDATA   #FIXED "Acme">
```

In the first example, although "Acme" is the default value for the company attribute, a Web document developer can override that value by typing a different company name. The second example forces the developer to accept the default company name. In both cases, however, if the company name is not entered, the Web processor uses the default value.

Remember that the asterisk (*) indicates that the expression within the parentheses can be used any number of times. Thus, an attribute list can include single values:

```
<!ATTLIST title size CDATA            "14">
```

and lists of values. These values can be followed by an attribute value default declaration (which specifies a default value):

```
<!ATTLIST title size (12|14|16|24)      "14">
```

or they can be followed by a keyword type of default declaration (which allows the user to choose from the list):

```
<!ATTLIST title size (12|14|16|24)      #IMPLIED>
```

Here's a more complete example:

```
<!ELEMENT    title (#PCDATA)>
  <!ATTLIST title
          name    CDATA                    #REQUIRED
          id      ID                       #REQUIRED
          font    (Helvetica|Arial Black)  "Helvetica"
          size    (12|14|16|24)            "14">
```

11

The attribute list follows the element declaration. Both the `name` and `id` attributes are required. `name` accepts character data, and `id` must be an ID type. For the `font` attribute, a developer is limited to two choices: Helvetica or Arial Black. Helvetica is the default value. The `size` attribute provides four choices of point sizes; 14 is the default.

Declaring Entities

An *entity* is simply a named chunk of information — ranging in size all the way from a single character to an entire book consisting of one file. An *entity reference* refers to an entity from within a document. When a browser or processor interprets the document, it identifies each entity reference and replaces it with the content of the entity — that is, the replacement text.

You can use entities to represent long or technical words, commonly used but difficult-to-type text, or text (such as a product name) that you think will change in the final document. For example, an entity allows you to use the nickname *fram* to avoid typing *The Frammis Manufacturing Organization, Inc.* too many times throughout a business plan or long report. You can compile a book using a series of chapter entities and other external documents. This has certain advantages: You can create boilerplate pages or documents that you can plug into all your books (and you can store the files in a central location), and you can show the underlying structure of the book without obstructing it with a great deal of text.

The two main categories of XML entities are general and parameter. A *general entity* occurs anywhere in the document, including some parts of the DTD, whereas a *parameter entity* occurs only within the DTD.

The text of a general entity replaces its reference as document content. In a document, a general entity reference is preceded by an ampersand (&) and succeeded by a semicolon (;).

The following example shows a typical general entity declaration:

```
<!ENTITY copyright "This document is
  copyrighted by the Eddy Group, Inc.">
```

In the example, `copyright` is the name of the entity. When the XML parser finds the entity reference `&copyright;` in the document, it replaces the reference with the text `This document is copyrighted by the Eddy Group, Inc.`

You can embed an entity within an entity. For example:

```
<!ENTITY eddy "Eddy Group, Inc.">
<!ENTITY copyright "This document is
  copyrighted by the &eddy;">
```

Just make sure that you declare the entity that is to be embedded before the entity that contains it.

● **NOTE** ─────────────────────────────────────

A typical processor or browser processes an XML document from top to bottom — from the first line to the last. If an entity declaration is located after a mixed-content element in which that entity appears, the processor or browser cannot correctly interpret the element's contents. Therefore, it's good practice to cluster all entities at the top of the DTD, above all element declarations. This ensures that all the entities included in mixed-content elements are always processed and replaced with replacement text before the XML parser interprets the elements.

Character entities are a particular type of general entity used to enter non-keyboard characters into an XML document. Say you're creating a cover letter in English and you want to incorporate accented *e*'s into the word *resume* to make *résumé*. Rather than incorrectly omitting the accented *e*'s or using a utility such as Windows Character Map to insert the accented *e*'s (which the processor or browser will probably misinterpret), you can declare entities for the character, as in this example:

```
<!ENTITY accent_e    "&#233;">
```

In a Web document, the character entity reference might look like this:

```
<p>
Enclosed is my r&#233;sum&#233;.
</p>
```

Remember that XHTML supports the entire Unicode character set. When you use a predefined entity name for the accented *e* (in this case, é), you can incorporate the accented *e*'s into the word without declaring an entity. For example:

```
<p>
Enclosed is my r&eacute;sum&eacute;.
</p>
```

The choice is yours.

If you use a certain special character constantly, consider explicitly declaring it in the DTD for the current document or for a set of documents. You can either look it up at the Unicode site or find it in one of the International Standards Organization (ISO) character sets. If you compile an entire set of commonly used character entities (or any other list of entities, such as all 50 states, your company's customers, and so on), either paste them into each of your DTDs or refer to them by using an external identifier.

A parameter entity (PE) is a string that is named in the DTD only. A PE is always parsed because it is part of the document markup. Use a PE to enhance the current DTD by inserting a chunk of another DTD or by importing a DTD that is a standard either for your industry or the type of document on which you are working. For example, if you develop a document that combines a standard set of elements defined in your main DTD and elements declared especially for this document, use a PE to import the standard DTD. You could copy and paste, but this would increase the size of the current DTD unnecessarily. Using a PE to import the DTD limits the number of lines; the PE serves as a comment, too.

A PE's syntax differs slightly from that of a general entity. For example:

```
<!ENTITY % InputType
"(TEXT | PASSWORD | CHECKBOX | RADIO
        | SUBMIT | RESET | FILE | HIDDEN
        | IMAGE | BUTTON)"
>
```

When an HTML processor reads the % InputType entity in the input element declaration, it replaces % InputType with the list of ten attributes. In other words, without the InputType entity, the number of lines in this very large element declaration would increase by ten.

You can learn a great deal about using entities — especially PEs — by studying the HTML 4.0 DTD. At the top of the DTD are pages of PEs, which either categorize child elements or name lists of attributes. For example, the events entity lists ten dynamic HTML attributes (onclick, ondblclick, onkeypress, and so forth), which are covered in the "Introducing XHTML Events" section (658) in Chapter 10. When you specify one of these attributes in an HTML document, you can link an event, such as clicking a mouse or pressing a key, with a particular action, such as changing a color. Most HTML elements support the events attributes, so you can imagine the size of the HTML DTD without these shortcuts. Many entities in the HTML DTD contain other entities. For example, the inline entity includes four subcategories of formatting entities (and allows an HTML developer to enter #PCDATA as well):

```
<!ENTITY % inline "#PCDATA | %fontstyle;
            | %phrase; | %special;
            | %formctrl;"
>
```

Both general entities and PEs support external entities: To use an external entity in an XHTML document or a DTD, simply refer to a URI for a standalone file that contains one or more entity declarations. An external general entity refers to content that will be inserted in the non-DTD part of an XHTML document, whereas an external PE refers to markup that will be inserted in a DTD. For example:

```
<?xml version="1.0"?>
<!DOCTYPE manual [
<!ELEMENT manual (#PCDATA)>
<!ENTITY  intro      SYSTEM "intro.doc">
<!ENTITY  chap01     SYSTEM "chap01.doc">
<!ENTITY  chap02     SYSTEM "chap02.doc">
<!ENTITY  chap03     SYSTEM "chap03.doc">
<!ENTITY  appxa      SYSTEM "appxa.doc">
]>
<manual>
&chap01;
&chap02;
&chap03;
&appxa;
</manual>
```

The entity declarations in the internal DTD subset (marked by the [and]> delimiters) name each part of the manual. The <manual> and </manual> tags mark the beginning and end of the document body, and the &chap01;, &chap02;, &chap03;, and &appxa; entity references indicate the location of each entity within the body.

Elements by HTML Version and Activity

H TML 4.0 includes most HTML 3.2 and HTML 2.0 elements (and some that have survived from the prior HTML versions: HTML, HTML+, HTML 1.0, and HTML 3.0), plus elements that have been added for this version by the member companies of the World Wide Web Consortium. In addition, companies and individuals have developed elements, known as extensions, which are not part of the HTML 4.0 standard.

This appendix lists all HTML 4.0 elements (Table A-1). Each entry includes a short description and the version from which it originated:

- 4.0 represents HTML 4.0. In other words, this element is new or revived from a previously obsolete standard, such as HTML, HTML+, HTML 1.0, or HTML 3.0 — but not HTML 3.2 or HTML 2.0.

- 3.2 and 2.0 represent HTML 3.2 and HTML 2.0, respectively. HTML 3.2, the previous standard, was made up of completely new elements, HTML 2.0 elements, and some extensions from the Netscape Communications Corporation and Microsoft Corporation.

- M indicates that this element was most recently a Microsoft extension.
- N indicates that this element was most recently a Netscape extension.

A

On the last pages of the appendix are three additional tables: current Netscape extensions (Table A-2), current Microsoft extensions (Table A-3), and current WebTV extensions (Table A-4). Also listed are elements deprecated as of HTML 4.0 and elements now obsolete as of HTML 4.0.

Table A-1   *HTML 4.0 Elements*

Element	Description	Version
! —	Comment	2.0
!DOCTYPE	Document type	2.0
a	Hypertext link	2.0
acronym	Acronym	4.0
address	Address	2.0
applet	Applet	3.2
area	Area	3.2
b	Bold text	2.0
base	Base URL	2.0
basefont	Base font	N, M
bdo	Bidirectional	4.0
big	Big text	3.2
blockquote	Define quote	2.0
body	Document body	2.0
br	Line break	2.0
button	3D form button	4.0
caption	Caption	3.2
center	Center text	3.2
cite	Citation	2.0
code	Source code	2.0
col	Column properties	M
colgroup	Column group	M
dd	Definition description	2.0

Element	Description	Version
del	Deleted text	4.0
dfn	Definition	3.2
dir	Directory list	2.0
div	Division	3.2
dl	Definition list	2.0
dt	Definition term	2.0
em	Emphasis	2.0
fieldset	Form fields set	4.0
font	Font	3.2
form	Form	2.0
frame	Frame	N, M
frameset	Frame set	N, M
h1	Level one heading	2.0
h2	Level two heading	2.0
h3	Level three heading	2.0
h4	Level four heading	2.0
h5	Level five heading	2.0
h6	Level six heading	2.0
head	Document head	2.0
hr	Horizontal rule	2.0
html	HTML document	2.0
i	Italic text	2.0
iframe	Floating frame	M
img	Inline image	2.0
input	Input form field	2.0
ins	Inserted text	4.0
isindex	Searchable index	2.0
kbd	Keyboard input	2.0
label	Form element label	4.0
legend	Fields set caption	4.0
li	List item	2.0
link	Link	2.0
map	Map	3.2

Continued

Table A-1 *Continued*

Element	Description	Version
menu	Menu list	2.0
meta	Meta	2.0
nobr	No break	M
noframes	No frames	N, M
noscript	No script	4.0
object	Multimedia object	M
ol	Ordered list	2.0
optgroup	Option group	4.0
option	Menu option	3.2
p	Paragraph	2.0
param	Parameter	3.2
pre	Preformatted text	2.0
q	Quote	4.0
s	Strikethrough	4.0
samp	Sample output	2.0
script	Script	N, M
select	Form selection list	2.0
small	Small text	3.2
span	Style text span	M
strike	Strikethrough	2.0
strong	Strong	2.0
style	Style	3.2
sub	Subscript	3.2
sup	Superscript	3.2
table	Table	3.2
tbody	Table body	M
td	Table data	3.2
textarea	Form text input	2.0
tfoot	Table footer	M
th	Table heading	3.2
thead	Table header	M
title	Document title	2.0

Element	Description	Version
tr	Table row	3.2
tt	Teletype text	2.0
u	Underlined	2.0
ul	Unordered list	2.0
var	Variable	2.0

Table A-2 *Netscape Extensions*

Element	Description
blink	Blink text
embed	Embed
ilayer	Inflow layer
keygen	Generate key
layer	Layer
multicol	Multiple columns
nobr	No break
noembed	No embed
nolayer	No layer
server	LiveWire script
spacer	Insert space
wbr	Word break

Table A-3 *Microsoft Extensions*

Element	Description
bgsound	Background sound
embed	Embed
marquee	Marquee
nextid	Create identifiers
nobr	No break

Continued

Table A-3 *Continued*

Element	Description
rt	Ruby text
ruby	Text explanation
wbr	Word break

Table A-4 *WebTV Extensions*

Element	Description
audioscope	Audioscope
bgsound	Background sound
blackface	Blackface text
embed	Embed
marquee	Marquee
nobr	No break
noembed	No embed
spacer	Insert space

Deprecated Elements

applet, basefont, center, dir, isindex, menu, s, strike, u

Obsolete Elements

LISTING, PLAINTEXT, XMP

Unicode Characters and Character Sets

In the past, software and electronic-document developers used the ASCII and Latin-1 characters. Now, XML (and its subset, XHTML) supports the entire Unicode character set. In addition to ASCII and Latin-1 characters, which are a small part of the Unicode character set, Unicode includes many other special characters and — to completely support the internationalization of XML and XHTML documents — alphabets from many languages. For more information about internationalization, refer to Appendix C, Internationalization: Country Codes and Language Codes (743).

This appendix is made up of sections for each character-class production in XML. Starting each section is one or more tables that illustrate and describe characters from character sets that are commonly used by English-speaking individuals. The "Other Supported Character Sets" sections contain information about supported characters within non-English character sets. For more information about non-English character sets, refer to the Unicode 2.0 Charts Web page (http://www. unicode.org/Unicode.charts/normal/Unicode2.0.html). This page lists all currently supported Unicode character sets and provides links for each.

Legal or special characters allow you to embed alphabetic characters, symbols, and non-keyboard characters in a document. XML's character-class productions support the special characters listed in the tables in this appendix. Table B-1 lists the character-class productions and briefly describes them.

Table B-1 *XML Character-Class Productions*

Production	Represents
BaseChar	base character
CombiningChar	combining character
Digit	digit
Extender	extender symbol
Ideographic	ideographic symbol or glyph
Letter	letter of the current alphabet

For more information about character-class productions, including the syntax and specific characters supported by each, see Section 2, XML Syntax.

●─NOTE

The `Char` production supports any Unicode character, including those documented in this part, but excluding #xFFFE and #xFFFF.

Tables B-2 through B-22 each include some or all of the following column headings:

Char (Character)	A typed character.
Glyph	An image of the character or symbol, the counterpart to Char.
UTC Code	The code assigned by the Unicode Organization's Unicode Technical Committee.
Entity Name	The approved syntax for the characters. In most cases, you should use this syntax instead of the numeric entry reference.

Numeric Entry Reference	A numeric code counterpart to the entity name.
Description	A brief description of the character.

●—NOTE

In addition to the characters specified in this part, XML also supports four standard control characters and the Euro character for the European Monetary Union:

#x9 (Unicode code #x0009), which inserts a tab (HT)
#xA (Unicode code #x000A), which inserts a line feed (LF)
#xD (Unicode code #x000D), which inserts a carriage return (CR)
#x20 (Unicode code #x0020), which inserts a space
#20AC, which inserts a Euro character

BaseChar Characters and Character Sets

This section covers the characters and character sets supported by the BaseChar production.

Latin 1 Uppercase and Lowercase

Table B-2 contains the alphabetic characters in the Special Characters — Latin 1 Uppercase and Lowercase set, in the BaseChar production.

Table B-2   *BaseChar Special Characters — Latin 1 Uppercase and Lowercase*

Char.	UTC Code	Char.	UTC Code	Char.	UTC Code	Char.	UTC Code
A	#x0041	N	#x004E	a	#x0061	n	#x006E
B	#x0042	O	#x004F	b	#x0062	o	#x006F
C	#x0043	P	#x0050	c	#x0063	p	#x0070
D	#x0044	Q	#x0051	d	#x0064	q	#x0071
E	#x0045	R	#x0052	e	#x0065	r	#x0072
F	#x0046	S	#x0053	f	#x0066	s	#x0073
G	#x0047	T	#x0054	g	#x0067	t	#x0074

Continued

Table B-2 *Continued*

Char.	UTC Code	Char.	UTC Code	Char.	UTC Code	Char.	UTC Code
H	#x0048	U	#x0055	h	#x0068	u	#x0075
I	#x0049	V	#x0056	i	#x0069	v	#x0076
J	#x004A	W	#x0057	j	#x006A	w	#x0077
K	#x004B	X	#x0058	k	#x006B	x	#x0078
L	#x004C	Y	#x0059	l	#x006C	y	#x0079
M	#x004D	Z	#x005A	m	#x006D	z	#x007A

Latin 1 Supplementary

Table B-3 contains the XML-supported characters in the Latin 1 Supplementary set, in the BaseChar production.

Table B-3 *BaseChar Special Characters — Latin 1 Supplementary*

Glyph	UTC Code	Entity Name	Numeric Entry Reference	Description
À	#x00C0	À	À	Grave Accent A
Á	#x00C1	&Aacute	Á	Acute Accent A
Â	#x00C2	Â	Â	Circumflex Above A
Ã	#x00C3	Ã	Ã	Tilde Above A
Ä	#x00C4	Ä	Ä	Umlaut Above A
Å	#x00C5	Å	Å	Ring Above A
Æ	#x00C6	Æ	Æ	Ligature AE
Ç	#x00C7	Ç	Ç	Cedilla C
È	#x00C8	È	È	Grave Accent E
É	#x00C9	É	É	Acute Accent E
Ê	#x00CA	Ê	Ê	Circumflex Above E
Ë	#x00CB	Ë	Ë	Umlaut Above E
Ì	#x00CC	Ì	&#204:	Grave Accent I
Í	#x00CD	Í	Í	Acute Accent I
Î	#x00CE	Î	Î	Circumflex Above I

Glyph	UTC Code	Entity Name	Numeric Entry Reference	Description
Ï	#x00CF	Ï	Ï	Umlaut Above I
Ð	#x00D0	Ð	Ð	Icelandic ETH
Ñ	#x00D1	Ñ	Ñ	Tilde Above N
Ò	#x00D2	Ò	Ò	Grave Accent O
Ó	#x00D3	Ó	Ó	Acute Accent O
Ô	#x00D4	Ô	Ô	Circumflex Above O
Õ	#x00D5	Õ	Õ	Tilde Above O
Ö	#x00D6	Ö	Ö	Umlaut Above O
Ø	#x00D8	Ø	Ø	Stroke or Slash O
Ù	#x00D9	Ù	Ù	Grave Accent U
Ú	#x00DA	Ú	Ú	Acute Accent U
Û	#x00DB	Û	Û	Circumflex Above U
Ü	#x00DC	Ü	Ü	Umlaut Above U
Ý	#x00DD	Ý	Ý	Acute Accent Y
Þ	#x00DE	Þ	Þ	Icelandic THORN
ß	#x00DF	ß	ß	Sharp s
à	#x00E0	à	à	Grave Accent a
á	#x00E1	á	á	Acute Accent a
â	#x00E2	â	â	Circumflex Above a
ã	#x00E3	ã	ã	Tilde Above a
ä	#x00E4	ä	ä	Umlaut Above a
å	#x00E5	å	å	Ring Above a
æ	#x00E6	æ	æ	Ligature ae
ç	#x00E7	ç	ç	Cedilla c
è	#x00E8	è	è	Grave Accent e
é	#x00E9	é	é	Acute Accent e
ê	#x00EA	ê	ê	Circumflex Above e
ë	#x00EB	ë	ë	Umlaut Above e

Continued

Table B-3 *Continued*

Glyph	UTC Code	Entity Name	Numeric Entry Reference	Description
ì	#x00EC	ì	ì	Grave Accent i
í	#x00ED	í	í	Acute Accent i
î	#x00EE	î	î	Circumflex Above i
ï	#x00EF	ï	ï	Umlaut Above i
ð	#x00F0	ð	ð	Icelandic eth
ñ	#x00F1	ñ	ñ	Tilde Above n
ò	#x00F2	ò	ò	Grave Accent o
ó	#x00F3	ó	ó	Acute Accent o
ô	#x00F4	ô	ô	Circumflex Above o
õ	#x00F5	õ	õ	Tilde Above o
ö	#x00F6	ö	ö	Umlaut Above o
ø	#x00F8	ø	ø	Stroke or Slash o
ù	#x00F9	ù	ù	Grave Accent u
ú	#x00FA	ú	ú	Acute Accent u
û	#x00FB	û	û	Circumflex Above u
ü	#x00FC	ü	ü	Umlaut Above u
ý	#x00FD	ý	ý	Acute Accent y
þ	#x00FE	þ	þ	Icelandic thorn
ÿ	#x00FF	ÿ	ÿ	Umlaut Above y

Extended Latin-A

Table B-4 contains the XML-supported characters in the Extended Latin-A set, in the BaseChar production.

Table B-4 *BaseChar Special Characters — Extended Latin-A*

Glyph	UTC Code	Entity Name	Description
Ā	#x0100	Ā	Macron A
ā	#x0101	ā	Macron a

Glyph	UTC Code	Entity Name	Description
Ă	#x0102	Ă	Breve Above A
ă	#x0103	ă	Breve Above a
Ą	#x0104	Ą	Ogonek A
ą	#x0105	ą	Ogonek a
Ć	#x0106	Ć	Acute Accent C
ć	#x0107	ć	Acute Accent c
Ĉ	#x0108	Ĉ	Circumflex Above C
ĉ	#x0109	ĉ	Circumflex Above c
Ċ	#x010A	Ċ	Dot Above C
ċ	#x010B	ċ	Dot Above c
Č	#x010C	Č	Caron C
č	#x010D	č	Caron c
Ď	#x010E	Ď	Caron D
ď	#x010F	ď	Caron d
Đ	#x0110	Đ	Stroke D
đ	#x0111	đ	Stroke d
Ē	#x0112	Ē	Macron E
ē	#x0113	ē	Macron e
Ĕ	#x0114	n/a	Breve Above E
ĕ	#x0115	n/a	Breve Above e
Ė	#x0116	Ė	Dot Above E
ė	#x0117	ė	Dot Above e
Ę	#x0118	Ę	Ogonek E
ę	#x0119	ę	Ogonek e
Ě	#x011A	Ě	Caron E
ě	#x011B	ě	Caron e
Ĝ	#x011C	Ĝ	Circumflex Above G
ĝ	#x011D	ĝ	Circumflex Above g
Ğ	#x011E	Ğ	Breve Above G

Continued

Table B-4 *Continued*

Glyph	UTC Code	Entity Name	Description
ğ	#x011F	ğ	Breve Above g
Ġ	#x0120	Ġ	Dot Above G
ġ	#x0121	ġ	Dot Above g
Ģ	#x0122	Ģ	Cedilla G
ģ	#x0123	n/a	Cedilla g
Ĥ	#x0124	Ĥ	Circumflex Above H
ĥ	#x0125	ĥ	Circumflex Above h
Ħ	#x0126	Ħ	Stroke H
ħ	#x0127	ħ	Stroke h
Ĩ	#x0128	Ĩ	Tilde Above I
ĩ	#x0129	ĩ	Tilde Above i
Ī	#x012A	Ī	Macron I
ī	#x012B	ī	Macron i
Ĭ	#x012C	n/a	Breve Above I
ĭ	#x012D	n/a	Breve Above i
Į	#x012E	Į	Ogonek I
į	#x012F	į	Ogonek i
İ	#x0130	İ	Dot Above I
ı	#x0131	ı	Dotless i
Ĵ	#x0134	Ĵ	Circumflex Above J
ĵ	#x0135	ĵ	Circumflex Above j
Ķ	#x0136	Ķ	Cedilla K
ķ	#x0137	ķ	Cedilla k
ĸ	#x0138	n/a	kra
Ĺ	#x0139	Ĺ	Acute Accent L
ĺ	#x013A	ĺ	Acute Accent l
Ļ	#x013B	Ļ	Cedilla L
ļ	#x013C	ļ	Cedilla l

Glyph	UTC Code	Entity Name	Description
Ľ	#x013D	Ľ	Caron L
ľ	#x013E	ľ	Caron l
Ł	#x0141	Ł	Stroke L
ł	#x0142	ł	Stroke l
Ń	#x0143	Ń	Acute Accent N
ń	#x0144	ń	Acute Accent n
Ņ	#x0145	Ņ	Cedilla N
ņ	#x0146	ņ	Cedilla n
Ň	#x0147	Ň	Caron N
ň	#x0148	ň	Caron n
Ŋ	#x014A	Ŋ	ENG
ŋ	#x014B	ŋ	eng
Ō	#x014C	Ō	Macron O
ō	#x014D	ō	Macron o
Ŏ	#x014E	n/a	Breve Above O
ŏ	#x014F	n/a	Breve Above o
Ő	#x0150	Ő	Double Acute Accent O
ő	#x0151	ő	Double Acute Accent o
Œ	#x0152	Œ	Ligature OE
œ	#x0153	œ	Ligature oe
Ŕ	#x0154	Ŕ	Acute Accent R
ŕ	#x0155	ŕ	Acute Accent r
Ŗ	#x0156	Ŗ	Cedilla R
ŗ	#x0157	ŗ	Cedilla r
Ř	#x0158	Ř	Caron R
ř	#x0159	ř	Caron r
Ś	#x015A	Ś	Acute Accent S
ś	#x015B	ś	Acute Accent s
Ŝ	#x015C	Ŝ	Circumflex Above S

Continued

Table B-4 *Continued*

Glyph	UTC Code	Entity Name	Description
ŝ	#x015D	ŝ	Circumflex Above s
Ş	#x015E	Ş	Cedilla S
ş	#x015F	ş	Cedilla s
Š	#x0160	Š	Caron S
š	#x0161	š	Caron s
Ţ	#x0162	Ţ	Cedilla T
ţ	#x0163	ţ	Cedilla t
Ť	#x0164	Ť	Caron T
ť	#x0165	ť	Caron t
Ŧ	#x0166	Ŧ	Stroke T
ŧ	#x0167	ŧ	Stroke t
Ũ	#x0168	Ũ	Tilde Above U
ũ	#x0169	ũ	Tilde Above u
Ū	#x016A	Ū	Macron U
ū	#x016B	ū	Macron u
Ŭ	#x016C	Ŭ	Breve Above U
ŭ	#x016D	ŭ	Breve Above u
Ů	#x016E	Ů	Ring Above U
ů	#x016F	ů	Ring Above u
Ű	#x0170	Ű	Double Acute Accent U
ű	#x0171	ű	Double Acute Accent u
Ų	#x0172	Ų	Ogonek U
ų	#x0173	ų	Ogonek u
Ŵ	#x0174	Ŵ	Circumflex Above W
ŵ	#x0175	ŵ	Circumflex Above w
Ŷ	#x0176	Ŷ	Circumflex Above Y
ŷ	#x0177	ŷ	Circumflex Above y
Ÿ	#x0178	Ÿ	Umlaut Above Y
Ź	#x0179	Ź	Acute Accent Z

Glyph	UTC Code	Entity Name	Description
ź	#x017A	ź	Acute Accent z
Ż	#x017B	Ż	Dot Above Z
ż	#x017C	ż	Dot Above z
Ž	#x017D	Ž	Caron Z
ž	#x017E	ž	Caron z

Extended Latin-B

Table B-5 contains the XML-supported characters in the Extended Latin-B set, in the BaseChar production.

Table B-5   *BaseChar Special Characters — Extended Latin-B*

Glyph	UTC Code	Description
b	#x0180	Stroke b
B	#x0181	Hook B
Ƃ	#x0182	Topbar B
ƃ	#x0183	Topbar b
ƅ	#x0184	Tone SIX
ƅ	#x0185	Tone six
Ɔ	#x0186	Open O
Ƈ	#x0187	Hook C
ƈ	#x0188	Hook c
Ɖ	#x0189	African D
Ɗ	#x018A	Hook D
Ƌ	#x018B	Topbar D
ƌ	#x018C	Topbard d
ƍ	#x018D	Turned delta
Ǝ	#x018E	Reversed E
Ə	#x018F	SCHWA
Ɛ	#x0190	Open E

Continued

Table B-5 *Continued*

Glyph	UTC Code	Description
Ƒ	#x0191	Hook F
ƒ	#x0192	Hook f
Ɠ	#x0193	Hook G
Ɣ	#x0194	GAMMA
ƕ	#x0195	hv
ɩ	#x0196	IOTA
Ɨ	#x0197	Stroke I
Ƙ	#x0198	Hook K
ƙ	#x0199	Hook k
ƚ	#x019A	Bar l
ƛ	#x019B	Stroke lambda
ɯ	#x019C	Turned M
Ɲ	#x019D	Left Hook N
ƞ	#x019E	Long Right Leg n
Ɵ	#x019F	Middle Tilde O
Ơ	#x01A0	Horn O
ơ	#x01A1	Horn o
Ƣ	#x01A2	OI
ƣ	#x01A3	oi
Ƥ	#x01A4	Hook P
ƥ	#x01A5	Hook p
Ʀ	#x01A6	YR
Ƨ	#x01A7	Tone TWO
ƨ	#x01A8	Tone two
Ʃ	#x01A9	ESH
ƪ	#x01AA	Reversed ESH Loop
ƫ	#x01AB	Palatal Hook t
Ƭ	#x01AC	Hook T
ƭ	#x01AD	Hook t

Glyph	UTC Code	Description
Ț	#x01AE	Retroflex Hook T
Ư	#x01AF	Horn U
ư	#x01B0	Horn u
Ʊ	#x01B1	UPSILON
ʊ	#x01B2	Hook V
Ƴ	#x01B3	Hook Y
ƴ	#x01B4	Hook y
Ƶ	#x01B5	Stroke Z
ƶ	#x01B6	Stroke z
ʒ	#x01B7	EZH
Ƹ	#x01B8	EZH Reversed
ƹ	#x01B9	ezh Reversed
ƺ	#x01BA	ezh Tail
ƻ	#x01BB	Stroke 2
Ƽ	#x01BC	Tone FIVE
ƽ	#x01BD	Tone five
ƾ	#x01BE	Stroke Inverted Glottal Stop
ƿ	#x01BF	Wynn
ǀ	#x01C0	Dental Click
ǁ	#x01C1	Lateral Click
ǂ	#x01C2	Alveolar Click
ǃ	#x01C3	Retroflex Click
Ǎ	#x01CD	Caron A
ǎ	#x01CE	Caron a
Ǐ	#x01CF	Caron I
ǐ	#x01D0	Caron i
Ǒ	#x01D1	Caron O
ǒ	#x01D2	Caron o
Ǔ	#x01D3	Caron U

Continued

Table B-5 *Continued*

Glyph	UTC Code	Description
ǔ	#x01D4	Caron u
Ǖ	#x01D5	Umlaut Above Macron U
ǖ	#x01D6	Umlaut Above Macron u
Ǘ	#x01D7	Umlaut Above Acute Accent U
ǘ	#x01D8	Umlaut Acute Accent u
Ǚ	#x01D9	Umlaut Above Caron U
ǚ	#x01DA	Umlaut Above Caron u
Ǜ	#x01DB	Umlaut Above Grave Accent U
ǜ	#x01DC	Umlaut Above Grave Accent u
ə	#x01DD	Turned e
Ǟ	#x01DE	Umlaut Above Macron A
ǟ	#x01DF	UmlautAbove Macron a
Ǡ	#x01E0	Dot Above Macron A
ǡ	#x01E1	Dot Above Macron a
Ǣ	#x01E2	Macron AE
ǣ	#x01E3	Macron ae
Ǥ	#x01E4	Stroke G
ǥ	#x01E5	Stroke g
Ǧ	#x01E6	Caron G
ǧ	#x01E7	Caron g
Ǩ	#x01E8	Caron K
ǩ	#x01E9	Caron k
Ǫ	#x01EA	Ogonek O
ǫ	#x01EB	Ogonek o
Ǭ	#x01EC	Ogonek Macron O
ǭ	#x01ED	Ogonek Macron o
Ǯ	#x01EE	Caron EZH
ǯ	#x01EF	Caron ezh
ǰ	#x01F0	Caron j

Glyph	UTC Code	Description
Ǵ	#x01F4	Acute Accent G
ǵ	#x01F5	Acute Accent g
Ǻ	#x01FA	Ring Above Acute Accent A
ǻ	#x01FB	Ring Above Acute Accent a
Ǽ	#x01FC	Acute Accent AE
ǽ	#x01FD	Acute Accent ae
Ǿ	#x01FE	Stroke Acute Accent O
ǿ	#x01FF	Stroke Acute Accent o
Ȁ	#x0200	Double Grave Accent A
ȁ	#x0201	Double Grave Accent a
Ȃ	#x0202	Inverted Breve A
ȃ	#x0203	Inverted Breve a
Ȅ	#x0204	Double Grave Accent E
ȅ	#x0205	Double Grave Accent e
Ȇ	#x0206	Inverted Breve E
ȇ	#x0207	Inverted Breve e
Ȉ	#x0208	Double Grave Accent I
ȉ	#x0209	Double Grave Accent i
Ȋ	#x020A	Inverted Breve I
ȋ	#x020B	Inverted Breve i
Ȍ	#x020C	Double Grave Accent O
ȍ	#x020D	Double Grave Accent o
Ȏ	#x020E	Inverted Breve O
ȏ	#x020F	Inverted Breve o
Ȑ	#x0210	Double Grave Accent R
ȑ	#x0211	Double Grave Accent r
Ȓ	#x0212	Inverted Breve R
ȓ	#x0213	Inverted Breve r
Ȕ	#x0214	Double Grave Accent U

Continued

Table B-5 *Continued*

Glyph	UTC Code	Description
ů	#x0215	Double Grave Accent u
Ȗ	#x0216	Inverted Breve U
ȗ	#x0217	Inverted Breve u

IPA Extensions

Table B-6 contains the XML-supported characters in the IPA Extensions set, in the BaseChar production.

Table B-6 *BaseChar Special Characters — IPA Extensions*

Glyph	UTC Code	Description
ɐ	#x0250	Turned a
ɑ	#x0251	alpha
ɒ	#x0252	Turned alpha
ɓ	#x0253	Hook b
ɔ	#x0254	Open o
ɕ	#x0255	Curl c
ɖ	#x0256	Tail d
ɗ	#x0257	Hook d
ɘ	#x0258	Reversed e
ə	#x0259	schwa
ɚ	#x025A	Hook schwa
ɛ	#x025B	Open e
ɜ	#x025C	Reversed Open e
ɝ	#x025D	Hook Reversed Open e
ɞ	#x025E	Closed Reversed Open e
ɟ	#x025F	Dotless Stroke j
ɠ	#x0260	Hook g
ɡ	#x0261	Script g

Glyph	UTC Code	Description
ɢ	#x0262	Small G
ɣ	#x0263	gamma
ɤ	#x0264	Rams horn
ɥ	#x0265	Turned h
ɦ	#x0266	Hook h
ɧ	#x0267	Hook heng
ɨ	#x0268	Stroke i
ɩ	#x0269	iota
ɪ	#x026A	Small I
ɫ	#x026B	Middle Tilde l
ɬ	#x026C	Belt l
ɭ	#x026D	Retroflex Hook l
ɮ	#x026E	lezh
ɯ	#x026F	Turned m
ɰ	#x0270	Turned Long leg m
ɱ	#x0271	Hook m
ɲ	#x0272	Left Hook n
ɳ	#x0273	Retroflex Hook n
ɴ	#x0274	Small N
ɵ	#x0275	Barred o
ɶ	#x0276	Small OE
ɷ	#x0277	Closed omega
ɸ	#x0278	Small PHI
ɹ	#x0279	Turned r
ɺ	#x027A	Turned Long Leg r
ɻ	#x027B	Hook Turned r
ɼ	#x027C	Long Leg r
ɽ	#x027D	Tail r
ɾ	#x027E	Fishhook r

Continued

Table B-6 *Continued*

Glyph	UTC Code	Description
ɿ	#x027F	Reversed Fishhook r
ʀ	#x0280	Small R
ʁ	#x0281	Inverted Small R
ʂ	#x0282	Hook s
ʃ	#x0283	esh
ʄ	#x0284	Stroke Hook Dotless j
ʅ	#x0285	Squat Reversed esh
ʆ	#x0286	Curl esh
ʇ	#x0287	Turned t
ʈ	#x0288	Retroflex Hook t
ʉ	#x0289	Bar u
ʊ	#x028A	upsilon
ʋ	#x028B	Hook v
ʌ	#x028C	Turned v
ʍ	#x028D	Turned w
ʎ	#x028E	Turned y
ʏ	#x028F	Small Y
ʐ	#x0290	Retroflex Hook z
ʑ	#x0291	Curl z
ʒ	#x0292	ezh
ʓ	#x0293	Curl ezh
ʔ	#x0294	Glottal Stop
ʕ	#x0295	Pharyngeal Voiced Fricative
ʖ	#x0296	Inverted Glottal Stop
ʗ	#x0297	Stretched C
ʘ	#x0298	Bilabial Click
ʙ	#x0299	Small B
ʚ	#x029A	Closed Open e

Glyph	UTC Code	Description
ɢ	#x029B	Small Hook G
ʜ	#x029C	Small H
ȷ	#x029D	Crossed-Tail j
ʞ	#x029E	Turned k
ʟ	#x029F	Small L
ɋ	#x02A0	Hook q
ʡ	#x02A1	Stroke Glottal Stop
ʢ	#x02A2	Stroke Reversed Glottal Stop
ʣ	#x02A3	dz Digraph
ʤ	#x02A4	dezh Digraph
ʥ	#x02A5	Curl dz Digraph
ʦ	#x02A6	ts Digraph
ʧ	#x02A7	tesh Digraph
ʨ	#x02A8	Curl tc Digraph

Spacing Modifier Letters

Table B-7 contains the XML-supported characters in the Spacing Modifier Letters set, in the BaseChar production.

Table B-7   *BaseChar Special Characters — Spacing Modifier Letters*

Glyph	UTC Code	Description
ʻ	#x02BB	Prime
ʼ	#x02BC	Double Prime
ʽ	#x02BD	Reversed Comma
ʾ	#x02BE	Right Half Ring
ʿ	#x02BF	Left Half Ring
ˀ	#x02C0	Glottal Stop
ˁ	#x02C1	Reversed Glottal Stop

Greek and Coptic

Table B-8 contains the XML-supported characters in the Greek and Coptic set, in the BaseChar production.

Table B-8 *BaseChar Special Characters — Greek and Coptic*

Glyph	UTC Code	Entity Name	Description
Ά	#x0386	n/a	Tonos ALPHA
Έ	#x0388	n/a	Tonos EPSILON
Ή	#x0389	n/a	Tonos ETA
Ί	#x038A	n/a	Tonos IOTA
Ό	#x038C	n/a	Tonos OMICRON
Ύ	#x038E	n/a	Tonos UPSILON
Ώ	#x038F	n/a	Tonos OMEGA
ΐ	#x0390	n/a	Dialytika Tonos iota
A	#x0391	&Agr;	ALPHA
B	#x0392	&Bgr;	BETA
Γ	#x0393	&Ggr;	GAMMA
Δ	#x0394	&Dgr;	DELTA
E	#x0395	&Egr;	EPSILON
Z	#x0396	&Zgr;	ZETA
H	#x0397	&EEgr;	ETA
Θ	#x0398	&THgr;	THETA
I	#x0399	&Igr;	IOTA
K	#x039A	&Kgr;	KAPPA
Λ	#x039B	&Lgr;	LAMBDA
M	#x039C	&Mgr;	MU
N	#x039D	&Ngr;	NU
Ξ	#x039E	&Xgr;	XI
O	#x039F	&Ogr;	OMICRON
Π	#x03A0	&Pgr;	PI
P	#x03A1	&Rgr;	RHO

Glyph	UTC Code	Entity Name	Description
Σ	#x03A3	&Sgr;	SIGMA
Τ	#x03A4	&Tgr;	TAU
Υ	#x03A5	&Ugr;	UPSILON
Φ	#x03A6	&PHgr;	PHI
Χ	#x03A7	&KHgr;	CHI
Ψ	#x03A8	&PSgr;	PSI
Ω	#x03A9	&OHgr;	OMEGA
Ϊ	#x03AA	n/a	Dialytika IOTA
Ϋ	#x03AB	n/a	Dialytika UPSILON
ά	#x03AC	n/a	Tonos alpha
έ	#x03AD	n/a	Tonos epsilon
ή	#x03AE	n/a	Tonos eta
ί	#x03AF	n/a	Tonos iota
ΰ	#x03B0	n/a	Dialytika Tonos upsilon
α	#x03B1	&agr;	alpha
β	#x03B2	&bgr;	beta
γ	#x03B3	&ggr;	gamma
δ	#x03B4	&dgr;	delta
ε	#x03B5	&egr;	epsilon
ζ	#x03B6	&zgr;	zeta
η	#x03B7	&eegr;	eta
θ	#x03B8	&thgr;	theta
ι	#x03B9	&igr;	iota
κ	#x03BA	&kgr;	kappa
λ	#x03BB	&lgr;	lambda
μ	#x03BC	&mgr;	mu
ν	#x03BD	&ngr;	nu
ξ	#x03BE	&xgr;	xi
ο	#x03BF	&ogr;	omicron

Continued

Table B-8 *Continued*

Glyph	UTC Code	Entity Name	Description
π	#x03C0	&pgr;	pi
ρ	#x03C1	&rgr;	rho
ς	#x03C2	&sfgr;	final sigma
σ	#x03C3	&sgr;	sigma
τ	#x03C4	&tgr;	tau
υ	#x03C5	&ugr;	upsilon
φ	#x03C6	&phgr;	phi
χ	#x03C7	&khgr;	chi
ψ	#x03C8	&psgr;	psi
ω	#x03C9	&ohgr;	omega
ϊ	#x03CA	n/a	Dialytika iota
ϋ	#x03CB	n/a	Dialytika upsilon
ό	#x03CC	n/a	Tonos omicron
ύ	#x03CD	n/a	Tonos upsilon
ώ	#x03CE	n/a	Tonos omega
ϐ	#x03D0	n/a	Beta Symbol
ϑ	#x03D1	n/a	Theta Symbol
ϒ	#x03D2	n/a	Hook Upsilon
ϓ	#x03D3	n/a	Acute Accent Hook Upsilon
ϔ	#x03D4	n/a	Umlaut Above Hook Upsilon
ϕ	#x03D5	n/a	Phi Symbol
ϖ	#x03D6	n/a	Pi Symbol
Ϛ	#x03DA	n/a	Stigma
Ϝ	#x03DC	n/a	Digamma
Ϟ	#x03DE	n/a	Koppa
Ϡ	#x03E0	n/a	Sampi
Ϣ	#x03E2	n/a	SHEI
ϣ	#x03E3	n/a	shei

Glyph	UTC Code	Entity Name	Description
ᕿ	#x03E4	n/a	FEI
ϥ	#x03E5	n/a	fei
ḅ	#x03E6	n/a	KHEI
ϭ	#x03E7	n/a	khei
Ϩ	#x03E8	n/a	HORI
ϩ	#x03E9	n/a	hori
Ϫ	#x03EA	n/a	GANGIA
ϫ	#x03EB	n/a	gangia
Ϭ	#x03EC	n/a	SHIMA
ϭ	#x03ED	n/a	shima
Ϯ	#x03EE	n/a	DEI
ϯ	#x03EF	n/a	dei
ϰ	#x03F0	n/a	Kappa Symbol
ϱ	#x03F1	n/a	Rho Symbol
ϲ	#x03F2	n/a	Lunate Sigma Symbol
ϳ	#x03F3	n/a	Yot

Additional Extended Latin

Table B-9 contains the XML-supported characters in the Additional Extended Latin set, in the BaseChar production.

Table B-9 *BaseChar Special Characters — Additional Extended Latin*

Glyph	UTC Code	Description
Ḁ	#x1E00	Ring Below A
ḁ	#x1E01	Ring Below a
Ḃ	#x1E02	Dot Above B
ḃ	#x1E03	Dot Above b
Ḅ	#x1E04	Dot Below B

Continued

Table B-9 *Continued*

Glyph	UTC Code	Description
ḅ	#x1E05	Dot Below b
B̲	#x1E06	Line Below B
ḇ	#x1E07	Line Below b
Ḉ	#x1E08	Cedilla Acute Accent C
ḉ	#x1E09	Cedilla Acute Accent c
Ḋ	#x1E0A	Dot Above D
ḋ	#x1E0B	Dot Above d
Ḍ	#x1E0C	Dot Below D
ḍ	#x1E0D	Dot Below d
Ḏ	#x1E0E	Line Below D
ḏ	#x1E0F	Line Below d
Ḑ	#x1E10	Cedilla D
ḑ	#x1E11	Cedilla d
Ḓ	#x1E12	Circumflex Below D
ḓ	#x1E13	Circumflex Below d
Ḕ	#x1E14	Macron Grave Accent E
ḕ	#x1E15	Macron Grave Accent e
Ḗ	#x1E16	Macron Acute Accent E
ḗ	#x1E17	Macron Acute Accent e
Ḙ	#x1E18	Circumflex Below E
ḙ	#x1E19	Circumflex Below e
Ḛ	#x1E1A	Tilde Below E
ḛ	#x1E1B	Tilde Below e
Ḝ	#x1E1C	Breve Above Cedilla E
ḝ	#x1E1D	Breve Above Cedilla e
Ḟ	#x1E1E	Dot Above F
ḟ	#x1E1F	Dot Above f
Ḡ	#x1E20	Macron G

Glyph	UTC Code	Description
ḡ	#x1E21	Macron g
Ḣ	#x1E22	Dot Above H
ḣ	#x1E23	Dot Above h
Ḥ	#x1E24	Dot Below H
ḥ	#x1E25	Dot Below h
Ḧ	#x1E26	Umlaut Above H
ḧ	#x1E27	Umlaut Above h
Ḩ	#x1E28	Cedilla H
ḩ	#x1E29	Cedilla h
Ḫ	#x1E2A	Breve Below H
ḫ	#x1E2B	Breve Below h
Ḭ	#x1E2C	Tilde Below I
ḭ	#x1E2D	Tilde Below i
Ḯ	#x1E2E	Umlaut Above Acute Accent I
ḯ	#x1E2F	Umlaut Above Acute Accent i
Ḱ	#x1E30	Acute Accent K
ḱ	#x1E31	Acute Accent k
Ḳ	#x1E32	Dot Below K
ḳ	#x1E33	Dot Below k
Ḵ	#x1E34	Line Below K
ḵ	#x1E35	Line Below k
Ḷ	#x1E36	Dot Below L
ḷ	#x1E37	Dot Below l
Ḹ	#x1E38	Macron Dot Below L
ḹ	#x1E39	Macron Dot Below l
Ḻ	#x1E3A	Line Below L
ḻ	#x1E3B	Line Below l
Ḽ	#x1E3C	Circumflex Below L
ḽ	#x1E3D	Circumflex Below l

Continued

Table B-9 *Continued*

Glyph	UTC Code	Description
Ḿ	#x1E3E	Acute Accent M
ḿ	#x1E3F	Acute Accent m
Ṁ	#x1E40	Dot Above M
ṁ	#x1E41	Dot Above m
Ṃ	#x1E42	Dot Below M
ṃ	#x1E43	Dot Below m
Ṅ	#x1E44	Dot Above N
ṅ	#x1E45	Dot Above n
Ṇ	#x1E46	Dot Below N
ṇ	#x1E47	Dot Below n
Ṉ	#x1E48	Line Below N
ṉ	#x1E49	Line Below n
Ṋ	#x1E4A	Circumflex Below N
ṋ	#x1E4B	Circumflex Below n
Ṍ	#x1E4C	Tilde Above Acute Accent O
ṍ	#x1E4D	Tilde Above Acute Accent o
Ṏ	#x1E4E	Umlaut Tilde Above O
ṏ	#x1E4F	Umlaut Tilde Above o
Ṑ	#x1E50	Macron Grave Accent O
ṑ	#x1E51	Macron Grave Accent o
Ṓ	#x1E52	Macron Acute Accent O
ṓ	#x1E53	Macron Acute Accent o
Ṕ	#x1E54	Acute Accent P
ṕ	#x1E55	Acute Accent p
Ṗ	#x1E56	Dot Above P
ṗ	#x1E57	Dot Above p
Ṙ	#x1E58	Dot Above R
ṙ	#x1E59	Dot Above r

Glyph	UTC Code	Description
Ṛ	#x1E5A	Dot Below R
ṛ	#x1E5B	Dot Below r
Ṝ	#x1E5C	Dot Below Macron R
ṝ	#x1E5D	Dot Below Macron r
Ṟ	#x1E5E	Line Below R
ṟ	#x1E5F	Line Below r
Ṡ	#x1E60	Dot Above S
ṡ	#x1E61	Dot Above s
Ṣ	#x1E62	Dot Below S
ṣ	#x1E63	Dot Below s
Ṥ	#x1E64	Acute Accent Dot Above S
ṥ	#x1E65	Acute Accent Dot Above s
Ṧ	#x1E66	Caron Dot Above S
ṧ	#x1E67	Caron Dot Above s
Ṩ	#x1E68	Dot Above Dot Below S
ṩ	#x1E69	Dot Above Dot Below s
Ṫ	#x1E6A	Dot Above T
ṫ	#x1E6B	Dot Above t
Ṭ	#x1E6C	Dot Below T
ṭ	#x1E6D	Dot Below t
Ṯ	#x1E6E	Line Below T
ṯ	#x1E6F	Line Below t
Ṱ	#x1E70	Circumflex Below T
ṱ	#x1E71	Circumflex Below t
Ṳ	#x1E72	Umlaut Below U
ṳ	#x1E73	Umlaut Below u
Ṵ	#x1E74	Tilde Below U
ṵ	#x1E75	Tilde Below u
Ṷ	#x1E76	Circumflex Below U

Continued

Table B-9 *Continued*

Glyph	UTC Code	Description
ṷ	#x1E77	Circumflex Below u
Ṹ	#x1E78	Tilde Above Acute Accent U
ṹ	#x1E79	Tilde Above Acute Accent u
Ṻ	#x1E7A	Macron Umlaut Above U
ṻ	#x1E7B	Macron Umlaut Above u
Ṽ	#x1E7C	Tilde Above V
ṽ	#x1E7D	Tilde Above v
Ṿ	#x1E7E	Dot Below V
ṿ	#x1E7F	Dot Below v
Ẁ	#x1E80	Grave Accent W
ẁ	#x1E81	Grave Accent w
Ẃ	#x1E82	Acute Accent W
Ẅ	#x1E84	Umlaut Above W
ẇ	#x1E87	Dot Above w
Ẉ	#x1E88	Dot Below W
Ẋ	#x1E8A	Dot Above X
ẍ	#x1E8D	Umlaut Above x
Ẕ	#x1E94	Line Below Z
ẕ	#x1E95	Line Below z
ẖ	#x1E96	Line Below h
ẗ	#x1E97	Umlaut Above t
ẙ	#x1E99	Ring Above y
aʾ	#x1E9A	Right Half Ring Above a
ẛ	#x1E9B	Dot Above Long s
Ạ	#x1EA0	Dot Below A
ạ	#x1EA1	Dot Below a
Ả	#x1EA2	Hook Above A
ả	#x1EA3	Hook Above a
Ấ	#x1EA4	Circumflex Above Acute Accent A

Glyph	UTC Code	Description
ấ	#x1EA5	Circumflex Above Acute Accent a
Ầ	#x1EA6	Circumflex Above Grave Accent A
ầ	#x1EA7	Circumflex Above Grave Accent a
Ẩ	#x1EA8	Circumflex Hook Above A
ẩ	#x1EA9	Circumflex Hook Above a
Ẫ	#x1EAA	Circumflex Tilde Above A
ẫ	#x1EAB	Circumflex Tilde Above a
Ậ	#x1EAC	Circumflex Above Dot Below A
ậ	#x1EAD	Circumflex Above Dot Below a
Ắ	#x1EAE	Breve Above Acute Accent A
ắ	#x1EAF	Breve Above Acute Accent a
Ằ	#x1EB0	Breve Above Grave Accent A
ằ	#x1EB1	Breve Above Grave Accent a
Ẳ	#x1EB2	Breve Hook Above A
ẳ	#x1EB3	Breve Hook Above a
Ẵ	#x1EB4	Breve Tilde Above A
ẵ	#x1EB5	Breve Tilde Above a
Ặ	#x1EB6	Breve Above Dot Below A
ặ	#x1EB7	Breve Above Dot Below a
Ẹ	#x1EB8	Dot Below E
ẹ	#x1EB9	Dot Below e
Ẻ	#x1EBA	Hook Above E
ẻ	#x1EBB	Hook Above e
Ẽ	#x1EBC	Tilde Above E
ẽ	#x1EBD	Tilde Above e
Ế	#x1EBE	Circumflex Above Acute Accent E
ế	#x1EBF	Circumflex Above Acute Accent e
Ề	#x1EC0	Circumflex Above Grave Accent E
ề	#x1EC1	Circumflex Above Grave Accent e

Continued

Table B-9 *Continued*

Glyph	UTC Code	Description
Ể	#x1EC2	Circumflex Hook Above E
ể	#x1EC3	Circumflex Hook Above e
Ễ	#x1EC4	Circumflex Tilde Above E
ễ	#x1EC5	Circumflex Tilde Above e
Ệ	#x1EC6	Circumflex Above Dot Below E
ệ	#x1EC7	Circumflex Above Dot Below e
Ỉ	#x1EC8	Hook Above I
ỉ	#x1EC9	Hook Above i
Ị	#x1ECA	Dot Below I
ị	#x1ECB	Dot Below i
Ọ	#x1ECC	Dot Below O
ọ	#x1ECD	Dot Below o
Ỏ	#x1ECE	Hook Above O
ỏ	#x1ECF	Hook Above o
Ố	#x1ED0	Circumflex Above Acute Accent O
ố	#x1ED1	Circumflex Above Acute Accent o
Ồ	#x1ED2	Circumflex Above Grave Accent O
ồ	#x1ED3	Circumflex Above Grave Accent o
Ổ	#x1ED4	Circumflex Hook Above O
ổ	#x1ED5	Circumflex Hook Above o
Ỗ	#x1ED6	Circumflex Tilde Above O
ỗ	#x1ED7	Circumflex Tilde Above o
Ộ	#x1ED8	Circumflex Above Dot Below O
ộ	#x1ED9	Circumflex Above Dot Below o
Ớ	#x1EDA	Horn Above Acute Accent O
ớ	#x1EDB	Horn Above Acute Accent o
Ờ	#x1EDC	Horn Above Grave Accent O
ờ	#x1EDD	Horn Above Grave Accent o

Glyph	UTC Code	Description
Ở	#x1EDE	Horn Hook Above O
ở	#x1EDF	Horn Hook Above o
Ỡ	#x1EE0	Horn Tilde Above O
ỡ	#x1EE1	Horn Tilde Above o
Ợ	#x1EE2	Horn Above Dot Below O
ợ	#x1EE3	Horn Above Dot Below O
Ụ	#x1EE4	Dot Below U
ụ	#x1EE5	Dot Below u
Ủ	#x1EE6	Hook Above U
ủ	#x1EE7	Hook Above u
Ứ	#x1EE8	Horn Above Acute Accent U
ứ	#x1EE9	Horn Above Acute Accent u
Ừ	#x1EEA	Horn Above Grave Accent U
ừ	#x1EEB	Horn Above Grave Accent u
Ử	#x1EEC	Horn Hook Above U
ử	#x1EED	Horn Hook Above u
Ữ	#x1EEE	Horn Tilde Above U
ữ	#x1EEF	Horn Tilde Above u
Ự	#x1EF0	Horn Above Dot Below U
ự	#x1EF1	Horn Above Dot Below u
Ỳ	#x1EF2	Grave Accent Y
ỳ	#x1EF3	Grave Accent y
Ỵ	#x1EF4	Dot Below Y
ỵ	#x1EF5	Dot Below y
Ỷ	#x1EF6	Hook Above Y
ỷ	#x1EF7	Hook Above y
Ỹ	#x1EF8	Tilde Above Y
ỹ	#x1EF9	Tilde Above y

Letterlike Symbols

Table B-10 contains the XML-supported characters in the Letterlike Symbols set, in the BaseChar production.

Table B-10 *BaseChar Special Characters – Letter-like Symbols*

Glyph	UTC Code	Description
Ω	#x2126	Ohm Sign
K	#x212A	Kelvin Sign
Å	#x212B	Angstrom Sign
e	#x212E	Estimated Symbol

Number Forms

Table B-11 contains the XML-supported characters in the Number Forms set, in the BaseChar production.

Table B-11 *BaseChar Special Characters — Number Forms*

Glyph	UTC Code	Description
ⅭⅮ	#x2180	Roman Numeral 1000
ⅅ	#x2181	Roman Numeral 5000
ⅭⅮ	#x2182	Roman Numeral 10000

Other Character Sets

Table B-12 lists other BaseChar character sets and the XML-supported characters for each.

●—NOTE—

Because it is difficult to use American fonts to display non-English special characters, the following table does not contain illustrations of the glyphs. To view the characters in this table, go to the Unicode Consortium's Web site (http://www.unicode.org/).

Table B-12   *Other BaseChar Character Sets*

Character Set	Supported Characters
Arabic Presentation Forms	#xFB50 - #xFBB1, #xFBD3 - #xFD3D, #xFD50 - #xFD8F, #xFD92 - #xFDC7, #xFDF0 - #xFDFB, #xFE70 - #xFE72, #xFE74, #xFE76 - #xFEFC
Arabic	#x0621 - #x063A, #x0641 - #x064A, #x0671 - #x06B7, #x06BA - #x06BE, #x06C0 - #x06CE, #x06D0 - #x06D3, #x06D5, #x06E5, #x06E6
Armenian	#x0531 - #x0556, #x0559, #x0561 - #x0586
Bengali	#x0985 - #x098C, #x098F, #x0990, #x0993 - #x09A8, #x09AA - #x09B0, #x09B2, #x09B6 - #x09B9, #x09DC, #x09DD, #x09DF - #x09E1, #x09F0, #x09F1
Bopomofo	#x3105 - #x312C
Cyrillic	#x0401 - #x040C, #x040E - #x044F, #x0451 - #x045C, #x045E - #x0481, #x0490 - #x04C4, #x04C7 - #x04C8, #x04CB - #x04CC, #x04D0 - #x04EB, #x04EE - #x04F5, #x04F8, #x04F9
Devanagari	#x0905 - #x0939, #x093D, #x0958 - #x0961
Georgian	#x10A0 - #x10C5, #x10D0 - #x10F6
Greek Extensions	#x1F00 - #x1F15, #x1F18 - #x1F1D, #x1F20 - #x1F45, #x1F48 - #x1F4D, #x1F50 - #x1F57, #x1F59, #x1F5B, #x1F5D, #x1F5F - #x1F7D, #x1F80 - #x1FB4, #x1FB6 - #x1FBC, #x1FBE, #x1FC2 - #x1FC4, #x1FC6 - #x1FCC, #x1FD0 - #x1FD3, #x1FD6 - #x1FDB, #x1FE0 - #x1FEC, #x1FF2 - #x1FF4, #x1FF6 - #x1FFC
Gujarati	#x0A8F - #x0A91, #x0A93 - #x0AA8, #x0AAA - #x0AB0, #x0AB2, #x0AB3, #x0AB5 - #x0AB9, #x0ABD, #x0AE0
Gurmukhi	#x0A05 - #x0A0A, #x0A0F, #x0A10, #x0A13 - #x0A28, #x0A2A - #x0A30, #x0A32, #x0A33, #x0A35, #x0A36, #x0A38, #x0A39, #x0A59 - #x0A5C, #x0A5E, #x0A72 - #x0A74, #x0A85 - #x0A8B, #x0A8D

Continued

Table B-12 *Continued*

Character Set	Supported Characters
Hangul Jamo	#x1100, #x1102 - #x1103, #x1105 - #x1107, #x1109, #x110B, #x110C, #x110E - #x1112, #x113C, #x113E, #x1140, #x114C, #x114E, #x1150, #x1154, #x1155, #x1159, #x115F - #x1161, #x1163, #x1165, #x1167, #x1169, #x116D, #x116E, #x1172, #x1173, #x1175, #x119E, #x11A8, #x11AB, #x11AE, #x11AF, #x11B7, #x11B8, #x11BA, #x11BC - #x11C2, #x11EB, #x11F0, #x11F9
Hangul Compatibility Jamo	#x3131 - #x318E
Hangul Syllables	#xAC00 - #xD7A3
Hebrew	#x05D0 - #x05EA, #x05F0 - #x05F2
Hiragana	#x3041 - #x3094
Kannada	#x0C85 - #x0C8C, #x0C8E - #x0C90, #x0C92 - #x0CA8, #x0CAA - #x0CB3, #x0CB5 - #x0CB9, #x0CDE, #x0CE0, #x0CE1
Katakana	#x30A1 - #x30FA
Lao	#x0E81, #x0E82, #x0E84, #x0E87, #x0E88, #x0E8A, #x0E8D, #x0E94 - #x0E97, #x0E99 - #x0E9F, #x0EA1 - #x0EA3, #x0EA5, #x0EA7, #x0EAA, #x0EAB, #x0EAD, #x0EAE, #x0EB0, #x0EB2, #x0EB3, #x0EBD, #x0EC0 - #x0EC4
Malayalam	#x0D05 - #x0D0C, #x0D0E - #x0D10, #x0D12 - #x0D28, #x0D2A - #x0D39, #x0D60, #x0D61
Oriya	#x0B05 - #x0B0C, #x0B0F, #x0B10, #x0B13 - #x0B28, #x0B2A - #x0B30, #x0B32, #x0B33, #x0B36 - #x0B39, #x0B3D, #x0B5C, #x0B5D, #x0B5F - #x0B61
Tamil	#x0B85 - #x0B8A, #x0B8E - #x0B90, #x0B92 - #x0B95, #x0B99, #x0B9A, #x0B9C, #x0B9E, #x0B9F, #x0BA3, #x0BA4, #x0BA8 - #x0BAA, #x0BAE - #x0BB5, #x0BB7 - #x0BB9
Telugu	#x0C05 - #x0C0C, #x0C0E - #x0C10, #x0C12 - #x0C28, #x0C2A - #x0C33, #x0C35 - #x0C39, #x0C60, #x0C61

Character Set	Supported Characters
Thai	#x0E01 - #x0E2E, #x0E30, #x0E32, #x0E33, #x0E40 - #x0E45
Tibetan	#x0F40 - #x0F47, #x0F49 - #x0F69

CombiningChar Characters and Character Sets

This section covers the characters and character sets supported by the CombiningChar production.

Combining Diacritical Marks

Table B-13 contains the XML-supported characters in the Combining Diacritical Marks set, in the CombiningChar production.

Table B-13 *CombiningChar Special Characters — Combining Diacritical Marks*

Glyph	UTC Code	Description
à	#x0300	Grave Accent Above
á	#x0301	Acute Accent Above
â	#x0302	Circumflex Above
ã	#x0303	Tilde Above
ā	#x0304	Macron Above
a̅	#x0305	Overline
ă	#x0306	Breve Above
ȧ	#x0307	Dot Above
ä	#x0308	Dieresis Above
ả	#x0309	Hook Above
å	#x030A	Ring Above
a̋	#x030B	Double Acute Accent
ǎ	#x030C	Caron Above

Continued

Table B-13 *Continued*

Glyph	UTC Code	Description
a̍	#x030D	Vertical Line Above
a̎	#x030E	Double Vertical Line Above
ȁ	#x030F	Double Grave Accent
a̐	#x0310	Candrabindu
ȃ	#x0311	Inverted Breve Above
a̒	#x0312	Turned Comma Above
a̓	#x0313	Comma Above
a̔	#x0314	Reversed Comma Above
a̕	#x0315	Comma Above Right
a̖	#x0316	Grave Accent Below
a̗	#x0317	Acute Accent Below
a̘	#x0318	Left Tack Below
a̙	#x0319	Right Tack Below
a̚	#x031A	Left Angle Above
a̛	#x031B	Horn
a̜	#x031C	Left Half Ring Below
a̝	#x031D	Up Tack Below
a̞	#x031E	Down Tack Below
a̟	#x031F	Plus Sign Below
a̠	#x0320	Minus Sign Below
a̡	#x0321	Palatalized Hook Below
a̢	#x0322	Retroflex Hook Below
ạ	#x0323	Dot Below
a̤	#x0324	Dieresis Below
ḁ	#x0325	Ring Below
a̦	#x0326	Comma Below
a̧	#x0327	Cedilla
ą	#x0328	Ogonek
a̩	#x0329	Vertical Line Below

Glyph	UTC Code	Description
a	#x032A	Bridge Below
a	#x032B	Inverted Double Arch Below
a	#x032C	Caron Below
a	#x032D	Circumflex Below
a	#x032E	Breve Below
a	#x032F	Inverted Breve Below
a	#x0330	Tilde Below
a	#x0331	Macron Below
a	#x0332	Low Line
a	#x0333	Double Low Line
a	#x0334	Tilde Overlay
a	#x0335	Short Stroke Overlay
a	#x0336	Long Stroke Overlay
a	#x0337	Short Solidus Overlay
a	#x0338	Long Solidus Overlay
a	#x0339	Right Half Ring Below
a	#x033A	Inverted Bridge Below
a	#x033B	Square Below
a	#x033C	Seagull Below
a	#x033D	X Above
a	#x033E	Vertical Tilde
a	#x033F	Double Overline
a	#x0340	Grave Tone Mark
a	#x0341	Acute Tone Mark
a	#x0342	Greek Perispomeni
a	#x0343	Greek Koronis
a	#x0344	Greek Dialytika Tonos
a	#x0345	Greek Ypogegrammeni
a	#x0360	Double Tilde
a	#x0361	Double Inverted Breve

Combining Diacritical Marks for Symbols

Table B-14 contains the XML-supported characters in the Combining Diacritical Marks for Symbols set, in the CombiningChar production.

Table B-14 *CombiningChar Special Characters — Combining Diacritical Marks for Symbols*

Glyph	UTC Code	Description
a̅	#x20D0	Left Harpoon Above
a̅	#x20D1	Right Harpoon Above
a̒	#x20D2	Long Vertical Line Overlay
a̓	#x20D3	Short Vertical Line Overlay
a̔	#x20D4	Anticlockwise Arrow Above
a̕	#x20D5	Clockwise Arrow Above
a̖	#x20D6	Left Arrow Above
a̗	#x20D7	Right Arrow Above
a̘	#x20D8	Ring Overlay
a̙	#x20D9	Clockwise Ring Overlay
a̚	#x20DA	Anticlockwise Ring Overlay
a̛	#x20DB	Three Dots Above
a̜	#x20DC	Four Dots Above
a̝	#x20E1	Left Right Arrow Above

CJK Symbols and Punctuation

Table B-15 contains the XML-supported characters in the CJK Symbols and Punctuation set, in the CombiningChar production.

●—**NOTE**————————————————————————

In this table, the lowercase *a* is in the background of each character to show the position of that character from the baseline.

Table B-15   *CombiningChar Special Characters — CJK Symbols and Punctuation*

Glyph	UTC Code	Description
ၛ	#x302A	Level Tone Mark
ä	#x302B	Rising Tone Mark
a˙	#x302C	Departing Tone Mark
a.	#x302D	Entering Tone Mark
ˌa	#x302E	Hangul Single Dot Tone Mark
ːa	#x302F	Hangul Double Dot Tone Mark

Other Character Sets

Table B-16 lists other CombiningChar character sets and the XML-supported characters for each.

●—NOTE

Because using American fonts to display non-English special characters is difficult, the following table does not contain illustrations of the glyphs. To view the characters in this table, go to the Unicode Consortium's Web site (http://www.unicode.org/).

Table B-16   *Other Combining Char Character Sets*

Character Set	Supported Characters
Cyrillic	#x0483 - #x0486
Hebrew	#x0591 - #x05A1, #x05A3 - #x05B9, #x05BB - #x05BD, #x05BF, #x05C1 - #x05C2, #x05C4
Arabic	#x064B - #x0652, #x0670, #x06D6 - #x06DC, #x06DD - #x06DF, #x06E0 - #x6E4, #x06E7 - #x06E8, #x06EA - #x06ED
Devanagari	#x0901 - #x0903, #x093C, #x093E - #x094C, #x094D, #x0951 - #x0954, #x0962 - #x963
Bengali	#x0981 - #x0983, #x09BC, #x09BE, #x09BF, #x09C0 - #x09C4, #x09C7 - #x09C8, #x09CB - #x09CD, #x09D7, #x09E2 - #x09E3

Continued

Table B-16 *Continued*

Character Set	Supported Characters
Gurmukhi	#x0A02, #x0A3C, #x0A3E, #x0A3F, #x0A40 - #x0A42, #x0A47 - #x0A48, #x0A4B - #x0A4D, #x0A70 - #x0A71
Gujarati	#x0A81 - #x0A83, #x0ABC, #x0ABE - #x0AC5, #x0AC7 - #x0AC9, #x0ACB - #x0ACD
Oriya	#x0B01 - #x0B03, #x0B3C, #x0B3E - #x0B43, #x0B47 - #x0B48, #x0B4B - #x0B4D, #x0B56 - #x0B57
Tamil	#x0B82 - #x0B83, #x0BBE - #x0BC2, #x0BC6 - #x0BC8, #x0BCA - #x0BCD, #x0BD7
Telugu	#x0C01 - #x0C03, #x0C3E - #x0C44, #x0C46 - #x0C48, #x0C4A - #x0C4D, #x0C55 - #x0C56
Kannada	#x0C82 - #x0C83, #x0CBE - #x0CC4, #x0CC6 - #x0CC8, #x0CCA - #x0CCD, #x0CD5 - #x0CD6
Malayalam	#x0D02 - #x0D03, #x0D3E - #x0D43, #x0D46 - #x0D48, #x0D4A - #x0D4D, #x0D57
Thai	#x0E34 - #x0E3A, #x0E47 - #x0E4E
Lao	#x0EB1, #x0EB4 - #x0EB9, #x0EBB - #x0EBC, #x0EC8 - #x0ECD
Tibetan	#x0F18 - #x0F19, #x0F35, #x0F37, #x0F39, #x0F3E, #x0F3F, #x0F71 - #x0F84, #x0F86 - #x0F8B, #x0F90 - #x0F95, #x0F97, #x0F99 - #x0FAD, #x0FB1 - #x0FB7, #x0FB9
Hiragama	#x3099, #x309A

Digit

This section covers the characters and character sets supported by the Digit production.

ISO 646 Digits

Table B-17 contains the XML-supported characters in the ISO 646 Digits set, in the Digit production.

Table B-17 *Digit Special Characters — ISO 646 Digits*

Glyph	UTC Code	Description
0	#x0030	Digit Zero
I	#x0031	Digit One
2	#x0032	Digit Two
3	#x0033	Digit Three
4	#x0034	Digit Four
5	#x0035	Digit Five
6	#x0036	Digit Six
7	#x0037	Digit Seven
8	#x0038	Digit Eight
9	#x0039	Digit Nine

Other Character Sets

Table B-18 lists other Digit character sets and the XML-supported characters for each.

●—NOTE

Because it is difficult to use American fonts to display non-English special characters, the following table does not contain illustrations of the glyphs. To view the characters in this table, go to the Unicode Consortium's Web site (http://www.unicode.org/).

Table B-18 *Other Digit Character Sets*

Character Set	Supported Characters
Arabic-Indic Digits	#x0660 - #x0669
Eastern Arabic-Indic Digits	#x06F0 - #x06F9
Devanagari Digits	#x0966 - #x096F
Bengali Digits	#x09E6 - #x09EF
Gurmukhi Digits	#x0A66 - #x0A6F
Gujarati Digits	#x0AE6 - #x0AEF

Continued

Table B-18 *Continued*

Character Set	Supported Characters
Oriya Digits	#x0B66 - #x0B6F
Tamil Digits (no zero)	#x0BE7 - #x0BEF
Telugu Digits	#x0C66 - #x0C6F
Kannada Digits	#x0CE6 - #x0CEF
Malayalam Digits	#x0D66 - #x0D6F
Thai Digits	#x0E50 - #x0E59
Lao Digits	#x0ED0 - #x0ED9
Tibetan Digits	#x0F20 - #x0F29

Extender

This section covers the characters and character sets supported by the Extender production.

Extender Special Characters

Table B-19 contains the XML-supported characters for the Extender production. The character sets in which the characters are located are within parentheses.

Table B-19 *Extender Special Characters*

Glyph	UTC Code	Description
.	#x00B7	Middle Dot (C1 Controls and Latin-1 Supplement)
:	#x02D0	Triangular Colon (Spacing Modifier Letters)
.	#x02D1	Half Triangular Colon (Spacing Modifier Letters)
⼌	#x3005	Ideographic Iteration Mark (CJK Symbols and Punctuation)
〱	#x3031	Vertical Kana Repeat Mark (CJK Symbols and Punctuation)
〲	#x3032	Vertical Kana Repeat with Voiced Sound Mark (CJK Symbols and Punctuation)

Glyph	UTC Code	Description
/	#x3033	Vertical Kana Repeat Mark Upper Half (CJK Symbols and Punctuation)
/∙	#x3034	Vertical Kana Repeat with Voiced Sound Mark Upper Half (CJK Symbols and Punctuation)
\	#x3035	Vertical Kana Repeat Mark Lower Half (CJK Symbols and Punctuation)

Other Character Sets

Table B-20 lists other Extender character sets and the XML-supported characters for each.

Table B-20   *Other Extender Character Sets*

Character Set	Supported Characters
Greek	#x0387
Arabic	#x0640
Thai	#x0E46
Lao	#x0EC6
Hiragana	#x309D - #x309E
Katakana	#x30FC - #x30FE

Ideographic

This section covers the characters and character sets supported by the Ideographic production.

CJK Symbols and Punctuation

Table B-21 contains the XML-supported characters for the Ideographic production.

Table B-21   *Ideographic Special Characters — CJK Symbols and Punctuation*

Glyph	UTC Code	Description
○	#x3007	Number Zero
〡	#x3021	Hangzhou Numeral One
〢	#x3022	Hangzhou Numeral Two
〣	#x3023	Hangzhou Numeral Three
〤	#x3024	Hangzhou Numeral Four
〥	#x3025	Hangzhou Numeral Five
〦	#x3026	Hangzhou Numeral Six
〧	#x3027	Hangzhou Numeral Seven
〨	#x3028	Hangzhou Numeral Eight
〩	#x3029	Hangzhou Numeral Nine

Additional Character Set

Table B-22 lists the additional Ideographic character set and its XML-supported characters.

● **NOTE**

Because it is difficult to use American fonts to display non-English special characters, the following table does not contain illustrations of the glyphs. To view the characters in this table, go to the Unicode Consortium's Web site (http://www.unicode.org/).

Table B-22   *Additional Ideographic Character Set*

Character Set	Supported Characters
CJK Unified Ideographs	#x4E00 - #x9FA5

in plain english in pl
sh in plain english in
glish in plain english
in plain english in pl
sh in plain english in
glish in plain english
in plain english in pl
glish in plain english
in plain english in pl
sh in plain english in
glish in plain english
in plain english in pl
sh in plain english in
glish in plain english
in plain english in pl
lish in plain english
in plain english in pl
sh in plain english in
glish in plain english
in plain english in pl
sh in plain english in
lish in plain english
in plain english in pl
glish in plain english

Internationalization: Language Codes and Country Codes

The World Wide Web is an international phenomena accessed by a worldwide population speaking many languages. As you know, the Web's original purpose was for scientists around the world to share research information. Now that the Web has grown to encompass many types of sites — commercial, educational, organizational, and personal — the developers of the Web have addressed the issue of *internationalization*, the support of non-English alphabets and special characters. Therefore, internationalization is the use of many languages — some included in single Web documents. When you create documents using multiple languages, you use different alphabets and symbols, all of which should be supported.

In the 2.0 and 3.2 versions of HTML, the supported character code was the International Standard ISO-8859, which was comprised of Latin character sets and special characters. Many international character sets and special symbols were not supported at all. Now, HTML 4.0 and XML support the International Standard ISO 10646-1, which includes ISO 8859, adds international characters and symbols, and supports the explicit setting of the direction of text output. Supported character sets include alphabets for many languages, punctuation marks, technical and mathematical characters, arrows, dingbats, and *diacritics*, which are marks that are added to a letter. Diacritics include acute and grave accents, breves, cedillas, circumflexes, macrons, tildes, and so on — components of many alphabets.

You can name a language for an XHTML document using a two-letter language code (see Table C-1) in the document's first line. For example:

```
<!DOCTYPE HTML PUBLIC
    "-//W3C//DTD HTML 4.0//EN">
```

The EN at the end of the line represents the English language.

Most XHTML elements support the LANG attribute, with which you can name the language used within the element's start tag and end tag:

```
<P LANG="DE">Erzeugnisse und Dienste</P>
```

As you might have guessed, the DE represents German.

You can also specify country codes and subcodes (see Table C-2), which refine a language or country (for example, British English versus American English or French French versus Canadian French).

Table C-1 lists language name codes based on those in the ISO 639: 1988 standard. Language names are listed alphabetically. Note that when you use a language code in a document, it is common practice to enter it in lowercase. In contrast, the country code is usually expressed in uppercase (see Table C-2).

Table C-1 *ISO 639 Language Codes*

Language	Code	Language	Code	Language	Code
Abkhazian	ab	Catalan	ca	Gujarati	gu
Afan	om	Chinese	zh	Hausa	ha
Afar	aa	Corsican	co	Hebrew	iw
Afrikaans	af	Croatian	hr	Hindi	hi
Albanian	sq	Czech	cs	Hungarian	hu
Amharic	am	Danish	da	Icelandic	is
Arabic	ar	Dutch	nl	Indonesian	in
Armenian	hy	English	en	Interlingua	ia
Assamese	as	Esperanto	eo	Interlingue	ie
Aymara	ay	Estonian	et	Inuktitut	iu
Azerbaijani	az	Faroese	fo	Inupiak	ik

Language	Code	Language	Code	Language	Code
Bashkir	ba	Fiji	fj	Irish	ga
Basque	eu	Finnish	fi	Italian	it
Bengali	bn	French	fr	Japanese	ja
Bhutani	dz	Frisian	fy	Javanese	jw
Bihari	bh	Gaelic (Scottish)	gd	Kannada	kn
Bislama	bi	Galician	gl	Kashmiri	ks
Breton	br	Georgian	ka	Kazakh	kk
Bulgarian	bg	German	de	Kinyarwanda	rw
Burmese	my	Greek	el	Kirghiz	ky
Byelorussian	be	Greenlandic	kl	Kirundi	rn
Cambodian	km	Guarani	gn	Korean	ko
Kurdish	ku	Punjabi	pa	Tamil	ta
Laotian	lo	Quechua	qu	Tatar	tt
Latin	la	Rhaeto-Romance	rm	Tegulu	te
Latvian	lv	Romanian	ro	Thai	th
Lingala	ln	Russian	ru	Tibetan	bo
Lithuanian	lt	Samoan	sm	Tigrinya	ti
Macedonian	mk	Sangho	sg	Tonga	to
Malagasy	mg	Sanskrit	sa	Tsonga	ts
Malay	ms	Serbian	sr	Turkish	tr
Malayalam	ml	Serbo-Croatian	sh	Turkmen	tk
Maltese	mt	Sesotho	st	Twi	tw
Maori	mi	Setswana	tn	Uigar	ug
Marathi	mr	Shona	sn	Ukrainian	uk
Moldavian	mo	Sindhi	sd	Urdu	ur
Mongolian	mn	Singhalese	si	Uzbek	uz
Nauru	na	Siswati	ss	Vietnamese	vi
Nepali	ne	Slovak	sk	Volapuk	vo
Norwegian	no	Slovenian	sl	Welsh	cy
Occitan	oc	Somali	so	Wolof	wo
Oriya	or	Spanish	es	Xhosa	xh

Continued

Table C-1   *Continued*

Language	Code	Language	Code	Language	Code
Oromo	om	Sudanese	su	Yiddish	ji
Pashto	ps	Swahili	sw	Yoruba	yo
Persian	fa	Swedish	sv	Zhuang	za
Polish	pl	Tagalog	tl	Zulu	zu
Portuguese	pt	Tajik	tg		

Table C-2 lists country name codes based on those in the ISO 3166 standard. Country names are listed alphabetically. Note that when you use a country code in a document, it is common practice to enter it in uppercase. In contrast, the language code is usually expressed in lowercase (see Table C-1).

Table C-2   *ISO 3166 Country Codes*

Country	Code	Country	Code
Afghanistan	AF	Botswana	BW
Albania	AL	Bouvet Island	BV
Algeria	DZ	Brazil	BR
American Samoa	AS	British Indian Ocean Territory	IO
Andorra	AD	Brunei	BN
Angola	AO	Bulgaria	BG
Anguilla	AI	Burkina Faso	BF
Antarctica	AQ	Burundi	BI
Antigua and Barbuda	AG	Cambodia	KH
Argentina	AR	Cameroon	CM
Armenia	AM	Canada	CA
Aruba	AW	Cape Verde	CV
Australia	AU	Cayman Islands	KY
Austria	AT	Central African Republic	CF
Azerbaijan	AZ	Chad	TD
Bahamas	BS	Chile	CL
Bahrain	BH	China	CN
Bangladesh	BD	Christmas Island	CX

Country	Code	Country	Code
Barbados	BB	Cocos Islands	CC
Belarus	BY	Colombia	CO
Belgium	BE	Comoros	KM
Belize	BZ	Congo	CG
Benin	BJ	Cook Islands	CK
Bermuda	BM	Costa Rica	CR
Bhutan	BT	Cote D'Ivoire	CI
Bolivia	BO	Croatia	HR
Bosnia Herzegovina	BA	Cuba	CU
Cyprus	CY	Greece	GR
Czech Republic	CZ	Greenland	GL
Denmark	DK	Grenada	GD
Djibouti	DJ	Guadeloupe	GP
Dominica	CM	Guam	GU
Dominican Republic	DO	Guatemala	GT
East Timor	TP	Guinea	GN
Ecuador	EC	Guinea-Bissau	GW
Egypt	EG	Guyana	GY
El Salvador	SV	Haiti	HT
Equatorial Guinea	GQ	Heard and McDonald Islands	HM
Eritrea	ER	Holy See (The Vatican)	VA
Estonia	EE	Honduras	HN
Ethiopia	ET	Hong Kong	HK
Falkland Islands	FK	Hungary	HU
Faroe Islands	FO	Iceland	IS
Fiji	FJ	India	IN
Finland	FI	Indonesia	ID
France	FR	Iran	IR
France, Metropolitan	FX	Iraq	IQ
French Guiana	GF	Ireland	IE
French Polynesia	PF	Israel	IL
French Southern Territories	TF	Italy	IT

Continued

Table C-2 *Continued*

Country	Code	Country	Code
Gabon	GA	Jamaica	JM
Gambia	GM	Japan	JP
Georgia	GE	Jordan	JO
Germany	DE	Kazakhstan	KZ
Ghana	GH	Kenya	KE
Gibraltar	GI	Kiribati	KI
Korea, North	KP	Mongolia	MN
Korea, South	KR	Montserrat	MS
Kuwait	KW	Morocco	MA
Kyrgyzstan	KG	Mozambique	MZ
Laos	LA	Myanmar (Burma)	MM
Latvia	LV	Namibia	NA
Lebanon	LB	Nauru	NR
Lesotho	LS	Nepal	NP
Liberia	LR	Netherland Antilles	AN
Libya	LY	Netherlands	NL
Liechtenstein	LI	New Caledonia	NC
Lithuania	LT	New Zealand	NZ
Luxembourg	LU	Nicaragua	NI
Macau	MO	Niger	NE
Macedonia	MK	Nigeria	NG
Madagascar	MG	Niue	NU
Malawi	MW	Norfolk Island	NF
Malaysia	MY	Northern Mariana Islands	MP
Maldives	MV	Norway	NO
Mali	ML	Oman	OM
Malta	MT	Pakistan	PK
Marshall Islands	MH	Palau	PW
Martinique	MQ	Palestinian Territory	PS
Mauritania	MR	Panama	PA
Mauritius	MU	Papua New Guinea	PG
Mayotte	YT	Paraguay	PY

Country	Code	Country	Code
Mexico	MX	Peru	PE
Micronesia	FM	Philippines	PH
Moldova	MD	Pitcairn	PN
Monaco	MC	Poland	PL
Puerto Rico	PR	Portugal	PT
Qatar	QA	St. Pierre and Miquelon	PM
Reunion	RE	Sudan	SD
Romania	RO	Suriname	SR
Russian Federation	RU	Svalbard and Jan Mayen Islands	SJ
Rwanda	RW	Swaziland	SZ
Saint Kitts and Nevis	KN	Sweden	SE
Saint Lucia	LC	Switzerland	CH
Saint Vincent and The Grenadines	VC	Syria	SY
Samoa	WS	Taiwan	TW
San Marino	SM	Tajikistan	TJ
Sao Tome and Principe	ST	Tanzania	TZ
Saudi Arabia	SA	Thailand	TH
Senegal	SN	Togo	TG
Seychelles	SC	Tokelau	TK
Sierra Leone	SL	Tonga	TO
Singapore	SG	Trinidad and Tobago	TT
Slovakia	SK	Tunisia	TN
Slovenia	SI	Turkey	TR
Solomon Islands	SB	Turkmenistan	TM
Somalia	SO	Turks and Caicos Islands	TC
South Africa	ZA	Tuvalu	TV
South Georgia and The South Sandwich Islands	GS	Uganda	UG
Spain	ES	Ukraine	UA
Sri Lanka	LK	United Arab Emirates	AE
St. Helena	SH	United Kingdom	GB

Continued

Table C-2   *Continued*

Country	Code	Country	Code
United States	US	United States Minor Outlying Islands	UM
Uruguay	UY	Wallis and Futuna Islands	WF
Uzbekistan	UZ	Western Sahara	EH
Vanuatu	VU	Yemen	YE
Venezuela	VE	Yugoslavia	YU
Vietnam	VN	Zambia	ZM
Virgin Islands, British	VG	Zimbabwe	ZW
Virgin Islands, U.S.	VI		

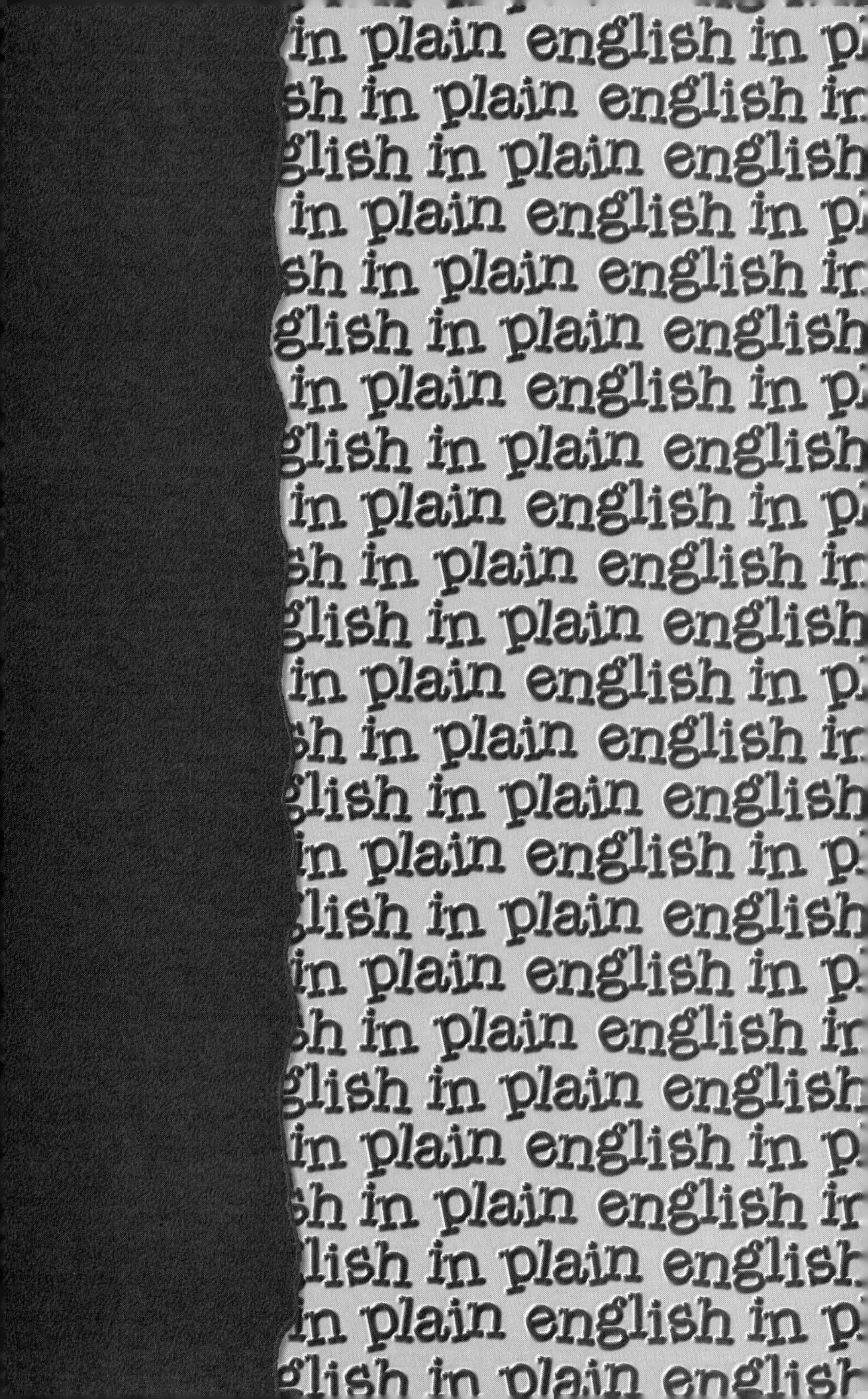
in plain english

EBNF Reference

The XML 1.0 recommendation uses Extended Backus-Naur Form (EBNF) notation to define XML documents and DTD syntax. Developer can then write a DTD to specify the elements, attributes, entities, and special characters for one document or a document set. A DTD also sets the rules, limitations, and values for each of the components. XHTML documents are associated with one of three DTDs: strict, transitional, or frameset.

This appendix contains tables of syntax. To learn about EBNF, refer to Page 522 in Chapter 2, *Constructing a Basic Document*, and Page 678 in Chapter 11, *Customizing XHTML*.

Table D-1 lists basic EBNF syntax used in the XML 1.0 specification. Under each entry is a short description.

Table D-1 *Continued*

Syntax	Description
#xN	Enter #x and N, a hexadecimal integer matching any UCS-4 code value in ISO/IEC 10646 standard.
[ ]	Brackets indicate that the grouped content within is optional.
[a-zA-Z], [#xN-#xN]	Enter one of the characters within the range a to z, A to Z, or #xN to #xN.
[^a-z], [^#xN-#xN]	Do *not* enter any of the characters within the range adjacent to the NOT character.
[^abc], [^#xN#xN#xN]	Do *not* enter any of the characters adjacent to the NOT character.
"string"|'string'	Enter the literal string enclosed within the quotation marks or single quote marks. Do *not* mix quotation marks and single quote marks in an expression.
( )	Parentheses contain an expression in the same way that you would write a mathematical expression.
(expression)	Enter an expression consisting of a combination of the previously listed parts of syntax in this table. To combine expressions, use the syntax in Table D-2.

Table D-2 lists the EBNF syntax for expressions and components, where A indicates an expression (within parentheses) or a component (without parentheses). With each entry is a short description.

Table D-2 *Extended Backus-Naur Form (EBNF) Expression Syntax*

Syntax	Description
A?	An expression or component followed by a question mark indicates that the expression is optional.
A B	One expression or component followed by another must be matched exactly.

Syntax	Description
A|B	Expressions or components separated by pipe symbols indicate ORs. Choose one expression OR the other—in other words, just choose one. In this book, pipes appear in a larger point size to differentiate them from pipe characters within elements.
A − B	The first expression or component must be present, and the expression or component following the minus sign must be absent. Note that a range (for example, A-B) contains no spaces, but the minus sign indicating an absent expression or component (A − B) is both preceded and succeeded by a space.
A+	An expression or component followed by a plus sign indicates that the expression *must* appear one or more times.
A*	An expression or component followed by an asterisk indicates that the expression *may* appear one or more times.

Table D-3 lists the symbols used as delimiters, connectors, and indicators within XML documents and DTDs. Under each entry is a short description. Note that some of these symbols have appeared in Tables D-1 and D-2.

Table D-3 *Extended Backus-Naur Form (EBNF) Symbols*

Symbols	Description
< and >	Delimits the start and end of a declaration or tag.
/	With < (for example, </), indicates the beginning of an end tag. With > (for example, />), indicates the end of an empty-element tag.
::=	Represents the formula for a production: symbol|Symbol ::= expression.
!	Indicates that a reserved keyword follows.
−	Indicates a range if the expressions (A-B) do not include spaces *or* subtraction if the expressions (A - B) include spaces.
^	Indicates that you must not select any of the characters that follow.
&	Starts a parsed general entity.
&#	Starts a decimal character reference.
&#x	Starts a hexadecimal character reference.

Continued

Table D-3 *Continued*

Symbols	Description
%	Starts a parameter entity or parameter entity reference.
;	Ends an entity.
?	Indicates that a content particle can occur up to one time.
+	Indicates that a content particle *must* occur one or more times.
*	Indicates that a content particle can occur an unlimited number of times.
|	Connects content particles and states that a Web page developer can select the listed components in any order. Within brackets, indicates a choice.
,	Connects content particles and states that a Web page developer *must* select the listed components in the order in which they appear.
/* and */	Delimits the start and end of a comment.
(and)	Delimits the start and end of an expression to be evaluated as a whole.
" and '	Delimits the start and end of a string. Do not mix quotation marks and single quote marks for the same string.
<? and ?>	Delimits the start and end of a processing instruction.
[and]	Delimits the start and end of a range; [delimits the start of an internal DTD.
]>	Delimits the end of an internal DTD.
<![and]]>	Delimits the start and end of a CDATA section.

D

Attributes in Depth

This bonus appendix which is located at www.mandtbooks.
com/extras/xhtmlipe contains an alphabetically arranged
list of XHTML 1.0 attributes, which are based on the XHTML
DTD. XHTML includes attributes for every element and extension. Each entry includes a brief description, usage notes, and
the elements under which the attribute is used.

Note that:

- HTML attributes are case-insensitive, and XHTML
  attributes are case-sensitive.
- Attribute values must be enclosed within quotation
  marks or single quotes.
- Attribute values can contain colons and underscores.

Glossary

absolute link
A link to another document using the complete URL or address, including the transfer protocol, the computer or network name, the directory or folder, and a filename (for example, `http://www.mispress.com/index.html`). See *relative link*.

address
An electronic location to which e-mail is sent; an electronic location on the Internet or on a network.

agent
Robot. A search index that finds information from all or part of the Internet or a network, sometimes at a regular time or date or when page content changes. Another definition of agent is anything (such as a browser) that processes user requests. See *search index* and *search tool*.

American National Standards Institute
See *ANSI*.

American Standard Code for Information Interchange
See *ASCII*.

761

anchor
The starting link that refers to another location within the current document or within another document; the ending link to which a starting link refers.

Anonymous FTP
See *FTP*.

ANSI
American National Standards Institute. A U.S. affiliate of the International Organization for Standardization (ISO), an organization that formulates many international standards for characters, numbers, and symbols; computing; telecommunicating; and so on. See *ISO*.

archive
A collection of information, usually from the past but sometimes from the present.

ASCII
American Standard Code for Information Interchange. A coding standard for characters, numbers, and symbols that is the same as the first 128 characters of the ASCII character set but differs from the remaining characters. See also *ASCII file*.

ASCII file
A text file or a text-only file. A file format that can be read by almost any word processor or text editor, allowing for transfer and viewing between individuals with dissimilar computers, operating systems, and programs. ASCII files contain characters, spaces, punctuation, end-of-line marks, and some formats._See also *ASCII*.

attributes
A World Wide Web Consortium (W3C) term for options, which are settings that affect formats, alignments, text enhancements, paragraphs, or other parts of an HTML document.

AU
A UNIX-based sound file format.

AVI
Audio Video Interleave; a popular Windows-based video file format.

base
See *absolute link*.

bit
Binary digit. The smallest unit of computer information, represented by a 1 (which represents *yes* or *on*) or 0 (representing *no* or *off*).

bit map
A graphic image made up of pixels (also known as "pels" in some circles). Bit map file formats include BMP, GIF, and JPEG.

block elements2
Elements that affect blocks of text, such as paragraphs and lists. Many block elements affect text in much the same way as paragraph formatting in a word processor.

bookmarks
Hot lists. URLs of sites that you regularly visit and that you have had your browser save. When you want to visit a bookmarked site, just select it from your browser's bookmark list.

browser
A program (such as Netscape Navigator, Microsoft Internet Explorer, or Mosaic) with which you can surf the World Wide Web as well as Gopher and FTP sites. Some browsers also provide e-mail and Telnet utilities. Other browsers are part of suites of Internet access programs.

CGI
Common Gateway Interface. A protocol that enables developers to write programs that create HTML in response to user requests; frequently used to connect databases to the World Wide Web.

client
A program (such as a browser) that is programmed to communicate with and ask for information from a server program (such as a World Wide Web or Gopher server), usually on a remote computer. See *browser* and *server.*

client pull
The automatic loading or reloading of a document at a specific time or time interval by a browser. You can either use the META element or write a CGI program to incorporate client pull features. See also *server push.*

Common Gateway Interface
See *CGI.*

declaration
A statement that defines the elements and attributes in a document without telling the computer how to use them. In HTML, an attribute (such as color) and its value (for example, blue) are declarations. In a cascading style sheet, a declaration specifies a property (for example, font style) and its value (for example, italic).

deprecated
An outdated element or attribute. Although it is still supported in the current HTML standard, it will eventually be obsolete. When you create or edit HTML documents, replace deprecated elements or attributes with fully supported elements or attributes. Deprecated elements in HTML 4.0, which is the foundation language for XHTML, are APPLET, BASEFONT, CENTER, DIR, FONT, ISINDEX, MENU, S, STRIKE, and U. See also *obsolete*.

dialup
A temporary network connection, made by dialing a telephone number with a modem and logging in with a user identifier (ID) and a password. This is the typical way that an individual gains access to the Internet. Since the dialup is not a dedicated (or permanent) connection, the individual can use the telephone line for other purposes.

Document Type Definition
See *DTD*.

domain
The two-or three-character codes for organizations (COM, EDU, INT, NET, GOV, MIL, NET) and for regions or countries (for example, the United States is US) in which the organization is located. At the time of this writing, new domains are under consideration.

domain name
The name for a site (for example, psu, which represents Pennsylvania State University, or lotus, which represents Lotus Development Corpora-tion) and its domain. A typical domain name is psu.edu or lotus.com.

Domain Name System
DNS. The system by which Internet sites are named; for example, www.lotus.com or eddygrp@sover.net.

download
The transfer of a file from a remote computer to your computer. The standard protocol for downloading files from the Internet is anonymous FTP (file transfer protocol). See *FTP* and *upload*.

DTD
Document Type Definition. A document, written in SGML, that specifies the elements (popularly known as *tags*), attributes (options), entities (special characters), and rules for creating documents using a particular HTML version or other SGML-related markup language. The !DOCTYPE comment, which names the DTD with which a document has been cre-ated, enables HTML validators to properly check a document. XML also uses DTDs.

dynamic HTML
A proposed standard that allows the appearance and content of an HTML document to change whenever a user interacts with it. Interactions that trigger document updating include moving the mouse, clicking, double-clicking, and pressing keys.

electronic mail
See *e-mail*.

element
The proper name for what is popularly known as a *tag*, one unit of a markup language. A command with which you define part of an HTML document. An element usually starts with a start tag, `<tagname>`, includes an element name, may contain attributes with which you vary the results of the element, and may end with an end tag, `</tagname>`. See *end tag* and *start tag*.

e-mail
Electronic mail. Messages (which may have files attached) sent from an individual to one or more individuals on a network or remote computer.

e-mail address
The electronic mailing address of an individual, group, or organization. For example, my e-mail address is `eddygrp@sover.net` (where *eddygrp* is the user ID, the @ (at) sign is a separator symbol, and *sover.net* is the name of the server computer to which my e-mail address is identified). My e-mail address is pronounced "Eddy Group at sover dot net."

end tag
The part of an HTML statement that indicates the end of an element and its attributes. The format of an end tag is `</elementname>`, in contrast to the start tag format, `<elementname>`. Sometimes, an end tag is either an optional or forbidden (that is, it must not be used) part of a statement. See *element* and *start tag*.

entity
A special character; a single unit or item.

extension
(1). An element that is not part of the current approved standard version of HTML. Netscape and Microsoft extensions are the best known. (2). Two or three characters (for example, DOC, TXT, HTM, GIF, PS, and so on) that identify a file type or format.

FAQ
Frequently Asked Questions. Documents that list commonly asked questions and their answers about almost any topic, including computing and the Internet. FAQs are designed to save those in the know the bother of responding to questions asked and answered many times before. First-time visitors to a newsgroup or support site should always read the FAQ (if one is provided) before asking questions.

File Transfer Protocol
See FTP.

firewall
A combination of a security program and hardware that creates a virtual wall between unwanted visitors and specified parts of a network.

fixed-width typeface
See *monospaced typeface*.

freeware
Public-domain programs. Programs you can download and use without making any payment to the software publisher. See also *shareware*.

Frequently Asked Questions
See *FAQ*.

FTP
File Transfer Protocol. A protocol, or set of rules, that allows the access, reading, and/or downloading of files from a remote computer. You can either log on to a remote computer using an assigned user identifier (ID) and password, or use anonymous FTP, which uses the word "anonymous" as the user ID, and the user's e-mail address as the password. With the growth of the World Wide Web, FTP login is becoming *transparent* to the user; that is, login is automatically enabled by the user clicking on a link in an HTML document.

GIF
Graphics Interchange Format. A format for graphics files used within World Wide Web documents. GIF files are larger than graphics files with the JPEG format. See also *JPEG*.

glyph
A graphic that represents a character, particularly in a typeface.

home page
The top hypertext document at a World Wide Web site or the document to which a user first goes when visiting a site. Typically, the home page provides an introduction to the site as well as links to the site's other pages. Most browsers are programmed to automatically go to a particular home page after your computer connects to the Internet.

host
A server. A computer that hosts other computers and provides information and services to client programs. See *client* and *server*.

HTML
HyperText Markup Language. A subset of SGML (Standard Generalized Markup Language); the language with which you typically mark up (or create) documents with hypertext links for the World Wide Web. HTML 4.0 is the current version. See *hypertext*, *link*, *SGML*, and *World Wide Web*.

HTML document
A document created using elements and attributes from HTML (HyperText Markup Language).

HTTP
HyperText Transport Protocol. The rules and standards that client programs use to read hypertext files on host computers. See *client*, *host*, *hypertext*, and *World Wide Web*.

hyperlink
See *link*.

hypermedia
See *multimedia*.

hypertext
A variety of media in a document. Hypertext includes links to other documents or sections of documents, text, graphics, audio, and video. See *link*, *multimedia*, and *World Wide Web*.

icon
A small button or graphic on which you click or double-click to open a folder, document, or file; to perform an action or issue a command, usually avoiding multiple steps; or to start a program.

IETF
Internet Engineering Task Force. An organization that evaluates and sets most standards for the Internet.

inline elements

Elements that affect characters. These elements affect text in much the same way as font or character formatting in a word processor. Most inline elements do not cause line breaks. One obvious exception is the inline element BR.

inline image

A graphic within an HTML document.

International Organization for Standardization

See *ISO*.

internet

Two or more networks connected into a single network.

Internet

The largest internet of all, comprised of networks connecting government agencies, private and public organizations, educational institutions, laboratories, and individuals.

Internet Engineering Task Force

See *IETF*.

Internet media type

IMEDIA. See *media type*.

Internet provider

An organization that provides user access to the Internet. Also known as *Internet access provider* and *Internet service provider*.

ISO

International Organization for Standardization. An international standards-setting organization. ISO sets standards for computing, telecommunicating, and so on. ANSI, the American National Standards Institute, is the U.S. affiliate. See *ANSI*.

JPEG

Joint Photographic Expert Group. A graphics file format with a JPG extension. JPEG graphics are usually smaller than GIF graphics. See also *GIF*.

keyword

A word or phrase stored in a META tag statement. Search indexes use keywords to compile and optionally rank lists of HTML documents. See *search index* and *search tool*.

link

A highlighted and/or underlined word or phrase or a graphic coded into an A element. Click on a link to go to another document or section of the current document. See *hypertext* and *World Wide Web*.

log in

Typing a user identifier (ID) and, optionally, a password to gain access to a file, program, computer, or network.

mailing list

An electronic mail distribution list for members of a discussion group.

man

Manual pages. Documentation for a program, such as UNIX.

markup

A document that includes commands to define attributes, such as formats and enhancements, and to describe the document. In an HTML document, the commands with which the document is marked up are known as *elements*. The term *markup* refers to the marks that editors make on manuscripts to be revised.

media type

The type of file and its contents, formatted as *file type/file format*. Examples include text/html and video/mpeg.

MIDI

Musical Instrumental Digital Interface. An audio standard for communications among computers, musical instruments, and synthesizers. MIDI files are commonly used to transfer musical information in a compact format.

MIME

Multipurpose Internet Mail Extensions or Multiple Internet Mail Extensions. A standard for sending and receiving messages that contain text, graphics, audio files, video files, and other multimedia files.

monospaced typeface

A font in which every character is a fixed width. A letter as wide as *w* or as narrow as *i* is the same width. Monospaced text, which often represents computer code and keyboard entries, is ideal for spacing table columns.

MPEG

Moving Pictures Experts Group. A standard for both video and audio files.

multimedia
Multiple media. A file composed of text, links, graphics, video files, and/or audio components.

Multiple Internet Mail Extensions
See *MIME*.

Multipurpose Internet Mail Extensions
See *MIME*.

Musical Instrumental Digital Interface
See *MIDI*.

National Center for Supercomputing Applications
NCSA. A center for computing and telecommunications at the University of Illinois; the developer of the pioneer Mosaic graphical browser.

nested
A command line (including attributes) that is inserted completely within another command line. For example, an IMG line, referring to an image used as a link, can be nested within the A line, which specifies the destination of the link.

newsgroup
A group devoted to discussing a particular topic, using mailing lists and other messages.

obsolete
An element or attribute that is no longer supported by the current HTML standard. Elements from the HTML 3.2 standard that are now obsolete in HTML 4.0 are LISTING, PLAINTEXT, and XMP. See also *deprecated*.

options
See *attributes*.

password
A hidden combination of characters and special symbols that a user types or that is automatically entered to gain access to a secure file, computer, directory, folder, or network.

pixel
Picture element; pel. A dot that represents the smallest part of an image displayed on a computer monitor or printed on paper.

post
Send a message electronically; add an HTML document to a server.

PostScript
A page description language developed by Adobe Systems; a standard for some Internet documents. If a document has a PS extension, it is a PostScript document.

protocol
Standards or rules that control the way in which a program and computer, two computers, a computer and network, two networks, and so on, communicate.

provider
See *Internet provider*.

rank
A score assigned to an entry in a list of results from a search index. A high rank indicates that several keywords or other attributes in the entry closely fit the keywords and other criteria that a user typed. A low rank indicates very few matches. See *search index* and *search tool*.

relative link
A link to a resource within the current document, directory or folder, or computer or network, using a partial URL or address (for example, /index.html). If your browser reads a partial URL or address, it will attempt to go to a relative link. See *absolute link*.

RFC
Request for Comments. Official standards developed by the Internet Engineering Task Force (IETF). See *IETF*.

search index
Search engine. A fill-out form in which you type one or more keywords, select or click on checkboxes and/or option buttons, optionally select other parameters for an Internet search, and click on a button to start the search. Examples of search indexes are AltaVista, Excite, Lycos, and Savvy Search. See *search tool*.

search tool
A search index (such as Savvy Search, AltaVista, Excite, Lycos, and many more) with which you search for Internet sites that closely match one or more keywords and other attributes that you select, or a master list or directory (such as Yahoo, the InterNIC Directory of Directories, or one of the World Wide Web Virtual Libraries), through which you can browse for Internet sites that you might want to visit. See *search index*.

selector
A string that identifies an element to which a declaration applies. For example, in HTML, the FONT element is a selector on which the SIZE, COLOR, and FACE attributes and their values can apply. Or, the H2 element is a selector that can be defined by other elements, their attributes, and values. See *declaration*.

server
A program (such as a World Wide Web or Gopher server) or computer that is programmed to communicate with and provide information to a client program (such as a browser). See *browser* and *client*.

server push
The automatic loading or reloading of a document or data at a specific time or time interval by a server. You can write a CGI program to incorporate server push features. See also *client pull*.

SGML
Standard Generalized Markup Language. An internationally accepted text-processing language. HTML is a subset of SGML. See *HTML*.

shareware
A complete or partial version of a program that you can download and try out before buying it for a small fee. If the downloaded program is not a complete version, the author will send you a complete version, a manual, and sometimes additional programs when you license it. See *freeware*.

site
A home page and its linked pages, all of which are located at a particular Internet address. See *home page*.

Standard Generalized Markup Language
See *SGML*.

start tag
The part of an HTML statement that indicates the start of an element and its attributes. The format of a start tag is *<elementname>*, in contrast to the end tag format, *</elementname>*. Occasionally, the start tag is an optional part of a statement. See *element* and *end tag*.

tag
See *element*. See also *end tag* and *start tag*.

Unicode
A standards organization that develops the Unicode Worldwide Character Standard, which supports characters comprising the principal written languages of the world, as well as symbols either within or outside character sets.

Uniform Resource Identifier
See *URI*.

Uniform Resource Locator
See *URL*.

upload
The transfer of a file from your computer to a remote computer. The standard protocol for uploading files is anonymous FTP (file transfer protocol). See *download* and *FTP*.

URI
Uniform Resource Identifier. The Internet address of an anchor. A URI can be either a URL (absolute link), a partial address (relative link), or a URN (Uniform Resource Name). See *URL* and *URN*.

URL
Uniform Resource Locator. An Internet address composed of the protocol type (such as `http:`, `ftp:`, `gopher:`, and so on), the name of the server to be contacted (such as `www.w3.org`), the directories or folders (such as `/pub/WWW/Provider/`), and the optional filename (for example, `homepage.xml`). See *URI* and *URN*.

URN
Uniform Resource Name. An identifier that can contain a variety of information, including one or more URLs. See *URI* and *URL*.

user agent
See *agent*.

W3C
World Wide Web Consortium. The organization that develops standards for the World Wide Web and contributes to HTML standards.

WAV
A Windows-supported sound file format.

World Wide Web

WWW, W3, or the Web. A hypertext-based information system that supports the use of multimedia, including text, links, graphics, video files, and sound files. The Web was developed at the European Laboratory for Particle Physics (CERN) in Switzerland.

XHTML

A subset of XML; a custom markup language that encompasses and extends HTML 4.0 to allow the definition of custom elements.

XML

Extensible Markup Language; a "child" of SGML and a language that coexists with both SGML and HTML. XML allows the creation of custom elements and attributes and will enable complex hyperlinks.

Index

Continued

Continued

Continued

Continued

Continued

Continued

Two Books in One!

CONCISE TUTORIALS
Each In Plain English guidebook delivers concise, targeted tutorials—no hand-holding, no coddling, just the skills you need to get up and running fast.

READY-REFERENCE HELP
Each book also features topic-sorted and A-to-Z reference sections that answer your questions quickly and help you get the job done, day after day.

In Plain English. All the tools you need to get up to speed—and get results.

Active Server™ Pages In Plain English
by Patricia Hartman & Timothy Eden
650 pages • $19.99
ISBN 0-7645-4745-3

C++ In Plain English, 3rd Edition
by Brian Overland
700 pages • $19.99
ISBN 0-7645-3545-5

Java™ In Plain English, 3rd Edition
by Brian Overland & Michael Morrison
750 pages • $19.99
ISBN 0-7645-3539-0

JavaScript™ In Plain English
by Sandra Eddy *Available Spring '01*
700 pages • $19.99
ISBN 0-7645-4792-5

XHTML™ In Plain English
by Sandra Eddy
750 pages • $19.99
ISBN 0-7645-4743-7

XML In Plain English, 2nd Edition
by Sandra Eddy
750 pages • $19.99
ISBN 0-7645-4744-5

For more information, visit our website at:
www.mandtbooks.com

my2cents.idgbooks.com

Register This Book — And Win!

Visit **http://my2cents.idgbooks.com** to register this book and we'll automatically enter you in our fantastic monthly prize giveaway. It's also your opportunity to give us feedback: let us know what you thought of this book and how you would like to see other topics covered.

Discover IDG Books Online!

The IDG Books Online Web site is your online resource for tackling technology — at home and at the office. Frequently updated, the IDG Books Online Web site features exclusive software, insider information, online books, and live events!

10 Productive & Career-Enhancing Things You Can Do at www.idgbooks.com

1. Nab source code for your own programming projects.

2. Download software.

3. Read Web exclusives: special articles and book excerpts by IDG Books Worldwide authors.

4. Take advantage of resources to help you advance your career as a Novell or Microsoft professional.

5. Buy IDG Books Worldwide titles or find a convenient bookstore that carries them.

6. Register your book and win a prize.

7. Chat live online with authors.

8. Sign up for regular e-mail updates about our latest books.

9. Suggest a book you'd like to read or write.

10. Give us your 2¢ about our books and about our Web site.

You say you're not on the Web yet? It's easy to get started with IDG Books' *Discover the Internet,* available at local retailers everywhere.